THE ATTORNEY'S HANDBOOK
on
SMALL BUSINESS REORGANIZATION
under
CHAPTER 11

HARVEY J. WILLIAMSON
Attorney at Law

ARGYLE PUBLISHING COMPANY
Glenwood Springs, Colorado

Other books published by Argyle Publishing Company:

The Attorney's Handbook on Consumer Bankruptcy and Chapter 13

The Bankruptcy Issues Handbook

The Attorney's Bankruptcy Code and Rules Book

Handbook on The Law of Small Business Enterprises

The Wills, Trusts and Estate Planning Handbook

Bonus Material Available at www.argylepub.com/bankruptcy-bonus-content

Twelfth Edition, 2016

ISBN 13: 978-1-880730-46-1
ISBN 10: 1-880730-46-4

Published and Distributed by
ARGYLE PUBLISHING COMPANY

P.O. Box 925
Glenwood Springs, Colorado 81602
(Website: www.argylepub.com)

Printed in the United States of America

CONTENTS

CHAPTER ONE

QUESTIONS AND ANSWERS ABOUT CHAPTER 11

CHAPTER TWO

ADVISING A FINANCIALLY-TROUBLED SMALL BUSINESS

CHAPTER THREE

PREPARING AND FILING A VOLUNTARY CHAPTER 11 CASE

EXHIBITS FOR CHAPTER THREE

CHAPTER FOUR

HANDLING A VOLUNTARY CHAPTER 11 CASE

EXHIBITS FOR CHAPTER FOUR

CHAPTER FIVE

REPRESENTING A CREDITOR IN A CHAPTER 11 CASE

EXHIBITS FOR CHAPTER FIVE

APPENDIXES

INTRODUCTION

Most Chapter 11 cases are small business cases. Many of these cases are filed and handled by attorneys who are not Chapter 11 specialists. This handbook was written for attorneys of this type. It is designed to serve as a reference and guide to attorneys in the handling of Chapter 11 cases for small business and individual clients. It contains all of the resource materials needed to handle typical cases of this sort except the local rules and forms, copies of which may be obtained from the website of the local bankruptcy court. The text and supplemental materials contained in this edition of the handbook incorporate all changes in the bankruptcy law and procedure through January 1, 2016.

The supplemental materials contained in this handbook include the following:

1. The text of all relevant chapters of the Bankruptcy Code, current through January 1, 2016.

2. The entire text of the Federal Rules of Bankruptcy Procedure, current through January 1, 2016.

3. Samples of frequently-used motions, applications, notices, and other forms, documents, and pleadings.

4. Samples of the bankruptcy petitions, schedules, statements, and lists needed in a typical small business Chapter 11 case.

Chapter one of the handbook contains questions and answers about Chapter 11 and Chapter 11 cases. It is intended to be useful to attorneys who are not familiar with Chapter 11 and to small business or individual clients. The questions and answers may be photocopied or scanned from the handbook and given to clients to aid in their understanding of the Chapter 11 process, if desired. They are also available on our downloadable Bankruptcy Documents.

Chapter two contains a discussion of the bankruptcy and non-bankruptcy remedies available to a financially-troubled small business. Included are discussions of workouts and other non-bankruptcy alternatives available to small businesses, as well as a discussion of the relative advantages and disadvantages to a small business client of the different chapters of the Bankruptcy Code.

Chapter three deals with the preparation and filing of a voluntary Chapter 11 case. It covers the employment and compensation of the debtor's attorney, the Chapter 11 eligibility requirements, and the preparation and filing of the initial Chapter 11 forms and documents. Chapter four covers the handling of a Chapter 11 case after the initial filing. It covers the operation of the debtor's business under Chapter 11, the preparation of a plan and a disclosure statement, the procedures for obtaining acceptance and confirmation of a plan, and the carrying out and consummation of a plan. Chapter five deals with the representation of creditors in Chapter 11 cases, including the representation of secured and unsecured creditors and the filing and handling of an involuntary Chapter 11 case.

This handbook is intended to serve as a guide and ready reference in the day-to-day representation of small business Chapter 11 debtors and in the representation of creditors in Chapter 11 cases. It is not necessarily intended for in-depth legal research associated with functions such as brief writing. However, the author has attempted to support each legal proposition with a citation of authority that should lead the reader to more extensive authority on the subject.

In using this handbook, the reader is encouraged to use the subject index found in the back of the book. The subject index will refer the reader to the appropriate page of text, and the paragraph notes appearing on each page of text will refer the reader to the appropriate paragraph.

CHAPTER ONE

QUESTIONS AND ANSWERS ABOUT CHAPTER 11 *

1. What is Chapter 11?

Chapter 11 is the chapter of the Bankruptcy Code that permits a person or business to reorganize while obtaining protection from creditors. Chapter 11 of the Bankruptcy Code is entitled "Reorganization." The Bankruptcy Code is the name given to that portion of the federal laws that deal with bankruptcy.

2. Who may file under Chapter 11?

Legally, anyone except a governmental agency, an estate, a nonbusiness trust, a stockbroker, a commodity broker, an insurance company, a bank, or an SBA-licensed small business investment company may file under Chapter 11. An individual may not file under Chapter 11 if he or she has had another bankruptcy case dismissed upon certain grounds within the last 180 days. As a practical matter, Chapter 11 is available to virtually any business or person able to afford the expenses of the case.

3. Are there any financial or insolvency requirements for filing under Chapter 11?

No. There are no financial or insolvency requirements for filing a voluntary Chapter 11 case other than the good faith requirement that the case be filed primarily for purposes of reorganization. A voluntary Chapter 11 debtor may be solvent or insolvent, its assets may exceed its liabilities by any amount (or vice versa), and its income may be substantial or nonexistent. The only financial restriction is the practical one of whether the cost of the case to the debtor is justified by the intended benefit. A voluntary Chapter 11 case is a Chapter 11 case filed by the debtor. An involuntary Chapter 11 case is a Chapter 11 case filed against the debtor by its creditors.

4. What is a debtor?

A debtor is a person or business concerning whom a case under the Bankruptcy Code has been commenced. A person or business who files a Chapter 11 case is referred to as a debtor. A debtor who qualifies may be treated as a small business debtor in a Chapter 11 case.

5. What is a small business debtor?

A small business debtor is a debtor who chooses to be treated as a small business debtor in a Chapter 11 case. To qualify as a small business debtor, a debtor must be engaged in a commercial or business activity (other than one whose primary activity is the business of owning or managing real property and activities incidental thereto) and the total amount of the debtor's noncontingent liquidated secured and unsecured debts must not exceed $2,490,925** when the case is filed.

6. How does a debtor get to be treated as a small business debtor?

A qualifying debtor who checks the appropriate box on the Chapter 11 petition will be treated as a small business debtor unless and until the court orders otherwise.

7. What are the advantages of being treated as a small business debtor?

Being treated as a small business debtor expedites the handling of a Chapter 11 case by dispensing with the necessity of a creditor's committee, by shortening the period for filing plans, and by simplifying the procedures for obtaining acceptance of a plan.

* These questions and answers may be reproduced or use by an attorney in the practice of law.

** Dollar amount subject to change on April 1, 2016.

8. Are there any restrictions on the size or type of business that may file under Chapter 11?

No. A business filing under Chapter 11 may be very large, very small, or anywhere in between. Under Chapter 11, a business may be a sole proprietorship, a partnership, a limited liability company or a corporation of any size. Only those entities listed in the answer to question 2 above are not eligible to file under Chapter 11.

9. Does a person have to be engaged in business to qualify for Chapter 11 relief?

A person does not have to be engaged in business in the traditional sense to obtain Chapter 11 relief. A consumer is legally eligible to file under Chapter 11. As a practical matter, however, the person filing under Chapter 11 must have something to reorganize, rehabilitate, or liquidate before Chapter 11 relief can be granted. A debtor with substantial personal investments or assets may use Chapter 11 to reorganize or liquidate his or her investments or assets, even if he or she is not engaged in business in the traditional sense.

10. What are the court costs in a Chapter 11 case?

The Chapter 11 filing fee is $1,717, which must be paid to the clerk of the bankruptcy court when the case is filed. In addition, there is a quarterly fee payable to the U.S. Trustee that is based on the amount disbursed during the quarter by the debtor during the Chapter 11 case until such time as a plan is confirmed. The amount of the quarterly fee varies from $325 to $30,000 per quarter, depending on the amount of money or property that is disbursed under the plan.

11. What is a United States Trustee and what does it do in a Chapter 11 case?

The United States Trustee is an employee of the United States Department of Justice and serves independently of the bankruptcy court. The function of the United States Trustee in a Chapter 11 case is to monitor the case, appoint one or more creditors' committees, call and preside at meetings of creditors, appoint a trustee in the case if ordered to do so by the bankruptcy court, and collect the quarterly fee. Generally, the United States Trustee takes appropriate action to insure that all reports and documents are filed, that all fees are paid, and that there is no undue delay in the case. Most Chapter 11 debtors are required to make periodic financial and operating reports to the United States Trustee during the course of the case, at least until a plan is confirmed. The United States Trustee should not be confused with the trustee that is sometimes appointed in a Chapter 11 case to operate the debtor's business and take possession of the debtor's property. A trustee in a Chapter 11 case is appointed by the United States Trustee, and is discussed in the answers to questions 28 and 29 below.

12. How much are the attorney's fees in a Chapter 11 case?

The amount charged by an attorney for handling a Chapter 11 case for a small business debtor varies greatly depending on such matters as the size of the business, the type and extent of relief needed by the debtor, the attitude of the debtor's creditors, the type of reorganization needed or contemplated by the debtor, and whether the owners of the business are in agreement or disagreement as to how the business should be reorganized. Unless the case is a simple one, most attorneys charge on an hourly basis and require a retainer to be paid in advance. The total fee charged for handling a small business Chapter 11 case may vary from $7,500 or less for a simple case to several times that amount for a complex case. All fees charged or collected by an attorney in connection with a Chapter 11 case, whether prior to or after the case is filed, must be approved by the bankruptcy court as being reasonable in amount.

13. What type of relief from creditors may a debtor obtain by filing under Chapter 11?

The filing of a Chapter 11 case automatically stays all foreclosures, collection actions, civil litigation, and creditor action of any kind against the debtor or the debtor's property. The only significant proceedings not stayed by the filing of a Chapter 11 case are criminal proceedings against the debtor, divorce-related proceedings, and proceedings by governmental agencies to enforce police or regulatory powers. All other proceedings and acts against the debtor or the debtor's property, whether in or out of court, are stayed. Even telephone calls or the sending of letters or bills to the debtor, if for the purpose of collecting a prepetition debt, are precluded by the automatic stay. An act or proceeding that is stayed is held in abeyance, and no further action may be taken in the matter without the approval of the bankruptcy court. The automatic stay that accompanies the filing of a Chapter 11 case normally gives the debtor a moratorium of several months on the payment of many of its debts.

14. What type of long-term relief may a debtor obtain under Chapter 11?

Long term relief in the form of either a reorganization of the debtor's business or an orderly, debtor-controlled liquidation of the debtor's assets may be obtained under Chapter 11. If the debtor's business is reorganized, it may continue to function either in its present form or in a revised form, and its present creditors will be permitted to satisfy their claims only to the extent provided in the debtor's plan of reorganization. A reorganization may consist of anything from an extension of time for the repayment of debts to a total restructuring of the business.

15. How long does a Chapter 11 case last?

A Chapter 11 case must be broken down into two phases: the pre-confirmation phase and the post-confirmation phase. The first phase, which is the phase prior to the confirmation of a plan, normally lasts from six to twelve months, although the time may vary depending on the condition of the debtor, the type of plan proposed by the debtor, and the reaction of creditors to the plan. The second phase, which is the phase where the confirmed plan is implemented and carried out by the debtor, normally lasts from three to five years, although it, too, may vary in duration. See the answer to question 52 below.

16. When does the debtor receive a discharge in a Chapter 11 case?

In the Chapter 11 case filed by a corporation, limited liability company, or other nonindividual, the debtor receives a discharge when a plan is confirmed by the court. The order of the court that confirms the plan also contains the debtor's Chapter 11 discharge. In a Chapter 11 case filed by an individual (i.e., a natural person), a discharge is granted by the court separately, after the completion of payments under the plan. A discharge is a court order relieving the debtor from liability for certain debts. A debt that is discharged is a debt for which the debtor is no longer liable, except as provided in the Chapter 11 plan.

17. What debts are discharged by a Chapter 11 discharge?

The debts discharged in a Chapter 11 case depend on whether the debtor is an individual (i.e., a natural person) or a nonindividual (i.e., a corporation, partnership, etc.). The discharge received by an individual debtor in a Chapter 11 case discharges the debtor from all pre-confirmation debts except those that would not be dischargeable in a Chapter 7 case filed by the same debtor. The discharge received by a nonindividual debtor in a Chapter 11 case depends on whether the plan confirmed is a plan of reorganization or a plan of liquidation. The discharge received in the confirmation of a plan of reorganization discharges a nonindividual debtor from all scheduled pre-confirmation debts without exception. However, if the plan confirmed is a plan of liquidation and if the debtor does not engage in business after consummation of the plan, a nonindividual debtor does not receive a discharge.

18. Is a Chapter 11 discharge valid if the debtor later fails to carry out the plan?

The validity of a Chapter 11 discharge granted to a nonindividual debtor is not affected by the subsequent failure of a debtor to carry out the plan. As long as the order of confirmation is not revoked by the court (which seldom happens), the discharge received by a debtor of this type is valid even if the debtor later fails to fulfill its obligations under the Chapter 11 plan. As explained in the answer to question 16 above, an individual debtor does not receive a discharge until the completion of payments under the plan. However, under certain circumstances an individual debtor who has not completed payments under the plan may also receive a Chapter 11 discharge.

19. How is a Chapter 11 case commenced?

A voluntary Chapter 11 case is commenced by filing a voluntary petition with the clerk of the bankruptcy court requesting relief under Chapter 11 of the Bankruptcy Code. A number of other documents are usually filed with the petition. However, if it is necessary to file the case before the other documents can be prepared, most of the other documents may be filed within 14 days after the petition is filed. The filing fee must usually be paid when the petition is filed, although an individual debtor may pay the filing fee in installments. As a practical matter, however, debtors who are unable to pay the filing fee when a Chapter 11 case is filed seldom succeed under Chapter 11.

20. Where is a Chapter 11 case filed?

A Chapter 11 case is filed with the clerk of the bankruptcy court in the district where the debtor either resides, has its principal place of business, or has its principal assets.

21. Is the public informed of the filing of a Chapter 11 case?

When a Chapter 11 case is filed, all of the debtor's creditors, shareholders, partners, and other persons directly involved with the debtor are notified. Notice of a Chapter 11 case is not normally published in newspapers or trade journals unless the filing of the case is considered newsworthy by the newspaper or journal. Generally, only the creditors, owners, and employees of a small business debtor are aware that the debtor has filed a Chapter 11 case.

22. Does a person or business filing under Chapter 11 have to continue to pay its debts after the case is filed?

Most Chapter 11 debtors receive a moratorium on the payment of most of their general unsecured debts for the period between the filing of the case and the confirmation of a plan. This period usually lasts for six to twelve months. During this period, however, it may be necessary to pay secured creditors and creditors whose property, goods, or services are needed to continue the debtor's business.

23. How does a Chapter 11 case proceed after it has been filed?

After a Chapter 11 case has been filed, the debtor must file documents with the court listing the names and addresses of all of its creditors and owners, describing all of its property and other assets, and disclosing its financial condition. The debtor, as a "debtor in possession," is usually permitted to continue to operate its business during the course of the case, but must comply with the requirements of Chapter 11 and the bankruptcy court in so doing. A creditor whose collateral is threatened may apply to the court for relief from the automatic stay or for adequate protection of its security interest. The debtor must prepare a Chapter 11 plan and file it with the court, usually within 180 days after the case is filed if the debtor is a small business debtor. The debtor must also prepare, file, and obtain court approval of a disclosure statement that adequately informs its creditors and interest holders of its financial condition and of its reorganizational plans. After the disclosure statement has been approved by the court, copies of the statement and the Chapter 11 plan are distributed to creditors and interest holders, who may then vote on whether to accept or reject the debtor's plan. If the plan is accepted by at least one class of creditors whose claims are impaired (i.e., not paid in full, see question 45 below) under the plan, the plan may be confirmed by the court. After the completion of voting, a confirmation hearing is held wherein the court must decide whether to confirm the plan. If the plan is confirmed by the court it becomes effective and must be carried out and consummated by the debtor. After the plan has been consummated, a final report is filed and the case is closed.

24. What is an interest holder and what is its role in a Chapter 11 case?

An interest holder is the holder of an equity interest in the debtor. In Chapter 11 cases interest holders are often referred to as equity security holders. A shareholder is an interest holder of a corporation and a member is an interest holder of a limited liability company. If the rights of interest holders are dealt with in a Chapter 11 plan, interest holders are treated like creditors and are permitted to file proofs of their interests, vote on the acceptance or rejection of a plan, and participate in distribution under the plan. However, most plans in small business Chapter 11 cases deal only with creditors and do not deal with the rights of interest holders.

25. What is a "debtor in possession" and what is required of it in a Chapter 11 case?

A "debtor in possession" is the debtor in a Chapter 11 case in which a trustee has not been appointed. As a debtor in possession, the debtor is legally charged with the rights, duties, and obligations of a trustee in dealing with the debtor's property and operating the debtor's business for the benefit of its creditors and interest holders. As a debtor in possession, the debtor must abide by the rules and standards of Chapter 11 and the orders of the bankruptcy court. The failure of a debtor in possession to perform its obligations and duties may result in the appointment of a trustee, a court order terminating the debtor's business, the conversion of the case to Chapter 7, or the dismissal of the case. A debtor ceases to be a debtor in possession when a plan is confirmed by the court.

26. What is cash collateral?

Cash collateral is cash or property that is easily converted to cash. Property such as bank accounts, checks, securities, and other cash equivalents constitutes cash collateral. Because it is easily disposed of, the use or sale of cash collateral is subject to strict rules in Chapter 11 cases. The use or sale of cash collateral is discussed in the answer to question 30 below.

27. Is the debtor permitted to operate its business during a Chapter 11 case?

Unless a trustee is appointed, the debtor may continue to operate its business during a Chapter 11 case as a debtor in possession. In operating its business during a Chapter 11 case, the debtor, as a debtor in possession, must abide by the requirements of Chapter 11 and the orders of the bankruptcy court.

28. What are the grounds for the appointment of a trustee in a Chapter 11 case?

There are three grounds for the appointment of a trustee in a Chapter 11 case: a trustee may be appointed for cause, if the appointment would be in the best interests of creditors, or if grounds exist to dismiss the case but the court determines that the appointment of a trustee, rather than dismissal, is in the best interests of creditors and the business. Cause for the appointment of a trustee includes substantial or continuing business or asset loss, gross mismanagement of the affairs of the debtor by current management, failure to comply with orders of the court, and several other grounds. A trustee is not appointed in most small business Chapter 11 cases.

29. What happens if a trustee is appointed in a Chapter 11 case?

If appointed, the trustee assumes most of the management functions of the debtor's business and takes control of the debtor's property. In effect, the trustee will replace the debtor's current management in the operation of the debtor's business during the course of the Chapter 11 case until a plan is confirmed. The trustee may also assume control over many aspects of the debtor's Chapter 11 case. When a trustee is appointed in a Chapter 11 case, the debtor ceases to be a "debtor in possession."

30. What limitations are placed on a debtor's right to use, sell, or lease its property during a Chapter 11 case?

For purposes of use, sale, or lease during a Chapter 11 case, a debtor's property is divided into two categories: cash collateral, and all other property. Until a plan is confirmed, the debtor, as a debtor in possession, may not use, sell, or lease cash collateral unless each creditor secured by the cash collateral consents to the proposed use, sale, or lease, or unless the court approves the proposed use, sale, or lease. Unless the court orders otherwise, the debtor may use, sell, or lease any of its property except cash collateral in the ordinary course of business during the case without prior notice to creditors or court approval. The debtor may use, sell, or lease property other than cash collateral outside the ordinary course of business during the case only after notice to any affected creditors and a court hearing.

31. May a debtor incur new debts and obtain new credit during a Chapter 11 case?

Yes. Unless the court orders otherwise, the debtor, as a debtor in possession, may obtain unsecured credit and incur unsecured debt in the ordinary course of business during a Chapter 11 case without court approval. Further, the unsecured credit or debt so obtained or incurred is payable as an administrative expense in the case, which means that those creditors get paid ahead of all other unsecured creditors. Court approval is required prior to obtaining or incurring any other type of credit or debt during the case. Thus, secured credit or unsecured credit not in the ordinary course of business may be obtained during the case only with the prior approval of the bankruptcy court.

32. May a debtor break its contracts or leases in a Chapter 11 case?

Yes. Under Chapter 11, the debtor, as a debtor in possession, may, at its option and without the consent of the other party, reject, assume, or assign most contracts or leases under which the debtor is obligated. This may be done either by motion during the Chapter 11 case or as part of a Chapter 11 plan.

33. What is a disclosure statement?

It is a document prepared by the proponent of a Chapter 11 plan that discloses financial and other information about the debtor and the proposed plan to the debtor's creditors. A disclosure statement must contain information that is sufficient to enable creditors to make an informed decision on whether to accept or reject a proposed plan. A disclosure statement must be approved by the court before it is distributed to creditors. In a small business case, the debtor's Chapter 11 plan may also serve as the disclosure statement if it contains adequate information about the debtor and the plan.

34. What is a Chapter 11 plan?

It is a written document that states the terms of how the debtor will deal with its creditors and, if necessary, interest holders. A Chapter 11 plan may be simple or complex, but it must comply with the legal requirements of Chapter 11. Most Chapter 11 plans are plans of reorganization, but a Chapter 11 plan may also be a plan of complete or partial liquidation, if desired.

35. How are secured creditors dealt with in a Chapter 11 plan?

Much depends on whether a creditor is fully secured or undersecured. The claim of a fully secured creditor must be paid in full in cash, and if deferred cash payments are made on the claim, interest must be paid to the creditor for not receiving its cash immediately. An undersecured creditor may elect to have its claim treated as being fully secured, and if such an election is made the claim must be paid in full in cash, but if deferred cash payments are made, interest does not usually have to be paid on the claim. If an undersecured creditor does not elect to have its claim treated as being fully secured, the secured portion of its claim must be paid in the same manner as a fully secured claim, while the unsecured portion may be paid as an unsecured claim.

36. What is the difference between a fully secured creditor and an undersecured creditor?

A fully secured creditor is the holder of a claim that is secured by property of a value that equals or exceeds the amount of the claim. An undersecured creditor is the holder of a claim that is secured by property of a value that is less than the amount of the claim. Suppose, for example, that the debtor has a truck valued at $10,000 that is subject to a $7,000 first mortgage held by Bank A and a $5,000 second mortgage held by Bank B. Because its $7,000 claim is secured by property valued at $10,000, Bank A's claim is fully secured. Bank B's $5,000 claim is undersecured because it is secured only by an interest in property valued at $3,000 (the $10,000 value of the truck less the $7,000 first mortgage lien against it). An undersecured creditor is treated as having two claims, one secured and the other unsecured. However, in a Chapter 11 case, an undersecured creditor may waive its unsecured claim and elect to have its claim treated as being fully secured by exercising what is called a Section 1111(b) election.

37. How are unsecured creditors dealt with in a Chapter 11 plan?

The answer depends on whether a creditor has a priority or a nonpriority claim. Priority claims must be paid in full in cash under a Chapter 11 plan, unless a creditor agrees otherwise. Further, all priority claims except tax claims must be paid when the plan is confirmed or shortly thereafter, unless a particular creditor agrees to accept payments under the plan. Tax claims may be paid in regular cash payments with interest over a period not exceeding 5 years from the date the case is filed. An unsecured creditor with a nonpriority claim must be paid at least as much as the creditor would have received had the debtor filed under Chapter 7, and the payments need not be in cash. Nonpriority claims may be paid in cash, property, or securities of the debtor or the successor to the debtor under the plan.

38. How does a priority unsecured claim differ from a nonpriority unsecured claim?

A priority unsecured claim is an unsecured claim that is given priority of payment under the Bankruptcy Code. Priority unsecured claims include the following types of claims: the administrative expenses of the Chapter 11 case, wage claims of up to $12,475* per employee, wage benefit claims of employees up to certain limits, consumer deposit claims of up to $2,775* each, most divorce-related claims, and tax claims. Administrative expenses include the fees of the debtor's attorney and unsecured debts incurred in the ordinary course of operating the debtor's business during the case. A nonpriority unsecured claim is a general unsecured claim incurred against the debtor prior to the filing of the Chapter 11 case. The claims of most trade creditors are nonpriority unsecured claims.

* Dollar amounts subject to change on April 1, 2016.

39. May someone other than the debtor file a Chapter 11 plan?

Yes, but only under certain conditions. If the debtor chooses to be treated as a small business debtor, only the debtor may file a plan for the first 180 days after the case is filed and creditors then have 120 days in which to file a plan. Otherwise, the debtor has the exclusive right to file a Chapter 11 plan for the first 120 days after the filing of the case, unless a trustee is appointed during the 120-day period. If the debtor files a plan during the 120-day exclusive period, the debtor must gain acceptance of its plan by creditors and interest holders within 180 days after the case is filed in order to retain the exclusive right to file a plan. A party other than the debtor may file a plan if a trustee is appointed in the case, if the debtor fails to file a plan within the exclusive period, or if the debtor fails to gain acceptance of a plan within 180 days after the case is filed.

40. Who may file a Chapter 11 plan if the debtor fails to do so?

If any of the conditions described in the answer to the previous question occur entitling a party other than the debtor to file a Chapter 11 plan, any party to the case may file a plan, including a creditor, an interest holder, or a creditors' committee. The United States Trustee may not file a plan.

41. What is a creditors' committee?

It is a committee appointed by the United States Trustee that represents the interests of creditors in the case. A creditor's committee must be appointed in a Chapter 11 case unless the debtor chooses to be treated as a small business debtor and requests that a creditors' committee not be appointed. While other committees may be appointed upon request, the only committee, if any, appointed in most small business cases is the unsecured creditors' committee, which represents the interests of nonpriority unsecured creditors in the case. The unsecured creditors' committee is usually composed of the seven largest unsecured creditors who are willing to serve on the committee.

42. What must a creditor do to become entitled to payment in a Chapter 11 case?

For a creditor to be entitled to payment in a Chapter 11 case, the creditor's claim must be filed and allowed by the court. If a creditor's claim is listed in the schedules filed by the debtor in the case, and is not listed as being disputed, contingent, or unliquidated, then the claim is considered to be filed in the case in the amount and priority listed on the debtor's schedules. Otherwise, a creditor must file a document called a "proof of claim" in order for its claim to be filed. Once a claim is filed, either by virtue of being included in the debtor's schedules or by the filing of a "proof of claim," the claim is automatically allowed by the court unless someone files an objection to the allowance of the claim, in which case the court must hold a hearing to determine whether to allow the claim. If a creditor's claim is correctly listed in the debtor's schedules and if no one files an objection to the claim, the claim will automatically be allowed in the case, even if the creditor does nothing. It is up to the creditor, however, to check and insure that its claim is correctly listed on the debtor's schedules.

43. When do creditors vote on whether to accept or reject a Chapter 11 plan?

Voting on a plan begins after the court approves or conditionally approves a disclosure statement prepared by the party proposing the plan. Each eligible creditor is mailed a ballot for voting on the plan. The ballot is accompanied by a copy of the disclosure statement and a copy or summary of the proposed plan. The court sets a deadline for voting on the plan, and a creditor's ballot must be filed with the court prior to the voting deadline in order to be counted.

44. What creditors are eligible to vote on the acceptance or rejection of a Chapter 11 plan?

Creditors must qualify both individually and by class in order to be permitted to vote on the acceptance or rejection of a plan. Individually, a creditor's claim must be allowed by the court in order to be eligible to vote. The allowance requirements for claims for purposes of voting are the same as the allowance requirements for purposes of payment, and are described in the answer to question 42 above. Except for certain priority claims, a Chapter 11 plan must put each claim in a class. To be eligible to vote on the acceptance or rejection of a plan, a class of claims must be impaired by the plan and must receive something under the plan. For a class of claims to be impaired by a plan, at least one claim in the class must be impaired under the plan. Classes of unimpaired claims are presumed to have accepted the plan and classes of claims receiving nothing under the plan are presumed to have rejected the plan. Creditors in these classes of claims do not vote on the acceptance or rejection of a plan. Creditors with allowed claims in all other classes of impaired claims are eligible to vote on the acceptance or rejection of a plan.

45. What is an impaired claim?

An impaired claim is a claim that is impaired by the terms of a Chapter 11 plan. A claim is impaired by a plan if the rights of the creditor to enforce its claim are diminished or materially changed by the plan. A claim that is not paid in full under a plan is an impaired claim. Even if a claim is paid in full under a plan, the claim is considered to be impaired if the original maturity date or any other obligation contained in the agreement upon which the claim is based is not met under the terms of the plan. However, a debtor is permitted to cure a defaulted note, mortgage, or other obligation so that the creditor's claim is no longer impaired. A defaulted obligation is deemed to be cured and not impaired by a plan if the obligation is made current, the creditor is compensated for any expenses incurred by reason of the debtor's default, and the rights of the creditor under the obligation are thereafter unaltered.

46. How is it determined whether a plan is accepted or rejected by creditors?

All voting on the acceptance or rejection of a plan is by class. The creditors in each class of impaired claims vote on whether the plan will be accepted by that class of claims. To be accepted by a class of claims, a plan must be accepted by creditors holding at least two-thirds in dollar amount and one-half in number of the claims in the class that actually vote on the acceptance or rejection of the plan. At least one class of impaired claims must vote to accept a plan before the plan can be confirmed by the court.

47. What happens when a plan is confirmed by the court?

To become legally effective, a Chapter 11 plan must be confirmed by the bankruptcy court. A plan is confirmed by the bankruptcy court when the bankruptcy judge signs an order approving the plan and ruling that the debtor and all creditors and interest holders are bound by the provisions of the plan.

48. When and under what circumstances may a plan be confirmed by the bankruptcy court?

After creditors and interest holders have voted on whether to accept or reject a proposed Chapter 11 plan, the bankruptcy court will hold a hearing for the purpose of determining whether to confirm the plan. This hearing is called the confirmation hearing. At the confirmation hearing, the party proposing the plan, which is usually the debtor, must present evidence showing that the plan complies with the Chapter 11 confirmation requirements. A plan may be confirmed by the court either through the regular confirmation method or through what is called a "cramdown." The regular method of confirmation is used when the plan has been accepted by the holders of every class of impaired claims and interests. The cramdown method of confirmation is used when the plan has been rejected by the holders of one or more classes of impaired claims or interests, but has been accepted by the holders of at least one class of impaired claims. A plan that has not been accepted by the holders of at least one class of impaired claims cannot be confirmed by the court.

49. How does confirmation of a plan under a "cramdown" differ from the regular method of confirmation?

When the holders of every class of impaired claims vote to accept a plan and confirmation is sought under the regular confirmation method, the plan will be confirmed by the court if the debtor proves that it has complied with the Chapter 11 confirmation requirements. When confirmation of a plan is sought under a cramdown, in addition to satisfying the Chapter 11 confirmation requirements, the debtor must show that the plan does not discriminate unfairly against any class of claims who have not accepted the plan and that the plan is fair and equitable with respect to each class of claims that has not accepted the plan. It is more difficult to obtain confirmation under a cramdown than under the regular confirmation method.

50. What happens if the court does not confirm a Chapter 11 plan?

If the court decides not to confirm a Chapter 11 plan, it will usually permit the party proposing the plan to modify the plan so that it can be confirmed. If a Chapter 11 plan is modified, it is usually necessary to hold another confirmation hearing on the modified plan. If the court refuses to confirm any plan, the Chapter 11 case must either be dismissed or converted to Chapter 7.

51. What happens after a Chapter 11 plan has been confirmed by the court?

After a Chapter 11 plan is confirmed by the court, the plan must be implemented and carried out, either by the debtor or by the successor to the debtor under the plan. If the plan calls for the debtor to be reorganized or for a new corporation to be formed, this function must be carried out first. If the plan calls for property to be transferred or for liens to be created or modified, this must also be done. And of course, the claims of creditors must be paid in the manner specified in the plan.

52. For how long a period may a Chapter 11 plan run?

There are no specified limits on the length of a Chapter 11 plan. A Chapter 11 plan must be long enough to convince the court and creditors that the debtor is making a good faith effort to pay as much of its debt as is realistically possible. On the other hand, the plan must not be so long that it does not appear feasible to the court. Typically, it takes from three to five years to carry out and consummate the Chapter 11 plan of a small business debtor.

53. What happens if the debtor is unable to comply with or carry out the provisions of a plan after it has been confirmed by the court?

If the debtor, or the successor to the debtor under the plan, is unable to comply with the provisions of a confirmed plan, the plan may be amended so that it can be complied with, if sufficient grounds exist for such an amendment. Otherwise, the Chapter 11 case may be dismissed or converted to Chapter 7. If the debtor, or the successor to the debtor under the plan, fails to carry out its obligations under the plan, creditors may sue, or foreclose on the property of, the debtor or its successor either in the bankruptcy court or in other courts.

54. What happens when all of the provisions and requirements of a Chapter 11 plan have been carried out?

When all of the provisions and requirements of a Chapter 11 plan have been fulfilled or carried out, the plan is said to have been consummated. When a plan has been consummated, a final report and accounting must be filed, and the case will be closed by the court.

CHAPTER TWO

ADVISING A FINANCIALLY TROUBLED SMALL BUSINESS

2.01 Chapter 11 - A General Description

Chapter 11, who may use

With only a few exceptions, any "person" who is entitled to be a debtor under Chapter 7 of the Bankruptcy Code may file a petition under Chapter 11. This includes limited liability entities such as LLCs and LLPs. Therefore, relief under Chapter 11 is available to virtually any individual or business entity able to afford the expenses of the proceeding. Only stockbrokers, commodity brokers, governmental units, insurance companies, most banks and credit unions, and SBA licensed small business investment companies are ineligible for Chapter 11 relief. Railroad reorganizations, which are dealt with in subchapter IV of Chapter 11, are not covered in this handbook. While the primary purpose of Chapter 11 is to facilitate business reorganization, it may also be used to carry out an orderly, debtor-controlled liquidation. And, it should be noted, there is no requirement that a voluntary Chapter 11 debtor be insolvent or unable to pay its debts.

Chapter 11 case, commencement of

A voluntary Chapter 11 proceeding is initiated by the filing of a petition by the debtor with the appropriate court, usually the bankruptcy court in the district where the debtor either lives, has its principal place of business, or has its principal assets. An involuntary Chapter 11 case is commenced by the filing of an involuntary petition by three or more creditors of the debtor who have claims totaling $15,325* or more, unless there are fewer than 12 creditors, in which case a single creditor with a claim of $15,325* or more may file the petition.

Chapter 11 case, consequences of filing

The filing of a voluntary Chapter 11 petition constitutes an order for relief under Chapter 11. In an involuntary case, the order for relief is entered after the trial on the petition, unless the petition is not timely controverted, in which case the order for relief is entered when the period for answering the petition expires. In either case, after the order for relief the debtor is required to timely file schedules of assets and liabilities, a statement of financial affairs, and other forms and documents with the court. Upon the filing of a voluntary petition, the debtor becomes a "debtor in possession" with most of the rights, powers, and duties of a trustee in bankruptcy. Unless the court orders otherwise, a Chapter 11 debtor, as a debtor in possession, may continue to operate its business during the course of the case.

automatic stay, effects of

The filing of a petition under Chapter 11 automatically stays virtually all litigation and creditor action against the debtor, and the debtor normally receives a moratorium of several months on the payment of many of its debts. However, secured creditors and important trade creditors may have to be paid during the moratorium, and relief from the automatic stay may be obtained by secured creditors whose collateral is threatened. It is often necessary for a debtor to "adequately protect" such creditors by means of cash payments, new liens, or otherwise, in order to retain the secured property.

debtor's right to use or sell property during case

A debtor may use, sell, or lease cash collateral during the case only with the consent of all creditors secured thereby, or with the prior approval of the court. A debtor may use, sell, or lease property other than cash collateral in the ordinary course of business during the case without prior notice or approval, but such property may be used, sold, or leased outside the ordinary course of business during the case only after notice and a hearing. While a debtor may obtain unsecured credit in the ordinary course of business during the case without court approval, any other credit obtained during the case requires prior court approval.

debtor's right to obtain credit during case

trustee, when appointed in Chapter 11 case

In most Chapter 11 cases the debtor remains in possession and control of its assets and business operation during the course of the case. Trustees are seldom appointed in Chapter 11 cases. A trustee may be appointed, however, for cause, if the appointment of a trustee is in the best interests of the creditors and the estate, or if grounds for dismissal or conversion exist and the court determines that the appointment of a trustee, rather than dismissal or conversion, would be in the best interests of creditors and the estate.

* Dollar amounts subject to change on April 1, 2016.

small business debtor, qualifications of

creditors' committee, appointment of

As soon as practicable after the order for relief under Chapter 11, the U.S. Trustee must appoint a committee of unsecured creditors, unless the debtor chooses to be treated as a small business debtor and requests that a creditors' committee not be appointed. A debtor may be treated as a small business debtor if it is engaged in a commercial or business activity (other than owning or operating real estate) and if the total amount of its debts do not exceed $2,490,925*. If appointed, the unsecured creditors' committee ordinarily consists of the seven largest unsecured creditors willing to serve. The U.S. Trustee may independently investigate the affairs of the debtor, and the debtor is normally required to file periodic financial and operating reports with the U.S. Trustee.

* Dollar amounts subject to change on April 1, 2016.

Chapter 11 plan, filing requirements

If the debtor chooses (by so designating on the petition) to be treated as a small business debtor in the case, the debtor has a 180-day exclusive period after the date of the order for relief in which to file a plan, and all plans must be filed within 300 days after the order for relief, unless the 180-day or the 300-day period is extended by the court. Otherwise, the debtor has the exclusive right to propose and file a plan during the first 120 days after the order for relief. If the debtor fails to file a plan within that period or if a filed plan has not been accepted within 180 days after the commencement of the case by the holders of each class of claims or interests impaired under the plan, then creditors and other parties in interest may propose and file plans. Whether submitted by the debtor or by another party in interest, a plan may be a plan of reorganization, a plan of liquidation, or a combination of thereof.

disclosure statement, filing and content requirements

After a plan has been prepared and filed with the court, the debtor or other plan proponent must prepare a disclosure statement, which must be approved by the court before it is distributed to creditors. However, if the debtor is a small business debtor, the court may conditionally approve a disclosure statement without a hearing, the hearing on the disclosure statement may be combined with the hearing on confirmation of the plan, and the plan may serve as a disclosure statement if it contains adequate information about the debtor and the plan. To be approved by the court, a disclosure statement must contain sufficient information about the proposed plan, and about the history and financial condition of the debtor, to enable a creditor or interest holder to make an informed decision on the acceptance or rejection of the plan.

acceptance of plan, solicitation of, when permitted

If the debtor is a small business debtor, acceptances of its plan may be solicited by the debtor based on a disclosure statement that has been conditionally approved by the court. Otherwise, the debtor or other plan proponent may solicit the acceptance of its plan only after the court has approved its disclosure statement and copies of the disclosure statement and copies or summaries of the proposed plan have been sent to all creditors and interest holders.

Chapter 11 plan, requirements of

A Chapter 11 plan must classify (i.e., place in a class) all claims and interests except certain priority claims, and a plan may be accepted or rejected only by classes of claims or interests. A class of claims or interests that is not impaired by a plan is deemed to have accepted the plan, and a class of claims or interests receiving nothing under a plan is deemed to have rejected the plan. The holders of claims or interests in classes that are impaired under a proposed plan must vote on the acceptance or rejection of the plan. A plan is accepted by a class of impaired claims if it is accepted by the holders of a majority in number and two-thirds in dollar amount of the claims in the class that actually voted on the plan. To be accepted by a class of interests, the holders of at least two-thirds of the interests voting on the plan must vote to accept the plan.

claims and interests, definition

A claim or interest is impaired by a plan if the holder's rights thereunder are diminished or materially changed by the plan. A claim is a right to payment, while an interest is the equity security right of a shareholder, limited partner, or other equity security holder. Thus, in Chapter 11 cases creditors have claims and equity security holders have interests.

Chapter 11 plan, who may vote on

In order to vote on the acceptance or rejection of a plan and in order to participate in distribution under a plan, the claim of a creditor or interest holder must be allowed. To be allowed, a proof of claim or interest must be filed, or deemed filed, with the court within the time specified by the court. Under Chapter 11, a proof of claim or interest is deemed filed for any claim or interest listed in the debtor's schedules, except claims or interests that are listed as disputed, contingent, or unliquidated. Once a proof of claim or interest is filed or deemed filed, the claim or interest is deemed allowed unless an objection to the claim or interest is filed, in which case the court must rule on the allowance of the claim or interest.

Chapter 11 plan, confirmation of

Even if it has been accepted by all classes of claims and interests, a Chapter 11 plan is not effective until it has been confirmed by the court. If a plan has been accepted by the holders of every class of impaired claims and interests, the court may confirm the plan upon a finding that the plan and the plan proponent have met and satisfied the Chapter 11 confirmation requirements.

Chapter 11 plan, confirmation of, cramdown requirements

If the holders of one or more classes of impaired claims do not vote to accept a proposed plan, the plan may nevertheless be confirmed by the court under the "cramdown" provisions of Chapter 11, provided that at least one class of impaired claims votes to accept the plan. If no class of impaired claims votes to accept a plan, the plan may not be confirmed under a cramdown or otherwise. To confirm a plan under a cramdown, the court must find that the statutory Chapter 11 confirmation requirements have been complied with and that the plan does not discriminate unfairly against, and is fair and equitable to, each class of impaired claims or interests that have not accepted the plan. To be fair and equitable, a plan must meet specific payment and security requirements with respect to each rejecting class of secured claims, and must satisfy the rule of absolute priority with respect to each rejecting class of unsecured claims. Under the rule of absolute priority, nothing may be paid to the holders of a junior class of claims or interests until all senior classes have been paid in full. In small business cases the absolute priority rule may be invoked to prevent the debtor's owners from retaining an interest in the reorganized debtor unless each class of impaired claims is paid in full under the plan or unless the owners contribute new capital under the plan in a manner that indicates that the owners are paying market value for their interests in the reorganized debtor.

Chapter 11 discharge, effect of

The confirmation by the court of a Chapter 11 plan of reorganization serves to discharge a corporate or other nonindividual debtor from all debts, except as provided in the plan. The confirmation of a Chapter 11 plan of liquidation, however, does not discharge a corporate or other nonindividual debtor if the debtor does not remain in business. An individual debtor receives a Chapter 11 discharge only after the completion of payments under the plan. A Chapter 11 discharge discharges an individual debtor from all debts except those that are not dischargeable in a Chapter 7 case, but a Chapter 11 discharge may be granted to an individual debtor even if he or she is not eligible for a Chapter 7 discharge.

Chapter 11 plan, impementation and consummation of

After obtaining confirmation of its plan, the debtor or reorganized debtor must implement the plan and carry out its provisions. The debtor must be reorganized as provided for in the plan, and any transfer of property, modification of lien, or other act called for under the plan must be carried out. Payments and other distributions must be made to the holders of allowed claims as provided for in the plan. Finally, the plan must be consummated, a final accounting made, a final order entered, and the case closed.

2.02 Gathering Information and Identifying The Problem

financially-troubled small businesses, basic issue

Most financially-troubled small businesses seek legal advice on the resolution of their financial problems because they are unable to meet their financial obligations as they become due. While this may be their reason for seeking legal advice, the real causes of their financial shortcomings are often less obvious and much more difficult to detect and remedy. Realistically, however, the underlying causes of a business's financial difficulties must be determined before meaningful legal or financial advice can be given.

small business, ascertaining cause of financial problems, importance of

Accordingly, one of the first tasks of an attorney representing a financially-troubled small business is to ascertain the causes of the business's financial difficulties. The extent to which the business's financial problems are caused by poor or dishonest management, disagreement among the business owners, a general slump in the field of the company's business, chronic undercapitalization, a general rise in the cost of labor or supplies, or other causes must be ascertained. Only when the underlying causes have been ascertained with a reasonable degree of certainty, can a sound decision be made on whether to reorganize, sell, liquidate, or abandon the business.

identifying financial problem, difficulty of

As might be expected, identifying the problem is seldom easy. And even when the problem has been identified, convincing the business owners may be difficult, especially if a significant portion of the problem is the management practices of one or more of the owners. Not surprisingly, identifying the problem can give rise to disputes among the business owners which, if not handled diplomatically, may further aggravate the financial and management ills of the business.

accurate financial data, necessity of

It will usually be necessary to obtain accurate financial and organizational data related to the business before an informed decision can be made as to the cause of its financial problems. Even if the business owners insist that they know the cause of their financial difficulties, the data should be obtained. It will be needed for two purposes: (1) to confirm (or refute) the owners' opinions; and (2) to justify any plan of reorganization that may later be proposed by or on behalf of the owners.

typical small business case, documents and information needed

The following data should be obtained by an attorney representing a financially-troubled small business:

(1) A complete list of all debts owed by the business, including the name and address of each creditor, the exact amount and current status of each debt, a description of any actual or threatened action taken by each creditor, a description of the collateral, if any, securing each debt, and the names and addresses of any other persons or entities liable with the business on each debt.

(2) Copies of all notes, mortgages, security agreements, finance statements, and other financial agreements of the business currently in effect.

(3) Copies of all leases and executory contracts under which the business is currently obligated.

(4) A detailed statement of the current status of the business's trade credit, relationships with commercial lenders, and general credit rating.

(5) A list of all court actions, executions, attachments, foreclosures, and other creditor action presently pending against the business in any court or forum, and a statement of the current status of each proceeding.

(6) A list of all bank accounts, deposits with financial institutions, negotiable instruments, documents of title, securities, or other sources of cash or cash equivalent currently owned or possessed by the business, together with a statement as to the amount or value and the secured status of each item listed.

(7) An accurate and up-to-date balance sheet and profit and loss statement for the business, and copies of all such documents issued by or on behalf of the business during the previous two years.

(8) Copies of the business's federal income tax returns for each of the last three years, and copies of any other documents available that show the income or expenses of the business during the last three years.

(9) Copies of the following: all documents under which the business was organized (e.g., articles of incorporation, bylaws, operating agreements, partnership agreements, etc.), minutes of all official meetings held by the business owners, and any agreements or other documents in any way dealing with the organizational or capital structure of the business.

(10) A list of all officers, directors, shareholders, partners, members, or other owners or persons in control of the business, and a description of the share of the business entity, if any, held by each person listed.

(11) A list of all significant management personnel of the business, a brief job description for each person listed, the compensation (current and deferred) paid to each, and copies of all employment contracts.

(12) A list of all other employees by class and a description of the compensation (current and deferred) paid to each class, together with a copy or complete description of the terms of any collective bargaining or similar agreements currently in effect.

(13) The names, addresses, and telephone numbers of all accountants, attorneys, and independent financial advisors employed or used by the business during the past two years.

(14) If the debtor is an individual, copies of any domestic support obligations under which the debtor may be obligated.

previous advisers of business, consultation with

It is a good practice to consult with any accountants, attorneys or independent financial advisors previously employed by the business, especially those employed recently. These persons may have a more objective opinion and a better understanding of the business and its financial or management problems than some of the business owners. In this regard, it may be necessary to prepare a written statement signed by one or more of the business owners authorizing an accountant, advisor, or attorney to release privileged or confidential information. When assembled, the information contained in the documents listed above should enable the business owners and their attorney to make an informed decision as to the underlying causes of the business's financial problems and, hopefully, to formulate a workable plan of reorganization for the business.

2.03 The Nonbankruptcy Alternatives

Once the underlying causes of a small business's financial difficulties have been ascertained, the problem of finding a suitable remedy may be addressed. Possible remedies for a financially-troubled small business include the following:

financially-troubled small business, possible remedies

(1) An out-of-court agreement between the business and its creditors whereby the creditors agree to extend the time for payment of their claims, to take less than the full amount in satisfaction of their claims, or a combination of both. An agreement of this type is often referred to as a "workout agreement," and it may include a reorganization of the business, provisions for the sale of assets, or other matters related to the future operation of the business. Workout agreements are discussed below in this section.

(2) Selling all or part of the business or its assets. This alternative, which may also be used in conjunction with a workout agreement, is discussed below in this section.

(3) Reorganizing the business under Chapter 11, Chapter 12, or Chapter 13 of the Bankruptcy Code. These alternatives are discussed in section 2.05, infra.

(4) Liquidating the business. This may be accomplished under Chapter 7, Chapter 11, Chapter 12, or Chapter 13 of the Bankruptcy Code, under the liquidation provisions of the state corporation, partnership, or limited liability company laws, under an assignment for the benefit of creditors, or informally, with or without an agreement with creditors. The bankruptcy alternatives are discussed in sections 2.04 and 2.05, infra, and the nonbankruptcy alternatives are discussed below in this section.

(5) Abandoning the business. This alternative is discussed below in this section.

workout agreement, definition and requirements

A workout agreement is the most common nonbankruptcy alternative for financially-troubled, but viable, small businesses. A workout agreement is a written agreement between a business and all or most of its creditors whereby the creditors agree to give the business some breathing room by extending the time for the repayment of debts, reducing the amount required for the satisfaction of debts, or a combination of both. A business must normally make a full disclosure of its financial condition to its creditors and has the burden of convincing its creditors that the proposed agreement is workable. Major creditors may insist on restricting the activities of a business during the term of the agreement, and may enforce such restrictions through veto powers or contract provisions governing certain activities of the business. Changes in the financial or management structure of a business may also be required by creditors as a condition to a workout agreement.

workout agreement, advantages of

The great advantage of a workout agreement, as opposed to the bankruptcy alternatives, is that it avoids the expenses, delays, and stigma inherent in bankruptcy proceedings. In certain fields, it should be noted, the bankruptcy alternatives may not be a viable option for a small business that wishes to reorganize. For example, a contractor who must obtain performance bonds in connection with its contracts may find it impossible to obtain such bonds if it files a bankruptcy proceeding. Also, in certain fields of commerce important customers or clients may prefer not to deal with a business that is involved in a bankruptcy proceeding, and this may render a reorganizational bankruptcy proceeding unworkable. Another advantage of a workout agreement is that because there are no judicial or statutory restrictions as to the methods or standards of debt satisfaction, there may be greater flexibility in devising repayment and reorganizational plans.

workout agreement, disadvantages of

The disadvantages of a workout agreement from the standpoint of a small business client are: (1) dissenting creditors cannot be bound by a workout agreement and a single dissenting creditor may be able to scuttle an otherwise workable agreement; (2) it may be difficult, logistically, to consummate an agreement if the creditors are either numerous or geographically widespread; (3) there is no method of preventing adverse creditor action while an agreement is being negotiated; and (4) a workout agreement can be superseded at any time by an involuntary bankruptcy proceeding or by a proceeding under state insolvency laws.

If a majority of all creditors, both in number and in amount of claims, are willing to accept a proposed workout agreement, but the implementation of the agreement is precluded by a few dissident creditors, it may be possible to force the agreement on the dissident creditors by drafting the workout agreement in the form of a Chapter 11 plan, obtaining written acceptances of the plan from a sufficient number of creditors to insure acceptance of the plan by all classes of impaired claims, and filing a Chapter 11 case. It should be noted, however, that prepetition acceptances of a plan are valid only if "adequate information" concerning the business and its financial affairs is given to the creditors. If the prepetition acceptances of the plan are valid and if the plan complies with the Chapter 11 requirements, neither a disclosure statement nor a cramdown should be required, and the Chapter 11 case should be a fairly simple proceeding. See sections 4.07 and 4.08, infra, for further reading on the Chapter 11 disclosure requirements.

workout agreement, use of as Chapter 11 plan, requirements

A significant disadvantage of a workout agreement from a creditor's standpoint is that it may be difficult to determine whether a business is making an accurate representation of its financial condition. It may also be difficult for creditors to detect and prevent fraudulent or preferential transfers by a business, especially to insiders. If there are dissident creditors who refuse to participate in a workout agreement, there is no effective method of preventing such creditors from gaining an advantage by seizing, or threatening to seize, newly-discovered assets, especially during the negotiation stage of a workout agreement.

workout agreement, other disadvantages

In practice, a workout agreement is most likely to be feasible when all or most of the following conditions exist:

workout agreement, when feasible

(1) most of the major creditors to whom the business is in default are either unsecured or substantially under secured;

(2) the major creditors are few in number and located in the same general geographical area;

(3) most of the major creditors are trade creditors or creditors who otherwise wish to see the business continue;

(4) all of the major creditors and a majority of all creditors are willing to participate in a workout agreement; and

(5) the business does not need the injunctive relief provided by the automatic stay in bankruptcy proceedings.

An attorney representing a small business client should undertake and substantially complete the following functions prior to the commencement of meaningful workout negotiations with creditors:

(1) Prepare a cash flow analysis of the business for the proposed period of the agreement to determine the amounts that can realistically be paid to creditors by the business. Any cash infusions to be received by the business, either under the workout agreement or as a condition of the agreement, should be included in the analysis.

attorney for small business, functions to perform

(2) Determine the approximate percentage of unsecured creditors, in amount of claims, that must become a party to the agreement for it to be workable. It is difficult to persuade every unsecured creditor to join in a workout agreement, and a figure of 85 to 90 percent of the total amount of all unsecured claims is usually a workable figure. Much, however, depends on the liquidity of the business and on the attitude and leverage of any nonaccepting creditors.

(3) Check the validity of the secured status of all significant secured or partially-secured claims. This may entail a uniform commercial code search, a check of the appropriate county or other public records, and an examination of the creditors' security agreements and other relevant documents.

(4) Determine the amounts and terms to be offered to each major creditor and to each class of minor creditors. It should be remembered here that while there is no legal reason to treat all creditors alike, the arrangement with each creditor will appear in the agreement thereby giving all creditors notice of the treatment accorded each creditor.

(5) If contractually possible, transfer the checking accounts and other cash deposits of the business to banks or institutions to whom the business is not indebted. While such actions will not endear the business to the creditor banks, it will remove some of their leverage by precluding the banks from unilaterally offsetting funds in the business's account against debts owed to the banks. This will give the business greater flexibility in the handling of its funds.

(6) Ascertain the status of all transfers of money or property made by the business within the bankruptcy preference periods (90 days for arms-length transfers and one year for transfers to insiders). If, for example, the business has repaid a substantial loan to a business owner within the last year, the possible liability of the owner for the funds received may affect the negotiating position of the business. A similar situation may arise as to recent payments to important trade creditors or on a debt that had been personally guaranteed by a business owner. The status of all potentially fraudulent transfers should also be ascertained. See section 3.03, infra, for further reading on preferential and fraudulent transfers.

(7) Prepare a disclosure statement showing the current financial status of the business. Included here should be an accurate and up-to-date list of all assets and liabilities of the business, together with a concise statement of the future plans and prospects of the business. The disclosure statement should be dated, signed, and verified by the chief executive officer of the business. While a disclosure statement is not legally required for a workout agreement, knowledgeable creditors may insist on such a statement before entering into meaningful negotiations.

(8) Devise a contingency plan for the business to follow should workout negotiations break down or should a major creditor attempt to scuttle the proposed agreement. The most important aspect of any contingency plan is to insure the availability of sufficient cash or working capital to enable the business to continue until corrective action, such as the filing of a bankruptcy petition, can be taken.

(9) Maintain communications with all major creditors so as to diminish the possibility of unfavorable creditor action that would render a workout agreement impossible. Unfavorable creditor action may include the repossession or seizure of important collateral, judicial attachments, an impounding or setoff of funds by a creditor bank, a cutoff of utility or telephone services, the closing of business premises by a taxing authority, and the filing of an involuntary bankruptcy petition against the business.

workout agreement, meeting of creditors

When the functions and procedures listed above have been accomplished, the next step is to approach the creditors and attempt to persuade them to accept the workout plan proposed by the business. The most effective method of initiating this step is to call a meeting of creditors at a specific time and place. If the number of creditors is not too large and if they are not too widespread geographically, all creditors should be invited to the meeting. If it is not feasible to invite all creditors to the meeting, only the larger creditors should be invited in hopes that they will later form a formal or informal creditors' committee and communicate with those not in attendance.

meeting of creditors, how to call

The use of a form letter is the simplest method of notifying creditors of the time and place of such a meeting. The letter should contain information sufficient to attract as many creditors as possible to the meeting, but insufficient to aid hostile creditors in collection or other unfavorable actions. In this regard, it is not a good practice to send a copy of the business's disclosure statement with the form letter announcing the meeting of creditors. Rather, the letter should state that a verified account of the current financial status of the business will be presented at the meeting.

workout agreement, treatment of creditors

When negotiating workout agreements with creditors, it is important to understand that it is not always necessary to treat all creditors alike, even those with identical claims. Some creditors may prefer to take substantially less than 100 cents on the dollar in return for early payment, while others may prefer to collect all or most of their claims over an extended period. The workout agreement, however, will disclose to all creditors how each creditor is being dealt with, and large discrepancies in creditor treatment may be difficult to justify.

The bargaining position of a small business client with a particular creditor is likely to be dependent upon two factors: (1) the creditor's ability to satisfy its claim in the absence of a workout agreement; and (2) the importance of the creditor to continuance of the business. If a creditor is fully secured, the business will have little bargaining power and the creditor will most likely have to be paid as contractually called for; although if a secured creditor is not hostile it may be possible to restructure the debt so as to give the business some immediate relief. If a creditor's claim is only partially secured, the bargaining position of the business will be proportionally stronger; and if the creditor's claim is completely unsecured, the business's bargaining position will, in the absence of other mitigating factors, be at its strongest. However, if the supplies or services provided by an unsecured creditor are essential to the continuance of the business, the business's bargaining position with the creditor may not be strong, especially if the business wishes to maintain its normal trade credit with the creditor during the period of the workout agreement.

workout agreement, bargaining with creditors

When negotiating with unsecured or undersecured creditors, a useful technique is to compute the liquidation value of the business and prorate it among the creditors so that each creditor will know what it would receive should the business be liquidated, either under Chapter 7 of the Bankruptcy Code or otherwise. Before attempting this technique, however, it should be ascertained whether any substantial preferential or fraudulent transfers that may be avoidable in bankruptcy have been made by or on behalf of the business. If so, the value of this device as a negotiating tool may be considerably diminished. A documentation of the delays, expenses, and impediments to collection inherent in a Chapter 11 case may also be a useful negotiating device.

workout agreement, negotiating techniques

As soon as negotiations have been successfully completed with all or a sufficient number of creditors to render the agreement workable, the workout agreement should be reduced to writing, signed on behalf of the business, and circulated among the creditors for signatures. It is important to prepare the agreement and obtain the necessary signatures without delay because a delay may give a reluctant creditor an excuse to pull out of the agreement. It is a good practice to obtain the signatures of reluctant or important creditors first.

workout agreement, obtaining signatures

Occasionally the illiquidity of a business can be cured by the sale of certain of its assets or by the sale of a portion of the business itself. In either case, whatever is being sold must not be vital to the continued operation of the business after the sale. Because such sales must normally be consummated within a short period of time, a fairly broad market should exist for the asset or business being sold in order to obtain full value. A sale of assets may also be used in conjunction with a workout agreement as a method of injecting cash into the business.

sale of business or assets, when feasible

If a sale of assets is contemplated, the possibility of a sale and leaseback arrangement should be considered. A sale and leaseback has the advantage of permitting a business to realize the value of an asset, while retaining the use of the asset. Under such an arrangement it may be possible to sell assets vital to the operation of the business without curtailing the income of the business.

sale and leaseback, when feasible

The two main detriments to the sale of either assets or a portion of the business as a means of raising working capital are encumbrances against assets and the difficulty of obtaining full value for whatever is being sold. In most cases any asset capable of being sold separately will have been mortgaged by the business, usually to the hilt and often in conjunction with other assets under a blanket mortgage. If the separate sale of an asset is permitted under the terms of a mortgage agreement, such a sale may relieve the business of all or a portion of an obligation, but it is likely to produce only a limited amount of cash or working capital. If the sale of a portion of the business is contemplated, the consent of the mortgagee of any asset being transferred in conjunction with the sale must usually be obtained before the sale can be consummated. And, of course, any encumbrance assumed by the purchaser of a business will be offset against the cash purchase price.

detriments to sale of business or assets

The "forced sale" nature of any sale by a financially-troubled business makes it difficult to obtain full value for whatever is being sold. Because the business's need for cash is invariably immediate and critical, there is usually insufficient time to properly market whatever is being sold. Further, purchasers are normally aware of the circumstances of such sales and seldom pay top dollar.

detriments to sale of business or assets

sale of business, when feasible

The possibility of selling a financially-troubled business in its entirety is realistic only if the business, despite its current financial difficulties, has either a potential for substantial future profits or assets that are likely to increase in value in the foreseeable future. In other words, the business must have an overall or going-concern market value that exceeds the amount of its present indebtedness. Businesses with substantial intangible assets are the most likely candidates for such a sale. Intangible assets include such items as favorable business locations, well known trade or brand names, a long record of successful and reputable business operation, and other forms of good will.

termination of business, liquidation or abandonment, factors to consider

If a workout agreement with creditors is not feasible, if neither the business nor its assets can be sold, and if the business cannot be reorganized or rehabilitated, the only alternative is the discontinuance and termination of the business. If a business is to be terminated, it must be decided whether to liquidate the business or simply abandon it. In making such a decision, three factors should be considered: (1) whether the business has significant unencumbered assets, (2) the extent to which the business owners are personally liable for the debts of the business, and (3) the ratio of the total amount of the business's debts to the total value of its assets. Generally, if a business has significant unencumbered assets, if the business owners are personally liable for substantial business debts, or if the ratio of the total amount of a business's debts to the total value of its assets is relatively low (lower than, say, 2 to 1), the business should be liquidated and not abandoned.

abandonment of business, when feasible

The abandonment alternative is widely used by small businesses that are hopelessly insolvent with all significant assets encumbered by valid liens or mortgages. Small, lightly capitalized corporations without significant marketable assets and whose shareholders and officers are not personally liable for substantial business debts are the best candidates for abandonment. Abandonment may also be a viable alternative for small businesses whose owners are personally liable for substantial business debts, provided that the owners are able to pay off, discharge, or otherwise deal with the business debts for which they are personally liable.

abandonment of business, informal arrangements with creditors

Under the abandonment alternative, it is not uncommon for business owners to make informal arrangements permitting certain creditors (usually those to whom they are personally liable) to satisfy their claims against what remains of the business's assets. Occasionally a business with significant assets will attempt to informally liquidate itself by distributing its assets to its creditors on a piecemeal basis. Such a procedure is fraught with exposure to personal liability for the business owners, however, and should be undertaken only with the concurrence of all major unsecured creditors.

abandonment of business, advantages and disadvantages

The advantages of the abandonment alternative are that it is inexpensive, is usually undertaken without notoriety, and avoids the stigma of bankruptcy. The principal disadvantage is that creditors often become suspicious and either file suit to hold the business owners personally liable for the debts of the business or file an involuntary petition against the business under Chapter 7 of the Bankruptcy Code.

liquidation of business, methods

If a formal liquidation of the assets of a business is desired, the business owners should consider the following options: (1) liquidating the business under Chapter 7, 11, 12, or 13 of the Bankruptcy Code, (2) liquidating the business under the state corporation or partnership laws, or (3) liquidating the business under an assignment for the benefit of creditors. The bankruptcy alternatives, which are dealt with in sections 2.04 and 2.05, infra, may be advantageous in situations where the business needs protection from creditors in order to carry out an orderly liquidation, where the business is a sole proprietorship and the business owner is eligible for a discharge, or where substantial business assets are located in more than one state.

The corporation and partnership laws of practically every state contain provisions dealing with the liquidation of corporations and partnerships organized under the laws of that state. In most states corporate liquidations may be either judicial or nonjudicial. Nonjudicial liquidations are carried out informally by the corporate officers without judicial supervision. Judicial liquidations normally entail the filing of a petition with the appropriate court, the appointment of a receiver, notification of creditors, the filing of claims, and other formalities. Because the laws of most states require all debts and obligations of a corporation to be either paid or provided for in a nonjudicial liquidation, insolvent corporations must usually be liquidated judicially. See Williamson, Handbook on The Law of Small Business Enterprises, supra, section 7.03, for further reading on the dissolution and liquidation of small business corporations.

liquidations under state corporation laws, judicial vs. nonjudicial

For businesses organized as partnerships, state liquidation proceedings are normally informal and carried out by a liquidating partner. However, because all claims of nonpartner creditors against a partnership must be paid, and because the partners are required to make contributions to the partnership sufficient to pay such claims, partnership liquidations are seldom feasible if the amount of a partnership's debts exceeds the value of its assets by a significant amount. See Williamson, Handbook on The Law of Small Business Enterprises, supra, section 3.09, for further reading on partnership liquidations.

liquidations under state partnership laws

The advantages of state liquidation proceedings are that they avoid the stigma of bankruptcy, they are usually sufficiently flexible so as to permit an orderly winding down of a business and a timely disposition of its assets, and, in judicial liquidations at least, creditors may be enjoined from seizing assets and may also receive a degree of protection from fraudulent or preferential transfers. The disadvantages are that it is difficult to acquire jurisdiction over and to administer business assets located in other states and dissatisfied creditors cannot be prevented from filing an involuntary bankruptcy petition against the business. The filing of an involuntary bankruptcy proceeding is especially likely if transfers of property or funds have occurred that may be avoidable under the Bankruptcy Code but not under state law, or if the distribution priorities under state law are less favorable to major creditors than those in the Bankruptcy Code. In general, state liquidation proceedings are a viable alternative only when the total value of a business's assets approaches the total amount of its debts, and time and judicial protection are needed to effect an orderly liquidation.

state liquidation proceedings, advantages and disadvantages

An assignment for the benefit of creditors is a proceeding under either the common law or a state statute whereby a debtor conveys substantially all of its property to a trustee, who is empowered to distribute the property to creditors in satisfaction of their claims. Statutes in many states regulate the form of such assignments, although assignments under the common law are also valid in such states unless the statutory proceeding is exclusive. Under both the common law and state statutes, however, a creditor must assent to such an assignment in order to be bound by it.

liquidating under assignment for benefit of creditors

The advantages of an assignment for the benefit of creditors are that it is less expensive and less time consuming than either state liquidation proceedings or bankruptcy proceedings, it avoids the stigma of bankruptcy, and it enables a business to continue to exist, though devoid of most of its assets. The disadvantages of such an assignment are that the consent of all significant creditors must be obtained for it to be effective, creditors are not fully protected from preferential or fraudulent transfers, and it may be superseded at any time by a bankruptcy proceeding.

assignment for benefit of creditors, advantages and disadvantages

Generally, an assignment for the benefit of creditors is a viable alternative only in the situation where there are relatively few creditors and the business has assets, such as accounts receivable or claims against third parties, that may be sufficient in time to satisfy most of its debts, but not as they become due.

assignment for benefit of creditors, when feasible

2.04 Chapter 11 vs. Chapter 7

Chapter 7 liquidation, description of

A Chapter 7 bankruptcy case is a liquidation proceeding wherein a trustee collects the debtor's nonexempt assets, converts it to cash, and pays the claims of creditors according to the priorities set forth in the Bankruptcy Code. While most individual debtors are eligible for discharge in a Chapter 7 case, corporations, partnerships, and other nonindividual debtors are not eligible for a Chapter 7 discharge. The business of a debtor who files under Chapter 7 must be terminated and liquidated, and, unless the debtor is an individual, a discharge of unpaid debts will not be granted. Chapter 7 is obviously not a viable alternative for a debtor who wishes to continue or reorganize its business.

liquidating business, the bankruptcy alternatives

If a debtor wishes to terminate and liquidate its business, it may, in addition to the nonbankruptcy alternatives discussed in section 2.03, supra, choose between Chapter 7, Chapter 11, and, in some cases, Chapter 12 or Chapter 13, of the Bankruptcy Code. This section deals only with the relative advantages and disadvantages of liquidating a business under Chapter 7 as compared to Chapter 11. The feasibility of liquidating a business under Chapter 12 or Chapter 13 is discussed in section 2.05, infra.

liquidating business under Chapter 11, when feasible

A debtor who wishes to liquidate its business in an orderly fashion may do so in a Chapter 11 case by filing a plan of liquidation and otherwise complying with the Chapter 11 requirements. See 11 U.S.C. 1123(b)(4). Because a Chapter 11 debtor has considerable flexibility in formulating and carrying out a plan for the liquidation or sale of its business, a small business debtor with assets that it wishes to liquidate is likely to find Chapter 11 preferable to Chapter 7, especially if the sale requires considerable time and expertise. Given the time and flexibility accorded debtors under Chapter 11, a debtor is likely to obtain a better price for its assets than a trustee in a Chapter 7 case. As a practical matter, however, the value of the debtor's assets must be fairly substantial to justify the expense of a Chapter 11 case.

sale of business under Chapter 11, when feasible

A debtor in a Chapter 11 case has the additional option of selling its business as a going concern, an alternative not normally available to a Chapter 7 trustee. The sale of the business itself (as opposed to the piecemeal sale of its assets) is most likely to be advantageous when the business has substantial intangible assets or other forms of good will, the value of which can only be realized through the sale of the business as a going concern. See Williamson, Handbook on The Law of Small Business Enterprises, supra, sections 2.03, 3.08, and 7.02 for further reading on the sale of small businesses.

nonindividual debtor, feasibility of Chapter 7

As a practical matter, filing under Chapter 7 is seldom advantageous for a corporate or other nonindividual small business debtor. One of the nonbankruptcy alternatives described in section 2.03, supra, is almost always preferable to Chapter 7 from the standpoint of an insolvent nonindividual debtor, who has little to gain by filing under Chapter 7. A solvent nonindividual debtor with substantial assets who wishes to liquidate and who needs the protection accorded debtors under the Bankruptcy Code to do so, will usually find a Chapter 11 liquidation proceeding preferable to Chapter 7.

individual debtor, feasibility of Chapter 7

Conversely, Chapter 7 is usually preferable to both Chapter 11 and the nonbankruptcy alternatives for an insolvent individual small business debtor who wishes to liquidate, provided that he or she can qualify for Chapter 7 relief under the means testing rules that are applicable to Chapter 7 debtors. Chapter 7 is especially attractive if the amount of an individual debtor's debts greatly exceeds the value of his or her nonexempt assets. A qualifying individual or family farmer with nonexempt assets who wishes to liquidate but needs the time and protection accorded debtors under the Bankruptcy Code in order to realize the full value of its assets, may find a Chapter 12 or Chapter 13 liquidation proceeding preferable to Chapter 7. See section 2.05, infra, for further reading. Finally, Chapter 7 may be the only alternative for individual owners of a corporate or partnership business who are exposed to extensive personal liability for business debts.

creditors, preference of Chapter 7

From a creditor's standpoint, Chapter 7 is usually preferable to both the nonbankruptcy alternatives and Chapter 11. The early appointment of a trustee and the other creditor-oriented features of Chapter 7 make it a favorite of creditors, especially those who suspect the existence of substantial preferential or fraudulent transfers to insiders or favored creditors that may be avoidable in bankruptcy. In such instances an involuntary Chapter 7 case may be the most practicable method for unsecured creditors to collect on their claims. See section 5.01, infra, for further reading on involuntary bankruptcy proceedings.

2.05 Chapter 11 vs. Chapter 13 or Chapter 12

A debtor filing under Chapter 13 of the Bankruptcy Code obtains protection from creditors, submits his or her nonexempt assets and future income to the jurisdiction and supervision of the bankruptcy court, and must, within 14 days after the filing of the case, file a plan for the repayment of all or a portion of his or her debts. Within 30 days after the filing of a proposed plan, the debtor must begin making regular payments to the Chapter 13 trustee, who collects the debtor's payments, deducts a fee of 10 percent of the amount collected, and makes payments to creditors as called for in the debtor's plan.

Chapter 13 case, general aspects

To become effective a debtor's plan must be confirmed by the bankruptcy court. A Chapter 13 plan is normally confirmed if the plan was proposed in good faith and constitutes the debtor's best effort, if each unsecured creditor will receive under the plan at least as much as it would have received had the debtor filed under Chapter 7, if it appears that the debtor will be able to make the prescribed payments and otherwise comply with the plan, and if each secured creditor has either accepted the plan, will retain its lien and be paid the full amount of its secured claim under the plan, will be given possession of its collateral under the plan, or will be paid outside the plan.

Chapter 13 plan, general aspects

In most Chapter 13 cases the debtor is required to pay all of his or her disposable income to the Chapter 13 trustee for the three-to-five year period of the plan. Disposable income is income not reasonably necessary for either the support of the debtor and his or her dependents or the operation of the debtor's business. For further reading on Chapter 13 proceedings see Williamson, The Attorney's Handbook on Consumer Bankruptcy and Chapter 13, supra, chap. 3.

Chapter 13 case, disposable income

To qualify as a debtor under Chapter 13, all of the following requirements must be met:

Chapter 13 eligibility requirements

(1) The debtor must be an individual (i.e., a natural person). Corporations, partnerships, limited liability companies, and other nonindividual debtors are not eligible to file under Chapter 13.

(2) The debtor must have regular income, which is defined as income sufficiently stable and regular so as to enable the debtor to make payments under a Chapter 13 plan.

(3) The debtor must have noncontingent, liquidated unsecured debts of less than $383,175* and noncontingent, liquidated secured debts of less than $1,149,525*.

(4) The debtor may not be a stockbroker or a commodities broker.

The above-described requirements obviously preclude the use of Chapter 13 by most small businesses. Only sole proprietorships (and husband and wife partnerships) with noncontingent, liquidated unsecured debts of less than $383,175* and noncontingent, liquidated secured debts of less than $1,149,525* qualify under Chapter 13. However, for those who qualify, Chapter 13 has several advantages over Chapter 11. First of all, a Chapter 13 proceeding is much simpler and less time-consuming than a Chapter 11 case. Unlike Chapter 11, it is not necessary under Chapter 13 for any class of unsecured creditors to approve the plan, and only the debtor may submit a plan. Also, the confirmation requirements for a plan under Chapter 13 are simpler and easier to comply with than those under Chapter 11. Finally, a Chapter 13 discharge is broader and more inclusive than a Chapter 11 discharge.

Chapter 13, when preferable to Chapter 11

In general, Chapter 13 is almost always preferable to Chapter 11 for a qualifying small business debtor who wishes to remain in business and either reorganize or rehabilitate his or her business. The three-to-five year length of most Chapter 13 plans is shorter than most Chapter 11 plans, and the legal expenses for a Chapter 13 case are normally only a fraction of those for a Chapter 11 case.

Chapter 13, when preferable to Chapter 11

* Dollar amounts subject to change on April 1, 2016.

liquidating under Chapter 13, feasibility of

It should be noted that Chapter 13 may also be used in lieu of either Chapter 7 or Chapter 11 by a qualifying small business debtor who wishes to liquidate. See 11 U.S.C. 1322(b)(8). This may be accomplished by filing under Chapter 13 and submitting a plan of liquidation as the debtor's Chapter 13 plan. It should be noted that in a liquidation proceeding under Chapter 13 it may not be necessary for the debtor to have "regular income" in the ordinary meaning of that phrase because most of the income under the plan will normally come from the sale of the debtor's assets. See In re Ratmansky, 7 B.R. 829, 832 (ED PA, 1980). Liquidating under Chapter 13 is less expensive and time consuming for the debtor than liquidating under Chapter 11. In addition, for a qualifying debtor with valuable nonexempt assets that he or she would lose in a Chapter 7 case, for a qualifying debtor who wishes to effect an orderly, debtor-controlled liquidation of his or her assets, and for a qualifying debtor in need of the broad discharge granted under Chapter 13, a Chapter 13 liquidation may be preferable to a Chapter 7 liquidation.

Chapter 12 eligibility requirements

Only a "family farmer" with regular annual income may be a debtor under Chapter 12 of the Bankruptcy Code. A "family farmer" may be an individual, an individual and spouse, a corporation, or a partnership. To qualify as a family farmer, a debtor's aggregate debts must not exceed $4,031,575* and 50 percent of the debtor's aggregate, noncontingent, liquidated debts must have arisen out of a farming operation. If the debtor is an individual, or an individual and spouse, the debtor must be engaged in a farming operation and more than 50 percent of the debtor's income for the preceding tax year must have come from the farming operation. If the debtor is a partnership or corporation, more than 50 percent of the debtor's equity or stock must be held by a family conducting a farming operation, and more than 80 percent of the value of the debtor's assets must be related to the farming operation. In most cases the debt for the principal residence of the debtor is not counted in the debt limitation requirement.

Chapter 12 case, general aspects

A Chapter 12 debtor is permitted to run the farming operation as a debtor in possession during the course of the case unless, for cause, the debtor is removed by the court as a debtor in possession. The debtor must file a plan within 90 days after the commencement of the case, and the plan must be confirmed by the court within 45 days thereafter. Only the debtor may file a plan under Chapter 12, and the plan may be confirmed by the court without the approval of unsecured creditors.

Chapter 12 plan, general aspects

The confirmation requirements for a Chapter 12 plan are the same as for a Chapter 13 plan (see supra, this section). Like Chapter 13, a Chapter 12 debtor must make periodic payments to a trustee, who collects the funds, assesses a fee, and distributes the balance of the funds collected to creditors in accordance with the debtor's plan. Also like Chapter 13, a Chapter 12 debtor must normally apply all of the debtor's disposable income toward payments under the plan during the three-to-five year period of the plan. A Chapter 12 debtor receives a discharge at the close of the case, although it should be noted that a Chapter 12 discharge is similar to a Chapter 7 discharge and is not as broad as a Chapter 13 discharge.

Chapter 12, when preferable to Chapter 11

Chapter 12 is usually preferable to Chapter 11 for a qualifying family farmer who wishes to remain in business and either reorganize or rehabilitate the farming operation. Chapter 12 plans are usually less complicated than Chapter 11 plans, and the legal expenses of a Chapter 12 case may be considerably less than those of a Chapter 11 case.

liquidating under Chapter 12, when feasible

A liquidating plan may be filed in a Chapter 12 case in the same manner as in a Chapter 13 case. See 11 U.S.C. 1222(b)(8). In addition, under Chapter 12 farmland and farm equipment may, with court approval, be sold free and clear of the interests of creditors, whose liens then attach to the proceeds of such a sale. See 11 U.S.C. 1206.

* Dollar amounts subject to change on April 1, 2016.

CHAPTER THREE

PREPARING AND FILING A VOLUNTARY CHAPTER 11 CASE

3.01 The Employment and Compensation of the Debtor's Attorney

attorney for debtor, general employment requirements

An attorney who contemplates representing a small business debtor in a voluntary Chapter 11 case should be aware that for employment and compensation purposes the attorney will be representing two distinct clients. Prior to the filing of the case the attorney will be representing the debtor in its ordinary capacity. After the case is filed the attorney will be representing a fiduciary entity known as a debtor in possession. Under the Bankruptcy Code a debtor automatically becomes a debtor in possession immediately upon the filing of a Chapter 11 petition. The Bankruptcy Code confers most of the rights, powers, functions and duties of a trustee in bankruptcy upon a debtor in possession. See 11 U.S.C. 1107(a). Therefore, after the filing of a Chapter 11 case the debtor's attorney effectively becomes an attorney for a bankruptcy trustee and must therefore comply with the employment and compensation requirements of the Bankruptcy Code that are applicable to attorneys for bankruptcy trustees.

debt relief agency, applicability to chapter 11 cases

It should be noted that the restrictions, disclosures and requirements imposed on "debt relief agencies" are not normally applicable to attorneys representing Chapter 11 debtors because such debtors do not normally qualify as an "assisted person," as that term is defined in 11 U.S.C. 101(3), because their debts are not primarily consumer debts and the value of their nonexempt property normally exceeds $186,825*. * Dollar amount subject to change on April 1, 2016.

prefiling compensation, reporting requirements

Prefiling services and compensation. The Bankruptcy Code contains no employment requirements or restrictions that are applicable to the prefiling representation of Chapter 11 debtors. Therefore, prefiling legal services may be performed for a debtor without notice to or the approval of the bankruptcy court. See Kressel v. Kotts, 34 BR 388, 392 (MN, 1983). However, any compensation paid or agreed to be paid to an attorney in contemplation of the case must be disclosed to and approved by the bankruptcy court after the filing of the case. See 11 U.S.C. 329(a). If the court then finds that an attorney's prefiling compensation exceeds the reasonable value of the services performed, the court may cancel the compensation agreement and order the return of any compensation paid to the extent excessive. See 11 U.S.C. 329(b) and Bankruptcy Rule 2017(a). Because the debtor's attorney must justify his or her prefiling compensation if called upon to do so by the court, it is important to maintain accurate records of all services performed for the debtor in contemplation of the filing of a Chapter 11 case.

attorney's prefiling disclosure requirements

11 U.S.C. 329(a) provides that, with respect to payments or agreements made within one year prior to the date the case was filed, an attorney representing a debtor must file with the court a statement disclosing the compensation paid or agreed to be paid for services rendered or to be rendered by the attorney in contemplation of or in connection with the case. The debtor's attorney must file this statement with the court and transmit it to the U.S. Trustee within 14 days after the order for relief. This statement must also set forth the specifics of any agreement by the attorney to share compensation with any other person, except members or regular associates of the attorney's law firm. The statement must be filed whether or not the attorney applies for compensation in the case and whether the attorney's compensation was paid, or is to be paid, by the debtor or by a third party. A supplemental statement must be filed with the court and transmitted to the U.S. Trustee within 14 days after the making of any payment or agreement that was not previously disclosed. See Bankruptcy Rule 2016(b).

Section 329(a) disclosure requirements, compliance with

The statement required by Section 329(a) may be filed separately, if desired, in which case Director's Form 2030, or a local substitute, should be completed and filed. In most Chapter 11 cases, however, the information required by Section 329(a) and Bankruptcy Rule 2016(b) is contained in the verified statement that an attorney representing a debtor in possession must file with the court. In most cases the attorney's verified statement will suffice as the Section 329(a) statement and a separate disclosure statement need not be filed. The local rules should be checked for specific disclosure statement requirements. Verified statements of attorneys are discussed below in this section.

attorney for debtor in possession, Code requirements

Postfiling services and compensation. As indicated above, the Bankruptcy Code imposes employment and compensation requirements on attorneys for Chapter 11 debtors in possession. Virtually all of the employment and compensation requirements that are applicable to an attorney for a trustee in bankruptcy are applicable to an attorney for a debtor in possession. See 11 U.S.C. 1107(a). The employment and compensation of an attorney representing a debtor in possession in a voluntary Chapter 11 case is governed by Sections 327, 328, 330, 331, 1107, and 1129(a)(4) of the Bankruptcy Code. The requirements established in these Code sections may be summarized as follows:

(1) The no-adverse-interest requirement whereby the attorney may not hold or represent an interest that is adverse to the interest of the estate or its creditors.

(2) The disinterested-person requirement whereby the attorney must be a "disinterested person," as that term is defined in the Bankruptcy Code.

(3) The approval-of-representation requirement whereby the attorney's representation of the debtor in possession must be approved by the bankruptcy court.

(4) The approval-of-compensation requirement whereby the attorney's compensation must be approved by the court prior to payment if he or she is being compensated by funds or property of the bankruptcy estate.

(5) The reasonable-amount-of-compensation requirement whereby the amount of the attorney's compensation must be reasonable under the circumstances.

disinterested person and no adverse interest requirements

The disinterested person and no-adverse-interest requirements. These requirements are imposed by 11 U.S.C. 327(a), which is made applicable to a debtor in possession by 11 U.S.C. 1107(a). Section 327(a) provides, in effect, that a debtor in possession may, with the approval of the court, employ one or more attorneys or other professionals who are disinterested persons and do not hold or represent an interest adverse to the estate. Section 328(c) provides that if at any time during his or her employment an attorney or other professional person is not a disinterested person or holds or represents an interest that is adverse to the estate, the court may deny compensation to that person.

adverse interest, what constitutes, effect of

The term "adverse interest" is not defined in the Bankruptcy Code. Most courts equate the term with "conflict of interest" in determining whether an adverse interest exists. See In re B H & P, Inc., 949 F.2d 1300 (CA 3, 1991), where the court stated that the factors to be considered in determining whether a conflict of interest exists include, but are not limited to, the nature of the disclosure of the conflict made at the time of appointment, whether the interests of the related estates or parties are parallel or conflicting, and the nature of the conflicting claims. See also, Rome v. Braunstein, 19 F.3d 54 (CA, 1994), where the court defined an adverse or conflicting interest as a competing interest sufficient to create either a meaningful incentive to act contrary to the best interests of the estate and its creditors or a reasonable perception of such an incentive. That the existence of either an actual or a potential conflict of interest can bar an attorney from representing a Chapter 11 debtor in possession, see In re Glenn Electric Sales Corp., 99 BR 596 (NJ, 1988), and In re American Printers & Lithographers, Inc., 148 BR 862 (ND IL, 1992). Adverse interests that are not disclosed by the attorney and are later discovered by the court are particularly offensive and almost always result in disqualification and denial of compensation. See In re Patterson, 53 BR 366 (NE, 1985), In re Michigan General Corp., 78 BR 479 (ND TX, 1987), and In re Pierce, 809 F.2d 1356 (CA 8, 1987). It should be noted that if an attorney holds or represents an interest adverse to the estate (i.e., has a conflict of interest), it is not a defense to show that no injury has resulted therefrom, and the court may deny all compensation to the attorney for services rendered in the case. See Matter of Futuronics Corp., 655 F. 2nd 463 (CA 2, 1981).

disinterested person, what constitutes

In 11 U.S.C. 101(14), a "disinterested person" is defined as a person who is not a creditor, equity security holder, or insider of the debtor, who has not been an officer, director, or employee of the debtor within two years prior to the commencement of the case, and who does not have an interest materially adverse to the interest of the estate or any class of creditors or equity security holders by reason of any direct or indirect relationship to, connection with, or interest in, the debtor or for any other reason. See 11 U.S.C. 101(14). An insider includes a relative, general partner, officer, director, or person in control of the debtor. See 11 U.S.C. 101(31).

attorney for debtor, when not a disinterested person

It is apparent from the above definition that an attorney who is an officer, director, or employee of the debtor, or who has been such during the two year period prior to the filing of the case, is not a disinterested person and should not represent the debtor in possession. Similarly, an attorney who is a shareholder, partner, relative, or person in control of the debtor is also not a disinterested person and should not represent the debtor in possession. While an attorney is not normally disqualified solely because he or she has previously represented the debtor, if the prior representation was of a nature that is not consistent with the interest of the estate in the Chapter 11 case, the attorney may be disqualified from representing the debtor in possession on that basis. See In re 419 Co., 133 B.R. 867 (ND OH, 1991). Also, the disqualification, for whatever reason, of a single attorney in a law firm normally disqualifies the entire firm from representing the debtor in possession. See In re Philadelphia Athletic Club, Inc., 20 B.R. 328 (ED PA, 1982). It should be noted that the disinterested person requirement is not applicable to attorneys employed on salary by the debtor and attorneys employed for a specific purpose. See 11 U.S.C. 327(b), (e).

attorney as creditor, effect of on disinterested person status

It is not uncommon for an attorney to be a creditor of the debtor when a Chapter 11 case is filed. It is clear that if the prepetition debt owed to the attorney is for nonbankruptcy legal services, the attorney is not a disinterested person and is therefore barred from representing the debtor in possession in the Chapter 11 case. See Electro-Wire Products v. Sirote & Permutt, P.C., 40 F.2d 356 (CA 11, 1994), and First Interstate Bank, N.A. v. CIC Invest. Corp., 175 BR 52 (BAP 9, 1994). However, if the claim for such legal services is waived, then the attorney may be eligible to represent the debtor in possession. See In re Adam Furniture Indus., 158 BR 291 (SD GA, 1993), and In re Watervliet Paper Co., 111 BR 131 (WD MI, 1989). Several courts have held that a prepetition debt owed to an attorney for legal services related to the bankruptcy case does not, without more, disqualify the attorney from representing the debtor in possession. See In re Watson, 94 BR 111 (SD OH, 1988), In re Gilmore, 127 BR 406 (MD TN, 1991), and In re Automend, Inc., 85 BR 173 (ND GA, 1988).

disinterested person, effect of retainer or security interest

What about attorneys who accept large prefiling retainers from Chapter 11 debtors or who take prefiling security interests in the debtor's property to secure the payment of their fees in the Chapter 11 case; are they "disinterested persons" under Section 327(a)? In In re Boro Recycling, Inc., 67 BR 3 (ED NY, 1986), a law firm that accepted a $10,000 retainer fee in contemplation of a Chapter 11 case was found not to be a disinterested person under Section 327(a). In In re Automend, Inc., 85 BR 173 (ND GA, 1988), the court stated that in an average case the retainer paid to its attorney by a Chapter 11 debtor should not be sufficient in amount to discharge all attorney's fees for the entire case, but should provide fees only for the early stages of the case. The receipt of a large prefiling retainer may also prevent an attorney from being a disinterested party on the grounds that the attorney is the transferee of a potentially avoidable transfer. See In re Intech Capital Corp., 87 BR 232 (CT, 1988), and In re Hathaway Ranch Partnership, 116 BR 208 (CD CA, 1990). That the acceptance of a significant prefiling security interest or mortgage in the debtor's property can prevent the accepting attorney from being a disinterested person under Section 327(a), see In re Pierce, 809 F.2d 1356 (CA 8, 1987), In re Martin, 817 F.2d 175 (CA 1, 1987), and In re Escalera, 171 BR 107 (ED WA, 1994).

debtor's attorney, effect of prior representation of creditor

It often happens that the debtor's attorney has previously represented or been employed by one or more of the debtor's creditors. Is such an attorney barred from representing the debtor in possession? Usually not, because 11 U.S.C. 327(c) provides that a professional person is not disqualified for employment by a trustee or debtor in possession solely because the person represented or was employed by a creditor of the debtor, unless a creditor or the U.S. Trustee objects to such employment, in which case the court may disapprove the employment if an actual conflict of interest exists. It would appear, then, that the prior representation of a creditor by the debtor's attorney does not prevent the attorney from representing the debtor in possession unless an objection is filed by a creditor or the U.S. Trustee and an actual conflict of interest is found to exist. See Graham v. Lennington, 74 BR 963 (SD IN, 1987). 11 U.S.C. 327(c), it should be noted, applies only to previous representations of creditors and does not permit an attorney to represent a creditor and the debtor in possession at the same time. See In re Oatka Restaurant and Lounge, Inc., 73 B.R. 84 (WD NY, 1987), and In re Plaza Hotel Corp., 123 BR 466 (BAP 9, 1990), where the court held that an attorney could not simultaneously represent the debtor and its controlling shareholders when the shareholders were being sued on their guarantees of the corporation's debts.

court approval of employment of attorney, requirement of

The approval-of-representation requirement. Even if an attorney is a disinterested person and does not hold or represent an interest that is adverse to the estate, court approval of the attorney's employment must be obtained if the attorney wishes to represent the debtor in possession in its Chapter 11 case. See 11 U.S.C. 327(a). If court approval is not obtained, the attorney may be denied compensation from the estate. See 11 U.S.C. 328(a) and In re THC Financial Corp., 837 F.2d 389 (CA 9, 1988). It should be noted that if the court approves the employment of either a law firm or a named attorney, any partner, member, or regular associate of the attorney's law firm may act as an attorney in the case without further order of the court. See Bankruptcy Rule 2014(b).

staff professionals, use of by debtor in possession

It should be understood that court approval is required only of attorneys and other professionals who are involved in the debtor's reorganization effort. Court approval need not be sought for staff professionals who are involved only in the regular operation of the debtor's business. See In re Pacific Forest Industries, Inc., 95 B.R. 740 (CD CA, 1989). Therefore, if the debtor has professionals on its regular payroll, or under some circumstances, on retainer, court approval need not be obtained in order to retain or replace these persons. See 11 U.S.C. 327(b) and In re Lowry Graphics, Inc., 86 B.R. 74 (SD TX, 1988).

application for approval of employment, requirements

In practice, one of the first tasks of the debtor's attorney is to file with the court and transmit to the U.S. Trustee, on behalf of the debtor in possession, an application requesting court approval of the employment of the attorney by the debtor in possession. The application should set forth the name of the proposed attorney, the reasons for the selection of the attorney, the professional services to be rendered, the compensation arrangements, and the attorney's connections, if any, with the debtor, creditors, or any other parties in interest, or their respective attorneys and accountants, or with the U.S. Trustee or any person employed in the office of the U.S. Trustee. See Bankruptcy Rule 2014(a). If a written employment agreement exists between the debtor and the proposed attorney, a copy of the agreement should be attached to the application. The application should be signed and verified by the proper officers or principals of the debtor.

application for approval of employment, when to file

An application for approval of employment of the attorney should be filed with the petition to open the case, or as soon as possible after the commencement of the case because in the absence of extraordinary circumstances legal services performed for a debtor in possession without prior court authorization are generally not compensable from the estate, even if they were performed in good faith. See In re Land, 943 F.2d 1265 (CA 10, 1991), and In re Offield, 128 BR 548 (WD MO, 1991), where the court approved a late-filed nonc pro tunc application because extraordinary circumstances were found to exist. In many districts the time for filing applications for approval of employment is governed by local rule.

application for approval of employment, service and filing requirements

A copy of the application for approval of employment of attorney should be transmitted to or served upon the U.S. Trustee. See Bankruptcy Rules 2014(a) and 9034. Unless the court or the local rules provide otherwise, it is not necessary to serve a copy of the application on, or to notify, any other party. See Bankruptcy Rule 2014(a). The service requirements for such applications are set forth in the local rules in some districts. In many districts the attorney seeking approval must also prepare the order approving the employment of the attorney. A sample Application For Order Approving Employment of Attorney is set forth in Exhibit 3-A at the end of this chapter.

verified statement of attorney, filing requirements

Bankruptcy Rule 2014(a) requires an application for an order of employment to be accompanied by a verified statement of the person to be employed setting forth the person's connections with the debtor, creditors, any other parties in interest, their respective attorneys and accountants, and the U.S. Trustee or any person employed in the office thereof. The attorney should review the list of creditors to insure that there are no disqualifying "connections" with a creditor. See In re Rusty Jones, Inc., 134 BR 321 (ND IL, 1991). If the attorney intends to share the compensation to be received in the case with any person other than members or regular associates of the attorney's law firm, the details of the sharing arrangement should be set forth in the verified statement. If a separate Section 329(a) disclosure statement is not being filed, the verified statement should also satisfy the fee disclosure requirements of Section 329(a), which are discussed above in this section. In preparing the application and verified statement, it should be remembered that the failure of an attorney to disclose facts giving rise to an actual or potential conflict of interest constitutes grounds for denial of compensation. A sample Verified Statement of Proposed Attorney is set forth in Exhibit 3-B at the end of this chapter.

The approval of compensation requirement. If, as is usually the case, the attorney for the debtor in possession is being compensated with funds from the estate, the attorney must file periodic applications for allowance of interim compensation during the course of the case, as well as an application for allowance of final compensation at the close of the case. Unless more frequent applications are allowed by local rule, an attorney may apply to the court not more than once every 120 days after the order for relief, or more often if the court permits, for compensation for services previously rendered and for reimbursement of expenses incurred. After notice and a hearing, the court may disburse to the applicant the allowable compensation and expenses. See 11 U.S.C. 331. That such compensation and expenses are allowable as an administrative expense in the case, see 11 U.S.C. 503(b)(2).

application for compensation, filing requirements

An application for allowance of compensation, whether interim or final, must set forth a detailed statement of the services rendered, time expended, and expenses incurred by the applicant, as well as a statement of the amount of compensation requested. The application must also list all payments previously made or promised to the applicant for services rendered or to be rendered in any capacity in connection with the case, state the source of all such compensation paid or promised, and indicate whether any compensation previously received has been shared and whether an agreement or understanding exists between the applicant and any other entity for the sharing of such compensation. If any compensation has been or is to be shared, the particulars of the sharing, or of the agreement or understanding therefor, must be set forth in the application, except that sharing arrangements with members or regular associates of the applicant's law firm need not be disclosed. See Bankruptcy Rule 2016(a). It should be noted that the foregoing requirements apply to applications for allowance of compensation for services rendered by an attorney or an accountant even if the application is filed by a creditor or other entity.

application for compensation, preparation requirements

Under 28 U.S.C. 536(a)(3)(A), the U.S. Trustee has the authority to review applications for allowance of compensation in bankruptcy cases. Bankruptcy Rule 2016(a) requires that a copy of each application for allowance of compensation be transmitted to the U.S. Trustee. Consequently, the Executive Office for United States Trustees has adopted guidelines for the preparation and review of applications for allowance of compensation that are applicable to all Chapter 11 cases. These guidelines are set forth in their entirety in the U.S. Trustee website (www.usdoj.gov/ust/guidelines.htm). The requirements of these guidelines should be followed in the preparation of all applications for allowance of compensation. A sample Application for Allowance of Compensation prepared in accordance with these guidelines is set forth in Exhibit 3-D at the end of this chapter.

guidelines for preparation of applications for allowance of compensation

Application for Allowance of Compensation, sample of

An application for allowance of compensation should be filed with the court and a copy transmitted to the U.S. Trustee. See Bankruptcy Rules 2016(a) and 9034. If the application seeks approval of $1,000 or more in compensation and expenses, the clerk, or such other person as the court may direct, must give at least 21 days notice by mail of the hearing on the application to the U.S. Trustee and to all creditors and any committees appointed in the case, unless the court orders that notice need be mailed only to the committees or their authorized agents and to the creditors and equity security holders who serve on the debtor in possession and file with the clerk a request that all notices be mailed to them. See Bankruptcy Rules 2002(a) and 2002(i). The notice must identify the applicant and state the amounts requested. See Bankruptcy Rule 2002(c)(2). The local rules should also be checked for notice requirements related to applications for allowance of compensation.

application for compensation, filing and notice requirements

If no objections to an application for allowance of compensation are filed, a hearing need not be held on the application. If a hearing is held on the application, the applicant should be prepared to present testimony and other evidence in support of the application. It is a good practice to present detailed time records kept in the ordinary course of the applicant's law practice or business to substantiate both the amount of time spent in performing the services and the quality of the services rendered. The documentary standards set forth in the U.S. Trustee Guidelines should be used as a guide in the presentment of evidence. If the application is opposed or if the requested compensation is substantial in amount, it may be advisable to present expert testimony in support of the application. The financial ability of the debtor in possession to pay the requested professional fees should also be established, if necessary, because if there is a question as to whether sufficient assets exist with which to pay the anticipated administrative expenses of the proceeding, the court may refuse to allow the requested fees in the full amount. See In re IML Freight, Inc., 52 B.R. 124 (UT, 1985).

application for compensation, conduct of hearing

attorney's fee, amount of retainer

In practice, most attorneys handling small business Chapter 11 cases collect a retainer at the start of their representation of the debtor. If a retainer is collected, it should be collected prior to the filing of the case (i.e., before the debtor becomes a debtor in possession). The amount of the retainer should be sufficient to cover the estimated value of the legal services to be performed during the early stages of the case. See In re Automend, Inc., 85 BR 173 (ND GA, 1988). An excessive retainer may disqualify the attorney from representing the debtor in possession in the case. See In re Boro Recycling, Inc., 67 B.R. 3 (ED NY, 1986). If the debtor's attorney intends to represent the debtor in possession during the case, the attorney should be compensated in advance for all services rendered prior to the filing of the case. Otherwise, the attorney will be a creditor of the debtor at the time of filing and may be ineligible to represent the debtor in possession. See 11 U.S.C. 327(a) and supra, this section. See In re Viscount Furniture Corp., 133 B.R. 360 (ND MS, 1991), and In re Fitzsimmons Trucking, Inc., 124 B.R. 556 (MN, 1991) for discussions of various types of retainers and the validity thereof in Chapter 11 cases.

professional person, terms of employment

The reasonable amount requirement. A debtor in possession, with the court's approval, may employ a professional person on any reasonable terms and conditions of employment, including on a retainer, on an hourly basis, on a fixed fee or percentage fee basis, or on a contingent fee basis. See 11 U.S.C. 328(a). While an hourly rate is often approved, especially in situations where the scope of legal services is not readily predictable, it is common in many districts for bankruptcy courts to approve an attorney's employment without compensation arrangements other than a reasonable fee as determined by the court upon application therefor. Typically, the attorney's compensation arrangement depends on the requirements and wishes of the debtor in this regard and on the relationship between the debtor and the attorney.

attorney's compensation, revision of by court

Regardless of the terms of employment that may have been agreed to by the parties and approved in advance by the court, the court may allow a different amount of compensation (usually a lesser amount) after the conclusion of the attorney's employment if the original terms and conditions of employment prove to be improvident in light of unanticipated developments. See 11 U.S.C. 328(a). Bankruptcy courts readily invoke this statute to reduce an attorney's compensation in situations where the results achieved by the attorney or the benefits to the estate are not commensurate with the amount of compensation as originally approved. See In re Reimers, 972 F.2d 1127 (CA 9, 1992). Thus, attorneys and other professionals should not expect compensation arrangements approved in advance by the bankruptcy court to be followed in every instance.

reasonableness of attorney's compensation, statutory provisions

The amount of compensation allowed to attorneys and other professionals in Chapter 11 cases is governed by 11 U.S.C. 330(a), which provides that the court may award reasonable compensation for actual necessary services rendered by a professional person. In determining the amount of reasonable compensation to be awarded, the court must consider the nature, the extent, and the value of the services taking into account all relevant factors, including (1) the time spent on the services, (2) the rates charged for the services, (3) the necessity of the services, (4) the reasonableness of the time spent on the services considering the complexity, importance and nature of the issues and problems addressed, (5) whether the attorney is board certified or otherwise has demonstrated skill and experience in the bankruptcy field, and (6) whether the compensation is reasonable based on the customary fees charged by comparably skilled practitioners in nonbankruptcy cases. See 11 U.S.C. 330(a)(3). The court may not allow compensation for unnecessary duplication of services or for services that are either not reasonably likely to benefit the debtor's estate or not necessary to the administration of the case. See 11 U.S.C. 330(a)(4)(A).

reasonable compensation, method of determining

As indicated above, the court may allow only a reasonable amount of compensation to a professional person. Not surprisingly, the courts have adopted various methods of determining the reasonableness of professional compensation. At least seven different methods of computing a reasonable fee have been employed. See In re Hutter Construction Co., 126 BR 1005 (ED WI, 1991) for a list. The most widely-used method is the so-called "lodestar" approach whereby the court determines the number of hours that were reasonably necessary to perform the services rendered, multiplies that number by a reasonable hourly rate, which may be adjusted up or down depending on several factors, including the nature of the services performed, the complexity and difficulty of the issues involved, the results achieved by the services, the ability of the estate to pay, the experience and standing of the applicant, and the time necessarily and actually expended by the applicant. See In re Apex Oil Co., 960 F.2d 728 (CA 8, 1992), In re Pearson, 156 BR 713 (MA, 1993), and In re Borger, 180 BR 326 (SD GA, 1995).

It is a common practice in many districts for a bankruptcy court to reduce interim allowances to attorneys representing debtors in possession (sometimes as much as 50 percent), usually with a proviso that the balance of the awardable compensation will be included in the allowance of final compensation. Such provisos, however, are usually based on a presumption that the debtor will prosper under the plan and have sufficient funds at the close of the case with which to pay the balance of the compensation. Such presumptions, which are not always realistic, are simply the court's method of forcing an attorney to share a portion of the financial risk inherent in a Chapter 11 case.

attorney's fees, allowance of, practical considerations

Whenever an attorney represents a debtor who is considering filing under Chapter 11, a written agreement should be prepared covering the attorney's employment and compensation. Such an agreement may become essential once the Chapter 11 case is filed. In addition to the usual factors of mutual understanding and clarity, a written agreement between the debtor and its attorney may later be of assistance to the court when ruling on the reasonableness of the compensation requested by the attorney, especially if unforeseen matters arise complicating the case and necessitating legal services in excess of those originally contemplated by the parties. Without a written agreement covering all aspects of the attorney's employment and compensation, embarrassing confrontations between the debtor and its attorney are more likely to arise during the course of the case, impairing their working relationship.

written employment agreement, advantages of

An employment agreement between a debtor and its attorney should describe the services to be performed by the attorney, provide for the method, rate, and source of payment, and, if desirable, provide for a guarantee of the attorney's compensation by a third party, often a principal owner of the debtor. If an employment agreement is entered into prior to the commencement of a Chapter 11 case, the agreement may provide for the payment of a retainer by the debtor and a method of billing against the retainer. If the attorney is to represent the debtor in possession after the filing of the case, the desire of the debtor in this regard should be set forth in the agreement, as should the post-filing compensation arrangements. A sample Agreement for Employment of Attorney is set forth in Exhibit 3-C, at the end of this chapter.

attorney's employment agreement, preparation of

3.02 The Chapter 11 Eligibility and Jurisdictional Requirements

Chapter 11 eligibility & jurisdictional requirements, general rules

To file under Chapter 11 a debtor must be eligible for Chapter 11 relief. In addition, the case or proceeding must be filed in a court of proper jurisdiction and venue. Generally, most individuals, corporations, partnerships and limited liability companies are eligible to file under Chapter 11, provided that the case is not filed in bad faith. Jurisdiction for Chapter 11 cases and proceedings lies in the United States District Court, where most such cases and proceedings are referred to the United States Bankruptcy Court in the local district. However, certain non-core bankruptcy proceedings must be heard in the district court unless the parties agree to have the proceeding heard in the bankruptcy court. The venue requirements for Chapter 11 cases are discussed in Section 3.05, infra.

Eligibility requirements.

Chapter 11 eligibility requirements

The Chapter 11 eligibility requirements for debtors may be summarized as follows:

(1) The debtor must be a "person," which includes individuals, partnerships, limited liability companies, and corporations, but does not include governmental units, estates, and nonbusiness trusts.

(2) The debtor may not be a stockbroker, a commodity broker, an insurance company, a bank, a savings institution, a small business investment company licensed by S.B.A., or, in some states, a defunct corporation.

(3) A Chapter 11 case must be filed by the debtor in good faith and not as a means of providing Chapter 11 relief to an ineligible entity or obtaining relief that the Bankruptcy Code was not intended to provide.

(4) If the debtor is an individual, he or she must not have been a debtor in another bankruptcy case that was dismissed under certain conditions within the preceding 180 days.

credit counseling requirement

(5) If the debtor is an individual, he or she must have received an individual or group briefing from an approved nonprofit budget and credit counseling agency within 180 days prior to the filing of the petition that outlined the opportunities for available credit counseling and assisted the debtor in performing a related budget analysis (unless this requirement is not applicable in the local district because the United States trustee has determined that an insufficient number of such agencies are available in the local district). See 11 U.S.C. 109(h).

"person", what constitutes

A "person" under the Bankruptcy Code includes an individual, a partnership, and a corporation, but does not include a governmental unit. See 11 U.S.C. 101(41). That an estate does not constitute a person, see Matter of 299 Jack-Hemp Associates, 20 B.R. 412 (SD NY, 1982). While a business trust is treated as a corporation under the Bankruptcy Code (see 11 U.S.C. 101(9)(A)(v)), a nonbusiness trust does not constitute a person under the Bankruptcy Code. See In re Dalton Lodge Trust No. 35188, 22 B.R. 918 (ND IL, 1982) and In re Cahill, 15 B.R. 639 (ED PA, 1981) for the general proposition and for the criteria used in determining whether a trust is business or nonbusiness.

Chapter 11, ineligible debtors

Only a railroad and a person that may be a debtor under Chapter 7 may be a debtor under Chapter 11, except that neither a stockbroker nor a commodity broker may be a Chapter 11 debtor. See 11 U.S.C. 109(d). Insurance companies, banks, savings banks, cooperative banks, savings and loan associations, building and loan associations, homestead associations, credit unions, and small business investment companies licensed by the Small Business Administration are precluded from filing under Chapter 7 and are therefore not eligible for Chapter 11 relief. See 11 U.S.C. 109(b). Railroad reorganizations, which are covered in subchapter IV of Chapter 11, are not covered in this handbook.

defunct corporations, eligibility under Chapter 11

Corporations whose charters have been revoked by the state for nonpayment of fees or failure to file reports may or may not be eligible for reorganizational relief under Chapter 11, depending upon the status of such corporations under local state law. See In re Vermont Fiberglass, Inc., 38 B.R. 151 (VT, 1984). The best practice, of course, is to reinstate the debtor's charter with the state prior to filing under Chapter 11.

individual debtor, previous title 11 case, effect on eligibility

An individual may not be a debtor under any chapter of the Bankruptcy Code if he or she has been a debtor in a bankruptcy case pending at any time during the preceding 180 days if: (1) the pending case was dismissed by the court for willful failure of the debtor to either abide by an order of the court or appear before the court, or (2) the debtor voluntarily dismissed the pending case following the filing of a request for relief from the automatic stay. See 11 U.S.C. 109(g). While this applies only to individual debtors, serial Chapter 11 filings by corporate or partnership debtors have been dismissed under the good-faith filing requirement described in the paragraphs below. See In re AT of Me., Inc, 56 BR 55 (ME, 1985).

filing of Chapter 11 case, good faith requirement

Good faith requirement. In addition to the statutory Chapter 11 eligibility requirements described above, there exists a judicially-imposed eligibility requirement that the case be filed in good faith and not primarily for purposes other than an effective reorganization. It is clear that a Chapter 11 case that is found to have been filed in bad faith is subject to dismissal for cause under 11 U.S.C. 1112(b). See Trident Assocs. Ltd. Partnership v. Metropolitan Life Ins. Co., 52 F.3d 127 (CA 6, 1995). Perhaps the clearest statement of the law on this subject is found in In re National Land Corp., 825 F.2d 296 (CA 11, 1987), where the court stated that in finding lack of good faith under 11 U.S.C. 1112(b), courts have emphasized the intent of the debtor to abuse judicial process and the reorganization purposes of Chapter 11. Factors indicating such an intent include the following: (1) the lack of a realistic possibility of an effective reorganization of the debtor's business; (2) evidence that the debtor seeks merely to delay or frustrate the legitimate efforts of secured creditors to enforce their rights; (3) evidence that the debtor is seeking to use Chapter 11 to create and organize a new business and not to reorganize or rehabilitate an existing business; (4) the timing of the debtor's relevant actions; (5) evidence that the debtor is merely a shell corporation; and (6) evidence that the debtor was created, or that important property was transferred to the debtor, for the sole purpose of obtaining protection under the automatic stay.

bad faith in filing case, what constitutes

A totality of the circumstances inquiry is required in determining whether a Chapter 11 case was filed in bad faith. See Cardin Corp. v. Miller, 886 F.2d 693 (CA 4, 1989), and March v. Marsch, 36 F.3d 825 (CA 9, 1994). That a Chapter 11 case may be dismissed for cause upon a finding that it was filed with an intent to abuse or misuse the reorganization process, see In re Kerr, 908 F.2d 400 (CA 8, 1990), and In re Humble Place Joint Venture, 936 F.2d 814 (CA 5, 1991). That a Chapter 11 case may be dismissed for cause on a finding that the case was filed primarily to frustrate creditors or prevent foreclosure, see Mac Elvain v. IRS, 180 BR 670 (MD AL, 1995), and In re Midway Invs., 187 BR 382 (SD FL, 1995). That a Chapter 11 case may be dismissed upon a finding that it was filed primarily to thwart collateral litigation in other forums, see In re Namer, 141 BR 603 (ED LA, 1992), and In re HBA East, Inc., 87 BR 248 (ED NY, 1988).

Chapter 11 debtor, financial and size requirements

Aside from the court-imposed requirement of good faith, no financial eligibility requirements are imposed on debtors seeking relief under Chapter 11. A Chapter 11 debtor may be solvent or insolvent, its assets may exceed its liabilities by any amount (or vice versa), and its income may be substantial or nonexistent. There are also no eligibility restrictions on the size of a business filing under Chapter 11. A business may be very large, very small, or anywhere in between. The only financial restrictions are the practical ones of whether the cost of the proceeding to the debtor is justified by the intended reorganizational benefit and whether the debtor has sufficient income or resources to obtain confirmation of a plan. Finally, Chapter 11 is available to an individual debtor who is not engaged in business because the Supreme Court has held that a debtor does not have to be engaged in an ongoing business to be eligible to file under Chapter 11. See Toibb v. Radloff, 501 U.S. 157, 115 L. Ed 2d 145, 111 S. Ct. 2197 (1991).

debtor not engaged in business, eligibility under Chapter 11

bankruptcy case, original jurisdiction

Jurisdictional requirements. Original and exclusive jurisdiction over all bankruptcy cases, including Chapter 11 cases, is vested in the United States districts courts. The district courts also have original, but not exclusive, jurisdiction over all civil proceedings arising under or related to bankruptcy cases. In addition, the district courts have exclusive jurisdiction over the property of the debtor as of the date of the filing of the petition and over property of the debtor's estate, regardless of where the property may be located. See 28 U.S.C. 1334(a),(b),(d). This does not mean that bankruptcy cases must be filed and heard in the district court, however, because district courts are empowered by 28 U.S.C. 157(a) to refer bankruptcy cases to bankruptcy courts. This practice is routinely followed in most districts.

bankruptcy case, referral to bankruptcy judge

bankruptcy case, authority of bankruptcy judge

Once a case is referred to a bankruptcy court, the authority of the bankruptcy court to enter final orders and judgments depends on whether the proceedings in the case are denominated as "core" or "non-core" proceedings. Upon referral from the district court, a bankruptcy court may hear and determine all bankruptcy cases and all core proceedings arising under the Bankruptcy Code or arising in a bankruptcy case, and may enter final orders and judgments in such cases and proceedings. See 28 U.S.C. 157(b)(1).

non-core proceedings, hearing of by bankruptcy judge

The district court, with the consent of all parties to the proceeding, may refer a related non-core proceeding to the bankruptcy court to hear and determine and enter final orders and judgments. See 28 U.S.C. 157(c)(2). Otherwise, a bankruptcy court may hear a non-core proceeding that is related to a bankruptcy case, but must submit proposed findings of fact and conclusions of law in such proceedings to the district court, who shall enter any final order or judgment after reviewing de novo those matters to which any party has timely and specifically objected. See 28 U.S.C. 157(c)(1). In essence, then, a bankruptcy judge sits as a court in core proceedings and in non-core proceedings referred with the consent of the parties under 28 U.S.C. 157(c)(2), and as a magistrate or special master in all other non-core proceedings.

non-core proceedings heard by bankruptcy court, procedure

The procedure in non-core proceedings heard by a bankruptcy court, other than proceedings referred with the consent of the parties under 28 U.S.C. 157(c)(2), is governed by Bankruptcy Rule 9033. In such proceedings, the clerk is required to forthwith mail copies of the bankruptcy court's proposed findings of fact and conclusions of law to all parties. See Bankruptcy Rule 9033(a). A dissatisfied party then has 14 days in which to file objections to specific findings or conclusions, which objections may then be responded to within 14 days by another party. The objecting party must arrange for the transcription of the record. See Bankruptcy Rule 9033(b). The district court may make a de novo review upon the transmitted record, or may take additional evidence in the case. The district court may accept, reject, or modify the proposed findings of fact or conclusions of law of the bankruptcy court, receive further evidence, or recommit the matter to the bankruptcy court with instructions. See Bankruptcy Rule 9033(d).

core proceeding, what constitutes

Generally speaking, a core proceeding is any matter arising under bankruptcy law in a bankruptcy case, while a non-core proceeding is any matter arising under nonbankruptcy law that is at issue in a bankruptcy case only because one of the litigants happens to be a debtor in the bankruptcy case. See Matter of Colorado Energy Supply, Inc., 728 F. 2nd 1283, 1286 (CA 10, 1984). A core proceeding is defined by example in 28 U.S.C. 157(b)(2), which contains a list of 15 types of proceedings that constitute core proceedings. The list is not all-inclusive, however, and proceedings not contained in the list may be core proceedings. Proceedings that do not meet the statutory definition of core proceedings are non-core proceedings.

adversary proceeding, core or non-core, pleading requirements

The bankruptcy court (and not the district court) must determine whether a proceeding is core or non-core. The determination may be made on the motion of a party or on the court's own motion. See 28 U.S.C. 157(b)(3). It appears that a ruling by a bankruptcy court on the issue of whether a proceeding is core or non-core is reviewable only by appeal. See 28 U.S.C. 158(a), and section 4.13, infra. It should be noted that proceedings involving the trial of personal injury tort and wrongful death claims must be heard by the district court. See 28 U.S.C. 157(b)(5).

proceeding, core or non-core, determination of

In an adversary proceeding in the bankruptcy court, the complaint, counterclaim, cross-claim, or third-party complaint must contain a statement that the proceeding is core or non-core, and, if non-core, that the pleader does or does not consent to the entry of final orders or judgment by the bankruptcy court. See Bankruptcy Rule 7008. A responsive pleading must admit or deny an allegation that the pleading is core or non-core. If the response is that the proceeding is non-core, the responsive pleading must include a statement that the party does or does not consent to the entry of final orders or judgment by the bankruptcy court. See Bankruptcy Rule 7012(b).

Once a case or proceeding has been referred to a bankruptcy court by the district court, the district court may withdraw the case or proceeding, in whole or in part, at any time for cause shown, either on the motion of a party or on its own motion. There are no statutory guidelines as to what constitutes cause for the withdrawal of a case or proceeding. In addition, the district court must, upon the timely motion of a party, withdraw a proceeding from the bankruptcy court upon a determination that the resolution of the proceeding requires consideration of both bankruptcy law and other federal laws regulating organizations or activities affecting interstate commerce. See 28 U.S.C. 157(d). The withdrawal of a referred proceeding or case from the bankruptcy court may be initiated by the filing of a motion under Bankruptcy Rule 5011, which governs the procedure in such matters.

bankruptcy case, withdrawal from bankruptcy court

In summary, then, jurisdiction for all bankruptcy cases and proceedings lies in the United States district courts, and bankruptcy courts may hear only such cases and proceedings as are referred to them by the district courts. In most districts virtually all bankruptcy matters are routinely referred by the district court to the bankruptcy court. Because such referrals are not mandated by statute, however, the local practice on the matter may vary and should be ascertained. In addition, a district court may not delegate to the bankruptcy court its jurisdiction over the trial of personal injury and wrongful death claims, or, if a party files a timely objection, over disputes involving questions of both bankruptcy law and other federal laws regulating organizations or activities affecting interstate commerce. See 28 U.S.C. 157(b)(5),(d), and In re Johns-Manville Corp., 45 B.R. 823 (SD NY, 1984).

bankruptcy jurisdiction, a summary

3.03 Gathering Information and Assessing the Case

Chapter 11 cases, types of debtors

Because small business debtors come in all sizes, conditions, forms, and degrees of disarray, small business Chapter 11 cases come in widely varying degrees of complexity. There are few stereotypes. Some cases are relatively simple, with no openly hostile creditors, no significant disputes among the business owners, sufficient cash flow to carry on the business, and only temporary creditor relief and a simple plan of reorganization is needed to get the business back on its feet. In other cases the creditors are on the brink of shutting down the business, the business owners are suing each other, cash flow has slowed to a trickle, and a reorganization plan in the nature of a miracle is needed to save the business. While most small business cases fall in the wide spectrum between these extremes, most are closer to the latter than the former.

Chapter 11 case, preliminary matters

Whatever the type of case, there are certain preliminary matters that must be ascertained and certain initial functions that must be performed if the case is to be handled in a professional manner by the debtor's attorney. These preliminary matters and functions are listed below, and each should be addressed by the debtor's attorney as soon after acceptance of the case as possible.

immediate bankruptcy relief, when needed

(1) Determining whether the debtor is in need of immediate bankruptcy relief. In most cases the key factor in this determination is the immediacy of the threat to the debtor's income or important assets posed by hostile creditors. If foreclosures, attachments, impoundment of funds, repossessions, or other creditor action that may curtail the debtor's income or deprive it of important assets are pending or likely to be carried out in the immediate future, then the debtor is probably in need of immediate bankruptcy relief. Such relief can be obtained only by filing a petition commencing a bankruptcy case, whereupon the debtor immediately receives the protection accorded by the automatic stay. See section 4.01, infra, for further reading on the extent and effect of the automatic stay in Chapter 11 cases.

immediate bankruptcy relief, preliminary matters

If a small business debtor is in need of immediate bankruptcy relief, two preliminary matters should be dealt with before filing a Chapter 11 petition: (1) it should be determined, preliminarily at least, whether Chapter 11 is an appropriate remedy for the debtor; and (2), the information needed to prepare and file the petition and other preliminary documents should be obtained.

Chapter 11, when appropriate for debtor

In emergency filing situations it may not be possible to gather sufficient information upon which to make a final determination on whether Chapter 11 is the best remedy for the debtor. Consequently, a preliminary decision may have to be made. In essence, it must be determined whether it appears to be feasible to reorganize or rehabilitate the debtor so that all or a portion of its business can be saved. If it does not appear to be feasible to save any portion of the debtor's business, it should be decided whether it is in the debtor's interest to carry out an orderly, debtor-controlled liquidation of its assets. If neither of these alternatives appear to be feasible, then Chapter 11 is not an appropriate remedy for the debtor and a Chapter 11 case should not be filed. See infra, this section, for further reading on determining the appropriateness of Chapter 11 for a small business debtor.

emergency bankruptcy relief, filing requirements

In emergency filing situations, the petition is usually filed without the schedules and statements. If the schedules and statements are not filed with the petition, a list containing the names and addresses of all the debtor's creditors, a list of the debtor's 20 largest unsecured creditors, excluding insiders, and such other documents as the local rules may require, must be prepared and filed with the petition. If the debtor is a corporation, partnership, or limited liability company it may be necessary to prepare and file a resolution authorizing the filing of the petition. If the debtor is an individual, a certificate under 11 U.S.C. 109(h)(3) must be filed requesting a temporary waiver of the required prefiling briefing on budget and credit counseling. See section 3.05, infra, for further reading on emergency filing requirements.

(2) Obtaining an understanding of the debtor's business and the reasons for its financial difficulties. Except when immediate bankruptcy relief is needed, the first task of an attorney for a financially-troubled small business debtor is to become familiar with every important aspect of the debtor's business operation. The attorney should become familiar with the debtor's purchasing, marketing, accounting, employment, and management practices, and with every other important function of the debtor's business. Normally this will entail considerably more than a couple of interviews with the principal owners of the business. Personal interviews with key employees or managers, preferably at their place of business, are essential in most cases. Such interviews will not only educate the attorney on the day-to-day business practices of the debtor, but will also acquaint the interviewees with the attorney and may help to dispel their apprehensions about the operation of the business and the payment of their salaries and wages during the pendency of the Chapter 11 case.

debtor's attorney, knowledge of debtor's business, necessity of

In the process of becoming educated on the operation of the debtor's business, an attorney will ordinarily learn much about the causes of its financial difficulties. More information may be required, however, to fully understand the problem. It may be necessary to consult with industry experts, important creditors, financial or tax consultants, former employees, and assorted other persons, especially in cases where conflicts exist as to the cause of the debtor's financial difficulties. In any event, it will usually be necessary to gather detailed financial and factual data related to the business in order to adequately determine the actual causes of its financial problems. See section 2.02, supra, for a list of the specific information that should be obtained by the debtor's attorney.

knowledge of debtor's business, how to obtain

(3) Determining whether Chapter 11 is the appropriate remedy for the debtor. There are several remedies, both bankruptcy and nonbankruptcy, available to financially-troubled small business debtors. These remedies, and the relative appropriateness of each, are discussed at length in sections 2.03, 2.04, and 2.05, supra. Once the debtor's attorney becomes familiar with the debtor's business operation and has investigated the causes underlying the debtor's financial difficulties, a final determination must be made as to whether Chapter 11 is the appropriate remedy for the debtor. Because it is invariably the most expensive and time-consuming of the available remedies, Chapter 11 is usually a remedy of last resort for small businesses debtors.

small business debtor, remedies available

There are several practical matters to consider when determining whether Chapter 11 is an appropriate remedy for a particular small business debtor. One such matter is the nature of the debtor's business. Chapter 11 does not lend itself to certain types of businesses. Businesses, such as construction companies, that require the obtaining of performance or surety bonds, businesses that perform public functions or projects extending over long periods, businesses that require public trust and confidence to survive, businesses that require the advance deposit or payment of money to the debtor for the performance of future services, and businesses in highly competitive fields are examples of businesses for which Chapter 11 may not be appropriate.

appropriateness of Chapter 11, nature of business

Another practical matter to consider is the effect of a Chapter 11 proceeding on the attitude and morale of the debtor's employees, especially key employees. Some employees prefer not to work for an employer that is "in bankruptcy," and are likely to seek other employment if a Chapter 11 case is filed. The attitude of key employees regarding such a filing should be sounded out beforehand, and they should be briefed on how the business will be run under Chapter 11, and on its chances for survival.

appropriateness of Chapter 11, morale of employees

The effect of a Chapter 11 case on the debtor's important creditors and customers should also be considered when making the decision on whether to file. In most instances it will be necessary to contact some or all of the debtor's important creditors and customers to ascertain their probable reaction to such a filing. If several important customers indicate an intention to cease doing business with the debtor if a Chapter 11 case is filed, or if one or more creditors from whom the debtor must obtain important supplies or services indicates an unwillingness to provide the supplies or services on terms affordable to the debtor, then Chapter 11 may not be feasible for the debtor. Even if the attitude of the debtor's important customers and creditors is favorable, it is a good practice to send a letter to them immediately after the filing of a Chapter 11 case in order to reassure them of the debtor's intentions. A sample of such a letter is set forth in Exhibit 3-L at the end of this chapter.

appropriateness of Chapter 11, effect on customers and creditors

appropriateness of Chapter 11, effect of case on business owners

Finally, the possible effects of the filing of a Chapter 11 case on the principal owners of the business should be investigated. If creditors or minority owners perceive fraud, dishonesty, incompetence, or gross mismanagement as a principal cause of the debtor's financial problems, they may seek to have a trustee appointed to assume many of the management functions of the debtor's business. Even if a trustee is not appointed, if either the creditors or the court distrusts those currently managing the debtor's business, it may become necessary for the debtor to institute significant management changes in order to obtain approval or confirmation of a plan of reorganization. Also, if significant preferential or fraudulent transfers have been made to one or more of the principal owners or key employees of the business, the filing of a Chapter 11 case may result in the setting aside of such transfers and repayment by the transferees. See infra, this section for further reading on preferential and fraudulent transfers.

determining affordability of Chapter 11 case

(4) Determining whether the debtor will have sufficient funds with which to pay the expenses of the case and operate its business during the case. It is important to determine whether the debtor can afford the expenses of a Chapter 11 case. In this regard it should be ascertained whether the debtor will have sufficient funds during the several months after the commencement of the case to both maintain its business activities and pay the expenses of a Chapter 11 proceeding. The effect on the debtor of the several-month moratorium on the payment of certain debts that follows the filing of a Chapter 11 case should be considered. Exactly which debts the debtor will have to pay during this period in order to stay in business and which debts will not have to be paid should be ascertained.

expenses of Chapter 11 case, what constitutes

For small business debtors, the principal expenses of a Chapter 11 proceeding are usually attorney and other professional fees, which are discussed below in this section. The anticipated amount of these fees, especially those that will have to be paid during the six-month period after the filing of the case, should be calculated and budgeted. Both the filing fee and the Chapter 11 quarterly fee payable to the U.S. Trustee during the pendency of the case should be taken into account (see section 3.05, infra, for the amount of these fees). The best method of ascertaining whether a Chapter 11 case will be financially feasible for the debtor is to prepare a cash flow analysis for the debtor during this period.

cash collateral, ability of debtor to use during case

Another important matter to be determined is the effect of the case on the debtor's post-filing supply of cash. Especially important here is the debtor's ability to use post-filing income to pay post-filing business and case expenses. The key issue here is the extent to which the debtor's post-filing income will constitute cash collateral under the Bankruptcy Code. To the extent that the debtor's post-filing income does not constitute cash collateral, it may be used by the debtor in the ordinary course of business. See 11 U.S.C. 363(c)(1). However, to the extent that the debtor's post-filing income constitutes cash collateral, it may not be used by the debtor without obtaining either the consent of each creditor secured by the cash collateral or the prior approval of the court. See 11 U.S.C. 363(c)(2). It is important, therefore, to determine the extent to which the debtor's post-filing income will constitute cash collateral and whether it will be feasible for the debtor to use its cash collateral for business purposes.

cash collateral, what constitutes

Cash collateral includes cash and properties such as bank deposits, securities and negotiable instruments that may be readily converted into cash. See 11 U.S.C. 363(a). It should be noted that while items such as accounts receivable, inventory, contract rights, and general intangibles are not cash collateral, they become cash collateral the instant they are converted into cash or the equivalent thereof by the debtor. See section 4.02, infra, for further reading on cash collateral and the use thereof by a Chapter 11 debtor in possession.

Chapter 11 case, professionals needed

(5) Determining how the professionals employed in the case are to be compensated. In many small business Chapter 11 cases the only professional is the debtor's attorney. Much, however, depends on the size and financial structure of the debtor's business and the type of reorganization contemplated. The services of an accountant, financial consultant, stockbroker, tax specialist, appraiser, or other professional may be needed in a particular case. If the creditors' committee retains an attorney or other professional, the expenses thereof may also be charged to the debtor's estate. See 11 U.S.C. 328(a). If either a trustee or an examiner is appointed in the case, their fees and those of any professionals employed thereby may also be assessed against the estate.

While it is impossible to know at the outset exactly what professional services may be needed during the course of a case, a good faith attempt should be made to anticipate the need for such services and the costs thereof. It is also important that a clear understanding exist between the debtor and each professional as to the role to be played in the case by the professional. See section 3.01, supra, for further reading on the employment and compensation of attorneys and other professionals in chapter 11 cases.

role of professionals in Chapter 11 case

The best practice is for the debtor to enter into a written agreement with each professional employed in the case. The agreement should cover such matters as the scope of services to be rendered by the professional, the professional's rate of compensation, the approximate total cost of the professional's services, the source of the funds from which the professional will be paid, the amount of the initial retainer, if any, to be paid to the professional, and the frequency of payments thereafter. In addition, if the professional's compensation is to be guaranteed by a third party, the specifics of the arrangement should be set forth. A sample Agreement for Employment of Attorney is set forth in Exhibit 3-C at the end of this chapter.

agreements with professionals, items to cover

(6) Explaining the Chapter 11 process to the debtor. The principal aspects of the Chapter 11 process must be understood by the owners and managers of a small business debtor in order for them to participate intelligently in the decision-making process and carry out the obligations of the debtor during the Chapter 11 case. First of all, the owners and managers of the business must understand the general legal principles of Chapter 11. Such matters as the effect and extent of the automatic stay, the acceptance or rejection of executory contracts, the handling of cash collateral, the obtaining of credit, the role played in the case by creditors and the court, the necessity of preparing an accurate disclosure statement, and the procedure for obtaining approval and confirmation of a plan must be understood by those who make the important decisions for the debtor. The owners and managers of a business should also understand how insiders are treated under Chapter 11. It may be advisable to make copies of the questions and answers appearing in chapter one of this handbook and distribute them to the owners and key employees of the business. Copies of section 2.01, supra (entitled, Chapter 11 - A General Description), may also be useful in this regard.

Chapter 11 process, understanding of by debtor, importance

Another aspect of Chapter 11 that the owners and managers of a small business debtor must understand is the extent of the rights, duties, and powers of a debtor in possession in a Chapter 11 case. If the debtor's business is to function on anything other than a crisis-to-crisis basis during the pendency of the case, those in charge of carrying out the debtor's day-to-day business activities must understand what can and cannot be done by a debtor in possession under Chapter 11. The owners and managers of the debtor must understand the fiduciary obligations of a debtor in possession. It is a good practice for the debtor's attorney to advise the debtor in writing of the specific responsibilities and obligations of a debtor in possession. A letter from the debtor's attorney explaining in plain language the rights, duties, and powers of a Chapter 11 debtor in possession is an effective method of advising the debtor. The letter should be delivered to the debtor immediately after the court has approved the employment of the attorney by the debtor in possession. A sample Attorney's Letter to Debtor in Possession may be found in Exhibit 3-E at the end of this chapter. See section 4.02, infra, for further reading on the obligations of a Chapter 11 debtor in possession.

debtor, necessity of understanding duties during case

A small business debtor should also understand the reorganizational alternatives available under Chapter 11. Because the owners and managers of the debtor are normally more knowledgeable than the debtor's attorney about the debtor's business operations, they should have considerable input in the formulation of a plan of reorganization. To enable them to formulate a creative and workable plan, however, they must be informed of the reorganizational requirements of Chapter 11. See sections 4.06, 4.08, and 4.09, infra, for further reading on the legal requirements of Chapter 11 plans.

reorganizational alternatives, knowledge of by debtor

preliminary plan, importance of

(7) Devising a preliminary plan of reorganization for the debtor. It is seldom possible to devise a final plan of reorganization until such matters as the attitude of creditors, court rulings on the debtor's rejection of executory contracts, creditors' requests for relief from the automatic stay and for adequate protection, the effect of the filing of the case on the debtor's business, and various other matters have been resolved. However, for purposes of cash flow projections, budgeting, employee and customer confidence, and determining the feasibility of Chapter 11 for the debtor, a preliminary plan of reorganization should be devised very early in the case. If possible, such a plan should be devised before the case is filed. It is important that the preliminary plan not be a farce, and that it be made in good faith. Otherwise, employee and customer confidence in the debtor may later be damaged, and important creditors may claim to have been misled. See section 4.06, infra, for further reading on the preparation of a Chapter 11 plan.

collecting information for case, method

(8) Collecting the information needed to prepare the Chapter 11 forms and documents for filing. The only proven method of gathering all of the information needed to prepare the Chapter 11 forms and documents for filing is to use work sheets or questionnaires that call for all of the required information without repetition or omission. Some attorneys use an extra copy of the Chapter 11 forms for this purpose, while others have devised work sheets of their own. Attorneys without work sheets of their own will find the Chapter 11 Work Sheets appearing in Exhibit 3-F at the end of this chapter useful.

information for case, how to assemble

The forms and documents that must be prepared and filed in a typical small business Chapter 11 case are described in section 3.05, infra. The specific information that must be gathered is listed in the Chapter 11 Work Sheets (Exhibit 3-F) and in the completed Chapter 11 forms and documents found in the exhibits at the end of this chapter. The source of the information needed to prepare the Chapter 11 forms and documents depends greatly on the debtor's size and organizational structure. If the debtor is small with few employees, the debtor's bookkeeper or accountant may provide most of the needed information. In the case of a larger debtor with several departments, it may be necessary to consult with employees in several departments in order to obtain the required information.

avoidable transfers, importance of discovering

(9) Discovering and handling preferential, fraudulent, and other avoidable transfers. It is important to discover all of the debtor's significant avoidable transfers early in the case for two reasons: (1) to determine the personal liability of the transferees (who are usually insiders or important creditors of the debtor) for the return of the funds or property transferred, and (2) to prevent such transfers from later becoming grounds for the appointment of a trustee in the case. Undisclosed preferential or fraudulent transfers, especially to insiders, may be grounds for the appointment of a trustee in the case, especially if the transfers were substantial and were known to and purposely not disclosed by the debtor's owners or management. See In re William H. Vaughan & Co., Inc., 40 B.R. 524 (ED PA, 1984), and section 4.12, infra.

preferential transfer, definition

A preferential transfer is a transfer of an interest by the debtor in property to or for the benefit of a creditor for payment of a debt owed by the debtor prior to the transfer that was made while the debtor was insolvent and within 90 days before the date of filing of the petition and that enables the creditor to receive more than it would have received in a Chapter 7 liquidation of the debtor's estate. The 90-day preferential look-back period is increased to one year for transfers to insiders of the debtor. See 11 U.S.C. 547(b).

insider, definition

In practice, small business debtors frequently make preferential transfers to insiders. If the debtor is a corporation, insiders include officers, directors, and persons in control of the debtor, as well as relatives of officers, directors, and persons in control. If the debtor is a partnership, insiders include general partners and persons in control of the debtor, and relatives of such persons. If the debtor is an individual, insiders include relatives of the debtor, partnerships in which the debtor is a general partner, fellow general partners of the debtor and their relatives, and corporations in which the debtor is an officer, director, or person in control. Regardless of the debtor's form of entity, insiders include affiliates of the debtor, insiders of such affiliates, and managing agents of the debtor. See 11 U.S.C. 101(31) for the statutory definition of "insider."

All significant transfers of funds or property to insiders of the debtor made within the 12-month period prior to filing should be closely scrutinized for preferential avoidability. If it appears that a significant transfer to an insider may be avoidable in bankruptcy, both the debtor and the transferee should be advised. With small business debtors such matters often have an important bearing on whether or when a Chapter 11 case should be filed. The situation may arise where it is in the best interest of the debtor to file the case immediately, while the interest of an insider-transferee is best served by postponing the filing for a few months in order to protect the transfer from avoidability. In such situations the debtor's attorney should be wary of a conflict of interest which may bar the attorney from representing the debtor in possession after the case is filed (see section 3.01, supra). The best practice is for the attorney to fully inform all parties of the situation and its possible ramifications, and request instructions from the debtor's management as to how and when to proceed.

avoidable transfers to insiders, how to handle

All transfers of funds or property by the debtor to anyone within 90 days prior to filing should be examined for preferential avoidability, especially if the transfer was not in the ordinary course of the debtor's business. It often happens with small business debtors that one or more of the principal owners is personally liable for an obligation paid off by a potentially avoidable preferential transfer. It may occasionally be necessary to delay the filing of the case in order to protect such a transfer, in which event the debtor's attorney should be wary of a conflict of interest similar to that described in the preceding paragraph.

preferential transfers, detection

Fraudulent transfers include transfers made with an actual intent to defraud creditors and transfers made for insufficient consideration. The look-back period for fraudulent transfers is 2 years. The Bankruptcy Code defines a fraudulent transfer as a transfer of an interest of the debtor in property or an obligation incurred by the debtor that was made or incurred within 2 years prior to the date of filing of the petition, if the debtor made the transfer or incurred the obligation with actual intent to hinder, delay, or defraud its present or future creditors, or received less than a reasonably equivalent value in exchange for the transfer or obligation, and was insolvent at the time of the transaction or became insolvent, undercapitalized, or unable to pay its debts as a result of the transaction. See 11 U.S.C. 548(a)(1). Transfers of cash or financial instruments by individuals to qualified charitable or religious entities, up to certain limits, are not considered fraudulent. See 11 U.S.C. 548(a)(2). Typical fraudulent transfers in small business Chapter 11 cases include transfers of property or money from the debtor to insiders, companies owned or controlled by insiders, or important creditors of the debtor (especially those to whom insiders are personally liable) for insufficient consideration. Transfers to or for the benefit of an insider under an employment contract are specifically avoidable under section 548(a).

fraudulent transfer, definition, examples

All significant transfers made or obligations incurred by the debtor within two years of the bankruptcy filing date should be examined for avoidability as fraudulent transfers. It is especially important to examine transfers and obligations that were made or incurred outside the ordinary course of the debtor's business. It is important to realistically evaluate the consideration received by the debtor for any such transfer or obligation, especially if the transferee or obligee is an insider. Foreclosure sales occurring within the last two years should also be examined because a foreclosure sale can be a fraudulent transfer if the value of the property received by the creditor exceeded the amount of the creditor's claim. See In re Lindsay, 98 B.R. 983 (SD CA, 1989).

fraudulent transfers, detection of

Other avoidable transfers that should be discovered prior to filing include transfers that may be avoidable under the "strong arm" provisions of 11 U.S.C. 544. Under Section 544(a), any lien, transfer of property or obligation incurred by the debtor is avoidable if the lien, transfer, or obligation could be avoided or set aside under local law by - (a) a creditor that extended credit to the debtor at the time the bankruptcy case was commenced and obtained, with respect to such credit, a judicial lien against the debtor's property, (b) a creditor that extended credit to the debtor at the time the bankruptcy case was commenced and obtained, with respect to such credit, an execution that was returned unsatisfied, or (c) a bona fide purchaser of real property from the debtor at the time the case was commenced who is permitted under local law to perfect the transfer. Under Section 544(a), then, transfers that are avoidable under local law by a judgment creditor or a bona fide purchaser of real estate are avoidable in bankruptcy, whether or not such a creditor or purchaser actually exists. The specific liens, transfers, and obligations that may be avoidable under Section 544(a) depend largely on the law of the local state. Under Section 544(b), transfers that are avoidable by unsecured creditors under local law, such as transfers made by the debtor in violation of state fraudulent conveyance or bulk sales laws, are avoidable in bankruptcy. See In re Landbank Equity Corp., 83 B.R. 362 (ED VA, 1987), and Butler v. Nations Bank, N.A., 58 F.3d 1022 (CA 4, 1995).

transfers avoidable under Section 544

3.04 Preparing the Initial Chapter 11 Forms and Documents

Official Bankruptcy Forms, use of

Bankruptcy Rule 1001 provides that the Rules of Bankruptcy Procedure and Official Bankruptcy Forms shall govern the procedure in bankruptcy cases, whether in the district court or in the bankruptcy court. Bankruptcy Rule 9009 provides that the Official Forms may be used with such alterations as may be appropriate and that the Official Forms may be combined and their contents rearranged to permit economies in their use.

local bankruptcy rules, adoption of

Bankruptcy Rule 9029 permits local courts to adopt rules governing the practice and procedure in bankruptcy cases, provided that the rules are not inconsistent with the Rules of Bankruptcy Procedure and do not prohibit or limit the use of the Official Bankruptcy Forms. Bankruptcy Rule 9029 permits either the local district court or, if authorized by the district court, the local bankruptcy court to make and adopt local rules of practice for bankruptcy cases. Bankruptcy Rule 9029 provides that in cases not provided for by rule, the court may regulate its practice in any manner not inconsistent with either the Rules of Bankruptcy Procedure or the local rules. In many districts the bankruptcy judges have adopted standing orders dealing with aspects of Chapter 11 cases not provided for by statute or rule. Single judge standing orders may not be inconsistent with either the Bankruptcy Rules or the local rules. See Committee Notes to Bankruptcy Rule 9029.

local bankruptcy rules, extent of

Both the Bankruptcy Code and the Rules of Bankruptcy Procedure leave many administrative and procedural aspects of Chapter 11 cases to the discretion of local courts. Consequently, nearly every district in the country has adopted local rules governing various aspects of its practice and procedure. Some courts have adopted only limited local rules and few, if any, local forms, while others have adopted extensive local rules and forms dealing with many aspects of Chapter 11 cases, including the initial filing requirements. In any event, it is important to obtain a copy of the local rules and copies of the local forms prior to preparing and filing a Chapter 11 case.

bankruptcy forms, general preparation requirements

The Rules of Bankruptcy Procedure contain several specific requirements relating to the preparation of forms and documents filed in a bankruptcy case. These requirements must be complied with if the forms and documents are to be properly prepared. When preparing Chapter 11 forms and documents, the following rules should be noted and their requirements complied with:

bankruptcy forms, verification requirements

(1) Bankruptcy Rule 1008 requires all petitions, lists, schedules, statements, and amendments thereto to be verified or to contain an unsworn declaration as provided in 28 U.S.C. 1746. Only the original copy of each document must be verified, however, if the copies are conformed to the original. See Bankruptcy Rule 9011(f). Other documents need not contain an unsworn declaration or be verified unless specifically required by a particular rule. See Bankruptcy Rule 9011(e).

bankruptcy forms, caption requirements

(2) Bankruptcy Rule 9004(b) requires every paper filed in a bankruptcy case to contain a caption setting forth the name of the court, the title of the case, the bankruptcy docket number, and a brief designation of the character of the paper. Bankruptcy Rule 1005 provides that the title of the case includes the debtor's name, the last 4 digits of his or her social security number, any other federal tax identification number, and all other names used by the debtor within the last eight years. A full caption contains all of the information described in the previous two sentences and must conform to Official Form 416A. A full caption is required on the petition and on documents relating to a Chapter 11 plan. The full caption is contained in block form on Official Form 101/201 (the petition). A short title caption conforming to Official Form 416B is required for general use in filing papers in bankruptcy cases. A short title caption containing the name of the court, the name of the debtor, and the case number and chapter, if known, may be used on statements, schedules, notices, motions, applications and other papers where a full caption is not required. Additional names, such as the name under which the debtor conducts business, may be included in the short title caption if necessary or desirable.

bankruptcy forms, signature of attorney, effect of

filing of document by attorney, effect of, sanctions for violations

(3) Bankruptcy Rule 9011(a) provides that every petition, pleading, motion, and other paper filed in a bankruptcy case by a party represented by an attorney, other than a list, schedule, statement, or amendments thereto, must be signed by at least one attorney of record in the attorney's individual name, with the attorney's office address and telephone number stated. An unsigned document will be stricken unless it is promptly signed. Bankruptcy Rule 9011(b) provides that by presenting to the court (whether by signing, filing, submitting, or advocating) a petition, pleading, motion, or other paper, an attorney is certifying that to the best of his or her knowledge, information and believe it is not being presented for an improper purpose, the claims, defenses and other legal contentions therein are not frivolous, the

allegations and other factual contentions have evidentiary support, and the denials of factual contentions are warranted on evidence or by a lack of information. Sanctions may be imposed on attorneys who violate this rule under the procedures set forth in Bankruptcy Rule 9011(c).

The following forms and documents may be needed in the initial stages of a voluntary Chapter 11 case of a typical small business debtor:

Chapter 11 case, forms and documents needed

Voluntary Petition (Official Form 101 for Individuals or Official Form 201 for Non-Individuals))
Schedules A/B through J or J-2 (Official Forms 106A/B through 106J or 106J-2 for Individuals or Official Forms 206A/B through 206J or 206J-2 for Non-Individuals)
Statement of Financial Affairs (Official Form 107 for Individuals or Official Form 207 for Non-Individuals)
Chapter 11 Statement of Your Current Monthly Income (Official Form 122B, if needed)
Your Statement About Your Social Security Numbers (Official Form 121, if needed)
The List of Creditors Who Have the 20 Largest Unsecured Claims Against You Who Are Not Insiders (Official Form 104 for Individuals or Official Form 204 for Non-Individuals)
Application for Order Approving Employment of Attorney
Verified Statement of Proposed Attorney
Preliminary List of Creditors (if necessary)
List of Equity Security Holders (if any exist)
Debtor's Resolution Authorizing Commencement of Case (if required)
Certificate as to Credit Counseling and debt repayment plans, if any (if needed)
Attorney's Letter to Debtor in Possession (if desired)
Debtor's Letter to Creditors and Customers (if desired)
Request for Order that Creditors' Committee Not Be Appointed (if necessary)
Declaration Regarding Electronic Filing (a local form, if needed)
Corporate Ownership Statement (if needed)
Debtor's most recent balance sheet, statement of operations, cash flow statement, and federal income tax return (see 11 U.S.C. 1116(1)).

Chapter 11 forms, where to obtain

In some districts the local rules or practices may require the filing of additional forms or documents. An informational summary sheet on a locally-prescribed form is sometimes required. The local rules should be checked for additional filing requirements in Chapter 11 cases. The required local forms, if any, are usually supplied by either the clerk of the bankruptcy court or the U.S. Trustee, and samples of them are often set forth in the local rules. The official forms can be found on the Argyle Publishing Company Bankruptcy Downloadable Forms. Most of the other forms and documents must be devised by the attorney. The exhibits at the end of this chapter may be used as guides in preparing the forms and documents listed above. The number of copies of each form or document required to be filed is determined by local rule, but usually only one copy of each form is needed because they are scanned immediately upon filing. The preparation of each form and document described above is discussed separately below.

Chapter 11 forms, number of copies to file

voluntary petition, preparation requirements

Voluntary Petition. The Voluntary Petition for Individuals Filing for Bankruptcy, as set forth in Official Form 101, is largely self-explanatory and simple to complete. Same goes for the Voluntary Petition for Non-Individuals Filing For Bankruptcy, which is set forth in Official Form 201. Each of the blanks appearing on the petition should contain a response. If the answer to a particular question or request for information is "none," or if the debtor has no information to provide for a particular box, the word "none" should be typed in the box. Use Exhibit 3-G at the end of this chapter as a guide in preparing this form (Form 201 is used in our example). Exhibit A (Form 201A) to the petition must be completed and attached only if the debtor has issued publicly-traded securities or bonds, which means that most small business debtors are not required to file Exhibit A. The appropriate box should be checked in the "type of debtor" square and the box indicating the debtor to be a small business debtor under 11 U.S.C. 101(51D) should be checked in most cases (see next paragraph).

small business case, definition, filing requirements

Bankruptcy Rule 1020(a) requires the debtor to state in the petition whether the debtor is a small business debtor. If the debtor indicates on the petition that the debtor is a small business debtor, the case shall be treated as a small business case unless and until the court enters an order finding that the debtor's statement is incorrect or until the United States trustee appoints a committee of unsecured creditors that is active in the case. See Bankruptcy Rule 1020(a), (c). The United States trustee or a party in interest has until 30 days after the conclusion of the meeting of creditors to file an objection to the debtor's small business designation. See Bankruptcy Rule 1020(b). To qualify as a small business debtor, the debtor must have noncontingent liquidated secured and nonsecured debts totaling $2,490,925* or less (excluding debts owed to affiliates or insiders) and must not be in the business of owning or operating real estate or activities incidental thereto. See 11 U.S.C. 101(51D). In a small business case the debtor must append to the petition its most recent balance sheet, statement of operations, cash-flow statement, and federal income tax return (or a sworn statement that such documents have not been prepared or filed). See 11 U.S.C. 1116(1). The advantages of being treated as a small business case are the elimination of a creditors' committee and plan and disclosure statement flexibility (see sections 4.06 and 4.07, infra). The disadvantages are increased reporting and deadline requirements (see section 4.02, infra).
* Dollar amount subject to change on April 1, 2016.

voluntary petition, authority to sign

In completing the voluntary petition, it is important to check the proper venue allegation. See section 3.05, infra, for a discussion of venue in Chapter 11 cases. The appropriate box indicating that the debtor intends to file a plan should also be checked. The petition should be signed by the debtor's attorney and by the debtor, or by a principal or chief executive officer thereof. Particularly if the debtor is a corporation, it is important to insure that the person signing the petition has been duly authorized to do so by a resolution of the appropriate corporate body. Either the board of directors or the shareholders may be the appropriate authorizing body, depending on local law and the debtor's articles of incorporation and bylaws. Corporate authorizations are discussed below in this section in connection with debtor's resolution authorizing commencement of the case.

partnership petition, signature and consent requirements

If the debtor is a partnership, the petition should be signed by at least one general partner, and all general partners should consent to the petition. If one or more general partners do not consent to the filing of the petition, the petition is deemed involuntary. See 11 U.S.C. 303(b)(3)(A). It is important, therefore, to obtain the written consent of all general partners to the filing of the petition. The best practice is for all general partners to sign the voluntary petition. If this is not practicable, a partnership resolution authorizing the signing and filing of the petition should be prepared and signed by each general partner. A sample of such a resolution is set forth in Exhibit 3-K at the end of this chapter. See below in this section for further reading on the authority needed to file a voluntary bankruptcy case for a partnership.

computer-generated petition, special rules

Special rules are applicable to the preparation of a computer-generated petition. If a box in the petition contains multiple choices, a computer-generated petition that shows only the choice made is acceptable for filing. All sections of the petition must be shown and completed, however, unless the instructions on the official form of the petition state that the box is applicable only to cases filed under a chapter other than the one selected by the debtor. If the debtor has no information to provide for a particular box, a computer-generated petition should so indicate by inserting the word "none" in the box. For example, if the debtor has no prior bankruptcies to report, the word "none" should appear in the appropriate location on the petition.

schedules of assets and liabilities, preparation of

Schedules A/B through J. Bankruptcy Rule 1007(b)(1) requires the debtor to file, unless the court orders otherwise, schedules of assets and liabilities, a schedule of current income and expenditures, a statement of executory contracts and unexpired leases, and a statement of financial affairs, prepared as prescribed by the appropriate Official Forms (which are Official Forms 106 (for Individuals) or 206 (for Non-Individuals) and 107 (for Individuals) or 207 (for Non-Individuals), respectively). For completed samples of these forms for individuals, see Williamson, The Attorney's Handbook on Consumer Bankruptcy and Chapter 13, Argyle Publishing Co., Exhibits 2-G to 2-Q. Official Forms 106/206 contains the following schedules:

official form 106/206, schedules included in

Schedule A/B - Property
Schedule C - Property Claimed as Exempt (for Individuals only)
Schedule D - Creditors Who Hold Claims Secured by Property
Schedule E/F - Creditors Who Have Unsecured Claims
Schedule G - Executory Contracts and Unexpired Leases
Schedule H - Your Codebtors
Schedule I - Your Income (for Individual Debtor(s) only)
Schedule J - Your Expenditures (for Individual Debtor(s) only)

Individual Chapter 11 debtors must normally complete all of the above schedules. In many districts corporate or partnership debtors are not required to complete Schedules I and J, and the local rules or standing orders should be checked in this regard. In addition, corporate or partnership debtors seldom have exempt property to list in Schedule C. All debtors, individual, corporate, or partnership, must complete schedules of assets and liabilities (i.e., Schedule A/B and Schedules D and E/F, respectively), the schedule of executory contracts and unexpired leases (Schedule G), and the schedule of codebtors (Schedule H).

corporate or partnership debtors, schedules required

The local rules in some districts may require the debtor to take an inventory of its assets for the purpose of accurately completing the schedules of assets and the statement of financial affairs. Bankruptcy Rule 2015(a)(1) contains a similar requirement, if the court so directs. If the court orders the taking of such an inventory, a copy of the inventory must be filed with the court and the U.S. Trustee. See Bankruptcy Rule 2015(a)(1). It should be noted that if the debtor is a partnership, the court may order any general partner of the debtor to file a statement of his or her personal assets and liabilities with the court within such time as the court may fix. See Bankruptcy Rule 1007(g).

inventory by debtor, necessity

If the debtor is an individual residing in a community property state, the debtor's interest in community property must be listed in the appropriate schedule of assets and the community creditors of the debtor and his or her spouse must be listed in the appropriate schedule of liabilities. It may be advisable to inform the debtor that an intentional failure to disclose assets in a bankruptcy case is a federal crime (concealment of assets) punishable by 5 years imprisonment and a $500,000 fine. See 18 U.S.C. 152.

community property, listing requirements

bankruptcy crime, penalty for

Every interest of the debtor in real property, including security interests in realty owned by others, should be listed on Schedule A/B. Both the street address (if any) and the legal description of each parcel of real property should be listed. Included here should be real property owned as a co-tenant or under community property laws, and real property in which the debtor has a life estate or a right or power excisable for the debtor's own benefit. However, real property interests resulting solely from executory contracts or unexpired leases should be listed in Schedule G and not on Schedule A/B. If a non-individual debtor owns no interest in any real property, the word "no" should be checked in Question 54 on Form 206A/B. If the debtor is an individual and a joint petition is being filed or if the debtor is married, indicate by the appropriate check box on Form 106A/B whether the property is owned by the husband, wife, jointly or, in community property states, as community property. The value of the property should be the estimated current market value of the property without regards to any encumbrances or exemptions. Only reduce the value based on the portion owned by the debtor.

Schedule A/B, preparation requirements

All interests of the debtor in personal property should also be listed in Schedule A/B, except interests resulting solely from executory contracts or unexpired leases, which should be listed on Schedule G. In completing Schedule A/B as to personal property, an answer should be indicated for each type of property that a question appears asking about. If the debtor has no property of a particular category, the word "no" should be checked in the appropriate location on the schedule. Property such as accounts receivable, licenses, office equipment, and inventory should be itemized with reasonable particularity (see Schedule A/B in Exhibit 3-J at the end of this chapter for an example).

Schedule A/B, preparation requirements

Schedule A/B, preparation requirements

If additional space is needed to list or describe a particular category of property appearing on the schedule, a separate sheet should be used. The sheet should be identified with the case name, case number (if known), and the schedule and category number and attached to the schedule. If the debtor is an individual and a joint petition is being filed or if the debtor is married, the appropriate box should be checked indicating whether the property is owned by the husband, wife, jointly, or, in community property states, as community property. The value to be shown is the estimated current market value of the property without regards to any encumbrances or exemptions.

Schedule C, preparation requirements

Schedule C is for the claiming of exempt property by the debtor and normally applies only to individual debtors. Corporations, partnerships, and other non-individual debtors are seldom, if ever, entitled to exemptions under federal or state exemption laws. If the debtor is an individual, see Williamson, The Attorney's Handbook on Consumer Bankruptcy and Chapter 13, supra, section 2.07 and 2.08 for further reading on the claiming of exemptions and for lists of exempt property.

schedule of liabilities, importance of

An accurate preparation of Schedules D and E/F is especially important in a Chapter 11 case because the schedules constitute prima facie evidence of the amount and status of each debt listed, except debts that are listed as disputed, contingent, or unliquidated. A proof of claim is deemed filed for each debt listed, except debts that are listed as disputed, contingent, or unliquidated, and a creditor is not required to file a proof of claim to protect its interest unless the creditor is dissatisfied with the amount or status of its claim as listed in the debtor's schedules of liabilities. See 11 U.S.C. 1111(a).

schedules of liabilities, how to list creditors

The schedules of liabilities (Schedules D and E/F) are largely self-explanatory, but may take some time to complete if the debtor has a large number of creditors. Additional or continuation sheets may be used if needed, provided that they are properly identified and attached. The creditors should be listed alphabetically by surname or firm name on each schedule, except Schedule E/F, where they should be listed alphabetically by type of priority claim as indicated on the official form. The local rules should be checked for additional reporting requirements for the schedules of liabilities.

schedules of liabilities, preparation requirements

The names and addresses of all creditors with claims secured in whole or in part by property of the debtor's estate or by a right of setoff should be listed in Schedule D. The names and addresses of all creditors holding claims entitled to priority under the Bankruptcy Code should be listed in Schedule E/F. The names and addresses of all creditors holding unsecured nonpriority claims against the debtor (i.e., creditors holding general unsecured claims) should also be listed in Schedule E/F. In completing the schedules of liabilities, each claim should be listed only once. If a claim is only partly secured or entitled to priority only in part, it should be listed only in Schedule D (if secured) or in Schedule E/F (if priority). However, if the same creditor has more than one claim, each claim should be listed separately on the appropriate schedule. Also, claims resulting from the breach by the debtor of executory contracts or unexpired leases should be listed in the appropriate schedule of liabilities.

correct addresses of creditors, necessity of

A debtor must use reasonable diligence in ascertaining the identity and correct addresses of its creditors. See In re Brown, 27 B.R. 151 (ND OH, 1982). It is important that no creditors be omitted from, and that the correct address of each creditor be listed on, the appropriate schedule, because if a creditor does not receive notice of the proceeding in time to file a proof of claim, its claim may not be dealt with under the plan and will most likely be nondischargeable in the case. See 11 U.S.C. 523(a)(3), and Omni Mfg. v. Smith, 21 F.3d 660 (CA 5, 1994). A creditor whose name and address is correctly listed on the debtor's schedules is presumed to have received timely notice of the case and may not claim nondischargeability under Section 523(a)(3). See L. F. Rothschild & Co. v. Angier, 84 BR 274 (MA, 1988). If a substantial creditor cannot be located, the feasibility of serving notice to the creditor by publication under Bankruptcy Rule 2002(l) should be considered.

If a claim listed on any of the schedules of liabilities is contingent, unliquidated, or disputed by the debtor, an "X" should be placed in the appropriate box on the schedule. A claim is contingent if the debtor's liability is determined by the happening or nonhappening of a future event. A claim is unliquidated if the debtor admits liability but the amount or value of the claim has not been established. A claim is disputed if the debtor has a defense or offset to all or a portion of the creditor's claim. See In re All Media Properties, Inc., 5 B.R. 126 (SD TX, 1980). If the debtor wishes to dispute a claim, it is only necessary to place an "X" in the appropriate box on the schedule; it is not necessary to file a detailed objection or give a statement as to why it is disputed by the debtor. It should be remembered that if a claim is listed as being contingent, unliquidated, or disputed, the creditor must file a proof of claim in order to have its claim allowed.

disputed, contingent, or unliquidated claims, definition of, how to list

It is important to properly identify the property securing each claim listed in Schedule D, but if the description of the property is lengthy, reference may be made to the appropriate schedule of assets for a complete description of the property. The market value of the secured property shown in Schedule D should be the estimated fair market value of the property as of the date of filing without deduction for encumbrances or exemptions against the property. If a creditor holds a claim that is only partially secured by property of the debtor's estate, the claim should be listed in Schedule D, with the estimated value of the security, the amount of the claim, and the estimated amount of the unsecured portion of the claim indicated in the appropriate columns. Such a claim should not be listed in Schedule E/F. A claim that is subject to a right of setoff should be listed as a secured claim in Schedule D, with the amount of the setoff shown as the security. See section 4.04, infra, for further reading on setoffs.

Schedule D, preparation of

All unsecured claims that are or may be entitled to priority of payment must be listed in Schedule E/F under the appropriate question. See section 4.04, infra, for a list of priority claims. The claims should be listed separately by type of priority, and the types of priority claims listed on the schedule should be indicated by checking the appropriate boxes at the beginning of the schedule. Schedule E/F should be completed in substantially the same manner as that described above for Schedule D, except that the amount of the claim entitled to priority should be shown in the specified column. The type of priority for each claim should also be indicated. If the debtor has no unsecured priority debts of any type, the appropriate box at the beginning of the schedule should be checked.

Schedule E/F, preparation requirements

All general unsecured claims should also be listed in Schedule E/F, including unsecured nonpriority claims resulting solely from breaches of executory contracts or unexpired leases (which should also be listed on Schedule G) and unsecured claims of codebtors and persons who have guaranteed or become liable for debts of the debtor. However, claims listed in Schedule D or Schedule E/F that are partially unsecured or partially without priority should not be repeated or duplicated in other areas of Schedule E/F. Accordingly, the unsecured portion of the claim of a partially-secured creditor should not be listed on Schedule E/F if the claim is listed in Schedule D.

Schedule E/F, preparation requirements

The creditors listed in Schedule E/F should be listed alphabetically by surname or firm name to the extent feasible under the appropriate question. If the claim has been assigned, the name and address of the assignee should also be listed in Question 4. If a person other than a spouse in an individual joint case is or may also be liable for a particular debt, an "X" should be typed in the appropriate box If a joint petition is being filed, the appropriate box should be checked to indicate which of the debtors is liable for each claim. If a particular claim is contingent, unliquidated, or disputed, an "X" should be typed in the appropriate box. The exact amount of each creditor's claim should be shown, if possible. If the exact amount cannot be ascertained and an estimated amount is shown, an appropriate notation should be made on the schedule. In showing when the claim was incurred, the month and year is normally sufficient.

Schedule E/F, preparation requirements

Schedule G, preparation requirements

executory contract, definition

All executory contracts or unexpired leases of real or personal property to which the debtor is a party should be included in the schedule of executory contracts (Schedule G). The listing of an executory contract or unexpired lease does not serve as either an acceptance or a rejection of the contract or lease by the debtor. An executory contract is a contract under which the obligations of both the debtor and the other party to the contract are unperformed to some extent. In other words, it is a contract on which performance remains due to some extent on both sides. If one party has completed its performance under the contract, the contract is no longer executory. See section 4.05, infra, for further reading on executory contracts and unexpired leases. If an executory contract or unexpired lease has been breached by the debtor, any existing or potential claims against the debtor resulting therefrom should be listed in the appropriate schedule of liabilities.

Schedule H, preparation requirements

Schedule H should contain the name and address of every person or entity, other than a spouse in a joint individual case, that is or may be liable with the debtor on any debt listed in Schedules D or E/F, including all guarantors. In community property states, a married debtor filing a single petition should include the name and address of the nondebtor spouse on this schedule (all names used by the nondebtor spouse during the last eight years should be listed). If there are no codebtors, the appropriate box should be checked.

Schedules I and J, necessity of filing

As indicated above, the schedules of current income and current expenditures (Schedules I and J) are required to be filed by 11 U.S.C. 521(1) and Bankruptcy Rule 1007(b)(1), unless the court orders otherwise. In most Chapter 11 cases the data provided in this document is of little use and is largely duplicitous. Especially if the debtor is actively engaged in business with many sources of current income and expenditures, the best practice is to file an application with the court requesting an order dispensing with the filing of this schedule. The local rules or standing orders in many districts dispense with the necessity of filing of these schedules in Chapter 11 cases filed by corporate or other nonindividual debtors.

Summary of Schedules, preparation of

Declaration Concerning Schedules, preparation of

When all of the schedules have been completed, the appropriate totals should be transposed to the Summary of Schedules, which, although it must of necessity be prepared last, should constitute the first page of the schedules when they are filed. The schedules that are being filed should be identified in the appropriate column on the Summary of Schedules and the number of sheets for each schedule should be listed in the indicated column. Finally, the Declaration Concerning Debtor's Schedules should be signed by the debtor or by an appropriate representative of the debtor, usually the person who signed the petition.

statement of financial affairs, preparation requirements

Statement of Financial Affairs. Bankruptcy Rule 1007(b) requires the debtor to file a statement of financial affairs unless the court orders otherwise. Official Form 107 (for Individuals) or 207 (for Non-Individuals) must be used for the statement of financial affairs. The questions appearing on the statement are largely self explanatory and should be answered completely. If additional space is needed to fully answer a question, a separate sheet may be used, provided that it is properly identified and attached to the statement. The signature of the debtor, or that of a principal or officer of the debtor if the debtor is not an individual, is required on the last page of the statement.

list of creditors holding 20 largest unsecured claims, preparation requirements

List of Creditors Holding 20 Largest Unsecured Claims. Use Exhibit 3-H at the end of this chapter as a guide in preparing this document. Bankruptcy Rule 1007(d) requires the filing of this list with the petition in all voluntary Chapter 11 cases, using Official Form 104 (for Individual Debtors) or 204 (for Non-Individual Debtors). This list must contain the names, addresses, and claims of the creditors holding the 20 largest unsecured claims against the debtor, excluding insiders. See 11 U.S.C. 101(31) and section 3.03, supra, for the definition of an insider. If there are fewer than 20 unsecured claims, the holders of all unsecured claims should be listed and the list appropriately noted. Undersecured creditors should be included on this list if the estimated amount of the unsecured portion of the claim renders the creditor one of the 20 largest unsecured creditors. Official Form 104/204 is self explanatory and relatively simple to complete. The unsecured creditors' committee is normally appointed from this list, if one is appointed in the case.

Application for Order Approving Employment of Attorney. Use Exhibit 3-A at the end of this chapter as a guide in preparing this document. See section 3.01, supra, for further reading on the requirements for and the preparation of this document. application for employment of attorney, preparation of

Verified Statement of Proposed Attorney. Use Exhibit 3-B at the end of this chapter as a guide in preparing this document. See section 3.01, supra, for further reading on the requirements for and the preparation of this document. verified statement of attorney, preparation of

Preliminary List of Creditors. This document will be needed only if the debtor's schedules of liabilities are not filed with the voluntary petition. See Bankruptcy Rule 1007(a)(1) and section 3.05, infra. This document must list the name and address of each creditor of the debtor; secured, unsecured, and priority. Use Exhibit 3-I at the end of this chapter as a guide in preparing this document. list of creditors, preparation of

List of Equity Security Holders. Use Exhibit 3-J at the end of this chapter as a guide in preparing this document. Bankruptcy Rule 1007(a)(3) requires the filing of this document within 14 days after the order for relief in all Chapter 11 reorganization cases, unless the court orders otherwise. This document should list the name and address of each holder of an equity security in the debtor. If there is more than one class or type of equity security holder, the holders should be listed by class or type. The number, percentage, and type or class of equity security held by each holder should be shown. If the debtor is a corporation, this document should show the number of shares held by each shareholder, the percentage of the total issued and outstanding stock of the debtor held by each shareholder, and the type or class of stock held by each shareholder (i.e., common stock, preferred stock, etc.). An equity security includes stock of a corporation, limited partnership interests, and the right to purchase, sell, or subscribe to either. See 11 U.S.C. 101(16),(17). If the debtor is an individual or a general partnership or other entity with no equity security holders, a statement that no equity security holders exist should be filed or appended to another document. list of equity security holders, preparation of

Debtor's Resolution Authorizing Commencement of Case. This document is required by local rule or standing order in many districts if the debtor is a corporation. It may also be required if the debtor is a partnership and one or more of the general partners does not sign the voluntary petition. The local rules should be checked in this regard. If the debtor is a partnership and it is not practicable for all of the general partners to sign the voluntary petition, this document should be prepared and executed by each general partner, even if the local rules do not so require. If the debtor is a limited liability company, the resolution should be executed by the company's manager or managers unless either the local LLC statute, the articles of organization, or the operating agreement requires membership approval, in which case the resolution should be ratified and signed by the members. If the debtor is an individual, this document is not required. Use Exhibit 3-K at the end of this chapter as a guide in preparing this document. resolution authorizing filing of case, execution of

If the debtor is a corporation, it is important that the authorizing resolution be issued by the appropriate corporate body. The court may dismiss a voluntary Chapter 11 petition filed by a corporation if the filing of the petition has not been properly authorized by the appropriate corporate body. See In re King Brand Food Products, Inc., 52 B.R. 109 (SD FL, 1985). The authority required to file a voluntary bankruptcy case for a corporation is determined by nonbankruptcy (i.e., state) law. See Price v. Gurney, 324 U.S. 100, 89 L. Ed. 776 (1945). Therefore, the corporation laws of the state of incorporation, the debtor's articles of incorporation and bylaws, and any applicable shareholders' agreements should be checked for relevant provisions dealing with this issue. corporate resolution authorizing filing of case, by whom issued

If the debtor is a partnership, the authority necessary to file a voluntary bankruptcy case is determined by nonbankruptcy (i.e., state) law. See Jolly v. Pittore, 170 B.R. 793 (SD NY, 1994). The Bankruptcy Code contains no provision specifying the manner in which a partnership commences a voluntary bankruptcy case, which means that state law governs the issue. The safest practice is for all of the general partners to sign a partnership resolution authorizing the filing of the Chapter 11 case. See Exhibit 3-K at the end of this chapter for sample resolution. partnership authorization to file case corporate resolution, by whom issued

If the debtor is a corporation the board of directors is the normally appropriate body to issue the authorizing resolution, unless the articles of incorporation, the bylaws, or a binding shareholders' agreement provide otherwise. If the debtor's articles of incorporation, bylaws, or a shareholders' agreement so provide, the authorizing resolution may have to be issued by the debtor's shareholders, and approved by the percentage of shareholders called for in the applicable article, bylaw, or agreement. In states having specialized close corporation laws, the chief corporate officer may have the authority to authorize the filing of a Chapter 11 case. To avoid confusion, the authorizing resolution should designate the corporate officer or officers who are to sign the petition and other bankruptcy documents.

attorney's letter to debtor in possession, preparation of

Attorney's Letter to Debtor in Possession. Use Exhibit 3-E at the end of this chapter as a guide in preparing this letter. This letter does not have to filed with the court and is not required by any statute or rule. It is recommended in most Chapter 11 cases, however, as a matter of good practice. The purpose of the letter is to advise the debtor of its duties and obligations as a debtor in possession once the case has been filed. See section 3.03, supra, for further reading on this document.

other required documents, preparation of

Debtor's Letter to Creditors and Customers. Use Exhibit 3-L at the end of this chapter as a guide in preparing this document. This letter does not have to be filed with the court and is not required by any statute or rule. It is recommended, however, as a matter of good practice, especially in cases where it is important that the debtor maintain good relations with creditors and customers after the filing of the case. The letter notifies the recipients of the filing of the case and advises them of the debtor's intentions. See section 3.03, supra, for further reading on this document.

other required documents, preparation of

Other Documents. The Statement of Social Security Number is required by Bankruptcy Rule 1007(f) if the debtor is an individual, in which case it must be filed with the petition. The form (Official Form 121) is self-explanatory and simple to complete. The Statement of Current Monthly Income is required by Bankruptcy Rule 1007(b)(5), but only for individual debtors. The form (Official Form 122B) is self-explanatory and simple to complete. Most of the information needed for this form is on Schedule I. The Declaration Regarding Electronic Filing is a local form that is required in most districts if the petition or any documents in the case are being filed electronically. The form can be downloaded from the website of the local bankruptcy court in most districts. This form is also self-explanatory and simple to complete. Bankruptcy Rules 1007(a)(1) and 7007.1 provide that if the debtor is a corporation, the debtor shall file with the petition a corporate ownership statement that identifies any corporation, other than a governmental unit, that directly or indirectly owns 10% or more of any class of the corporation's equity interests or states that there are no entities to report under this subdivision. This statement must be prepared by the debtor's attorney as there are no official forms for it. The certificate as to credit counseling is a local form that is needed only for individual chapter 11 debtors. It must be completed by the credit counseling agency.

amendments to bankruptcy forms, preparation of

amendments to schedule of liabilities or list of creditors, fee

Amendments. A voluntary petition, list, schedule, statement of financial affairs, or statement of executory contracts may be amended by the debtor as a matter of course at any time before the case is closed. See Bankruptcy Rule 1009(a). The debtor is required to give notice of an amendment to the trustee, if one is serving, and to any entity affected by the amendment. The clerk is responsible for sending copies of amendments to the U.S. Trustee. See Bankruptcy Rule 1009(a), (c). On the motion of a party in interest and after notice and a hearing, the court may order a voluntary petition, list, schedule, or statement to be amended and the clerk shall give notice of the amendment to the entities designated by the court. See Bankruptcy Rule 1009(a). An amended document or form must be verified or contain an unsworn declaration if such was required on the original document. See Bankruptcy Rule 1008. The fee for amending a schedule of liabilities or list of creditors after the notice to creditors has been sent is $30 for each amendment, provided that the court may, for good cause, waive the charge. See P.L. 103-21, Title IV, §406(a), 107 Stat. 1165 (also in notes to 28 U.S.C. 1930). No fee is charged for other amendments. The local rules should be checked for provisions dealing with amendments.

3.05 Filing a Voluntary Chapter 11 Case

A voluntary Chapter 11 case is commenced by filing a voluntary petition in the proper district seeking relief for the debtor under Chapter 11 of the Bankruptcy Code. If a bankruptcy clerk has been appointed for the district, the petition should be filed with the bankruptcy clerk. Otherwise, the petition should be filed with the clerk of the United States district court. See Bankruptcy Rules 1002 and 9001.

voluntary petition, where to file

Bankruptcy Rule 1007(c) provides that the schedules and statements must be filed with the petition in a voluntary case, or, if the petition is accompanied by a list of the names and addresses of all of the debtor's creditors, within 14 days thereafter. The List of Creditors Holding 20 Largest Unsecured Claims must be filed with the petition. See Bankruptcy Rule 1007(d). The number of copies of any form or document required to be filed in a bankruptcy case is governed by local rule, but only one copy of each document is normally required for scanning if the case is not being filed electronically. However, the local rules should be checked in this regard.

schedules & statements, when to file

bankruptcy forms, number of copies to file

Venue Requirements. A Chapter 11 case should be filed in a district in which the domicile, residence, principal place of business, or principal assets of the debtor have been located for the 180-day period immediately prior to the commencement of the case. If the domicile, residence, principal place of business, or principal assets of a debtor have been located in more than one district during the 180-day period, the proper venue is in the district in which the debtor's domicile, residence, principal place of business, or principal assets has been located for the longest portion of such 180-day period. See 28 U.S.C. 1408(1).

voluntary petition, venue requirements

The district in which there is pending a bankruptcy case involving an affiliate, general partner, or partnership of the debtor is also a proper venue. See 28 U.S.C. 1408(2). An affiliate includes an entity that owns 20 percent or more of the debtor's stock, a corporation 20 percent or more of whose stock is owned or controlled by the debtor, a person whose business is leased or operated by the debtor, and an entity that operates the debtor's business. See 11 U.S.C. 101(2). It is not uncommon in Chapter 11 cases for venue to lie in more than one district.

venue, affiliates and partners

If a Chapter 11 case is filed in an improper district, the court may, upon the timely filing of a motion by a party in interest and after a hearing on notice, either transfer the case to a district of proper venue or dismiss the case, whichever the court determines is more convenient for the parties or in the interest of justice. See 28 U.S.C. 1406, 1412 and Bankruptcy Rule 1014(a)(2). Even if a case is filed in a proper district, the court may, upon the timely motion of a party in interest and after notice and a hearing, transfer the case to another district if such a transfer if found to be in the interest of justice or for the convenience of the parties. See Bankruptcy Rule 1014(a)(1). If two or more cases are filed in different districts by or against the same debtor, or by or against a partnership and one or more of its general partners, or two or more general partners, or a debtor and an affiliate, on a motion filed in the district in which the petition first filed is pending, and after a hearing on notice, the court may determine which case or cases shall proceed. Unless otherwise ordered by the court in the district in which the petition first filed is pending, the proceedings in the other courts are stayed until a venue determination is made. See Bankruptcy Rule 1014(b).

improper venue, consequences, procedure

two or more cases, same debtor, procedure

Even though 28 U.S.C. 1412 specifically uses the term "district court" when referring to the transfer of cases, it appears that bankruptcy courts have the authority to rule and enter final orders on motions for change of venue. See In re Thomasson, 60 B.R. 629 (MD TN, 1986), In re Eleven Oaks Tower, Ltd. Partnership, 59 B.R. 626 (ND IL, 1986), and In re Leonard, 55 B.R. 106 (DC, 1985). The reason given for such authority is that venue matters concern the administration of an estate and are therefore core proceedings under 28 U.S.C. 157(b). Motions for change of venue, therefore, should be filed with the bankruptcy court, if the case has been referred to the bankruptcy court by the district court. Finally, it should be understood that venue is not jurisdictional in bankruptcy cases and that if a party fails to raise a timely objection to venue, the objection may be deemed to have been waived. See In re Potts, 724 F. 2nd 47 (CA 6, 1984), and Advisory Committee Notes to Bankruptcy Rule 1014.

motion for change of venue, where to file

objection to venue, waiver of

Chapter 11 case, filing fee

Chapter 11 fees. The filing fee for any Chapter 11 case except a railroad reorganization case is $1,167 plus a $550 administrative fee, for a total filing fee of $1,717.00. See 28 U.S.C. 1930(a)(3). The fee must be paid when the petition is filed, normally by the debtor's attorney as the clerk is not likely to accept the debtor's check. If the case is filed electronically, the filing fee will be charged against a previously approved credit card filed in the clerk's office by the debtor's attorney, unless the filing fee is to be paid in installments (which is rare in Chapter 11 cases). Some districts require the completion of a simple form or questionnaire when the case is filed, reciting such matters as the name and address of the debtor and its attorney.

Chapter 11 filing fee, payment in installments

While it is legally permissible for an individual chapter 11 debtor to file an application to pay the filing fee in installments when the case is filed, it is seldom practicable to do so for two reasons: (1) if the debtor cannot afford to pay the filing fee it may be difficult to convince the court and creditors that he or she will be able to successfully reorganize under Chapter 11, and (2) no payments can be made to the debtor's attorney in connection with the case until the filing fee has been paid in full, and few attorneys will handle a Chapter 11 case on such a basis. See 28 U.S.C. 1930(a) and Bankruptcy Rule 1006(b).

Chapter 11 case, quarterly fee

It should be noted that in addition to the filing fee paid to the clerk, a Chapter 11 debtor must pay a quarterly fee to the U.S. Trustee for each quarter, or fraction thereof, that the case is pending until a plan is closed, the case is dismissed, or the case is converted to another chapter. See 28 U.S.C. 1930(a)(6). The fee is payable to the U.S. Trustee on the last day of the calendar month following the calendar quarter for which the fee is owed. The Chapter 11 quarterly fees are set forth in the following chart:

Total Amount of Disbursements in Quarter	Quarterly Fee
Less than $15,000	$325
$15,000 to $74,999.99	$650
$75,000 to $149,999.99	$975
$150,000 to $224, 999.99	$1,625
$225,000 to $299,999.99	$1,950
$300,000 to $999,999.99	$4,875
$1,000,000 to $1,999,999.99	$6,500
$2,000,000 to $2,999,999.99	$9,750
$3,000,000 to $4,999,999.99	$10,400
$5,000,000 to $14,999,999.99	$13,000
$15,000,000 to $29,999,999.99	$20,000
$30,000,000 or more	$30,000

Documents to file. If a Chapter 11 case is not being filed on an emergency basis, the following forms and documents should be filed with the voluntary petition:

Chapter 11 case, documents to file with petition

Schedules A/B through J, or such schedules as may be required in the case
Statement of Financial Affairs
List of Creditors Holding 20 Largest Unsecured Claims
List of Equity Security Holders (if any exist)
Debtor's Resolution Authorizing Commencement of Case (if required locally)
Statement of Current Monthly Income (if debtor is an individual)
Statement of Social Security Number (if debtor is an individual)
Certificate as to Credit Counseling and debt repayment plan (if debtor is an individual)
Corporate Ownership Statement (if debtor is a corporation)
Declaration Regarding Electronic Filing (if case is filed electronically)
Debtor's most recent balance sheet, statement of operations, cash flow statement, and federal income tax return (see 11 U.S.C. 1116(1)).

debtor's attorney, documents to file

See section 3.04, supra, for instructions on the preparation of the forms and documents listed above. If the debtor's attorney intends to represent the debtor in possession during the case, an Application for Order Approving Employment of Attorney should be filed either with the petition or shortly thereafter. A Verified Statement of Proposed Attorney should be filed with the application. See section 3.01, supra, for further reading on the necessity for and the preparation of these documents.

If a debtor is in need of emergency bankruptcy relief, it may be necessary to file the case before all of the forms and documents described above can be prepared. In such instance, the voluntary petition may be filed accompanied only by a preliminary list of creditors, a list of creditors holding the 20 largest unsecured claims, a resolution of the debtor authorizing the commencement of the case (if required locally), and any other locally-required forms or documents. If the debtor is an individual a certificate as to credit counseling or a certification under 11 U.S.C. 109(h)(3) that the required could not be obtained, a statement of Current Monthly Income, and a Statement of Social Security Number must also be filed.

emergency filing of Chapter 11 case, documents to file

Time and notice requirements. If the schedules and statements are not filed with the petition, they must be filed within 14 days thereafter. See Bankruptcy Rule 1007(c). A list of the debtor's interest holders must also be filed within 14 days after the filing of the petition, unless otherwise ordered by the court. See Bankruptcy Rule 1007(a)(3). If the debtor holds an equity interest of 20% or more in any other entities, the debtor should file Form 26 (Periodic Report Regarding Value, Operations and Profitability of Entities in Which the Debtor's Estate Holds a Substantial or Controlling Interest) either with the petition or at least seven days prior to the date set for the meeting of creditors. Any further extension of time for the filing of the schedules, statements, or lists may be granted by the court only on motion for cause after a hearing on notice. See Bankruptcy Rules 1007(a)(4) and 1007(c). However, in a small business case the schedules and statement must be filed within 30 days after the order for relief, absent extraordinary and compelling circumstances. See 11 U.S.C. 1116(3).

bankruptcy forms, filing deadlines

bankruptcy forms, extension of time for filing

It should be noted that if the debtor in a voluntary Chapter 11 case fails to file, within 14 days after the filing of the petition or within such additional time as the court may allow, the required schedules, statements and lists, the court, on the request of the U.S. Trustee, may dismiss the case or convert the case to a case under Chapter 7, whichever is in the best interests of creditors and the estate. See 11 U.S.C. 1112(e). Dismissal or conversion under Section 1112(e) may be ordered only after notice and hearing. See Bankruptcy Rule 1017(d). This provision conflicts with the 30 days allowed small business debtors under 11 U.S.C. 1116(3).

dismissal or conversion of case for nonfiling of schedules

The clerk, or some other person as the court may direct, must give the debtor, all creditors and equity security holders, and any indenture trustees notice by mail of the order for relief. See Bankruptcy Rules 2002(d),(f). The filing of a voluntary Chapter 11 petition constitutes an order for relief under Chapter 11. See 11 U.S.C. 301, 302. In most districts these notices are sent by the clerk of the bankruptcy court, but in some districts it may be the responsibility of the debtor and its attorney. The local rules should be consulted to ascertain the practice of the local court on the sending of such notices.

order for relief, what constitutes, notice requirement

If it is necessary to deliver immediate notice of the commencement of the case to a creditor or other party, either a certified copy of the filed petition or a certificate of commencement of case signed by the clerk (if available locally) should be obtained and served on the appropriate party. In this regard, it is a good practice to obtain a few certified copies of the filed petition from the clerk's office when the case is filed and to promptly deliver at least one copy thereof to the debtor.

notice of case, how to deliver

Electronic Case Filing. The Administrative Office of the United States Courts has established an electronic case file and management system for the U.S. Bankruptcy Courts. Under this system case files are maintained in an electronic format rather than in a paper format as in the past. This means that all court documents (with only limited exceptions for items such as bulky exhibits) must be either filed electronically or converted to an electronic format immediately upon filing via the electronic scanning of filed paper documents. To implement this system the bankruptcy court in each district has established a website through which bankruptcy documents may be filed electronically over the internet. This electronic case file and management system may be used by attorneys who have been given a password that will enable them to access the system. To obtain a password an attorney must complete a training session to acquaint the attorney with the electronic case file and management system. To file a bankruptcy case electronically, an attorney must have an approved credit card on file in the clerk's office and the filing fee will be charged to the attorney's credit card. In most districts an attorney who files a case electronically must file a written declaration with the court stating that the case has been filed electronically.

electronic case filing, general requirements

UNITED STATES BANKRUPTCY COURT
NORTHERN DISTRICT OF INDIANA

IN RE	HARDTIMES SUPPLY CO., INC.,	)	
	an Indiana Corporation,	)	Case No. ______________
		)	
	Debtor	)	Chapter 11

APPLICATION FOR ORDER APPROVING EMPLOYMENT OF ATTORNEY

Hardtimes Supply Co., Inc., the Debtor, applies to the Court for an order authorizing the employment of Leo E. Lawnoer of Reddy, Willing & Able as attorney for the Debtor in this Chapter 11 case.

In support of this application, the Debtor shows and represents as follows:

1. On January 5, 2016 the Debtor filed a voluntary petition for relief under Chapter 11 of the Bankruptcy Code. The Debtor has remained in possession of its assets and is now operating its business as a debtor in possession.

2. The Debtor has retained Leo E. Lawnoer, attorney at law, and the law firm of Reddy, Willing & Able to represent it in carrying out its duties under the Bankruptcy Code.

3. The Debtor proposes to employ the attorney for the following purposes;

a. to represent the Debtor in this Chapter 11 case and to advise the Debtor as to its rights, duties and powers as a debtor in possession;

b. to prepare and file all necessary statements, schedules, and other documents and to negotiate and prepare one or more plans of reorganization for the Debtor;

c. to represent the Debtor at all hearings, meetings of creditors, conferences, trials, and other proceedings in this case; and

d. to perform such other legal services as may be necessary in connection with this case.

4. The Debtor has made careful and diligent inquiry and is satisfied that the attorney is qualified and competent to represent the Debtor in this case for the following reasons:

a. the attorney has represented the Debtor previously and is familiar with the Debtor's business operations and financial affairs;

b. the attorney has prepared and filed the petition and related documents initiating this Chapter 11 case; and

c. the attorney is admitted to practice before this court, and is experienced in bankruptcy practice and Chapter 11 proceedings.

5. The Debtor has entered into a written employment agreement with the attorney dated January 3, 2016 with respect to the services to be performed by the attorney and the compensation to be paid to the attorney. A copy of the agreement is attached to this application and the Debtor proposes to compensate the attorney as provided in the agreement, subject to the approval of the court after the rendering of such services.

6. The Debtor is informed and believes that the attorney has no connection with the Debtor, creditors, or any other party in interest, or their respective attorneys or accountants, except that the attorney has represented the Debtor previously, is acquainted with the Debtor's management, and is familiar with the Debtor's business operations and financial affairs. The Debtor is informed and believes that the attorney does not hold or represent an interest adverse to the estate with respect to the matters on which they are employed, and that the employment of the attorney is in the best interest of the estate.

7. The appointment of a trustee has not been requested in this case and notice of this application need be given only to the United States trustee for this district and a hearing need not be held on this application unless promptly requested by the United States trustee.

WHEREFORE, the Debtor respectfully requests this honorable court to enter an order approving the employment of Leo E. Lawnoer and the law firm of Reddy, Willing & Able as attorneys for the Debtor in this case.

Dated: January 10, 2016

Hardtimes Supply Co., Inc., The Applicant

by ______________________________
Joseph P. Jones, President

Approved:

Reddy, Willing & Able

by __________________________

Leo E. Lawnoer
Attorneys for Debtor
1000 First Street
Gary, IN 46407
Telephone: 219-272-1100

UNITED STATES BANKRUPTCY COURT
NORTHERN DISTRICT OF INDIANA

IN RE HARDTIMES SUPPLY CO., INC.,	)		
an Indiana Corporation,	)	Case No. ______________	
	)		
Debtor	)	Chapter 11	

VERIFIED STATEMENT OF ATTORNEY

Pursuant to 11 U.S.C. 329(a) and Bankruptcy Rules 2014(a) and 2016(b), Leo E. Lawnoer (the Attorney), on behalf of himself and the law firm of Reddy, Willing & Able (the Firm), being of lawful age, states and declares under penalty of perjury as follows:

1. The Attorney is admitted to practice law in the State of Indiana and before the United States District Court for the Northern District of Indiana, and is a partner in the Firm at the address shown below.

2. Both the Attorney and the Firm are disinterested persons, as that term is defined in the Bankruptcy Code, and do not hold or represent an interest adverse to the estate with respect to the matter on which we are to be employed.

3. The Firm has entered into a written agreement dated January 5, 2016 with Hardtimes Supply Co., Inc., the Debtor, regarding the services to be performed for the Debtor in connection with this case and the compensation to be paid for such services. A copy of this agreement is attached to the Debtor's Application For Order Approving Employment of Attorney that has been filed with the court. Pursuant to this agreement, the Debtor paid the Firm a retainer of $10,000 on January 5, 2016. The agreement has been guaranteed by John J. Jones and Sarah S. Smith, the principal shareholders of the Debtor.

4. Neither the Attorney nor the Firm have shared or agreed to share any portion of the compensation paid or to be paid in connection with this case with any other persons except members or associates of the Firm.

5. To the best of my knowledge, the Firm (including the Attorney) has the following connections with the Debtor, its creditors, other parties in interest, their respective attorneys and accountants, the United States Trustee, and persons employed in the office of the United States Trustee:

The Debtor. The Firm has represented the Debtor for approximately one year on general business matters, the defense of a foreclosure proceeding filed by Big Bank of Boston, N.A., and the initiation of this Chapter 11 case. All fees owed by the Debtor to the Firm for such representation have been paid or forgiven and the Firm is not a creditor of the Debtor.

The Creditors of the Debtor. The Firm represented Happy Home Builders, Inc., a creditor of the Debtor, for a period that ended approximately 2 years ago on matters that are unrelated to this case. Conflicts of interest waivers signed by the Debtor and by Happy Home Builders, Inc. are attached to this statement. The Firm does not consider its previous representation of Happy Home Builders, Inc. to be an actual conflict of interest.

Other Parties in Interest. The Firm has represented John J. Jones, a principal owner of the Debtor, on personal matters for approximately 10 years. Because the interests of Mr. Jones and the Debtor are substantially the same with respect to matters related to this case, the Firm does not consider its representation of Mr. Jones to constitute an actual conflict of interest. Mr. Jones has personally guaranteed the payment of the Firm's compensation for services rendered in this case.

Attorneys and Accountants. The Firm has no connections with the attorneys or accountants of any party in interest.

United States Trustee. The Firm has no connections with the United States Trustee or any person employed in the office of the United States Trustee.

6. Both the Attorney and the Firm understand that there is a continuing duty to disclose any adverse interest that may arise or be discovered during the course of this case.

Dated: January 10, 2016

Reddy, Willing & Able

by ____________________________________

Leo E. Lawnoer
Attorneys for Debtor
1000 First Street
Gary, IN 46407
Telephone: 219-222-1100

Subscribed and sworn to before me this ___________ day of ______________, 2016 by Leo E. Lawnoer.

____
Notary Public

AGREEMENT FOR EMPLOYMENT OF ATTORNEY

Hardtimes Supply Co., Inc., an Indiana corporation (hereinafter, the client), and Leo E. Lawnoer, attorney at law and the law firm of Reddy, Willing & Able (hereinafter collectively, the attorney), agree as follows:

1. The client hereby employs the attorney to represent, advise, and perform legal services for the client on matters related to any reorganization, workout agreement, bankruptcy proceeding, or similar transaction contemplated or entered into by the client, including the filing of a voluntary petition under Chapter 11 of the United States Bankruptcy Code.

2. The services to be performed by the attorney under this contract include the following:

a. Provide legal advice to and representation for the client with respect to any reorganization, workout agreement, bankruptcy proceeding, or other agreement or transaction proposed or entered into by the client.

b. Prepare any instruments, agreements, pleadings, or other documents necessary to effectuate any reorganization, workout agreement, bankruptcy proceeding, or other agreement or transaction proposed or entered into by the client.

c. Represent the client in any action, proceeding, trial, conference, meeting, hearing, negotiation, or other proceeding or transaction in which the client is or becomes involved as a result of any reorganization, workout agreement, bankruptcy proceeding, or other agreement or transaction proposed or entered into by the client.

d. Should the client file a voluntary petition under Chapter 11 of the United States Bankruptcy Code, the attorney shall, with the assistance and cooperation of the client and its agents and employees, perform the following services:

A. prepare and file on behalf of the client all petitions, schedules, statements, plans, and other documents or pleadings;

B. attend and represent the client at all meetings of creditors, hearings, trials, conferences, negotiations, and other proceedings, whether in or out of court;

C. provide legal advice to the client as to the rights, duties, and powers of the client as a Chapter 11 debtor in possession, and as to other matters arising in or related to the Chapter 11 case, including the formulation, presentation and confirmation of a plan of reorganization; and

D. otherwise assist, advise, and represent the client on matters related to the Chapter 11 case as requested by the client.

3. The client agrees to reimburse the attorney for all necessary expenses incurred by the attorney in the performance of services under this contract and to compensate the attorney for services performed under this contract as follows:

a. $250 per hour for time spent in court;

b. $225 per hour for other time spent by the attorney; and

c. $60 per hour for paralegal time spent by paralegals employed by the attorney.

4. The client agrees to pay the attorney, within two days after the date of this contract, a retainer of $10,000 for services performed or to be performed under this contract. The attorney shall apply the retainer toward the first $10,000 of services rendered or expenses incurred under this contract. Thereafter, the attorney shall bill the client on or about the final day of each month for services performed and expenses incurred under this contract during that

month. The client shall promptly pay such bills from its general funds, except that if a bankruptcy case is filed, such bills shall not be paid unless allowed by the bankruptcy court.

5. The attorney warrants that the attorney is knowledgeable in the fields of law to be dealt with in the performance of this contract; that the attorney is experienced in bankruptcy practice and Chapter 11 reorganization proceedings; that the attorney has no connection with the client, the client's creditors, any other party in interest, their respective attorneys and accountants, the United States trustee, or any person employed in the office of the United States trustee that would preclude the attorney from representing the client as a debtor in possession in a Chapter 11 case; and that the attorney does not hold or represent an interest that would be adverse to the interest of the client's estate in a chapter 11 case.

6. The parties agree that the attorney may retain other attorneys as consultants on matters related to this contract, and the client agrees to compensate these attorneys for services rendered on the client's behalf at the rates set forth in paragraph 3 of this contract, provided that no services shall be performed by any other attorney without the prior written consent of the client to the employment of the other attorney.

7. The attorney agrees to fully account for all attorney and paralegal time performed under this contract and to permit the client to periodically review the work performed under this contract and the records thereof maintained by the attorney.

8. Either party may terminate this contract at any time, subject to the approval of the bankruptcy court, if necessary.

IN WITNESS WHEREOF, the parties have executed this contract on the 3rd day of January, 2016 in Gary, Indiana.

Reddy, Willing & Able
Attorneys at Law

by ______________________________
Leo E. Lawnoer
1000 First Street
Gary, Indiana 46407

Hardtimes Supply Co., Inc.

by ______________________________
Joseph P. Jones, President
4455 West 39th Avenue
Gary, Indiana 46404

GUARANTY

The undersigned, being the principal shareholders of Hardtimes Supply Co., Inc., an Illinois corporation, in consideration of the benefits to be received by reason of the performance of the above agreement and to induce Leo E. Lawnoer and the law firm of Reddy, Willing & Able, to enter into the said agreement, hereby do personally guaranty to Leo E. Lawnoer and the law firm of Reddy, Willing & Able the payment of all funds due or to become due under the above Agreement For Employment of Attorney.

Dated: January 3, 2016

____
John J. Jones

____
Sarah S. Smith

UNITED STATES BANKRUPTCY COURT
NORTHERN DISTRICT OF INDIANA

IN RE	HARDTIMES SUPPLY CO., INC.,	)	
	an Indiana Corporation,	)	Case No. ______________
		)	
	Debtor	)	Chapter 11

FIRST APPLICATION FOR ALLOWANCE OF INTERIM COMPENSATION AND EXPENSES

Reddy, Willing & Able, the Applicant, hereby applies to the court pursuant to 11 U.S.C. 330, 331, and 503(b), and Rule 2016 of the Federal Rules of Bankruptcy Procedure for the allowance of compensation for services rendered and reimbursement of expenses as attorney for the Debtor. In support of this application the following is shown:

Background Information.

1. The voluntary petition initiating this case was filed on January 5, 2016.

2. The order approving the employment of the attorney was entered on January 20, 2016. The services for which interim compensation is sought were rendered on behalf of the Debtor as a debtor in possession. Compensation is being sought as an allowable administrative expense of the estate under 11 U.S.C. 503(b).

3. The terms of employment are compensation at the hourly rates set forth in the Fee Agreement dated January 5, 2016, a copy of which was filed with the court on January 10, 2016. A retainer of $10,000.00 was paid to the Applicant on January 1, 2016, all of which was earned prior to the filing of the petition. No caps or limitations have been imposed on any fees or charges payable to the applicant in this case.

4. The professionals and paraprofessionals requesting fees in this application and their respective hourly rates are:

Leo E. Lawnoer, attorney	$250 per hour for court time $225 per hour for other time
Mary E. Poppins, paralegal	$60 per hour

The hourly rates shown above are those specified in the Fee Agreement of January 5, 2016. The rates customarily charged by the applicant to nonbankruptcy clients for similar services are the same as those set forth above.

5. This is the applicant's first application for interim compensation. The amount of interim compensation previously paid to the applicant since the filing of this case is none.

6. The time period of the services and expenses covered by this application is from January 10, 2016 to May 1, 2016. The total amount of compensation sought by this application is $6,990.00. Copies of the firm's billing statements are attached hereto.

Case Status.

1. The amount of cash presently on deposit and available to the estate is $35,770.40, of which $26,780.00 is unencumbered.

2. The following administrative expenses are presently accrued and unpaid:

   State sales taxes - $1,227.75
   Wages and salaries - $6,788.40

3. A plan of reorganization has been prepared and filed by the applicant on behalf of the Debtor. A disclosure statement has also been prepared and filed on behalf of the debtor. All quarterly fees have been paid to the United States Trustee and all monthly operating reports have been filed.

Project Summaries. Not required by concurrence of the United States Trustee because of the size of the case.

Evaluation Standards. The application has performed the services set forth in Exhibit A to this application at the times shown in Exhibit A at the hourly rates specified on Exhibit A. Exhibit A contains a chronological itemization of the time and services performed by each involved agent or employee of the applicant for the period covered by this application. The listings on Exhibit A are not itemized by project. A Summary Sheet summarizing the services performed by the applicant is attached as Exhibit B.

Expenses. The expenses for which reimbursement is sought in this application are itemized on Exhibit A to this application. The total amount of expenses for which reimbursement is sought is $214.77.

Certification. The application certifies that the Debtor has received a copy of this application, has reviewed the application, and has approved the application. The applicant also certifies that the expenses for which reimbursement is sought were actually incurred and paid by the applicant.

WHEREFORE, the applicant requests that interim compensation and expense reimbursement in the combined amount of $7,204.77 be allowed to the applicant under Sections 331 and 503(b) of the Bankruptcy Code.

Dated: May 9, 2016

Reddy, Willing & Able, Applicant

by ______________________________

Leo E. Lawnoer
Attorneys for Debtor
1000 First Street
Gary, Indiana 46407
Telephone: 219-222-1100

CERTIFICATE OF TRANSMITTAL TO UNITED STATES TRUSTEE

The undersigned certifies under penalty of perjury that he or she has on the date shown below, by first class mail addressed to the entity's local address of record, transmitted a true copy of this document and the attachments thereto to the United States Trustee and all other interested parties.

Date: ________________________ ________________________

(Attorney's Letter to Debtor in Possession)

Joseph P. Jones, President
Hardtimes Supply Co., Inc.
4455 West 39th Avenue
P.O. Box 2227
Gary, Indiana 46404

[DATE]

RE: Bankruptcy Case No. 15-00017, Chapter 11 Reorganization of Hardtimes Supply Co., Inc.
Instructions and Guidelines for Debtor in Possession

Dear Mr. Jones:

Hardtimes Supply Co., Inc. is a debtor in possession in the Chapter 11 case that I recently filed on its behalf in the United States Bankruptcy Court for the Northern District of Indiana. There are certain duties and obligations in the operation of a business by a debtor in possession of which you and your employees should be aware. The purpose of this letter is to inform you of these duties and obligations. To that end, this letter should serve as a general guideline for you and your employees in the management and operation of your business as a debtor in possession during the course of the Chapter 11 case.

In a voluntary Chapter 11 case such as yours, the party filing the case is referred to as the debtor. Upon the filing of a voluntary Chapter 11 case, the debtor automatically becomes a debtor in possession unless the court orders otherwise. Accordingly, Hardtimes Supply Co., Inc. is now a debtor in possession in its Chapter 11 case. A debtor in possession has most of the legal rights, duties, and powers of a trustee in bankruptcy. This means that until a plan is confirmed, Hardtimes Supply Co., Inc. is deemed to be holding its property and conducting its business primarily for the benefit of its creditors. A debtor in possession must abide by the rules and standards of Chapter 11 and by the orders of the bankruptcy court. A failure to abide by these rules, standards, and orders may result in the appointment of a trustee to manage the debtor's business and property, a court order converting the Chapter 11 case to a Chapter 7 liquidation case, or a court dismissing the Chapter 11 case. It is important, therefore, that Hardtimes Supply Co., Inc., perform its duties and obligations as a debtor in possession in a manner acceptable to the bankruptcy court.

Hardtimes Supply Co., Inc. should open new bank accounts and start new bookkeeping records as of the date the Chapter 11 case was filed. There should be a general operating bank account, a separate bank account for the employees' withholding and trust fund taxes, and a separate bank account for any other taxes (including sales taxes) that are being collected. Each bank account should be named or identified as follows: "Hardtimes Supply Co., Inc., as Debtor in Possession in Bankruptcy Case no. ____________." Also, such items as insurance policies, supply contracts, and utility service accounts should be changed to show the debtor in possession as the owner or responsible party.

As a Chapter 11 debtor in possession, Hardtimes Supply Co., Inc. may incur unsecured debt and obtain unsecured credit in the ordinary course of business without court approval. Any other debt or credit should not be obtained without first obtaining the approval of the bankruptcy court. This means that goods, services and supplies normally obtained in the ordinary course of operating the business may be purchased on unsecured credit if that is the customary method. If other credit is needed, prior court approval must be obtained. As far as possible, the business should be operated on a cash basis. All goods and supplies should be paid for within 30 days of purchase.

In the payment of debts, it is extremely important to separate the debts incurred prior to the filing of the case from those incurred after the filing of the case. Debts incurred prior to filing should not be paid, as they are to be paid under the Chapter 11 plan later in the case. Debts incurred in the ordinary course of business after the date of filing may be paid as they become due, provided that sufficient funds are available, adequate records are kept, and payment thereof is approved by the bankruptcy court. If it becomes necessary to pay a particular prefiling debt, prior court approval must be obtained.

A debtor in possession must abide by certain rules in using, leasing, or selling its property. The first rule is that cash collateral may not be used, leased or sold unless each creditor secured by the cash collateral consents to the proposed use, lease, or sale, or unless the bankruptcy court approves the proposed use, lease, or sale. Cash collateral is cash or property easily converted into cash. Bank accounts, checks, securities, and bank drafts are examples of cash collateral. Unless the court orders otherwise (which it has not done in this case), property other than cash collateral owned by the debtor in possession may be used, leased, or sold in the ordinary course of business without court approval. Property owned by the debtor in possession may be used, leased, or sold other than in the ordinary course of business only after notice to any affected creditors and a court hearing. Thus, you may use or sell inventory and trade goods in the normal course of operating your business, but other property should not be used, sold or leased without prior court approval.

In general, you may continue to operate the business as you have in the past, subject to the restrictions described above. For example, you may hire whatever employees you deem necessary at the wage or salary of your choice. You may charge whatever price for your products or services that you deem appropriate. You may contract for goods and supplies in the ordinary course of business at whatever price you may deem to be appropriate. However, before doing anything that might be deemed outside the ordinary course of business (such as opening a new place of business), it may be necessary to obtain court approval. Also, your salary and the salary of any other owner-employee may have to be approved before it is paid.

A Chapter 11 debtor in possession is required to file monthly operating reports with the United States Trustee. These reports must be filed on forms provided by the United States Trustee, copies of which will be provided to you. These reports should be prepared and forwarded to the United States Trustee no later than 21 days after the last day of the preceding month. Generally, these reports are self-explanatory and can be prepared from the company's bookkeeping records. To be safe, however, the first set of these reports should be forwarded to me for approval before they are filed with the United States Trustee.

This letter is only a general guide as to the operation of a business by a debtor in possession. If questions arise that are not covered or answered by this letter, please contact me. I suggest that you photocopy this letter and distribute it to any employees whose activities may be affected by the filing of your Chapter 11 case.

Yours truly,

____

Leo E. Lawnoer
Attorney at Law

CHAPTER 11 WORK SHEETS

GENERAL INFORMATION: The questions in these work sheets should be answered by or on behalf of the debtor. In these work sheets, the debtor is the entity for whom a Chapter 11 bankruptcy case is being filed. The DEBT FORM referred to below is located on the last page of these work sheets.

INSTRUCTIONS: Answer each question completely and truthfully. If more space is needed to completely answer a question, complete the answer on a separate sheet of paper or on the back of the work sheet. If you do not understand a question write "Don't Understand" after the question. Do not guess at the answer to any question. The value listed for any item should be the estimated present market value of the item without regard to any lien, mortgage, encumbrance or exemption. If a joint case is being filed, a separate set of these work sheets should be completed by each spouse.

ADVISEMENT TO DEBTOR: Official Bankruptcy Forms will be completed using the information given in these work sheets and the debtor, or an officer thereof, will be required to sign a declaration stating under penalty of perjury that the information is true and correct. A failure to disclose assets in a bankruptcy case is a federal crime punishable by imprisonment for up to five years and by a fine of up to $500,000. In addition, if the bankruptcy forms do not contain complete and accurate information, the case may be dismissed or converted to Chapter 7 by the bankruptcy court.

Preliminary Information

1. List the name of the person or persons completing these work sheets ____________________

____

2. List the date or dates upon which these work sheets were completed. ____________________

Petition Information

3. List the debtor's full name. ____________________

4. What other names has the debtor used during the last 8 years (include married or maiden names, trade names, and names under which the debtor has conducted business)? ____________________

____

5. What is the debtor's social security or tax identification number? ____________________

6. What is the debtor's street address? ____________________
   no. & street city state zip code

7. In what county is the debtor's residence or principal place of business located? ____________________

8. What is the debtor's mailing address? ____________________

9. Where are the debtor's principal business assets located? ____________________

10. Where has the debtor resided or been domiciled for the last 180 days? ____________________

11. Is there a bankruptcy case pending involving one or more of the debtor's general partners or a partnership of the debtor? __________ If so, in what district is the case pending? ____________________

12. Is there a bankruptcy case now pending filed by the spouse, a partner, or an affiliate of the debtor? __________

    If so, attach papers showing the particulars of the case and list the following information about the pending case:
    Name of debtor ____________________
    Case number, district and judge ____________________ Date case filed __________
    Relationship of debtor in pending case with debtor in this case ____________________

13. Has the debtor issued publicly-traded equity securities or debt instruments? ____________________
    If so, list the types of instruments that were issued and the dates of issuance. ____________________

____

Schedule A/B Information - Property (Real Estate)

14. Does the debtor own or have an interest in any real estate? ____________

15. If the answer to question 14 is yes, complete the following showing each parcel of real estate that the debtor owns or has an interest in:

Address of property	Legal description of property	Nature of debtor's interest in the property	Date property acquired	Estimated market value of property	Amount of each mortgage or lien against property

Schedule A/B Information - Property (Personal Property)

16. How much cash will the debtor have on hand when this case is filed? $__________________

17. Does the debtor have any accounts, deposits, or shares in any bank or financial institution? ____________________ If so, complete the following for each account, deposit or share:

Name and address of of financial institution	Name or names under which the account, deposit or shares are registered	Amount of deposit or account, or value of shares

18. Does the debtor have any security deposits with a landlord, telephone company, utility company, or anyone else?____________ If so, list the amount of each deposit and the name and address of the holder of each deposit. ___

____

19. Does the debtor own any household goods or furnishings, including audio, video, or computer equipment? ________________ If so, using a separate sheet or the back of this sheet, list each item or group of items and show the location and estimated market value of each. State the total market value of all of these items. $_________________

20. Does the debtor own any books, pictures, art objects, antiques, stamp, coin, record, tape, compact disc, or other collections or collectibles? __________________________ If so, describe each item and list its location and estimated market value. ____

____

____

21. Does the debtor own any wearing apparel? $____________ If so, using a separate sheet or the back of this sheet, list each item of wearing apparel that has a market value of $20 or more. Include such items as watches and similar articles that are not made of gold or silver or set with gems.

22. Does the debtor own any furs or jewelry? ____________ If so, identify each item and list its location and market value. ____________

____

23. Does the debtor own any firearms, sports equipment, photographic equipment, or other hobby equipment? ________ If so, identify each item and list its location and estimated market value. ____________

____

24. Does the debtor own an interest in a life insurance policy? ____________ If so, identify each policy by policy number, owner, name of insurance company, amount of death benefit, and name of beneficiaries, and list the cash surrender or refund value of each policy. ____________

____

25. Does the debtor own or have an interest in an annuity? ____________ If so, identify each annuity by number, owner, and issuer and list the value and terms of each annuity. ____________

____

26. Does the debtor have an interest in an IRA, ERISA, Keogh, or other retirement, pension, or profit-sharing plan or in an education IRA or state tuition plan? ____________ If so, identify each plan or account and list the amount of the debtor's interest in each plan. ____________

27. Does the debtor own any stock in a corporation or an interest in any partnership, joint venture, or other business? ____________ If so, describe the stock or interest and list its estimated market value. ____________

____

28. Does the debtor own any government or corporate bonds or similar instruments? ____________ If so, describe each instrument and list its location, and market value. ____________

29. Does the debtor own any accounts receivable? ____________ If so, describe them and list their estimated value. ____

____

30. Is the debtor owed any accrued and unpaid alimony, maintenance, support, or property settlement payments? ____________ If so, how much is owed, by whom is it owed, and what is the nature of the obligation? $ ____________ ____________

31. Is the debtor owed any liquidated debts, including tax refunds? ____________ If so, identify each debt, state the amount owed, and list the name and address of the entity that owes it. ____________

____

____

32. Does the debtor own or have an equitable or future interest in any property? ____________ If so, describe each interest and list its present market value. ____________

____

33. Does the debtor own or have an interest of any kind in the estate of a deceased person, in a death benefit plan, in the death benefits in a life insurance policy, or in a trust? ________ If so, describe each interest and list its present market value.

____

34. Does the debtor have any contingent or unliquidated claims of any nature, including tax refunds, counterclaims, or rights of setoff? ____________ If so, describe each claim, identify its owners, and estimate its present value.

____

____

35. Does the debtor own or have an interest in any patents, copyrights, or other intellectual property? ________________ If so, describe each interest and list its value. ________________

36. Does the debtor own or have an interest in any license, franchise, or other general intangibles? ________________ If so, describe each interest and list its estimated market value. ________________

36a. Does the debtor own or possess any customer lists or other compilations containing personally identifiable information that were provided to the debtor in connection with the sale of personal or household products or services? ________ If so describe each list or compilation. ________________

37. Does the debtor own or have an interest in any automobiles, trucks, trailers, or other vehicles or accessories? ________ If so, describe each vehicle or accessory and list its location, vehicle identification number, if any, and estimated market value. ________________

38. Does the debtor own or have an interest in any boats, motors, or accessories? ____________ If so, describe each item and list its location and market value. ________________

39. Does the debtor own or have an interest in any aircraft or accessories? ____________ If so, identify each item and list its location and market value. ________________

40. Does the debtor own any office equipment, office furnishings, or office supplies? ____________ If so, using a separate sheet or the back of this sheet, list each item or group of items and show the location and market value of each. The total market value of these items is $____________.

41. Does the debtor own or have an interest in any machinery, fixtures, equipment, or supplies used in business? ____________ If so, using a separate sheet or the back of this sheet, list each item or group of items and show the location and market value of each. The total market value of these items is $____________.

42. Does the debtor own in any inventory? ____________ If so, describe the inventory and list its location and market value. ________________

43. Does the debtor own or have an interest in any animals? ________________ If so, describe each animal or group of animals and list their location and market value. ________________

44. Does the debtor own or have an interest in any growing or harvested crops? ____________ If so, describe the crops and list their market value. ________________

45. Does the debtor own or have an interest in any farming equipment or implements? ____________ If so, using a separate sheet or the back of this work sheet, describe each item and list its location and market value.

46. Does the debtor own any farm supplies, chemicals, or feed? ____________ If so, describe each item or group of items and list their market value. ________________

47. Does the debtor own or have an interest in any other personal property of any kind that has not been listed above in these work sheets? ____________ If so, describe the property and list its location and market value. ________________

Schedule D Information - Secured Debts

48. Complete a separate DEBT FORM for each debt owed by the debtor that is secured by a mortgage or other lien on property of the debtor. When a DEBT FORM has been completed for each secured or partially secured debt, complete the following: The total number of all secured or partially secured debts owed by the debtor is __________. The total amount of these debts is $__________.

Schedule E/F Information - Unsecured Debts (Priority)

49. Does the debtor owe any debts to employees for wages, salaries, or commissions, including vacation, severance, or sick leave pay? _____________ If so, complete a DEBT FORM for each such debt listing the name and address of each employee, the amount owed to each employee and the date that the wages, etc. were earned. The total number of these debts is _____________. The total amount of these debts is $_____________.

50. Does the debtor owe any debts for unpaid employer's contributions to employee benefit plans? __________________ If so, complete a DEBT FORM for each such debt identifying the employees and the plan and listing the amount owed and the dates that the services were rendered for the unpaid contributions. The total number of these debts is _____________. The total amount of these debts is $_____________.

51. Does the debtor operate a grain storage facility or a fish produce storage or processing facility? __________________ If so complete a DEBT FORM for each debt incurred in the operation of such a facility.

52. Does the debtor owe any debts for the return of deposits made for the purchase, lease, or rental of property or services that were not provided? __________ If so, complete a DEBT FORM for each debt of this kind. The total number of these debts is _____________. The total amount of these debts is $_____________.

53. Does the debtor owe any debts for alimony, maintenance or support? __________ If so, complete a DEBT FORM for each debt of this kind. The total number of these debts is __________ . The total amount of these debts is $__________ .

54. Does the debtor owe any debts to any local, state, or federal governmental entity for taxes, customs, duties, or penalties? _____________ If so, complete a DEBT FORM for each debt showing the governmental agency or department to whom the debt is owed and the date that the debt first became due. The total number of these debts is _____________. The total amount of these debts is $_____________.

55. Does the debtor have a commitment to the FDIC or other insuror to maintain the capitol of a federally insured bank or savings institution? __________ If so, explain: ____

Schedule E/F Information - Unsecured Debts (Without Priority)

56. Complete a separate DEBT FORM for each debt owned by the debtor that is not secured by property of the debtor and is not entitled to priority. When a DEBT FORM has been completed for each unsecured nonpriority debt, complete the following: The total number of all unsecured, nonpriority debts owed by the debtor is _____________. The total amount of these debts is $_____________.

Schedule G Information - Executory Contracts and Unexpired Leases

57. Is the debtor a party to any executory contract or unexpired lease? _____________ If so, describe each such contract or lease and list the name and address of all parties to each contract or lease. Attach a copy of each contract or lease, if possible. ____

____

____

Schedule H Information - Codebtors

58. Is anyone beside the debtor liable for any of the debtor's debts? _______________ If so, the name and address of codebtor should appear in item 5 of the DEBT FORM filled out for that debt. List the name and address of each codebtor.____

____

Statement of Financial Affairs Information

59. How much gross income has the debtor received from the debtor's business in this calendar* year? $____________

60. How much gross income did the debtor receive from the debtor's business during each of the last two calendar* years? Last year: $____________ Year before: $____________

* If the debtor operates the its business on a fiscal year other than the calendar year, substitute fiscal year for calendar year and identify the fiscal year.

61. How much income has the debtor received from sources other than the debtor's business during the last two years? $ ____________ What were the sources of this income?

62. Complete the following showing each creditor to whom the debtor has paid more than $600 in the last 90 days.

Name of creditor	Address of creditor	Dates of payment	Aggregate amount paid in last 90 days	Amount still owing

63. Complete the following showing all payments made by the debtor within the last 365 days to or for the benefit of creditors who were or are insiders.

Name and address of creditor	Relationship of creditor to debtor	Date(s) of payment(s)	Total amount paid	Amount still owing

64. Complete the following showing all lawsuits to which the debtor has been a party during the last 365 days.

Name of case and case number	Nature of case	Court	Status or disposition of case

65. Complete the following describing all money or property of the debtor that has been attached, garnished or seized under any legal or equitable process within the last 365 days.

Name and address of creditor	Date of seizure	Description of property seized	Value of property

66. Complete the following showing all property owned by the debtor that within the last 365 days has been repossessed by a creditor, foreclosed upon, or otherwise returned to the seller.

Name and address of creditor or seller	Date of repossession, foreclosure or return	Description of property	Value of property

67. Has the debtor made an assignment for the benefit of creditors within the last 120 days? ____________ If so, attach copies of all papers related to the assignment.

68. Has any of the debtor's property been held by a custodian, receiver, or other court-appointed official during the last 365 days? ____________ If so, attach copies of all papers related to the proceeding.

69. Complete the following showing all gifts or charitable contributions made by the debtor within the last 365 days, except ordinary gifts to family members totalling less than $200 per recipient and charitable contributions of less than $100 per recipient.

Name and address of recipient	Relationship of recipient to debtor	Date of gift	Description of gift	Value of gift

70. Complete the following showing any losses from fire, theft, or other casualty, or from gambling, incurred by the debtor during the last 365 days.

Type of loss	Description of Property lost	Date of loss	Amount of loss	Covered by insurance?

71. Complete the following showing all transfers of money or property within the last 365 days by or on behalf of the debtor to attorneys or other persons for consultation concerning debt counseling or the filing of a bankruptcy case.

Name and address of person paid	Date of payment	Name of entity who made payment	Amount paid or value and description of property transferred

72. Complete the following showing all other transfers of money or property made by the debtor within the last 2 years, other than transfers made in the ordinary course of the debtor's business or financial affairs.

Name and address of transferee	Relationship of transferee to debtor	Date of transfer	Description of property transferred	Value of property transferred

72a. Identify by amount and date all property or money transferred by the debtor within the last 10 years to a trust created by the debtor and of which the debtor is a beneficiary. ____________________

____

73. Complete the following showing all checking, savings, or other financial accounts, certificates of deposits, and shares in banks, credit unions or other financial institutions that the debtor has closed, transferred, or sold during the last 365 days.

Name and address of financial institution	Name of account, account number and type of account	Amount of final balance of account	Date of sale, if any, and amount received

74. Complete the following showing all safety deposit boxes or other boxes or depositories in which the debtor has kept cash, securities, or other valuables within the last 365 days.

Name and address of bank or depository	Names and address of all persons with access to box or depository	Description of contents	Date of transfer or surrender, if any

75. Has any creditor, including a bank, made a setoff against a debt or deposit of the debtor within the last 90 days? __________ If so, list the name and address of the creditor and the date and amount of the setoff.

____

____

76. Does the debtor hold or control any property owned by another person? __________ If so, list the name and address of the owner, describe the property, and list its value and location. ____________________

____

77. Has the debtor moved during the last 24 months? ____________ If so, give the address of each place that the debtor has occupied during that period, the name or names used by the debtor at each address, and the dates of occupancy at each address. ______________________________

____

____

78. If the debtor is an individual, using a separate sheet or the back of this sheet list the names and addresses of all businesses in which the debtor was an officer, director, partner or managing executive of a corporation, partnership, sole proprietorship, or was a self-employed professional within the last two years, or in which the debtor owned 5 percent or more of the voting or equity securities within the last two years.

If the debtor is a partnership, using a separate sheet or the back of this sheet list the names and addresses of all businesses in which the debtor was a partner, or owned 5 percent or more of the voting securities, within the last two years.

If the debtor is a corporation, using a separate sheet or the back of this sheet list the names and addresses of all businesses in which the debtor was a partner, or owned 5 percent or more of the voting securities, within the last two years.

Note: The following questions should be answered for any business listed in the answer to question 78.

79. List the names and addresses of, and the dates services were rendered by, any bookkeepers or accountants who kept or supervised the keeping of the books and records of the debtor's business within the last six years.

____

____

____

80. List the names and addresses of, and the dates services were rendered by, any firms or persons who, within the last two years, have audited the books and records of the debtor's business or prepared a financial statement for the debtor. ____

____

____

81. List the names and addresses of all firms or persons who now have possession of the debtor's business books and records. If any of the debtor's business books and records are not available, explain why. ______________________________

____

____

82. List the name and address of all financial institutions, creditors, trade agencies, and other parties to whom the debtor has issued a financial statement within the last two years and the date each statement was issued.

____

____

83. Complete the following showing the last two inventories taken of the debtor's property.

Date of inventory	Inventory supervisor	Amount of inventory in dollars	Basis of inventory (cost, market value, etc.)	Name and address of person having custody of inventory records

84. If the debtor is a partnership or limited liability company, list the nature and percentage of the ownership interest of each partner or member.

Name of partner	Address of partner	Nature of interest	Percentage of interest

85. If the debtor is a corporation, list all officers and directors of the corporation, and each stockholder who directly or indirectly owns, controls, or holds 5 percent or more of the voting securities of the corporation.

Name	Address	Title	Nature and percentage of stock ownership

86. If the debtor is a partnership or limited liability company, list each member who withdrew from the partnership or company within the last 365 days.

Name	Address	Date of withdrawal

87. If the debtor is a corporation, list all officers or directors whose relationship with the corporation was terminated within the last 365 days.

Name	Address	Title	Date of termination

88. If the debtor is a partnership, limited liability company, or corporation, list all withdrawals or distributions credited or given to an insider, including compensation in any form, bonuses, loans, stock redemptions, options exercised and any other perquisite during the last 365 days.

Name & address of recipient	Relationship to debtor	Date and purpose withdrawal	Amount of money or description and value of property

DEBT FORM

Instructions: Complete one of these forms for each debt of any kind. If possible, attach a copy of the creditor's most recent statement or bill to the completed form. Respond to every question on this form. Write "N/A" in the blank after each question that does not apply to a particular debt. If more space is needed to answer a question, use the back of the form.

1. List the complete name and address of the party to whom this debt is owed. ______________________________ \
name
____
address
____
city state zipcode

2. What is the creditor's account number for this debt? ______________________________

3. Is this debt covered or secured by a mortgage, lien, pledge, or other security interest on any property? ____________
If so, is this property listed elsewhere in these Work Sheets? ____________ In what question? ____________
If it is not listed in these Work Sheets, describe the property and list its owner, value and location. ____________
____

4. Is this debt entitled to priority of payment under the Bankruptcy Code? _______ If so, describe the type of priority (wage claim, tax claim, etc.; see questions 69-73). ______________________________

5. Is anyone beside the debtor liable for this debt? ____________ If so, list that person's name and address.
____

6. Has this debt been turned over to anyone for collection? _______ If so, to whom? ____________
name
____
address city state zipcode

7. When was this debt incurred? Month ______________ Year _______

8. What did the debtor receive in consideration for this debt? ______________________________
____

9. Does this creditor owe the debtor a debt? _____ If so, can the creditor's debt be setoff against this debt? ____________

10. Is this debt contingent upon anything? _______ If so, explain ______________________________
____

11. Has the final amount of this debt been determined? _______

12. Does the debtor admit liability for the full amount of this debt? _______ If not, explain. ____________
____

13. Do the debtor and the creditor agree on the amount of this debt? _______ If not, explain. ____________
____

14. Has the debtor given a written financial statement in connection with this debt? _______ If so, attach a copy of the statement to this form and state to whom and when the statement was given. ____________
____

15. If this debt is a continuing obligation, are the payments on this debt current or delinquent? ____________
If delinquent, what is the total amount of the arrearage? $____________

16. Is this a debt of someone else that the debtor has guaranteed, secured, or otherwise became liable for? __________
If so, list the other person's name, address and relationship to the debtor. ______________________________
name
____
address city state zipcode

17. What is the total amount of this debt? $____________

Fill in this information to identify the case:

United States Bankruptcy Court for the:

Northern District of Indiana (State)

Case number (If known): ______ Chapter 11

☐ Check if this is an amended filing

Official Form 201

Voluntary Petition for Non-Individuals Filing for Bankruptcy 12/15

If more space is needed, attach a separate sheet to this form. On the top of any additional pages, write the debtor's name and the case number (if known). For more information, a separate document, *Instructions for Bankruptcy Forms for Non-Individuals,* is available.

1. **Debtor's name** Hardtimes Supply Co., Inc.

2. **All other names debtor used in the last 8 years** Hardtimes Supply Company

   Include any assumed names, trade names, and *doing business as* names

3. **Debtor's federal Employer Identification Number** (EIN) 87-0778225

4. **Debtor's address**

   Principal place of business

   4455 West 39th Avenue.
   Number Street

   Gary IN 46405
   City State ZIP Code

   Lake
   County

   Mailing address, if different from principal place of business

   Number Street

   P.O. Box 3355
   P.O. Box

   Gary IN 46404
   City State ZIP Code

   Location of principal assets, if different from principal place of business

   Number Street

   City State ZIP Code

5. **Debtor's website** (URL) www.HardtimesSupplyCompany.com

6. **Type of debtor**

   ☒ Corporation (including Limited Liability Company (LLC) and Limited Liability Partnership (LLP))
   ☐ Partnership (excluding LLP)
   ☐ Other. Specify: ______

Debtor Hardtimes Supply Co., Inc. Case number (if known)__________
Name

7. Describe debtor's business

A. *Check one:*

- ☐ Health Care Business (as defined in 11 U.S.C. § 101(27A))
- ☐ Single Asset Real Estate (as defined in 11 U.S.C. § 101(51B))
- ☐ Railroad (as defined in 11 U.S.C. § 101(44))
- ☐ Stockbroker (as defined in 11 U.S.C. § 101(53A))
- ☐ Commodity Broker (as defined in 11 U.S.C. § 101(6))
- ☐ Clearing Bank (as defined in 11 U.S.C. § 781(3))
- ☒ None of the above

B. *Check all that apply:*

- ☐ Tax-exempt entity (as described in 26 U.S.C. § 501)
- ☐ Investment company, including hedge fund or pooled investment vehicle (as defined in 15 U.S.C. § 80a-3)
- ☐ Investment advisor (as defined in 15 U.S.C. § 80b-2(a)(11))

C. NAICS (North American Industry Classification System) 4-digit code that best describes debtor. See http://www.uscourts.gov/four-digit-national-association-naics-codes .

2 3 8 9

8. Under which chapter of the Bankruptcy Code is the debtor filing?

Check one:

- ☐ Chapter 7
- ☐ Chapter 9
- ☒ Chapter 11. *Check all that apply*:
  - ☒ Debtor's aggregate noncontingent liquidated debts (excluding debts owed to insiders or affiliates) are less than $2,490,925 (amount subject to adjustment on 4/01/16 and every 3 years after that).
  - ☒ The debtor is a small business debtor as defined in 11 U.S.C. § 101(51D). If the debtor is a small business debtor, attach the most recent balance sheet, statement of operations, cash-flow statement, and federal income tax return or if all of these documents do not exist, follow the procedure in 11 U.S.C. § 1116(1)(B).
  - ☐ A plan is being filed with this petition.
  - ☐ Acceptances of the plan were solicited prepetition from one or more classes of creditors, in accordance with 11 U.S.C. § 1126(b).
  - ☐ The debtor is required to file periodic reports (for example, 10K and 10Q) with the Securities and Exchange Commission according to § 13 or 15(d) of the Securities Exchange Act of 1934. File the *Attachment to Voluntary Petition for Non-Individuals Filing for Bankruptcy under Chapter 11* (Official Form 201A) with this form.
  - ☐ The debtor is a shell company as defined in the Securities Exchange Act of 1934 Rule 12b-2.
- ☐ Chapter 12

9. Were prior bankruptcy cases filed by or against the debtor within the last 8 years?

If more than 2 cases, attach a separate list.

☒ No

☐ Yes. District ________ When ________ Case number ________
MM / DD / YYYY

District ________ When ________ Case number ________
MM / DD / YYYY

10. Are any bankruptcy cases pending or being filed by a business partner or an affiliate of the debtor?

List all cases. If more than 1, attach a separate list.

☒ No

☐ Yes. Debtor ________ Relationship ________

District ________ When ________
MM / DD / YYYY

Case number, if known ________

Debtor Hardtimes Supply Co., Inc. Case number *(if known)*______
Name

11. Why is the case filed in *this district*?

Check all that apply:

☒ Debtor has had its domicile, principal place of business, or principal assets in this district for 180 days immediately preceding the date of this petition or for a longer part of such 180 days than in any other district.

☐ A bankruptcy case concerning debtor's affiliate, general partner, or partnership is pending in this district.

12. Does the debtor own or have possession of any real property or personal property that needs immediate attention?

☒ No

☐ Yes. Answer below for each property that needs immediate attention. Attach additional sheets if needed.

Why does the property need immediate attention? (*Check all that apply.*)

☐ It poses or is alleged to pose a threat of imminent and identifiable hazard to public health or safety.

What is the hazard? ______

☐ It needs to be physically secured or protected from the weather.

☐ It includes perishable goods or assets that could quickly deteriorate or lose value without attention (for example, livestock, seasonal goods, meat, dairy, produce, or securities-related assets or other options).

☐ Other ______

Where is the property?______
Number Street

______

______ City ______ State ______ ZIP Code

Is the property insured?

☐ No

☐ Yes. Insurance agency ______

Contact name ______

Phone ______

Statistical and administrative information

13. Debtor's estimation of available funds

Check one:

☒ Funds will be available for distribution to unsecured creditors.

☐ After any administrative expenses are paid, no funds will be available for distribution to unsecured creditors.

14. Estimated number of creditors

☐ 1-49	☐ 1,000-5,000	☐ 25,001-50,000
☒ 50-99	☐ 5,001-10,000	☐ 50,001-100,000
☐ 100-199	☐ 10,001-25,000	☐ More than 100,000
☐ 200-999		

15. Estimated assets

☐ \$0-\$50,000	☐ \$1,000,001-\$10 million	☐ \$500,000,001-\$1 billion
☐ \$50,001-\$100,000	☐ \$10,000,001-\$50 million	☐ \$1,000,000,001-\$10 billion
☒ \$100,001-\$500,000	☐ \$50,000,001-\$100 million	☐ \$10,000,000,001-\$50 billion
☐ \$500,001-\$1 million	☐ \$100,000,001-\$500 million	☐ More than \$50 billion

Debtor Hardtimes Supply Co., Inc.
Name

Case number (if known)

16. Estimated liabilities

- ☐ $0-$50,000
- ☐ $50,001-$100,000
- ☐ $100,001-$500,000
- ☒ $500,001-$1 million
- ☐ $1,000,001-$10 million
- ☐ $10,000,001-$50 million
- ☐ $50,000,001-$100 million
- ☐ $100,000,001-$500 million
- ☐ $500,000,001-$1 billion
- ☐ $1,000,000,001-$10 billion
- ☐ $10,000,000,001-$50 billion
- ☐ More than $50 billion

Request for Relief, Declaration, and Signatures

WARNING -- Bankruptcy fraud is a serious crime. Making a false statement in connection with a bankruptcy case can result in fines up to $500,000 or imprisonment for up to 20 years, or both. 18 U.S.C. §§ 152, 1341, 1519, and 3571.

17. Declaration and signature of authorized representative of debtor

The debtor requests relief in accordance with the chapter of title 11, United States Code, specified in this petition.

I have been authorized to file this petition on behalf of the debtor.

I have examined the information in this petition and have a reasonable belief that the information is true and correct.

I declare under penalty of perjury that the foregoing is true and correct.

Executed on 01/05/2016
MM / DD / YYYY

✘ /s/ Joseph Jones
Signature of authorized representative of debtor

Joseph Jones
Printed name

Title President

18. Signature of attorney

✘ /s/ Leo Lawnoer, Esq.
Signature of attorney for debtor

Date 01/05/2016
MM / DD / YYYY

Leo Lawnoer, Esq.
Printed name

Reddy, Willing & Able, P.C.
Firm name

1000 First St., Suite 600
Number Street

Gary
City

IN
State

46407
ZIP Code

219-222-1109
Contact phone

llawnoer@rwapc.com
Email address

12-23409
Bar number

IN
State

Fill in this information to identify the case:

Debtor name Hardtimes Supply Co., Inc.

United States Bankruptcy Court for the: Northern District of Indiana (State)

Case number (If known): ____________

☐ Check if this is an amended filing

Official Form 204

Chapter 11 or Chapter 9 Cases: List of Creditors Who Have the 20 Largest Unsecured Claims and Are Not Insiders

12/15

A list of creditors holding the 20 largest unsecured claims must be filed in a Chapter 11 or Chapter 9 case. Include claims which the debtor disputes. Do not include claims by any person or entity who is an *insider*, as defined in 11 U.S.C. § 101(31). Also, do not include claims by secured creditors, unless the unsecured claim resulting from inadequate collateral value places the creditor among the holders of the 20 largest unsecured claims.

	Name of creditor and complete mailing address, including zip code	Name, telephone number, and email address of creditor contact	Nature of the claim (for example, trade debts, bank loans, professional services, and government contracts)	Indicate if claim is contingent, unliquidated, or disputed	Amount of unsecured claim If the claim is fully unsecured, fill in only unsecured claim amount. If claim is partially secured, fill in total claim amount and deduction for value of collateral or setoff to calculate unsecured claim.		
					Total claim, if partially secured	Deduction for value of collateral or setoff	Unsecured claim
1	Ace Factoring, Inc. 9000 Easy Street Chicago, IL 60639	Sam Malone Vice President 312-227-9911 smalone@acefactor.com	Loan				$66,712.98
2	Harris Lumber 1721 Cedar Lane Gary, IN 46405	Dan Harris President 219-321-6598 dan.harris@harrislumber.com	trade debt				$29,768.35
3	Action Accounts Company 1200 South Side Street Overland Park, KS 66044	Sam Action Vice President 329-649-8213 actionaccounts@gmail.com	loan				$29,768.35
4	Baker & Baker Attorneys at Law 400 Equitable Bldg. Baltimore, MD 21202	Joseph Baker Partner 509-82-2389 joseph.baker@bakerbaker.com	legal service				$12,892.03
5	Last National Bank 300 Wazee Street Denver, CO 80202	Ben Banker 329-649-8213 banker@LNB.com	loan				$29,986.39
6	Davidson Computer Service 1100 South Broadway Cheyenne, WY 82001	Sam Davidson President 202-93-2358 davidson@dcs.com	computer service				$9,039.04
7	East Coast Computers, Inc. 2100 Boyleston Street Boston, MA 02105	George Computer Vice President 505-08-3456 george@computersrus.com	internet service				$10,768.35
8	Friendly Finance Co. 777 West Fifth Ave. Dallas, TX 75211	Geoff Friendly Vice President 329-649-8213 friendly@financefriendly.com	cash advance				$10,349.00

Debtor Hardtimes Supply Co., Inc. Case number (if known)____________
Name

	Name of creditor and complete mailing address, including zip code	Name, telephone number, and email address of creditor contact	Nature of the claim (for example, trade debts, bank loans, professional services, and government contracts)	Indicate if claim is contingent, unliquidated, or disputed	Amount of unsecured claim If the claim is fully unsecured, fill in only unsecured claim amount. If claim is partially secured, fill in total claim amount and deduction for value of collateral or setoff to calculate unsecured claim.		
					Total claim, if partially secured	Deduction for value of collateral or setoff	Unsecured claim
9	Great Western Sugar Co. 1234 Teller Street Pueblo, CO 81004	Sam Sugar President 312-328-9865 sugar@westernsugar.com	trade debts				$14,412.98
10	Henry's Automotice Co. 1144 Outside Ave. Wayside, TX 78444	Henry Smith President 312-112-3298 hsmith@gmail.com	services				$13,712.98
11	Ivy, Ivy & Jones, CPA 2600 Highrise Building Chicago, IL 60606	James Ivy Partner 934-239-7453 jivy@ivyivyjones.com	professional CPA				$12,712.98
12	Jackson's Service Supply 4455 Maple Street Akron, CO 80566	John Jackson Vice President 439-438-7658 jackson@jacksonservice.com	trade debts				$7,712.98
13	Katz Furniture Company 700 Broadway Denver, CO 80203	Brad Katz President 312-234-6658 bkatz@katzfurniture.com	equipment				$6,398.56
14	Cole Janitorial Service P.O. Box 444 Pueblo, CO 81001	Janice Cole President 312-340-6651 cole@gmail.com	Services				$4,712.98
15	Manley's Automotive Co. 12233 East Elm Street San Francisco, CA 94122	Tracy Manley Vice President 303-444-3387 tracy@manleyauto.com	Services				$3,598.56
16	Nancy's Temps 900 Sixth Street, N.E. Omaha, NE 68107	Joy Johnson President 312-394-0098 jjohnson@tempservices.com	Services				$4,985.47
17	Old Time Music Company P.O. Box 2233 Nashville, TN 37222	John Fosenberg Vice President 312-222-9998 jfosman@gmail.com	Loan				$3,712.98
18	Perfect Computer Company 2000 Broadway South Portland, OR 97211	Josh Peterson Vice President 313-222-4465 jp@perfectcomputers.com	Services				$5,712.98
19	Rockville Envelope Co. 2100 North Smith St Rockville, MD 20850	James Tracy Vice President 309-448-3987 tracy@rockville.com	Loan				$4,712.98
20	Schenectady Manufacturing Co. 234 Front Street Schenectady, NY 12305	Sam Schenectady Vice President 317-398-3765 schenectady@gmail.com	Goods				$3,712.98

UNITED STATES BANKRUPTCY COURT
NORTHERN DISTRICT OF INDIANA

IN RE	HARDTIMES SUPPLY CO., Inc.	)	
	An Indiana corporation,	)	Case No. ______________
		)	
	Debtor	)	Chapter 11

LIST OF EQUITY SECURITY HOLDERS

The following constitutes a list of all holders of equity security interests in Hardtimes Supply Co., Inc., the debtor, as of January 15, 2016:

John J. Jones 3201 East Pine Avenue Gary, IN 46407	500 shares of Common Stock
Sarah S. Smith 117 Country Club Road Gary, IN 46402	500 shares of Common Stock
Joseph P. Jones 4737 South Fifth Ave. Gary, IN 46407	300 shares of Common Stock

VERIFICATION

I, Joseph P. Jones, the President Hardtimes Supply Co., Inc. the debtor, declare under penalty of perjury that I am informed, that I have read the above list of equity security holders, and that the list is complete, true, and correct.

Dated: January 15, 2016

____
Joseph P. Jones, President
Hardtimes Supply Co., Inc.

CERTIFICATE OF CORPORATE RESOLUTION
AUTHORIZING COMMENCEMENT OF CHAPTER 11 CASE

I, Mary M. Jones, the Secretary of HARDTIMES SUPPLY CO, INC., an Illinois corporation, hereby certify and declare under penalty of perjury that the following is a true and correct excerpt from the official records and minutes of the said corporation, truly and correctly reflecting the matters transacted by the board of directors of the said corporation at a special meeting duly called and held on January 3, 2016:

WHEREAS, from the information presented to the board of directors it appears that the corporation is no longer able to pay or meet its debts and obligations as they become due, that the corporation qualifies as a debtor under Chapter 11 of the United States Bankruptcy Code, and that it is in the best interest of the corporation to file a petition under Chapter 11; therefore,

IT WAS UNANIMOUSLY RESOLVED and voted by the board of directors of HARDTIMES SUPPLY CO., INC., an Illinois corporation, that the corporation should file a petition under Chapter 11 of the United States Bankruptcy Code and thereafter file a plan to reorganize its business under Chapter 11.

IT WAS FURTHER RESOLVED and voted by the board of directors of the corporation that Leo E. Lawnoer, Attorney at Law, and the law firm of Reddy, Willing & Able be retained to represent the corporation on all matters related to the Chapter 11 case, including the filing of the petition and initial pleadings.

IT WAS FURTHER RESOLVED and voted that Joseph P. Jones, the President of the corporation, be authorized and directed to execute any and all petitions, statements, schedules, plans, and other necessary documents in the Chapter 11 case on behalf of the corporation.

The foregoing matters were transacted and approved on behalf of the corporation by the entire board of directors at a special meeting duly called and held on the 3rd day of January, 2016.

Certified under penalty of perjury this 5th day of January 2016 by

____

Mary M. Jones, Secretary

PARTNERSHIP RESOLUTION AUTHORIZING COMMENCEMENT OF CHAPTER 11 CASE

WHEREAS, at a special meeting of the general partners duly called and held, it appeared to the general partners of the SMITH BROTHERS SUPPLY COMPANY, a general partnership engaged in the oil field supply business, that the partnership is no longer able to meet its debts and obligations as they become due, that the partnership qualifies as a debtor under Chapter 11 of the United States Bankruptcy Code, and that the best interest of the partnership would be served by filing a petition under Chapter 11 and reorganizing its business thereunder; therefore,

IT IS UNANIMOUSLY RESOLVED by the general partners of the SMITH BROTHERS SUPPLY COMPANY that the partnership file a petition under Chapter 11 of the United States Bankruptcy Code and thereafter file a plan of reorganization for the partnership business.

IT WAS FURTHER RESOLVED by the general partners that John H. Jones, Attorney at Law, be retained to represent the partnership on all matters related to the Chapter 11 case and that Sidney S. Smith be authorized and appointed to execute any and all petitions, schedules, statements, plans, and other necessary documents in the Chapter 11 case on behalf of the partnership.

The foregoing matters were transacted and unanimously approved by all of the general partners on behalf of the partnership at a special meeting duly called and held on this 10th day of January, 2016.

____________________________	____________________________	____________________________
Joseph P. Smith General Partner	Sidney S. Smith General Partner	Henry H. Smith General Partner

CERTIFICATION

I, Joseph P. Smith, a general partner of the SMITH BROTHERS SUPPLY COMPANY, a general partnership, certify and declare under penalty of perjury that the above is a true and correct account of a resolution duly passed and adopted by the partnership on the date therein reflected.

Certified under penalty of perjury on this 12th day of January, 2016 by

____

Joseph P. Smith, General Partner,
Smith Brothers Supply Company

(Debtor's Letter to Creditors and Customers)

To: The Creditors and Customers of Hardtimes Supply Co, Inc.

Re: Chapter 11 Reorganization Case No. 16-000019, United States Bankruptcy Court for the Northern District of Indiana; Hardtimes Supply Co., Inc.,debtor

Dear Creditor or Customer:

Hardtimes Supply Co., Inc. has filed a voluntary petition in the United States Bankruptcy Court for the Northern District of Indiana seeking relief under Chapter 11 of the United States Bankruptcy Code. We felt it necessary to file the Chapter 11 case in order to protect our assets and property from foreclosures and to prevent other litigation while we attempt to reorganize the business. We would prefer to spend our resources reorganizing the business and paying the claims of our creditors, rather than defending lawsuits and foreclosures.

It is important to understand that the bankruptcy proceeding we have filed is a reorganization case and not a liquidation case, and that it is our intention to stay in business, treat our creditors fairly, and continue to provide products and services for our customers. The filing of the Chapter 11 case will give us a moratorium on the payment of some of our debts, and we intend to use this moratorium to reorganize our financial resources so that we can continue in business and ultimately repay as much of our debts as possible. We intend to continue to operate our business as a debtor in possession during the course of the Chapter 11 case, and we hope that you will continue to conduct business with us during the course of the case. Debts incurred in the ordinary course of business during the case will be paid in full as administrative expenses.

We intend to file a fair and equitable plan of reorganization in the Chapter 11 case within the required period. Our creditors will soon receive a notice from the clerk of the bankruptcy court advising them of certain matters in the case, including the time and place of the first meeting of creditors. Some of you may soon be contacted by the United States trustee and asked to serve on a creditors' committee in the case. We hope that you will accept this invitation to serve on the creditors' committee, as we look forward to working closely with the creditors' committee in order to insure the fair treatment of our creditors in the Chapter 11 case.

Our attorney in the Chapter 11 case is Leo E. Lawnoer, Attorney at Law, 1000 First St., Gary, Indiana 46407 (telephone number: 219-222-1100; email: LLawnoer@lawnoer.com). If any of you, or your attorneys, have questions concerning any aspect of the Chapter 11 case, please contact our attorney at your convenience.

In summary, we have filed under Chapter 11 because we felt that a Chapter 11 case represented the only method of dealing with our present financial difficulties that would permit us to remain in business and thereby have a chance to pay our creditors. We hope that you will accept this decision and work with us to insure a satisfactory reorganization of our business and a fair treatment of our creditors and customers. We look forward to your cooperation during the course of the case.

Yours truly,

January 10, 2016

____

Joseph P. Jones, President,
Hardtimes Supply Co., Inc.

CHAPTER FOUR

HANDLING A VOLUNTARY CHAPTER 11 CASE

4.01 The Automatic Stay and Relief Therefrom

The automatic stay is one of the fundamental protections accorded debtors under the Bankruptcy Code. It gives debtors a breathing spell from creditors by stopping virtually all collection efforts, foreclosures, and other creditor action. It permits a debtor some time in which to formulate and attempt a repayment or reorganizational plan. The basic purposes of the automatic stay are to protect the debtor from hostile creditor action and harassment and from expensive and widespread litigation in a multitude of forums, prevent piecemeal liquidation or dismemberment of the debtor's property by creditors, and freeze the respective rights of creditors as of the date the bankruptcy petition was filed. See H.R. Report No. 595, p. 340 (1977), 1978 Code Cong. & Ad. News 5963, 6296. It should be noted that the automatic stay protects creditors as well as debtors by preventing aggressive creditors from acting unilaterally to obtain payment from the debtor to the detriment of other creditors. See Borman v. Raymark Industries, Inc., 946 F.2d 1031 (CA 3, 1991).

automatic stay, purpose of

Acts affected by the automatic stay. The filing of a voluntary Chapter 11 petition operates as a stay, applicable to all entities, of the following acts:

automatic stay, matters stayed by

(1) The commencement or continuation of a judicial, administrative, or other proceeding against the debtor that was or could have been commenced before the filing of the petition to recover a claim against the debtor that arose before the commencement of the case. See 11 U.S.C. 362(a)(1). This section basically prohibits collection and other activities by unsecured creditors. Proceedings stayed include arbitration, license revocation, administrative, judicial, and other civil proceedings, even if they are not before governmental tribunals. See In re Del Mission, Ltd., 998 F.2d 756 (CA 9, 1993).

stay of collection activities

(2) The enforcement against the debtor or against property of the estate of a judgment obtained before the commencement of the case. See 11 U.S.C. 362(a)(2). This section prohibits not only executions, levies, attachments, and garnishments, but also such matters as warrants of eviction issued in the course of enforcing a judgment. See In re Butler, 14 B.R. 532 (SD NY, 1981).

stay of judgment enforcement

(3) Any act to obtain possession of property of the estate or of property from estate or to exercise control over property of the estate. See 11 U.S.C. 362(a)(3). As to what constitutes property of the estate, see 11 U.S.C. 541(a) and section 4.02, infra. The purpose of this section is to prevent dismemberment of the estate and it applies to all creditors (including postpetition creditors) and other persons regardless of the nature of their right or activity. This section has been held to preclude the cancellation or revocation of such items as licenses and insurance policies. See In re Aegean Fare, 35 B.R. 923 (MA, 1983), and In re Cahokia Downs, Inc., 5 B.R. 529 (SD IL, 1980). This section applies equally to property acquired by the estate after the commencement of the case, property of the estate in the possession of third parties, and property of third parties in the possession of the estate.

stay of acts against property

(4) Any act to create, perfect, or enforce any lien against property of the estate. See 11 U.S.C. 362(a)(4). This section applies to both judicial and nonjudicial lien enforcement activities, and applies to all liens whenever obtained, including postpetition liens.

stay of lien enforcement against estate property

stay of lien enforcement against exempt or abandoned property

(5) Any act to create, perfect, or enforce against property of the debtor any lien to the extent that the lien secures a claim that arose before the commencement of the case. See 11 U.S.C. 362(a)(5). This section applies mainly to exempt property and property abandoned by the estate.

stay of acts to collect claims against debtor

(6) Any act to collect, assess, or recover a claim against the debtor that arose before the commencement of the case. See 11 U.S.C. 362(a)(6). This section prohibits such acts as telephone calls to the debtor, the sending of letters or bills to the debtor, deductions from a debtor's postpetition earnings, and all other acts, both judicial and nonjudicial, designed to enhance the collection of a prepetition claim. See In re Olson, 38 B.R. 515 (IA, 1984), and In re Warden, 36 B.R. 968 (UT, 1984).

stay of setoff activities

(7) The setoff of any debt owing to the debtor that arose before the commencement of the case against any claim against the debtor. See 11 U.S.C. 362(a)(7). This section does not abolish a creditor's right of setoff under 11 U.S.C. 553; it merely postpones it by prohibiting a creditor from unilaterally exercising a right of setoff. This section has been held to prevent a loan creditor with whom the debtor has funds deposited from unilaterally offsetting the debtor's deposited funds against the outstanding balance of the debtor's loan after the filing of the case. See In re Patterson, 967 F.2d 505 (CA 11, 1992). However, it has been held that this section does not preclude a creditor bank from refusing to turn over to the debtor funds upon which it has a right of setoff. Compare Kenney's Franchise Corp. v. Central Fidelity Bank, 22 B.R. 747 (WD VA, 1982) with In re Executive Associates, Inc., 24 B.R. 171 (SD TX, 1982). See section 4.04, infra, for further reading on setoffs.

stay of tax court proceedings

(8) The commencement or continuation of a proceeding before the United States Tax Court concerning a corporate debtor's tax liability for a taxable period the bankruptcy court may determine or concerning the tax liability of an individual debtor for a taxable period ending prior to the order for relief in the bankruptcy case. See 11 U.S.C. 362(a)(8).

automatic stay, effect on periods to perform acts

statute of limitations, effect of stay on

It should be understood that the automatic stay, as described in the preceding paragraphs, does not create substantive nonbankruptcy rights and applies only to affirmative acts of creditors and other persons. For example, the automatic stay does not prevent the running of a redemption period following a foreclosure. See Johnson v. First Nat'l Bank, 719 F. 2nd 270 (CA 8, 1983). However, such periods may be extended under 11 U.S.C. 108, which provides that such periods expire either at the time they would ordinarily expire or 30 days after notice of the termination or expiration of the automatic stay with respect to the claim, whichever date is later. See 11 U.S.C. 108(c). It is also clear that the automatic stay tolls the statute of limitations against a debtor if the creditor is precluded by the automatic stay from proceeding on its claim. See Wekell v. U.S., 14 F.3d 32 (CA 9, 1994).

Acts not affected by the automatic stay. The filing of a petition under any chapter of the Bankruptcy Code by or against a debtor does not operate as a stay of the following activities or events:

acts not affected by automatic stay

(1) The commencement or continuation of a criminal action or proceeding against the debtor. See 11 U.S.C. 362(b)(1).

(2) The commencement or continuation of a civil action or proceeding for the establishment of paternity, for the establishment or modification of an order for domestic support obligations, concerning child custody or visitation, for the dissolution of a marriage (except to the extent that the proceeding seeks to determine the division of estate property), or regarding domestic violence. See 11 U.S.C. 362(b)(2)(A).

(3) The collection of a domestic support obligation from property that is not property of the estate. See 11 U.S.C. 362(b)(2)(B).

(4) The withholding of income that is property of the estate or the debtor for payment of a valid domestic support obligation. See 11 U.S.C. 362(b)(2)(C).

(5) The withholding, suspension or restriction of a driver's license, a professional or occupational license, or a recreational license. See 11 U.S.C. 362(b)(2)(D).

(6) The reporting of overdue child support owed by a parent to any consumer reporting agency. See 11 U.S.C. 362(b)(2)(E).

(7) The interception of a tax refund. See 11 U.S.C. 362(b)(2)(F).

(8) The enforcement of a medical obligation. See 11 U.S.C. 362(b)(2)(G).

(9) Any act to perfect an interest in property to the extent that the trustee's rights and powers are subject to such perfection under 11 U.S.C. 546(b) or to the extent that such act is accomplished within the period provided under 11 U.S.C. 547(e)(2)(A). See 11 U.S.C. 362(b)(3).

(10) The commencement or continuation of an action or proceeding by a governmental unit to enforce its police and regulatory power, including the enforcement of a nonmonetary judgment obtained in an action or proceeding by the governmental unit to enforce its police or regulatory power. This provision is also applicable to organizations exercising authority under the Convention on the Prohibition of the Development, Production, Stockpiling and Use of Chemical Weapons and on Their Destruction. See 11 U.S.C. 362(b)(4).

(11) The setoff of certain debts and claims relating to dealings in commodity contracts, forward contracts, or securities contracts. See 11 U.S.C. 362(b)(6).

(12) The setoff by a repo participant of certain debts and claims in connection with repurchase agreements. See 11 U.S.C. 362(b)(7).

(13) The commencement of foreclosure actions by the Secretary of Housing and Urban Development on certain mortgages or deeds of trust insured under the National Housing Act. See 11 U.S.C. 362(b)(8).

(14) Various tax activities by governmental units, including audits to determine tax liability, the issuance of tax deficiency notices, demands for tax returns, and the making of tax assessments and issuing notices of and demands for payment of the assessments. See 11 U.S.C. 362(b)(9).

(15) Any act by a lessor of the debtor under a lease of nonresidental real property that has terminated by the expiration of its term before the commencement of or during the case to obtain possession of the property. See 11 U.S.C. 362(b)(10).

(16) The presentment of a negotiable instrument and the giving of notice of and protesting dishonor of such an instrument. See 11 U.S.C. 362(b)(11).

(17) Certain setoffs by swap participants, certain actions by educational accrediting agencies, certain actions by state educational licensing bodies, and certain actions by the Secretary of Education or guaranty agencies regarding the eligibility of the debtor to participate in certain programs. See 11 U.S.C. 362(b)(14)-(17).

(18) The creation or perfection of a statutory lien for an ad valorem property tax, or a special tax or special assessment on real property, imposed by a political subdivision of a state, if the tax becomes due after the filing of the petition. See 11 U.S.C. 362(b)(18).

(19) The withholding of income from a debtor's wages and collection of amounts withheld under the debtor's agreement authorizing the withholding and collection for the benefit of a pension, profit-sharing, stock bonus, or other tax-qualified plan, to the extent that the amounts withheld and collected are used solely to repay a loan from the plan or a loan from a thrift savings plan. See 11 U.S.C. 362(b)(19).

(20) Any act to enforce a lien against or security interest in real property if, within 2 years in a prior bankruptcy case the court found that the case was filed as part of a scheme to delay, hinder or defraud creditors; provided that the debtor may move for relief from the order based upon changed circumstances or other good cause. See 11 U.S.C. 362(b)(20).

(21) Any act to enforce a lien against or a security interest in real property if the debtor is an ineligible debtor under 11 U.S.C. 109(g) or if the present bankruptcy case was filed in violation of a bankruptcy court order in a prior case prohibiting the debtor from filing another bankruptcy case. See 11 U.S.C. 362(b)(21).

(22) The continuation of an eviction, unlawful detainer, or similar proceeding by a lessor against the debtor involving residential property in which the debtor resides as a tenant under a lease or rental agreement against which the lessor had obtained a judgment of possession prior to the filing of the bankruptcy case. See 11 U.S.C. 362(b)(22). However, the debtor can reinstate the stay by following the procedures set forth in 11 U.S.C. 362(l).

(23) An eviction action that seeks possession of residential property leased to the debtor based on endangerment of the property or the illegal use of a controlled substance on the property if the lessor files a sworn certification of such use. See 11 U.S.C. 362(b)(23). However, the debtor can reinstate the stay by following the procedures set forth in 11 U.S.C. 362(m).

(24) Any transfer that is not avoidable under 11 U.S.C. 544 and 11 U.S.C. 549 (i.e., postpetition transfers that are avoidable under local law). See 11 U.S.C. 362(b)(24).

(25) Certain acts and actions by securities self regulatory organizations. See 11 U.S.C. 362(b)(25).

(26) The setoff of an income tax refund by a government unit under certain conditions. See 11 U.S.C. 362(b)(26).

(27) The setoff of mutual debts and claims under a master netting agreement under certain conditions. See 11 U.S.C. 362(b)(27).

(28) The exclusion by the Secretary of Health and Human Services of the debtor from participation in the medicare and other Federal health care programs. See 11 U.S.C. 362(b)(28).

perfection of security interests, automatic stay

The exception to the automatic stay listed in (9) above permits, under section 9-301(2) of the Uniform Commercial Code, the perfection of a purchase money security interest within 30 days after delivery of the collateral to the debtor, if the debtor's bankruptcy petition is filed during the 30 day period. See 11 U.S.C. 547(e)(2)(A). Similarly, a mechanic's lien may be perfected if the petition is filed during the period provided for perfection under state law. See In re Fiorillo & Co., 19 B.R. 21 (SD NY, 1982).

Governmental acts not stayed by automatic stay

The exceptions to the automatic stay listed in (5) and (10) above permit governmental units to enforce their police and regulatory powers. These exceptions are generally given a broad construction by the courts. See Penn Terra Ltd. v. Dept. of Environmental Resources, 733 F. 2nd 267 (CA 3, 1985). This exception to the automatic stay can be important to a small business debtor because it permits governmental action that may affect the debtor's right to conduct business. Governmental action on such items as liquor licenses, utility franchises, and construction permits are excepted from the automatic stay under this exception. See Eddleman v. U.S. Dept. of Labor, 923 F.2d 782 (CA 10, 1991).

effect of automatic stay on government acts, general rules

The general rule is that while governmental units are permitted to pursue actions enforcing their police or regulatory powers, they are not permitted to pursue actions related primarily to their pecuniary interests in violation of the stay. See Ohio v. Kovacs, 469 U.S. 274, 105 S. Ct. 705, 83 L. Ed. 2nd 649 (1985). However, the distinction between actions enforcing the pecuniary interest of a governmental unit and actions enforcing its police or regulatory powers can be a fine one. See generally, State of Missouri v. U.S. Bankruptcy Court, 647 F. 2nd 768 (CA 8, 1981), and Commodity Futures Trading Comm. v. Co Petro Marketing, 700 F. 2nd 1279 (CA 9, 1983). Generally, if a governmental unit is pursuing primarily monetary remedies, the action is stayed by the automatic stay, while if primarily nonmonetary remedies are being pursued the action is not stayed.

automatic stay, effect on acts of debtor and on counterclaims against debtor

It should be understood that the automatic stay is not applicable to claims brought by the debtor or acts initiated by the debtor. Therefore, actions previously filed by the debtor to collect accounts are not stayed by the automatic stay, even if counterclaims filed in the action by the other party are stayed. See Maritime Electric Co. v. United Jersey Bank, 959 F.2d 1194 (CA 3, 1991). An attempt by a creditor to dismiss a pending action previously brought by the debtor may also be a violation of the automatic stay as an attempt to control estate property without obtaining relief from the stay. Compare In re General Associated Investors, Ltd., 159 BR 552 (AZ, 1993), with U.S. v. Inslaw, Inc., 932 F.2d 1467 (CA DC, 1991). That the automatic stay does not apply to sales or transfers of property initiated by the debtor, see In re Schwartz, 954 F.2d 569 (CA 9, 1992).

The automatic stay applies only to acts against the debtor or the debtor's property and does not apply to acts against third parties. Therefore, the automatic stay does not protect guarantors, officers, employees, codefendants, or other nondebtor parties from actions brought against them. See U.S. v. Dos Cabezas, 995 F.2d 1486 (CA 9, 1993), Credit Alliance Corp. v. Williams, 851 F.2d 119 (CA 4, 1988), and In re CCDC Fin. Corp., 143 BR 946 (KS, 1992). The automatic stay also does not protect the general partners of a partnership debtor from actions to collect partnership debts. See In re Cloud Nine, Ltd., 3 B.R. 202 (NM, 1980). However, a bankruptcy court may issue injunctions under 11 U.S.C. 105(a) prohibiting certain acts against third parties in order to prevent irreparable harm to estate, especially if there is an identity between the debtor and the third party. See In re Arrow Huss, Inc., 51 B.R. 853 (UT, 1985). For example, if such relief is necessary to protect an otherwise effective reorganization, a creditor may be enjoined from proceeding in a state court against the president of a corporate Chapter 11 debtor on personal guarantees of the corporation's debts. See In re Otero Mills, Inc., 25 B.R. 1018 (NM, 1982).

automatic stay, effect on acts of third parties

Injunctions, when issued by bankruptcy court

Violations of the automatic stay. An individual debtor injured by a willful violation of the automatic stay may recover actual damages, including costs and attorney's fees, and, under appropriate circumstances, punitive damages. See 11 U.S.C. 362(k)(1). Corporate and other nonindividual debtors may not recover under Section 362(k)(1) and must seek relief for willful violations of the automatic stay through contempt proceedings. See In re Chateaugay Corp., 920 F.2d 183 (CA 2, 1990). Actions seeking damages for violations of the automatic stay may be maintained and enforced even after the bankruptcy case has been closed or otherwise terminated. See Price v. Rochford, 947 F.2d 820 (CA 7, 1991). It should be noted that governmental entities are not immune from monetary damages for willful violations of the automatic stay. See 11 U.S.C. 106(a)(1). However, punitive damages may not be assessed against a governmental entity. See 11 U.S.C. 106(a)(3). For further reading on the recovery of damages for violations of the automatic stay, see Williamson, The Bankruptcy Issues Handbook, Art. 1.15 (Argyle Pub. Co.).

willful violation of automatic stay, debtor's remedies

A willful violation of the automatic stay does not require a specific intent by the offending party to violate the stay. A showing that the offending party knew of the stay and intentionally committed the act that violated the stay will support an award of damages for intentional violation of the stay. See In re Landsdale Family Restaurants, Inc., 977 F.2d 826, 829 (CA 3, 1992), and In re Bloom, 875 F.2d 224, 227 (CA 9, 1989). A creditor's good faith belief that its acts did not constitute a violation of the stay is not a defense, even if its belief was based on the advice of legal counsel. See In re Taylor, 884 F.2d 478, 483 (CA 9, 1989).

willful violation of automatic stay, what constitutes

If a creditor unintentionally or unknowingly violates the automatic stay, the creditor action taken in violation of the stay is voidable at the request of the debtor or trustee, and the parties will be reinstated to the positions they held when the bankruptcy case was filed. See Matter of Lee, 35 B.R. 452 (ND GA, 1983). Acts committed in an intentional violation of the automatic stay are not only voidable, but void. See In re Schwartz, 954 F.2d 569 (CA 9, 1990).

unintentional violation of automatic stay, voidability of act

Duration of automatic stay. In the absence of a court order terminating the stay, the automatic stay continues as to acts against property of the estate until such property is no longer property of the estate. See 11 U.S.C. 362(c)(1). For individual chapter 11 debtors who have had other bankruptcy cases pending in the year prior to the filing of the present case, the stay may terminate 30 days after the date of filing of the present case if the conditions described in 11 U.S.C. 362(c)(3) exist. The stay against lien enforcement is not terminated by disposal of the property, however, and if property of the estate is sold, abandoned, set aside as exempt, or otherwise disposed of by the trustee or debtor in possession prior to confirmation, creditors with prepetition claims may not pursue lien enforcement remedies against the property without court approval. See In re Gassaway, 28 B.R. 842 (ND MS, 1983), and In re Brady Mun. Gas Corp., 936 F.2d 212 (CA 5, 1991).

automatic stay, when terminated

The BAPCPA added a new subsection (n) to 11 U.S.C. 362 which may significantly limit the applicability of the automatic stay in small business Chapter 11 cases. Under the new subsection (n), the automatic stay does not apply in a small business case if the debtor has a current case pending or filed the case within two years of either dismissal or confirmation of a previous small business case. A small business debtor can be excepted from this rule if it can prove that the new Chapter 11 petition resulted from circumstances beyond the debtor's control that were not foreseeable at the time the previous case was filed. The debtor must also prove that it is more likely than not that the court will confirm a feasible plan in the current case in a reasonable time. The burden of proof is a preponderance of the evidence.

automatic stay, BAPCPA amendments

automatic stay, BAPCPA amendments

The new subsection (n) also applies to entities that acquire previous small business Chapter 11 debtors through asset or business acquisitions. However, the exclusion from automatic stay protection may be overcome if the purchasing entity can prove that it acquired the assets or business of the previous small business debtor in good faith and not for the purpose of evading the provisions of the new subsection (n). The level of proof required is a preponderance of the evidence.

automatic stay, when terminated

Unless earlier terminated by the court, all aspects of the automatic stay, other than those relating to acts against property of the estate, terminate at the earliest of: (1) the closing of the case, (2) the dismissal of the case, or (3) the granting or denial of an individual debtor's discharge. See 11 U.S.C. 362(c)(2). Because in Chapter 11 cases a debtor's discharge is effective upon confirmation of the plan, all aspects of the automatic stay, except as it relates to acts against property of the estate, ordinarily terminate upon confirmation of the plan. See In re James Wilson Assocs., 965 F.2d 160 (CA 7, 1992). It should be noted, however, that even if the automatic stay is terminated by the discharge inherent in an order of confirmation, the post-discharge stay under 11 U.S.C. 524(a) becomes effective and prevents certain activities against the debtor and certain property of the debtor. See section 4.10, infra, for further reading on the effect of the post-discharge stay.

relief from stay, grounds for

Relief from the automatic stay. The court may grant relief from the automatic stay to any party in interest by terminating, annulling, modifying, or conditioning the stay on three grounds: (1) for cause, including the lack of adequate protection of an interest of such party in property, (2) with respect to the stay of acts against property, upon a showing that the debtor has no equity in the property and that the property is not necessary for an effective reorganization, or (3) with respect to the stay of acts against real property, if the court finds that the filing of the case was part of scheme to delay, hinder or defraud creditors. See 11 U.S.C. 362(d)(3) for provisions dealing with relief from the stay against single asset real estate.

relief from stay, equity of debtor in property

Under the second ground for relief described above, which is used mainly by secured creditors seeking to reach their collateral, the creditor must show that the debtor has no equity in the property constituting the collateral. See 11 U.S.C. 362(d)(2). This is normally accomplished by showing that the total amount of all valid liens and encumbrances against the property exceeds the value of the property. Not surprisingly, the key issue is often that of valuing the property in question. Value is determined on a case-by-case basis, taking into account the nature of the debtor's business, market conditions, the debtor's prospects for rehabilitation, and the type of collateral. See In re Sutton, 904 F.2d 327, 330 (CA 5, 1990). The party opposing the motion for relief from the stay (usually the debtor) will normally attempt to establish a high value for the property and the party seeking relief (usually a creditor) will attempt to establish a lower value. The burden of proof on the issue of valuation is on the party seeking relief from the stay. See 11 U.S.C. 362(g)(1).

valuation of property, factors

relief from stay, necessity of property for reorganization

On the second issue under 11 U.S.C. 362(d)(2), that of whether the property is necessary for an effective reorganization, the burden of proof is on the party opposing the relief (usually the debtor) to show that the property is in fact necessary for an effective reorganization. See 11 U.S.C. 362(g)(2). To establish that the property is necessary for an effective reorganization, it must be shown that (1) there is a reasonable possibility of an effective reorganization within a reasonable period, and (2) the property is necessary to effectively reorganize and run the debtor's business. It is important to establish both of these factors if relief from the stay is to be successfully avoided. It is, of course, easier to convince the court of the possibility of a successful reorganization if the debtor has timely proposed a realistic plan and has met the other Chapter 11 deadlines. See In re Canal Place Ltd. Partnership, 921 F.2d 569 (CA 5, 1991), and In re Anderson, 913 F.2d 530 (CA 8, 1990). To establish the necessity of the property in the debtor's reorganization, it must be shown that the property is "essential" and has a "part to play" in the reorganization. See In re Mikole Developers, Inc., 14 B.R. 524 (ED PA, 1981), and In re T-H New Orleans Ltd. Partnership, 148 BR 456 (ED LA, 1992).

relief from stay, when granted under section 362(d)(2

On the other hand, if it is shown that the debtor has no equity in the secured property and either that the property is not necessary for the operation of the debtor's business or that there is no reasonable possibility of an effective reorganization of the debtor's business within a reasonable period, then relief from the stay may be granted and the creditor may reclaim its collateral. See In re Trina-Dee, Inc., 26 B.R. 152 (ED PA, 1983).

relief from stay, lack of adequate protection

Relief from stay for lack of adequate protection. In Chapter 11 cases relief from the automatic stay is most often sought for cause, which includes lack of adequate protection of an interest in property of the party seeking the relief. See 11 U.S.C. 362(d)(1). While cause for lifting the stay may include other grounds (see infra, this section), the lack of adequate protection of an interest in property is the grounds most commonly alleged for seeking relief from the automatic stay. Indeed, as judged by the number of reported cases on the issue, it may be the most heavily litigated matter in all of bankruptcy. Demands for adequate protection can be expected at any stage of the case prior to the confirmation of a plan. While any party with an interest in property of the estate may seek relief from automatic stay for lack of adequate protection, in practice this ground is used almost exclusively by secured creditors.

relief from stay, adequate protection, extent of

A secured creditor seeking relief from the automatic stay on the grounds of lack of adequate protection has the burden of proving the validity of its lien or security interest. See In re Sports Enterprises, 38 B.R. 282 (NH, 1984). Further, a secured creditor is entitled to adequate protection of only its interest in the property, not for the full value of the property. See In re George Ruggiere Chrysler-Plymouth, Inc., 727 F. 2nd 1017 (CA 11, 1984). Adequate protection is not meant to enhance the position of a secured creditor, its purpose is only to enable the creditor to maintain during the course of the case the position it held when the case was filed. A creditor with a security interest on an apartment building that was almost completely occupied, that was protected under a full maintenance contract, and that had sufficient cash flow to pay operating expenses was held not to be entitled to adequate protection in In re Marion Street Partnership, 108 BR 218 (MN, 1989). Creditors with valueless junior liens or unsecured deficiency claims are not entitled to adequate protection. See In re Lopez-Soto, 764 F.2d 23 (CA 1, 1985).

adequate protection of oversecured creditor, equity cushion theory

Historically, whether or not an oversecured creditor was entitled to adequate protection depended largely on the amount and stability of its so-called "equity cushion." The equity cushion is the amount by which the value of a creditor's collateral exceeds the amount of its claim. Because of the valuation problems inherent in applying the equity cushion theory and because of the Supreme Court's ruling in United Savings Assn. of Texas v. Timbers of Inwood Forest Assocs., Ltd., infra, the use of the equity cushion theory as the primary determinant in deciding whether an oversecured creditor is entitled to adequate protection has fallen into disfavor. However, the existence of a reasonable equity cushion may still be a valid reason for denying adequate protection to an oversecured creditor. See In re 495 Central Park Ave. Corp., 136 B.R. 626 (SD NY, 1992).

oversecured creditor, adequate protection of, important factors

In determining whether an oversecured creditor is entitled to adequate protection, the court is likely to be primarily concerned with the value of the creditor's collateral and whether or not that value is decreasing. See In re James River Assocs., 148 B.R. 790 (ED VA, 1992). If the value of its collateral is not decreasing, an oversecured creditor is not likely to be entitled to adequate protection, even if interest is accruing on its claim. See In re Lane, 108 B.R. 6 (MA, 1989). The basis of these rulings is the Supreme Court's holding in United Savings Assn. of Texas v. Timbers of Inwood Forest Assocs., Ltd., infra, that for purposes of adequate protection, a creditor's protected interest in property is the value of its collateral and not contractual or other legal rights such as the right to accrue interest or the right to foreclose and reinvest the proceeds. See In re Marion Street Partnership, 108 B.R. 218 (MN, 1989).

undersecured creditor, adequate protection

The issue of adequate protection most often arises with respect to undersecured creditors. A undersecured creditor is a creditor whose allowed claim exceeds the value of its collateral. A undersecured creditor is almost always entitled to adequate protection (or a lifting of the stay in the absence thereof) upon a showing that the value of its collateral is declining. The decline in value of its secured claim caused by an increase in the amount of senior liens against the property may also entitle a undersecured creditor to adequate protection. See Ridgewood Apt. Assocs., Ltd. v. Atlanta English Village Ltd., 110 B.R. 77 (ND GA, 1988) affirmed in 890 F. 2d 1166 (CA 11, 1989).

United Savings Assoc. v. Timbers of Inwood Forest, holding of case

In United Savings Assn. of Texas v. Timbers of Inwood Forest Assocs., Ltd., 484 U.S. 365, 98 L. Ed. 2d 740, 108 S.Ct. 626 (1988), the debtor, the owner of an apartment project, had borrowed money from a lender to finance the project and gave the lender a security interest in the project. When the debtor later filed under Chapter 11 the lender applied for relief from the automatic stay on the grounds of lack of adequate protection of its security interest. In the bankruptcy court it was established that the lender was an undersecured creditor and that the value of its collateral was appreciating slightly. The bankruptcy court held that even though its security interest was not depreciating the lender was entitled to adequate protection on the grounds that it had been prevented by the filing of the bankruptcy case from foreclosing on the property and obtaining possession thereof. The bankruptcy court therefore ordered the debtor to make monthly payments to the lender amortizing the amount that the lender would have received on a foreclosure sale of the property. The Supreme Court reversed the bankruptcy court ruling holding that an undersecured creditor whose security interest is not depreciating in value is not entitled to relief from the stay on the grounds of lack of adequate protection.

undersecured creditor, entitlement to adequate protection payments

Specifically, in Timbers of Inwood Forest the Supreme Court held that the phrase "value of such entity's interest" in 11 U.S.C. 361 means the value of its collateral only and not the value of the creditor's foreclosure rights under state law. Therefore, an undersecured creditor whose collateral is not depreciating is not entitled to postpetition interest as compensation for the delay in foreclosing on its collateral. However, an undersecured creditor whose collateral is declining in value is entitled to adequate protection payments as compensation for the decline in the value of its collateral. See Ridgemont Apartment Assocs. Ltd. v. Atlanta English Village, Ltd., 890 F.2d 1166 (CA 11, 1989).

adequate protection vs. relief from stay, which to grant

adequate protection, burden of proof

Upon a finding that the interest of a creditor in its collateral is not adequately protected, the court may either require the debtor to adequately protect the interest of the creditor in the property or grant relief from the stay and permit the creditor to proceed against the property. If the property is of value to the debtor and necessary for the rehabilitation of its business, the court will normally permit the debtor to adequately protect the creditor. However, it is usually up to the debtor to affirmatively propose the form and extent of any adequate protection, as the burden of proof on the issue of adequate protection is on the party opposing relief from the stay. See 11 U.S.C. 362(g).

11 U.S.C. 361 provides, in part, that when adequate protection of an interest of an entity in property is required under 11 U.S.C. 362, 363, or 364, it may be provided by:

adequate protection, form of

(1) requiring debtor in possession to make a cash payment or periodic cash payments to the entity, to the extent that the stay results in a decrease in the value of the entity's interest in the property;

(2) providing to the entity an additional or replacement lien to the extent that the stay results in a decrease in the value of the entity's interest in the property; or

(3) granting such other relief, other than entitling the entity to compensation under 11 U.S.C. 503(b)(1) as an administrative expense, as will result in the realization by the entity of the indubitable equivalent of the entity's interest in the property.

adequate protection, policy considerations

Section 361 and the concept of adequate protection is based on the policy that secured creditors should not be deprived of the benefit of their bargain in a bankruptcy proceeding. However, there may be situations where giving a secured creditor an absolute right to its bargain may be impossible or seriously detrimental to the bankruptcy laws. Therefore, Section 361 recognizes the availability of alternate means of protecting a secured creditor's interest. Though a creditor might not receive its bargain in kind, the purpose of Section 361 is to ensure that a secured creditor receives in value essentially what it bargained for. The examples of adequate protection given in Section 361 are neither exclusive nor exhaustive. See H.R. Report No. 595, p. 339 (1977), 1978 U.S. Code Cong. & Ad. News, 5963, 6295.

adequate protection, utility service

The practioner representing a small business debtor should be aware of the holding in In re Lucre, Inc., 333 BR 151 (WD MI, 2005). The case was decided shortly after the effective date of the revisions to the Bankruptcy Code mandated by the BAPCPA. The court ruled that it has no discretion under Section 366 (utility service) to continue an automatic stay against a utility provider past 30 days simply because the utility provider did not respond to the debtor's offers of adequate assurance of payment. The court ruled that an offer of adequate assurance of payment made to a utility binds the utility to continue service to the debtor only through the 30th day following the filing of a petition. The practitioner must act quickly after the case is filed to comply with the new Section 366 requirements and the "In re Lucre, Inc." holding. If nothing is done and the utility is not satisfied with an offer of adequate assurance, it could cut off service without first seeking court approval or relief from the automatic stay.

As indicated in Section 361, adequate protection may be in the form of a single cash payment, periodic cash payments, providing a replacement or additional lien, or such other relief as will give the creditor the indubitable equivalent of its interest in the collateral. However, both the form and the extent of adequate protection may vary with the circumstances of the case. For example, if a creditor's collateral is steadily declining in value, periodic cash payments in an amount approximately equal to the periodic decline in value of the collateral may be an appropriate form of adequate protection. See In re W.S. Sheppley & Co., 45 B.R. 473 (ND IA, 1984). Under other circumstances, if it is necessary to sell a creditor's collateral, adequate protection may be provided by permitting the creditor's lien to attach to the proceeds of the sale. See Matter of Wilhoit, 34 B.R. 14 (MD FL, 1983). Adequate protection in the form of the debtor's future business prospects may be accepted by court if it is shown that the debtor's business is likely to improve in the near future. See In re Snowshoe Co., 789 F. 2d 1085 (CA 4, 1986).

adequate protection, form of

As indicated in Section 361(3), adequate protection is not limited to the forms listed in the statute. Unconditional guarantees by third parties with means have been held to constitute adequate protection, especially if the guarantees are secured. See In re Greenwood Building Supply, Inc., 23 B.R. 720 (WD MO, 1982). Unsecured or conditional personal guarantees by third parties without substantial means, however, do not constitute adequate protection. See In re Mary Harpley Builders, Inc., 44 B.R. 151, (ND OH, 1984). FHA insurance and a VA guarantee on a loan have both been held to constitute adequate protection for a lender. See In re Roane, 8 B.R. 997 (ED PA, 1981), and In re DiBona, 9 B.R. 121 (ED PA, 1981). Similarly, a lien on unencumbered future crops may constitute adequate protection, as may a lien on the proceeds of an oil well drilled in a proven oil field. See In re Ahlers, 794 F.2d 388 (CA 8, 1986) (reversed on other grounds in 485 U.S. 1987), and In re O'Connor, 808 F.2d 1393 (CA 10, 1987).

adequate protection, what constitutes

It is clear in Section 361(3) that granting a creditor a claim as an administrative expense does not constitute adequate protection. If, however, the court grants adequate protection to a creditor and such protection later proves inadequate, the resulting unsecured claim for damages by the inadequately-protected creditor is a superpriority unsecured claim payable ahead of all other unsecured claims, including administrative expenses. See 11 U.S.C. 507(b).

adequate protection, insufficiency of, superpriority claim

Relief from stay for other cause. Relief from the automatic stay may also be granted for cause other than lack of adequate protection. See 11 U.S.C. 362(d)(1). Generally, when cause other than lack of adequate protection is alleged, the courts tend to look to the purposes of the stay and determine whether the granting of relief from the stay will defeat those purposes. See In re Tucson Estates, Inc., 912 F. 2d 1162 (CA 9, 1990), and Pursifull v. Eakin, 814 F. 2d 1501 (CA 10, 1987). If the purposes of the stay will not be substantially defeated by the granting of the requested relief and if the party seeking the relief can show a real need for the relief, the relief is likely to be granted. See In re Unioil, 54 B.R. 192 (CO, 1985). Similarly, if lifting the stay will not substantially harm the debtor or other creditors and will not interfere with the administration of the case, the relief is likely to be granted. See In re Central Hobron Associates, 36 B.R. 106 (HI, 1983).

relief from stay, cause other than lack of adequate protection

Bankruptcy courts often lift the automatic stay for cause to permit the continuation of a pending personal injury action against the debtor when the debtor is covered by liability insurance. See Matter of Holtkamp, 669 F. 2nd 505 (CA 7, 1982). Under proper circumstances, relief from the stay may be granted to permit a creditor to liquidate its claim in a nonbankruptcy forum. See Elliott V. Hardison, 26 B.R. 305 (ED VA, 1982). If the debtor is merely a nominal party in a nonbankruptcy action between third parties, the bankruptcy court may lift the stay and permit the action to proceed. See In re Columbia Ribbon & Carbon Mfg. Co., Inc., 13 B.R. 276 (SD NY, 1981). Family law disputes, if not excluded from the stay by 11 U.S.C. 362(b)(2), are often permitted to continue in state courts, usually because of the superior ability of state courts to resolve such matters. See Schulze v. Schulze, 15 B.R. 106 (SD OH, 1981). The stay may also be lifted to permit the continuation of nonbankruptcy proceedings in which the debtor is a fiduciary. See H.R. Report No. 595, p. 343 (1977), 1978 U.S. Code Cong. & Ad. News, 5963, 6300.

cause for relief from stay, what constitutes

cause for relief from stay, what constitutes

Relief from the automatic stay may also be granted for cause when it is shown that the bankruptcy case was filed by the debtor in bad faith. See 11 U.S.C. 362(d)(4) and In re Little Creek Dev. Co., 779 F. 2d 1068 (CA 5, 1986). Similarly, if the debtor is guilty of misconduct or mismanagement during the case, the stay may be lifted for cause. See In re CGR, Ltd., 56 B.R. 305 (SD TX, 1985), and In re Holly's, 140 B.R. 643 (WD MI, 1992). Secured and unsecured creditors alike may seek relief from the stay where cause other than lack of adequate protection is the grounds for the relief. See In re Westwood Broadcasting, Inc., 35 B.R. 47 (HI, 1983). Relief from the stay may also be obtained on the grounds of abstention. See 28 U.S.C. 1334(c), In re Tucson Estates, Inc., 912 F.2d 1162 (CA 9, 1990), and section 4.13, infra.

motion for relief from stay, procedure

Procedure for obtaining relief from stay. The procedure for seeking relief from the automatic stay is governed by 11 U.S.C. 362(e),(f), and (g) and Bankruptcy Rules 4001(a), 9013, and 9014. Obtaining relief from the automatic stay is a contested matter, and relief is sought by filing a motion under Bankruptcy Rule 9014. See Bankruptcy Rule 4001(a)(1). A motion seeking relief from the automatic stay must state with particularity the grounds therefor and must set forth the relief or order sought. See Bankruptcy Rule 9013. A copy of the motion must be served by first class mail or personal service upon the trustee or debtor in possession, any committee appointed in the case or, if no committee has been appointed, upon the creditors listed in the debtor's list of creditors holding the 20 largest unsecured claims, and upon such other persons as the court may direct. See Bankruptcy Rule 4001(a)(1). Unless the court orders otherwise, a response to the motion is not required. See Bankruptcy Rules 9013 and 9014. A fee is charged for the filing of a motion seeking relief from the automatic stay. The local rules should be checked for requirements pertaining to motions for relief from the automatic stay. A sample Motion for Relief From Stay of Acts Against Property is set forth in Exhibit 4-A at the end of this chapter.

motion for relief from stay, filing fee, sample

motion for relief from stay, who may file

Motions seeking relief from the automatic stay are core proceedings and are handled by the bankruptcy court, once the case has been referred by the district court. See 28 U.S.C. 157(b)(2)(G). A motion seeking relief from the automatic stay must be filed by a party in interest. See 11 U.S.C. 362(d). This means that the moving party must be either a direct creditor of the debtor or the legal holder of the right sought to be enforced by the motion. See In re Comcoach Corp., 698 F. 2nd 571 (CA 2, 1983). Once the party seeking relief has established a cause for lifting the stay, the burden of proof is on the party opposing relief from the stay (usually the debtor) to show why the relief should not be granted. See 11 U.S.C. 362(g). It should be noted that an order granting relief from the automatic stay is itself automatically stayed for 14 days after entry of the order unless the court orders otherwise or unless the order was entered ex parte. See Bankruptcy Rule 4001(a)(3).

order granting relief, stay of

motion for relief from stay, hearing requirements

Bankruptcy courts are required to resolve motions for relief from the automatic stay expeditiously, especially those filed by secured creditors seeking to reach or protect their collateral. A final hearing on a motion for relief from the stay as to acts against property of the estate must be commenced within 30 days after the motion is filed, unless the court, during that 30-day period, holds a preliminary hearing and orders the stay continued pending the final hearing. The court may continue the stay pending the final hearing only if it finds that there is a reasonable likelihood that the party opposing the relief will prevail at the final hearing. If a hearing is not held within the 30-day period, the stay is deemed terminated with respect to the moving party. See 11 U.S.C. 362(e)(1). If the debtor is an individual, the stay terminates 60 days after the request for relief is filed unless a final decision is rendered during the 60-day period or the 60-day period is extended. See 11 U.S.C. 362(e)(2). The preliminary hearing does not necessarily have to be an evidentiary hearing. See Satter v. KDT Industries, Inc., 28 B.R. 374 (SD NY, 1982). If a preliminary hearing is held, the final hearing must be concluded within 30 days after the conclusion of the preliminary hearing, unless the 30-day period is extended with consent of the parties in interest or for a specific period which the court finds is required by compelling circumstances. See 11 U.S.C. 362(e)(1). The courts, it should be noted, occasionally use their injunctive powers to reinstate the automatic stay after its expiration. See 11 U.S.C. 105, Matter of Martin Exploration Co., 731 F. 2nd 1210 (CA 5, 1984).

motion for relief from stay, hearing deadlines

motion for relief from stay, applicability of hearing deadlines

The deadlines described in the preceding paragraphs apply only to motions seeking relief from the stay as to acts against property of the estate. Accordingly, they ordinarily apply only to motions for relief from the stay filed by secured creditors seeking to reach or protect their collateral. They do not apply to unsecured creditors seeking relief from the stay for cause other than lack of adequate protection. See In re Small, 38 B.R. 143 (MD, 1984).

Because hearings on motions for relief from the automatic stay as to acts against property of the estate must be disposed of expeditiously, it is impossible to permit extended discovery and other pretrial proceedings prior to the hearing. Such hearings are usually limited to matters relating directly to the issue of relief from the stay. Often, however, the debtor has setoffs or counterclaims against the creditor, or other affirmative defenses to the creditor's claim, that, in effect, challenge the existence, validity, or amount of the very claim that the creditor seeks to enforce or protect by its motion for relief. Normally in such instances, only the issues directly related to the amount or validity of a creditor's claim are considered by the court at the hearing on a motion for relief from the stay. Any issues indirectly related to the amount or validity of the claim are held in abeyance and litigated at the trial on the allowance of the claim. See In re Bialac, 694 F. 2nd 625 (CA 9, 1982). Unfortunately, it is often difficult to determine which issues relate directly to the amount or validity of a claim and which do not.

motion for relief from stay, matters considered at hearing

At any hearing on a motion for relief from the automatic stay as to any act precluded by the stay, the party seeking the relief (usually a creditor) has the burden of proof on the issue of whether the debtor has an equity in the property in question, if that is an issue in the case. The party opposing the relief (usually the debtor) has the burden of proof on all other issues. See 11 U.S.C. 362(g). This procedural rule is, of course, applicable to motions seeking relief from the stay on the grounds of lack of adequate protection of an interest in property. Once a creditor has raised the issue in its motion, it becomes the responsibility of the debtor to show that the interest of the creditor in the property is adequately protected. See 11 U.S.C. 362(g). Further, it is usually incumbent upon the debtor to propose and establish the form and extent of the adequate protection, because it is not necessarily the function of the court to formulate what will serve as adequate protection in a case. See In re Monroe Park, 17 B.R. 934 (DE, 1982).

motion for relief from stay, burden of proof

In summary, relief from the automatic stay may be sought on two grounds: (1) cause, including lack of adequate protection, and (2) no equity by the debtor in property not needed for reorganization. See 11 U.S.C. 362(d). Proof of either ground will suffice to either lift the stay or secure adequate protection. Unless the debtor's equity in the collateral is beyond dispute, most secured creditors will allege both grounds in their motions for relief from the stay. The debtor has the burden of proof on all issues except its equity in the property in question. See 11 U.S.C. 362(g).

relief from stay, summary of grounds for

Occasionally it may become necessary for a creditor to seek relief from the automatic stay ex parte. Upon the motion of a party in interest, the court, with or without a hearing, may grant such relief from the stay as is necessary to prevent irreparable damage to the interest of an entity in property, if such interest will suffer damage before there is an opportunity for notice and a hearing. See 11 U.S.C. 362(f). To obtain ex parte relief from the automatic stay, the party seeking the relief must present, by affidavit or verified motion, specific facts showing the immediacy of the irreparable damage. Also, the party's attorney must certify to the court in writing as to the efforts which have been made to give notice and the reasons why further notice should not be required. If ex parte relief from the stay is granted, the party obtaining the relief must give immediate oral notice thereof to the debtor and must forthwith mail or deliver a copy of the order granting the relief to the debtor. On two days notice to the party obtaining the relief, or on shorter notice if the court permits, the debtor may move for reinstatement of the stay, in which event the court must expeditiously hear and determine the motion. See Bankruptcy Rule 4001(a)(2).

ex parte relief from stay, when granted, procedure

If the debtor enters into an agreement with a creditor to provide adequate protection, to prohibit or condition the use, sale, or lease of property, to modify or terminate the automatic stay, to use cash collateral, or for the creation of a senior or equal lien, it will be necessary to file a motion under Bankruptcy Rule 4001(d)(1) in order to obtain court approval of the agreement. If such a motion is filed, a copy or notice of the motion and notice of the time for filing objections to the agreement must be mailed to any committee appointed in the case or its authorized agent, or, if no committee has been appointed, to the creditors listed in the list of 20 largest unsecured creditors filed by the debtor, and to such other entities as the court may direct. If no objection to the agreement is filed, the court may enter an order approving or disapproving the agreement without a hearing. If an objection is filed, a hearing on not less than five days notice must be held on the motion. See Bankruptcy Rule 4001(d)(1), (2), (3). If the agreement is in settlement of a motion, the service, notice, and hearing requirements may be waived by the court if it is determined that the motion provided adequate notice to the parties. See Bankruptcy Rule 4001(d)(4).

agreements with creditors, court approval of, when necessary, procedure

4.02 Operating a Business Under Chapter 11

debtor in possession, matters of concern

After the filing of a Chapter 11 case, the debtor, as a debtor in possession, must operate its business in accordance with the restrictions and requirements imposed by the Bankruptcy Code. Of particular concern to most newly-filed Chapter 11 debtors are the initial functions of a debtor in possession and the right of a debtor in possession to use cash collateral, sell or use estate property, and obtain credit during the pendency of the case. Each of these matters is discussed separately below in this section.

debtor in possession, what constitutes

The rights and duties of a debtor in possession. Upon the entry of an order for relief under Chapter 11, an entity referred to in the Bankruptcy Code as a "debtor in possession" comes into existence. In a Chapter 11 case, the debtor is the debtor in possession, except when a trustee is serving in the case. See 11 U.S.C. 1101(1). Even though the debtor and the debtor in possession are the same entity in physical and practical terms, for purposes of the Bankruptcy Code the debtor in possession is generally regarded as a legal entity separate and apart from the debtor. See In re General Coffee Corp., 32 B.R. 23 (SD FL, 1983).

debtor in possession, rights, powers, and duties

A Chapter 11 debtor in possession has all of the rights, powers, and duties of a trustee except the right to compensation and the duty to investigate the affairs of the debtor. See 11 U.S.C. 1107(a). Thus, a debtor in possession must set aside its own fraudulent or preferential transfers and may reject its own executory contracts. For practical purposes, then, the debtor in possession in a Chapter 11 case in which no trustee is serving has the rights, powers, and duties of a trustee in the operation of the debtor's business and the handling of the debtor's property. A failure to perform such duties may result in the appointment of a trustee, the termination of the debtor's business, or the conversion or dismissal of the case.

debtor in possession, right to operate debtor's business

Unless a trustee is appointed in the case or unless the court, on the request of a party in interest and after notice and a hearing, orders otherwise, the debtor as a debtor in possession may operate its business during the course of a Chapter 11 case. See 11 U.S.C. 1108. It is not necessary for the court to enter an order permitting the debtor to operate its business as a debtor in possession because this right exists by statute. Further, the court may not, on its own motion, enter an order directing the debtor to cease its business operation, because such an order may be entered only upon the request of a party in interest. See 11 U.S.C. 1108.

The following duties for a Chapter 11 debtor in possession are set forth in 11 U.S.C. 1106(a) and 1107:

debor in possession, statutory duties

(1) Account for all property of the debtor's estate.

(2) If a purpose would be served, examine proofs of claim and object to the allowance of improper claims.

(3) Unless the court orders otherwise, furnish such information concerning the estate and its administration as may be requested by a party in interest.

(4) File with the court, the U.S. Trustee, and any appropriate governmental taxing authorities, periodic reports and summaries of the operation of the debtor's business, including a statement of receipts and disbursements, and such other information as the U.S. Trustee or the court may require.

(5) Make a final report and file a final account of the administration of the estate with the court and with the U.S. Trustee.

(6) As soon as practicable, either file a plan under 11 U.S.C. 1121, file a report as to why a plan will not be filed, recommend conversion of the case to another chapter, or recommend dismissal of the case.

(7) For any year for which the debtor has not filed a tax return required by law, furnish to the taxing authority, without personal liability, any required information that is available.

(8) After confirmation of a plan, file such reports as are necessary or as the court may order.

(9) If with respect to the debtor there is a claim for a domestic support obligation, provide the notice specified in 11 U.S.C. 1106(c).

(10) If, when the case was commenced, the debtor (or any entity designated by the debtor) served as the administrator of an employee benefit plan, continue to perform the obligations required of the administrator.

(11) If the debtor is in the health care business, comply with the patient transfer requirements of 11 U.S.C. 704(a)(12).

In a small business case, the following additional duties are imposed on a debtor in possession by 11 U.S.C. 1116:

additional duties of small business debtor

(1) Append to the voluntary petition or, in an involuntary case, file not later than 7 days after the date of the order for relief, the debtor's most recent balance sheet, statement of operations, cash-flow statement, and Federal income tax return, or a statement made under penalty of perjury that no balance sheet, statement of operations, or cash-flow statement has been prepared and no Federal tax return has been filed with respect to the debtor.

(2) Attend, through its senior management personnel and counsel, meetings scheduled by the court or the United States trustee, including initial debtor interviews, scheduling conferences, and meetings of creditors convened under 11 U.S.C. 341, unless the court, after notice and a hearing, waives that requirement upon a finding of extraordinary and compelling circumstances.

(3) Timely file all schedules and statements of financial affairs, unless the court, after notice and a hearing, grants an extension, which shall not extend the time for filing to a date later than 30 days after the date of the order for relief, absent extraordinary and compelling circumstances.

(4) File all postpetition financial and other reports required by the Federal Rules of Bankruptcy Procedure or by local rule of the district court.

(5) Subject to the cash collateral provisions of 11 U.S.C. 363(c)(2), maintain insurance customary and appropriate to the industry.

(6) Timely file tax returns and other required government filings and, subject to the cash collateral provisions of 11 U.S.C. 363(c)(2), timely pay all taxes entitled to administrative expense priority except those being contested by appropriate proceedings being diligently prosecuted.

(7) Allow the United States trustee, or a designated representative of the United States trustee, to inspect the debtor's business premises, books, and records at reasonable times, after reasonable prior written notice, unless notice is waived by the debtor.

monthly reporting requirements of small business debtor

In addition to the above, a small business debtor is required to file monthly financial and other reports with the court and the United States trustee containing information regarding the debtor's profitability, including reasonable approximations of the debtor's projected cash receipts and disbursements over a reasonable period, comparisons of actual cash receipts and disbursements with projections in prior reports, a statement as to whether the debtor is in compliance with the postpetition requirements imposed on the debtor by the Bankruptcy Code and the Federal Rules of Bankruptcy Procedure, and as to whether tax returns and other required government filings have been timely filed and paid and, if the debtor is not in compliance, what the failures are and how and when the debtor intends to remedy the failures, and such other matters as are in the best interests of the debtor and creditors. See 11 U.S.C. 308(b) and Bankruptcy Rule 2015(a)(6). The monthly reports should be transmitted using Federal Bankruptcy Form 425(C) (Small Business Monthly Operating Report). See Exhibit 4-F.

periodic reports of equity interests

In addition to the monthly reporting requirements, if the debtor owns 20% or more of another entity, the debtor must timely file Federal Bankruptcy Form 26 (Periodic Report Regarding Value, Operations and Profitability of Entities in Which the Debtor's Estate Holds a Substantial or Controlling Interest). See Bankruptcy Rule 2015.3. The first periodic report must be filed no later than 7 days before the first meeting of creditors under 11 U.S.C. § 341. Subsequent reports must be filed at least every 6 months thereafter until the plan becomes effective or the case is closed. Copies of the report must be served on the trustee, any creditors' committee, and any other party in interest that has requested a copy. The report must list all entities in which the debtor has a substantial or controlling interest in the table on the first page of the form. Reports for each listed entity should be placed behind separate tabs and must include three exhibits: Exhibit A must provide valuation information, Exhibit B must provide financial statements, and Exhibit C must provide a description of operations. The exhibits should also include a statement of compliance with the Bankruptcy Rules, tax filings, and any other governmental requirements. See Exhibit 4-T.

A Chapter 11 debtor in possession is required by Bankruptcy Rule 2015(a) to perform the following functions:

debtor in possession, other duties

(1) If the court so directs, file with the court and transmit to the U.S. Trustee a complete inventory of the debtor's property within 30 days after qualifying as a debtor in possession, unless such an inventory has already been filed.

(2) Keep a record of the receipt and disposition of all money and property.

(3) File with the court, the U.S. Trustee, and any governmental taxing authorities, periodic reports and summaries of the operation of the debtor's business, including a statement of receipts and disbursements and such other information as the U.S. Trustee or the court may require and, if payments are made to employees, a statement of the amounts deducted for the employees' taxes and the place where these amounts were deposited.

(4) As soon as possible after the commencement of the case, if such notice has not previously been given, give notice of the case to every entity known to be holding money or property subject to the order or withdrawal of the debtor.

(5) On or before the last day of the month after each calendar quarter until a plan is confirmed or the case is converted or dismissed, file with the clerk of the bankruptcy court and transmit to the U.S. Trustee a statement of the disbursements made during the preceding calendar quarter and a statement of the amount of the quarterly fee required under 28 U.S.C. 1930(a)(6) that has been paid for that calendar quarter. See section 3.05, supra, for further reading on the quarterly fee in Chapter 11 cases.

quarterly report and fee, filing requirements

(6) In a chapter 11 small business case, unless the court, for cause, sets another reporting interval, file and transmit to the United States trustee for each calendar month after the order for relief, a report on the appropriate Official Form as required by 11 U.S.C. 308. If the order for relief is within the first 15 days of a calendar month, a report must be filed for the portion of the month that follows the order for relief. If the order for relief is after the 15th day of a calendar month, the period for the remainder of the month must be included in the report for the next calendar month. Each report must be filed no later than 21 days after the last day of the calendar month. See Exhibit 4-F.

The debtor's bankruptcy estate. As indicated above, a principal duty of the debtor in possession is to account for and administer all property of the debtor's estate. The debtor's estate includes the following property, wherever located:

debtor's estate, property included in

(1) all legal or equitable interests of the debtor in property as of the commencement of the case, except as provided in 11 U.S.C. 541(b) and 541(c)(2), which exceptions are described below in this section;

(2) all interests of the debtor and the debtor's spouse in community property as of the commencement of the case that is under the sole, equal, or joint management and control of the debtor or that is liable for an allowable claim against the debtor or against the debtor and the debtor's spouse, to the extent of such liability;

(3) any interest in property recovered under 11 U.S.C. 329(b), 363(n), 543, 550, 553, or 723;

(4) any interest in property preserved for the benefit of the estate or transferred to the estate under 11 U.S.C. 510(c) or 551;

(5) any interest in property that would have been property of the estate if held by the debtor on the date the petition was filed if the debtor acquires or becomes entitled to acquire such property within 180 days after the date of filing by bequest, devise, or inheritance, as a result of a divorce decree or property settlement agreement with the debtor's spouse, or as a beneficiary of a life insurance policy or death benefit plan;

(6) any proceeds, product, offspring, rents, or profits of or from property of the estate; and

(7) any interest in property that the estate acquires after the commencement of the case. See 11 U.S.C. 541(a).

If the debtor is an individual, property of the estate also includes property of the types described above that the debtor acquires after the commencement of the case and before the case is closed, dismissed or converted and earnings from services performed by the debtor after the commencement of the case and before the case is closed, dismissed or converted. See 11 U.S.C. 1115.

individual debtor, additional property of estate

Under 11 U.S.C. 541(b), property of the debtor's bankruptcy estate does not include the following:

property not included in bankruptcy estate

(1) Any power that the debtor may exercise solely for the benefit of another.

(2) Any interest of the debtor as a lessee of nonresidential real property wherein the lease expired prior to the commencement of the case, and ceases to include any such interest upon the expiration of the stated term of the lease during the case.

(3) Certain rights of the debtor as an educational institution.

(4) Certain rights of the debtor in oil and gas interests.

(5) Funds placed in Education IRAs or used to purchase tuition credit accounts, up to certain limits.

(6) Amounts withheld or received by an employer as contributions to employee benefit plans.

(7) Any interest of the debtor in pledged property held by a licensed pledgee as collateral for a loan that the debtor is not obligated to repay.

(8) Certain interests of the debtor in the proceeds of the sale of money orders.

11 U.S.C. 541(c)(2) provides that a restriction on the transfer of a beneficial interest of the debtor in a trust that is enforceable under applicable nonbankruptcy law is enforceable in a Chapter 11 case. This provision has been held to prevent the debtor's interest in an ERISA-qualified retirement plan from becoming property of the bankruptcy estate. See Patterson v. Shumate, 504 U.S. 753, 119 L. Ed. 2d 519, 112 S.Ct. 2242 (1992).

debtor's estate, property not included in

If property of the estate is in the hands of a third party, it may be necessary for the debtor to file an action to compel the turnover of the property to the estate. If, during the case, an entity other than a custodian is in possession, custody, or control of property that the debtor may use, sell, or lease under 11 U.S.C. 363, or that the debtor may exempt, the entity is required to account for and deliver the property, or the value thereof, to the debtor, unless the property is of inconsequential value or benefit of the estate. See 11 U.S.C. 542(a). The turnover of property by a custodian is governed by 11 U.S.C. 543. A custodian is a receiver or trustee appointed in a nonbankruptcy case or an assignee under a general assignment for the benefit of creditors. See 11 U.S.C. 101(11). See infra, this section for a discussion of the use, sale, or lease of property under 11 U.S.C. 363.

debtor in possession, action to compel turnover of property

The turnover of money or property of the estate that was repossessed, seized, or otherwise obtained from the debtor by a creditor prior to the commencement of the case may be compelled under 11 U.S.C. 542(a). See In re California Gulf Partnership, 48 B.R. 959 (ED LA, 1984), and In re H. Wolfe Iron & Metal Co., 64 B.R. 754 (WD PA, 1986). Non-creditor third parties may also be compelled under Section 542(a) to turn over property or funds in their possession, if the property or funds are found to constitute property of the estate. See In re Pied Piper Casuals, Inc., 50 B.R. 549 (SD NY, 1985). It is usually necessary for a debtor in possession to provide adequate protection to a creditor before the creditor can be compelled to turn over property in which it has a security interest. See United States v. Whiting Pools, Inc., 462 U.S. 198, 103 S.Ct. 2309, 76 L. Ed. 2nd 515 (1983). See section 4.01, supra, for further reading on adequate protection. See section 4.13, infra, for further reading on litigation related to bankruptcy proceedings.

turnover action by debtor in possession, property subject to

The debtor's initial post-filing functions. Promptly after the filing of a Chapter 11 case, certain functions must be performed by or on behalf of a debtor in possession in order to comply with the general provisions of the Bankruptcy Code and Rules and, in some districts, the local rules. Included among these functions are the following:

debtor in possession, functions to perform at start of case

(1) Establish one or more new bank accounts in the name of the debtor in possession.

(2) Amend such items as insurance policies, utility contracts, and agreements with suppliers to show the debtor in possession (as opposed to the debtor) as the responsible party.

(3) Make arrangements for the payment of necessary business expenses, including, if necessary, payment of the debtor's employees for services performed prior to the commencement of the case.

(4) Make arrangements for the preparation and filing of any operating or financial reports required locally by the U.S. Trustee or the court.

(5) Obtain prior approval of any post-filing compensation to be paid to debtor's owners or officers, if required locally.

(6) Obtain court approval for the employment by the debtor in possession of any professionals to be employed in the case.

(7) Take a complete inventory of the debtor's property if directed to do so by the court or if required under a local rule.

(8) File a copy or notice of the petition in the real estate transfer recording office in each county where real estate of the debtor is located.

(9) Investigate and take necessary action regarding the assumption or rejection of any executory contracts or unexpired leases of the debtor.

debtor in possession, bank accounts of

The filing of a Chapter 11 case normally serves to freeze the funds in the debtor's prefiling bank accounts. Banks often refuse to honor checks or drafts written on a debtor's prefiling account, even if the checks were written prior to the filing of the case. The best practice is for the debtor in possession to open one or more new bank accounts promptly after the case is filed. Any funds received by the debtor after the filing of the case should be deposited in the new bank accounts. The opening and use of new bank accounts will also aid in the important function of segregating the debtor's prefiling and postfiling funds and receipts. When opening a bank account for a debtor in possession, it is a good practice to require at least two signatures on each check, and for the checks to bear a notice that the check is void if not presented within a specified time, say 60 days.

debtor in possession, insurance policies and contracts

Unless a trustee is appointed, the debtor in possession becomes the effective "owner" of the debtor's property and business immediately upon the filing of the case. Accordingly, insurance policies insuring the debtor's property, utility contracts, and agreements with suppliers should be amended to show the debtor in possession as the insured or responsible party. Such amendments will also help to distinguish the debtor's prefiling debts and obligations from its postfiling obligations (see infra, this section). Postfiling agreements and bank accounts should identify the debtor in possession in the following manner: "(name of debtor), as debtor in possession in Case No. (case number)."

utility service, right to continuance of

It should be noted that a debtor has a right to continued service from a utility company if a prefiling debt owed to the utility is not paid when due. To retain this right, however, the debtor must, within 20 days after the date of filing, furnish to the utility adequate assurance of payment for future services in the form of a deposit or other security, the amount of which may be determined by the court if so requested. See 11 U.S.C. 366(a), (b). However, in a Chapter 11 case a utility may alter, refuse, or discontinue service if the utility does not receive, within 30 days after the date of filing, adequate assurance of payment for utility service that is satisfactory to the utility. See 11 U.S.C. 366(c)(2) and In re Lucre, Inc., 333 BR 151 (WD MI, 2005). Assurance of payment must be a cash deposit, a letter of credit, a certificate of deposit, a surety bond, a prepayment of utility consumption, or another form of security that is mutually agreed on between the utility and the debtor, but may not be an administrative expense priority. See 11 U.S.C. 366(c)(1). Upon the request of a party in interest and after notice and a hearing, the court may modify the amount of assurance of payment, but in determining the modification may not consider the absence of security prior to the filing of the case, timely payments made by the debtor prior to filing, or the availability of an administrative expense priority. See 11 U.S.C. 366(c)(3). Finally, notwithstanding any other provision of law, a utility may recover or set off its claim against a prefiling deposit made by the debtor without notice or a court order. See 11 U.S.C. 366(c)(4).

debtor's employees, prefiling wages, method of payment

If sufficient time and funds exist, the best practice is to pay the debtor's employees their prefiling wages and salaries prior to the filing of the case. Such payments should be made in the form of cash, cashier's checks, or some other device that does not include checks or drafts written on a bank account of the debtor (which are likely to be "frozen" when the case is filed). If cash is used, written receipts should be obtained from the employees.

In most cases it will be either impossible or impracticable to pay all accrued prefiling wages and salaries to the debtor's employees prior to the filing of the case. If prefiling compensation is owed to current employees of the debtor, it will be necessary for the debtor in possession to apply to the court shortly after the case is filed for an order authorizing the payment of prefiling wages and salaries. While the payment of such prefiling claims may appear to constitute preferential treatment, the court will normally authorize such payments of up to $12,475* per employee because most employees are entitled to a $12,475* priority claim for wages, salaries, commissions, and fringe benefits. See 11 U.S.C. 507(a)(4), (5). A sample Application for Allowance of and for Authorization to Pay Claims of Debtor's Employees for Prefiling Wages and Salaries is set forth in Exhibit 4-B at the end of this chapter. It may also be necessary to prepare proofs of claims on behalf of the employees (see section 4.04, infra).

prefiling wages of debtor's employees, payment after filing, procedure

* Dollar amounts subject to change on April 1, 2016.

In a small business case the debtor in possession is required to file the reports specified in 11 U.S.C. 308 and Bankruptcy Rule 2015(a). These reports are described above in this section. If the debtor is not a small business debtor, the local office of the U.S. Trustee may require a debtor in possession to file periodic operating and financial reports, usually either monthly or bi-weekly. The purpose of such reports is to enable the U.S. Trustee to monitor the business operations of debtors in possession. Accordingly, the local reporting requirements should be ascertained and promptly complied with. The failure to file such reports may, by itself, constitute sufficient cause for a court order terminating the debtor's business operations. See In re Modern Office Supply, Inc., 28 B.R. 943 (WD OK, 1983). In either event, it is important that these reports be prepared and filed in a timely manner.

United States trustee, reports required by

The local rules in many districts provide that officers of a debtor in possession may not be compensated in a Chapter 11 case until their compensation has been approved by the U.S. Trustee or the court. If necessary, an application or similar document seeking approval of officers' compensation should be prepared and filed with the appropriate office soon after the case is filed. A local form may be provided by the U.S. Trustee for this purpose. It should be noted that the compensation of highly paid officers of a debtor in possession is often required to be reduced following the filing of a Chapter 11 case.

officers of debtor in possession, approval of compensation of

It is usually necessary to file one or more applications with the court seeking approval of the employment of professional persons by the debtor in possession. Court approval is required for both the employment and compensation of attorneys, accountants, appraisers, and other professionals. The requirements and procedures for the filing of an application by a debtor in possession to employ an attorney or other professional person are set forth in sections 3.01 and 3.04, supra. The substantive and procedural requirements described in section 3.01, supra, for the employment and compensation of attorneys are also applicable to the employment and compensation of other professionals.

application to employ attorney or other professional, requirements

The local rules in some districts require a debtor in possession to take an inventory of its property and assets immediately after the filing of a Chapter 11 case for the purpose of adequately preparing its schedules and statement of affairs. The local rules should be checked for such requirements. Bankruptcy Rule 2015(a) contains a similar requirement, if the court so directs.

debtor in possession, duty to take inventory

The assumption or rejection of executory contracts and unexpired leases is covered in section 4.05, infra. Most executory contracts and unexpired leases may be rejected, assumed, or assigned at any time during the case or under a plan. However, if a debtor in possession does not assume or reject an unexpired lease of nonresidential real property under which the debtor is the lessee prior to the date of the order confirming the plan or within 120 days after the order for relief, whichever is earlier, or within such additional time as the court, for cause within the 120-day period, fixes, the lease is deemed rejected and the premises must be surrendered. See 11 U.S.C. 365(d)(4). A debtor in possession also has certain duties with respect to unexpired leases of equipment and other non-household personal property. See 11 U.S.C. 365(d)(5). See section 4.05, infra, for further reading on this matter.

executory contracts, assumption or rejection of, time limits

cash collateral, definition

Use of cash collateral. To obtain funds to meet its payroll or other business expenses, it is usually necessary for a debtor in possession to use cash collateral during a Chapter 11 case, often early in the case. Cash collateral includes cash, negotiable instruments, documents of title, securities, deposit accounts, or other cash equivalents, whenever acquired, in which both the estate and another entity have an interest. See 11 U.S.C. 363(a). If the security agreement so provides, the proceeds, products, offspring, rents, or profits of property subject to a security interest, whether existing before or after the commencement of the case, may also be included as cash collateral. See 11 U.S.C. 363(a), 552(b)(1). It is important to note that a debtor in possession is required to segregate and account for all cash collateral that is at any time in its possession, custody, or control. See 11 U.S.C. 363(c)(4).

cash collateral, existence of, duty to segregate

cash collateral, what constitutes

Cash collateral normally exists when a secured creditor has a security interest in cash or the equivalent of cash. The creditor's lien may have originally been on the cash collateral itself (e.g., on a bank account or securities of the debtor), on property (such as accounts receivable) that is later turned into cash, or on real or personal property of the debtor that later produces profits or rents. Cash collateral normally includes receipts from prepetition accounts receivable that have been assigned by the debtor, receipts from the sale of prepetition inventory upon which a creditor's security interest exists, and cash or securities in prepetition bank accounts upon which a security interest exists. If the security agreement so provides, the postpetition proceeds, rents or profits from secured property may also constitute cash collateral. Cash collateral also includes postpetition rents from hotels and other lodgings unless the court rules otherwise.

proceeds of secured property, when cash collateral

Generally, if a creditor has a prefiling security interest, the security interest does not attach to property of the debtor's estate acquired after the commencement of the case, even if the security agreement contains an after-acquired property clause. See 11 U.S.C. 552(a). However, if a creditor has a prepetition security interest in property of the estate and if the security interest created by the security agreement extends to proceeds, product, offspring, rents, or profits of the property, then the creditor's security interest extends to the proceeds, product, offspring, rents, or profits of the secured property acquired by the estate after the commencement of the case, except to the extent that the court, based on the equities of the case, orders otherwise. See 11 U.S.C. 363(a), 552(b)(1). Thus, postpetition proceeds, rents, or income from secured property may constitute cash collateral, but only if there is a security agreement that so provides, and only if the court, based on the equities of the case, does not order otherwise. If a creditor's prefiling security agreement provides that the creditor's security interest attaches to rents of secured property or to fees charged for the use of hotel or motel rooms, then the creditor's security interest attaches to any such rents or fees collected by the debtor after the filing of the case unless the court, based on the equities of the case, rules otherwise. See 11 U.S.C. 552(b)(2). These rules are important in determining whether cash or other property received by the debtor after the commencement of the case constitutes cash collateral.

hotel rents as cash collateral

debtor in possession, use of cash collateral by, requirements

Because it can be so easily converted by a debtor, the Bankruptcy Code treats cash collateral differently than other types of collateral. A debtor in possession may not use, sell, or lease cash collateral unless each entity that has an interest in the cash collateral consents to such use, sale, or lease, or unless the court, after notice and a hearing, authorizes such use, sale, or lease. See 11 U.S.C. 363(c)(2). A debtor in possession may use, sell or lease cash collateral (and other estate property) only in accordance with applicable nonbankruptcy law governing the transfer of property by a corporation or trust that is not a moneyed, business, or commercial corporation or trust. See 11 U.S.C. 363(d)(1). If a debtor in possession wishes to use cash collateral, the safest practice is to obtain either the prior written consent of each creditor having a valid security interest in the cash collateral or a court order authorizing the proposed use. In practice, however, many Chapter 11 debtors continue to use cash collateral after the filing of the case without obtaining either creditor consent or court approval. If a creditor does not object to the use or request adequate protection, the debtor is not usually retroactively penalized for using the cash collateral. See In re Kain, 86 B.R. 506 (WD MI, 1988) and In re Broomall Printing Corp., 131 B.R. 32 (MD, 1991).

debtor in possession, motion to use cash collateral, procedure

If a creditor with an interest in cash collateral which the debtor proposes to use will not consent to the proposed use, the debtor will have to file a motion under Bankruptcy Rule 4001(b) to obtain authority to use the cash collateral. A motion for authority to use cash collateral is a contested matter governed by Bankruptcy Rule 9014. The motion must be transmitted to the U.S. Trustee and served by personal service or first class mail on every entity having an interest in the cash collateral, on any creditors' committee appointed in the case or its authorized agent, or, if no committee has been appointed, on the creditors listed in the list of creditors holding the 20 largest unsecured claims filed by the debtor, and upon such other entities as the court may direct. See Bankruptcy Rules 4001(b)(1) and 9034.

A motion for authority to use cash collateral is required to include the following: (1) the amount of cash collateral sought to be used, sold, or leased, (2) the name and address of each entity having an interest in the cash collateral, (3) the name and address of the entity in control of or having possession of the cash collateral, (4) the facts demonstrating the need to use the cash collateral, and (5) the nature of the protection to be provided to those having an interest in the cash collateral. In addition, if a preliminary hearing is desired, the motion should include a request for such a hearing and should show the amount of cash collateral sought to be used pending the final hearing and the protection to be provided to creditors pending such hearing. See Advisory Committee's Notes to Bankruptcy Rule 4001(b).

motion to use cash collateral, preparation of

If an emergency or immediate need to use cash collateral exists, a motion for authority to use cash collateral should contain a request for a preliminary hearing and the debtor should be prepared to show at such a hearing that the creditors secured by the cash collateral will be adequately protected and that the estate will suffer immediate and irreparable damage if preliminary relief is not granted. See 11 U.S.C. 363(c)(3) and Bankruptcy Rule 4001(b)(2). A sample Motion for Authority to Use Cash Collateral is set forth in Exhibit 4-C at the end of this chapter.

emergency use of cash collateral, procedure

motion to use cash collateral, sample of

Most creditors secured by cash collateral will demand adequate protection of their interest in the cash collateral as a condition of any proposed use or other disposition thereof by the debtor. See 11 U.S.C. 363(e), which provides that the court shall prohibit or condition any proposed use, sale, or lease of property to the extent necessary to provide adequate protection of an interest in property. Adequate protection in such situations may be in the form of restrictions on the debtor's use of the cash collateral, the making of regular payments to the creditor, providing insurance on the property, the payment of interest for the use of the cash collateral, segregating and accounting for the cash collateral, the granting of additional liens, or other affirmative actions by the debtor. It should be noted that the debtor has the burden of proof on the issue of adequate protection in any hearing where the issue arises. See 11 U.S.C. 363(p). See section 4.01, supra, for further reading on the subject of adequate protection.

use of cash collateral, necessity of adequate protection

The hearing on a motion for authority to use cash collateral may be a preliminary hearing or may be consolidated with a hearing on a creditor's request for adequate protection. If the hearing is a preliminary hearing, the court may authorize the use, sale, or lease of cash collateral only if it finds that there is a reasonable likelihood that the debtor will prevail on the issue of adequate protection at the final hearing. See 11 U.S.C. 363(c)(3).

motion to use cash collateral, hearing requirements

The court is required to act promptly on a motion for authority to use cash collateral, and the hearing on such a motion must be scheduled in accordance with the needs of the debtor. See 11 U.S.C. 363(c)(3). While the final hearing on a motion for authority to use cash collateral may not be held earlier than 14 days after service of the motion, the court may conduct a preliminary hearing at an earlier date, if the motion so requests. At a preliminary hearing the court may authorize the use of only that amount of cash collateral as is necessary to avoid immediate and irreparable harm to the debtor's estate pending the final hearing on the motion. See Bankruptcy Rule 4001(b)(2).

motion to use cash collateral, hearing, when held

Notice of the hearing on a motion for authority to use cash collateral must be given to the parties upon whom service of the motion is required (see supra, this section), and to such other entities as the court may direct. See Bankruptcy Rule 4001(b)(3). If feasible, the best practice is to obtain a hearing date when the motion is filed and serve notice of the hearing with the motion. It should be noted that notice of the preliminary and final hearings may be combined and that Bankruptcy Rule 4001(b) does not limit the authority of the court to schedule hearings appropriate under circumstances and in accordance with the needs of the debtor. See Committee Notes to Bankruptcy Rule 4001(b). The provision in 11 U.S.C. 363(c)(3) requiring hearings to be scheduled in accordance with the needs of the debtor has been held to permit a hearing with only 72 hours notice to creditors, if the needs of the debtor so dictate. See In re Sheehan, 38 B.R. 859 (SD, 1984). It should be noted that a stipulation to use cash collateral must comply with Bankruptcy Rules 4001(d) and 9034.

motion to use cash collateral, notice requirements

It is common for creditors whose security may be threatened by a proposed use or other disposition of cash collateral by the debtor to seek relief from the automatic stay for the purpose of protecting or reclaiming their security. Such a motion may be heard by the court in conjunction with a motion by the debtor to use cash collateral. Orders approving the use or lease of property, including the use of cash collateral, are core proceedings and may be issued by the bankruptcy court. See 28 U.S.C. 157(b)(2)(M).

motion to use cash collateral, motion for relief from stay, consolidation of unauthorized use of cash collateral, penalties for

An unauthorized use of cash collateral by a debtor may result in a replacement lien being given to a creditor damaged by such use, by an award of damages, by the appointment of a trustee, or in other civil sanctions being imposed against the debtor by the court under 11 U.S.C. 105(a). See Hester v. NCNB Texas Nat. Bank, 899 F. 2d 361 (CA 5, 1990). However, it has been held that if the unauthorized use of cash collateral was a violation of a statute and not a court order, the debtor may not be held in contempt of court for such use. See In re Continental Marine Corp., 35 B.R. 990 (ED MO, 1984).

selling estate property, general rules

Selling estate property. In many Chapter 11 cases it becomes necessary, often early in the case, to sell property of the estate. Estate property may be sold either prior to confirmation or under the debtor's plan after confirmation. Estate property may be sold for any legitimate purpose, including raising funds with which to operate the debtor's business, downsizing the business, or ridding the business of unprofitable assets. Preconfirmation sales of estate property are governed by Section 363 of the Bankruptcy Code and postconfirmation sales are provided for in Section 1123. If desired, a Chapter 11 plan may be a liquidating plan that calls for the sale of all of the estate property. See 11 U.S.C. 1123(a)(5)(B), (D) and 1123(b)(4). Some courts, however, have refused to confirm Chapter 11 plans that call for complete liquidation from the outset. See In re Lyons Transportation Lines, Inc., 123 BR 526 (WD PA, 1991).

sales of estate property, types of sales

The Bankruptcy Code divides preconfirmation sales of estate property (other than cash collateral) into two categories: (1) sales made in the ordinary course of the debtor's business, and (2) sales made other than in the ordinary course of business. Substantially different rules are applicable to each type of sale. Postconfirmation sales of estate property must be made in the manner provided for in the plan.

sale of estate property, general requirements

Unless the court orders otherwise, a debtor in possession may sell estate property (other than cash collateral), in the ordinary course of business without notice or a hearing. See 11 U.S.C. 363(c)(1). If a sale of estate property is not in the ordinary course of business, the sale may be made only after notice and a hearing. See 11 U.S.C. 363(b)(1). It should be noted that a debtor in possession may use, sell, or lease property of the estate (including cash collateral) only in accordance with applicable nonbankruptcy law governing the transfer of property by a corporation or trust that is not a moneyed, business, or commercial corporation or trust and only to the extent that such use, sale, or lease is not inconsistent with any relief from the automatic stay granted to a creditor by the court. See 11 U.S.C. 363(d).

sale in ordinary course of business, what constitutes

In the case of preconfirmation sales, it is obviously important to determine prior to the sale whether the proposed sale will qualify as having been made in the ordinary course of the debtor's business. In making such a determination, much depends on the nature of the debtor's business. The term "ordinary course of business" generally refers to the debtor's day-to-day business affairs. See In re Cascade Oil Co., Inc., 51 BR 877, 882 (KS, 1985). In most instances sales of inventory and products normally sold by the debtor to its customers and little else are deemed to be made in the ordinary course of business. See In re Dant & Russell, Inc., 853 F.2d 700 (CA9, 1988). Sales of other assets, or even unusually large sales of products or inventory, are normally deemed to be other than in the ordinary course of business. See In re Selgar Realty Corp., 85 BR 235 (ED NY, 1988).

sales not in the ordinary course of business, procedure

Sales of estate property that are made other than in the ordinary course of the debtor's business are governed by 11 U.S.C. 363(b)(1), which provides that a debtor in possession may use, sell, or lease estate property other than in the ordinary course of business only after notice and a hearing. If such a sale is effected without the required notice and hearing, the sale may subsequently be attacked and set aside by a creditor or the U.S. Trustee. See In re Cavalieri, 142 BR 710 (ED PA, 1992). In addition, such a sale, especially to an insider, may constitute grounds for the appointment of a trustee or a denial of confirmation of the debtor's plan. See In re Sir Julian, Inc., 95 BR 851 (SD FL, 1989), and In re Brookfield Clothes, Inc., 31 BR 978 (SD NY, 1983). In the least, the faith of the court in the debtor is likely to be damaged by such a sale. It should be noted that 11 U.S.C. 363(b)(1) contains restrictions on the transfer of personally identifiable information about individuals and persons not affiliated with the debtor.

As indicated above, estate property may be sold other than in the ordinary course of business either prior to confirmation under Section 363(b) of the Bankruptcy Code or after confirmation in the manner provided for in the debtor's plan. Before attempting to sell significant estate assets other than in the ordinary course of business, it is important to consider both methods of sale and determine which method is preferable in the case at hand. If an emergency situation exists where it is important that the sale be consummated quickly, then a Section 363(b) sale prior to confirmation is clearly preferable because of the time constraints associated with the Chapter 11 confirmation process. However, if time is not of the essence, an asset sale under the debtor's plan may be preferable to a preconfirmation sale under Section 363(b). The primary reason favoring an asset sale under the plan over a Section 363(b) sale is that many bankruptcy courts are reluctant to approve a Section 363(b) sale of a substantial portion of the estate assets, especially if the sale is opposed by the U.S. Trustee or a creditor, unless it can be established that an emergency situation exists, no collusion or bad faith exists in connection with the proposed sale, and adequate consideration will be paid. See In re Abbotts Dairies of Pa., Inc., 788 F.2d 143 (CA 3, 1986), and In re Ancor Exploration Co., 30 BR 802 (ND OK, 1983). The reason for such reluctance is that such a sale can be the most significant event in the case and may render the confirmation process essentially meaningless. It should be noted that the U.S. Trustee is likely to oppose a Section 363(b) sale of significant estate assets unless it is shown early on that an emergency situation truly exists and no collusion or bad faith is present.

Section 363(b) sale vs. sale under plan, factors

If it is decided to conduct a Section 363(b) sale, the "notice and a hearing" requirement of Section 363(b)(1) must be complied with. Under the Bankruptcy Code, the phrase "after notice and a hearing" means "after notice but without a hearing unless someone asks for one." See 11 U.S.C. 102(1) and In re Northern Star Industries, 38 B.R. 1019 (ED NY, 1984). Thus, once notice is given of an intention to use, sell, or lease estate property outside the ordinary course of business, a hearing must be held only if a creditor or other party in interest timely requests one. If a hearing is not requested, the debtor in possession may carry out the proposed use, sale, or lease without a court order.

notice and a hearing, what constitutes

At least 21 days notice by mail must be given of any proposed use, sale, or lease of estate property outside the ordinary course of business to all creditors, creditors' committees, and the U.S. Trustee, unless the court, for cause, shortens the time or directs another method of giving notice. See Bankruptcy Rules 6004(a), 2002(a)(2), 2002(i), and 2002(k). In lieu of sending notice to all creditors, the court may order that notice need be mailed only to the creditors' committee (if one has been appointed) or its authorized agent and to such creditors or equity security holders who serve on the trustee or debtor in possession and file with the clerk a request that all notices be mailed to them. See Bankruptcy Rule 2002(i). If the proposed sale constitutes the sale of all or substantially all of the debtor's assets, notice of the sale must also be given to equity security holders, unless the court orders otherwise. See Bankruptcy Rule 2002(d). The local rules should be checked for other requirements related to such notices, including the person responsible for sending the notices.

sales not in the ordinary course of business, notice requirements

The notice should identify and describe the property proposed to be used, sold, or leased outside the ordinary course of business. However, a general description of the property is sufficient, and a full legal description of real estate is not usually required. The notice should specify the date, time, and place of any proposed public sale, or the terms and conditions of any proposed private sale. It should also specify the time for filing objections to the proposed transaction. See Bankruptcy Rule 2002(c)(1). The date of the hearing to be held should objections be filed may also be set forth in the notice. See Bankruptcy Rule 6004(e). Objections to the proposed use, sale, or lease transaction must be filed and served not less than seven days before the date set for the proposed transaction, unless the court fixes another time. The filing of an objection to the proposed use, sale, or lease of property creates a contested matter that is governed by Bankruptcy Rule 9014, which requires a motion, notice, and a hearing. See Bankruptcy Rule 6004(b). A sample Notice of Proposed Sale of Estate Property Not in the Ordinary Course of Business is set forth in Exhibit 4-D at the end of this chapter.

notice of proposed sale of estate property, contents

objections to proposed sale of estate property, when filed

adequate protection, when required, burden of proof

At any time, on the request of an entity that has an interest in property used, sold, or leased, or proposed to be used, sold, or leased, by a debtor in possession, the court, with or without a hearing, may prohibit or condition such use, sale, or lease as is necessary to provide adequate protection to such entity's interest in property. See 11 U.S.C. 363(e). Thus, a debtor in possession should be prepared to adequately protect any creditor whose security may be affected by a proposed use, sale, or lease of estate property, whether in or outside of the ordinary course of business. As always, the debtor in possession has the burden of proof on the issue of adequate protection at any hearing. See 11 U.S.C. 363(o). Adequate protection can often be provided by having the lien of the secured creditor attach to the proceeds of the proposed sale or lease. However, if the proceeds of the transaction are other than cash, additional protection may be necessary. See Matter of Wilhoit, 34 B.R. 14 (MD FL, 1983). See section 4.01, supra, for further reading on the subject of adequate protection.

debtor in possession, recovering expenses of preserving or selling secured property

A debtor in possession may recover from property securing an allowed secured claim the reasonable and necessary costs and expenses of preserving or disposing of the property, to the extent of any benefit to the secured creditor. See 11 U.S.C. 506(c). This provision should be remembered when secured property is being sold, because the debtor in possession may be permitted to surcharge the property and recover some or all of the expenses incurred in preserving or selling the property. See section 5.02, infra, for further reading on the recovery of costs and expenses under 11 U.S.C. 506(c).

small estate, general notice of intent to sell

If all nonexempt property of the debtor's estate has an aggregate gross value of less than $2,500, a general notice of intent to sell the property other than in the ordinary course of business may be given. Objections to such a sale must be filed and served within 14 days of the date the notices were mailed, unless the court fixes a different time. See Bankruptcy Rule 6004(d). This may be a useful procedure for selling the property of a small estate.

sales not in ordinary course of business, conduct of sale

The conduct of sales outside the ordinary course of business are governed by Bankruptcy Rule 6004(f). Such sales may be private or by public auction, whichever appears to be more beneficial to the estate. Unless it is impracticable, an itemized statement of the property sold, the name of each purchaser, and the price received for each item or lot or for the property as a whole if sold in bulk, must be filed with the clerk and transmitted to the U.S. Trustee upon completion of the sale. The debtor in possession must file this statement unless the property is sold by an auctioneer, in which case the auctioneer must file the statement with the clerk and transmit copies to the U.S. Trustee and the debtor in possession. See Bankruptcy Rule 6004(f)(1). The debtor or debtor in possession, as the case may be, may be required to execute any instruments necessary to effectuate the transfer of property to the purchasers. See Bankruptcy Rule 6004(f)(2). Finally, it should be noted that unless the court orders otherwise, an order authorizing the use, sale or lease of property other than cash collateral is automatically stayed for 14 days after entry of the order. See Bankruptcy Rule 6004(h). See Bankruptcy Rule 6004(g) for the procedures governing sales of personally identifiable information.

secured creditor, bidding on property at sale

avoidance of sale, when permitted

order authorizing sale, effect of appeal

Unless the court orders otherwise, the holder of an allowed claim secured by a lien on property of the estate being sold outside the ordinary course of business may bid on the property at the sale, and if the creditor purchases the property it may offset its claim against the purchase price of the property. See 11 U.S.C. 363(k), and section 5.02, infra. The debtor in possession may avoid any sale wherein the sales price was controlled by an agreement among potential bidders, or may recover damages from the parties to such an agreement. See 11 U.S.C. 363(n). Finally, the reversal or modification on appeal of an order authorizing a sale or lease of property does not affect the validity of a good-faith sale or lease unless the authorization order was stayed pending the appeal. See 11 U.S.C. 363(m). See section 4.13, infra, for further reading on appeals.

When estate property subject to a lien or security interest is sold, the best price can usually be obtained by selling the property free and clear of all liens or security interests. Under 11 U.S.C. 363(f), a debtor in possession may sell estate property free and clear of the interest in the property of any entity other than the estate only if one or more of the following conditions exist:

free and clear sale of estate property, when permitted

(1) applicable nonbankruptcy law permits the sale of the property free and clear of such interests;

(2) the other entity or entities having an interest in the property consent to a sale free and clear of their interests;

(3) the other interests in the property are liens and the price at which the property is to be sold exceeds the aggregate value of all liens on the property;

(4) the other interests in the property are the subject of a bona fide dispute; or

(5) the other entities with an interest in the property could be compelled in a legal or equitable dispute to accept a money satisfaction of their interests.

Most free and clear sales are outside the ordinary course of business, which means that the notice and hearing requirements described above for such sales must be complied with. Under the proper circumstances, free and clear sales may also occur in the ordinary course of business, in which case neither notice nor a hearing is required. As in any sale, however, a creditor whose security is threatened by a free and clear sale, whether in or outside of the ordinary course of business, may seek to prohibit or condition the sale on the grounds of lack of adequate protection. See 11 U.S.C. 363(e).

free and clear sale, rules governing

For free and clear sales outside the ordinary course of business, a motion for authority to sell property free and clear of liens and other interests must be filed in accordance with Bankruptcy Rule 9014 and served on all parties holding liens or other interests in the property to be sold. See Bankruptcy Rule 6004(c), which governs the procedure for such motions. Notice of such a motion must be given as specified in Bankruptcy Rules 2002(a)(2), 2002(c)(1), 2002(i), and 2002(k). The notice must include the date of the hearing and the time for filing objections to the proposed sale.

free and clear sale, procedure

Sales of property that is co-owned by the estate and another entity are governed by 11 U.S.C. 363(h). A debtor in possession may sell, either in or outside of the ordinary course of business, as the case may be, both the interest of the estate and the interest of any co-owner in property in which the debtor had, at the time of the commencement of the case, an undivided interest as a tenant in common, joint tenant, or tenant by the entirety, provided that all of the following conditions exist:

sale of co-owned property, when permitted

(1) partition in kind of the property among the estate and the co-owners is impracticable;

(2) sale of the estate's undivided interest in the property would realize significantly less for the estate than the sale of such property free of the interests of co-owners;

(3) the benefit to the estate of a sale of the property free of the interests of co-owners outweighs the detriment, if any, to the co-owners; and

(4) the property is not used in the production, transmission, or distribution, for sale, of electric energy or natural or synthetic gas for heat, light, or power. See 11 U.S.C. 363(h).

Prior to the consummation of any sale of co-owned property, the co-owner of the property has the right to purchase the property at the price at which the sale is to be consummated. See 11 U.S.C. 363(i). After consummation of a sale of co-owned property to another entity, the debtor in possession must distribute to the co-owners their share of the sales proceeds, less their share of the costs and expenses of the sale, not including any compensation owing to the trustee or debtor in possession. See 11 U.S.C. 363(j).

sale of co-owned property, rights of co-owner

Obtaining postpetition credit. Most Chapter 11 debtors are short on cash. In fact, short term lack of cash and stalemates with lenders are the precipitating causes of most Chapter 11 filings. Even with the moratorium on the payment of prepetition debts following the filing of a Chapter 11 case, most debtors are unable to pay all of their business and legal expenses out of cash and current income. It is generally necessary, then, for a debtor to obtain credit or borrow funds during the course of the case in order to remain in business. More often than not, borrowing will become necessary early in the case.

Chapter 11 debtor, need for credit

The Bankruptcy Code permits a debtor in possession to obtain the following types of credit or incur the following types of debt:

(1) Unsecured credit or debt in the ordinary course of business. Unless the court orders otherwise, a debtor in possession may obtain unsecured credit and incur unsecured debt in the ordinary course of business, and the claims therefor are allowable as administrative expenses under 11 U.S.C. 503(b)(1). See 11 U.S.C. 364(a). Neither notice nor a hearing is required for this type of credit or debt, unless the court so orders. This type of credit is most often obtained from the debtor's customary trade suppliers. However, suppliers with substantial prepetition claims against the debtor are often reluctant to extend this type of credit after the case is filed.

unsecured credit in ordinary course of business, how to obtain unsecured credit not in ordinary course of business, requirements

(2) Unsecured credit or debt outside the ordinary course of business. The court, after notice and a hearing, may authorize a debtor in possession to obtain unsecured credit or incur unsecured debt other than in the ordinary course of business, the claim for which is allowable as an ordinary administrative expense under 11 U.S.C. 503(b)(1). See 11 U.S.C. 364(b). As a practical matter, most unsecured lines of credit that were available prior to the filing of the case become unavailable after the case is filed. Therefore, if a debtor in possession is unable to obtain unsecured credit or debt allowable as an ordinary administrative expense under 11 U.S.C. 503(b)(1), the court, after notice and a hearing, may authorize the obtaining of unsecured credit or the incurring of unsecured debt, the claim for which has priority over all other administrative expenses. See 11 U.S.C. 364(c)(1). This claim is one of the two superpriority claims created under the Bankruptcy Code. Until a superpriority claim has been paid, the debtor in possession may be precluded from paying administrative expenses in the case, including attorney's fees. See In re Flagstaff Foodservice, Inc., 739 F. 2nd 73 (CA 2, 1984).

superpriority claim for unsecured credit, when allowed

junior secured credit, how to obtain

(3) Junior secured credit or debt. If a debtor in possession is unable to obtain unsecured credit or debt that is allowable as an ordinary administrative expense under 11 U.S.C. 503(b)(1), the court, after notice and a hearing, may authorize the obtaining of credit or the incurring of debt secured either by a lien on property of the estate that is not otherwise subject to a lien or by a junior lien on estate property that is already subject to a lien. See 11 U.S.C. 364(c)(2), (3). To obtain court approval of financing arrangements of this type it must normally be shown that (1) the debtor was unable to obtain unsecured credit, (2) the proposed credit is necessary to preserve the estate, and (3) the terms of the proposed credit are fair, reasonable and adequate. See In re The Crouse Group, Inc., 71 BR 544 (ED PA, 1987). In determining whether the proposed credit is fair, reasonable and adequate, most courts apply the so-called business judgment rule whereby the debtor's business judgment on the matter is presumed valid and will not be interfered with in the absence of bad faith or abuse of discretion. See In re Ames Dept. Stores, Inc., 115 BR 34 (SD NY, 1990), and In re St. Mary's Hospital, 86 BR 393 (ED PA, 1988), where the court refused to approve a financing arrangement with the debtor's parent company because of a lack of good faith.

senior secured credit, how to obtain

(4) Senior secured credit or debt. The court, after notice and a hearing, may authorize the obtaining of credit or the incurring of debt secured by a senior or equal lien on property of the estate that is subject to a prior lien, but only if the debtor in possession is unable to obtain such credit or debt otherwise and there is adequate protection of the interest of the prior lienholder. See 11 U.S.C. 364(d)(1). In any hearing on the granting of such a senior or equal lien, the debtor in possession has the burden of proof on the issue of adequate protection. See 11 U.S.C. 364(d)(2). The requirements for obtaining court approval of financing of this type are generally the same as that described in the preceding paragraph with respect to junior secured credit except that it must also be shown that existing lienholders will be adequately protected.

prefiling and postfiling debts, importance of segregating

As indicated above, unsecured debts and obligations incurred in the ordinary course of business by a debtor in possession after the commencement of the case are given priority and treated as administrative expenses, while similar debts and obligations incurred by the debtor prior to filing are treated merely as unsecured claims. It is important, therefore, for a debtor in possession to segregate prefiling debts and obligations from those incurred after the commencement of the case.

allowable postfiling debt, what constitutes

It may be difficult at times to determine whether a particular obligation was incurred prior to or after the date of filing. Agreements negotiated or entered into prior to filing but performed by the other party or breached by the debtor after the filing of the case are examples. Generally, an allowable postpetition obligation is an obligation beneficial to the estate which is incurred directly by the debtor in possession either by affirmatively entering into an agreement with the creditor or by using the creditor's property. See Matter of Jartran, Inc., 732 F. 2nd 584 (CA 7, 1984), and In re Mammoth Mart, Inc., 536 F. 2nd 950 (CA 1, 1976). A postpetition obligation for rent may be incurred when leased property is used by the debtor in possession for the benefit of the estate in the absence of a postpetition lease (i.e., under a prepetition lease agreement). The amount of the administrative rental obligation is the fair rental value of the property, which is rebuttably presumed to be the rental specified in the debtor's prepetition lease. See In re GHR Energy Corp., 41 B.R. 668 (MA, 1984).

postfiling claim under prefiling lease

A debtor in possession who wishes to obtain credit other than in the ordinary course of business should take certain steps in order to enhance its chances of obtaining it. The first step is for the creditor to examine and evaluate the status of its assets and property. It should be determined, for example, whether the debtor has any unencumbered assets that could serve as collateral for the credit. Assets acquired since the filing of the case and less obvious assets such as causes of action and leasehold interests should be considered. The status of the security interests of existing creditors on the debtor's assets should be examined. If an existing lien is not fully perfected it may be avoidable in the Chapter 11 case and the debtor's chances of obtaining new credit will be improved. Unencumbered assets or property owned by the principals of the debtor should also be considered as sources of collateral for credit.

obtaining postpetition credit, steps to take

A Chapter 11 debtor seeking postpetition credit will also need appraisals made on any significant assets that are to be used as collateral for the credit. The appraisals will be needed both to convince prospective lenders that actual value exists to secure new credit and to convince the court that excess value exists for purposes of providing adequate protection to existing lienholders. In addition, the debtor will need updated operating statements, balance sheets, cash-flow statements, anticipated budgets, and related financial statements. These documents will be needed for both the prospective lenders and the court. These documents should accompany the motion seeking court approval of the financing.

obtaining postpetition credit, necessity of appraisals and financial statements

A debtor seeking postpetition secured financing is required to make a good-faith effort to obtain unsecured credit as a condition of court approval of secured credit. See 11 U.S.C. 364(c), (d)(1)(A). The extensiveness of the debtor's effort required in this regard depends on the facts of the case at hand. See In re 495 Central Park Ave. Corp., 136 BR 626 (SD NY, 1992). Most courts require debtors to have attempted to obtain unsecured credit only from conventional sources of credit, such as local banks and institutional lenders in the area. See In re Snowshoe Co., 789 F.2d 1085 (CA 4, 1986). While most courts do not require attempts to be made to secure financing from nonconventional sources of credit, such sources can be a fruitful source of credit for some debtors. Nonconventional sources include principals and other insiders of the debtor, equity financing, suppliers of the debtor, and other non-financial creditors. The latter can be productive sources of short-term credit, especially if the continued existence of the debtor as a customer is important to the supplier or creditor or if the creditor stands to suffer a significant financial loss should the debtor's reorganization efforts fail.

nonavailability of unsecured credit, necessity of showing

When a debtor in possession wishes to obtain credit or incur debt outside the ordinary course of business, a motion for authority to obtain credit or a similarly-entitled motion should be filed under Bankruptcy Rule 4001(c). A motion of this type is a contested matter governed by Bankruptcy Rule 9014. The motion must be transmitted to the U.S. Trustee and served by personal service or first class mail on any committee appointed or its authorized agent, or, if no committee has been appointed, on the creditors listed in the debtor's list of creditors holding the 20 largest unsecured claims, and on such other entities as the court may direct. A copy of the proposed credit agreement should accompany the motion. See Bankruptcy Rules 4001(c)(1) and 9034. A sample Motion for Authority to Obtain Credit Not in the Ordinary Course of Business is set forth in Exhibit 4-E at the end of this chapter.

motion to obtain credit, procedure

A final hearing on a motion for authority to obtain credit may be held not earlier than 14 days after service of the motion. However, if the motion so requests, a preliminary hearing may be held at an earlier date wherein the court may authorize the obtaining of credit only to the extent necessary to avoid immediate and irreparable harm to the estate pending a final hearing. See Bankruptcy Rule 4001(c)(2). Notice of any hearing must be given to the parties specified above for service of the motion and to such other entities as the court may direct. See Bankruptcy Rule 4001(c)(3). Sufficient notice of the proposed credit transaction must be given to permit creditors to make a meaningful investigation into the need for and the terms of the proposed borrowing. See In re Sullivan Ford Sales, 2 B.R. 350 (ME, 1980).

motion to obtain credit, hearing and notice requirements

It should be noted that even if the debtor enters into an agreement with one or more creditors regarding the obtaining of credit and related matters, it may be necessary to file, and transmit to the U.S. Trustee, a motion for court approval of the agreement, especially if the agreement affects the rights of unsecured creditors. See Bankruptcy Rule 4001(d), which governs the procedure for such motions, and Bankruptcy Rule 9034.

agreements with creditors, necessity of court approval

authorization to obtain credit, effect of appeal

The reversal or modification on appeal of an authorization to obtain credit or incur debt, or the granting of a priority or a lien, does not affect the validity of any debt so incurred, or any priority or lien so granted, to an entity that extended such credit in good faith, whether or not the entity knew of the pendency of the appeal, unless such authorization and the incurring of such debt, or the granting of such priority or lien, were stayed pending the appeal. See 11 U.S.C. 364(e). See section 4.13, infra, for further reading on appeals.

4.03 Creditors' Committees and Meetings of Creditors

unsecured creditors' committee, when not appointed in small business cases

As soon as practicable after the order for relief under Chapter 11, the U.S. Trustee is required to appoint a committee of creditors holding unsecured claims. See 11 U.S.C. 1102(a)(1). However, if the debtor is a small business debtor, upon the request of a party in interest and for cause the court may order that a committee of creditors not be appointed in the case. See 11 U.S.C. 1102(b)(3). Therefore, if the debtor is a small business, the debtor may request the court to order that a creditor's committee not be appointed in the case if there is a valid reason for doing so. While there are no reported cases on the issue, it would seem that the saving of estate funds would constitute sufficient cause in most small business cases. The request should be made early in the case.

unsecured creditors' committee, composition of

meeting of creditors, when not held

Unless the court orders otherwise, an unsecured creditors' committee will be appointed by the U.S. Trustee as a matter of course and the filing of a request for the appointment of the committee is not required. The committee normally consists of the persons, willing to serve, holding the seven largest unsecured, nonpriority claims against the debtor. In most cases the unsecured creditors' committee is appointed from the list of creditors holding the 20 largest unsecured claims filed by the debtor. See Bankruptcy Rule 1007(d). However, if the debtor has filed a plan as to which the debtor has solicited acceptances prior to the commencement of the case, the court, on the request of a party in interest and after notice and a hearing, may, for cause, order the United States trustee not to convene a meeting of creditors. See 11 U.S.C. 341(e).

other committees, when appointed

committee of retired employees, appointment of

While additional committees are seldom appointed in small business Chapter 11 cases, the U.S. Trustee may appoint such additional committees of creditors or equity security holders as may be deemed appropriate. See 11 U.S.C. 1102(a)(1). A committee of equity security holders ordinarily consists of the debtor's seven largest equity security holders who are willing to serve. See 11 U.S.C. 1102(b)(2). If the debtor wishes to modify or not pay certain retiree benefits, a committee of retired employees may be appointed by the court under certain circumstances. See 11 U.S.C. 1114(c),(d), and section 4.06, infra. It is important to note that a committee of retired employees is appointed by the court and not by the U.S. Trustee.

debtor in possession, relationship with committee

The debtor in possession is required to meet with the creditors' committee as soon as practicable after the committee is appointed to transact such business as may be necessary and proper. See 11 U.S.C. 1103(d). Thereafter, it is important for the committee to maintain communications with the debtor in possession and its attorney and other agents. It is customary in many districts for the debtor in possession's attorney to send proposed orders and other pleadings to the committee or its attorney for approval before submitting them to the court.

creditors' committee, statutory duties & functions

The duties and functions of a creditors' committee are set forth in 11 U.S.C. 1102(b)(3) and 1103(c). They include the following:

(1) Provide access to information for and solicit and receive comments from creditors who hold claims of the kind represented by the committee and are not appointed to the committee, and be subject to court orders compelling additional reports or disclosures to be made to such creditors.

(2) Consult with the trustee or debtor in possession concerning the administration of the case.

(3) Investigate the acts, conduct, assets, liabilities, and financial condition of the debtor, the operation of the debtor's business, the desirability of continuing the debtor's business, and any other matter relevant to the case or to the formulation of a plan.

(4) Participate in the formulation of a plan, advise those whom the committee represents of the committee's determination as to any plan formulated, and collect and file with the court acceptances or rejections of a proposed plan.

(5) Request the appointment of a trustee or examiner if grounds exist.

(6) Perform such other services as are in the interest of those whom the committee represents.

creditors' committee, rights of

A creditors' committee may raise, and may appear and be heard on, any issue in a Chapter 11 case. See 11 U.S.C. 1109(b). A creditors' committee may bring an action to set aside an avoidable transfer, may intervene as a matter of right in an adversary proceeding brought by a third party, and as a party in interest, may request the court to convert a Chapter 11 case to Chapter 7. See Matter of Marin Motor Oil, Inc, 689 F. 2nd 445 (CA 3, 1982) and In re Graf Brothers, Inc., 19 B.R. 269 (ME, 1982). Generally, however, a committee has standing to bring an independent action on behalf of the estate only when the trustee or debtor in possession unjustifiably fails to do so. See In re Toledo Equipment Co., 35 B.R. 315 (ND OH, 1983).

creditors' committee, filing of plan by

A creditors' committee may file a plan of its own with the court if a trustee is appointed in the case, if the debtor fails to file a plan within 120 days after the order for relief, or if a filed plan has not been accepted within 180 days after the order for relief. See 11 U.S.C. 1121(c). If a committee files a plan, it must also prepare and file a disclosure statement and otherwise comply with the requirements necessary to obtain acceptance and confirmation of a plan.

creditors' committee, employment of professionals by

Committees often employ attorneys, accountants, and other professionals to aid the committee in carrying out its functions. At any scheduled meeting of a committee which is attended by a majority of its members, the committee may, with the approval of the court, select and authorize the employment of one or more attorneys, accountants, or other agents, to represent or perform services for the committee. See 11 U.S.C. 1103(a). Most of the rules that govern the conduct and compensation of attorneys and other professionals employed by a trustee or debtor in possession apply to attorneys and other professionals employed by a committee. See section 3.01, supra, for further reading on the conduct and compensation of attorneys and other professionals in Chapter 11 cases.

committee members, reimbursement of expenses

The members of a creditors' committee may be reimbursed from the estate for their actual, necessary expenses. See 11 U.S.C. 503(b)(3)(F). This means that committee members may be reimbursed from the estate for the travel, lodging, and other personal expenses incurred by reason of their service on the committee. Committee members may not, however, be reimbursed for professional services rendered by or to committee members. See 11 U.S.C. 503(b)(3).

meeting of creditors, when and where held

Meetings of Creditors. The U.S. Trustee is required to call a meeting of creditors to be held not less than 21 nor more than 40 days after the order for relief. See Bankruptcy Rule 2003(a) and 11 U.S.C. 341(a). However, if there is an appeal from or a motion to vacate the order for relief, or if a motion to dismiss the case is filed, a later time may be set for the meeting. The meeting may be held at the courthouse or at a more convenient place within the district if so designated by the U.S. Trustee. If the U.S. Trustee designates a place for the meeting that is not regularly staffed, the meeting may be held not more than 60 days after the order for relief. See Bankruptcy Rule 2003(a).

meeting of creditors, order of business

The U.S. Trustee, or a designee thereof, must convene and preside at the meeting of creditors, which is often referred to as the Section 341(a) meeting. The order of business of the meeting, which the debtor is required to attend, includes an examination, under oath, of the debtor by creditors, indenture trustees, the trustee if one is serving in the case, and the U.S. Trustee. See 11 U.S.C. 343 and Bankruptcy Rule 2003(b)(1). The bankruptcy judge may neither preside at nor attend any meeting of creditors or equity security holders. See 11 U.S.C. 341(c). Because the U.S. Trustee is not a judicial officer, if contested legal issues arise during a meeting of creditors, the meeting may have to be adjourned and the issues taken before the bankruptcy judge for a ruling. Any examination under oath at the meeting must be recorded by the U.S. Trustee, preserved for at least two years, and made available to any entity. See Bankruptcy Rule 2003(c). The meeting of creditors may be adjourned from time to time by announcement at the meeting and without further written notice. See Bankruptcy Rule 2003(e). The U.S. Trustee may call a special meeting of creditors on the request of a party in interest or on its own initiative. See Bankruptcy Rule 2003(f).

meeting of equity security holders, when held

The U.S. Trustee may also call a meeting of equity security holders, if necessary. See 11 U.S.C. 341(b) and Bankruptcy Rule 2003(b)(2). While meetings of equity security holders are seldom called in small business cases, if such a meeting is desired the procedure is to request the U.S. Trustee to call a meeting of equity security holders. If the request is refused, a motion should be filed under Bankruptcy Rule 9014 to compel the U.S. Trustee to call the meeting. See Bankruptcy Rule 2020.

In Chapter 11 reorganization cases the scope of examination at the meeting of creditors is broader than in liquidation cases. Inquiry into the liabilities and financial condition of the debtor, the operation of the debtor's business, the desirability of continuing the business, and any matters relevant to the formulation of a plan is normally permitted. See Bankruptcy Rule 2004(b). To this end, it is important that knowledgeable representatives of the debtor attend the meeting. If the debtor is a corporation, the president and other appropriate executive officers are usually required to attend the meeting. If the debtor is a partnership or limited liability company, one or more of the general partners or managers should be in attendance. It should be noted that attendance for examination at the meeting of creditors of any person or other entity may be compelled, as may the production of documentary evidence. See Bankruptcy Rule 2004(c).

meeting of creditors, scope of debtor's examination

For the debtor, the meeting of creditors is a convenient, and often the first, opportunity to clarify and personally explain the debtor's situation to its creditors. A clear and realistic explanation of the debtor's financial condition, prospects, and plans may answer some of the creditors' questions and may help to shorten the time of the debtor's examination. If permitted by the presiding officer and if a significant number of creditors are in attendance, it is a good practice for a representative of the debtor or the debtor's attorney to begin the meeting of creditors with an opening statement touching on the following matters:

meeting of creditors, importance of

(1) The status of the debtor's present financial condition and the underlying reasons for its financial problems.

(2) The prospects for the debtor's business in the foreseeable future and a description of the obstacles that must be overcome if the business is to succeed.

(3) The debtor's reasons for seeking reorganizational relief under Chapter 11.

(4) The reorganizational alternatives being considered by the debtor.

meeting of creditors, opening statement

It is important for the debtor to create a favorable reaction to its reorganizational effort among its creditors. By so doing the debtor can help to ensure continuing business relationships with important creditors, diminish the potential for contested matters during the course of the case, and increase the chances for creditor acceptance of its reorganizational plan. With careful preparation and a proper attitude, a knowledgeable debtor can make a significant stride toward accomplishing its reorganizational objectives at the meeting of creditors.

meeting of creditors, importance of

As a class, unsecured creditors, who usually receive little or nothing in liquidation proceedings, tend to favor reorganization as opposed to liquidation. For significant unsecured creditors, the meeting of creditors is an opportunity to determine the reorganizational alternatives that will result in the most favorable treatment of their claims. When examining the debtor, unsecured creditors are generally most concerned with matters pertaining to the condition of the debtor's business, its prospects for the future, and the reorganizational alternatives being considered by the debtor. If the unsecured creditors' committee has been appointed, the presiding officer will often permit the committee's chairperson or attorney to examine the debtor on the committee's behalf.

unsecured creditors, matters of concern at meeting of creditors

Fully-secured creditors tend to be hostile to reorganization because liquidation of the debtor's assets will usually satisfy their claims. The enthusiasm of undersecured creditors toward reorganization tends to be directly proportional to the degree of their undersecurity. At the meeting of creditors, a secured creditor is likely to examine the debtor on matters pertaining to the condition of the creditor's collateral, whether the collateral is deteriorating, whether it is covered by insurance, whether taxes against it have been paid, and what steps are being taken to protect and preserve the property. Secured creditors are also likely to question the debtor as to the role their collateral will play in any reorganizational plans being considered by the debtor.

secured creditors, matters of concern at meeting of creditors

The meeting of creditors serves the practical function of bringing the debtor and many of its creditors together in the same room on a face-to-face basis. As such, it presents an opportunity for the parties to begin negotiating on the practical issues that are likely to arise during the course of the case. Such matters as adequate protection for secured creditors, the use of cash collateral by the debtor in possession, and the formulation of a mutually-acceptable plan of reorganization can be discussed in a professional atmosphere. Negotiations that later produce a workable reorganizational plan often begin at the meeting of creditors.

meeting of creditors, practical aspects

4.04 Handling Claims, Security Interests, and Setoffs

amount and status of claims, importance of determining

In small business cases it is often difficult to prepare a plan of reorganization that is both feasible for the debtor and acceptable to creditors until the status and amount of all significant claims have been determined. This includes secured claims, priority claims, and general unsecured claims. For purposes of both distribution and voting, the status of disputed, contingent, or unliquidated claims must be determined, and damage claims resulting from the rejection of executory contracts or unexpired leases must be fixed. The allowed amount of each secured claim must usually be determined before a realistic plan can be proposed. The status and amount of any priority claims must be ascertained because such claims, with only limited exception, must be paid in full on the effective date of the plan.

proof of claim, filing of, when required

Filing Proofs of Claims. In a Chapter 11 case, if a claim or interest is listed in the debtor's schedules of liabilities, proof of the claim or interest is deemed filed unless the claim or interest is listed in the schedules as disputed, contingent, or unliquidated. See 11 U.S.C. 1111(a). If a claim or interest is listed in the schedules as disputed, contingent, or unliquidated, or is omitted from the schedules, a proof of claim or interest must be filed for the claim or interest to be allowed for purposes of voting and distribution. See Bankruptcy Rule 3003(c)(2). This rule applies to both secured and unsecured claims, and to interests. For purposes of clarification, it should be noted that in Chapter 11 cases creditors have claims and equity security holders have interests. See 11 U.S.C. 501(a), and section 4.06, infra.

proof of claim, importance of filing

In Chapter 11 cases a creditor is not notified of either the amount of its claim as listed in the debtor's schedules of liabilities or whether the claim is listed in the schedules as disputed, contingent, or unliquidated. It is the creditor's responsibility to determine whether its claim is accurately listed in the debtor's schedules, both as to status and amount. Unfortunately, it is the practice of some attorneys to list all claims as either disputed, contingent, or unliquidated, or to intentionally understate the amount of claims. Therefore, it is important that a creditor either examine the debtor's filed schedules or file a proof of claim. Because it is usually easier to prepare and file a proof of claim than to examine the filed schedules, and because a proof of claim filed by a creditor supersedes any claim deemed filed by the debtor's schedules, the best and safest practice is for a creditor to file a proof of claim. Equity security holders should also either examine the schedules or file a proof of interest, especially if they are not insiders.

proof of claim, time for filing, requirements

In a Chapter 11 case the court must fix a time within which proofs of claims or interests must be filed. See Bankruptcy Rule 3003(c)(3). The time for filing proofs of claims or interests, which is referred to as the "bar date," may be fixed upon the motion of a party in interest or on the court's own motion. A proof of claim or interest that is not listed in the schedules, or that is listed as disputed, contingent, or unliquidated, must be filed prior to the bar date or the claim or interest will be barred for purposes of voting and distribution. See Bankruptcy Rule 3003(c)(2). An exception to this rule exists for claims of infants or incompetent persons, claims arising from the entry of a judgment, and claims arising from the rejection of executory contracts or unexpired leases. A governmental unit must have at least 180 days after the date of the order for relief in which to file a claim. See 11 U.S.C. 502(b)(9). Also, the court may for cause shown extend the bar date. See Bankruptcy Rule 3003(c)(3). The filing of a proof of claim after the bar date may be permitted upon a showing of excusable neglect, provided that other parties in interest are not prejudiced by the late filing. See Pioneer Investment Services Co. v. Brunswick Associates, 507 U.S. 380, 113 S.Ct. 1489, 123 L. Ed. 2d 74 (1993).

bar date, when to establish

If the court does not promptly do so on its own motion, the attorney for the debtor in possession should file a motion early in the case requesting the court to set a bar date. Otherwise, it may be difficult to properly plan and administer the case. For practical purposes, the bar date should normally be prior to the date of the hearing on the disclosure statement. It should be noted that the clerk, or some other person as the court may direct, must give all creditors at least 21 days notice by mail of the bar date. See Bankruptcy Rule 2002(a)(7).

A proof of claim is, by definition, a written statement setting forth a creditor's claim. A proof of claim of any kind must conform substantially to Official Form 410. See Bankruptcy Rule 3001(a). A proof of claim must be signed by the creditor or the creditor's authorized agent, unless the claim is filed by the debtor, the trustee, or a guarantor, surety, endorser, or codebtor of the debtor. See Bankruptcy Rule 3001(b). A proof of claim should be filed with the clerk of the bankruptcy court. See Bankruptcy Rule 3002(b). A sample Proof of Claim is set forth in Exhibit 5-C at the end of chapter five, infra.

proof of claim, preparation of

proof of claim, sample

If a claim, or an interest in property of the debtor securing a claim, is based on a writing, the original copy of the writing, or a duplicate, must be filed with the proof of claim. If the writing has been lost or destroyed, a statement of the circumstances of the loss or destruction must be filed with the proof of claim. See Bankruptcy Rule 3001(c). If a security interest in property of the debtor is claimed, the proof of claim must be accompanied by evidence that the security interest has been perfected. See Bankruptcy Rule 3001(d). A proof of claim for a transferred claim must comply with the requirements of Bankruptcy Rule 3001(e). The withdrawal of claims is governed by Bankruptcy Rule 3006.

claim based on writing, secured claim, proof of

transferred claims, proof of

If a creditor does not file a proof of claim, the debtor may, within 30 days after the bar date, file a claim in the name of the creditor. See 11 U.S.C. 501(c) and Bankruptcy Rule 3004, which governs the filing of such claims. If a creditor fails to timely file a proof of claim, an entity that is liable to the creditor with the debtor, or that has secured the creditor, may, within 30 days after the bar date, file a proof of claim and an acceptance or rejection of a plan in the name of the creditor. See 11 U.S.C. 501(b) and Bankruptcy Rule 3005, which governs the filing of such claims and acceptances or rejections.

proof of claim filed by debtor, trustee, or codebtor, requirements

Objections to claims. A proof of claim is, in essence, a request for the allowance of a claim. For a creditor to collect on or enforce a claim, the claim must be allowed by the court. A properly executed and filed proof of claim constitutes prima facie evidence of the validity and amount of the claim. See Bankruptcy Rule 3001(f). A properly filed proof of claim is deemed allowed unless a party in interest objects to the allowance of the claim. See 11 U.S.C. 502(a). It is important, therefore, that objections to disputed claims be made and filed on behalf of the debtor. The foregoing statements apply equally to proofs of interest.

proof of claim, when deemed allowed

An objection to the allowance of a claim must be in writing and must be filed with the court. A copy of the objection, together with notice of the hearing thereon, must be mailed or delivered to the claimant, the debtor, the trustee (if one is serving), and, if required locally, the U.S. Trustee. See Bankruptcy Rules 3007 and 9034(k). If an objection to a claim is joined with a request to determine the validity, priority, or extent of a lien or other interest in property, the proceeding becomes an adversary proceeding requiring the filing of a complaint and compliance with Part VII of the Rules of Bankruptcy Procedure. See Bankruptcy Rule 7001(2). Otherwise, a proceeding on an objection to the allowance of a claim is a contested matter governed by Bankruptcy Rule 9014. See Bankruptcy Rule 3007. Again, the foregoing statements apply equally to proofs of interests.

objection to allowance of claim, procedure

One of the duties of the attorney for a debtor in possession is to examine proofs of claims or interests and file objections to the allowance of improper claims or interests. If it is not done online through the court's website, examining proofs of claims and interests may require a trip to the clerk's office and should be performed soon after the bar date. If the allowance of a secured claim is objected to on the ground that the lien securing the claim is invalid, an adversary proceeding under Part VII of the Bankruptcy Rules must be commenced to determine the validity of the lien. See Bankruptcy Rules 3007, 7001(2). If an objection to a secured claim challenges only the valuation of the creditor's collateral, adversary proceedings are not necessary. See Bankruptcy Rule 3012, and infra, this section. A sample Objection to Allowance of Claim and Notice is set forth in Exhibit 4-G at the end of this chapter.

objection to allowance of claim, type of proceeding

objection to allowance of claim, when filed and heard

The Bankruptcy Rules contain no time limit for filing objections to the allowance of claims. Thus, an objection to the allowance of a claim may be filed at any time, even after the claim has been paid, in which case any distributions to the creditor may be recovered if the claim is disallowed. See Advisory Committee's Notes to Bankruptcy Rule 3007. In practice, most objections to the allowance of unsecured claims are filed after the confirmation of a plan, and hearings on such objections are often consolidated and heard by the court at a single hearing. The local rules should be checked for requirements relating to the filing of proofs of claims or interests, the filing of objections to disputed claims, and the establishment of a reserve for the payment of disputed claims.

allowance of claim, burden of proof

Allowance of claims. If an objection to the allowance of a claim is filed, the court, after notice and a hearing, must determine the amount of such claim in dollars and cents as of the date the petition was filed and allow the claim in that amount, except to the extent that the claim is not allowable. See 11 U.S.C. 502(b). Because a properly filed proof of claim constitutes prima facie evidence of its allowability, the party objecting to the allowance of a claim must present evidence of disallowability. See In re Woodmere Investors Ltd. Partnership, 178 B.R. 346 (SD NY, 1995). The mere filing of an objection will not suffice. However, once the objecting party produces credible evidence of disallowability, the burden shifts to the creditor to prove the allowability of its claim. See In re Lewis, 80 B.R. 39 (ED PA, 1987).

In determining the allowability of claims, it should be noted that the following claims are not allowable under the Bankruptcy Code:

claims not allowable in bankruptcy cases

(1) Claims that are unenforceable against the debtor or property of the debtor by reason of an agreement or applicable law for any reason other than because a claim is contingent or unliquidated, are not allowable. See 11 U.S.C. 502(b)(1). This provision has the effect of giving the estate the benefit of any defenses to a claim that the debtor may possess. See 11 U.S.C. 558.

(2) Claims for unmatured interest are not allowable. See 11 U.S.C. 502(b)(2). This provision has the effect of denying unsecured creditors postpetition interest on their claims.

(3) Claims for taxes assessed against property of the estate are not allowable to the extent that the claim exceeds the value of the estate's interest in the property. See 11 U.S.C. 502(b)(3).

(4) Claims of insiders or attorneys of the debtor are not allowable to the extent that the claim exceeds the reasonable value of such services. See 11 U.S.C. 502(b)(4).

(5) Claims for unmatured alimony, maintenance, or support are not allowable to the extent that the claim is nondischargeable. See 11 U.S.C. 502(b)(5). This provision essentially bars claims for postpetition alimony, maintenance, or support.

(6) Claims of lessors for damages resulting from the termination of leases of real property are not allowable to the extent that the claim exceeds certain limits. See 11 U.S.C. 502(b)(6), and see section 4.05, infra, for the specific limits and further reading.

(7) Claims of employees for damages resulting from the termination of employment contracts are not allowable to the extent that the claim exceeds certain limits. See 11 U.S.C. 502(b)(7), and see section 4.05, infra, for the specific limits and further reading.

(8) Claims resulting from a reduction, due to late payment, in the amount of an otherwise applicable credit available to the debtor in connection with an employment tax on wages, salaries, or commissions earned from the debtor are not allowable. See 11 U.S.C. 502(b)(8). This provision applies mainly to claims of governmental units for unemployment taxes.

(9) Claims that are not timely filed, except to the extent that the tardy filing of a claim is permitted under paragraphs (1), (2) or (3) of 11 U.S.C. 726(a) or under the Federal Rules of Bankruptcy Procedure and except that a governmental unit may file a claim within 180 days after the date of the order for relief. See 11 U.S.C. 502(b)(9).

In addition to the above, a claim of an entity from which property is recoverable by the estate or that is a transferee of an avoidable transfer is not allowable unless the entity has turned over the recoverable property or paid the amount for which it is liable. See 11 U.S.C. 502(d). Also, a claim for reimbursement or contribution by a codebtor or guarantor of the debtor is not allowable to the extent that the primary creditor's claim is disallowed, the claim for contribution or reimbursement is contingent, or the entity seeks to subrogate itself to the rights of the primary creditor. See 11 U.S.C. 502(e)(1). Essentially, then, for a codebtor or guarantor of the debtor to have an allowable claim, it must have actually paid an allowable claim and must not seek to collect its claim elsewhere.

allowability of claims, restrictions

The general rule is that only claims that exist against the debtor at the time the petition is filed are allowable. However, the fact that a claim is contingent, unliquidated, or unmatured when the petition is filed does not prevent its allowance. The court must estimate, for purposes of allowance, any right of payment arising from a right to an equitable remedy for breach of performance and any contingent or unliquidated claim, the fixing or liquidation of which would unduly delay the administration of the case. See 11 U.S.C. 502(c).

unliquidated claims, allowability

It should be noted here that the liquidation or estimation of a contingent or unliquidated personal injury tort or wrongful death claim against the estate for purposes of distribution is not a core proceeding. See 28 U.S.C. 157(b)(2)(B). Further, it appears that such a claim may not be referred to a bankruptcy judge as a non-core proceeding. See 28 U.S.C. 157(b)(5), and Matter of Poole Funeral Chapel, Inc., 63 B.R. 527, 532 (ND AL, 1986). In such claims, the claimant may be entitled to a jury trial and the discretionary abstention provisions of 28 U.S.C. 1334(c)(1) may be applicable. See 28 U.S.C. 1411, and In re White Motor Credit, 761 F. 2nd 270 (CA 6, 1985). See sections 3.02, supra, and 4.13, infra, for further reading.

personal injury or wrongful death claims, allowability, procedure

As indicated above, the general rule is that postpetition claims against the debtor are not allowable. However, this general rule is subject to the following exceptions:

postpetition claims, allowability of

(1) A claim for reimbursement or contribution by a codebtor or guarantor of the debtor that pays an allowable claim after the filing of the petition is allowable as if the claim had arisen before the filing of the petition. See 11 U.S.C. 502(e)(2).

claims of codebtor or guarantor

(2) A gap claim arising in the ordinary course of the debtor's business during the gap between the filing of the petition and the order for relief or the appointment of a trustee in an involuntary case is allowable as of the date the claim arises. See 11 U.S.C. 502(f). This provision has the effect of giving a gap creditor an allowable claim, which, if the claim is unsecured, is a third priority claim. See 11 U.S.C. 507(a)(3).

gap claims in involuntary cases, allowability

(3) A claim arising from the rejection by the trustee or debtor in possession of an executory contract or unexpired lease is allowable as if the claim had arisen prior to the filing of the petition. See 11 U.S.C. 502(g), and see section 4.05, infra, for further reading.

claims from rejection of executory contracts

(4) A claim arising from the recovery of money or property by the trustee or debtor in possession is allowable as if the claim had arisen before the petition was filed. See 11 U.S.C. 502(h). Thus, if property is recovered from a transferor of the debtor during the course of the case, the transferor's claim against the debtor is allowable as a prefiling claim even though the claim actually arose after the filing of the petition.

claims from recovery of property

postpetition tax claims

(5) A tax claim against the debtor arising after the filing of the petition that would have been a priority claim had it arisen prior to the filing of the petition is allowable as if the claim had arisen prior to filing. See 11 U.S.C. 502(i). This provision has the effect of giving a taxing authority an eighth priority claim for postpetition taxes against the debtor instead of a second priority administrative claim. However, postpetition taxes based solely on the activities of a trustee or debtor in possession are treated as administrative claims. See 11 U.S.C. 364(a), and In re EMC Industries, Inc., 27 B.R. 696 (SC, 1983).

postpetition claims from operation of debtor's business, treatment of

On the subject of postpetition claims, it is important to understand that claims against the debtor in possession that arise in the ordinary course of operating the debtor's business after the commencement of the case are not treated as postpetition claims. Instead, claims of this type are treated as administrative expenses and constitute second priority claims. See 11 U.S.C. 364(a), 503(b), and section 4.02, supra.

secured claim, definition, allowability

Allowance of secured claims. A secured claim is an allowed claim of a creditor secured by a lien on property in which the estate has an interest, or an allowed claim that is subject to a setoff. Further, a claim is a secured claim only to the extent of the value of the creditor's interest in the estate's interest in the property, or to the extent of the amount subject to setoff. See 11 U.S.C. 506(a)(1). Therefore, the allowability of a secured claim depends on three factors: the allowability of the underlying claim against the debtor, the validity of the creditor's lien, and the value of the collateral or the amount of the setoff. See infra, this section for further reading on setoffs.

lien securing disallowed claim, validity of

If a claim secured by a lien is not allowable in whole or in part, the lien securing the claim is void to the extent that the claim is not allowed, unless the claim is not allowed solely because of a failure to timely file a proof of claim or unless the claim is disallowed as either a claim for an unmatured domestic support obligation or a claim for reimbursement or contribution by a codebtor or guarantor of the debtor. See 11 U.S.C. 506(d). In all other instances, a lien securing a disallowed claim is void. Thus, if a claim secured by an otherwise valid lien is not allowed for any reason other than those listed above in this paragraph, both the claim and lien are unenforceable, both during the case and thereafter. See In re Watson, 49 B.R. 23 (MD AL, 1985). However, if no action is taken on a secured claim and the claim is neither allowed nor disallowed in the proceeding, the lien survives the proceeding and is enforceable after the case to the extent permitted under state law. See 11 U.S.C. 506(d)(2) and Johnson v. Home State Bank, 501 U.S. 78, 115 L. Ed. 2d 66, 111 S. Ct. 2150 (1991). It should be noted here that the lien of an undersecured creditor may not be "stripped down" under Section 506(d) to the value of the collateral. See Dewsnup v. Timm, 502 U.S. 410, 116 L. Ed. 2d 903, 112 S. Ct. 773 (1992). This means that the unsatisfied portion of the lien of an undersecured creditor may survive the bankruptcy case.

lien securing undersecured claim, validity of

types if liens securing claim, validity of

If the underlying claim is allowed, the lien securing the claim must be valid under both bankruptcy and nonbankruptcy law in order for the claim to be secured. There are three basic types of liens that secure claims in bankruptcy cases: consensual liens created by security agreements; judicial liens created through legal or equitable proceedings; and statutory liens created by statutes. Whatever the type of lien, it must be valid against the avoiding powers of the trustee or debtor in possession or the secured claim will not be allowed. If a lien or security interest has not been perfected, is preferential or fraudulent, is the result of an invalid judicial proceeding, is an invalid statutory lien, or is otherwise vulnerable in bankruptcy, the secured claim will be disallowed and the lien avoided and the creditor will have only an unsecured claim.

fully secured claim, definition, allowance of interest and fees

If the underlying claim is allowed and if the lien securing the claim is valid, then the question of the value of the collateral becomes important. If the value of the estate's interest in the property securing the claim equals or exceeds the amount of the claim, and if there are no senior liens or surcharges against the property, then the claim is fully secured and the creditor should be able to realize the full value of its claim. Further, if the value of the collateral exceeds the amount of the claim plus any expenses chargeable against the property by the debtor in possession for preserving or disposing of the property, the creditor may also be allowed to collect interest on the claim and any reasonable fees, costs, or charges provided for in the agreement under which the claim arose. See 11 U.S.C. 506(b),(c). See section 5.02, infra, for further reading on the right of a secured creditor to collect interest and other charges and the right of a debtor in possession to surcharge secured property for the expenses of preserving or disposing of the property.

If the Section 1111(b) election is not exercised and if the value of a creditor's interest in its collateral is less than the amount of its claim, the creditor's secured claim is allowable only to the extent of the value of its interest in its collateral, and the balance of its claim is allowable only as an unsecured claim. See 11 U.S.C. 506(a). In most cases, then, the amount of a creditor's secured claim may not exceed the value of its collateral. Similarly, a creditor with a right of setoff is secured only to the extent of the amount of its setoff. If the Section 1111(b) election is exercised, the claim of an undersecured creditor is treated as being fully secured and must be dealt with accordingly. See 11 U.S.C. 1111(b)(2). It should also be noted that unless the collateral is sold, a non-recourse creditor is treated as a recourse creditor in Chapter 11 cases. See 11 U.S.C. 1111(b)(1)(A). See sections 4.09 and 5.02, infra, for further reading on Section 1111(b) and the election thereunder.

undersecured claim, allowable amounts of

Valuation of property. In determining the amount of an allowed secured claim, the valuation of the creditor's collateral is obviously an important function. The Bankruptcy Code provides that the value of property securing a claim shall be determined in light of the purpose of the valuation and in light of the proposed disposition or use of the property. See 11 U.S.C. 506(a). In valuations for purposes of determining the amount of an allowed secured claim, the debtor in possession normally favors a low valuation, while the creditor usually seeks to establish a high value for the collateral. This, it should be noted, constitutes a reversal of the positions normally taken by the parties in valuations for purposes of adequate protection. See section 4.01, supra.

secured claims, valuation of collateral

The value of property securing a claim may be determined in conjunction with a hearing on the disposition or use of the property, or in conjunction with a hearing on a plan affecting a secured creditor's interest in the property. See 11 U.S.C. 506(a). The value of property securing a claim may also be determined in a separate hearing. Upon the motion of a party in interest, the court, after a hearing on notice to the holder of the claim and such other entities as the court may direct, may determine the value of a claim secured by a lien on property of the estate. See Bankruptcy Rule 3012. If the proceeding involves only the issue of valuing the collateral securing the claim, it is a contested matter governed by Bankruptcy Rule 9014. If the validity, priority, or extent of a lien is at issue, the proceeding is an adversary proceeding governed by Part VII of the Rules of Bankruptcy Procedure. See Bankruptcy Rule 7001(2). Generally, adversary proceedings are required only when the validity of a lien or its application to particular property is being challenged. See Advisory Committee's Notes to Bankruptcy Rule 3012.

valuation of collateral, procedure

The admissibility of evidence in a valuation hearing is governed by Rules 701 to 704 of the Federal Rules of Evidence. In the valuation of most types of property, especially real estate, it is generally held that the owner of the property (or the CEO of a corporate or other nonindividual owner) is competent, without qualifying as an expert witness, to express an opinion as to the value of the property. See U.S. v. 10,031.98 Acres of Land, 850 F.2d 634 (CA 10, 1988). While the debtor's schedules and financial statements may constitute evidence of value, it is usually necessary to produce expert testimony to establish the value of property whose value is not readily ascertainable. See In re Savannah Gardens-Oaktree, 146 BR 306 (SD GA, 1992), and In re SM 104, Ltd., 160 BR 202 (SD FL, 1993).

value of property, admissible evidence of

In valuing inventory, such factors as the age and condition of the stock, the season of the year, and the general state of the trade are considered. See In re Total Technical Services, Inc., 150 BR 893 (DE, 1993), and In re Taxman Clothing Co., 905 F.2d 166 (CA 7, 1990). Plants and equipment are valued at their actual market value and not on book value. See In re Ascher, 146 BR 764 (ND IL, 1992), and In re David Jones Builder, Inc., 129 BR 682 (SD FL, 1991). The face value of accounts receivable are likely to be discounted to reflect uncollectability and delays in collection. See In re Total Technical Services, supra. Motor vehicles are usually valued at their wholesale value. See In re Mitchell, 954 F.2d 557 (CA 9, 1992). However, if the vehicle is essential to the debtor's business, replacement (i.e., retail) cost may be used as value. See In re Johnson, 117 BR 577 (ID, 1990). Replacement cost is especially likely to be used if the vehicle is not being liquidated or sold. See In re Johnson, 145 BR 108 (SD GA, 1992), and In re Green, 151 BR 501 (MN, 1993).

valuation of personal property, types of, general rules

codebtor or guarantor, rights of

Limitations on the allowance of claims. Except as noted below in this paragraph, an entity that is liable with the debtor on a claim (i.e., a codebtor) or that has secured a claim (i.e., a guarantor), and that pays the claim, is subrogated to the rights of the paid creditor to the extent of such payment. See 11 U.S.C. 509(a). However, the codebtor or guarantor is not subrogated to the rights of the paid creditor to the extent that its own claim for reimbursement or contribution on account of such payment is allowed, independently disallowed, or subordinated to the claim of another. See 11 U.S.C. 509(b).

subordination of claims, definition

The bankruptcy court has the authority to subordinate the claims of certain creditors to the claims of other creditors under appropriate circumstances. When the court subordinates a claim it is not disallowing the claim; it is allowing the claim but, because of the subordination, it is denying the claim the priority to which it would ordinarily be entitled.

subordination of claims, types of subordination

There are three types of subordination recognized under the Bankruptcy Code: contractual subordination, security holder subordination, and equitable subordination. See 11 U.S.C. 510. Contractual subordination occurs when an agreement between creditors calls for the subordination of one claim to another. Such agreements are enforceable in bankruptcy cases to the same extent that they are enforceable under nonbankruptcy law. See 11 U.S.C. 510(a). Security holder subordination essentially prevents a security holder of the debtor from being elevated to the status of a creditor by rescinding a stock purchase agreement and filing a claim for damages resulting therefrom. See 11 U.S.C. 510(b).

equitable subordination, general aspects

After notice and a hearing, the court may, under the principles of equitable subordination, subordinate for purposes of distribution, all or part of an allowed claim to all or part of another allowed claim, or the court may order that a lien securing a subordinated claim be transferred to the estate. See 11 U.S.C. 510(c). Under the doctrine of equitable subordination, the court has broad powers to subordinate claims as the equities of the case may dictate. To invoke the doctrine of equitable subordination it must be shown that the creditor to be subordinated engaged in inequitable conduct, that such conduct either gave the creditor an unfair advantage or resulted in injury to the debtor, to other creditors, or to the estate, and that the requested subordination is consistent with the purposes of the Bankruptcy Code. See Matter of Missionary Baptist Foundation of America, 712 F. 2nd 206 (CA 5, 1983).

equitable subordination, when applied, procedure

The doctrine of equitable subordination is most often applied to the claims of insiders, especially in situations where the debtor was undercapitalized and insiders acted illegally or fraudulently to give their claims an advantage in bankruptcy. See Stoumbos v. Kilimnik, 988 F.2d 949 (CA 9, 1993), and In re Formaggio Mfg., Inc., 23 B.R. 688 (RI, 1982). A proceeding to subordinate a claim or interest is an adversary proceeding requiring the filing of a complaint, unless the subordination is provided as a part of a Chapter 11 plan, in which case the subordination is imposed through the normal plan confirmation process. See Bankruptcy Rule 7001(8).

reconsideration of allowance of claims

A claim that has been allowed or disallowed may be reconsidered by the court for cause. See 11 U.S.C. 502(j). A party in interest may move for reconsideration of an order allowing or disallowing a claim, and the court, after a hearing on notice, must enter an appropriate order. See Bankruptcy Rule 3008. If a previously disallowed claim is allowed on a motion to reconsider, no further distribution may be made to creditors in the reconsidered creditor's class until the reconsidered creditor has received payments on its claim proportionate in value to that previously received by other creditors in the class. See 11 U.S.C. 502(j).

Handling Setoffs. A right of setoff is an important right in a Chapter 11 case. A creditor with a right of setoff is treated as a secured creditor under the Bankruptcy Code. See 11 U.S.C. 506(a). Whether a creditor has a right of setoff is initially a question of state law, as the Bankruptcy Code contains no definition of the term. Generally, a setoff is a right that exists between two parties to net their respective debts, where each party, as a result of unrelated transactions, owes the other an ascertainable amount. See In re IML Freight, Inc., 65 B.R. 788 (UT, 1986). To qualify as a setoff, then, the two debts (or claims, depending on the perspective) must arise independently and not out of the same transaction.

right of setoff, what constitutes

It is important to distinguish a setoff from a recoupment. If the mutual obligations arose out of the same transaction, a creditor may assert its claim against the debtor as a defense or counterclaim to the debtor's claim under the doctrine of recoupment. See In re H. Wolfe Iron & Metal Co., 64 B.R. 754 (WD PA, 1986). Recoupments are not subject to the automatic stay and may be made by a creditor unilaterally after the filing of the case, provided, of course, that both claims arose out of the same transaction. See In re Holford, 896 F.2d 165 (CA 5, 1990).

recoupment, definition of, right of creditor to

As indicated above, the Bankruptcy Code generally allows a creditor with a right of setoff to offset mutual prepetition obligations. However, a creditor's right of setoff is subject to the following exceptions:

(1) A creditor may not exercise a right of setoff against the debtor after the bankruptcy case has been filed without first obtaining relief from the automatic stay. See 11 U.S.C. 362(a)(7). This exception prohibits banks with whom the debtor has funds on deposit from unilaterally withdrawing the debtor's deposited funds after the filing of the case to cover outstanding prepetition debts owed to the bank by the debtor without first obtaining relief from the automatic stay. However, some courts permit banks to temporarily freeze the debtor's deposited funds if the bank promptly applies for relief from the stay. See In re Learn, 95 BR 495 (ND OH, 1989), and In re Wilde, 85 BR 147 (NM, 1988).

right of setoff, necessity of obtaining relief from stay

(2) A creditor's right of setoff may be denied if the debtor provides adequate protection to the creditor for its right of setoff. In effect, a creditor with a right of setoff is treated as a secured creditor for purposes of adequate protection. See 11 U.S.C. 363 and section 4.01, supra.

right of setoff, adequate protection of

(3) A creditor may not manipulate its rights of setoff against the debtor during the 90-day period prior to the filing of the case so as to enhance its setoff rights after the filing of the case. See 11 U.S.C. 553(a). Setoffs exercised by the debtor within 90 days of bankruptcy in violation of Section 553(a) may be recovered by the debtor in possession. See 11 U.S.C. 553(b). Exceptions are made for setoffs by financial brokers, repo participants, and swap participants.

right of setoff, prohibited activities

As indicated above, after the filing of a bankruptcy case a creditor may not unilaterally enforce its right of setoff against the debtor. To exercise and enforce a right of setoff after the case has been filed, a creditor should proceed in the following manner:

right of setoff, how to exercise

(a) file a proof of claim as a secured creditor and assert the right of setoff in the proof of claim;

(b) file a motion for relief from the automatic stay either to enforce the right of setoff or, if desired, to obtain adequate protection; and

(c) if the right of setoff is to be exercised against a bank account, funds, or other property that may be used, sold, or leased by the debtor, do not permit the debtor to use, sell, or lease the property unless adequate protection is first provided.

Administrative claims. Unless the court orders otherwise, postpetition claims against the debtor in possession arising in the ordinary course of operating the debtor's business are allowable as administrative expenses in Chapter 11 cases. See 11 U.S.C. 364(a). Postpetition claims for compensation filed by attorneys and other professionals, if approved by the court under 11 U.S.C. 330, are also treated as administrative expenses under 11 U.S.C. 503(b)(2). The allowance of administrative expenses is governed by 11 U.S.C. 503, which requires the filing of a request and notice and a hearing. The Rules of Bankruptcy Procedure contain no specific procedures for filing and obtaining approval of claims for administrative expenses, other than postpetition claims for compensation of attorneys and other professionals under Bankruptcy Rule 2016.

administrative expenses of case, what constitutes, allowability administrative expenses, allowance procedure

Unless the local rules set forth a different procedure, the best method of obtaining court approval of administrative expenses, other than compensation of attorneys and other professionals, is to apply to the court for allowance of the administrative expense. An application for allowance of the expense should be filed with the court and notice of the application given to the creditors' committee (if one is appointed in the case), the U.S. Trustee, and such other parties in interest as the court may direct. If an objection to the allowance of the expenses is filed, a hearing should be scheduled. Otherwise a hearing is not usually necessary. Applications for the allowance of compensation for attorneys and other professionals are covered in section 3.01, supra. A sample Application for Allowance of Administrative Expenses is set forth in Exhibit 4-H, at the end of this chapter.

priority of claims and interests, importance of

The order of priority of claims and interests. The priority of a claim or interest is an important factor in determining the classification of the claim or interest in a plan. The priority of claims and interests becomes even more important if confirmation of a plan is sought under the cramdown provisions of 11 U.S.C. 1129(b) and the rule of absolute priority must be complied with. Under the Bankruptcy Code, claims and interests are entitled to payment in the following order of priority:

priority of claims and interest under Bankruptcy Code

(1) Secured claims. Secured claims take priority over unsecured claims of any kind. The only exception is that a trustee or debtor in possession may recover from secured property the costs and expenses of preserving or disposing of the property, to the extent of any benefit to the secured creditor. See 11 U.S.C. 506(c).

(2) Superpriority claims. There are two superpriority claims that must be paid ahead of all other unsecured claims, including expenses of administration. One of the superpriority claims is created when a secured creditor is granted adequate protection by the court that later proves to be inadequate. The claim of such a creditor for damages for lack of adequate protection is a superpriority claim. See 11 U.S.C. 507(b), and section 4.01, supra. The other superpriority claim is created when the court grants such a claim to a person that extends credit to the trustee or debtor in possession during the course of the case. See 11 U.S.C. 364(c)(1), and section 4.02, supra. The second superpriority claim has priority over the first. See 11 U.S.C. 364(c)(1).

(3) Priority unsecured claims in the order set forth in 11 U.S.C. 507(a), which is as follows:

First: Claims for domestic support obligations
Second: Expenses of administration
Third: Unsecured gap claims in involuntary cases
Fourth: Wage and commission claims of employees and certain independent sales representatives of up to $12,475* per person earned within 180 days prior to bankruptcy
Fifth: Employee benefit plan claims up to $12,475* per employee
Sixth: Grain producer's and U.S. fisherman's claims up to $6,150* per person
Seventh: Consumer deposit claims up to $2,775* per person
Eighth: Certain unsecured tax claims of governmental units
Ninth: Unsecured claims of a federal depository institutions regulatory agency
Tenth: Claims for personal injury or death resulting form the unlawful operation of a motor vehicle or vessel by the debtor while intoxicated.

* Dollar amounts subject to change on April 1, 2016.

(4) Nonpriority unsecured claims. Such claims, which are often referred to as general unsecured claims, have neither security nor a priority, but they may be divided into separate classes and treated differently under a plan if a valid reason exists for doing so. See section 4.06, supra.

(5) Subordinated nonpriority unsecured claims. These are claims that have been subordinated to other nonpriority unsecured claims for purposes of distribution by the court under 11 U.S.C. 510. See supra, this section, for further reading on the subordination of claims.

(6) Interests. The interests of equity security holders have the lowest priority of payment. Under applicable nonbankruptcy law, under the debtor's charter, or under a plan, the interests of certain interest holders may have priority over the interests of other interest holders. For example, the holders of preferred stock in the debtor may have priority over the holders of common stock.

4.05 Handling Executory Contracts and Unexpired Leases

A Chapter 11 debtor is likely to have burdensome contracts or leases that must be terminated or renegotiated if the debtor's business is to survive. The debtor may have entered into ill-advised contracts to sell property or services at prices so low that it can no longer comply with the contracts and remain in business. The rejection or renegotiation of such contracts is often a principal reason for filing under Chapter 11. On the other hand, the debtor may have entered into beneficial contracts or leases that it wishes to preserve or assign to third parties for a profit. By permitting a debtor in possession to unilaterally assume, reject, or assign executory contracts or unexpired leases, the Bankruptcy Code fosters considerable flexibility in the handling of such contracts or leases.

executory contracts, general aspects

A typical small business debtor is likely to be a party to one or more of the following types of executory contracts or unexpired leases:

(1) leases on one or more of the premises from which it conducts its business,

(2) leases of equipment used in the conduct of its business,

(3) contractual obligations to provide products or services in the future,

(4) contractual obligations to purchase supplies, inventory, equipment, or other goods or services,

(5) employment contracts with key employees,

(6) maintenance agreements, or

(7) franchise or licensing agreements.

executory contracts, typical types of

Right of debtor to assume or reject. A chapter 11 debtor in possession has the unilateral option, subject to the court's approval, of either assuming or rejecting most of the debtor's executory contracts and unexpired leases. See 11 U.S.C. 365(a). Specifically, a debtor in possession may assume or reject an executory contract or unexpired lease of residential real property or personal property of the debtor at any time prior to confirmation of a plan, but the court, on the request of a party to the contract or lease, may order the debtor in possession to determine within a specified period whether to assume or reject the contract or lease. See 11 U.S.C. 365(d)(2). In the Chapter 11 case of an individual debtor wherein the debtor is a lessee of personal property, the lease is deemed rejected if it is not assumed in the plan confirmed by the court. See 11 U.S.C. 365(p)(3). An unexpired lease of nonresidential real property under which the debtor is a lessee is deemed rejected (and must be surrendered to the lessor) unless the trustee or debtor in possession assumes or rejects the lease within 120 days after the date of the order for relief or the date of the confirmation order, whichever is earlier. See 11 U.S.C. 365(d)(4). The 120 period may be extended by the court, for cause, for an additional 90 days. However, any extension past the additional 90 days requires the consent of the lessor. See 11 U.S.C. 365(d)(4)(B).

executory contracts, right of debtor to assume or reject

While a debtor in possession is not required to assume or reject most executory contracts or unexpired leases until confirmation, the debtor has the option of acting sooner if desired. Further, the rights and obligations of a debtor in possession under an assumed contract or lease may be assigned to a third party, if desired. An executory contract or unexpired lease that is neither rejected nor assumed by the debtor in possession continues in effect and passes with the other property of the debtor to the reorganized debtor. See In re Parkwood Realty Corp., 157 B.R. 687 (WD WA, 1993).

executory contracts, general aspects

If a debtor in possession assumes an executory contract or unexpired lease, the debtor must cure any prepetition defaults and thereafter perform its obligations under the contract or lease, unless its rights and obligations under the contract or lease are validly assigned to another entity. If the debtor rejects an executory contract or unexpired lease, the other party to the contract is entitled to a claim against the estate in the amount of the damages caused by the rejection. The other party's claim for damages may be secured or unsecured depending on the terms of the contract or lease and on whether the other party has a right of setoff.

executory contracts, consequences of assumption or rejection for debtor

executory contracts, rights and obligations of debtor under

The other party to an executory contract or unexpired lease is required to fulfill its obligations under the contract or lease until it is rejected by the debtor. See In re Public Service, 884 F.2d 11 (CA 1, 1989). If necessary, the debtor can compel performance by the other party pending the assumption or rejection of the contract by the debtor. See In re Whitcomb & Keller Mfg. Co., 715 F.2d 375 (CA 7, 1983). However, the debtor may not require a lessor to provide services incidental to a defaulted lease before assumption of the lease unless the lessor is compensated for the services under the terms of the lease. See 11 U.S.C. 365(b)(4). After the filing of the case the debtor, whether as a lessee or lessor, must timely perform all of its obligations under any unexpired lease of nonresidential real property until the lease is assumed or rejected, provided that the court may extend the time for performance to a time not to exceed 60 days from the date of filing. See 11 U.S.C. 365(d)(3). Also, the debtor must, within 60 days from date of filing, perform all obligations under any unexpired lease of equipment or other non-household personal property until the lease is assumed or rejected, unless the court orders otherwise. See 11 U.S.C. 365(d)(5).

executory contract, what constitutes

Types of contracts. Only "executory" contracts may be assumed or rejected by a debtor in possession. Therefore the first order of business is to determine where a particular contract is executory. The Bankruptcy Code does not define the term "executory contract." The generally-accepted definition is that an executory contract is a contract under which performance remains due to some extent by both (or all) of the contracting parties. See In re Streets & Beard Farm Partnership, 882 F.2d 233 (CA 7, 1989), and In re Sundial Asphalt Co., Inc., 147 B.R. 72 (ED NY, 1992). If one party has completed performance, the contract is no longer executory. A promissory note, for example, is not an executory contract because performance by one party has been completed.

executory contract, effect of termination

A contract that has been validly and permanently terminated prior to the filing of the case is not "executory" and may not be assumed or rejected by the debtor. See In re Gourmet Services, Inc., 142 BR 216 (SD OH, 1992). However, if the pre-filing termination is subject to reversal or reconsideration under state law, the contract may be executory. See In re Mako, Inc., 102 BR 814 (ED OK, 1988). It should be noted that after the filing of the case the other party to an executory contract or unexpired lease is normally precluded by the automatic stay from taking action to terminate the contract or lease.

executory contract v. financing arrangement, factors, significance of

To be treated as an executory contract or unexpired lease under the Bankruptcy Code, the arrangement between the parties must actually be contractually executory. If the relationship between the parties is deemed by the court to be that of debtor-creditor instead of lessee-lessor, the court is likely to find the relationship to be a "disguised financing arrangement" instead of a "true lease," even if the controlling document purports to be a lease or contract. See In re Torgerson Co., 114 BR 899 (SD TX, 1990). In making such a determination the court must apply state law and will consider such factors as the intent of the parties and the circumstances and economic realities surrounding the transaction in question. See In re Chateaugay Corp., 112 BR 335 (SD NY, 1989). Equipment leases are most likely to be scrutinized on this ground. If the arrangement is found not to be a true contract or lease, the ownership of the property may be deemed to have passed to the debtor, subject only to a perfected or unperfected security interest in the other party and the rights of the other party will be substantially reduced.

ipso facto clauses, effect of in bankruptcy case

Many contracts and leases contain clauses providing that the contract or lease is automatically terminated upon the filing of a bankruptcy petition by or against one of the parties, upon the appointment of a trustee, or upon the insolvency of a party. Such clauses, which are often referred to as "ipso facto clauses," are unenforceable against a debtor in possession after the commencement of a bankruptcy case, and a contract or lease may not be terminated or modified by the other party after the commencement of a case by reason of such a clause. See 11 U.S.C. 365(e)(1). Further, a debtor in possession is not required to cure any default that is a breach of an ipso facto clause. See 11 U.S.C. 365(b)(2).

It is generally held that a debtor must assume or reject an executory contract in its entirety. See In re Royster Co., 137 BR 530 (MD FL, 1992). The debtor may not bifurcate a contract and assume the favorable terms and reject the unfavorable. See In re Patella Const. Corp., 114 BR 53 (NJ, 1990). However, if a single writing actually contains more than one contract, each contract may be assumed or rejected separately. See In re Holly's, Inc., 140 BR 643 (WD MI, 1992). Arbitration clauses and covenants not to compete have been found to be separate contracts under this theory. See In re Chorus Data Sys. Inc., 122 BR 845 (NH, 1990), and In re Hirschorn, 156 BR 379 (ED NY, 1993).

executory contract, rejection of entire contract, when required

Assuming an executory contract. A debtor in possession may, with the approval of the bankruptcy court, assume virtually any executory contract or unexpired lease of the debtor that has not been terminated prior to the filing of the case. See 11 U.S.C. 365(a). The only types of executory contracts or unexpired leases that may not be assumed by a debtor in possession are:

executory contracts, debtor's right to assume

(1) Unexpired leases of nonresidential real property, under which the debtor is the lessee, which were not assumed by the debtor prior to the order of confirmation or within 120 days after the filing of the case, whichever is earlier, or within any additional period allowed by the court. See 11 U.S.C. 365(d)(4).

executory contracts, types not assumable

(2) Certain types of contracts the assumption or assignment of which is forbidden under 11 U.S.C. 365(c). Included here are personal services contracts, contracts to lend money, and terminated leases of nonresidential real property. These contracts are discussed below in this section in connection with the assignment of executory contracts.

If the debtor is not in default under the executory contract or unexpired lease that it wishes to assume, the Bankruptcy Code imposes no conditions to the assumption other than the requirement that the assumption be in the best interests of the estate and its creditors. See In re Currivan's Chapel of the Sunset, 51 BR 27 (CD CA, 1985). If the court finds that the debtor's motion was timely filed and that the debtor has exercised reasonable business judgment in assuming the contract or lease, the assumption will be approved by the court and will thereafter be effective and enforceable. See In re TS Industries, Inc., 117 BR 682 (UT, 1990).

executory contract, debtor not in default, assumption requirements

It frequently happens that the debtor is in default on an executory contract or unexpired lease that it wishes to assume. The first matter to check is whether the contract or lease has been effectively terminated by the other party. If so, the contract or lease no longer exists and may not be assumed. If the other party has not taken the steps necessary to terminate the contract or lease prior to the filing of the Chapter 11 case, the debtor may assume the contract or lease by curing the default in the manner described below.

defaulted executory contracts, debtor's right to assume

If there has been either a prepetition or postpetition default of an executory contract or unexpired lease by the debtor, the debtor may assume the contract or lease only if, at the time of assumption, the debtor (1) has cured the default or provides adequate assurance that the default will be promptly cured (other than certain nonmonetary defaults under unexpired leases of real property), (2) compensates the other party to the contract for any actual pecuniary loss incurred by the party as a result of the default, or provides adequate assurance that such compensation will be promptly provided, and (3) provides adequate assurance of future performance under the contract or lease. See 11 U.S.C. 365 (b)(1).

executory contracts, curing defaults in, requirements

If the debtor's default under the assumed contract or lease has not been cured by the time of the hearing on the motion to assume (or at the time of the confirmation hearing if the assumption is being made under the plan), the debtor must present competent evidence that the default will be "promptly" cured. "Promptly" has been held to mean immediately under some circumstances and over an extended period under other circumstances. Much depends on the type of contract, the circumstances of the respective parties, and other relevant facts of the particular case. See In re World Skating Ctr., Inc., 100 BR 147 (CT, 1989), and In re Carlisle Homes, Inc., 103 BR 524 (NJ, 1988).

executory contract, default by debtor, prompt curing of, what constitutes

executory contract, default by debtor, actual pecuniary losses, what constitutes

In determining the actual pecuniary losses, if any, incurred by the other party as a result of the debtor's default under the contract or lease, the burden of proof is on the other party. To be entitled to compensation, the other party must establish (1) that it incurred additional expenses or costs that were directly or indirectly related to the debtor's default, (2) that the expenses were in fact necessary to either cure the debtor's default or to adequately protect or indemnify the other party from further damages, and (3) that the expenses were reasonable in amount. See In re French, 131 BR 138 (ED MO, 1991), and In re Westworld Community Healthcare, Inc., 95 BR 730 (CD CA, 1989). Some courts require the expenses to be authorized by the terms of the contract or lease in question. See In re F & N Acquisition Corp., 152 BR 304 (WD WA, 1993). Such expenses as late charges, interest payments, and attorney's fees may be recovered, especially if the contract or lease so provides. See In re Hillsborough Holdings Corp., 126 BR 895 (MD FL, 1991), and In re Eagle Bus Mfg., Inc., 148 BR 481 (SD TX, 1992).

adequate assurance of future performance, what constitutes

Of the three requirements for assuming a defaulted executory contract or unexpired lease, the requirement of adequate assurance of future performance is often the most troublesome from a legal standpoint. While the Bankruptcy Code contains a detailed description as to what constitutes adequate assurance of future performance of a defaulted shopping center lease (see 11 U.S.C. 365(b)(3)), it is silent as to what constitutes adequate assurance of future performance for other types of leases and contracts. Consequently, the degree of adequate assurance required depends greatly on the facts and circumstances of a particular case. See In re Joshua Slocum, Inc., 922 F.2d 1081 (CA 3, 1990). Adequate assurance can range from COD terms for a supply contract to the posting of a performance bond. See In re Docktor Pet. Ctr. Inc., 144 BR 14 (MA, 1992), and Matter of Wesmac Computer Systems, Inc., 59 B.R. 87 (NJ, 1986). The court has considerable discretion in the matter, and the necessity of the assumption to the rehabilitation of the debtor's business is often a factor. See Richmond Leasing v. Capital Bank, 762 F.2d 1303 (CA 5, 1985).

assumption of executory contract, what constitutes, effect of

The assumption of an executory contract normally requires judicial approval. However, it has been held that the acceptance by the debtor of the benefits of an executory contract during the course of the case constitutes a binding assumption of the contract by the debtor. See In re California Steel Co., 24 B.R. 185 (ND IL, 1982). Evidence of an implied assumption must be clear, however, as it has been held that the mere occupancy during the case of a premises leased by the debtor or the making of lease payments during the case by the debtor are insufficient to create a binding assumption. See In re Belize Airways, Ltd., 12 B.R. 387 (SD FL, 1981), and In re Florida Airlines, Inc., 73 B.R. 64 (MD FL, 1987). It should be understood that once the assumption of an executory contract has been approved by the court, the debtor may not later reject the contract in the absence of fraud or unusual circumstances. See In re City Stores Co., 21 B.R. 809 (SD NY, 1982).

executory contract, right of debtor in possession to assign

Assigning an executory contract. It frequently happens that a debtor in possession wishes to assign an executory contract or unexpired lease to a third party. To assign an executory contract or unexpired lease, the debtor must first assume the contract or lease in accordance with the requirements set forth above in this section. See 11 U.S.C. 365(f)(2)(A). Then the debtor must provide adequate assurance of future performance of the contract or lease by the assignee, whether or not there has been a default under the contract or lease. See 11 U.S.C. 365(f)(2)(B). The providing of financial information showing the ability of the assignee to perform or adequately compensate the other party in the event of a default will normally suffice as adequate assurance of future performance by an assignee. See In re Jewelcor, Inc., 178 B.R. 640 (MD PA, 1995), and In re Embers 86th St., 184 B.R. 892 (SD NY, 1995).

executory contracts, types of that may not be assigned by debtor

A debtor in possession is precluded by Section 365(c) of the Bankruptcy Code from assigning certain types of executory contracts and unexpired leases. Specifically, a debtor in possession may not assign the following types of contracts or leases:

personal services contracts, prohibited assignment of

(1) Contracts under which state or federal law excuses the other party to the contract from accepting performance from anyone but the debtor, unless the other party consents to assignment. See 11 U.S.C. 365(c)(1). Under this exception the other party to the contract may not be compelled to accept the assignment of a contract whereunder the debtor is obligated to render personal services, if state law so provides. See In re Ewing, 147 BR 970 (NM, 1992). Whether an executory contract is a contract for personal services depends on the nature and subject matter of the contract, including the type of services to be provided, and the intention of the parties. See In re Fastrax, Inc., 129 BR 274 (MD FL, 1991). While a literal reading of Section 365(c)(1) would indicate that personal service contracts of the debtor may not be assumed or assigned, it has been held that such a contract may be assumed by the debtor as long as it is not assigned. See In re Fastrax, Inc., supra.

lending and credit contracts, prohibited assignment of

(2) Contracts requiring the other party to lend money or extend credit to the debtor and contracts to issue securities of the debtor. Contracts of this type may be neither assumed nor assigned by a debtor in possession. See 11 U.S.C. 365(c)(2), and In re Thomas B. Hamilton Co., 115 BR 384 (ND GA, 1990).

nonresidential real property leases, prohibited assignment of

(3) Leases of nonresidential real property that have been terminated under applicable nonbankruptcy law prior to the filing of the case. Leases of this kind may not be assumed or assigned by a debtor in possession. See 11 U.S.C. 365(c)(3).

executory contract, right to assign

It should be noted that an otherwise assumable executory contract or unexpired lease may be assigned by a debtor in possession despite the inclusion in the contract or lease, or in applicable nonbankruptcy law, of a provision prohibiting, restricting, or conditioning assignment thereof. See 11 U.S.C. 365(f)(1). Further, contract provisions permitting the other party to terminate or modify the contract in the event of an assignment are also ineffective as against a debtor in possession. See 11 U.S.C. 365(f)(3).

assignment of executory contract, effect of

The assignment of an assumed executory contract or unexpired lease by a debtor in possession relieves the debtor and the estate from liability for any breach of the contract or lease occurring after the assignment. See 11 U.S.C. 365(k). If an unexpired lease under which the debtor is the lessee is assigned, the lessor may require a deposit or other security for the performance of the debtor's obligations under the lease that is substantially the same as what the lessor would have required upon the initial leasing to a similar tenant. See 11 U.S.C. 365(l).

debtor in possession, right to reject executory contract

Rejecting an executory contract. While debtors in possession have broad powers to assume executory contracts and unexpired leases, they have even broader powers to reject such contracts or leases. A Chapter 11 debtor in possession may reject virtually any executory contract or unexpired lease of the debtor not previously assumed. See 11 U.S.C. 365(a). Conditions are imposed only on the right of a debtor in possession to reject collective bargaining agreements and contracts licensing rights to intellectual property. See 11 U.S.C. 365(n), 1113.

rejection of executory contract, claim for damages

The rejection of an executory contract or unexpired lease by a debtor in possession constitutes a breach (as opposed to a rescission) of the contract or lease, entitling the other party to a claim for damages for breach of contract. See 11 U.S.C. 365(g). While the other party's claim for damages actually arises at the time of rejection, which is after the commencement of the case, the claim is treated as if it had arisen prior to the filing of the petition. See 11 U.S.C. 365(g)(1), 502(g). In most instances this relation back has the effect of giving the other party a nonpriority unsecured claim against the estate. However, if the damaged party is secured by a lien or setoff or is entitled to a priority independent of the rejection, it may be entitled to a secured or priority claim for all or part of its damages. See In re Crouthamel Potato Chip Co., 52 B.R. 960 (ED PA, 1985).

breach of assumed contract, damages

rejected contract, right to assume

If an executory contract or unexpired lease is assumed and later breached by the debtor in possession, the resulting claim of the other party is not related back to the filing of the petition, but is treated as a first priority administrative expense in the case. See 11 U.S.C. 365(g)(2)(A). Special rules apply to previously assumed contracts in cases that are converted from one chapter to another. See 11 U.S.C. 365(g)(2)(B). Finally, once a contract has been rejected or deemed rejected by a failure to assume, the debtor in possession may not assume the contract without the consent of the other party. See In re Tompkins, 95 B.R. 722 (BAP 9, 1989).

damages for rejection of executory contract, allowability, restrictions

Most claims arising from the rejection of executory contracts and unexpired leases are allowable to the full extent of the damages incurred as determined under state law. However, the Bankruptcy Code imposes limitations and other restrictions on damage claims arising from the rejection of executory contracts and unexpired leases in the following instances:

rejection of real property lease, limitation of landlord's damages

(1) Landlord's damages for termination of real property lease. A landlord's claim for damages resulting from the termination of a lease of real property (residential or nonresidential) may not exceed an amount equal to the amount of any unpaid rent due under the lease without acceleration, plus the greater of the amount of rent due under the lease, without acceleration, for one year or 15 percent of the total amount due under the remaining term of the lease, which may not exceed three years. All damages are computed as of the earlier of the date of termination of the lease or the date the petition was filed. See 11 U.S.C. 502(b)(6). Rent under the Section 502(b)(6) cap may include, in addition to base rent, such items as utilities, taxes, insurance, and maintenance charges if they are payable by the debtor under lease. See In re William Brittingham, Inc., 39 BR 575 (DE, 1984). The damages recoverable under this paragraph are in addition to any amounts owing to the landlord for the use and occupancy of the premises by the debtor in possession between the date the petition was filed and the date the lease was rejected. See In re Conston Corp., 130 BR 449 (ED PA, 1991).

rejection of employment contract, limitation of damages

(2) Employee's damages for termination of employment contract. The claim of an employee of the debtor resulting from the termination of an employment contract may not exceed an amount equal to the compensation provided by the contract, without acceleration, for one year following the earlier of the date of filing of the petition or the date of termination of the contract, plus any unpaid compensation due under the contract, without acceleration, on such date. See 11 U.S.C. 502(b)(7).

rejection of real property lease, tenant's rights

(3) Tenant's rights upon termination of real property lease. If the debtor is a lessor and rejects a lease of real property (residential or nonresidential), the tenant has the option of vacating the premises and filing a claim for damages incurred by reason of the rejection, or of remaining on the leased premises for the balance of the term plus any enforceable renewals or extensions thereof. If the tenant elects to remain on the premises, it must continue to pay the rent as provided in the lease, except that it may offset against the rent any damages incurred after the rejection resulting from any nonperformance by the debtor under the lease, but the tenant may not file a claim against the estate for such damages. See 11 U.S.C. 365(h)(1). Similar provisions are applicable to a purchaser of a timeshare interest under a timeshare plan. See 11 U.S.C. 365(h)(2).

rejection of contract to purchase real property, rights of purchaser

(4) Rights of contract purchasers of real property. If the debtor rejects an executory contract for the sale of real property under which the purchaser is in possession, the purchaser may either treat the contract as terminated or remain in possession of the property. See 11 U.S.C. 365(i)(1). If the purchaser remains in possession, it must continue to make the payments due under the contract, but may offset against such payments any damages incurred after the date of rejection as the result of any nonperformance by the debtor, but may not file a claim against the estate for such damages. The trustee or debtor in possession must deliver title to the property to the purchaser as called for in the contract, but is relieved of all other obligations under the contract. See 11 U.S.C. 365(i)(2). If a contract purchaser of real property, whether or not it is in possession of the property, elects to treat the contract as terminated, the purchaser has a lien on the debtor's interest in the property for the recovery of any portion of the purchase price that the purchaser has paid. See 11 U.S.C. 365(j). Thus, a terminating contract purchaser of real property, whether or not the purchaser is in possession of the property, has a potential secured claim for the return of its purchase money and an unsecured claim for any other damages incurred by reason of the rejection. The provisions of this paragraph apply equally to a contract purchaser of a timeshare interest under a timeshare plan. See 11 U.S.C. 365(i).

rejection of collective bargaining agreement, general aspects, procedure

(5) Collective bargaining agreements. The rejection of a collective bargaining agreement in a Chapter 11 case in governed by the provisions of 11 U.S.C. 1113. A trustee or debtor in possession may not unilaterally reject a collective bargaining agreement prior to complying with the provisions of 11 U.S.C. 1113. See 11 U.S.C. 1113(f). To file an application to reject a collective bargaining agreement, a trustee or debtor in possession must first make a postpetition attempt to renegotiate the agreement by making a proposal to the union, providing the union with sufficient relevant information with which to evaluate the proposal, and bargaining with the union in good faith. See 11 U.S.C. 1113(b). Once the proposal is made, the trustee or debtor in possession may file an application to reject the collective bargaining agreement. Within 14 days thereafter a hearing must be held on at least 10 days notice to all parties. During the period between the filing of the application to reject and the hearing (which may be extended beyond 7 days), the parties must continue to negotiate. The court may permit rejection of the collective bargaining agreement only upon a finding that the trustee or debtor in possession has made a bona fide attempt to renegotiate necessary modifications to the agreement, that the union has rejected the proposed modifications without good cause, and that the equities of the case favor a rejection of the agreement. See 11 U.S.C. 1113(c). The court must rule on the application to reject within 30 days after the commencement of the hearing, unless the parties agree otherwise. See 11 U.S.C. 1113(d)(2). The collective bargaining agreement remains in effect until the court authorizes its rejection, but emergency relief may be granted upon a showing of irreparable damage. See 11 U.S.C. 1113(e). An application to reject a collective bargaining agreement is made by the filing of a motion under Bankruptcy Rule 6006(a). A motion to reject creates a contested matter under Bankruptcy Rule 9014, and service on the union is made under Bankruptcy Rule 7004. See Advisory Committee's Notes to Bankruptcy Rule 6006. The foregoing is only a cursory explanation of matters relating to the rejection of collective bargaining agreements. The reader should consult other authorities before proceeding.

rejection of intellectual property contract, effect of

(6) Executory contracts licensing rights to intellectual property. If the debtor in possession rejects an executory contract under which it is a licensor of a right to intellectual property, the provisions of 11 U.S.C. 365(n) are applicable. See 11 U.S.C. 101(35A) for a definition of "intellectual property." If such a contract is rejected, the licensee may elect either to treat the contract as terminated (if such rejection would permit termination under nonbankruptcy law) or to redeem its rights under the contract. If the licensee elects to retain its rights under the contract, the debtor must allow the licensee to exercise its rights and the licensee must make all royalty payments due under the contract and is deemed to have waived any right of setoff with respect to the contract and any right to an administrative claim arising from the performance of the contract. See 11 U.S.C. 365(n)(2). If the licensee elects to retain its rights under the contract, upon the written request of the licensee, the debtor must, to the extent contractually permissible, provide to the licensee the intellectual property held by the debtor and not interfere with the contractual rights of the licensee. See 11 U.S.C. 365(n)(3). Further, unless and until the debtor rejects the contract, upon the written request of the licensee, the trustee must either perform the contract or provide the licensee with the intellectual property held by the debtor and not interfere with the contractual rights of the licensee. See 11 U.S.C. 364(n)(4), and In re Prize Frize, Inc., 32 F.3d 426 (CA 9, 1994).

executory contract, rejection or assumption, procedure

Procedure for assuming or rejecting executory contracts. An executory contract or unexpired lease may be assumed, rejected, or assigned in a Chapter 11 plan or by motion under Bankruptcy Rule 6006. If an executory contract or unexpired lease is assumed, rejected, or assigned as part of a plan, a separate proceeding or hearing to consider the proposed action is unnecessary because the matter will be handled in the ordinary course of the plan confirmation process. If the debtor in possession wishes to assume, reject, or assign an executory contract or unexpired lease other than as part of a plan, the proceeding is a contested matter governed by Bankruptcy Rule 9014. See Bankruptcy Rule 6006(a). In either event, however, court approval of any proposed assumption, rejection, or assignment is required. See 11 U.S.C. 365(a).

executory contracts, time limits for motions to assume or reject

A debtor in possession may file a motion to assume, reject, or assign any type of executory contract or unexpired lease except an unexpired lease of nonresidential real property under which the debtor is the lessee at any time before confirmation of a plan. See, supra, this section for the requirements for assuming or rejecting unexpired leases of nonresidential real property. If a debtor in possession wishes to assume an unexpired lease of nonresidential real property prior to confirmation, it must file a motion to do so within the required period or any extension thereof, but court approval of the assumption does not have to be obtained within that period. See By-Rite Distributing, Inc., 55 B.R. 740 (UT, 1985).

executory contract, motion to compel rejection or assumption

As stated above, on the request of any party to an executory contract or unexpired lease, the court may order the debtor in possession to determine within a specified period of time whether to assume or reject the contract or lease. See 11 U.S.C. 365(d)(2). If a status conference is held in the case, the court may at the conference set a date by which the debtor must assume or reject an executory contract or unexpired lease. See 11 U.S.C. 105(d)(2)(A). It is important to understand that the other party to a contract may only compel the debtor to decide within a specified period whether to assume or reject the contract, and may not compel its assumption or its rejection.

motion to compel assumption or rejection of executory contract, procedure

A proceeding to compel a debtor in possession to determine whether to assume or reject an executory contract or unexpired lease is a contested matter governed by Bankruptcy Rule 9014, which requires the filing of a motion. See Bankruptcy Rule 6006(b). When such a motion is filed, the court must set a hearing on notice to the other party to the contract or lease, the U.S. Trustee, and other parties in interest as the court may direct. See Bankruptcy Rule 6006(c).

motion to assume or reject executory contract, procedure, hearing, notice

sample motions, where located

When a debtor in possession files a motion to assume or reject an executory contract or unexpired lease, the court must set a hearing on notice to the other party to the contract or lease, the U.S. Trustee, and other parties in interest as the court may direct. See Bankruptcy Rule 6006(c). A proceeding to assume, reject or assign an executory contract or unexpired lease is governed by Bankruptcy Rule 9014. See Bankruptcy Rule 6006(a). The motion must be served as provided in Bankruptcy Rule 7004 (which includes service by first class mail). A Sample Motion For Approval of Assumption of Executory Contract is set forth in Exhibit 4-I at the end of this chapter. A sample Motion for Approval of Rejection of Executory Contract is set forth in Exhibit 4-J at the end of this chapter.

assumption or rejection of contract, business judgment rule

The test applied by the courts in deciding whether to approve motions to assume or reject executory contracts and unexpired leases is the so-called business judgment rule. Under this rule, if all of the legal requirements for assumption or rejection have been complied with and if the debtor, in the exercise of prudent business judgment, elects to assume or reject an executory contract or unexpired lease, the court will not substitute its business judgment for that of the debtor. See In re Orion Pictures Corp., 4 F.3d 1095 (CA 2, 1993). However, the burden of proof in satisfying the business judgment standard is on the debtor. See In re Continental Country Club, Inc., 114 BR 73 (MD FL, 1990).

assumption of executory contract, requirements

Should the debtor wish to assume an executory contract or unexpired lease, court approval may be obtained, under the business judgment rule, by showing that performance of the contract or lease will be advantageous to the estate and that the debtor in possession will be able to perform its obligations under the contract or lease. See In re Sundial Asphalt Co., 147 BR 72 (ED NY, 1992). Of course, it must also be shown that any cure or other legal requirement for the assumption of the contract or lease has been performed.

rejection of executory contract, requirements

If the debtor in possession desires to reject an executory contract or unexpired lease, the only question, under the business judgment rule, is whether the proposed rejection is in the best interest of the estate and creditors. See In re Brada Miller Freight System, Inc., 702 F. 2nd 890 (CA 11, 1983). The general rule is that fairness or injury to the other party to the contract or lease is not considered in determining whether to approve the rejection of an executory contract. See In re Chi-Feng Huang, 23 B.R. 798 (BAP 9, 1982), and In re A.J. Lane & Co., 107 B.R. 435 (MA, 1989).

4.06 Preparing and Filing a Plan of Reorganization

The most important aspect of most small business Chapter 11 cases is the preparation, proposal, and confirmation of a plan. While most Chapter 11 plans are plans of reorganization, a good-faith plan of liquidation may also be proposed and confirmed. Because most Chapter 11 plans are plans of reorganization, this section deals specifically with plans of reorganization. However, most of the requirements, rules, and procedures set forth in this section apply equally to plans of liquidation. applicability of section

The Chapter 11 plan process may be divided into the following distinct steps: (1) the preparation and filing of a plan, (2) the preparation and approval of a disclosure statement, (3) the acceptance or rejection of a plan by creditors and equity security holders, and (4) the confirmation of an accepted plan by the court. This section deals with the first step described above: the preparation and filing of a plan. The preparation and approval of a disclosure statement is covered in section 4.07, infra. The acceptance or rejection of a plan by creditors and equity security holders is covered in section 4.08, infra, and the confirmation of a plan is dealt with in section 4.09, infra. It is important to understand that each step must be properly followed in order for a plan to be confirmed by the court. One of the things a court does at the confirmation stage is to examine the process that led to confirmation. Therefore, no step should be omitted or cut short, except as noted below in small business cases. Chapter 11 plan process, steps

In a small business case, the court may rule that the plan itself provides adequate information and that a separate disclosure statement is not necessary. See 11 U.S.C. 1125(f)(1). In addition, in a small business case, the court may approve a disclosure statement and confirm a plan that conforms substantially to the appropriate Official Form or other standard form approved by the court. See Bankruptcy Rule 3016(d). The Official Forms for both a disclosure statement (Form 25B) and Plan of Reorganization (Form 25A) are included in Exhibits 4-L and 4-K respectively. They are also available in a Microsoft Word format on the Argyle Publishing Company Bankruptcy Downloadable Forms. small business case, plan requirements

Practical aspects of plan preparation. While this section deals primarily with the legal aspects of Chapter 11 plans, in many cases the most difficult aspect of preparing a Chapter 11 plan is the practical or financial aspect. Such basic matters as how the debtor should restructure its business, how much money the debtor will be able to put into a plan, when funds will be available for use under a plan, and the amounts and terms that creditors will accept in satisfaction of their claims, must be resolved before a realistic plan can be devised. In resolving these matters, input should come from four sources: the debtor's owners and management, the debtor's financial consultants, the attorney for the debtor or other plan proponent, and the debtor's principal creditors, secured and unsecured. Chapter 11 plan, practical aspects

The debtor's owners and management should start by disclosing to the debtor's principal creditors a realistic account of the debtor's financial situation, the extent of the debtor's resources, and the debtor's plans or intentions for reorganizing. It is important to involve creditors in the plan preparation process for two reasons: (1) the holders of at least one class of impaired claims must accept the plan if it is to be confirmed, and (2) discontented creditors can make a Chapter 11 case both difficult and expensive for a debtor by opposing the debtor at every opportunity, including such matters as the use of cash collateral, the use or sale of secured property, the obtaining of credit, and, most importantly in many cases, the right of the debtor's owners to maintain their ownership interest in the reorganized business. If the debtor's principal creditors are involved in the preparation of the debtor's plan, they are more likely to be cooperative during the course of the case. preparation of plan, importance of involving creditors

Especially if the debtor has not previously done so, it is often a good practice to meet with the principal creditors, preferably after the debtor has had a few weeks of operational experience under Chapter 11. The purpose of such a meeting is to commence working on a compromise that, hopefully, will ultimately result in a mutually acceptable plan. The primary objectives of the debtor at such a meeting should be to convince creditors of the soundness of the decision to file under Chapter 11 and to create a favorable impression among the creditors as to the debtor's intent and ability to reorganize. These tasks can be best accomplished if those in attendance on behalf of the debtor have a thorough understanding of both the present condition of the debtor and what the debtor intends to accomplish under Chapter 11. debtor, meeting with creditors, importance of, objectives

Chapter 11 plan, general requirements

A Chapter 11 plan must comply with the mandatory plan requirements set forth in 11 U.S.C. 1123(a) and must satisfy the Chapter 11 confirmation requirements set forth in 11 U.S.C. 1129(a). In addition, a Chapter 11 plan may contain the permissive (or optional) provisions set forth in 11 U.S.C. 1123(b). The local rules should also be checked for any additional plan provisions that may be required locally. The Chapter 11 plan confirmation requirements and the optional plan provisions are listed separately on subsequent pages in this section. The mandatory Chapter 11 plan requirements are listed immediately below.

Chapter 11 plan, mandatory provisions

Required plan provisions. The mandatory Chapter 11 plan provisions are set forth in 11 U.S.C. 1123(a), which provides that a Chapter 11 plan must:

(1) designate classes for all claims and interests other than certain priority claims (which are described below in this section);

(2) specify the classes of claims or interests that are not impaired under the plan;

(3) specify the treatment to be accorded under the plan to each class of impaired claims or interests;

(4) provide the same treatment to each claim or interest in a particular class, unless the holder of a particular claim or interest agrees to less favorable treatment;

(5) provide an adequate means of implementing and carrying out the plan;

(6) if the debtor is a corporation, provide for the inclusion in the debtor's charter of certain provisions relating to the issuance of stock, voting rights, and dividends;

(7) contain only provisions that are consistent with the interests of creditors and equity security holders and with public policy with respect to the manner of selecting officers, directors, or trustees under the plan; and

(8) if the debtor is an individual, provide for the payment to creditors under the plan of all or such portion of the debtor's earnings from personal services performed after the commencement of the case or other future income as is necessary for the execution of the plan.

In addition, Bankruptcy Rule 3016(c) provides that if a plan provides for an injunction against conduct not otherwise enjoined under the Bankruptcy Code, the plan must describe in specific and conspicuous language (bold, italic, or underlined text) all acts that are to be enjoined and identify the entities that would be subject to the injunction.

The BAPCPA implemented a new bankruptcy form for small business reorganization plans in December 2008. The new form (Form 25A) is included at Exhibit 4-K and is also on the accompanying downloadable forms. The form may be used when the debtor is a small business debtor under 11 U.S.C. § 101(51D). Form 25A is intended to be used in conjunction with the small business chapter 11 disclosure statement discussed infra. Because the type of debtor and the specific details will vary from case to case, the form is intended to provide a guide for preparing a plan, rather than a specific prescription for a plan in any particular case. Basic instructions for completing the form are as follows:

(1) Summary: The summary should describe the manner in which the plan will be consummated and the source of funds for payments to be made under the plan. The treatment of the various classes of claimants should also be described in this article.

(2) Classification of Claims and Interests: The proponent should describe each class of claimants that will receive a distribution under the plan. The first class will consist of claimants entitled to priority pursuant to 11 U.S.C. § 507 other than those entitled to priority under 11 U.S.C. § 507(a)(2), (3), or (8). The next class or group of classes will consist of those creditors holding allowed secured claims. Secured creditors are usually listed individually, with each secured creditor being placed in its own class. The next class will be unsecured creditors not entitled to priority. Additional classes of unsecured creditors may be added as needed. The final class will be equity security holders.

(3) Administrative Expense Claims, U.S. Trustee Fees, and Priority Tax Claims. This article specifies how the various classes of claims will be treated under the plan. Priority claimants other than those allowed under 11 U.S.C. § 503 and § 507(a)(8) must be classified and paid in full unless the claimant agrees otherwise. Each secured creditor is placed in its own class. 11 U.S.C. § 1129(a)(9)(D) provides that a secured tax claim which would otherwise meet the description of a priority tax claim under 11 U.S.C.

§ 507(a)(8) is to be paid in the same manner and over the same period as described in 11 U.S.C. § 507(a)(8). The proponent should describe the treatment of general unsecured claims. An administrative convenience class may be created here under 11 U.S.C. § 1122(b). Finally, describe the treatment of equity securities.

(4) Allowance and Disallowance of Claims. This article of the plan deals with the treatment of disputed claims. No distribution will be made on account of a disputed claim unless such claim is allowed.

It is important to understand the distinction between claims and interests. Under the Bankruptcy Code a claim is a right to payment or a right to an equitable remedy in lieu of payment. See 11 U.S.C. 101(5). While the term "interest" is not defined in the Bankruptcy Code, as used in the context of a Chapter 11 plan the term refers to the equity security rights of shareholders and limited partners. See 11 U.S.C. 101(16), (17). Although the Bankruptcy Code does not so provide, it would seem that limited liability company members would also be interest holders in most instances. In Chapter 11 cases creditors have claims and equity security holders have interests. See 11 U.S.C. 501(a).

claim, definition

interest, definition

In most small business Chapter 11 cases the equity security holders are the individual business owners and their equity security interests are not ordinarily dealt with in the plan. Thus, in most small business cases the plan deals exclusively with creditors and does not affect the interests of equity security holders. However, if the debtor's business is to be transferred to a new entity under the plan, if additional stock is to be issued under the plan, or if the plan proposes the buy out or termination of the equity interests of certain owners, then the interests of equity security holders may have to be dealt with in the plan. Also, if the plan is to be confirmed under the cramdown provisions of 11 U.S.C. 1129(b), and if the claims of a nonaccepting class of creditors are not paid in full under the plan, the rule of absolute priority may render it necessary for the plan to eliminate the interests of equity security holders unless they contribute new capital under the plan. See section 4.09, infra, for further reading on the absolute priority rule.

small business Chapter 11 case, role of holders interest

In preparing a Chapter 11 plan it should be noted that the Bankruptcy Code imposes no time limit on the duration of Chapter 11 plans. Thus, a Chapter 11 plan may, within reason, extend for as long a period as is necessary to carry out the desired reorganization, rehabilitation, or liquidation. The only time limit imposed is that imposed by the court under the feasibility requirement of 11 U.S.C. 1129(a)(11). To be confirmed, a Chapter 11 plan must appear to the court to be feasible, and a plan that extends for too long a period may not appear feasible to the court. See section 4.09, infra, for further reading on the feasibility requirement.

Chapter 11 plan, duration of, requirements

Classifying claims. As noted above, the one exception to the rule requiring the classification of claims is that certain priority claims may not be classified. Claims for administrative expenses, unsecured gap claims arising in involuntary cases, and unsecured tax claims of governmental units may not be classified in a Chapter 11 plan. See 11 U.S.C. 1123(a)(1). All other claims and interests, including other priority claims, must be separated into appropriate classes or the Chapter 11 plan is defective and may not be confirmed. See In re Mastercraft Record Plating, Inc., 32 B.R. 106 (SD NY, 1983).

priority claims, classification of

In classifying claims and interests, the first rule is that a plan may place a claim or interest in a particular class only if the claim or interest is substantially similar to the other claims or interests in the class. See 11 U.S.C. 1122(a). Under this rule, claims of different rank, or claims of the same rank but secured by different properties, should not be placed in the same class. Thus, unsecured, nonpriority claims should not be placed in the same class as either secured claims or priority claims, even if they are receiving identical treatment under the plan. Similarly, a claim secured by a first mortgage against property of the estate should not be placed in the same class as a claim secured by a second mortgage against the same property, even if it appears that both are fully secured. Finally, claims secured by different properties of the estate should be placed in different classes. See In re Commercial Western Finance Corp., 761 F. 2nd 1329 (CA 9, 1985). Therefore, in small business cases each fully or partially secured claim should normally be placed in a separate class. In classifying undersecured claims, the provisions of 11 U.S.C. 1111(b) permitting the holder of an undersecured claim to elect to have its claim treated as being fully secured should be taken into account. See sections 4.09 and 5.02, infra, for further reading on the Section 1111(b) election.

classification of claims, requirement of similarity

secured claims, classification requirements

small claims, classification of

The one exception to the rule requiring a class to consist of substantially similar claims or interests is that a plan may designate a separate class of claims consisting only of every unsecured claim that is less than or reduced to an amount that the court approves as reasonable and necessary for administrative convenience. See 11 U.S.C. 1122(b). Typically, small creditors are offered payment in full to avoid the expense of mailing ballots and a series of small checks to them. Other creditors may be offered the opportunity to reduce their claims to the small creditor amount and to take that amount as payment in full. The small creditor amount, which must be approved by the court as reasonable and necessary, may vary somewhat depending on the size of the estate and the number of small creditors. In small business cases a small creditor amount of $300 or less is typically approved, although the amount customarily approved by the local court should be ascertained.

unsecured claims, types of in typical case

Classifying unsecured claims. In small business Chapter 11 cases it is not uncommon for a debtor to have a substantial number of trade creditors whose claims are relatively small and one or two large secured creditors (usually financial institutions) whose claims are significantly undersecured. Frequently the unsecured portions of a large claim will exceed the total amount of the trade creditors' claims. In a typical situation the debtor may have 20 trade creditors whose debts total, say, $100,000 and a $350,000 debt owed to a bank or other institutional lender that is secured by collateral (often inventory and accounts receivable) worth $150,000. The debtor, then, has $300,000 in unsecured debts of which $200,000 is owed to a single creditor. It is apparent that if the trade claims and the unsecured portion of the bank's claim are placed in the same (and only) class of unsecured impaired claims, the bank has the voting power to block the confirmation of any plan that it does not like.

unsecured trade claims, classification of in plan

In cases such as this the debtor will often seek to put its unsecured trade creditors in one class and the unsecured portion of the bank's claim in another. The reasons for this proposed classification are two-fold: First, the trade creditors, who individually have little leverage in the Chapter 11 case and who will receive little or nothing if the debtor goes out of business or liquidates under Chapter 7, will normally vote to accept a plan that calls for a smaller payment on their claims than will the bank, who because of the size of its unsecured claim has leverage in the case. Secondly, if the debtor wishes to effect a cramdown on the bank's claim, there must be at least one class of impaired claims that votes to accept the plan and by putting the trade creditors, who are likely to vote for acceptance of the plan, in a separate class, that requirement can usually be satisfied. The question is, must the claims of the trade creditors and the unsecured portion of the bank's claim be placed in the same class under the plan or may the claims be classified separately?

similar unsecured claims, classification requirements

11 U.S.C. 1122(a) requires all claims in a class to be substantially similar. However, it does not by its wording require all substantially similar claims to be placed in the same class. The court-imposed general rule is that claims of equal rank or priority should be placed in the same class unless there is a valid reason for not doing so other than the debtor's motive of securing acceptance of its plan by a class of impaired claims. See In re Greystone III Joint Venture, 948 F.2d 134 (CA 5, 1991). Accordingly, classifications based solely on the size of the creditors' claims are usually disapproved unless there is a valid reason for the separate classification other than the debtor's desire to create a class of claims that will accept its plan. See In re Windsor on the River Associates, Ltd., 7 F.3d 127 (CA 8, 1993), and In re Bryson Properties, XVIII, 961 F.2d 496 (CA 4, 1992), where the court held that while the separate classification of similar claims is not prohibited, it may only be undertaken for reasons independent of the debtor's motivation to secure the vote of an impaired class of claims.

substantially similar claims, what constitutes

To gain acceptance of a plan that segregates unsecured claims into separate classes, then, it is incumbent upon the debtor to show that the claims are not substantially similar. See In re Boston Post Rd. Ltd. Part., 21 F.3d 477 (CA 2, 1994). Substantially similar claims are claims that share common priority and rights against the debtor's estate. See In re Greystone III Joint Venture, 948 F.2d 134 (CA 5, 1991). It is not sufficient to show that the claims are of different sizes or that they are being treated differently under the plan. See In re Lumber Exchange Limited Partnership, 125 BR 1000 (MN, 1991). Also, the fact that a third party may be liable for a claim if it is not paid under the plan has also been held to be an insufficient reason to classify the claim separately from other unsecured claims. See In re Holywell Corp., 913 F.2d 873 (CA 11, 1990).

However, if it can be shown that the rights of a particular unsecured creditor against the estate are different from the rights of the other creditors, then the claim may be separately classified and dealt with under the plan. See In re Briscoe Enterprises, Ltd., 994 F. 2d 1160 (CA 5, 1993), where the debtor was permitted to separately classify the unsecured portion of a city's claim against the estate because the city had noncreditor interests in the estate under its urban renewal program and contributed $20,000 per month to the estate in rental assistance. In Steelcase, Inc. v. Johnston, 21 F.3d 323 (CA 9, 1994), the debtor was permitted to separately classify the unsecured portion of a large undersecured claim because the creditor was engaged in litigation against the debtor that could in the future give the creditor a right of setoff against the debtor. See also In re Pattni Holdings, 151 BR 628 (ND GA, 1992), and In re Schoeneberg, 156 BR 963 (WD TX, 1993).

unsecured claims, when not substantially similar

If the debtor or other plan proponent wishes to separate substantially similar unsecured claims into different classes and treat the classes in a substantially different manner under the plan, care should be taken to ensure either that any class of claims discriminated against under the plan will vote to accept the plan or that the discrimination will be found not to be unfair. If a class of impaired claims or interests rejects the plan and confirmation is sought under a cramdown, a finding that the plan does not discriminate unfairly with respect to each rejecting class of impaired claims or interests is required. See 11 U.S.C. 1129(b)(1). See section 4.09, infra, for further reading on this issue. The application of the rule of absolute priority should also be kept in mind when classifying unsecured claims, if the owners of the debtor wish to retain their ownership interests in the reorganized debtor. If the application of this rule is to be avoided, the debtor should attempt to classify and deal with its unsecured claims in such a manner that each class will vote to accept the plan. The absolute priority rule is discussed in sections 4.09 and 5.03, infra.

similar claims, different classes, requirements

While priority administrative claims, involuntary gap claims, and tax claims may not be put into a class, even with other claims of equal priority, other priority claims must be classified in a Chapter 11 plan. See 11 U.S.C. 1123(a)(1). If priority wage claims, wage benefit claims, grain farmer and U.S. fisherman claims, consumer deposit claims, or claims for alimony, maintenance or support exist, they must be put into classes and treated as classes of claims in the plan. A separate class should be created for each type of priority claim, however, because the priority of each type of claim is different. See 11 U.S.C. 507(a). A wage claim, for example, has a higher priority than a consumer deposit claim.

priority claims, classification of

In classifying claims, it should be noted that a subordination agreement is enforceable in a Chapter 11 case to the same extent that it is enforceable under nonbankruptcy law. See 11 U.S.C. 510(a). Thus, if by agreement one creditor's claim is subordinated to the claim of another, the claims should be put into different classes. Also, under the doctrine of equitable subordination the court may subordinate for purposes of distribution all or part of a claim to all or part of another claim. See 11 U.S.C. 510(c). This doctrine is most often used in Chapter 11 cases to subordinate the claims of insiders to the claims of other creditors. See In re Beverages Intern., Ltd., 50 B.R. 273 (MA, 1985). See section 4.04, supra, for further reading on the subordination of claims.

classification of claims, effect of subordination

Claim-related confirmation requirements. When designating and treating classes of claims and interests in a plan, it is important to be cognizant of the Chapter 11 confirmation requirements that pertain to the treatment of claims in a plan. These confirmation requirements are set forth in 11 U.S.C. 1129 and are discussed in section 4.09, infra. The reader should review section 4.09 prior to drafting a plan.

Chapter 11 confirmation requirements, importance of in drafting plan

A Chapter 11 plan should be drafted so as to comply with the following claim-related confirmation requirements:

(1) Each holder of a claim or interest in an impaired class must either accept the plan or be paid under the plan a value that is not less than what the holder would have received had the debtor been liquidated under Chapter 7 on the effective date of the plan. See 11 U.S.C. 1129(a)(7)(A). In other words, the holder of each impaired claim must receive under the plan a value that is at least equal to what the holder would receive in a Chapter 7 liquidation of the debtor. This minimum payment requirement is referred to as the "best interests" test, and it must usually be complied with under the plan because creditors seldom vote to accept a plan that provides less than what they would receive under a Chapter 7 liquidation. It may be necessary to compute a hypothetical liquidation of the debtor in order to determine the liquidation value for each claim. See section 4.09, infra, for further reading on this matter.

best interests test, importance of in drafting plan

Section 1111(b) election, importance of in drafting plan

(2) Each holder of an undersecured claim who makes an election under 11 U.S.C. 1111(b) to have its claim treated as a fully secured claim must receive or retain under the plan a value, as of the effective date of the plan, that is not less than the value of the holder's interest in the estate's interest in the property securing the claim. See 11 U.S.C. 1129(a)(7)(B). Thus, each creditor exercising the Section 1111(b) election must receive under the plan a present value equal to the value of its interest in its collateral. In a cramdown, however, an electing creditor is normally entitled to receive deferred cash payments totalling the full amount of its allowed secured claim after the election, and such a creditor will normally reject any plan that provides substantially less than this amount. See 11 U.S.C. 1129(b)(2)(A)(i)(II). See sections 4.09, and 5.02, infra, for further reading on the Section 1111(b) election.

administrative and gap claims, payment requirements in plan

(3) Unless a particular claimant agrees otherwise, all allowed administrative claims and all allowed gap claims in an involuntary case must be paid in full in cash on the effective date of the plan. See 11 U.S.C. 1129(a)(9)(A).

tax claims, plan requirements

(4) Unless a particular claimant agrees otherwise, each allowed secured and unsecured tax claim of a governmental unit must be paid in full in regular installment payments in cash within 5 years after the date of the order for relief. See 11 U.S.C. 1129(a)(9)(C).

other priority claims, payment requirements in plan

(5) Unless a particular claimant agrees otherwise, each allowed priority claim, other than those described in (3) and (4) above, must be paid in full in cash on the effective date of the plan, except that a class of such claims may accept a plan that provides for deferred cash payments with a present value equal to the allowed amount of each claim. See 11 U.S.C. 1129(a)(9)(B). In other words, priority claims, other than administrative and tax claims, must be paid in full on the effective date of the plan unless a particular claim holder agrees to accept payment in full with interest over a period of time after confirmation.

cramdown requirements, nonaccepting classes of claims or interests

(6) If confirmation of the plan is to be obtained through a cramdown, the plan must be fair and equitable to, and must not discriminate unfairly with respect to, any class of impaired claims or interests that has not accepted the plan. See 11 U.S.C. 1129(b)(1). To be fair and equitable, a plan must permit a secured creditor to retain its lien and be paid the full value of its secured claim, and must follow the rule of absolute priority in the payment of unsecured claims and interests. See 11 U.S.C. 1129(b)(2). Under the rule of absolute priority, a class of senior claims or interests must be paid in full before any payments are made to a junior class of claims or interests, except that an individual debtor may retain his or her after-acquired property and post-filing earnings. See 11 U.S.C. 1129(b)(2)(B). If the debtor is a corporation, the rule of absolute priority may require the cancellation or surrender of the owners' stock or other ownership interests in the debtor if a nonaccepting class of unsecured claims is not paid in full under the plan. See section 4.09, infra, for further reading on cramdowns and the absolute priority rule.

classification disputes, procedure for handling

If there is a dispute as to the propriety of a proposed classification of a claim in a plan, it may be advantageous to obtain a court ruling on the matter prior to the confirmation hearing. This can be accomplished by filing a motion under Bankruptcy Rule 3013, which provides that for purposes of the plan and its acceptance, the court may, on motion after a hearing on such notice as the court may direct, determine classes of creditors and equity security holders pursuant to 11 U.S.C. 1122. If a classification issue arises in a case, obtaining a preconfirmation ruling on the issue may assist the debtor in obtaining creditor approval of its plan because the creditors will then know for certain where they stand under the plan when they vote on its acceptance.

impaired claims and interests, treatment of in plan

A Chapter 11 plan must specify the treatment to be given under the plan to every class of impaired claims and interests. The plan should specify in detail the consideration or value that each class of impaired claims, secured and unsecured, is to receive under the plan. For nonpriority unsecured claims, this is often accomplished by specifying either the percentage that will be paid on the allowed claims in the class or the total amount that will be paid for pro-rata distribution to the holders of all allowed claims in the class. The plan should also specify when the payment or payments will be made and the form of payment (i.e., cash, stock, property, etc.). If a particular class is to be paid nothing on its claims under the plan, it should be so stated in the plan. Priority claims, with the exceptions noted above, must be paid in full in cash, unless the holder of a particular claim agrees otherwise. See 11 U.S.C. 1129(a)(9). See section 4.09, infra, for further reading on the payment of priority claims under a plan.

Great flexibility is permitted in dealing with impaired nonpriority unsecured claims in a Chapter 11 plan. Such claims may be paid in cash, in property of the estate, in securities of the debtor or a successor to the debtor, or by a combination of the above. Payment of such claims may be made on the effective date of the plan, in installments over a period of time, or at a specified later time. The only restrictions imposed on the payment of impaired unsecured claims is the confirmation requirement of not less than liquidation value, the cramdown requirements of no unfair discrimination and compliance with the rule of absolute priority, and the practical requirement of gaining acceptance of the proposed plan by at least one class of impaired claims. If one or more classes of impaired claims is expected to reject the plan and confirmation is to be obtained through a cramdown and if interest holders (i.e., owners) of the debtor wish to retain their ownership interests in the reorganized debtor, then the rule of absolute priority may require each class of unsecured claims to be paid an amount sufficient to induce plan acceptance if the interests of the debtor's owners are to survive the proceeding. See sections 4.09 and 5.03, infra, for further reading on the rule of absolute priority and its effect on interest holders.

general unsecured claims, treatment of in plan

Impairment disputes. A Chapter 11 plan must specify the classes of claims or interests that are not impaired under the plan. See 11 U.S.C. 1123(a)(2). This is an important function in many Chapter 11 cases because only impaired classes of claims may vote on the acceptance or rejection of the plan. Unimpaired classes of claims are conclusively presumed to have accepted the plan. See 11 U.S.C. 1126(f). Further, by keeping a secured creditor from being impaired, the debtor can often save a low interest mortgage or preserve a favorable and otherwise unobtainable financing arrangement.

unimpaired classes of claims, treatment in plan, rights of

Under 11 U.S.C. 1124, a claim or interest is deemed not impaired by a Chapter 11 plan if:

claim or interest, when not impaired by Chapter 11 plan

(1) the legal, equitable, and contractual rights of the holder of the claim or interest are unaltered by the plan; or

(2) notwithstanding any law or contract provision entitling the holder of a claim or interest to receive accelerated payment after the occurrence of a default, the debtor's default is cured, the original maturity is reinstated, the holder of the claim or interest is compensated for any damages incurred as a result of the holder's reasonable reliance on the law or contract provision permitting acceleration, and, once cured, the legal, equitable, and contractual rights of the holder are unaltered.

If either of the above requirements are complied with in the plan with respect to a claim or interest, the claim or interest is deemed not impaired by the plan. In addition to the above cure requirements, a debtor can avoid the impairment of a secured claim, if desired, by turning the collateral over to the secured creditor. See In re Wise, 34 B.R. 444, (WD LA, 1983). Also, it should be noted that defaults resulting from the breach of contractual ipso facto provisions related to the insolvency or financial condition of the debtor, the commencement of a bankruptcy case, or the appointment of a trustee or custodian do not constitute defaults in Chapter 11 cases and do not have to be cured. See 11 U.S.C. 1124(2)(A).

secured claim, return of collateral, nonimpairment

Section 1124 refers to the impairment of classes of claims or interests, and at least one of the nonimpairment requirements listed above must be met with respect to each claim or interest in a particular class in order for the class to be deemed not impaired. Thus, if there are ten claims in a particular class and only one of the claims is impaired, the class is deemed to be an impaired class of claims. As a practical matter, however, a claim over which there is an impairment dispute is usually put into a separate class.

class of claims, nonimpairment requirements

In practice there are seldom disputes over the impairment of unsecured claims or of secured claims that are either cashed out or completely unaffected by the proposed plan. Impairment disputes usually arise in the context of a debtor's attempt to cure a default on a secured claim under the plan, a practice permitted under 11 U.S.C. 1124(2), which is requirement (2) listed above. Disputes of this nature are typically referred to as "cure to avoid impairment" disputes, or, simply, impairment disputes. Acceleration clauses in mortgages or security agreements triggered by the debtor's default are the most common sources of impairment disputes.

impairment disputes, curing of defaults

impairment dispute, possibility of curing defaults

The first issue in an impairment dispute is whether a cure of the debtor's default is legally possible. The fact that a mortgage or security agreement has been accelerated by a prepetition default does not, without more, prevent a cure. See In re Entz-White Lumber and Supply, Inc., 850 F.2d 1338 (CA 9, 1988). Even if the secured party has foreclosed and the foreclosure has gone to judgment, the debtor may still cure the default and reinstate the agreement in most cases. See In re Madison Hotel Associates, 749 F. 2nd 410 (CA 7, 1984), and Valente v. Savings Bank of Rockville, 34 B.R. 362 (CT, 1983). As long as the creditor has not disposed of the collateral to a bonafide purchaser, the debtor can usually cure the default and save the claim from impairment. However, if the creditor has legitimately disposed of the collateral, a cure is not legally possible. See U.S. v. Whiting Pools, Inc., 462 U.S. 198, 76 L. Ed. 2nd 515, 103 S.Ct. 2309 (1983).

impairment dispute, cure of defaults, requirements

If it is legally possible to cure a default, the next issue is how to effect the cure. 11 U.S.C. 1123(d) provides that if it is proposed in a plan to cure a default, the amount necessary to cure the default shall be determined in accordance with the underlying agreement and applicable nonbankruptcy law. The debtor must bring the principal and interest payments current and may be required to pay additional interest to compensate the creditor for the lateness of any defaulted contract payments at the interest rate provided for in the agreement or under local law. The debtor is also obligated to compensate the creditor for any damages incurred as a result of any reasonable reliance by the creditor on the contract provision or law that permitted the acceleration. See 11 U.S.C. 1124(2)(C). This damage provision is strictly construed by the courts. See In re Manville Forest Products Corp., 43 B.R. 293 (SD NY, 1984). A creditor is not entitled to recover lost opportunity damages under this provision. See In re Kizzac Management Corp., 44 B.R. 496 (SD NY, 1984). Such expenses as collection costs and reasonable attorney's fees may be collected under this provision, however. See In re Orlando Tennis World Development Co., Inc., 34 B.R. 558 (MD FL, 1983), and In re Centre Court Apartments, Ltd., 85 B.R. 651 (ND GA, 1988).

impairment dispute, cure of defaults, time limits

effective date of plan, definition

The final issue is when must the debtor complete the cure in order to avoid impairing the claim? The statute (11 U.S.C. 1124(2)(A)) is silent on the matter. Most courts require the cure to have been completed by the effective date of the plan in order to avoid impairment of the claim. See In re Jones, 32 B.R. 951 (UT, 1983). The term "effective date of the plan" is not defined in the Bankruptcy Code, but it is usually held to be the date upon which the order of confirmation becomes final and can no longer be appealed. See In re Jones, 32 B.R. 951 (UT, 1983).

cure of defaults, nonmonetary requirements

To avoid impairment, a cure must also reinstate the original maturity date of the agreement and not otherwise alter the legal, equitable, or contractual rights of the creditor. See 11 U.S.C. 1124(2)(B), (D). This means that such nonmonetary defaults as defaulted maintenance or insurance requirements must also be cured in order to avoid impairment. See In re Masnorth Corp., 36 B.R. 335 (ND GA, 1984). Nonmonetary defaults that do not harm the creditor or its claim may be overlooked by the court, however. See In re Orlando Tennis World Development Co., Inc., 34 B.R. 558, 562 (MD FL, 1983).

impairment dispute, resolution of, procedure

A court ruling on an impairment dispute may be obtained by filing a motion under Bankruptcy Rules 3013 and 9014. Otherwise, a ruling on such a dispute may be obtained either at the disclosure statement hearing or at the confirmation hearing. Because it is usually easier to finalize and gain creditor acceptance of a plan if impairment disputes are disposed of beforehand, an early ruling may be advantageous to the debtor.

cure of default vs. cramdown, similarity and difference in treatment of secured claims

Under Chapter 11, a debtor has two effective methods of dealing with recalcitrant secured creditors. One method is through the cure to avoid impairment provisions of 11 U.S.C. 1124 as described immediately above in this section. The other method is through a cramdown under 11 U.S.C. 1129(b), which is discussed at length in section 4.09, infra. Under each method the debtor can save collateral over the objection of the secured creditor. It is important, however, to understand the differences in the two methods and not to confuse them. The two methods are quite different in both approach and execution, although the results are similar.

In a cramdown, the debtor does not have to comply with the maturity dates and other terms of the original contract and must, in effect, offer a secured creditor future payments with a present value equal to the value of the secured claim. A cramdown essentially permits the debtor to pay off a secured claim over an extended period, regardless of the terms of the original agreement, while allowing the creditor to retain its lien until the claim is paid. Under the cure to avoid impairment method, the debtor must reinstate the original agreement prior to the effective date of the plan and thereafter comply with the terms of the agreement. A principal function of the debtor's attorney in many Chapter 11 cases is to determine whether the cramdown or the cure to avoid impairment method is preferable for the debtor with respect to each secured creditor to whom the debtor is in default.

secured claims, treatment of, in cramdown, in cure of default procedure

Implementing plan. A Chapter 11 plan must provide an adequate means of implementing the plan. See 11 U.S.C. 1123(a)(5). Methods of implementing a Chapter 11 plan may include, but are not limited to, any or all of the following:

Chapter 11 plan, methods of implementing

(1) retention by the debtor of all or any part of the property of the estate;

(2) transferring all or any part of the property of the estate to one or more entities, whether organized before or after confirmation of the plan;

(3) a merger or consolidation of the debtor with one or more persons;

(4) the sale of all or any part of the property of the estate, either subject to or free of any lien, or the distribution of all or any part of the estate property among those having an interest therein;

(5) satisfying or modifying any lien;

(6) cancelling or modifying any indenture or similar instrument;

(7) the curing or waiving of any default;

(8) extending a maturity date or changing an interest rate or other term of any outstanding securities;

(9) amending the debtor's charter; or

(10) issuing securities of the debtor, or of any entity referred to in (2) or (3) above, for cash, for property, for existing securities, or in exchange for claims or interests, or for any other appropriate purpose. See 11 U.S.C. 1123(a)(5)(A)-(J).

In practice, many small business Chapter 11 debtors implement their plans by simply retaining the property of the estate and continuing the debtor's business, sometimes supplemented by an infusion of capital in exchange for stock or other equity interests in the debtor. If the debtor's business is to be scaled down or modified in the reorganization, it may be necessary to transfer property of the estate to other entities in exchange for cash, property, the release of a lien, the satisfaction of a claim, or other value. In summary, few legal limits are placed on the imagination of business owners and attorneys with respect to the implementation of Chapter 11 plans. The overriding requirement is that the proposed implementation must appear to the court to be feasible. See 11 U.S.C. 1129(a)(11).

methods of implementing plan, practical aspects

If the debtor is a corporation, or if the debtor's plan proposes a conveyance of property to, or a merger or consolidation with, a corporation, the plan must provide for inclusion in the corporate charter (the articles of incorporation in most states) of provisions prohibiting the issuance of nonvoting equity securities, providing for an appropriate distribution of voting power among the classes of voting stock, and providing adequate provisions for the election of directors by holders of preferred stock in the event of a default in the payment of dividends to such holders. See 11 U.S.C. 1123(a)(6). These mandatory plan provisions are designed mainly for publicly held corporations with several classes of stock. It is seldom a problem for small business debtors to comply with such provisions.

corporate debtor, required plan provisions

Chapter 11 plan, restrictions on future changes in management

A Chapter 11 plan must contain only provisions that are consistent with the interests of creditors and equity security holders and with public policy with respect to the manner of selection of any officer, director, or trustee under the plan and their successors. See 11 U.S.C. 1123(a)(7). This requirement should be read together with the confirmation requirement of disclosing the identity of the debtor's officers, directors, voting trustees, affiliates, successors, and insiders. See 11 U.S.C. 1129(a)(5). The apparent purpose of these provisions is to prevent the debtor from making future changes in management to the detriment of creditors and equity security holders. In essence, these requirements give creditors and equity security holders the opportunity to accept or reject a plan based on the debtor's current management.

individual debtor, payment of earnings under plan

Finally, if the debtor is an individual, the plan must provide for the payment to creditors under the plan of all or such portion of the debtor's earnings from personal services performed by the debtor after the commencement of the case, or other future income of the debtor as is necessary for the execution of the plan. See 11 U.S.C. 1123(a)(8).

Optional plan provisions. In addition to the mandatory plan provisions described above, a Chapter 11 plan may, if desired, contain provisions that:

Chapter 11 plan, permissive plan provisions

(1) impair or leave unimpaired any class of secured claims, unsecured claims, or interests;

(2) provide for the assumption, rejection, or assignment of any executory contract or unexpired lease not previously rejected;

(3) provide for the settlement or adjustment of any claim or interest belonging to the debtor or the estate, or for the retention and enforcement of any such claim or interest;

(4) provide for the sale of all or substantially all of the property of the estate and for distribution of the proceeds therefrom among the debtor's creditors and interest holders;

(5) modify the rights of holders of secured claims, other than claims that are secured only by a security interest in real property that is the debtor's principal residence, and modify the rights of holders of unsecured claims, or leave unaffected the rights of holders of any class of claims; and

(6) include any other appropriate provision that is not inconsistent with the applicable provisions of the Bankruptcy Code. See 11 U.S.C. 1123(b)(1)-(6).

permissive plan provisions, general aspects

home mortgage, modification of by plan

Most of the permissive or optional plan provisions described immediately above are self-explanatory. Any or all of these provisions may be incorporated into a plan. The standards and rules for dealing with executory contracts and unexpired leases under a plan are the same as under 11 U.S.C. 365. The reader is referred to section 4.05, supra, for further reading on the handling of executory contracts and unexpired leases. If the debtor has outstanding claims against third parties that are unresolved as of the effective date of the plan, the method of handling such claims and the disposition of the proceeds therefrom should be fully spelled out in the plan. It may be necessary to appoint a special representative or creditors' committee to prosecute the claims to conclusion and distribute the proceeds. 11 U.S.C. 1123(b)(4) makes it clear that a plan of liquidation may be proposed and confirmed in a Chapter 11 case. 11 U.S.C. 1123(5) is identical to the Chapter 13 provision dealing with home mortgages and means that a Chapter 11 plan may not modify the rights of a mortgagee who is secured only by a mortgage on the debtor's principal residence. This provision does not apply to commercial property used as the debtor's principal residence. See In re Hammond, 27 F. 3d 52 (CA 3, 1994).

Chapter 11 plan, provisions retaining jurisdiction of bankruptcy court

Because the extent of the bankruptcy court's jurisdiction after confirmation is not clear under the Bankruptcy Code, it is a good practice to include in the plan one or more provisions which expressly retain the jurisdiction of the bankruptcy court to interpret the confirmed plan, enter orders in aid of consummation of the plan, and hear any other specific matter deemed necessary in the case. If litigation is pending or threatened at the time of confirmation or if there is a possibility of future litigation in the case, the plan should contain a provision specifically retaining the jurisdiction of the bankruptcy court to hear the matter. See section 4.10, infra, for further reading on the order of confirmation.

If the debtor wishes to modify or not pay a retiree benefit, the plan (and the debtor) must comply with the provisions of 11 U.S.C. 1114. See 11 U.S.C. 1129(a)(13). Under Section 1114, if the debtor wishes to modify or not pay a retiree benefit, the debtor must first attempt to negotiate with the authorized representative of the retired employees. The debtor may then file an application with the court to modify or not pay the retiree benefit. The court may approve a modification of retiree benefits only upon a finding that - (1) the debtor has made a fair and equitable offer which was refused by the authorized representative of the retirees without good cause, and (2) the modification is necessary to permit the reorganization of the debtor, assures that all creditors, the debtor, and all other affected parties will be treated fairly and equitably, and is clearly favored by a balance of the equities. See 11 U.S.C. 1114(g). See 11 U.S.C. 1114(a) for a definition of "retiree benefits." Section 1114 is lengthy and sets forth specific procedures and requirements. If the debtor wishes to modify or not pay a retiree benefit, the debtor's attorney should examine Section 1114 closely before proceeding.

retiree benefits, modification of, requirements and procedures

If the debtor is an individual, a plan proposed by an entity other than the debtor may not provide for the use, sale, or lease of property exempted under 11 U.S.C. 522 unless the debtor consents thereto. See 11 U.S.C. 1123(c). This provision protects the exempt property of individual debtors in Chapter 11 cases.

individual debtor, exempt property, plan restrictions

Filing a plan. The debtor may file a plan with the voluntary petition or at any time during the case in either a voluntary or an involuntary Chapter 11 case. See 11 U.S.C. 1121(a). Unless a trustee is appointed in the case, the debtor has the exclusive right to file a plan for the first 120 days after the date of the order for relief. See 11 U.S.C. 1121(b). If a status conference is held in the case, the court may set a date at the conference for the filing of a plan. See 11 U.S.C. 105(d)(2)(B).

debtor's right to file plan, time limits

In a small business case the following rules apply: (1) Only the debtor may file a plan during the first 180 days after the date of the order for relief, unless the period is extended in the manner described in (4) below, or unless the court, for cause, orders otherwise. See 11 U.S.C. 1121(e)(1). (2) The plan and a disclosure statement (if needed) must be filed not later than 300 days after the date of the order for relief, unless the period is extended in the manner described in (4) below. See 11 U.S.C. 1121(e)(2). (3) The order on confirmation must be entered within 45 days after the plan is filed, unless the period is extended in the manner described in (4) below. See 11 U.S.C. 1129(e). (4) Any of the periods described above may be extended only if the debtor, after providing notice to the parties in interest (including the U.S. trustee), demonstrates by a preponderance of the evidence that it is more likely than not that the court will confirm a plan within a reasonable period. In addition, a new deadline must be imposed to replace the deadline that is being extended and the order extending the period must be signed by the court prior to expiration of the existing deadline. See 11 U.S.C.1121(e)(3).

small business case, time limits for filing plan

A debtor loses the exclusive right to file a plan upon the occurrence of any of the following events:

debtor's right to file plan, when lost

(1) the appointment of a trustee in the case;

(2) the failure of the debtor to file a plan within 120 days after the order for relief; or

(3) the failure of the debtor, within 180 days after the order for relief, to gain acceptance of its plan by each class of claims or interests impaired under the plan. See 11 U.S.C. 1121(c).

Upon the request of a party in interest made within the respective period, and after notice and a hearing, the court may, for cause, reduce or increase the 120-day or 180-day period described above, provided that the 120-day period may not be extended beyond 18 months after the date of the order for relief and the 180-day period may not be extended beyond 20 months after the order for relief. See 11 U.S.C. 1121(d). Cause for extending the 120-day exclusive period for filing a plan at the request of the debtor includes extraordinary events or circumstances that have impeded the debtor's ability to formulate a plan. See In re Swatara Coal Co., 49 B.R. 898 (ED PA, 1985). A dispute with a major creditor is usually an insufficient cause for extending the exclusive periods. See Matter of Lake in the Woods, 10 B.R. 338 (ED MI, 1981). Because it is not clear whether an order extending the 120-day period also extends the 180-day period, the best practice is to seek extensions of both periods simultaneously. It should be noted that an order reducing or increasing the time to file a plan under 1121(d) may be appealed as a matter of right even though the order is interlocutory in nature. See 28 U.S.C. 158(a)(2) and section 4.13, infra.

time limit for debtor to file plan, extension of

filing of plan by other parties, when permitted, who may file

If the debtor loses its exclusive right to file a plan, any party in interest, including the debtor, the trustee, a creditors' committee, an equity security holders' committee, a creditor, an equity security holder, or an indenture trustee, may file a plan. See 11 U.S.C. 1121(c). The U.S. Trustee, it should be noted, may not file a plan. See 11 U.S.C. 307. As indicated above, the debtor may file a plan at any time during the case. See 11 U.S.C. 1121(a).

modifying plan prior to confirmation, requirements

Modifying a plan prior to confirmation. The proponent of a plan may modify its plan as a matter of right at any time prior to confirmation, but may not modify the plan so that it fails to meet the requirements of Chapter 11. After the modification of a plan is filed with the court, the plan as modified becomes the plan. See 11 U.S.C. 1127(a). While prior court approval is not required to modify a filed plan prior to confirmation, the proponent must comply with the plan requirements set forth in 11 U.S.C. 1121-1128, including the disclosure and solicitation requirements of 11 U.S.C. 1125, and the confirmation requirements of 11 U.S.C. 1129. See 11 U.S.C. 1127(c), (f)(1). Modifying a plan prior to acceptance is normally a simple matter, unless the modification occurs after the court has approved the disclosure statement, in which case the disclosure statement may have to be amended and another disclosure statement hearing scheduled if the modification renders the previous disclosure statement insufficient. The modification of a plan after acceptance is covered in section 4.09, infra, and the modification of a plan after confirmation is covered in section 4.11, infra.

Chapter 11 plan, identification of, filing of two or more plans

Every proposed plan or modification thereof must be dated and identified with the name of the entity or entities submitting or filing it. See Bankruptcy Rule 3016(a). A disclosure statement must be filed with the plan or within a time fixed by the court, unless, in a small business case, the plan is intended to provide adequate information and a separate disclosure statement is not required. See Bankruptcy Rule 3016(b). If more than one plan is filed, the court may submit more than one plan to creditors and equity security holders for approval, provided that each plan is accompanied by an approved disclosure statement. However, the court may confirm only one plan, and in choosing between approved plans, the court must consider the preferences of creditors and equity security holders. See 11 U.S.C. 1129(c). The plan, as modified, becomes the plan only after there has been such disclosure under 11 U.S.C. 1125 as the court may direct, notice and a hearing, and the modification is approved. See 11 U.S.C. 1127(f)(2).

Chapter 11 plan, number of copies to file

The number of copies of the Chapter 11 plan to be initially filed with the court may depend on whether the plan proponent or the clerk is required to send notices of the hearing on the disclosure statement. The local rules and practices should be checked in this regard. If the plan is lengthy or complex, it may be necessary to prepare a summary of the plan for distribution to creditors and parties in interest after court approval of the disclosure statement. The summary must be approved by the court prior to distribution. See Bankruptcy Rule 3017(d).

4.07 Preparing and Obtaining Approval of a Disclosure Statement

One of the fundamental precepts of Chapter 11 is that creditors and equity security holders may not be required to accept or reject a proposed plan until they have been provided with information sufficient to enable them to make an informed decision on the matter. The party or person proposing a Chapter 11 plan is required to provide this information in the form of a disclosure statement. To ensure that the disclosure statement contains accurate and sufficient information, the statement may not be distributed to creditors and equity security holders until it has been approved by the court.

disclosure statement, general aspects

The Bankruptcy Code provides that after the commencement of a Chapter 11 case, the acceptance or rejection of a plan by a creditor may not be solicited until there is transmitted to the creditor a written disclosure statement that has been approved by the court and a copy or summary of the proposed plan. See 11 U.S.C. 1125(b). However, an acceptance or rejection of a plan may be solicited from a creditor or interest holder prior to the commencement of the case, if the solicitation complies with applicable nonbankruptcy law. See 11 U.S.C. 1125(g).

disclosure statement, when required

In a small business case the court may determine that the plan itself provides adequate information and that a separate disclosure statement is not necessary. See 11 U.S.C. 1125(f)(1). In a small business case the court may also approve a disclosure statement submitted on standard forms approved by the court or adopted pursuant to 28 U.S.C. 2075 and may conditionally approve a disclosure statement subject to final approval after notice and a hearing. See 11 U.S.C. 1125(f)(2), (3)(A). Acceptances or rejections of a plan may be solicited based on a conditionally approved disclosure statement if adequate information is provided to each person solicited. The hearing on the disclosure statement may be combined with the hearing on confirmation of the plan. See 11 U.S.C. 1125(f)(3)(B), (C) and Bankruptcy Rule 3016(d).

small business case, disclosure requirements

Adequate information. The primary requirement of a disclosure statement is that it must contain adequate information. The term "adequate information" means information of a kind, and in sufficient detail, as far as is reasonably practicable in light of the nature and history of the debtor and the condition of the debtor's books and records, including a discussion of the potential material Federal tax consequences of the plan to the debtor, any successor to the debtor, and a hypothetical investor typical of the holders of claims or interests in the case, that would enable such a hypothetical investor of the relevant class to make an informed judgment about the plan. In determining whether a disclosure statement provides adequate information, the court must consider the complexity of the case, the benefit of additional information to creditors and other parties in interest, and the cost of providing additional information. See 11 U.S.C. 1125(a)(1). The term "investor typical of holders of claims or interests of the relevant class" means an investor having a claim or interest of the relevant class, having the same relationship with the debtor as the holders of other claims or interests of the class generally have, and having the same ability to obtain information from sources other than the disclosure statement as holders of claims or interests of the class generally have. See 11 U.S.C. 1125(a)(2). As indicated above, in a small business case the court may approve a disclosure statement that is submitted on standard forms that have been approved by the court or adopted under 28 U.S.C. 2075. See 11 U.S.C. 1125(f)(2) and Bankruptcy Rule 3016(d).

disclosure statement, adequate information, what constitutes

Obviously, the question of what constitutes adequate information is very important in the preparation of a disclosure statement. The standard of adequate information is a flexible one, to be applied on a case by case basis. The standard is subjective and not objective. Both the words and the legislative history of 11 U.S.C. 1125(a) reflect an intent to establish a variable standard on the degree of information required. It is clear, however, that the standard of adequate information in a disclosure statement is not controlled by federal or state securities laws and regulations. See 11 U.S.C. 1125(d). See In re Malek, 35 B.R. 443 (ED MI, 1983) for a discussion of the minimum requirements for disclosure statements.

standard of adequate information, flexibility of

disclosure statement, segments of

Contents of statement. A well-written disclosure statement should be divided into three general segments. The first segment should consist of a history of the debtor's business and a description of its present business operation. The second segment should consist of factual and financial information about the debtor and its business operations. The third segment should consist of an explanation and summary of the debtor's proposed plan. The first segment is normally best prepared by the debtor's management personnel. The second segment should ordinarily be prepared, at least initially, by the debtor's accountant or other financial recordkeeper. The third segment should be prepared by the attorney for the debtor or other plan proponent.

drafting of disclosure statement, general considerations

When an acceptable draft of each segment of the disclosure statement has been prepared, a general meeting of all persons involved in the preparation of the statement should be held to discuss and resolve any conflicts, discrepancies, duplications, or omissions contained in the various drafts. In most cases the disclosure statement is the most voluminous and expensive document prepared in the case. Consequently, the final draft of the statement should be thoroughly edited to remove any duplicitous or surplus materials.

disclosure statement, contents, general requirements

The BAPCPA provides for a new standard form for disclosure statements in small business cases. The new form implements § 433 of the BAPCPA. The new form (Form 25B) is included at Exhibit 4-L and is also contained on the downloadable forms accompanying this text. Form 25B is intended to be used in conjunction with the new Bankruptcy Form 25A, which is a form of small business plan of reorganization. The new forms are not mandatory, but are instead intended to provide an illustrative format for disclosure to interested parties. If the standard form disclosure statement is used, the statement may be conditionally approved, with final approval granted at the confirmation hearing. Bankruptcy Rule 3016 specifies the manner in which the disclosure statement is to be filed. Bankruptcy Rule 3017 specifies the manner in which the court will consider it. Bankruptcy Rule 3017.1 specifies the procedures for granting conditional approval of a disclosure statement in a small business case.

Instructions for completing Form 25B are as follows:

(1) Introduction. This section describes the purpose of the disclosure statement and provides procedural information pertaining to confirmation of the plan of reorganization. The purpose of this section is to orient the reader. This section directs the preparer to include a full copy of the plan with the disclosure statement as Exhibit A.

(2) Background. In this section the plan's proponent should provide a brief synopsis of the debtor's business and the events that led to the debtor's bankruptcy filing. Identify the people who managed the debtor before, during, and after the proposed confirmation of the plan. Any third party guarantors of the debtor's obligations should be identified. Itemize any current or pending litigation by or against the debtor. The proponent should disclose the debtor's intentions regarding any avoidance actions. If an avoidance action is anticipated against a specific creditor, disclose that fact. If the debtor is uncertain as to which, if any, avoidance actions may be brought, that fact should also be stated. A schedule of all of the debtor's material assets, along with the basis for their valuation should be attached as Exhibit B. Attach the debtor's most recent financial statements as Exhibit C. Attach the most recent monthly operating reports of the debtor as Exhibit D.

(3) Summary. This section describes how various creditors and equity interest holders will be treated under the plan. Although the form suggests monthly payments, this is not mandatory. The proponent should describe the method and timing of proposed plan payments and describe the source of funds for payments. The source of funds for payments to be made on the effective date of the plan should be listed in Exhibit F. The post-confirmation management structure must be detailed pursuant to 11 U.S.C. § 1129(a)(5). The proponent should also list any risk factors that could affect the debtor's ability to make payments under the plan. This section should also include any material executory contracts that will be assumed or rejected by the debtor. To the extent possible, the tax consequences of the plan should also be summarized in this section.

(4) Confirmation Requirements and Procedures. In this section, the plan's proponent should inform creditors and equity interest holders of what class they are in, whether they are entitled to vote, and the amount of their claim allowed for voting purposes. A liquidation analysis of the debtor should be attached as Exhibit E. Profitability and cash flow projections for the debtor should be attached as Exhibit G.

(5) Effect of Plan Confirmation. Describe the effect of the proposed plan's confirmation. If the plan provides for property of the estate to vest in someone other than the debtor after confirmation, identify such person or entity.

In drafting a disclosure statement it is important to remember that the statement should contain as many facts and as few opinions as possible. A disclosure statement containing too much opinion and too little fact is not likely to be approved by the court. While opinions must, of necessity, be rendered on such matters as the value of property and anticipated future income, such opinions should be supported by fact and rendered by persons competent to do so.

disclosure statement, opinions contained in

The name of the party submitting the disclosure statement should be clearly set forth, usually on either the cover sheet or the first page of the statement. The local rules should be checked for requirements relating to the preparation and filing of disclosure statements. A sample Disclosure Statement conforming to Official Form 25B is set forth in Exhibit 4-L at the end of this chapter. It may be used as a guide in the preparation of a disclosure statement.

disclosure statement, form of, sample of

Filing requirements. The disclosure statement must be filed with the court with the Chapter 11 plan or within a time fixed by the court for the filing of the disclosure statement. See Bankruptcy Rule 3016(b). If a status conference is held in the case, the court may set a date at the conference for the filing of the disclosure statement and plan. See 11 U.S.C. 105(d)(2)(B)(i). In a small business case wherein the plan is intended to provide adequate information, the plan must be filed as if it was a disclosure statement and the disclosure statement filing requirements must be complied with. See Bankruptcy Rule 3016(b). If the plan is not intended to provide adequate information, the best practice is to file the plan and the disclosure statement at the same time. However, if the debtor's exclusive period for the filing of a plan is nearing an end and the disclosure statement is not prepared, application should be made to the court to fix a different time for the filing of the disclosure statement. In fixing the time it should be remembered the debtor must gain acceptance of its plan within 180 days after the order for relief in order to retain the exclusive right to file a plan, so the filing of the disclosure statement should not be delayed any longer than necessary.

disclosure statement, filing requirements

As indicated above, in a small business case, the court may, on application of the plan proponent or on its own initiative, conditionally approve a disclosure statement subject to its final approval after notice and a hearing. In a small business case, then, the debtor must file the disclosure statement with the plan or within a time fixed by the court and file an application for conditional approval of the disclosure statement. If the plan itself contains adequate information and a separate disclosure statement is not filed, the plan may be conditionally approved as a disclosure statement. See Bankruptcy Rules 3017.1(a) and 3016(b). Upon conditional approval of the disclosure statement (or plan) by the court, the debtor may solicit acceptances of the plan based on the conditionally-accepted disclosure statement as long as the debtor provides adequate information to each creditor or interest holder that is solicited. The conditionally-approved disclosure statement must be mailed to each creditor or interest holder at least 25 days prior to the confirmation hearing, and the court may combine the disclosure statement hearing with the confirmation hearing. See 11 U.S.C. 1125(f)(3). On or before conditional approval of the disclosure statement the court must (1) fix a deadline for voting on the acceptance of the plan, (2) fix a deadline for filing objections to the disclosure statement, (3) set a date for the disclosure statement hearing to be held if an objection to the statement is timely filed, and (4) set a date for the confirmation hearing. See Bankruptcy Rule 3017.1(a).

small business debtor, disclosure statement procedure

Notice requirements. After the disclosure statement has been filed in a case that is not a small business case, the court must hold a hearing on the statement on not less that 28 days notice to the debtor, creditors, the U.S. Trustee, any committees appointed in the case, and other parties in interest. See Bankruptcy Rule 3017(a). The court normally enters an order fixing the time of the disclosure statement hearing, fixing the time for filing objections to the disclosure statement, and ordering the distribution of the disclosure statement. This order must conform to Official Form 312. Notice as prescribed by the court must also be given to interest holders, unless the court orders otherwise. See Bankruptcy Rule 2002(d)(5). It should be noted that if a status conference is held in the case, the court may enter an order fixing the scope and format of the notice of the disclosure statement hearing, and may order that the disclosure statement hearing be combined with the hearing on confirmation of the plan. See 11 U.S.C. 105(d)(2)(B)(v), (vi). A status conference may be held in a Chapter 11 case at the request of a party in interest or upon the court's own motion. See 11 U.S.C. 105(d)

hearing on disclosure statement, notice requirements

status conference orders, disclosure statement hearing

small business debtor, disclosure statement notice requirements

In a small business case, not less than 28 days notice of the time fixed for filing objections to the disclosure statement and of the date set for the hearing to consider final approval of the disclosure statement if an objection is timely filed, or to consider a determination that the plan provides adequate information and that a separate disclosure statement is not necessary, must be given to the debtor, all creditors and the U.S. Trustee. See Bankruptcy Rules 3017.1(c)(1), 2002(b), 2002(k). This notice may be combined with notice of the confirmation hearing, if desired. See Bankruptcy Rule 3017(c)(1).

notice of disclosure statement hearing, requirements

disclosure statement, number of copies to file

In sending notices of the disclosure statement hearing, a copy of the plan and the disclosure statement must be mailed with the notice only to the debtor (if the debtor is not the plan proponent), the trustee (if one is serving in the case), any committee appointed in the case, the Securities and Exchange Commission, the U.S. Trustee, and any party in interest who requests in writing a copy of the statement or plan. See Bankruptcy Rules 3017(a). All other parties need only be sent a notice of the hearing. If the debtor or other plan proponent is not required to send notices of the hearing, sufficient copies of both the plan and the disclosure statement must be filed to permit the clerk to send copies of them to the required parties. If the debtor or other plan proponent is required to send the notices of the disclosure statement hearing, two copies of both the plan and the disclosure statement should be filed unless either the court or the local rules require a different number.

objection to disclosure statement, filing of

Objection requirements. Objections to the disclosure statement must be filed with the court and served on the debtor, the trustee (if one is serving in the case), any committee appointed in the case, the U.S. Trustee, and any other entity designated by the court. Unless an earlier date is fixed by the court, such objections may be filed and served at any time prior to the approval (or final approval in the case of a conditionally-approved statement) of the disclosure statement by the court. See Bankruptcy Rules 3017(a), 3017.1(c)(2).

disclosure statement, resolving disputes over

If a creditor objects to certain matters contained in (or omitted from) the disclosure statement, the best practice in most cases is to attempt to accommodate the creditor by revising the statement so as to include the requested matter. A practical method of accomplishing this is to ask the objecting creditor or (more often) its attorney to provide specific language for inclusion in the statement. If at all possible the suggested language should then be included in the disclosure statement. The object here is to avoid extended litigation over the adequacy of the disclosure statement. Most courts will appreciate this because they understand that in cases involving small businesses the disclosure statement is usually more formality than substance and that most creditors pay little attention to it.

disclosure statement hearing requirements

Hearing requirements. In cases that are not treated as small business cases, the court must hold a hearing on the disclosure statement. See Bankruptcy Rule 3017(a). However, if a status conference is held in the case, the disclosure statement hearing may be combined with the confirmation hearing. See 11 U.S.C. 105(d)(2)(B)(vi). In small business cases, the court must hold a disclosure statement hearing only if a timely objection to the conditionally approved disclosure statement is filed and may combine the disclosure statement hearing with the confirmation hearing. See Bankruptcy Rule 3017.1(c)(3) and 11 U.S.C. 1125(f)(3).

disclosure statement hearings, general aspects

Most objections considered at disclosure statement hearings relate to the adequacy of the information contained in the statement or to the sufficiency or validity of the opinions or conclusions set forth in the statement. A practical method of resolving disputes over opinions asserted in a disclosure statement is for the court to order the statement amended by inserting a counter opinion of the objecting party. It should be noted here that a disclosure statement may be approved by the court without a valuation of the debtor or an appraisal of the debtor's assets. See 11 U.S.C. 1125(b). Even if no objections to a disclosure statement are filed, the court may on its own motion disapprove the statement or require amendments to the statement as a condition of approval. See In re Medley, 58 B.R. 255 (ED MO, 1986).

Most disclosure statement hearings consist mainly of legal arguments by counsel over the adequacy of the statement. Only rarely is it necessary to call witnesses and produce evidence. However, the attorney for the debtor or other plan proponent should be prepared to place the disclosure statement into evidence (if that is the local practice) and, depending on the nature of the objections and what is at issue in the case, present testimony regarding the correctness and extent of the information contained in the statement. If necessary, testimony as to the condition of the debtor's books and records should be presented, and the cost of obtaining more extensive or detailed information established. Testimony laying a reasonable foundation or basis for any contested opinions contained in the statement should also be presented, if necessary. If the plan provides for an injunction against conduct not otherwise enjoined under the Bankruptcy Code and an entity that would be subject to the injunction is not a creditor or equity security holder, the court at the disclosure statement hearing must consider procedures for providing the entity with (1) at least 28 days notice of the time fixed for filing objections to the plan and the confirmation hearing and, (2) to the extent feasible, a copy of the plan and disclosure statement. See Bankruptcy Rule 3017(f).

disclosure statement hearing, conduct of

Following the hearing, the court must determine whether the disclosure statement should be approved. See Bankruptcy Rule 3017(b). If the court does not approve the statement as submitted, it may direct that certain amendments to the statement be made and may enter an order of approval conditioned on the amendments. If, after the court has approved the disclosure statement, the plan is modified so as to render the approved disclosure statement inadequate, it may be necessary to schedule another hearing to obtain court approval of the revised disclosure statement. When the disclosure statement is approved the court must fix a time within which the holders of claims or interests may accept or reject the proposed plan and may fix a date for the confirmation hearing. See Bankruptcy Rule 3017(c). Typically, all of these matters are combined in a single order, a sample of which is set forth in Exhibit 4-M at the end of this chapter. In a small business case, these functions are performed on or before conditional approval of the disclosure statement by the court. See Bankruptcy Rule 3017.1(a).

disclosure statement, approval of by court, order

4.08 Obtaining Acceptance of a Plan by Creditors and Interest Holders

acceptance or rejection of plan, general aspects

The next step in the confirmation process after court approval of the disclosure statement is acceptance of the plan by creditors and, if they are dealt with in the plan, by interest holders. Creditors and interest holders are not permitted to vote on the acceptance or rejection of a plan, however, until they have been provided with a court-approved disclosure statement and related documents. When voting on the acceptance or rejection of a plan does take place, it is by class: that is, the vote of a particular creditor is counted only in the class of claims in which the plan places the claim.

Pre-voting functions. After the court has approved or conditionally approved the disclosure statement, unless the court orders otherwise with respect to one or more unimpaired classes of creditors or interest holders, the debtor in possession, plan proponent, or clerk, as ordered by the court, must mail the following materials to all creditors and interest holders:

materials to be mailed to creditors and interest holders

(1) the plan, or a court-approved summary thereof;

(2) the disclosure statement as approved or conditionally approved by the court;

(3) notice of the time within which acceptances or rejections of the plan may be filed;

(4) notice of the time fixed for filing objections to the plan and of the date and time fixed for the hearing on confirmation of the plan;

(5) a ballot for accepting or rejecting the plan, which must conform to Official Form 314; and

(6) such other information as the court may direct, including any opinion of the court approving the disclosure statement or a court-approved summary of such opinion. See Bankruptcy Rules 3017(d), 3017.1(b).

plan solicitation documents, to whom transmitted

The materials described in subparagraphs (1), (2), (3), and (6) above must also be transmitted to the U.S. Trustee. For the purposes of mailing the above-described documents, creditors and interest holders include holders of stock, bonds, debentures, notes, and other securities of record as of the date that the order approving the disclosure statement was entered. See Bankruptcy Rule 3017(d).

plan injunction, notice requirements

If the plan provides for an injunction against conduct not otherwise enjoined under the Bankruptcy Code, the notice described in subparagraph (4) above must include in conspicuous language (bold, italic, or underlined text) a statement that the plan proposes such an injunction. The notice must also describe briefly the nature of the injunction and identify the entities that would be subject to the injunction. See Bankruptcy Rule 2002(c)(3). At least 28 days notice must be given to parties in interest of the events described in this notice. See Bankruptcy Rule 2002(b).

small business debtor, solicitation of acceptances of plan by

In a small business case, the court may conditionally approve a disclosure statement without a hearing and acceptances of a plan may be solicited based on the conditionally-approved disclosure statement as long as adequate information is provided to each creditor. However, a copy of the conditionally-approved disclosure statement must be mailed to each solicited creditor at least 28 days prior to the confirmation hearing. In such cases the hearing on the disclosure statement may be combined with the hearing on confirmation of the plan. See 11 U.S.C. 1125(f).

holders of unimpaired claims, mailing requirements

If the court orders that the disclosure statement and the plan or summary of the plan shall not be mailed to the holders of an unimpaired class of claims or interests, notice that the class is designated in the plan as unimpaired and notice of the name and address of the person from whom and at whose expense the plan or summary of the plan and disclosure statement may be obtained upon request shall be mailed to members of the unimpaired class together with the notice of the time fixed for filing objections to the plan and the date and time fixed for the hearing on confirmation of the plan. See Bankruptcy Rule 3017(d).

The materials described above must be transmitted to creditors and interest holders before acceptances or rejections of the plan may be solicited. See 11 U.S.C. 1125(b). If the debtor or other plan proponent is directed by the court to mail the above materials, the usual and best practice is to send the materials with a cover letter explaining the purpose of the various documents and soliciting acceptance of the plan. A sample of such a letter in contained in Exhibit 4-N at the end of this chapter. If a creditors' committee is appointed in the case and if the committee approves of the plan, a letter from the committee soliciting the acceptance of the plan should also be included in the mailing.

debtor's letter soliciting acceptance of plan, sending of

If the opinion of the court approving the disclosure statement is not transmitted or if only a summary of the plan is transmitted, the opinion of the court and the full plan must be provided, at the expense of the plan proponent, upon the request of any party in interest. See Bankruptcy Rule 3017(d). If the disclosure statement is too lengthy or technical to be readily understood by a typical creditor, the court may approve a summary of the disclosure statement to be mailed with the disclosure statement. See Advisory Committee's Notes to Bankruptcy Rule 3017(d). Ballots need only be mailed to those creditors and interest holders who are entitled to vote on the plan. See Bankruptcy Rule 3017(d). Therefore, ballots need not be mailed to creditors or interest holders in unimpaired classes of claims or interests or to creditors or interest holders in classes receiving nothing under the plan, because the former are deemed to have accepted the plan and the latter are deemed to have rejected it. See 11 U.S.C. 1126(f), (g).

materials provided to creditors, miscellaneous aspects

The attorney for the debtor or other plan proponent should check to be sure that the order approving the disclosure statement has been signed by the bankruptcy judge and then follow up to ensure that the required materials have been mailed to creditors and equity security holders and transmitted to the U.S. Trustee. Then, any active solicitation of the acceptance of the plan that is to be undertaken should be immediately commenced because the date of the confirmation hearing and voting deadline is likely to be only about a month after the date of the order approving the disclosure statement.

debtor's attorney, responsibilities after approval of disclosure statement

Solicitation of votes. The solicitation of acceptances (or rejections) of a plan may be by mail, telephone, or direct personal contact. Logic dictates that the most critical classes of creditors should receive the most attention. These are normally the classes receiving the least under the plan. Holders of unimpaired claims and holders of claims or interests receiving nothing under the plan cannot vote and need not be contacted. The persons doing the actual soliciting should be cautioned not to exaggerate either the provisions of the plan or the financial ability of the reorganized debtor because such representations might result in accusations that a creditor's vote was not procured in good faith or that the plan itself was not proposed in good faith. See 11 U.S.C. 1126(e), 1129(a)(3). All solicitation letters should be approved by the attorney for the plan proponent prior to mailing.

solicitation of acceptance of plan, general considerations

The attorney for the debtor or other plan proponent should be aware of the deadline for filing acceptances or rejections of the plan. A failure to obtain and file the necessary acceptances by that date may preclude confirmation of the plan. It should be noted that if the holders of a class of claims or interests fail to cast any votes either for or against the plan, the plan is deemed to have been rejected by the class because it was not accepted. See 11 U.S.C. 1126(c),(d). If the local court requires the proponent's attorney to prepare and file a compilation of acceptances and rejections prior to or at the confirmation hearing, this must also be accomplished. In summary, the proponent's attorney must keep a close check on all matters related to the case during the period between the disclosure statement hearing and the confirmation hearing, or, in a small business election case, during the period between conditional approval of the disclosure statement by the court and the confirmation hearing.

attorney for plan proponent, matters to consider

If securities of the reorganized debtor are to be issued under the plan, it should be noted that a person who offers or sells such securities, or solicits the acceptance or rejection of a plan, in good faith and in compliance with the applicable provisions of the Bankruptcy Code is not liable for the violation of any law, rule, or regulation governing the offer, issuance, sale, or purchase of securities or the solicitation of acceptances or rejections of a plan. See 11 U.S.C. 1125(e). This means, in essence, that if the debtor or another person selling or offering securities of the debtor issued pursuant to a Chapter 11 plan complies with the requirements of the Bankruptcy Code, that person is not liable for any violation of a federal or state securities law or regulation.

securities of reorganized debtor, applicability of securities laws

acceptance or rejection of plan, who may vote on

Voting procedures. The holder of any impaired claim or interest that has been allowed (or deemed allowed) under 11 U.S.C. 502 may vote to accept or reject a plan within the time fixed by the court. See 11 U.S.C. 1126(a) and Bankruptcy Rule 3018(a). However, as indicated above, only creditors and interest holders of record as of the date of the entry of the order approving the disclosure statement are entitled to vote. See Bankruptcy Rule 3017(d). Also, a creditor or interest holder whose claim is based on a security of record must be the holder of record of the security on the date of the order approving the disclosure statement or on another date fixed by the court in order to be entitled to vote on the acceptance or rejection of a plan. See Bankruptcy Rule 3018(a).

acceptance or rejection of plan, change or withdrawal of vote

For cause shown and within the time fixed for voting on the plan, the court may, after notice and a hearing, permit a creditor or interest holder to change or withdraw an acceptance or rejection of a plan. See Bankruptcy Rule 3018(a). Also, unless the court orders otherwise, an authorized withdrawal of a claim constitutes the withdrawal of any acceptance or rejection of a plan previously filed by the creditor. See Bankruptcy Rule 3006.

voting by codebtor or guarantor

voting by United States

If a claim has been filed in the name of a creditor by a codebtor or guarantor of the debtor, the codebtor or guarantor may file an acceptance or rejection of a plan in the creditor's name, unless the creditor timely files either a proof of claim or a notice of its intention to act in its own behalf. See Bankruptcy Rule 3005(b). If the United States is a creditor or interest holder, the Secretary of Treasury may accept or reject a plan on behalf of the United States. See 11 U.S.C. 1126(a).

voting on plan, temporary allowance of claim for

If an objection has been filed to the allowance of a claim or interest, the court, after notice and a hearing, may temporarily allow the claim or interest in an amount which the court deems proper for the purpose of accepting or rejecting a plan. See Bankruptcy Rule 3018(a). It should be noted that the allowance or disallowance of claims, including unliquidated personal injury tort and wrongful death claims, for the purpose of confirming a Chapter 11 plan is a core proceeding and may be performed by the bankruptcy court. See 28 U.S.C. 157(b)(2)(B).

objection to allowance of claim, when to file

If the debtor intends to file an objection to the allowance of a substantial claim, the vote of which is likely to result in the plan being rejected by the class, an objection should be filed and a ruling obtained on the objection prior to the commencement of voting. On the other hand, if the debtor intends to object to the allowance of the claim of a creditor who is expected to vote for acceptance of the plan, it may be prudent to file the objection after the voting deadline. See section 4.04, supra, and section 4.11, infra, for further reading on the handling of claims and the filing of objections thereto.

ballot accepting or rejecting plan, requirements

partially-secured creditor, right to vote on plan

An acceptance or rejection of a plan must be in writing, must identify the plan accepted or rejected, must be signed by the creditor or interest holder or an authorized agent thereof, and must conform to Official Form 314. If more than one plan is transmitted, a creditor or interest holder may file an acceptance or rejection for each plan and may indicate a preference among the plans accepted. See Bankruptcy Rule 3018(c). An undersecured creditor whose claim has been allowed in part as a secured claim and in part as an unsecured claim may accept or reject a plan in both capacities if both claims are impaired under the plan. See Bankruptcy Rule 3018(d). A sample Acceptance or Rejection of Plan may be found in Exhibit 4-O at the end of this chapter.

acceptance of plan by class of creditors, what constitutes

Voting requirements. Acceptance of a plan by a class of claims occurs when the plan is accepted by creditors holding at least two-thirds in dollar amount and more than one-half in number of the allowed claims in the class that were voted in the election. See 11 U.S.C. 1126(c). Both acceptance requirements must be satisfied if the plan is to be deemed accepted by the class. Thus, a failure to obtain either the two-thirds in amount requirement or the one-half in number requirement results in a rejection of the plan by the class. The acceptance requirements are calculated on the amount and number of claims that were actually voted in the election, and not on the amount and number of claims in the class. Thus, a failure to vote on the plan constitutes neither an acceptance nor a rejection of the plan, but a plan receiving no votes for either acceptance or rejection is deemed rejected because it has not been accepted. Acceptances or rejections which are found by the court, after notice and a hearing, not to have been exercised in good faith or not to have been solicited or procured in good faith or in accordance with the Bankruptcy Code are not counted. See 11 U.S.C. 1126(c),(e).

Acceptance of a plan by a class of interests occurs when the plan is accepted by the holders of at least two-thirds in amount of the allowed interests in the class that were actually voted in the election. See 11 U.S.C. 1126(d). Again, a nonvote counts nothing and acceptances or rejections not solicited or procured in good faith or in accordance with the Bankruptcy Code are not counted. See 11 U.S.C. 1126(d),(e).

acceptance of plan by class of interests, what constitutes

It is not unusual for a small business debtor to obtain the acceptance of a plan from one or more creditors prior to the commencement of the case. The most common situation in which prepetition acceptances of a plan are obtained is where the debtor files a Chapter 11 case primarily to force a prepetition workout agreement on a dissident creditor (see section 2.03, supra). To be deemed valid, acceptances (or rejections) of a plan obtained before the commencement of the case must comply with the requirements of 11 U.S.C. 1126(b) and Bankruptcy Rule 3018(b), which are discussed below.

acceptance of plan before filing of case, requirements

An acceptance or rejection of a plan executed prior to the commencement of the case is valid only if: (1) solicitation of the acceptance or rejection was in compliance with any applicable nonbankruptcy law, rule, or regulation governing the adequacy of disclosure in connection with the solicitation, or (2) if no such law, rule, or regulation exists, the acceptance or rejection was solicited after disclosure to the creditor or interest holder of "adequate information" as that term is defined in 11 U.S.C. 1125(a). See 11 U.S.C. 1126(b). Further, 11 U.S.C. 1125(g) provides that an acceptance or rejection of a plan may be solicited from the holder of a claim or interest if the solicitation complies with applicable nonbankruptcy law and if the holder was solicited before the commencement of the case in a manner complying with applicable nonbankruptcy law. Thus, it appears that acceptances of a plan solicited prior to the commencement of the case are valid as long as the solicitation complied with the requirements of nonbankruptcy law.

acceptance of plan before filing of case, when valid

Prepetition acceptances or rejections of a plan may be filed with the court on behalf of any creditor or interest holder who is qualified to vote on the plan. However, such acceptances or rejections are not valid if the court finds, after notice and a hearing, that the plan was not transmitted to substantially all creditors and interest holders of the same class, that an unreasonably short time was prescribed for such creditors and interest holders to accept or reject the plan, or that solicitation of the acceptance was not in compliance with 11 U.S.C. 1126(b). See Bankruptcy Rule 3018(b). Thus, when obtaining prepetition acceptances of a plan the debtor should give a copy of the plan to the holder of each claim or interest, give each holder a reasonable period of time in which to study the plan before soliciting its acceptance, and provide each holder with "adequate information" as that term is defined in 11 U.S.C. 1125(a). Finally, if a claim or interest is based on a security of record, the creditor or interest holder must be the holder of record of the security on the date specified in the solicitation in order for the creditor's prepetition acceptance to be valid. See Bankruptcy Rule 3018(b).

requirements for prepetition acceptances of plan

4.09 Obtaining Confirmation of a Plan

confirmation of plan, general aspects

After acceptance of a plan by creditors and interest holders, the next, and final, step in the confirmation process is that of obtaining confirmation of the plan by the court. In essence, confirmation of a plan means court approval of the plan in accordance with the requirements of Chapter 11. Before confirming a plan the court must hold a hearing and must give all parties in interest an opportunity to object to the plan and to otherwise oppose its confirmation. The party proposing the plan has the burden of proof on the issue of confirmation and must prove that the plan meets the confirmation requirements of Chapter 11. At the close of the confirmation hearing the court must decide whether or not to confirm the plan. It should be noted that in a small business case, or if a status conference is held, the court may combine the disclosure statement hearing with the confirmation hearing. See 11 U.S.C. 1125(f)(3)(C), 105(d)(2).

objection to confirmation, who may file, grounds

Objections to confirmation. A creditor or interest holder may express its opposition to a Chapter 11 plan in two ways: by voting to reject the plan and by filing an objection to confirmation of the plan. To oppose a Chapter 11 plan on its merits, an objection to confirmation should be filed. Any party in interest may object to the confirmation of a plan. See 11 U.S.C. 1128(b). Therefore, even if a class of creditors votes to accept a plan, a dissatisfied member of that class may file an objection to confirmation of the plan. Objections may be filed challenging any aspect of the confirmation process. A sample Objection to Confirmation is set forth in Exhibit 4-P at the end of this chapter.

objections to confirmation, time for filing, notice

All interested parties must be given at least 28 days notice of the time fixed for filing objections to confirmation. See Bankruptcy Rules 2002(b),(k) and 3017(d). Notice, as prescribed by the court, must also be given to interest holders, unless the court orders otherwise. See Bankruptcy Rule 2002(d)(6). Notice of the time fixed for filing objections to confirmation is usually incorporated in the combined order and notice sent following the court's approval of the disclosure statement. This practice is permissible under Bankruptcy Rule 3017(d).

objection to confirmation, procedure after filing, effect of failure to file

Objections to confirmation must be filed with the court within the time fixed by the court and served on the debtor, all committees, the U.S. Trustee, and any other entity designated by the court. An objection to confirmation creates a contested matter governed by Bankruptcy Rule 9014. See Bankruptcy Rule 3020(b)(1). While objections based on the failure of the plan proponent to comply with the statutory confirmation requirements can usually be raised at any time, even after the time fixed for filing objections, it has been held that affirmative objections to confirmation, such as objections based on fraud, are deemed waived if an objection to confirmation is not timely filed. See In re Total Transportation Services, Inc., 43 B.R. 8 (SD OH, 1984). Regardless of when they are filed, objections to confirmation are heard by the court at the confirmation hearing, unless an earlier hearing is requested.

modification of plan after acceptance, procedure

Modification of plan after voting. It occasionally becomes necessary for the debtor or other plan proponent to modify the plan after its acceptance has been voted upon by creditors and interest holders but before confirmation. In such event, the proponent must file the desired modification and the court must hold a hearing on notice to all committees and any other entity designated by the court, to determine whether the proposed modification adversely changes the treatment of any claim or interest the holder of which has not accepted the proposed modification. The plan requirements of 11 U.S.C. 1121-28, including the disclosure requirements of 11 U.S.C. 1125, and the confirmation requirements of 11 U.S.C. 1129 are applicable to the modification. See 11 U.S.C. 1127(c), (f)(1). If the court finds that the proposed modification does not adversely affect such claims or interests, the modification shall be deemed accepted by all creditors and interest holders who have previously accepted the plan. See Bankruptcy Rule 3019(a).

modification of plan after acceptance, rights of creditors, notice requirements

A creditor or interest holder who has previously rejected the plan or who has previously accepted the plan but the treatment of whose claim or interest is found to be adversely affected by the proposed modification, may change its previous acceptance or rejection within the time fixed by the court for doing so. Otherwise, the previous acceptance or rejection will apply to the modification. See 11 U.S.C. 1127(d), and Bankruptcy Rule 3019(a). The debtor and all creditors and other interested parties must be given at least 21 days notice by mail of the time fixed by the court for accepting or rejecting a proposed plan modification. See Bankruptcy Rule 2002(a)(5). Notice must also be given to interest holders, unless the court orders otherwise. See Bankruptcy Rule 2002(d)(7).

After the plan proponent files a modification of its plan with the court, the plan as modified becomes the plan. However, the modified plan must meet the requirements of Chapter 11 plans generally. See 11 U.S.C. 1127(a). See section 4.06, supra, for a discussion of these requirements. As indicated above, the proponent of a modification must also comply with the disclosure requirements of 11 U.S.C. 1125. See 11 U.S.C. 1127(c). If the modification renders the proponent's disclosure statement inadequate, the statement may have to be revised and another disclosure statement hearing held. In such case, the proponent should stop soliciting acceptances of the plan until a revised disclosure statement is approved by the court. See section 4.07, supra, for further reading on disclosure statements. The plan, as modified, becomes the plan only after there has been such disclosure under 11 U.S.C. 1125 as the court may direct, notice and a hearing, and the modification is approved. See 11 U.S.C. 1127(f)(2). The modification of a plan prior to acceptance is covered in section 4.06, supra, and the modification of a plan after confirmation is covered in section 4.11, infra.

modification of plan after acceptance, general requirements

Confirmation hearings. After notice, the court must hold a hearing on the confirmation of a proposed plan. See 11 U.S.C. 1128(a). The confirmation hearing must be held whether or not it is requested by a party in interest, whether or not an objection to confirmation has been filed, and even if the plan has been accepted by every creditor and equity security holder. See Bankruptcy Rule 3020(b)(2). The court must make an independent determination as to whether the Chapter 11 confirmation requirements have been complied with even if no one objects to the plan. See In re Wallace, 61 B.R. 54 (WD AR, 1986). However, if no objection to confirmation is timely filed, the court may find that the plan has been proposed in good faith and not by any means forbidden by law without receiving evidence on those issues. See Bankruptcy Rule 3020(b)(2). It has been held that if a plan is patently not in compliance with Chapter 11 or was obviously filed in bad faith, the court may disapprove the plan without a hearing. See In re Weathersfield Farms, Inc., 34 B.R. 435 (VT, 1983). Also, a confirmation hearing on a plan that has been rejected by all classes of impaired claims would appear to be a fruitless endeavor, unless the plan proponent intends to challenge the voting results.

confirmation hearing, necessity of, general requirements

The debtor and all creditors and other interested parties must be given at least 28 days notice of the confirmation hearing. See Bankruptcy Rules 2002(b),(k) and 3017(d). Unless otherwise ordered by the court, notice of the confirmation hearing must also be given to interest holders. See Bankruptcy Rule 2002(d)(6). Notice of the confirmation hearing is often given in the combined order and notice issued following the court's approval of the disclosure statement. See Bankruptcy Rule 3017(d).

confirmation hearing, notice of

Confirmation hearings come in two categories: in the first category are hearings on plans that have been accepted by all impaired classes of claims and interests; in the second category are hearings on plans that have been rejected by one or more impaired classes of claims or interests. In cases of the second category, the plan proponent must confirm the plan under the cramdown provisions of 11 U.S.C. 1129(b). In the first category of cases, the only opposition to the plan is normally from minority creditors in classes of claims that have accepted the plan. In cases of the second category, which are usually referred to as "cramdown cases," the plan proponent must get the plan confirmed over the opposition of one or more classes of creditors or interest holders. In cases of the first category, the plan proponent must meet the requirements of 11 U.S.C. 1129(a) in order to obtain confirmation of its plan. In the second category of cases, in addition to complying with all but one of the requirements of 11 U.S.C. 1129(a), usually over heavier opposition, the plan proponent must also comply with the confirmation requirements of 11 U.S.C. 1129(b).

confirmation hearings, categories of

In either category of cases, the court must hold a hearing and the plan proponent must present evidence to show that the plan is confirmable. The conduct of a particular confirmation hearing will depend greatly on the extent of the opposition to the plan, on the nature of any unruled-upon objections to confirmation, and on the scope and provisions of the proposed plan. Generally, however, at a confirmation hearing in either category of case the attorney for the plan proponent should be prepared to present evidence and legal arguments designed to establish the following matters:

confirmation hearing, conduct of

(1) That the notice requirements of the hearing have been complied with. A certificate of service or affidavit of mailing should suffice to satisfy the notice requirements in most cases. The notice requirements for confirmation hearings are set forth above in this section.

plan proponent, matters to establish at confirmation hearing

(2) That the plan complies with the confirmation requirements of 11 U.S.C. 1129(a). These requirements are set forth and discussed at length below in this section.

(3) That the issues of fact or law raised in any unruled-upon objections to confirmation and any unresolved impairment disputes should be resolved in the proponent's favor.

deposit of funds, when required

(4) That any required deposits have been or will be made. Prior to the entry of an order of confirmation in a Chapter 11 case, the court may order the deposit of any funds or other consideration required under the plan to be distributed upon confirmation. See Bankruptcy Rule 3020(a). If such a deposit has been ordered in the case, evidence that the deposit has been or will be made should be presented at the hearing. Even if a deposit has not been ordered, the plan proponent should be prepared to show the ability of the debtor to make any payments required upon confirmation of the plan. A deposit is sometimes required to establish a reserve for either disputed claims or contingent or unliquidated claims.

confirmability of plan, necessity of independent determination

A determination on the confirmability of a plan under 11 U.S.C. 1129(a) must be independently made by the court regardless of whether any objections to confirmation have been filed and regardless of whether any class of creditors or equity security holders has rejected the plan. A plan that fails to meet the statutory confirmation requirements may not be confirmed, even if no party in interest objects. See In re S & W Enterprise, 37 B.R. 153 (ND IL, 1984). Further, the plan proponent always has the burden of proof on the issue of whether the confirmation requirements of 11 U.S.C. 1129(a) have been satisfied. See In re Agawan Creative Marketing Associates, Inc., 63 B.R. 612 (MA, 1986).

Confirmation without cramdown. The 13 confirmation requirements of 11 U.S.C. 1129(a) are as follows:

confirmation requirement, compliance of plan with Bankruptcy Code

(1) The plan must comply with the applicable provisions of the Bankruptcy Code. See 11 U.S.C. 1129(a)(1). Under this provision the court may examine such matters as whether the plan includes all of the mandatory provisions required under 11 U.S.C. 1123(a), whether the plan classifies claims and interests as required by 11 U.S.C. 1122, and whether any modifications of the plan were carried out in compliance with 11 U.S.C. 1127. See In re Haardt, 65 B.R. 697 (ED PA, 1986). The court may also determine whether the plan violates any applicable provision in any other chapter of the Bankruptcy Code. For example, if the plan calls for a payment to an attorney in violation of 11 U.S.C. 330, for the payment of an administrative expense in violation of 11 U.S.C. 503, or for the payment of a claim that is not allowable under 11 U.S.C. 502(b), then the plan may not be confirmable. See In re Eller Bros., Inc., 53 B.R. 10 (MD TN, 1985).

confirmation requirement, compliance of plan proponent with Bankruptcy Code

(2) The proponent of the plan must have complied with all applicable provisions of the Bankruptcy Code. See 11 U.S.C. 1129(a)(2). Under this provision the court may examine such matters as whether the proponent has complied with the disclosure and solicitation requirements of 11 U.S.C. 1125 and 1126(b), whether the plan was filed in violation of 11 U.S.C. 1121, and whether the proponent has complied with the plan modification requirements of 11 U.S.C. 1127. Unless the proponent has modified the plan since the entry of the order approving the disclosure statement or unless an objection to confirmation is filed alleging improper disclosure or illegal solicitation of acceptances, the court will not normally inquire into disclosure matters because they were considered by the court at the disclosure statement hearing. However, in a small business case, disclosure statement matters may be considered at the confirmation hearing if an objection to the disclosure statement was timely filed. See Bankruptcy Rule 3017.1(c)(3).

(3) The plan must have been proposed in good faith and not by any means forbidden by law. See 11 U.S.C. 1129(a)(3). This is an omnibus clause giving the court the power to deny confirmation if it finds that any illegal activity or bad faith exists in connection with the case. However, if no objection is timely filed, the court may determine that the plan was proposed in good faith and not by any means forbidden by law without receiving evidence on such issues. See Bankruptcy Rule 3020(b)(2). Thus, evidence of good faith and legal activity need only be presented if the issue is raised either by an objection to confirmation or on the motion of the court. Generally, a plan is proposed in good faith when there is a reasonable likelihood that the plan will achieve a result consistent with the objectives and purposes of the Bankruptcy Code. See Matter of Madison Hotel Associates, 749 F. 2nd 410 (CA 7, 1984). However, if the court finds that the primary purpose of a plan is to avoid taxes, settle a contract dispute, or achieve an objective other than reorganization or liquidation, a lack of good faith may be found. See In re Belco Vending, Inc., 67 B.R. 234 (MA, 1986), and In re Coastal Cable T.V., Inc., 709 F. 2nd 762 (CA 1, 1983).

confirmation requirement, plan proposed in good faith

(4) Any payment made or to be made by the plan proponent, by the debtor, or by a person issuing securities or acquiring property under the plan, for services or for costs and expenses in or in connection with the case, or in connection with the plan and incidental to the case, must have been approved by, or be subject to the approval of, the court as being reasonable. See 11 U.S.C. 1129(a)(4). This provision applies not only to attorneys and other professionals employed in the case, but also to such entities as investment bankers, underwriters, consultants, and other persons and organizations employed in connection with the case by anyone issuing securities or receiving property under the plan. See section 3.01, supra, for further reading on the payment of compensation to attorneys and other professionals. The plan proponent should be prepared to justify any previously unapproved payments made, or to be made, to attorneys or other persons involved in the case.

confirmation requirement, court approval of payments

(5) The proponent of the plan must have disclosed the identity and affiliations of all directors, officers, voting trustees, affiliates and successors of the debtor after confirmation, the appointment or continuance in office of such persons must be consistent with the interests of creditors and equity security holders and with public policy, and the identity of all insiders and their compensation must have been disclosed. See 11 U.S.C. 1129(a)(5). This provision must be read in connection with the required plan provision relating to the manner of selecting officers and directors. See 11 U.S.C. 1123(a)(7), and section 4.06, supra. The basic purpose of this provision is to require the plan proponent to disclose the identity of the management, persons in control, and insiders of the reorganized debtor so that creditors and equity security holders can vote intelligently on whether to accept the proposed plan. Generally, the court will inquire into the competency of a reorganized debtor's management only if an objection is made and a prima facie case established. See In re Lyon & Reboli, Inc., 24 B.R. 152 (ED NY, 1982). The disclosures required by this provision are normally included in the disclosure statement. If such disclosures were not contained in the disclosure statement, independent evidence of such disclosures may have to be presented at the confirmation hearing.

confirmation requirement, disclosure of management and insiders

(6) Any governmental regulatory commission with jurisdiction, after confirmation of the plan, must have approved any rate change provided for in the plan, or the rate change provided for in the plan must be expressly conditioned on commission approval. See 11 U.S.C. 1129(a)(6). If the debtor is subject to regulatory commission jurisdiction and if the plan calls for a rate change, the rate change must be approved by the commission prior to confirmation, as the court has no jurisdiction to regulate such rates. See In re Auto-Train Corp., 6 B.R. 510 (DC, 1980). However, if the plan is not to be implemented until the rate change is approved, then prior approval of the rate change is not required.

confirmation requirement, approval of rate change

(7) Each creditor in each class of impaired claims not exercising the Section 1111(b) election must have either accepted the plan or will receive or retain under the plan a value, as of the effective date of the plan, that is not less than what the creditor would have received had the debtor been liquidated under Chapter 7 on such date. See 11 U.S.C. 1129(a)(7). The term "effective date of the plan" is not defined in the Bankruptcy Code, but it is generally held to be the date upon which an order of confirmation becomes final and can no longer be appealed or when an appeal of such an order is resolved. See In re Jones, 32 B.R. 951 (UT, 1983).

confirmation requirement, best interests test

effective date of plan, definition

best interests test, when applicable

This is the so-called "best interests" test that is applied to unsecured creditors, whereunder it must be shown that each non-accepting unsecured creditor will receive under the plan a value that is at least equal to what the creditor would receive in a Chapter 7 liquidation of the debtor's estate. This test must be satisfied in every Chapter 11 case except where the plan is accepted by every creditor in every impaired class, or where there are no impaired classes of claims. Thus, even if every impaired class of claims votes to accept the plan, the best interests test must still be satisfied if a single creditor in any accepting class either did not vote or voted to reject the plan. While this test is also applicable to interest holders, in small business cases interest holders typically would receive nothing in a Chapter 7 liquidation and receive nothing under the plan, so the test is usually moot as to them. It may be applicable, however, if one of the purposes of the plan is to eliminate a class of interest holders.

best interests test, how to satisfy

hypothetical liquidation of debtor, evidence required

In applying the best interests test, the plan proponent must produce evidence showing what the various classes of claims would receive in a hypothetical Chapter 7 liquidation of the debtor on the effective date of the plan. To do this it is usually necessary to show the amount of money that would be generated by the sale of the debtor's assets in a Chapter 7 liquidation proceeding and how the money so received would be allocated among the creditors. The testimony required to establish values in a hypothetical liquidation of the debtor depends greatly on the amount and type of assets and property owned by the debtor. Usually, however, auctioneers or other valuation experts are needed to testify as to the liquidation value of such items as inventory, receivables, equipment, real estate, and other tangible property. Intangible property is difficult to evaluate and seldom brings much in liquidation proceedings. In determining distributions to creditors in a hypothetical Chapter 7 liquidation of the debtor, it should be remembered that any executory contracts being assumed in the Chapter 11 case may have to be rejected in a Chapter 7 case, thus increasing the amount of claims to be paid. In partnership cases, the liability of general partners for partnership debts and their ability to pay such debts in a Chapter 7 case must also be considered. If the debtor has extensive holdings of property, the application of the best interests test can be an involved procedure.

best interests test, present value of deferred cash payments, how to establish

If the plan calls for creditors to receive deferred payments on their claims, the best interests test requires the present value approach to be used in computing the value that creditors are to receive under the plan. The theory behind the present value approach is that a dollar received in the future is worth less than a dollar received today. Therefore, the present value of any deferred cash payments to be made under the plan must be computed using an appropriate discount or interest rate. The appropriate rate may be the current market rate on commercial paper, or any other justifiable rate. See In re Gramercy Twins Assocs., 187 B.R. 112 (SD NY, 1995), and In re 203 N. LaSalle St. Ltd. Partnership, 190 B.R. 567 (ND IL, 1995).

best interests test, Section 1111(b) election

If a class of undersecured claims has made an election under 11 U.S.C. 1111(b) to have their claims treated as being fully secured, the best interests test requires that each creditor in the class receive or retain under the plan property of a value, as of the effective date of the plan, that is not less than the value of the creditor's interest in its collateral. See 11 U.S.C. 1129(a)(7)(B). Again, the present value approach must be used in computing the value to be received by each creditor under the plan. See infra, this section and section 5.02, infra, for further reading on the Section 1111(b) election.

confirmation requirement, acceptance of plan by each impaired class

acceptance of plan by each impaired class, necessity to avoid cramdown

(8) Each class of claims or interests must have either accepted the plan or not be impaired under the plan. See 11 U.S.C. 1129(a)(8). Unless the voting results are stipulated to or the court takes judicial notice thereof, evidence of the results of the voting on the acceptance or rejection of the plan may have to be presented to satisfy the requirements of this provision. See In re Wallace, 61 B.R. 54 (WD AR, 1986). The voting requirements for acceptance of a Chapter 11 plan by impaired classes of claims and interests are set forth in section 4.08, supra. See 11 U.S.C. 1126(c), (d). Impairment disputes may also arise under this provision, and such disputes may have to be ruled on by the court prior to confirmation. It should be remembered that a claim may be impaired even if it is being paid in full if the maturity date or any other contract provision is not complied with, and that a class of claims is deemed impaired if a single claim in the class is impaired. See 11 U.S.C. 1124. See section 4.06, supra, for further reading on impairment of claims. It should be noted that a plan may be confirmed under the cramdown provisions of 11 U.S.C. 1129(b) even if one or more impaired classes of claims or interests does not accept the plan, provided that at least one class of impaired claims accepts the plan. See 11 U.S.C. 1129(b), (a)(10). Therefore, 11 U.S.C. 1129(a)(8) must be complied with only if a cramdown is to be avoided.

(9) Except to the extent that a particular creditor has agreed otherwise, the plan must provide for payment in full in cash on the effective date of the plan of all administrative expenses and gap claims, and of all other priority claims except tax claims, unless a class of such claims has accepted a plan calling for deferred cash payments equal in value, as of the effective date of the plan, to the allowed amount of each such claim. Except to the extent that a particular creditor agrees otherwise, the plan must provide for the payment of each priority unsecured tax claim of a governmental unit in regular installment payments in cash of a total value, as of the effective date of the plan, equal to the allowed amount of the claim over a period ending not later than 5 years after the date of the order for relief and in a manner not less favorable than the most favored nonpriority unsecured claim provided for by the plan. See 11 U.S.C. 1129(a)(9).

confirmation requirement, payment of priority claims

Administrative expenses include, among other things, fees awarded to attorneys and other professionals and ordinary postpetition operating expenses of the debtor's business. If a Chapter 11 debtor is operating an active business, a literal reading of this provision would require that all employees and suppliers extending credit be paid in full on the effective date of the plan, regardless of the debtor's normal business practices on the payment of such expenses. In reality such payment is seldom required, and the debtor is usually permitted to continue its normal business practice on the payment of such expenses. If a debtor is short of funds at confirmation time, a priority creditor, such as a postpetition supplier or the debtor's attorney, may agree to accept payment of its administrative claim at a later time. If deferred cash payments are to be made to tax creditors or to accepting classes of other priority creditors, the present value approach must be used in computing the required amount of deferred cash payments to be made under the plan, and an appropriate discount or interest rate must be used.

administrative expenses, necessity of payment

(10) If one or more classes of claims is impaired under the plan, at least one class of impaired claims must have accepted the plan as determined without including any acceptance of the plan by an insider. See 11 U.S.C. 1129(a)(10). The voting requirements of 11 U.S.C. 1126(c) must be satisfied with respect to any accepting class, except that any acceptances of the plan by insiders must be excluded in determining whether a class of claims has accepted the plan for purposes of this provision. See 11 U.S.C. 101(31) and section 3.03, supra, for the definition of an insider. A plan must be affirmatively accepted by noninsiders in order to comply with the provision. Thus, if, after excluding acceptances by insiders, there are no votes for either acceptance or rejection of the plan, then the class is deemed to have rejected the plan for purposes of this provision. This provision is important because if it is not complied with, a cramdown may not be implemented. See 11 U.S.C. 1129(b)(1). It should be noted that if 11 U.S.C. 1129(a)(8) is complied with, then 11 U.S.C. 1129(a)(10) is also complied with unless the Section 1129(a)(8) compliance was accomplished with respect to a class of impaired claims only through acceptances of the plan by insiders.

confirmation requirement, acceptance of plan by one class of impaired claims

(11) Confirmation of the plan must not be likely to be followed by the liquidation, or the need for further financial reorganization, of the debtor or any successor to the debtor under the plan, unless such liquidation or reorganization is called for in the plan. See 11 U.S.C. 1129(a)(11). This is the feasibility requirement for Chapter 11 plans. Under this requirement, both the plan and the debtor's ability to implement it must appear to the court to be feasible before the plan can be confirmed. The courts are reluctant to send a financially weak debtor back out into the business world to injure yet another group of creditors.

confirmation requirement, feasibility of plan

Feasibility includes the ability of the debtor to make the payments and meet the other obligations called for in the plan and the ability of the debtor to survive for a reasonable period (unless a future liquidation, merger, or other reorganization is provided for in the plan). The factors considered by the court in determining the feasibility of a plan include the reorganized debtor's earning capacity, the adequacy of its capital structure, the current and projected economic conditions affecting its business or industry, and the adequacy of its management. See In re Apple Tree Partners, 131 B.R. 380 (WD TN, 1991), and In re U.S. Truck Co., Inc., 800 F. 2nd 581 (CA 6, 1986).

feasibility of plan, matters considered by court

Especially if feasibility has been put into issue by the filing of an objection to confirmation on such grounds, the plan proponent should be prepared to present at the confirmation hearing expert testimony and other evidence relating to the feasibility of the plan. Testimony may be presented from investment or market experts, from economists, and from the debtor's management on such matters as the projected earnings and cash flow of the reorganized debtor, the projected market and industry conditions, the experience and competency of the reorganized debtor's management, and the probability of the reorganized debtor's financial success in its field or market.

feasibility of plan, how to establish

deferred payment plans, feasibility of

Especially troublesome for many debtors is establishing the feasibility of a so-called negative amortization plan wherein the payment of all or part of the interest due on a secured claim is deferred until a later date, when the deferred interest together with all or a portion of the principal is payable in the form of a balloon payment. Such plans are often not confirmed. To establish the feasibility of these and other deferred-payment plans, the debtor must present believable evidence of its future ability to make the required payments. See Great W. Bank v. Sierra Woods Group, 953 F. 2d 1174 (CA 9, 1992), and In re James Wilson Assocs., 965 F. 2d 160 (CA 7, 1992).

confirmation requirement, payment of fees

(12) All fees payable under 28 U.S.C. 1930, as determined by the court at the confirmation hearing, must have been paid or the plan must provide for the payment of all such fees on the effective date of the plan. See 11 U.S.C. 1129(a)(12). The fees payable under this provision include the filing fee and the quarterly fee payable to the U.S. Trustee. See section 3.05, supra, for the amount of the quarterly fee. If such fees have been paid, in whole or in part, evidence of payment in the form of receipts, cancelled checks, or an acknowledgement of such by the U.S. Trustee, should be presented at the hearing. Because the amount of the quarterly fee is based on the amount disbursed during the quarter by the debtor in possession, evidence of the amount of such disbursements during any quarter for which payment is due may have to be presented at the hearing.

confirmation requirement, retiree benefits

(13) The plan must provide for the continuation, after its effective date, of the payment of all retiree benefits at the level established under 11 U.S.C. 1114 for the duration of the period for which the debtor has obligated itself to provide such benefits. See 11 U.S.C. 1129(a)(13). This provision is applicable only if the debtor seeks to modify a retiree benefit, as that term is defined in 11 U.S.C. 1114(a). If such a modification has been approved by the court or agreed to by the authorized representative of the retirees, the provisions as modified must be incorporated into the plan. See section 4.06, supra, for further reading.

confirmation requirement, domestic support obligations

(14) If the debtor is required by a judicial or administrative order, or by statute, to pay a domestic support obligation, it must be shown that the debtor has paid all amounts payable under the order or statute that first became due after the filing of the bankruptcy case. See 11 U.S.C. 1129(a)(14). This requirement is applicable only to individual chapter 11 debtors. An individual debtor who is subject to a domestic support obligation should be prepared to show that all post-filing obligations have been paid.

confirmation requirement, individual debtor, disposable income requirement

(15) In a case in which the debtor is an individual and in which the holder of an allowed unsecured claim objects to confirmation of the plan, it must be shown that the value, as of the effective date of the plan, of the property to be distributed under the plan on account of such claim is not less than the amount of the claim or that the value of the property to be distributed under the plan is not less than the projected disposable income of the debtor (as defined in 11 U.S.C. 1325(b)(2)) to be received during the 5-year period beginning on the date that the first payment is due under the plan, or during the period for which the plan provides payments, whichever is longer. See 11 U.S.C. 1129(a)(15). As indicated, this requirement applies only to individual Chapter 11 debtors. The term "disposable income" means current monthly income received by the debtor (with certain exclusions) less amounts reasonably necessary to be expended for the maintenance or support of the debtor and his or her dependents, charitable contributions (up to 15 percent of the debtor's gross income), and, if the debtor is engaged in business, for the payment of expenditures necessary for the continuation, preservation, and operation of the debtor's business. The debtor's current monthly income should appear on the Statement of Current Monthly Income that individual Chapter 11 debtors are required to file. If the debtor's current monthly income multiplied by 12 exceeds the median family income for the debtor's state and family size, the debtor is required to use the National and Local Standards established by the Internal Revenue Services as his or her expenses in computing his or her disposable income. See 11 U.S.C. 1325(b)(2) and 707(b)(2). This procedure is identical to the procedure used to determine disposable income in Chapter 13 cases. The reader is referred to Williamson, The Attorney's Handbook on Consumer Bankruptcy and Chapter 13, section 3.07, for further reading on this matter. It should be noted that this requirement is applicable only if an unsecured creditor files an objection to confirmation. If such an objection is filed, the debtor should be prepared to show either that the creditor's claim is being paid in full under the plan (which is unlikely) or that the value of the payments being made under the plan are equal to or greater than the debtor's projected disposable income for the applicable period.

(16) All transfers of property of the plan must be made in accordance with any applicable provisions of nonbankruptcy law that govern the transfer of property by a corporation or trust that is not a moneyed, business, or commercial corporation or trust. See 11 U.S.C. 1129(a)(16). This requirement means that any property transfers made under the plan must comply with state law requirements for property transfers by nonprofit corporations and trusts.

property transfer requirements under plan

Even if all other statutory requirements for confirmation have been complied with, the court, on the request of a party in interest that is a governmental unit, may not confirm a plan if the principal purpose of the plan is the avoidance of taxes or the avoidance of the application of section 5 of the Securities Act of 1933 (15 U.S.C. 77e). The governmental unit has the burden of proof on the issue of avoidance in any hearing on the matter. See 11 U.S.C. 1129(d). However, even if a governmental unit does not object to confirmation, the court apparently has the authority to deny confirmation under the good faith provision of 11 U.S.C. 1129(a)(3) if it finds that the principal purpose of the plan is to avoid taxes. See In re Maxim Industries, Inc., 22 B.R. 611 (MA, 1982).

avoidance of taxes or securities laws, effect on confirmation of plan

Confirmation by cramdown. If all of the confirmation requirements of Section 1129(a) are complied with except the provision of paragraph (8) requiring acceptance of the plan by all impaired classes of claims and interests, the plan may be confirmed by the court under Section 1129(b), if the cramdown requirements of that section are complied with. It should be noted here that the term "cramdown" is not found in the Bankruptcy Code. It is a term used in Chapter 11 cases to refer to the process under Section 1129(b) by which a plan is confirmed notwithstanding the rejection of the plan by one or more classes of impaired creditors or interest holders. Because interest holders seldom play a significant role in small business Chapter 11 cases, cramdowns are usually required to obtain confirmation over the objection of one or more classes of secured or unsecured creditors.

confirmation of plan through cramdown, when necessary

cramdown, definition

It is important to understand that while a cramdown may be implemented if the provision of Section 1129(a)(8) requiring plan acceptance by all impaired classes of claims and interests is not complied with, the provision of Section 1129(a)(10) requiring plan acceptance by at least one class of impaired claims by noninsiders must be satisfied before a cramdown may be implemented. See 11 U.S.C. 1129(b)(1). It should also be understood that a cramdown may not be implemented against a creditor who is secured only by a security interest in real property that is the debtor's principal residence. See 11 U.S.C. 1123(b)(5) and Nobleman v. American Savings Bank, 508 U.S. 324 , 124 L.Ed. 2d 228, 113 S.Ct. 2106 (1993).

cramdown, requirement of acceptance of plan by 1 class of impaired creditors

The court, on the request of the plan proponent, may confirm a Chapter 11 plan under the cramdown provisions of Section 1129(b) if the plan does not discriminate unfairly and is fair and equitable with respect to each impaired class of claims or interests that has not accepted the plan. See 11 U.S.C. 1129(b)(1). Thus, to implement a cramdown the debtor or other plan proponent must request confirmation under Section 1129(b). Such a request may be made in the plan, in a separate written motion or application, or, in appropriate circumstances, orally at the confirmation hearing. The local rules should be checked for requirements relating to requests for confirmation under Section 1129(b).

confirmation by cramdown, statutory requirements

As indicated in the previous paragraph, the two basic requirements for a cramdown are that the plan not discriminate unfairly with respect to any impaired class of claims or interests that has not accepted the plan, and that the plan be fair and equitable with respect to each nonaccepting class of claims or interests. See 11 U.S.C. 1129(b)(1). The unfair discrimination requirement normally relates to the classification of claims and the relative treatment given the nonaccepting class (or classes) under the plan. In a cramdown, the court may examine any differences in treatment under the plan given a nonaccepting class as compared to other classes of claims of the same rank or priority. Generally, the unfair discrimination requirement ensures that any nonaccepting class will receive under the plan a relative value equal to that received by other similarly-situated classes of claims. See Matter of Johns-Manville Corp., 68 B.R. 618 (SD NY, 1986). All discrimination is not prohibited, however, only unfair discrimination is prohibited, and if a valid reason exists for treating a nonaccepting class less favorably than another class of the same rank or priority, the plan may be confirmed. The payment of unequal interest rates to secured creditors can be an unfair discrimination unless there is a valid reason for doing so. See In re Buttonwood Partners, Ltd., 111 B.R. 57 (SD NY, 1990), and In re Dilts, 100 BR 759 (WD PA, 1989).

cramdown, basic requirements

unfair discrimination, what constitutes

cramdown of secured claims, fair and equitable requirement

To confirm a plan under a cramdown, the court must also find that the plan is fair and equitable with respect to each nonaccepting class of impaired claims or interests. The fair and equitable requirement is defined differently in the Bankruptcy Code for secured claims, unsecured claims, and interests. 11 U.S.C. 1129(b)(2)(A) provides that a plan is fair and equitable with respect to a nonaccepting class of impaired secured claims if it provides for any of the following methods of treatment:

(1) The secured creditor retains the full extent of the lien securing its claim, whether or not the debtor retains the property subject to the lien, and the creditor receives on account of its secured claim deferred cash payments totalling at least the allowed amount of its secured claim and having a value, as of the effective date of the plan, at least equal to the value of the creditor's lien.

(2) The sale, subject to 11 U.S.C. 363(k), of the collateral, free and clear of the creditor's lien, with the lien attaching to the proceeds of the sale, and the creditor's allowed secured claim treated as described in paragraph (1) above or paragraph (3) below.

(3) The secured creditor receives the indubitable equivalent of its allowed secured claim.

cramdown, deferred cash payments, present value requirement

The deferred cash payments called for in paragraph (1) above must have a present value, as of the effective date of the plan, at least equal to the value of the creditor's collateral. Therefore, the payments must be discounted to present value using an appropriate discount or interest rate, which is normally the current market rate. All payments must be in cash; securities or other property will not suffice. The requirement of cash payments with a present value at least equal to the value of a secured creditor's interest in its collateral is the key to giving a secured creditor the full value of its allowed secured claim and is essential to the cramdown of a secured claim. The value of a secured creditor's collateral must be determined by the court if the parties cannot agree on a value. See sections 4.01 and 4.04, supra, for further reading on the valuation of collateral.

cramdown, sale of secured property, requirements

The alternative described in paragraph (2) above is identical to the alternative in paragraph (1) above except that the lien is transferred from the secured property to the proceeds from the sale of the property, subject to 11 U.S.C. 363(k), which permits a secured creditor to bid on and purchase the secured property at any sale and to offset its allowed secured claim against the purchase price of the property. The matters set forth in the preceding paragraph apply equally to this alternative.

cramdown, indubitable equivalent, what constitutes

The "indubitable equivalent" alternative described in paragraph (3) above is apparently intended to lend flexibility to cramdowns. By substituting collateral at least equal in quality and value to the original collateral and giving the creditor the required deferred cash payments, a plan may provide a secured creditor with the indubitable equivalent of its claim. See In re Monnier Bros., 755 F. 2nd 1336 (CA 8, 1985). The turnover of a secured creditor's collateral to the creditor may also constitute the realization of the indubitable equivalent of the creditor's claim. See In re Coral Petroleum, Inc., 60 B.R. 377 (SD TX, 1986). However, if the creditor secured by the property is an undersecured creditor who has exercised the Section 1111(b) election, the indubitable equivalent test cannot be satisfied by turning the secured property over to the creditor. See In re Griffiths, 27 B.R. 873 (KS, 1983).

cramdowns, application of Section 1111(b)

nonrecourse secured creditor, definition

The Section 1111(b) election. In cramdowns involving either undersecured claims or nonrecourse secured claims, the parties should be aware of the provisions of 11 U.S.C. 1111(b). Section 1111(b) provides that in a Chapter 11 case a nonrecourse secured creditor is treated as a recourse creditor unless the collateral is sold, either under 11 U.S.C. 363 or under the plan, or unless the creditor exercises the Section 1111(b) election to have its claim treated as being fully secured. See 11 U.S.C. 1111(b)(1)(A). A nonrecourse secured creditor is a creditor who, under nonbankruptcy law, has rights only against the collateral and not against the debtor.

Section 1111(b) election, exercise of in small business cases

Section 1111(b), it should be noted, refers to classes of secured claims. In small business cases, however, each secured claim is almost always classified separately, so the election is normally available to each qualifying creditor separately. Accordingly, the Section 1111(b) election may be exercised by any undersecured creditor, recourse or nonrecourse, unless the creditor's interest in the collateral is of inconsequential value or unless the creditor is a recourse creditor and the property is sold, either under the plan or under 11 U.S.C. 363. See 11 U.S.C. 1111(b)(1)(B) and Bankruptcy Rule 3014.

If an undersecured creditor exercises the Section 1111(b) election, the creditor's allowed claim is treated as being fully secured and must be dealt with accordingly; in a cramdown and otherwise. In essence, by exercising the Section 1111(b) election an undersecured creditor waives the unsecured portion of its claim (and the right to contest or block confirmation of the plan in a cramdown) in return for payment in full of the allowed amount of its claim under the plan without interest. The decision on whether to exercise the Section 1111(b) election can be complicated and a creditor should consider all of the consequences of the election before exercising it. See section 5.02, infra, for further reading on the Section 1111(b) election.

Section 1111(b) election, effect of

Cramdowns of unsecured claims. The fair and equitable cramdown requirement is defined quite differently in the Bankruptcy Code with respect to unsecured claims as compared to secured claims. A plan is fair and equitable with respect to a nonaccepting class of impaired unsecured claims if it provides for either of the following methods of treatment:

cramdown of unsecured claims, fair and equitable requirement

(1) for each unsecured creditor in the class to receive or retain on account of its claim property of a value, as of the effective date of the plan, equal to the allowed amount of its claim; or

(2) for the holders of any claims or interests that are junior to the nonaccepting class to receive or retain nothing on their claims or interests, except that an individual chapter 11 debtor may retain estate property acquired during the pendency of the case and earnings from services performed by the debtor during the pendency of the case, if the debtor has paid all domestic support obligations that became due after the commencement of the case. See 11 U.S.C. 1129(b)(2)(B).

Thus, to be fair and equitable with respect to a nonaccepting class of unsecured claims, a plan must either pay each claim in the class in full or pay nothing to any junior classes of claims or interests. As indicated in the next paragraph, this requirement is referred to as the rule of absolute priority. In determining whether an unsecured claim in a nonaccepting class is being paid in full under the plan the value of any deferred cash payments to be made under the plan must be discounted to present value as of the effective date of the plan. This means that an appropriate discount or interest rate must be used. It should be noted that it is not necessary to pay unsecured creditors in cash; payment may consist of property, which includes securities of the reorganized debtor. If securities are to be used for payment, they may have to be valued by the court to determine whether full compensation is being paid. To value such securities, the court may require a going-concern valuation of the reorganized debtor.

cramdown of unsecured claims, methods of payment

The rule of absolute priority. The cramdown requirement that a nonaccepting class of unsecured claims be paid in full under the plan or that nothing be paid or retained by any junior class of claims or interests is known as the rule of absolute priority. In small business cases this rule is most often invoked to prevent the debtor's owners (as junior interest holders) from retaining an interest in the reorganized business unless each nonaccepting class of impaired unsecured claims is paid in full under the plan. Otherwise stated, the rule of absolute priority requires payment in full of unsecured creditors who have not accepted the plan if the owners of the debtor are to retain ownership of the reorganized debtor. This rule gives great leverage to large unsecured creditors in small business cases. It should be understood that this rule is applicable only in cramdowns (i.e., confirmations under Section 1129(b)) and only with respect to claims or interests that are junior to the nonaccepting class.

absolute priority rule, explanation of

The absolute priority rule is applicable to all Chapter 11 debtors seeking confirmation by cramdown, regardless of the type of business entity involved. It is applicable to debtors who are sole proprietorships, partnerships, limited liability companies, and corporations. See Unruh v. Rushville State Bank, 987 F.2d 1506 (CA 10, 1993) and Kham & Nate's Shoes No. 2, Inc. v. First Bank, 908 F.2d 1351 (CA 7, 1990). Because small businesses are usually unable to pay unsecured claims in nonaccepting classes in full, because the expertise of the business owners is often essential to the continuation of the business, and because there is usually little incentive to reorganize if the owners are to lose control and ownership of the reorganized business, the absolute priority rule can be a major impediment to the reorganization of a small business under Chapter 11. It should be noted that there is an exception to the rule of absolute priority for individual debtors whereby such debtors may retain their postpetition property acquisitions and earnings in a cramdown. See 11 U.S.C. 1129(b)(2)(B)(ii).

absolute priority rule, application of

absolute priority rule, new value exception

The hardships imposed on small business debtors by the absolute priority rule are eased somewhat, in some districts at least, by the application of the so-called "new value" exception to the rule of absolute priority. Under the new value exception the debtor's owners may, by contributing new capital to the business under the plan, retain their ownership interest in the reorganized debtor even if one or more classes of unsecured claims are not paid in full under the plan. This exception was first recognized by the Supreme Court in Case v. Los Angeles Lumber Products Co., 308 U.S. 106, 60 S.Ct. 1, 84 L. Ed. 110 (1939), which was a case under a prior bankruptcy act.

new value exception to absolute priority rule, requirements

The Supreme Court ruled on the new value exception to the rule of absolute priority in Bank of America v. 203 N. La Salle Street Partnership, 526 U.S. 434, 119 S. Ct. 1411, 143 L. Ed. 2d 607 (1999). In that case the court held that a plan permitting former business owners to retain their interest in the reorganized debtor by contributing money (i.e., new value) to the business could not be confirmed in a cramdown because the equity in the reorganized business that was being conveyed to the former owners was exclusive to the former owners and not offered to other potential buyers. The court stated that plans providing junior interest holders with exclusive opportunities free from competition and without the benefit of market valuation are in violation of the absolute priority rule and may not be confirmed. If the former business owners are to retain an interest in the reorganized debtor they must contribute new value in amounts and in a manner that is market tested and open to other potential investors.

new value exception to absolute priority rule, how value is determined

In In re Union Financial Services Group, Inc., 303 B.R. 390 (MO, 2003), the court held that the marketing process provided for in the plan was sufficient to satisfy the new value rules adopted by the Supreme Court in the La Salle Street case. Under the plan, independent directors managed the marketing process with the assistance of independent counsel and professional financial advisors. The court held that these additional components of the plan were sufficient to ensure that a true market test occurred and that the value contributed by the former owners was market tested. On the other hand, in In re Global Ocean Carriers, Inc., 251 B.R. 31 (DE, 2000), the court held that the debtor's plan violated the absolute priority rule by allowing the debtor's controlling shareholder to exclusively determine, without the benefit of public auction or competing plans, who would own the equity in the reorganized debtor and how much they would pay for it. See In re MJ Metal Products, Inc., 292 B.R. 702 (WY, 2003), for a similar ruling.

retention of ownership by former owners, requirments

If the former owners wish to retain their interest in the reorganized debtor under the new value exception to the rule of absolute priority, it is clear that the plan must provide a method of determining the value of ownership interests in the reorganized debtor that exposes the interests to the market place and permits others to compete for the interests. It is clearly not sufficient for a plan to permit the former owners to determine the value of the interests in the reorganized debtor and who should be permitted to acquire the interests. The public and other potential investors, including senior creditors, must be permitted to compete for the ownership interests in the reorganized debtor and, if desired, propose competing plans of reorganization.

cramdown of interests, rule of absolute priority

If a debtor has more than one class of interest holders it should be noted that 11 U.S.C. 1129(b)(2)(C) provides that a plan is fair and equitable with respect to a nonaccepting class of interests if the plan provides (1) for each interest holder in the nonaccepting class to receive or retain property with a present value equal to the allowed amount of any applicable fixed liquidation preference, any applicable fixed redemption price, or the value of the holder's interest, whichever is greatest, or (2) for junior interests to receive or retain nothing under the plan. Thus, the rule of absolute priority is also applicable to nonaccepting classes of interests, and the treatment required of interests in cramdowns is similar to that described above for unsecured claims.

order of confirmation, entry of

If, after the presentation of evidence, the court is satisfied that the confirmation requirements of 11 U.S.C. 1129(a) and, in the event of a cramdown, 11 U.S.C. 1129(b), have been satisfied, an order of confirmation may be entered. If more than one plan has met the confirmation requirements, the court must consider the preferences of creditors and interest holders in determining which plan to confirm, as the court may confirm only one plan. See 11 U.S.C. 1129(c).

4.10 The Order of Confirmation

The order of confirmation culminates the confirmation process and, of course, confirms the plan. In addition, the confirmation order has the following significant effects on the case: (1) it terminates the estate and reverts the estate property to the reorganized debtor, (2) it terminates the "debtor in possession" status of the debtor, (3) it discharges the debtor, and (4) it terminates the automatic stay.

order of confirmation, effect of

The order of confirmation, which must conform to Official Form 315, should contain rulings on the confirmation requirements of Sections 1129(a) and, if necessary, 1129(b) of the Bankruptcy Code. If the disclosure statement hearing was combined with the confirmation hearing under 11 U.S.C. 1125(f)(3), then the order should also contain a provision approving the disclosure statement, unless a separate order is issued approving the disclosure statement. Notice of entry of the confirmation order must be promptly mailed or transmitted to the debtor, all creditors and interest holders, the U.S. Trustee, and other parties in interest. See Bankruptcy Rule 3020(c). If the plan provides for an injunction against conduct not otherwise enjoined under the Bankruptcy Code, the order of confirmation must (1) describe in reasonable detail all acts enjoined, (2) be specific in its terms regarding the injunction, and (3) identify the entities that are subject to the injunction. Notice of entry of the order must be mailed to any identified entity that may be subject to the injunction described above. See Bankruptcy Rule 3020(c). A sample Order of Confirmation is set forth in Exhibit 4-Q at the end of this chapter.

order of confirmation, form, notice of entry

Even though an order of confirmation is a final judgment, it possesses many of the characteristics of a contract, and the courts often employ rules of contract construction (including the parol evidence rule) in construing or interpreting the provisions of a confirmed plan. See In re Stratford of Texas, Inc., 635 F. 2nd 365 (CA 5, 1981). Further, even though an order of confirmation is a final judgment for purposes of appeal and otherwise, a confirmed plan may, under certain circumstances, be modified by the plan proponent or the reorganized debtor prior to substantial confirmation of the plan. See 11 U.S.C. 1127(b). See section 4.11, infra, for further reading on the modification of a confirmed plan. Finally, unless the court orders otherwise, an order of confirmation is automatically stayed for 14 days following entry of the order. See Bankruptcy Rule 3020(e). This means that unless the court orders otherwise, any transfer of assets, cash distributions, or other acts provided for in the plan may not be made until the expiration of the 15-day period. See Bankruptcy Rule 3021.

order of confirmation, rules of construction, stay of

Effect of confirmation order. The confirmation of a plan binds the debtor and all parties to the terms of the plan regardless of whether the claim or interest of a party is impaired under the plan and regardless of whether the party has accepted the plan. See 11 U.S.C. 1141(a). An order of confirmation is a final judgment and constitutes res judicata with respect to all issues that were or that could have been litigated in the proceeding. See In re Penn-Dixie Industries, Inc., 32 B.R. 173 (SD NY, 1983). Thus, a creditor or other party in interest cannot later, either in the bankruptcy court or in another forum, pursue claims or raise defenses that could have been maintained or raised in the confirmation process. See In re St. Louis Freight Lines, Inc., 45 B.R. 546 (ED MI, 1984). An order of confirmation also bars the debtor from later asserting against third parties claims that the debtor failed to disclose prior to confirmation. See In re Heritage Hotel Partnership I, 160 B.R. 374 (BAP 9, 1993).

confirmed plan, binding effect

order of confirmation, res judicata effect

Because a Chapter 11 order of confirmation serves to discharge the debtor, it has the effect of terminating the automatic stay, except as it applies to acts against property of the estate. See 11 U.S.C. 362(c). However, a Chapter 11 discharge operates as a permanent injunction against the commencement or continuation of an action, the employment of process, or any act to collect, recover, or offset a discharged debt as a personal liability of the debtor, whether or not discharge of the debt is waived. See 11 U.S.C. 524(a)(2), (3). It should be understood that this injunction does not prevent creditors from enforcing their rights under the plan. For example, if the debtor defaults on an obligation set forth in the plan, a secured creditor may foreclose on its lien without obtaining relief from either the automatic stay or the permanent injunction. See In re Ernst, 45 B.R. 700 (MN, 1985).

order of confirmation, termination of stay, permanent injunction

Except as otherwise provided in the plan or in the order confirming the plan, the confirmation of a plan vests all property of the estate in the debtor. See 11 U.S.C. 1141(b). Thus, if there is estate property that is not dealt with in the plan or in the order of confirmation, ownership of the property is vested in the debtor after confirmation. See In re Ford, 61 B.R. 913 (WD WI, 1986). An order of confirmation also terminates the "debtor in possession" status of the debtor. See In re WRMJ Johnson Fruit Farm, Inc., 107 B.R. 18, (WD NY, 1989).

confirmation of plan, vesting of property

property not dealt with in plan, effect of confirmation order

Except as otherwise provided in the plan or in the order confirming the plan, after confirmation of a plan the property dealt with by the plan is free and clear of all claims and interests of creditors and interest holders. See 11 U.S.C. 1141(c). However, property not dealt with by the plan remains subject to the same encumbrances or other interests to which it was subject at the time the petition was filed, even if a creditor secured thereby accepts the plan as an unsecured creditor and has its unsecured claim discharged by the order of confirmation. See In re Snedaker, 39 B.R. 41 (SD FL, 1984). Likewise, executory contracts not dealt with in the plan or in the order of confirmation pass through a Chapter 11 case unaltered, preserving the rights thereunder of the nondebtor party. See Matter of Central Watch, Inc., 22 B.R. 561 (ED WI, 1982). It is important, therefore, that either the plan or the order of confirmation contain a provision dealing with the disposition or treatment of property, contracts, and other interests of the debtor not specifically dealt with under the plan.

order of confirmation, effect of on interest holders

Except as otherwise provided in the plan or the order, a confirmation order terminates the rights of interest holders who are dealt with under the plan. See 11 U.S.C. 1141(d)(1)(B). Thus, a confirmation order that deals with the rights of interest holders, in effect, substitutes the rights set forth in the plan for the prepetition rights of the interest holders. For example, if the plan terminates the rights of the debtor's shareholders and does not provide them with an interest in the reorganized debtor, then the interests of the shareholders are terminated by the order of confirmation. However, if the plan is silent as to the rights of the debtor's interest holders, then their prepetition rights in the debtor survive the Chapter 11 case unchanged.

chapter 11 discharge, general provisions

The Chapter 11 discharge. Except as provided below, and except as otherwise provided in the plan or in the order confirming the plan, the confirmation of a chapter 11 plan discharges the debtor from any debt that arose or is deemed to have arisen prior to confirmation, whether or not a proof of claim based on the debt was filed, whether or not a claim for the debt was allowed, and whether or not the creditor has accepted the plan. See 11 U.S.C. 1141(d)(1). The exceptions to chapter 11 discharge provisions stated above are listed below.

chapter 11 discharge, individual debtor, debts not dischargeable

(1) A chapter 11 discharge does not discharge an individual debtor from any debt that is excepted from discharge under 11 U.S.C. 523. This means that any debt that is nondischargeable in a chapter 7 case is also nondischargeable in a chapter 11 case. See 11 U.S.C. 1141(d)(2).

chapter 11 discharge, plan of liquidation

(2) The confirmation of a chapter 11 plan does not discharge a debtor (individual or nonindividual) if the plan provides for the liquidation of all or substantially all of the property of the estate, if the debtor does not engage in business after consummation of the plan, and if the debtor would be denied a discharge in a chapter 7 case. See 11 U.S.C. 1141(d)(3). This means that if the chapter 11 plan is a plan of liquidation and the debtor goes out of business after the liquidation of its assets and would be denied a discharge in a chapter 7 case, confirmation of the plan does not discharge the debtor. The provision is mainly applicable to corportate and other nonindividual liquidating debtors who are not eligible for a chapter 7 discharge. It may also be applicable to a liquidating individual debtor who is not eligible for a chapter 7 discharge.

chapter 11 discharge, individual debtor, plan payment requirements

(3) Unless, after notice and a hearing and for cause, the court orders otherwise, the confirmation of a chapter 11 plan does not discharge an individual debtor from any debt provided for in the plan until the court grants the debtor a discharge upon the completion of all payments under the plan. See 11 U.S.C. 1141(d)(5)(A). However, at any time after confirmation of the plan, and after notice and a hearing, the court may grant a discharge to an individual debtor who has not completed payments under the plan if the value, as of the effective date of the plan, of property actually distributed under the plan an account of each allowed unsecured claim is not less than the amount that would have been paid on such claim in a chapter 7 case of the debtor on the effective date of the plan, and if modification of the chapter 11 plan is not practicable. See 11 U.S.C. 1141(d)(5)(B). An individual debtor who has completed all payments under the plan should, as a matter of course, receive a chapter 11 discharge unless the court, for cause and after notice and a hearing, orders otherwise. An individual debtor who is unable to complete the payments required under the plan may obtain a chapter 11 discharge only by filing a request for the discharge and establishing at the hearing on the request that each unsecured creditor received not less than what the creditor would have received in a chapter 7 case and by showing that modification of the plan is not practicable.

(4) An individual debtor may not receive a chapter 11 discharge unless the court, after notice and a hearing held not more than 10 days before the date of the order of discharge, finds that there is no reasonable cause to believe that the debtor has been, or may in a pending case be, convicted of a felony which demonstrates that the filing of the bankruptcy case was an abuse of the Bankruptcy Code, or owes a debt arising from a violation of a Federal or state securities law or regulation, from securities fraud, from a civil remedy for racketeering under 18 U.S.C. 1964, or from a criminal act or intentional or reckless conduct that caused serious injury or death to another person within the last 5 years. See 11 U.S.C. 1141(d)(5)(C).

chapter 11 discharge, individual debtor, when not granted

(5) The confirmation of a chapter 11 plan does not discharge a corporate debtor from certain fraud debts and from tax debts that resulted from the making of a fraudulent tax return or willful evasion of the tax. See 11 U.S.C. 1141(d)(6). This provision applies only to chapter 11 debtors that are corporations.

chapter 11 discharge, corporate debtor, debts not discharged by

If a nonindividual debtor fails to list a creditor on its schedules, the debt owed to that creditor is not discharged by the order of confirmation unless the creditor had notice or actual knowledge of the confirmation proceeding in the Chapter 11 case in time to file a claim and participate in the proceeding. That an unscheduled debt of a reorganizing nonindividual debtor owed to a creditor that had neither notice nor knowledge of the confirmation proceeding is, on constitutional grounds, not discharged by a Chapter 11 order of confirmation, see Reliable Electric Co. v. Olson Construction Co., 726 F. 2nd 620 (CA 10, 1984), and In re Sullivan Ford Sales, Inc., 25 B.R. 400 (ME, 1982). It should be noted that the dischargeability of unscheduled debts of individual debtors is governed by 11 U.S.C. 523(a)(3), which provides that such debts are not discharged unless the creditor had notice or actual knowledge of the case in time to file a proof of claim. See 11 U.S.C. 1141(d)(2). If requested, the court may approve a written waiver of discharge executed by the debtor after the order for relief under Chapter 11. See 11 U.S.C. 1141(d)(4).

nonindividual debtor, unscheduled debt, dischargeability

individual debtor, unscheduled debt, dischargeability

waiver of discharge

Except for certain matters related to community property, the discharge of a debt of the debtor does not affect the liability of any other entity on, or the liability of the property of any other entity for, a discharged debt. See 11 U.S.C. 524(e). However, in attempting to gain as much from the order of confirmation as possible, Chapter 11 plans often contain language providing that confirmation of the plan shall serve to discharge or release from liability any guarantors of the debtor's obligations. Provisions in a confirmed plan releasing or discharging guarantors have been upheld under the doctrine of res judicata. See Stoll v. Gottlieb, 305 U.S. 165, 59 S. Ct. 134, 83 L. Ed. 104 (l938), and Levy v. Cohen, 19 Cal. 3rd 165, 137 Cal. Rep. 162, 561 P. 2nd 252 (1977). Other courts, however, have refused to uphold such provisions on the theory that the discharge of a debt is a matter of federal bankruptcy law and not a matter of contract. See Union Carbide Corp. v. Newboles, 686 F. 2nd 593 (CA 7, 1982), In re Western Real Estate Fund, Inc., 922 F.2d 592 (CA 10, 1990), and Underhill v. Royal, 769 F.2d 1426 (CA 9, 1985). The discharge of a guarantor is more likely to be upheld if the creditor expressly consents to the discharge of the guarantor, as opposed to merely voting in favor of the plan. See In re Monroe Well Service, Inc., 80 B.R. 324 (ED PA, 1987). It is clear, however, that a creditor who votes to reject the plan does not, by virtue of a plan provision so providing, release a guarantor from post-confirmation liability. See In re Consolidated Motor Inns, 666 F.2d 189 (CA 5, 1982).

Chapter 11 discharge, effect on guarantors

guarantor discharge provisions in plan, effect of

If a confirmed plan calls for the payment in full of unpaid withholding taxes to the Internal Revenue Service over a period of up to five years as permitted under 11 U.S.C. 1129(a)(9)(C), and if the Internal Revenue Service later attempts to collect the 100 percent penalty provided in 26 U.S.C. 6672 against responsible officers of the debtor, most bankruptcy courts will enjoin such collection attempts, especially if the imposition of such a penalty would substantially harm the debtor's rehabilitation efforts. See In re Steel Products, Inc., 47 B.R. 44 (WD WA, 1984), and Matter of Driscoll's Towing Service, Inc., 43 B.R. 647 (SD FL, 1984).

IRS, collection of taxes from third party, enjoined from

revocation of discharge, grounds, time limits

Revocation of confirmation. On the request of a party in interest at any time before 180 days after the date of the entry of the order of confirmation, and after notice and a hearing, the court may revoke the order of confirmation if, and only if, the order was procured by fraud. See 11 U.S.C. 1144. It should be noted that an order of confirmation may only be revoked; it cannot be voided or stricken. See In re Modern Steel Treating Co., 130 BR 60 (ND IL, 1991). An order of confirmation in a Chapter 11 case may be revoked only upon the grounds that confirmation of the plan was procured by fraud and only if the proceeding to revoke confirmation is commenced within 180 days after the date of the order of confirmation. Once the 180-day period after confirmation has run, confirmation cannot be revoked even if fraud is then discovered. See Matter of Newport Harbor Assoc., 589 F. 2nd 20 (CA 1, 1978). If the plan has been modified, the 180-day period is measured from confirmation date of the modified plan. See In re TM Carlton House Partners, Ltd., 110 BR 185 (ED PA, 1990). However, if the fraud complained of related only to the procuring of the original confirmation order and was not related to the modified order, then the 180-day period is measured from the date of the original order. See In re Orange Tree Associates, Ltd., 961 F.2d 1445 (CA 9, 1992).

revocation of discharge, type of fraud

Actual fraud must be shown to justify the revocation of an order of confirmation. The appearance of impropriety or something less than actual fraud will not suffice. Further, the fraud must relate to the procurement of confirmation. Fraudulent activity by the debtor in the management of its business affairs will not suffice unless confirmation of the plan resulted from such activity. See In re Hertz, 38 B.R. 215 (SD NY, 1984), and In re D.F.D., Inc., 43 B.R. 393 (ED PA, 1984). However, a misrepresentation made by the debtor as to the value of property of the estate has been held to constitute actual fraud for purposes of Section 1144. See In re Kostoglou, 73 BR 596 (ND OH, 1987). It should be noted that the same requirements apply regardless of whether revocation of confirmation is sought by a creditor or by the debtor. See In re Errington, 39 B.R. 968 (MN, 1984).

revocation of confirmation, procedure

order of revocation, requirements

revocation of discharge

A proceeding to revoke an order of confirmation is an adversary proceeding requiring the filing of a complaint and the other notice, pleading, and hearing requirements of Part 7 of the Rules of Bankruptcy Procedure. See Bankruptcy Rule 7001(5). Rule 9 of the Federal Rules of Civil Procedure govern the proceeding, which means that allegations of fraud must be stated with particularity. See In re Longardner & Assocs., Inc., 855 F.2d 455 (CA 7, 1988). If an order revoking confirmation of a plan is entered, the order must contain such provisions as are necessary to protect any entity acquiring rights in good faith reliance on the order of confirmation, and such an order must also revoke the discharge of the debtor. See 11 U.S.C. 1144. Thus, the revocation of an order of confirmation also revokes the debtor's Chapter 11 discharge.

4.11 Postconfirmation Matters - Implementation, Distribution and Consummation

While the confirmation of a plan is the principal objective of most Chapter 11 cases, the entry of an order of confirmation does not signal the end of the case. To the contrary, in many small business cases there are nearly as many functions to be performed after confirmation as before. The plan must be implemented and its provisions carried out. The claims of creditors must be reviewed, objected to, and allowed, and distributions must be made on the allowed claims as provided for in the plan. Finally, the plan must be consummated, a final decree entered, and the case closed.

postconfirmation matters, general aspects

Postconfirmation jurisdiction. The extent of the postconfirmation jurisdiction of the bankruptcy court can be a troublesome matter in Chapter 11 cases. 11 U.S.C. 1142 provides that the debtor and any entity organized to carry out the plan shall comply with the orders of the court and that the court may direct the debtor or any other necessary party to execute or deliver any instrument of transfer required under the plan and to perform any act necessary for consummation of the plan. 11 U.S.C. 105(a) provides that the court may issue orders necessary to carry out the provisions of the Bankruptcy Code. Bankruptcy Rule 3020(d) provides that notwithstanding the order of confirmation, the court may enter all orders necessary to administer the estate, but the Federal Rules of Bankruptcy Procedure cannot confer jurisdiction. See Bankruptcy Rule 9030. It is generally held, however, that even in the absence of a plan provision on the matter, a bankruptcy court retains sufficient postconfirmation jurisdiction to interpret and administer a confirmed plan. See In re Johns Manville Corp., 97 B.R. 174 (SD NY, 1989), and Goodman v. Phillip R. Curtis Enterprise, Inc., 809 F.2d 228 (CA 4, 1987).

bankruptcy court, postconfirmation jurisdiction

In an attempt to resolve the postconfirmation jurisdiction issue, Chapter 11 plans and orders of confirmation often contain provisions retaining the jurisdiction of the bankruptcy court on particular issues or matters. For example, it is common for Chapter 11 plans to retain the jurisdiction of the bankruptcy court to interpret the plan, to enter orders in aid of consummation, and to hear specific litigation related to the implementation or consummation of the plan. That a retention of jurisdiction in a plan is valid if within reason, see In re Malden Mills, Inc., 35 B.R. 71 (MA, 1983). That plan provisions retaining the jurisdiction of the bankruptcy court to continue to hear litigation pending at the time of confirmation and to entertain litigation directly related to the implementation or consummation of the plan are valid, see In re Jennings, Inc., 46 B.R. 167 (ED PA, 1985).

bankruptcy court, retention of jurisdiction

The two most questionable areas of postconfirmation bankruptcy court jurisdiction are those involving the postconfirmation supervisory powers of the court over the property and business operations of the reorganized debtor and litigation related solely to postconfirmation defaults by the reorganized debtor. It is clear that the supervisory powers of bankruptcy courts are substantially reduced after confirmation. Unless the plan or the confirmation order provides otherwise, after confirmation the reorganized debtor may enter into contracts, obtain secured or unsecured credit, open business bank accounts in its own name without reference to the Chapter 11 case, buy and sell property, and pay professional fees, all without the approval of the bankruptcy court. However, if desired, the plan or confirmation order may provide for the continued supervision of the bankruptcy court over one or more of the postconfirmation activities of the reorganized debtor. See In re NTG Industries, Inc., 118 B.R. 606 (ND IL, 1990).

bankruptcy court, postconfirmation jurisdiction, questionable areas

On the issue of the jurisdiction of the bankruptcy court to hear postconfirmation disputes not directly related to the implementation or consummation of the plan, most cases hold that while the bankruptcy court has the jurisdiction to hear most matters of this sort, especially if the plan contains a broad reservation of bankruptcy court jurisdiction, its jurisdiction is not exclusive. See In re Paradise Valley Country Club, 31 B.R. 613 (CO, 1983), and In re Morgan & Morgan, Inc., 24 B.R. 518 (SD NY, 1982). Much, however, depends on whether there is any relationship between the litigation and the consummation of the plan. One case held that the bankruptcy court had no jurisdiction to hear a postconfirmation trademark infringement case against the debtor, while another case held that the bankruptcy court had jurisdiction to enter an injunction prohibiting suppliers from refusing to deal with the reorganized debtor. See, respectively, Matter of Pan American School of Trade, Inc., 47 B.R. 242 (SD NY, 1985), and In re Blackwelder Furniture Co., Inc., 7 B.R. 328 (WD NC, 1980).

bankruptcy court, jurisdiction over postconfirmation litigation postconfirmation litigation, general aspects

Typical postconfirmation litigation involving the reorganized debtor or the debtor's successor under the plan are breach of contract actions, eviction actions, and lien foreclosure actions resulting from the failure of the debtor or its successor to comply with the requirements of the plan. That a secured creditor under the plan may foreclose on its lien in a nonbankruptcy forum without first obtaining relief from either the automatic stay or the permanent injunction that accompanies the discharge of a debtor, see In re Ernst, 45 B.R. 700 (MN, 1985).

Postconfirmation functions. While it is convenient to break postconfirmation matters down into categories such as implementation, distribution, and consummation, in practice such clear-cut categories of activities seldom exist. In reality postconfirmation activities take the form of functions that must be performed if the plan is to become effective and its provisions carried out. The postconfirmation functions to be performed by the reorganized debtor or the debtor's successor under the plan in a typical small business Chapter 11 case include the following:

postconfirmation functions in typical small business case

(1) Prepare and file any postconfirmation reports required by the court or the U.S. Trustee.

(2) Perform the acts or functions, if any, upon which the implementation of the plan is expressly conditioned or contingent.

(3) Distribute the deposit or other funds or property required under the plan to be distributed upon confirmation.

(4) If necessary, prepare the corporate and other documents needed to revise or restructure the reorganized debtor, incorporate or otherwise organize the successor to the debtor under the plan, or complete any merger, consolidation, or other reorganization required under the plan.

(5) Prepare any documents needed to transfer assets or property of the debtor as provided in the plan, and, if necessary, prepare the documents needed to transfer the assets or liabilities of the debtor to the successor to the debtor under the plan.

(6) If necessary, prepare the pleadings and other documents needed to extinguish, modify, or create liens or other security interests in accordance with the provisions of the plan.

(7) Examine all claims and interests that have been filed or deemed filed, file objections to the allowance of claims or interests where necessary, resolve each objection either by negotiation or court ruling, and prepare a final list of claims and interests for each class of claims and interests provided for in the plan.

(8) Prepare, file, and obtain court approval of any necessary modifications to the confirmed plan. See infra, this section, for further reading on postconfirmation plan modifications.

(9) Substantially consummate the plan and, if desired, obtain an order of substantial consummation.

(10) Prepare and file a final report and a final account of the administration of the debtor's estate with the court and U.S. Trustee.

(11) After the completion of all matters provided for in the plan and the confirmation order, obtain from the court a final decree and an order closing the case.

conditions to implementation of plan, performance of

If, under the plan, there are conditions or contingencies to the implementation of the plan, the first matter of business after confirmation should be to fulfill the required conditions or contingencies. For example, if implementation of the plan is contingent upon the approval of a specified rate change for the debtor by a governmental regulatory commission, the initiation of a proceeding to obtain approval of the rate change should be the first order of business after confirmation. Other contingencies to the implementation of a plan might be the resolution of certain pending litigation or the obtaining of a particular patent, copyright, or contract.

As soon as any contingencies or conditions precedent to implementation of the plan have been satisfied, any funds or property distributable upon confirmation of the plan should be distributed in accordance with the plan. If the debtor was required, under Bankruptcy Rule 3020(a), to deposit funds or property prior to confirmation, distributions should be made from the deposit. Otherwise, the debtor must provide the funds or property to be distributed.

implementation of plan, distribution of funds

Implementation of plan. After complying with any contingencies or conditions precedent to implementation, the actual implementation of the plan may be commenced. Such matters as the formation of the entity that is to be the successor to the debtor under the plan, or the restructuring of the debtor as required under the plan, are normally the first matters to be performed in implementing the plan. In this regard it should be noted that notwithstanding any otherwise applicable nonbankruptcy law, rule, or regulation relating to financial condition, the debtor or any entity organized for the purpose of carrying out the plan may carry out the plan and comply with the orders of the bankruptcy court. See 11 U.S.C. 1142(a). Thus, if the reorganized debtor or its successor under the plan cannot comply with any state laws or rules relating to net capitalization or reserve requirements, the debtor or other entity may nevertheless be organized, at least for purposes of carrying out the plan.

implementation of plan, general requirements

Implementation usually includes such matters as conveyances of property, either to the successor to the debtor under the plan or to creditors, the extinguishment or modification of liens, the creation of new liens, and the payment of claims. In this regard it should be noted that the court may direct the debtor or any other necessary party to execute or deliver, or to join in the execution or delivery of, any instrument required to effect a transfer of property dealt with by a confirmed plan, and to perform any other act, including the satisfaction of any lien, that is necessary for consummation of the plan. See 11 U.S.C. 1142(b). Depending on the local practice on the handling of matters such as the transfer of assets and lien extinguishments, it may be necessary to present the required documents to the court for approval in the form of a motion and order in aid of consummation, with such notice to other parties as the court may direct.

implementation of plan, power of court, order in aid of consummation

In making distributions under a plan it should be noted that if a plan requires presentment or surrender of a security or the performance of any other act as a condition to participation in distribution under the plan, such matters must be performed not later than five years after the date of the order of confirmation for the party to be entitled to distribution under the plan. See 11 U.S.C. 1143. Thus, if the plan requires a creditor to surrender property or relinquish a lien as a condition to payment and if the creditor fails to do so within five years after confirmation, the creditor is not entitled to distribution under the plan. Similarly, if a shareholder is required to surrender shares of stock in the debtor in return for shares of stock in the reorganized debtor and fails to surrender the old stock within the required five-year period, the shareholder is not entitled to stock in the reorganized debtor.

distributions under plan, conditions, time limits

Allowance of claims. A principal task of the debtor and its attorney in most small business Chapter 11 cases is the preparation of the final list of creditors. A final list of interest holders must also be prepared if they are dealt with in the plan. The best practice is to start with the list of creditors shown in the debtor's schedule of liabilities, and then check the bankruptcy clerk's file for any proofs of claim filed by or on behalf of creditors. If differences exist between the amount of a creditor's claim as shown in the schedule of liabilities and as shown on the proof of claim, the creditor should be contacted and an attempt made to resolve the difference. If a resolution of the difference is not possible, an objection to the allowance of the claim in the requested amount should be filed. In preparing the final list of creditors it should be remembered that it is not necessary for a creditor to file a proof of claim in a Chapter 11 case unless the creditor's claim is either not scheduled or listed in the debtor's schedule of liabilities as contingent, disputed or unliquidated. See 11 U.S.C. 1111(a) and Bankruptcy Rule 3003(c)(2).

final list of creditors, preparation of

If a proof of claim has been filed for any claim listed on the debtor's schedules as disputed, contingent, or unliquidated, an appropriate objection should be filed unless an agreement can be reached with the creditor as to the amount and status of the claim. It should be noted that the claims dealt with at this stage of the case are usually nonpriority unsecured claims, because the allowance of secured and priority claims is normally determined prior to confirmation. See section 4.04, supra, for further reading on the handling of claims and the filing of objections to the allowance thereof.

objection to allowance of claim, filing of

objection to allowance of claims, common hearing

When all objections to the allowance of claims have been prepared, the best practice in most districts is to file and serve notice of the objections as a group, and, if possible, obtain a common hearing date for all of the objections. See section 4.04, supra, for the required notice and hearing requirements. When all such objections have been ruled upon by the court, a final list of claims may be prepared for each class of claims provided for in the plan. If the rights of interest holders are dealt with in the plan, a final list of interest holders must also be prepared.

distributions to creditors, how to handle

After the confirmation of a plan, distributions must be made to creditors whose claims have been allowed. See Bankruptcy Rule 3021. Especially if there are a large number of claims to be paid, the best practice is to obtain a court order in aid of consummation authorizing distribution in accordance with the plan to creditors as set forth in the final list of creditors. Disbursement checks should contain a notice stating that the check is void if not presented for payment within a specified period, such as 60 days from the date of the check. After all distributions have been made, the debtor or its attorney should file an affidavit with the court confirming that distributions have been made in accordance with the plan and orders of the court.

distributions to creditors, when made

Normally distributions should not be made to creditors until all objections to the allowance of claims have been ruled upon and the final list of creditors has been approved by the court. However, if appeals or other delays prevent the finalization of the final list of creditors for a prolonged period, the court may grant permission to make an earlier distribution to the holders of allowed claims, provided that sufficient funds or other property is reserved for the later payment of contested claims.

modification of plan after confirmation, requirements

Modifying plan after confirmation. The proponent of a plan or the reorganized debtor may, for cause shown, modify a confirmed plan at any time prior to substantial consummation of the plan. See 11 U.S.C. 1127(b). The modification of a confirmed plan is usually attempted when the reorganized debtor is unable to perform its obligations under the existing plan, but could perform under a modified plan. A postconfirmation modification may also be warranted in situations where certain provisions or matters were inadvertently omitted from a confirmed plan. See Goodman v. Phillip R. Curtis Enterprises, Inc., 809 F. 2nd 228 (CA 4, 1987).

modification of plan, individual debtor

If the debtor is an individual, the plan may be modified at any time after confirmation of the plan but before the completion of payments under the plan, whether or not the plan has been substantially consummated, upon request of the debtor, the trustee, the United States trustee, or the holder of an allowed unsecured claim, to increase or reduce the amount of payments on claims of a particular class provided for by the plan, to extend or reduce the time period for such payments, or to alter the amount of the distribution to a creditor whose claim is provided for by the plan to the extent necessary to take account of any payment of such claim made other than under the plan. See 11 U.S.C. 1127(e).

substantial consummation of plan, what constitutes

A plan is deemed to be substantially consummated when: (1) substantially all of the property proposed to be transferred under the plan has been transferred, (2) the reorganized debtor or the successor to the debtor under the plan has assumed the business or the management of all or substantially all of the property dealt with by the plan, and (3) distribution under the plan has commenced. See 11 U.S.C. 1101(2). Once substantial consummation of a plan has occurred, the plan may not be modified. See In re Northampton Corp., 37 B.R. 110 (ED PA, 1984). Whether substantial confirmation has occurred is a question of fact to be determined on a case-by-case basis. See In re Jorgenson, 66 B.R. 104 (BAP 9, 1986), In re Modern Steel Treating Co., 130 BR 60 (ND IL, 1991), and In re Fansal Shoe Corp., 119 BR 28 (SD NY, 1990). Under plans that provide for transfers of property or money upon confirmation or shortly thereafter and for distributions to creditors from earnings over an extended period, substantial confirmation is generally held to require completion or near completion of the former but only commencement of the latter. See In re Hayball Trucking, Inc., 67 B.R. 681 (ED MI, 1986), and In re Bedford Springs Hotel, Inc., 99 B.R. 302 (WD PA, 1989).

Even if substantial consummation has not occurred, a confirmed plan may not be modified as a matter of course. A proposed modification becomes effective only if circumstances warrant such modification and the court, after notice and a hearing, confirms the plan as modified. See 11 U.S.C. 1127(b). Thus, the proponent of a postconfirmation modification must show cause to obtain the modification. Generally, significant unforeseen and uncontrollable intervening circumstances must be shown in order to justify the modification of a confirmed plan over the objection of adversely affected creditors. See In re Ernst, 45 B.R. 700 (MN, 1985). Much depends upon the extent of the proposed modification, however, and if the debtor seeks only to add a creditor to the list of creditors, a lesser showing may be required. See In re Heatron, Inc., 34 B.R. 526 (WD MO, 1983). It should be noted that only the debtor and the plan proponent have standing to seek modification of a confirmed plan. See 11 U.S.C. 1127(b), and In re Charterhouse, Inc., 84 BR 147 (MN, 1988).

modification of plan after confirmation, grounds for

If substantial consummation has not occurred and if sufficient cause is shown to warrant modification of a confirmed plan, the modified plan must comply with the classification requirements of 11 U.S.C. 1122 and the plan provision requirements of 11 U.S.C. 1123. Also, the plan, as modified, must be reconfirmed by the court under 11 U.S.C. 1129, after notice and a hearing. See 11 U.S.C. 1127(b). In addition, the proponent of a postconfirmation modification must comply with the disclosure and solicitation requirements of 11 U.S.C. 1125 with respect to the modified plan. See 11 U.S.C. 1127(c). Thus, a proposed modification of a confirmed plan may have to be accompanied by a revised disclosure statement if the modification is sufficient to render the previous disclosure statement inadequate.

modification of plan after confirmation, requirements

Creditors and interest holders who have previously accepted or rejected the plan are deemed to have similarly accepted or rejected the modified plan, unless, within the time fixed by the court, a creditor or interest holder changes its previous acceptance or rejection. See 11 U.S.C. 1127(d). All creditors and other interested parties must be given at least 21 days notice by mail of the time fixed by the court for accepting or rejecting the proposed modification. See Bankruptcy Rule 2002(a)(6). Notice, as prescribed by the court, must also be given to interest holders, unless the court orders otherwise. See Bankruptcy Rule 2002(d)(7). The plan, as modified, becomes the plan only after there has been such disclosure under 11 U.S.C. 1125 as the court may direct, notice and a hearing, and court approval of the modification. See 11 U.S.C. 1127(f)(2).

modification of plan after confirmation, procedure

Closing the case. When a plan has been substantially consummated, it is a good practice for the debtor or other plan proponent to file a motion for an order of substantial consummation, although the filing of such a motion is not required by either the Bankruptcy Code or the Rules of Bankruptcy Procedure. Substantial consummation is a significant event in a Chapter 11 case in that it denotes that substantially all of the provisions of the plan have been complied with and that only minor or ministerial matters are yet to be performed. As noted above, a confirmed plan may not be modified after substantial consummation. See 11 U.S.C. 1127(b).

order of substantial consummation, necessity of

When all of the statutory requirements for substantial consummation, as listed above in this section, have been satisfied, a motion for an order of substantial consummation may be filed. The motion should comply with the notice and other requirements of Bankruptcy Rule 9014, and the local rules and practices should be checked for requirements relating to the filing of such a motion.

order of substantial consummation, motion for

The debtor is required to make a final report and file a final account of the administration of the estate with the court and with the U.S. Trustee. See 11 U.S.C. 1106(a)(1), 704(9), which are made applicable to a debtor in possession by 11 U.S.C. 1107(a). The final account may normally be filed after substantial consummation of the plan. The local rules should be checked for requirements and forms relating to the filing of the final report and final account.

final report and account, when filed

After an estate has been fully administered, the court, on its own motion or on the motion of a party in interest, must enter a final decree closing the case. See Bankruptcy Rule 3022 and 11 U.S.C. 350(a). A case may be reopened in the court in which the case was closed to administer assets, to accord relief to the debtor, or for other cause. See 11 U.S.C. 350(b). In many districts the final decree in a Chapter 11 case customarily contains a broad injunction prohibiting parties from asserting preconfirmation claims or interests against the reorganized debtor or against the property or assets of the reorganized debtor.

final decree, when entered, effect of

application for final decree, when filed, provisions

An application for a final decree may be filed, if desired, when all matters requiring court approval or court action have been resolved, and when the jurisdiction of the bankruptcy court is no longer needed in the rehabilitation of the debtor or the consummation of the plan. If certain minor provisions of the plan have yet to be completed, the application should set forth such matters and request the court to retain jurisdiction with respect to such matters. In small business cases the application for a final decree is often filed with the final account of the debtor.

4.12 The Appointment of a Trustee or Examiner

appointment of trustee, general rule

In the vast majority of small business Chapter 11 cases neither a trustee nor an examiner is appointed. The general rule in both voluntary and involuntary Chapter 11 cases is that the debtor is to remain in possession and control of its assets and business during the course of the case. See In re Casco Bay Lines, Inc., 25 B.R. 747 (BAP 1, 1982). Further, in any proceeding for the appointment of a trustee in a Chapter 11 case, there is a strong presumption in favor of retaining the debtor in possession. See In re Colorado-Ute Electric Assn., 120 B.R. 164 (CO, 1990).

appointment of trustee, grounds for

Appointment of trustee. The grounds for the appointment of a trustee in a Chapter 11 case are set forth in 11 U.S.C. 1104(a), which provides that at any time after the commencement of a case but before confirmation of a plan, on the request of a party in interest or the U.S. Trustee, and after notice and a hearing, the court may order the appointment of a trustee on any of the following grounds:

(1) For cause, including fraud, dishonesty, incompetence, or gross mismanagement of the affairs of the debtor by current management, either before or after the commencement of the case, or similar cause, but not including the number of holders of securities of the debtor or the amount of assets or liabilities of the debtor. See 11 U.S.C. 1104(a)(1).

(2) If such appointment is in the interests of creditors, equity security holders, and other interests of the estate, without regard to the number of holders of securities of the debtor or the amount of assets or liabilities of the debtor. See 11 U.S.C. 1104(a)(2).

(3) If grounds exist to convert or dismiss the case under 11 U.S.C. 1112, but the court determines that the appointment of a trustee is in the best interests of creditors and the estate. See 11 U.S.C. 1104(a)(3).

appointment of trustee, cause for, what constitutes

Thus, the court may order the appointment of a trustee either for cause or if the appointment would be in the best interests of creditors, equity security holders, and the estate. As the statute indicates, cause for the appointment of a trustee is not limited to fraud, dishonesty, incompetence, or gross mismanagement, and may include other grounds as well. See In re McCall, 34 B.R. 68 (ED PA, 1983). For example, the death of an individual Chapter 11 debtor may constitute cause for the appointment of a trustee. See In re Martin, 26 B.R. 39 (SD WV, 1982). However, in determining whether cause exists for the appointment of a trustee, the court may not consider either the number of holders of securities of the debtor or the amount of the debtor's assets or liabilities. See 11 U.S.C. 1104(a)(1).

appointment of trustee, cause for, what constitutes

U.S. Trustee, when required to move for appointment of trusts

The debtor's failure to disclose postpetition income and liabilities may constitute cause for the appointment of a trustee. See In re Deena Packaging Industries, Inc., 29 B.R. 705 (SD NY, 1983). The debtor's failure for a prolonged period to file tax returns and pay taxes may also constitute cause for the appointment of a trustee. See In re Great Northeastern Lumber & Millwork Corp., 20 B.R. 610 (ED PA, 1982). Similarly, a trustee may be appointed if the debtor fails to bring an action against its president to recover a large preferential transfer. See In re William H. Vaughan & Co., Inc., 40 B.R. 524 (ED PA, 1984). If, during the case, the debtor fails to keep adequate books and records and does not maintain its property, a trustee may be appointed. See In re Hotel Associates, Inc., 3 B.R. 343 (ED PA, 1980). It should be noted that the United States trustee is required to move for the appointment of a trustee under 11 U.S.C. 1104(a) if there are reasonable grounds to suspect that current members of the governing body of the debtor, the debtor's chief executive or chief financial officer, or members of the governing body who selected the debtor's chief executive or chief financial officer, participated in actual fraud, dishonesty, or criminal conduct in the management of the debtor or the debtor's public financial reporting. See 11 U.S.C. 1104(e).

In the absence of cause, the court may order the appointment of a trustee if the appointment is in the best interests of creditors, interest holders, and other interests of the estate. See 11 U.S.C. 1104(a)(2). This ground for the appointment of a trustee is usually referred to as the "best interests" grounds. A trustee may be appointed under the "best interests" grounds where the loyalty of the debtor's management to the debtor's reorganization is in doubt. See In re Concord Coal Corp., 11 B.R. 552 (SD WV, 1981).

appointment of trustee, best interests grounds

In deciding whether to appoint a trustee on the "best interests" grounds, the court may balance the added expense of a trustee against any possible savings to the estate and creditors that may result from the appointment of a trustee, and if such an appointment would impose a substantial financial hardship, a trustee will not be appointed. See In re Crescent Beach Inn, Inc., 22 B.R. 155 (ME, 1982). In deciding whether to appoint a trustee on the "best interests" grounds, the court again may not consider either the number of security holders of the debtor or the amount of the debtor's assets or liabilities. See 11 U.S.C. 1104(a)(2).

appointment of trustee, best interests grounds, balancing expenses

As indicated above, a trustee may also be appointed if grounds exist to convert or dismiss the case, but the court determines that the appointment of a trustee, rather than conversion or dismissal, is in the best interests of creditors and the estate. See 11 U.S.C. 1104(a)(3). Under this ground, the proponent of the appointment must establish that grounds exist for the conversion or dismissal of the case under 11 U.S.C. 1112 and that the appointment of a trustee, rather than conversion or dismissal, is in the best interests of creditors and the estate. See section 4.14, infra, for a discussion of the grounds for conversion or dismissal of a chapter 11 case under 11 U.S.C. 1112.

appointment of trustee in lieu of conversion or dismissal

The appointment of a trustee is a highly significant event in a Chapter 11 case for a number of reasons. First of all, unless the court orders otherwise the trustee dispossesses the debtor or the debtor's current management of any authority to operate the debtor's business or administer the estate. See 11 U.S.C. 1108. Second, the appointment of a trustee terminates the debtor's exclusive right to file a plan. See 11 U.S.C. 1121(c). Third, the trustee, immediately upon appointment, has the exclusive right to control all litigation, pending and potential, by and against the debtor, including the right to bring actions against the debtor's owners and management. See 11 U.S.C. 323 and Bankruptcy Rule 6009. Fourth, the trustee has the right to file a plan of either reorganization or liquidation in the case. See 11 U.S.C. 1121(c). Fifth, the debtor loses its right to convert the case to a case under Chapter 7. See 11 U.S.C. 1112(a)(1). Sixth, as a party in interest, the trustee may move to dismiss the case or have it converted to a case under Chapter 7. See 11 U.S.C. 1112(b).

appointment of trustee, effect of

A proceeding to appoint a trustee may be initiated by a party in interest or the U.S. Trustee at any time before confirmation of a plan. See 11 U.S.C. 1104(a). A proceeding to appoint a trustee is a contested matter governed by Bankruptcy Rule 9014 and is initiated by the filing of a motion requesting the appointment of a trustee. See Bankruptcy Rule 2007.1(a). The motion should state the grounds for the requested appointment, and a copy of the motion must be served on the debtor in possession, the U.S. Trustee, and such other entities as the court may direct. See Bankruptcy Rules 9013 and 9034. Unless the court orders otherwise, a response to the motion is not required. See Bankruptcy Rule 9014.

appointment of trustee, procedure

A hearing must be held on a motion for the appointment of a trustee upon such notice as the court deems appropriate to the U.S. Trustee and to such other parties as the court may direct. See 11 U.S.C. 1104(a), 102(1), and Bankruptcy Rules 9007 and 9034. At the hearing on a motion for the appointment of a trustee, the moving party has the burden of proof and must present evidence in support of its motion sufficient to overcome a strong presumption that the debtor is to remain in possession. See In re Harlow, 34 B.R. 668 (ED PA, 1983). A clear and convincing case must be presented before a trustee will be appointed in a Chapter 11 case. See In re Tyler, 18 B.R. 574 (SD FL, 1982).

motion to appoint trustee, hearing, notice, burden of proof

If the court finds that a trustee should be appointed, the court will order the appointment of a trustee in the case and will direct the U.S. Trustee to make the appointment. The U.S. Trustee, after consultation with parties in interest, must then appoint one disinterested person other than the U.S. Trustee to serve as trustee in the case. However, the person so chosen is subject to court approval. See 11 U.S.C. 1104(d). A Chapter 11 trustee need not be appointed from the panel of private trustees. See 28 U.S.C. 586(a)(1). A Chapter 11 trustee may be elected by creditors, if desired. See 11 U.S.C. 1104(b)(1), which provides that on the request of a party in interest made not later than 30 days after the court orders the appointment of a trustee, the U.S. Trustee shall convene a meeting of creditors for the purpose of electing a Trustee. The election of a Chapter 11 trustee is governed by 11 U.S.C. 702(a), (b), (c). The trustee elected at the meeting replaces the trustee appointed by the U.S. Trustee. See 11 U.S.C. 1104(b)(2).

trustee, appointment of, approval

election of trustee, procedure for

Chapter 11 trustee, qualifications

Functions of trustee. A Chapter 11 trustee must be a "disinterested person" and may not be the U.S. Trustee. See 11 U.S.C. 1104(c). See 11 U.S.C. 101(14) for the definition of a "disinterested person." A Chapter 11 trustee must also be competent to perform the duties of a trustee, and, if the trustee is a corporation, it must be authorized by its charter or bylaws to act as a trustee. See 11 U.S.C. 321(a). A person that has served as an examiner in the case may not serve as trustee. See 11 U.S.C. 321(b). To qualify, the person selected to serve as trustee must file a bond in favor of the United States with the court within five days after being selected and before beginning its official duties. See 11 U.S.C. 322(a). The U.S. Trustee must determine the amount of the bond and the sufficiency of the surety on the bond. See 11 U.S.C. 322(b)(2).

trustee, rights and powers

Once appointed, the trustee is the official representative of the debtor's estate and has the capacity to sue and be sued. See 11 U.S.C. 323. Unless the court, on the request of a party in interest and after notice and a hearing, orders otherwise, the trustee may operate the debtor's business. See 11 U.S.C. 1108. The trustee, with the court's approval, may employ one or more attorneys, accountants, appraisers, auctioneers, or other professional persons to represent or assist the trustee in the performance of its duties. See 11 U.S.C. 327(a). The court may also authorize the trustee to act as the attorney or accountant for the estate. See 11 U.S.C. 327(d). The requirements applicable to attorneys and other professional persons serving in a Chapter 11 case are set forth in section 3.01, supra.

The duties of a Chapter 11 trustee are set forth in 11 U.S.C. 1106(a). Generally, the duties of a trustee are the same as the duties of a debtor in possession (see the list in section 4.02, supra), except that a trustee is required under 11 U.S.C. 1106(a) to perform the additional duties listed below.

trustee, duties of

(1) If the debtor has not done so, file the list, schedules, and statement required by 11 U.S.C. 521(1).

(2) Except as the court orders otherwise, investigate the affairs of the debtor, the operation of the debtor's business, the desirability of continuing such business, and any other matter relevant to the case or to the formulation of a plan.

(3) As soon as practicable, file a statement of its investigation with the court and transmit a copy or summary of such statement to any committee serving in the case and to such other entity as the court may designate.

(4) As soon as practicable, file a plan, file a report as to why the trustee will not file a plan, or recommend conversion of the case to a case under chapter 7, 12, or 13 or dismissal of the case.

(5) For any year for which the debtor has not filed a tax return required by law, furnish, without personal liability, such information as may be required by the governmental unit with which such tax return was to be filed, in light of the condition of the debtor's books and records and the availability of such information.

(6) After confirmation of a plan, file such reports as are necessary or as the court orders.

(7) If with respect to the debtor there is a claim for a domestic support obligation, provide the notice specified in 11 U.S.C. 1106(c).

compensation of trustee, approval of, amount

After a hearing on notice to any parties in interest and the U.S. Trustee, the court may award a trustee reasonable compensation for actual and necessary services rendered in the case and reimbursement for actual and necessary expenses incurred in the case. See 11 U.S.C. 330(a). A trustee may apply to the court not more than once every 120 days after the order for relief, or more often if the court permits, for interim compensation and expense reimbursement during the course of the case. See 11 U.S.C. 331. After a hearing on notice, the court may allow and disburse such compensation and expense reimbursement. The trustee's fee in a Chapter 11 case may not exceed the percentage fees set forth in 11 U.S.C. 326(a), which are: 25 percent of the first $5,000, 10 percent of the next $45,000, and 5 percent of the next $950,000 and 3 percent of the balance of all moneys disbursed or turned over in the case by the trustee to parties in interest other than the debtor.

At any time before confirmation of a plan, on the request of a party in interest or the U.S. Trustee, and after notice and a hearing, the court may terminate the trustee's appointment and restore the debtor to possession and management of the property of the estate and the operation of the debtor's business. See 11 U.S.C. 1105. The court, after notice and a hearing, may also remove a trustee for cause. See 11 U.S.C. 324(a). If a trustee is removed, or if a trustee resigns or dies during the case, the U.S. Trustee, after consultation with parties in interest and with the approval of the court, must appoint another disinterested person to serve as trustee in the case. See 11 U.S.C. 1104(d) and Bankruptcy Rule 2012.

trustee termination of appointment, procedure

Appointment of examiner. If the court does not order the appointment of a trustee in the case, then on the request of a party in interest or the U.S. Trustee at any time before the confirmation of a plan, and after notice and a hearing, the court may order the appointment of an examiner to conduct an investigation of the debtor. See 11 U.S.C. 1104(c). Thus, an examiner may be appointed only if a trustee is not serving in the case. Like the appointment of a trustee, the appointment of an examiner in a Chapter 11 case is extraordinary and should be done only if there are grounds clearly justifying the appointment. See In re Table Talk, Inc., 22 B.R. 706 (MA, 1982).

examiner, appointment of

An examiner may be ordered appointed in a Chapter 11 case if such appointment is found to be in the interests of creditors, equity security holders, and other interests of the estate or if the debtor's fixed, liquidated, unsecured debts, other than debts for goods, services, or taxes, or owing to an insider, exceed $5,000,000. See 11 U.S.C. 1104(c)(1), (2). The standards for the appointment of an examiner are similar to those for the appointment of a trustee under the "best interests" grounds in 11 U.S.C. 1104(a)(2); namely, protection of the interests of creditors and the estate must be needed, and the expenses to be incurred by such an appointment must not be disproportionately high. In other words, the benefit to the estate and creditors to be provided by an examiner must outweigh the expenses of such an appointment. See In re Gilman Services, Inc., 46 B.R. 322 (MA, 1985). Obviously, the court has considerable discretion on the matter.

appointment of examiner, grounds for

The role of an examiner in a Chapter 11 case is primarily investigatory. Examiners are traditionally required to investigate allegations of fraud, dishonesty, incompetence, misconduct, mismanagement, or irregularity in the management of the debtor's affairs by current or former management. See 11 U.S.C. 1104(c). An examiner is a disinterested and nonadversarial person who answers solely to the court, although an examiner's findings are not binding on the court. See Matter of Baldwin-United Corp., 46 B.R. 314 (SD OH, 1985). Unlike a trustee, an examiner does not displace the debtor in possession, who continues to operate the business and otherwise conduct its affairs, subject only to whatever functions the court removes from the debtor in possession and assigns to the examiner.

examiner, role in Chapter 11 case

A proceeding to appoint an examiner may be commenced by a party in interest or the U.S. Trustee at any time before the confirmation of a plan. See 11 U.S.C. 1104(c). A proceeding to appoint an examiner is a contested matter governed by Bankruptcy Rule 9014, and is initiated by the filing of a motion for the appointment of an examiner. See Bankruptcy Rule 2007.1(a). The procedure under a motion for the appointment of an examiner is similar to the procedure under a motion for the appointment of a trustee, which is described above in this section. If an examiner is sought to investigate alleged fraud, dishonesty, or misconduct by the debtor or its management, evidence of the basis of such allegations or grounds must be presented at the hearing, as mere unsupported allegations are insufficient to warrant the appointment of an examiner. See In re American Bulk Transport Co., 8 B.R. 337 (KS, 1980).

appointment of examiner, procedure, burden of proof

If the court orders the appointment of an examiner in the case, the court must direct the U.S. Trustee to make the appointment. The U.S. Trustee, after consultation with parties in interest, must then appoint one disinterested person, other than the U.S. Trustee, to serve as an examiner in the case. See 11 U.S.C. 1104(d). See 11 U.S.C. 101(14) for the definition of "disinterested person."

examiner, appointment of, approval

4.13 Handling Related Litigation and Appeals

Chapter 11 debtor, typical litigation

It is common for a small business debtor to have civil litigation of some sort pending when its Chapter 11 case is filed. Collection and foreclosure actions against the debtor and its property are the most commons types of pending litigation, but other proceedings by, against, or involving the debtor may also be pending. In addition, Chapter 11 debtors often have claims or causes of actions against others that must be filed and litigated during the course of the case. Also, contractual and other nonbankruptcy disputes involving the operation of the debtor's business during the case may arise, and such disputes may have to be litigated. Finally, it may be necessary to appeal an order, judgment, or decree entered by the bankruptcy or district court during the course of a Chapter 11 case. As the foregoing suggests, the handling of related litigation and appeals can play an important role in the handling of a small business Chapter 11 case.

doctrine of abstention, definition

abstention, title 11 case

Before beginning a discussion of the various types of related litigation, a matter common to most bankruptcy-related litigation should be discussed. That matter is the doctrine of abstention as practiced in bankruptcy cases. Abstention is the doctrine whereby a federal court abstains from hearing a proceeding over which it has jurisdiction in order to avoid needless conflict with the administration by a state of its own affairs. In bankruptcy proceedings, the doctrine of abstention may be applied by the court in deciding whether to hear a bankruptcy case, a proceeding arising under the Bankruptcy Code, or a proceeding arising in or related to a bankruptcy case.

abstention, types of in proceedings in title 11 cases

The abstention provisions applicable to the decision of a bankruptcy court on whether to hear a bankruptcy case are set forth in 11 U.S.C. 305, and are discussed in section 4.14, infra. There are two types of abstention applicable to proceedings that arise under the Bankruptcy Code or that arise in or are related to bankruptcy cases: discretionary abstention, and mandatory abstention. See 28 U.S.C. 1334(c)(1),(2). Discretionary abstention is also variously referred to by commentators and courts as permissive abstention or voluntary abstention.

discretionary abstention, definition, when exercised

Discretionary abstention. Discretionary abstention is defined in 28 U.S.C. 1334(c)(1), which provides that a district court may, in the interest of justice or in the interest of comity with state courts or respect for state law, abstain from hearing a particular proceeding arising under the Bankruptcy Code or arising in or related to a bankruptcy case. Discretionary abstention may be exercised by the court in either core or non-core proceedings. See Matter of Republic Oil Corp., 51 B.R. 355 (WD WI, 1985). Discretionary abstention may be sought in a proceeding by the filing of a motion for abstention under Bankruptcy Rule 5011. The procedure under such a motion is governed by Bankruptcy Rule 9014. See Bankruptcy Rule 5011(b).

discretionary abstention, when exercised

In exercising discretionary abstention, the courts in bankruptcy cases have traditionally elected to abstain from proceedings involving questions of divorce or family law. See In re Boyd, 31 B.R. 591 (MN, 1983). Proceedings involving unique, unsettled, or unresolved questions of state law are often left to the state courts to decide, if the resolution of the proceeding will not be unduly delayed. See In re Tucson Estates, Inc., 912 F.2d 1162 (CA 9, 1990). However, a court will not abstain merely because it would have to pass on issues of state law. See Matter of Republic Oil Corp., 51 B.R. 355 (WD WI, 1985). Similarly, if a related proceeding involves primarily issues of bankruptcy law, discretionary abstention will not be exercised. See In re Meyer, 59 B.R. 16 (SD OH, 1985).

discretionary abstention, when exercised

If the related proceeding is in a specialized court, such as the Armed Forces Board of Contract Appeals, the court in a bankruptcy case is likely to abstain from hearing the proceeding. See Matter of Gary Aircraft Corp., 698 F. 2nd 775 (CA 5, 1983). If litigation related to a Chapter 11 case is pending in a state court, discretionary abstention may be exercised because litigating the matter again in the bankruptcy court would be a needless expense. See In re Richards, 59 B.R. 541 (ND NY, 1986). Also, if the related proceeding has a minimal impact on the estate, discretionary abstention is likely to be exercised. See In re Jodan's Pro Hardware, 49 B.R. 976 (ED WI, 1985).

Mandatory abstention. Mandatory abstention is defined in 28 U.S.C. 1334(c)(2), which provides as follows:

> "Upon the timely motion of a party in a proceeding based upon a State law claim or State law cause of action, related to a case under title 11 but not arising under title 11 or arising in a case under title 11, with respect to which an action could not have been commenced in a court of the United States absent jurisdiction under this section, the district court shall abstain from hearing such proceeding if an action is commenced, and can be timely adjudicated, in a State forum of appropriate jurisdiction. Any decision to abstain or not to abstain made under this subsection is not reviewable by appeal or otherwise by the court of appeals under section 158(d), 1291, or 1292 of this title or by the Supreme Court of the United States under section 1254 of this title. This subsection shall not be construed to limit the applicability of the stay provided for by section 362 of title 11, United States Code, as such section applies to an action affecting the property of the estate in bankruptcy."

mandatory abstention, definition

For mandatory abstention to be exercised in a Chapter 11 case, each of the following requirements must be satisfied:

mandatory abstention, conditions to be satisfied

(1) A motion for mandatory abstention must be timely filed by a party to the related proceeding. The motion should be filed with the clerk of the bankruptcy court, and, unless a district judge rules otherwise, will be heard by the bankruptcy judge. See Bankruptcy Rule 5011 and the Advisory Committee's Notes thereto.

(2) The related proceeding must be based on a claim or cause of action arising only under state law.

(3) The proceeding must be related to the bankruptcy case but must not arise under the Bankruptcy Code or arise in the bankruptcy case. This means, for example, that mandatory abstention is likely to be applied to a proceeding filed by a debtor in possession to enforce a purely state law claim or cause of action against a third party.

(4) No independent grounds for federal jurisdiction must exist for the related proceeding. In other words, but for the existence of the bankruptcy case the related proceeding could not have been commenced in or removed to a federal court. This means that neither the federal question nor the diversity of citizenship plus amount in controversy grounds for federal jurisdiction must exist in the related proceeding. It should be noted, however, that a finding of independent federal jurisdiction in a related proceeding does not prevent a court from exercising discretionary abstention. See In re Counts, 54 B.R. 730 (CO, 1985).

(5) The related proceeding must be commenced and timely adjudicated in the state court. It has been held that mandatory abstention does not apply if a state court proceeding has not been commenced or if the proceeding cannot be timely heard in the state court. See Matter of Krupke, 57 B.R. 523 (WD WI, 1986) and In re DeLorean Motor Co., 49 BR 900 (ED MI, 1985).

(6) The related proceeding must not involve the liquidation or estimation of a contingent or unliquidated personal injury tort or wrongful death claim against the estate for purposes of distribution in the bankruptcy case. See 28 U.S.C. 157(b)(4), which provides that proceedings of this sort are not subject to mandatory abstention.

(7) The related proceeding must be a non-core proceeding. It has been held that mandatory abstention applies only to non-core proceedings. See Harley Hotels, Inc., v. Rain's International, Ltd., 57 B.R. 773 (MD PA, 1985). See section 3.02, supra, for further reading on what constitutes a non-core proceeding. For the application of these seven requirements for mandatory abstention, see Bowen Corp. v. Security Pacific Bank Idaho, FSB, 150 BR 777 (ID, 1993).

mandatory abstention, effect on automatic stay

The mandatory abstention statute does not limit the applicability of the automatic stay as it applies to actions affecting property of the estate. See 28 U.S.C. 1334(c)(2). This apparently means, among other things, that if mandatory abstention is granted in a related proceeding and a judgment against the debtor is obtained, the other party to the proceeding may not execute against property of the estate without first obtaining relief from the stay in the bankruptcy court.

motion for abstention, procedure under

A motion for abstention in a related proceeding should be filed with the clerk of the bankruptcy court. A motion for abstention, whether discretionary or mandatory, is governed by Bankruptcy Rule 9014 and must be served on the parties to the proceeding. See Bankruptcy Rule 5011(b). The filing of a motion for abstention does not stay the bankruptcy proceeding unless the court so orders. See Bankruptcy Rule 5011(c). It should be noted that a decision by the court to abstain or not to abstain from mandatory abstention is not reviewable by appeal or otherwise. See 28 U.S.C. 1334(c)(2).

pending litigation against debtor, handling of

Prepetition litigation. A principal task in the administration of many Chapter 11 cases is the handling and disposition of litigation that was pending against the debtor when the Chapter 11 case was commenced. Of course, the automatic stay that accompanies the filing of a Chapter 11 petition stays virtually all civil proceedings pending against the debtor. See 11 U.S.C. 362(a)(1) and section 4.01, supra. The automatic stay only stays such proceedings, however; it does not resolve them. Pending actions against the debtor must be resolved on a case-by-case basis. The manner of resolving of a pending case depends largely on the nature of the claim or cause of action, the type of action filed, and the forum wherein the action is pending.

collection and foreclosure actions, handling of

Collection proceedings against the debtor are usually resolved through the claim allowance procedure in Chapter 11 cases. See section 4.04, supra, for further reading. Foreclosure actions are normally resolved through the efforts of secured creditors to obtain relief from the automatic stay and through the claim allowance procedure. See sections 4.01, 4.04, and 4.11, supra, for further reading. In this regard, it should be noted that all proceedings for the allowance or disallowance of claims, except certain personal injury tort and wrongful death claims, are core proceedings. See 28 U.S.C. 157(b)(2)(B). Therefore, unless the court abstains from a particular proceeding, such proceedings are handled by the bankruptcy court. See 28 U.S.C. 157(b)(1).

personal injury or wrongful death claims, handling of

jury trial in bankruptcy court, right to

The method of handling personal injury tort and wrongful death claims pending against the debtor may depend on whether the debtor has insurance coverage for the claim. If the debtor has insurance coverage to the extent that the claim poses no threat to the estate, then the court is likely to abstain from the proceeding and permit the case to be resolved in the court wherein the case was pending when the Chapter 11 petition was filed. If the debtor has inadequate or no insurance against a pending personal injury tort or wrongful death claim, the case may be tried either in the state or federal court in which the case is pending, or in the United States district court, either in the district in which the Chapter 11 case is pending or in the district where the claim arose, as determined by the court in the district in which the Chapter 11 case is pending. See In re White Motor Credit, 761 F. 2nd 270 (CA 6, 1985), 28 U.S.C. 1334(c)(1), 28 U.S.C. 157(b)(5). That a proceeding for the liquidation or estimation of a personal injury tort or wrongful death claim for purposes of distribution is a non-core proceeding, see 28 U.S.C. 157(b)(2)(B). That the filing of a Chapter 11 case does not affect the right of any party to a trial by jury in such a case, see 28 U.S.C. 1411(a). It should be noted if the right to a jury trial exists in a proceeding that may be heard by a bankruptcy judge, the bankruptcy judge may conduct the jury trial if the bankruptcy judge is specially designated to do so by the district court and if all parties consent thereto. See 28 U.S.C. 157(e).

removal of proceeding to district court, when permitted

remand to state court, grounds for

Removal. It may be necessary for the debtor in possession in a Chapter 11 case to remove a pending case involving the debtor from a state court to the United States district court. A party may remove any claim or cause of action in a civil action, other than a proceeding before the United States Tax Court or a civil action by a governmental unit to enforce its police or regulatory power, to the United States district court for the district where the civil proceeding is pending if the district court has jurisdiction over the claim under 28 U.S.C. 1334. See 28 U.S.C. 1452(a). The district court to which a claim or cause of action is removed may remand the proceeding back to the state court on any equitable grounds, and any such order to remand or not to remand is not reviewable by appeal or otherwise. See 28 U.S.C. 1452(b).

In this regard, it should be noted that the United States district courts have original, but not exclusive, jurisdiction over all civil proceedings arising under the Bankruptcy Code, or arising in or related to bankruptcy cases, except that the U.S. district courts have exclusive jurisdiction of all property of the debtor (as of the commencement of the case) and of the estate and over all claims related to the employment of professional persons in the case. See 28 U.S.C. 1334(b), (e). Thus, any civil proceeding involving the debtor or the estate that arises under the Bankruptcy Code, that arises in a bankruptcy case, or that is related to a bankruptcy case may be removed to the federal district court, except proceedings before the United States Tax Court and civil actions by governmental units to enforce their police or regulatory powers. See section 4.01, supra, for a discussion of what constitutes an action by a governmental unit to enforce its police or regulatory powers.

related proceedings, jurisdiction of district court

Although 28 U.S.C. 1452(a) provides only for removal to the district court for the district where the nonbankruptcy case is pending, after removal the case may be transferred to the district where the Chapter 11 case is pending, and there referred by the district court to the bankruptcy judge. See 28 U.S.C. 1412, 157(a), and Bankruptcy Rule 9027(e), which governs the procedure after removal. Once in the bankruptcy court, the removed proceeding becomes an adversary proceeding governed by Part VII of the Rules of Bankruptcy Procedure. See Bankruptcy Rules 7001(10) and 9027(g).

transfer of proceeding to bankruptcy court, procedure

A removal proceeding is commenced by filing a notice of removal with the clerk of the bankruptcy court in the appropriate district and division. See Bankruptcy Rule 9027(a)(1). The application must be filed within the longest of the following periods: (1) 90 days after the order for relief in the bankruptcy case; (2) 30 days after the entry of an order terminating a stay, if the proceeding has been stayed by the automatic stay; or (3) 30 days after a trustee qualifies in a Chapter 11 case, but not later than 180 days after the order for relief. See Bankruptcy Rule 9027(a)(2). Removal proceedings are governed by Bankruptcy Rule 9027, which contains extensive provisions dealing with such proceedings. A party seeking to remove a case should examine and follow the provisions of Bankruptcy Rule 9027.

application for removal, where filed, time limits

removal proceeding, procedure

Postpetition litigation. The automatic stay precludes the postpetition filing of civil actions against the debtor or the estate based on prepetition claims or causes of action, except actions by governmental units to enforce their police or regulatory powers. See 11 U.S.C. 362(a), (b)(5), and section 4.01, supra. Thus, postpetition litigation against the debtor or the estate based on prepetition claims or causes of action, other than actions by governmental units to enforce their police or regulatory powers, must originate in the bankruptcy court, normally as a proof of claim, a motion for relief from the automatic stay, or a motion for abstention. See section 4.04, supra, for further reading on the filing of proofs of claim. See section 4.01, supra, for further reading on obtaining relief from the automatic stay. See supra, this section, for further reading on abstention.

postpetition litigation, handling of

Postpetition claims or causes of action against the estate or the debtor in possession that are related to or arise out of the Chapter 11 case may have to be defended during the course of the case. Actions of this type typically include claims or causes of action of third parties arising out of the operation of the debtor's business during the course of the case. The venue for such proceedings is set forth in 28 U.S.C. 1409(e), which provides that related proceedings based on postpetition claims arising from the operation of the debtor's business may be commenced either in the district where the state or federal court sits in which the party commencing the proceeding may, under applicable nonbankruptcy venue provisions, have brought an action on such claim, or in the district in which the Chapter 11 case is pending.

postpetition claims, venue requirements

State court actions based on postpetition claims or causes of action may be removed to the appropriate United States district court if the removal proceeding is initiated within 30 days after receipt of the initial pleading or summons in the state court case. See Bankruptcy Rule 9027(a)(3). The removal procedure in such proceedings is similar to that described above in this section for the removal of prepetition actions. See generally, Bankruptcy Rule 9027.

postpetition claims, removal to district court

actions by debtor in possession, where filed

It is often necessary for the debtor in possession to file actions against third parties to enforce claims or causes of action of the debtor or the estate, or to compel the turnover of property under 11 U.S.C. 542(a). If the defendant in such a proceeding is domiciled in the local district, the action can normally be filed in the bankruptcy court as an adversary proceeding under Part VII of the Rules of Bankruptcy Procedure. See Bankruptcy Rule 7001(1). However, if the defendant in such a proceeding is domiciled in another state or district, the venue requirements of 28 U.S.C. 1409 must be complied with. The applicable venue requirements are as follows:

actions by debtor in possession, venue requirements

(1) A debtor in possession may commence a proceeding arising under the Bankruptcy Code or arising in or related to a bankruptcy case that is based on a claim arising from the postpetition operation of the debtor's business only in the district court for the district where a state or federal court sits in which, under applicable nonbankruptcy venue provisions, an action on such a claim may have been brought. See 28 U.S.C. 1409(d).

(2) Except for postpetition claims arising out of the operation of the debtor's business, an action or proceeding by a debtor in possession to recover money or property valued at less than $1,250*, or to recover a consumer debt of less than $18,675*, or a debt other than a consumer debt against a noninsider of less than $12,475* may be commenced only in the district court for the district in which the defendant resides. See 28 U.S.C. 1409(b). * Dollar amounts subject to change on April 1, 2016.

(3) Related proceedings by a debtor in possession to collect property of the estate valued at $1,250* or more ($18,675* or more if the property is a consumer debt), or to avoid the transfer of an interest in property under 11 U.S.C. 544(b), may be commenced in the district court for the district where a state or federal court sits in which, under applicable nonbankruptcy venue provisions, the debtor or creditors, as the case may be, could have commenced an action on which the proceeding is based if the bankruptcy case had never been filed. See 28 U.S.C. 1409(c). Such proceedings may also be commenced in the district court in which the bankruptcy case is pending. See 28 U.S.C. 1409(a). * Dollar amounts subject to change on April 1, 2016.

(4) All other proceedings arising under the Bankruptcy Code, or arising in or related to a bankruptcy case, may be commenced in the district court in which the bankruptcy case is pending. See 28 U.S.C. 1409(a).

related proceedings, core or non-core, pleading requirements

If a related proceeding is deemed by the bankruptcy court to be a core proceeding, the bankruptcy court may enter final orders and judgments in the proceeding. See 28 U.S.C 157(b)(1). If the related proceeding is deemed a non-core proceeding, all final orders and judgments must be entered by the district court, unless the district court and the parties consent to permit the bankruptcy court to enter final orders and judgments in the proceeding. See 28 U.S.C. 157(c) and Bankruptcy Rule 9033.

adversary proceeding, core or non-core determination

In an adversary proceeding in a bankruptcy court, the complaint, counterclaim, cross-claim, or third-party complaint must contain a statement that the proceeding is core or non-core, and, if non-core, that the pleader does or does not consent to the entry of final orders or judgment by the bankruptcy court. See Bankruptcy Rule 7008. A responsive pleading must admit or deny an allegation that the proceeding is core or non-core. If the response is that the proceeding is non-core, it shall include a statement that the party does or does not consent to the entry of final orders or judgment by the bankruptcy court. See Bankruptcy Rule 7012(b). See section 3.02, supra, for further reading on what constitutes a core proceeding.

actions by debtor in possession, abstention

It should be remembered that discretionary abstention may be exercised by the court, if warranted, in related proceedings commenced by a debtor in possession. See 28 U.S.C. 1334(c)(1). Further, if a claim or cause of action asserted by a debtor in possession is based solely on state law, the mandatory abstention provisions of 28 U.S.C. 1334(c)(2) may be applicable to the proceeding. See, supra, this section for further reading on abstention.

If a person against whom the debtor in possession has a claim or cause of action files a proof of claim in the Chapter 11 case, the debtor in possession may file a counterclaim against that person in the bankruptcy court, even if the person is a nonresident. In such event, regardless of the type of claim or cause of action asserted in the counterclaim, the proceeding thereunder is a core proceeding in which the bankruptcy court may enter final orders and judgments. See 28 U.S.C. 157(b)(2)(C), and Bedford Computer Corp. vs. Ginn Publishing, Inc., 63 B.R. 79 (NH, 1986). Because proceedings on counterclaims against persons filing claims are core proceedings, the mandatory abstention provisions of 28 U.S.C. 1334(c)(2) are not applicable. See In re Answerfone, Inc., 67 B.R. 167 (ED AR, 1986). Permissive abstention may be exercised in such proceedings, however. See 28 U.S.C. 1334(c)(1), and In re Sun West Distributors, Inc., 69 B.R. 861 (SD CA, 1987).

counterclaim by debtor in possession, jurisdiction of bankruptcy court

Appeals. Because litigation is common in Chapter 11 cases, appeals are also common. Most appeals in bankruptcy cases are governed by 28 U.S.C. 158 and Part VIII of the Federal Rules of Bankruptcy Procedure. Generally, the method of handling an appeal in a Chapter 11 case depends on three factors: (1) whether the order, judgment, or decree appealed from was entered by the bankruptcy court or the district court; (2) whether a bankruptcy appellate panel has been established in the local circuit and whether appeals thereto are authorized in the local district; and (3) whether the order, judgment, or decree appealed from is final or interlocutory in nature.

appeal in Chapter 11 case, general aspects

It is important, initially, to distinguish between an appeal to the district court and the entry of a final order or judgment by the district court in a non-core proceeding. An appeal to the district court requires the filing of a notice of appeal by the dissatisfied party and must comply with the procedural requirements of Part VIII of the Rules of Bankruptcy Procedure. The entry of a final order or judgment by the district court in a non-core proceeding, on the other hand, is done as a matter of course, and the dissatisfied party need only file specific objections to the findings of fact and conclusions of law proposed by the bankruptcy judge. See 28 U.S.C. 157(c)(1) and Bankruptcy Rule 9033. In an appeal, the district court is bound by the findings of fact of the bankruptcy court unless such findings are clearly erroneous. In entering a final order or judgment in a non-core proceeding, the district court must review the objected-to proceeding de novo, may take additional evidence, and is not bound by the bankruptcy court's proposed findings of fact even if such findings are not clearly erroneous. See Bankruptcy Rule 9033(d), and Matter of Campbell, 812 F. 2nd 1465 (CA 4, 1987).

appeal vs. final order in non-core proceeding, distinction

If the order, judgment, or decree appealed from was entered by the district court in a non-core proceeding, the appeal must be taken to the circuit court of appeals in the manner and upon the grounds prescribed for appeals from the district court to the court of appeals generally. Final orders of district courts in non-core proceedings may be appealed as a matter of right to the circuit court of appeals, while interlocutory orders of district courts in such proceedings may be appealed to the same extent that such matters may be appealed in nonbankruptcy actions. See 28 U.S.C. 1291, 1292. It should be noted that the procedure for appeals to the circuit court of appeals is governed by the Federal Rules of Appellate Procedure and not by Part VIII of the Rules of Bankruptcy Procedure.

non-core proceeding, appeal of order in, requirements

Because most orders, judgments, and decrees in Chapter 11 cases are entered by the bankruptcy court, most orders, judgments, or decrees appealed from are those of bankruptcy courts. Appeals from final or interlocutory orders, judgments, or decrees of bankruptcy courts are taken to either the United States district court in the same district or, if one is established and appeals thereto are authorized locally, to the circuit bankruptcy appellate panel. It should be noted that an appeal from an order or judgment of a bankruptcy court is taken in the same manner regardless of whether the order or judgment appealed from was entered in a core proceeding or in non-core proceeding wherein the bankruptcy court was authorized under 28 U.S.C. 157(c)(2) to enter final orders and judgments.

appeals from bankruptcy judges, general aspects

bankruptcy appellate panel, appeals to, requirements

Under 28 U.S.C. 158(b), a bankruptcy appellate panel may be established in a district. To the author's knowledge, such a panel has been created only in the 1st, 6th, 8th, 9th, and 10th circuits. A bankruptcy appellate panel consists of three bankruptcy judges, provided that a judge on such a panel may not hear an appeal from within the district from which the judge was appointed. Before appeals from a particular district may be taken to the bankruptcy appellate panel, the district judges of that district must, by majority vote, authorize the referral of appeals from that district to the bankruptcy appellate panel. Finally, even if appeals to the bankruptcy appellate panel are authorized in a particular district, an appeal may be taken to the bankruptcy appellate panel only with the consent of all parties to the proceeding. See 28 U.S.C. 158(b), (c).

appeals from orders of bankruptcy judges, when permitted

Final vs. interlocutory orders. A final order, judgment, or decree of a bankruptcy court or an interlocutory order increasing or decreasing the time for filing a plan may be appealed as a matter of right to the district court or the bankruptcy appellate panel. Other interlocutory orders and decrees of bankruptcy courts may be appealed to the district court or the bankruptcy appellate panel only with leave of the appellate court. See 28 U.S.C. 158(a). Therefore, when appealing a decision of a bankruptcy court, it must first be determined whether the order, judgment, or decree appealed from is final or interlocutory in nature.

order of bankruptcy judge, final or interlocutory, how to determine

Determining whether an order, judgment, or decree of a bankruptcy judge is final or interlocutory for purposes of appeal can be difficult. Because there are no statutory guidelines, the case law on the subject must be resorted to for guidance. The general rule is that a final order or judgment is one that ends the litigation. See In re Alchar Hardware, 730 F. 2nd 1386 (CA 11, 1984). In bankruptcy cases, however, this rule is applied separately to the various disputes or proceedings within the case, and not just to the bankruptcy case as a whole. The following factors are usually considered in determining whether an order is a final order for purposes of appeal:

(1) Whether the order directly affects the final disposition of estate assets; if so it is a final order.

(2) Whether the order determines the final outcome of a particular proceeding; if so it is a final order.

(3) Whether the order irrevocably determines or disposes of a party's property right; if so it is a final order.

(4) Whether the order conclusively determines a particular issue or dispute; if so it is a final order.

(5) Whether the order requires further action by the court with regard to the issue decided; if so it is not a final order.

See Kubick v. Apex Oil Co., 123 BR 671 (ME, 1991), and In re Murray, 116 BR 6 (MA, 1990).

final order, what constitutes, cases

Orders dismissing a case, confirming a plan, or dismissing an adversary complaint are final orders. See Southerland v. Smith, 136 BR 565 (MD FL, 1992). An order denying confirmation of a plan is not a final order. See In re M Corp. Fin., Inc., 139 BR 820 (SD TX, 1992). An order allowing or denying a claim is normally considered a final order for purposes of appeal. See In re Olson, 730 F. 2nd 1109 (CA 8, 1984). However, an order allowing a claim is not a final order if it allows the claim but does not specify the amount. See Matter of Fox, 762 F. 2nd 54 (CA 7, 1985). While orders granting or denying motions to amend pleadings and documents are usually interlocutory, if an order denying a motion to amend a proof of claim results in the denial of the claim, the order is a final order for purposes of appeal. See In re Sambo's Restaurants, Inc., 754 F. 2nd 811 (CA 9, 1985).

order granting relief from stay, final or interlocutory

An order granting relief from the automatic stay is normally a final order for purposes of appeal. See In re Sun Valley Foods Co., 801 F. 2nd 186 (CA 6, 1986). An order denying relief from the automatic stay may be final or interlocutory, depending on the reason the relief was denied. See In re Chateaugay Corp., 880 F.2d 1509 (CA 2, 1989). If relief was denied because the court found the creditor's lien to be invalid, the order denying relief is a final order. See In re Leimer, 724 F. 2nd 744 (CA 8, 1984). If relief from the stay was denied because the court found the creditor to be adequately protected, the order denying relief is interlocutory. See In re Alchar Hardware, 730 F. 2nd 1386 (CA 11, 1984).

While an order dismissing a case is a final order, an order denying a motion to dismiss a case is an interlocutory order. See In re Hebb, 53 B.R. 1003 (MD, 1985). An order granting a motion to cure defaults is also an interlocutory order. See In re 405 N. Bedford Dr. Corp., 778 F. 2nd 1374 (CA 9, 1985). Likewise, an order granting interim compensation is an interlocutory order. See In re W.J. Serv., Inc., 139 BR 824 (SD TX, 1992). An order determining a debt to be nondischargeable is a final order. See In re Bathlater, 951 F.2d 349 (CA 6, 1991). An order authorizing the employment of professionals is also a final order. See In re Middleton Arms Ltd., 934 F.2d 723 (CA 6, 1991).

interlocutory order, what constitutes

As indicated above, interlocutory orders may be appealed only with leave of the appellate court. See 28 U.S.C. 158(a). The general rule is that an interlocutory order is eligible for appellate review if (1) the order conclusively determines a disputed question that is collateral to the merits of the overall action, and (2) the disputed question will be otherwise effectively unreviewable on appeal. See Cohen v. Beneficial Industrial Loan Corp., 337 U.S. 541, 69 S.Ct. 1221 , 93 L. Ed. 1528 (1949). In other words, the party seeking review must show that denial of leave to appeal will result in irreparable harm that cannot later be undone in an appeal of the overall action.

appeal of interlocutory order, basis for

Appellate procedure. The procedure for appealing orders, judgments, and decrees of a bankruptcy court is governed by Part VIII of the Rules of Bankruptcy Procedure. Part VIII was comprehensively rewritten in 2015 to bring the bankruptcy appellate rules in closer alignment with the Federal Rules of Appellate Procedure. An appeal of right taken from a final order, judgment, or decree of the bankruptcy court to the district court or bankruptcy appellate panel is initiated by the filing of a notice of appeal with the bankruptcy clerk, if one has been appointed in the district, otherwise with the clerk of the district court. See Bankruptcy Rules 8001(a), 9001(3). A notice of appeal must conform substantially to Official Form 417, and must be filed within 14 days of the date of the entry of the order, judgment, or decree appealed from. See Bankruptcy Rules 8002(a). If a timely motion is filed by a party requesting the bankruptcy court to reconsider the order, judgment, or decree, the time for appeal runs from the date of the court's ruling on such motion. See Bankruptcy Rule 8002(b). Unless otherwise provided by a local rule, the consent of a party to have an appeal heard by the District Court may be set forth in the notice of appeal or given in a separate signed statement. See Bankruptcy Rule 8005(a). The applicable filing fee must be paid with the notice of appeal.

final orders of bankruptcy judge, appeal of, procedure

notice of appeal, requirements, time for filing, fee

An appeal from an interlocutory order or decree of a bankruptcy court is initiated by the filing of a notice of appeal in the manner described in the preceding paragraph, accompanied by a motion for leave to appeal. See Bankruptcy Rule 8004(a). A motion for leave to appeal must contain the following: (1) a statement of the facts necessary to an understanding of the questions to be presented by the appeal; (2) a statement of the questions to be presented by the appeal and of the relief sought; (3) a statement of the reasons why an appeal should be granted; and (4) a copy of the order or decree complained of and of any opinion or memorandum relating thereto. See Bankruptcy Rule 8004(b). Copies of the motion for leave to appeal must be served on all parties to the appeal and proof of service thereof must be filed with the clerk of the appellate court. See Bankruptcy Rules 8003(c) and 8008.

interlocutory orders of bankruptcy judge, appeal of, procedure

motion for leave to appeal, requirements

It is often necessary for a party to an appeal to obtain a stay or other relief pending the appeal in order to protect its interests during the appeal. A motion for a stay of the order, judgment, or decree of a bankruptcy judge, for approval of a supersedeas bond, or for other relief pending appeal must ordinarily be presented to the bankruptcy judge in the first instance. The bankruptcy judge may suspend or order the continuation of other proceedings in the bankruptcy case or make any other appropriate order during the pendency of an appeal on such terms as will protect the rights of all parties in interest. If a party is not satisfied with the relief granted by the bankruptcy judge, the party may file a similar motion, or a motion for modification or termination of any relief granted by the bankruptcy judge, with the district court or bankruptcy appellate panel. Such a motion must show why the relief requested was not granted by the bankruptcy judge. The district court or bankruptcy appellate panel may condition any relief granted upon the filing of a bond or other appropriate security with the bankruptcy court. See Bankruptcy Rule 8007.

stay or relief pending appeal, how to obtain

doctrine of mootness, importance of in appeals

A party to an appeal should be aware of the doctrine of mootness. If, pending an appeal, an event occurs which makes it impossible for the appellate court to grant any effective relief or that makes a decision on the appeal unnecessary, the appeal may be dismissed on the grounds of mootness. This doctrine is often applied to appeals of orders of confirmation where a stay is not obtained pending the appeal and the plan is substantially consummated before the appeal is heard. See In re Roberts Farms, Inc., 652 F. 2nd 793 (CA 9, 1981), and In re AOV Industries, Inc., 792 F. 2nd 1140 (CA DC, 1986). The doctrine of mootness may also be applicable to appeals of orders authorizing the sale or lease of property, orders authorizing the obtaining of credit, orders granting relief from the automatic stay, and similar orders where an irrevocable change of position occurs prior to the determination of the appeal if a stay or other relief pending the appeal is not obtained. See 11 U.S.C. 363(m), 364(e), and Matter of Combined Metals Reduction Co., 557 F. 2nd 179 (CA 9, 1977). In cases of this sort the appellant's motion for a stay or other relief pending the appeal is a vital part of the appeal, because if such relief is not obtained the appeal is likely to be dismissed under the doctrine of mootness.

appeals, procedure, standard of review

"clearly erroneous," definition

As stated above, Part VIII of the Rules of Bankruptcy Procedure covers the procedural aspects of appeals from both final and interlocutory orders, judgments, and decrees of bankruptcy judges. Any party to such an appeal should examine these rules closely and comply with all requirements therein. It should be noted that in a bankruptcy proceeding an appellate court may overturn a finding of fact by a bankruptcy judge only if the finding is clearly erroneous. See, e.g., In re Chase & Sanborn Corp., 904 F.2d 588 (11th Cir. 1990). A finding of fact is clearly erroneous when, although there is evidence to support it, the reviewing court on the entire evidence is left with the definite and firm conviction that a mistake has been committed. The reviewing court may not reverse a finding of fact simply because it is convinced that it would have decided the case differently. See In re Pearson Bros. Co., 787 F. 2nd 1157 (CA 7, 1986). Conclusions of law are reviewed de novo.

appeals to court of appeals, when permitted

An appellate decision of a district court or bankruptcy appellate panel on a final order, judgment or decree of a bankruptcy judge may be further appealed to the circuit court of appeals. See 28 U.S.C. 158(d). Appeals to the circuit court of appeals are governed by the Federal Rules of Appellate Procedure and not by Part VIII of the Rules of Bankruptcy Procedure. The decision of a district court or bankruptcy appellate panel on an appeal of an interlocutory order or decree of a bankruptcy judge may not be further appealed. See 28 U.S.C. 158(d) and Matter of UNR Industries, 725 F. 2nd 1111 (CA 7, 1984). Thus, appeals of interlocutory orders and decrees of bankruptcy judges, if allowed at all, end at the first appellate level, while final orders of bankruptcy judges may be further appealed to circuit court of appeals.

4.14 Dismissal or Conversion to Another Chapter

Not all small business Chapter 11 cases end with the consummation of a confirmed plan. In fact, most do not. If the purpose of Chapter 11 is to prevent a sinking business from drowning, many have taken on too much water and cannot be kept afloat. While the reasons for unsuccessful Chapter 11 cases are as varied as there are debtors whose cases have failed, the result of an unsuccessful case is either dismissal of the case or conversion of the case to another chapter, usually Chapter 7. It is important to understand that a Chapter 11 debtor does not have an absolute to dismiss its case and may seek the dismissal of its case only for cause under 11 U.S.C. 1112(b).

unsuccessful case, how terminated

Voluntary conversion to Chapter 7. A Chapter 11 debtor may, as a matter of right, convert a Chapter 11 case to a case under Chapter 7 unless: (1) the debtor is not a debtor in possession, (2) the case was originally commenced as an involuntary Chapter 11 case, or (3) the case was previously converted to Chapter 11 from another chapter other than on the request of the debtor. See 11 U.S.C. 1112(a). If none of the three exceptions apply, the debtor may convert its Chapter 11 case to a case under Chapter 7 for any reason and at any time prior to confirmation. Because the confirmation of a plan terminates the "debtor in possession" status of a debtor, it is doubtful that a debtor can voluntarily under Section 1112(a) convert a Chapter 11 case to Chapter 7 after confirmation. If one or more of the exceptions listed above is applicable, the debtor may convert its Chapter 11 case to Chapter 7 only for cause under 11 U.S.C. 1112(b).

conversion of case to Chapter 7 by debtor, requirements

11 U.S.C. 1112(a) contains no hearing requirements, and proceedings thereunder are governed by Bankruptcy Rule 1017(d), which requires that a motion be filed and served as provided in Bankruptcy Rule 9013. Bankruptcy Rule 9013 requires a written motion and service of the motion on the trustee (if one is serving) and on such other entities as the court may direct. A copy of the motion must also be served on the U.S. Trustee. See Bankruptcy Rule 9034. A voluntary conversion proceeding under 11 U.S.C. 1112(a) is not a contested matter, therefore Bankruptcy Rule 9014 is not applicable and a hearing is not required unless the court so directs. See Bankruptcy Rule 1017(d) and the Advisory Committee's Notes thereto. A sample Motion to Convert Case to Chapter 7 Under Section 1112(a) is set forth in Exhibit 4-R at the end of this chapter.

conversion of case to Chapter 7 by debtor, procedure

Conversion or dismissal for cause. On the request of a party in interest, and after notice and a hearing, absent unusual circumstances specifically identified by the court that establish that the requested conversion or dismissal is not in the best interests of creditors and the estate, the court may convert a Chapter 11 case to a case under Chapter 7 or dismiss the case, whichever is in the best interest of creditors and the estate, if the movant establishes cause. See 11 U.S.C. 1112(b)(1). That the debtor, as a party in interest, may seek the dismissal or conversion of its Chapter 11 case under this section., see In re Taylor Transport, Inc., 28 B.R. 832 (ND OH, 1983). Cause for conversion or dismissal under 11 U.S.C. 1112(b)(1) includes the following:

conversion to chapter 7 or dismissal of case for cause, general rules

cause for dismissal or conversion of case, what constitutes

(1) substantial or continuing loss to or diminution of the estate and the absence of a reasonable likelihood of rehabilitation;

(2) gross mismanagement of the estate;

(3) failure to maintain appropriate insurance that poses a risk to the estate or to the public;

(4) unauthorized use of cash collateral substantially harmful to one or more creditors;

(5) failure to comply with an order of the court;

(6) unexcused failure to timely satisfy any filing or reporting requirement established by the Bankruptcy Code or by any rule applicable to a Chapter 11 case;

(7) failure to attend the meeting of creditors convened under 11 U.S.C. 341(a) or an examination ordered under Bankruptcy Rule 2004 without good cause;

(8) failure timely to provide information or attend meetings reasonably requested by the United States trustee;

(9) failure to timely pay taxes owed after the date of the order for relief or to file tax returns due after the date of the order for relief;

(10) failure to file a disclosure statement, or to file or confirm a plan, within the time fixed by the Bankruptcy Code or by order of the court;

(11) failure to pay the Chapter 11 filing fees or charges;

(12) revocation of an order of confirmation;

(13) inability to effectuate substantial consummation of a confirmed plan;

(14) material default by the debtor with respect to a confirmed plan;

(15) termination of a confirmed plan by reason of the occurrence of a condition specified in the plan; and

(16) failure of the debtor to pay any domestic support obligation that first becomes payable after the date of the filing of the petition.

dismissal or conversion of case, when not granted

Unless unusual circumstances specifically identified by the court exist establishing that the relief requested by the objecting party is not in the best interests of creditors and the estate, the court may not order the dismissal or conversion of a chapter 11 case if the debtor or another party in interest objects to the dismissal or conversion and establishes that there is a reasonable likelihood that a plan will be timely confirmed and that the grounds for dismissal or conversion include an act or omission of the debtor (other than the 16 causes for dismissal or conversion listed above) for which there is a reasonable justification and that will be cured within a reasonable time fixed by the court. See 11 U.S.C. 1112(b)(2). Further, a chapter 11 case may not be dismissed or converted if the best interest of creditors and the estate would be served by the appointment of a trustee or examiner. See 11 U.S.C. 1104(a)(3). Also, the court may not convert a chapter 11 case to a case under chapter 7 if the debtor is a farmer or a nonprofit corporation, unless the debtor requests the conversion. See 11 U.S.C. 1112(c). Finally, a chapter 11 case may not be converted to a case under another unless the debtor qualifies as a debtor under the other chapter. See 11 U.S.C. 1112(f).

cause for dismissal or conversion of case, lack of good faith by debtor

The 16 causes for conversion or dismissal of a Chapter 11 case listed above are not exclusive. See 11 U.S.C. 102(3), In re Denver, 338 B.R. 494 (CO, 2006) and In re Becker, 38 B.R. 913 (MN, 1984). Thus, other causes for conversion or dismissal under 11 U.S.C. 1112(b) may be alleged and proven. While not specifically enumerated in the amended Section 1112(b)(4), conversion or dismissal of a Chapter 11 is still appropriate if the court finds that the proposed reorganization plan is not feasible. See In re Ram, Inc., 343 B.R. 113 (ED PA, 2006). The most common nonlisted cause for the dismissal or conversion of a Chapter 11 case is lack of good faith by the debtor, either in filing the case or during the course of the case. That a Chapter 11 case may be dismissed or converted to Chapter 7 if it was not filed in good faith, see In re Elmwood Dev. Co., 964 F.2d 508 (CA 5, 1992). If the debtor's conduct during a Chapter 11 case is fraudulent or lacking in good faith, the court may also dismiss the case or convert it to Chapter 7. See In re Kerr, 908 F.2d 400 (CA 8, 1990). Even the bad faith proposal of a plan may justify dismissal or conversion to Chapter 7 for cause. See In re Abijoe Realty Corp., 943 F.2d 121 (CA 1, 1991). See section 3.02, supra, for further reading on the good faith requirement in Chapter 11 cases.

dismissal for loss or diminution of estate, cases

Among the 16 causes for dismissal or conversion listed in 11 U.S.C. 1112(b), the cause most commonly alleged is that in paragraph (1), which is "substantial or continuing loss to or diminution of the estate and the absence of a reasonable likelihood of rehabilitation." Especially if dismissal is sought on this ground early in the case, the burden of proving both a continuing loss to or diminution of the estate and the absence of a reasonable likelihood of rehabilitating the debtor's business is squarely on the moving party. See In re Brown, 951 F.2d 564 (CA 3, 1991). Even if it is shown that the debtor's business is losing money, if a reasonable possibility exists of rehabilitating the business, cause for dismissal or conversion on this ground is not established. See In re Brown, 951 F.2d 564 (CA 3, 1991). Further, even if the debtor has a negative cash flow, if there are estate assets that are appreciating in value sufficient to offset the debtor's business losses, then the estate is not diminishing and cause for dismissal or conversion is not established. See In re Route 202 Corp., 37 B.R. 367 (ED PA, 1984), and In re Petralex Stainless, Ltd., 78 B.R. 738 (ED PA, 1987). On the other hand, the passage of time in a Chapter 11 case often works against the debtor, and facts that may have been insufficient early in the case might be sufficient for dismissal or conversion later in the case, especially if the debtor has failed to file a plan for a prolonged period. See In re Powell Brothers Ice Co., 37 B.R. 104 (KS, 1984), and In re ABEPP Acquisition Corp., 191 B.R. 365 (ND OH, 1996).

A troublesome issue in some Chapter 11 cases is whether the court may dismiss or convert a Chapter 11 case for cause on its own motion or only on the motion of a party in interest or the U.S. Trustee. 11 U.S.C. 1112(b) clearly states that dismissals thereunder must be on the request of a party in interest. Nevertheless, many courts have held that a bankruptcy court has the inherent power under 11 U.S.C. 105(a) to dismiss or convert a Chapter 11 case on its own motion, especially on such grounds as bad faith, frivolity, and lack of jurisdiction. See In re Toibb, 902 F.2d 14 (CA 8, 1990), In re Pedro Abich, Inc., 165 B.R. 5 (PR, 1994), and Pleasant Pointe Apartments, Ltd. v Kentucky Housing Corp., 139 B.R. 828 (WD KY, 1992), where the court held that the language in 11 U.S.C. 105(a) clearly gives the bankruptcy court the authority to enter sua sponte orders of this type.

dismissal or conversion of case on motion of court, legality of

A proceeding to dismiss or convert a Chapter 11 case for cause under 11 U.S.C. 1112(b) is a contested matter governed by Bankruptcy Rule 9014. See Bankruptcy Rule 1017(f). Such a proceeding must be initiated by the filing of a motion, which, together with at least 20 days notice of the hearing thereon, must be served on the debtor, all creditors, and the U.S. Trustee. See Bankruptcy Rules 2002(a)(5),(k) and 9034. Unless the court orders otherwise, such notice as the court may direct must also be given to the debtor's interest holders. See Bankruptcy Rule 2002(d)(4). The hearing must be held not later than 30 days after the filing of the motion and a ruling on the motion must be rendered within 15 days after the commencement of the hearing, unless the moving party expressly consents to a continuance for a specific period or compelling circumstances prevent the court from meeting these time limits. See 11 U.S.C. 1112(b)(3). At the hearing, the burden of proof as to existence of cause for dismissal or conversion is on the moving party. See In re Route 202 Corp., 37 B.R. 367 (ED PA, 1984). A sample Motion For Dismissal or Conversion of Case For Cause Under Section 1112(b) is set forth in Exhibit 4-U at the end of this chapter.

dismissal or conversion of case for cause, procedure

motion for dismissal, burden of proof

Once cause had been established for the dismissal or conversion of a Chapter 11 case under 11 U.S.C. 1112(b), the court must decide whether to dismiss the case, convert it to a case under Chapter 7, or order the appointment of a trustee or examiner. The best interests of creditors and the estate is the criterion used by the court in making such a determination. See 11 U.S.C. 1112(b). Failed Chapter 11 cases are usually converted to Chapter 7 in order to protect the interests of creditors, if dismissal is prior to confirmation. Only when a Chapter 11 debtor is clearly solvent, when there are no creditors to protect, or when there would be no assets available to creditors in a Chapter 7 case, is a failed Chapter 11 case likely to be dismissed. See In re Danehy Development Corp., 27 B.R. 727 (SD FL, 1983). However, if the court finds that neither dismissal nor conversion are in the best interests of creditors and the estate, it is not required to do either and may appoint a trustee or examiner or do nothing. See In re HRP Auto Ctr. Inc., 130 BR 247 (ND OH, 1991).

conversion or dismissal, criterion used by court

Occasionally the dismissal or conversion of a Chapter 11 case is sought after confirmation. Because after confirmation neither conversion nor dismissal are normally beneficial to creditors and the estate, courts seldom grant the requested relief. The reason for denying conversion to Chapter 7 after confirmation is that the confirmation of a plan vests the property of the estate in the reorganized debtor, which means that the estate is essentially an empty shell containing no assets for a Chapter 7 trustee to administer. See In re T.S. Note Co., 140 BR 812 (KS, 1992). Only if there are assets such as avoidable transfers for a Chapter 7 trustee to pursue and administer is the court likely to convert a confirmed Chapter 11 case to Chapter 7. See In re TSP Industries, Inc., 120 BR 107 (ND IL, 1990). Dismissals after confirmation are seldom granted because it would not be in the best interests of creditors and would serve no purpose other than to revest the property of the estate, if any exists, in the original debtor whose discharge would not be affected by the dismissal, unless the debtor is an individual. See In re Page, 118 BR 456 (ND TX, 1990), and In re Depew, 115 BR 965 (ND IN, 1989).

dismissal or conversion after confirmation, when granted

Conversion to Chapter 12 or 13. Under certain circumstances a debtor may convert its Chapter 11 case to a case under Chapter 12 or Chapter 13. Under 11 U.S.C. 1112(d), (f), the court may convert a Chapter 11 case to a case under Chapter 12 or Chapter 13 if:

conversion of case to Chapter 12 or 13, requirements

(1) the debtor requests the conversion;

(2) the debtor has not received a discharge in the Chapter 11 case;

(3) in the case of a conversion to Chapter 12, if such conversion is equitable; and

(4) if the debtor qualifies as a debtor under the Chapter to which conversion is requested.

conversion of case to Chapter 12, when equitable

In determining whether a requested conversion from Chapter 11 to Chapter 12 is equitable, the court must consider the likelihood of the debtor's success under Chapter 12, what action has occurred in the Chapter 11 case, and whether creditors and other parties in interest who have relied on the Chapter 11 case will be adversely affected by a conversion to Chapter 12. See In re Anderson, 70 B.R. 883 (UT, 1987).

conversion of case to another Chapter, procedure, treatment of expenses

Conversion Procedure. The conversion of a Chapter 11 case to another chapter constitutes an order for relief under the new chapter, but does not change the date of the filing of the petition, the date of the commencement of the case, or the date of the order for relief. See 11 U.S.C. 348(a). Appropriate notice of the conversion to the new chapter must be given, and the time for assuming or rejecting executory contracts under the new chapter is extended. See 11 U.S.C. 348(c) and Bankruptcy Rule 2002(f)(2). Administrative expenses incurred during the Chapter 11 case are treated as administrative expenses in the case under the new chapter, but no other claims in the Chapter 11 case are given priority in the case under the new chapter. See 11 U.S.C. 348(d). If a Chapter 11 case is converted to Chapter 7, the administrative expenses of the Chapter 7 case take priority over the administrative expenses of the converted Chapter 11 case. See 11 U.S.C. 726(b). Thus, the payment of legal fees and other expenses incurred in the Chapter 7 case take priority over similar unpaid expenses that were incurred in the Chapter 11 case. The conversion of a Chapter 11 case to another chapter terminates the service of any trustee or examiner serving in the Chapter 11 case. See 11 U.S.C. 348(e). The procedure following conversion to Chapter 7 is set forth in Bankruptcy Rule 1019.

dismissal of case, effect of

Unless the court, for cause, orders otherwise, the dismissal of a Chapter 11 case does not bar the discharge, in a later case under any chapter of the Bankruptcy Code, of any debts that were dischargeable in the Chapter 11 case. Further, the dismissal of a Chapter 11 case does not prejudice the debtor with regard to the filing of a subsequent petition under any chapter of the Bankruptcy Code except as provided in 11 U.S.C. 109(g), which deals with repetitive filings. See 11 U.S.C. 349(a). An order of dismissal in a Chapter 11 case does not divest the bankruptcy court of jurisdiction over pending matters (such as an application for the allowance of professional fees) if the order of dismissal expressly provides for the retention of such jurisdiction. See Matter of Mandalay Shores Co-op. Housing Assn., 60 B.R. 22 (MD FL, 1986).

UNITED STATES BANKRUPTCY COURT
NORTHERN DISTRICT OF INDIANA

IN RE HARDTIMES SUPPLY CO., INC.,	)		
an Indiana Corporation,	)	Case No. 16-00019	
	)		
Debtor	)	Chapter 11	

MOTION FOR RELIEF FROM STAY OF ACTS AGAINST PROPERTY

COMES NOW the Last National Bank (the "Creditor"), a secured creditor of the above-named debtor, by its attorney and, pursuant to 11 U.S.C. 362(d) and Bankruptcy Rules 4001(a) and 9014, moves this honorable court to grant relief from the automatic stay so as to permit the Creditor to foreclose on and take possession of certain property of the estate described below. In support of this motion the Creditor represents as follows:

1. On January 10, 2016, the debtor initiated this case by filing a voluntary petition under Chapter 11 of the Bankruptcy Code, and the automatic stay that accompanied the order for relief in this case has prevented the Creditor from foreclosing on, obtaining possession of, or otherwise protecting its interest in the property of the estate securing its claim.

2. The Creditor is the holder of a valid and perfected secured claim against the debtor in the amount of $124,500.00, as evidenced by the debtor's promissory note dated April 1, 2012, a copy of which is attached to this motion and marked as Exhibit A.

3. The Creditor has a valid perfected security interest in a warehouse and lot located at 2455 Oak Street, Muncie, Indiana (the "Collateral"), which Collateral is property of the estate and is more specifically described in the deed of trust dated April 1, 2012, a copy of which is attached to this motion and marked as Exhibit B. The attached deed of trust has been duly recorded and otherwise perfected.

4. The Creditor is entitled to adequate protection of its interest in the Collateral. The Creditor does not have and has not been offered adequate protection of its interest in the Collateral. The Collateral is deteriorating in value and is not being adequately maintained or protected by the debtor, and as a result thereof the value of the Creditor's secured claim is deteriorating.

5. The Collateral now has a fair market value of less than $124,500.00, the debtor has no equity in the Collateral, and the Collateral is not needed by the debtor for an effective reorganization.

6. The Creditor will suffer irreparable damage and loss unless relief from the automatic stay is granted and the Creditor is permitted to foreclose on and obtain possession of the Collateral.

WHEREFORE, the Creditor prays for the entry of an order granting relief from the automatic stay permitting the Creditor to foreclose on and take possession of the property described in Exhibit B, or, in the alternative, that the Creditor be granted adequate protection of its interest in the Collateral, and for such other relief as may be just.

Dated: January 20, 2016

____
Joseph J. Jackson
Attorney for Last National Bank
2400 Main Street
Kokomo, IN 46901

---

*Note - Use a local form for noticing requirements and calendaring the proposed hearing dates for all motions or applications.

UNITED STATES BANKRUPTCY COURT
NORTHERN DISTRICT OF INDIANA

IN RE	HARDTIMES SUPPLY CO., INC., an Indiana Corporation,	)	Case No. 16-00019
	Debtor	)	Chapter 11

APPLICATION FOR ALLOWANCE OF AND FOR AUTHORITY TO PAY CLAIMS OF DEBTOR'S EMPLOYEES FOR PRE-FILING WAGES AND SALARIES.

The debtor in possession (the "Debtor"), by its attorney, represents as follows:

1. On January 10, 2016, the Debtor filed a voluntary petition under Chapter 11 of the Bankruptcy Code and is presently operating its business as a debtor in possession.

2. The Debtor was unable to pay its employees the wages and salaries earned during the ten-day period prior to the commencement of this case. Said employees are still employed by the Debtor and are necessary for the continued operation and reorganization of the Debtor's business.

3. None of the employees for whom payment is sought by this application is an owner, shareholder, director or officer of the Debtor, and the claim of each such employee is less than $12,475 and is therefore entitled to priority of payment under 11 U.S.C. 507(a)(3).

4. The Debtor's normal practice is to pay its employees on the first and 15th day of each month. The employees are in need of their unpaid wages and salaries, and the nonpayment of such wages and salaries will result in low morale and a possible disruption in the Debtor's business operation.

5. The name and address of each employee for whom payment is sought, and the amount of the claim for each employee, is listed on the attached Exhibit A.

6. The Debtor has funds available for the payment of such claims and the payment of such claims will not deplete the Debtor's estate.

WHEREFORE, the Debtor, by its attorney, prays for the entry of an order allowing the pre-filing wage and salary claims of the Debtor's employees as priority claims under 11 U.S.C. 507(a)(3) and authorizing the Debtor to forthwith pay such claims.

Dated: January 10, 2016

Reddy, Willing & Able

by ______________________________

Leo E. Lawnoer
Attorneys for Debtor in Possession
1000 First Street
Gary, Indiana 46407

CERTIFICATE OF TRANSMITTAL TO UNITED STATES TRUSTEE

The undersigned certifies under penalty of perjury that he or she has, on the date shown below, by first class mail addressed to their respective addresses of record in this case, transmitted and served a true copy of this document to the United States Trustee at its local address of record, and all other interested parties as shown on the attached copy of the creditors' matrix.

Date: ______________________________ ______________________________

UNITED STATES BANKRUPTCY COURT
NORTHERN DISTRICT OF INDIANA

IN RE	HARDTIMES SUPPLY CO., INC.,	)	
	an Indiana Corporation,	)	Case No. 16-00019
		)	
	Debtor	)	Chapter 11

MOTION FOR AUTHORITY TO USE CASH COLLATERAL

The debtor in possession (the "Debtor"), by its attorney, represents as follows:

1. On January 10, 2016 the Debtor filed a voluntary petition initiating this Chapter 11 case and is now operating its roofing supply business as a debtor in possession.

2. By this motion the Debtor seeks authority to use cash collateral in the amount of $20,000.00. The cash collateral sought to be used consists of a funds on deposit in an account with the Last National Bank of LaPorte, Indiana.

3. The name and address of each entity having an interest in the cash collateral sought to be used is: The Last National Bank of LaPorte, 100 Main Street, LaPorte, Indiana 46350. The name and address of the entity having possession of the cash collateral sought to be used is the Last National Bank of LaPorte, 100 Main Street, La Porte, IN 46350.

4. The Debtor needs to use the cash collateral described above in this motion in order to meet its payroll and to purchase inventory and supplies needed in the operation of its business. The Debtor has no other funds with which to pay such expenses and if such expenses are not paid the Debtor will be unable to continue its business operations.

5. The Debtor proposes to protect the interest of the Last National Bank in the cash collateral sought to be used by providing the said bank with a lien on the account owed to the Debtor by The Rustic Building Company of 300 Second Street, Fort Wayne, Indiana, which account is in the total amount of $26,345.45, of which $15,000 is payable on January 31, 2016, with the balance payable on or before April 1, 2016. There are no other liens against the account.

6. The Debtor hereby requests a preliminary hearing on this motion. The amount of cash collateral sought to be used pending the final hearing on this motion is $15,800. The protection to be provided to creditors pending the final hearing is the protection described in paragraph 5 above.

WHEREFORE, the Debtor prays for the entry of an order authorizing the Debtor to use cash collateral in the amount and in the manner described above in this motion and for such other relief as may be just and proper.

Dated: January 20, 2016

Reddy, Willing & Able

by ______________________________
Leo E. Lawnoer
Attorneys for Debtor in Possession
1000 First Street
Gary, Indiana 46407

CERTIFICATE OF TRANSMITTAL AND SERVICE BY MAIL

The undersigned certifies under penalty of perjury that he or she has, on the date shown below, by first class mail addressed to their respective addresses of record in this case, transmitted and served a true copy of this document to the United States Trustee, the creditors listed in the above document, the unsecured creditors' committee, and their respective attorneys of record.

Date: ______________________________ ______________________________

UNITED STATES BANKRUPTCY COURT
NORTHERN DISTRICT OF INDIANA

IN RE HARDTIMES SUPPLY CO., INC.,	)		
an Indiana Corporation,	)	Case No. 16-00019	
	)		
Debtor	)	Chapter 11	

NOTICE OF PROPOSED SALE OF ESTATE PROPERTY
NOT IN ORDINARY COURSE OF BUSINESS AND OF HEARING

TO: All Creditors and Other Parties in Interest

PLEASE TAKE NOTICE that Hardtimes Supply Co., the debtor in possession, proposes to sell property of the estate described in the following paragraph at a private sale on February 19, 2016 to the Jones Bros. Supply Company of 7777 Maple Avenue, Chicago, Illinois upon the terms set forth in an Agreement of Sale dated January 12, 2016, a copy of which is attached to this Notice.

The property proposed to be sold is a 10,000 square-foot warehouse located at 2300 Oak Street, East Chicago, Indiana. The legal description of the property is set forth in the attached Agreement of Sale.

The property is subject to a first mortgage in favor of the Last National Bank of East Chicago, Indiana, and to a second mortgage in favor of the Fast Finance Company of Joliet, Illinois. The sale is to be free and clear of all liens and encumbrances, with all liens and encumbrances to be transferred and attached to the proceeds of the sale. The proposed sales price of the property exceeds the amount of all liens and encumbrances against the property. The purposes of the proposed sale are to raise funds for the operation of the Debtor's business and to rid the estate of an unneeded asset.

Objections to the proposed sale must be filed with the clerk of the bankruptcy court and served upon the undersigned attorney for the debtor in possession not less than seven days before the date of the proposed sale (i.e., by February 12, 2016). If an objection to the proposed sale is filed, a hearing on such objection shall be held on February 17, 2016, at 10:00 A.M. in Division 2 of the United States Bankruptcy Court for the Northern District of Indiana.

If no objections to the proposed sale are filed and served within the time set forth above, a hearing will not be held and the sale shall be consummated as set forth in the attached Agreement of Sale. Additional information regarding the proposed sale may be obtained from the undersigned attorney for the debtor in possession.

Dated: January 23, 2016

Reddy, Willing & Able

by ______________________________

Leo E. Lawnoer
Attorneys for Debtor in Possession
1000 First Street
Gary, Indiana 46407

CERTIFICATE OF TRANSMITTAL AND SERVICE BY MAIL

The undersigned certifies under penalty of perjury that he or she has, on the date shown below, by first class mail addressed to their respective addresses of record in this case, transmitted and served a true copy of this document to the United States Trustee, all creditors, the unsecured creditors' committee, and their respective attorneys of record.

Date: ______________________________ ______________________________

UNITED STATES BANKRUPTCY COURT
NORTHERN DISTRICT OF INDIANA

IN RE	HARDTIMES SUPPLY CO., INC.,	)	
	an Indiana Corporation,	)	Case No. 16-00019
		)	
		)	
	Debtor	)	Chapter 11

MOTION FOR AUTHORITY TO OBTAIN CREDIT NOT IN THE ORDINARY COURSE OF BUSINESS

The Debtor in Possession (the “Debtor”), by its attorney, represents as follows:

1. On January 10, 2016 the Debtor filed a voluntary petition initiating this Chapter 11 case and is now operating its roofing supply business as a debtor in possession.

2. The Debtor’s business is seasonal and during the months of February and March it is necessary to contract to purchase shingles and other roofing supplies in order to be ready for the busy season that begins in April. It is the practice of manufacturers in the roofing supply business to require a deposit of at least 25 percent on all orders of shingles and other roofing supplies. In order to meet these deposit requirements it will be necessary for the Debtor to borrow the sum of $25,000.

3. The Last National Bank of South Bend, Indiana has agreed to lend the sum of $25,000 to the Debtor upon the following terms: interest on the unpaid portion of the loan shall be at the rate of five percent per month; the loan shall be repayable at the rate of $5,000 per month beginning on the first day of June, 2016; the loan shall be secured by a senior lien on all accounts payable to the Debtor beginning on June 1, 2016; and the loan shall be personally guaranteed by John J. Jones, the principal shareholder of the Debtor. A letter from the Last National Bank of South Bend confirming the loan agreement is attached to this motion.

4. The Debtor’s accounts receivable are currently subject to a security interest in favor of the Ace Factoring Company of Chicago, Illinois, which security interest the Debtor proposes to subordinate to the lien of the First National Bank of South Bend. The Debtor proposes to adequately protect the interest of Ace Factoring in the accounts receivable by extending the duration of Ace Factoring’s security interest to cover accounts receivable received after August 15, 2016, which is when its present security interest expires.

5. The Debtor as a Debtor in possession is unable to obtain unsecured credit allowable as an administrative expense and is unable to obtain credit other than by granting a senior lien as described above in this motion. The borrowing requested herein is in the best interest of the estate and the Debtor expects to be able to repay the borrowed funds as called for in the agreement from the sale of the supplies purchased with the borrowed funds. Unless the Debtor is permitted to borrow the funds herein requested, the Debtor will be unable to continue in business.

WHEREFORE, the Debtor prays for the entry of an order authorizing the Debtor to borrow the funds herein requested upon the terms herein set forth.

Reddy, Willing & Able

Dated January 22, 2016.

by ____________________________

Leo E. Lawnoer
Attorneys for Debtor in Possession
1000 First Street
Gary, Indiana 46407

CERTIFICATE OF TRANSMITTAL AND SERVICE BY MAIL

The undersigned certifies under penalty of perjury that he or she has, on the date shown below, by first class mail addressed to their respective addresses of record in this case, transmitted and served a true copy of this document to the United States Trustee, Ace Factoring Company, and the unsecured creditors’ committee, and their respective attorneys of record.

Date: ____________________________ ____________________________

B 25C (Official Form 25C) (12/08) 1

UNITED STATES BANKRUPTCY COURT

In re Hardtimes Supply Co., Inc., Case No. 16-19031-HRT
Debtor

Small Business Case Under Chapter 11

SMALL BUSINESS MONTHLY OPERATING REPORT

Month: February 2016 Date filed: 03/10/16

Line of Business: Hardware Supply NAISC Code: 8895

IN ACCORDANCE WITH TITLE 28, SECTION 1746, OF THE UNITED STATES CODE, I DECLARE UNDER PENALTY OF PERJURY THAT I HAVE EXAMINED THE FOLLOWING SMALL BUSINESS MONTHLY OPERATING REPORT AND THE ACCOMPANYING ATTACHMENTS AND, TO THE BEST OF MY KNOWLEDGE, THESE DOCUMENTS ARE TRUE, CORRECT AND COMPLETE.

RESPONSIBLE PARTY:

____
Original Signature of Responsible Party

John Jones, President
Printed Name of Responsible Party

Questionnaire: *(All questions to be answered on behalf of the debtor.)*	**Yes**	**No**
1. IS THE BUSINESS STILL OPERATING?	☑	☐
2. HAVE YOU PAID ALL YOUR BILLS ON TIME THIS MONTH?	☑	☐
3. DID YOU PAY YOUR EMPLOYEES ON TIME?	☑	☐
4. HAVE YOU DEPOSITED ALL THE RECEIPTS FOR YOUR BUSINESS INTO THE DIP ACCOUNT THIS MONTH?	☑	☐
5. HAVE YOU FILED ALL OF YOUR TAX RETURNS AND PAID ALL OF YOUR TAXES THIS MONTH?	☑	☐
6. HAVE YOU TIMELY FILED ALL OTHER REQUIRED GOVERNMENT FILINGS?	☑	☐
7. HAVE YOU PAID ALL OF YOUR INSURANCE PREMIUMS THIS MONTH?	☑	☐
8. DO YOU PLAN TO CONTINUE TO OPERATE THE BUSINESS NEXT MONTH?	☑	☐
9. ARE YOU CURRENT ON YOUR QUARTERLY FEE PAYMENT TO THE U.S. TRUSTEE?	☑	☐
10. HAVE YOU PAID ANYTHING TO YOUR ATTORNEY OR OTHER PROFESSIONALS THIS MONTH?	☑	☐
11. DID YOU HAVE ANY UNUSUAL OR SIGNIFICANT UNANTICIPATED EXPENSES THIS MONTH?	☐	☑
12. HAS THE BUSINESS SOLD ANY GOODS OR PROVIDED SERVICES OR TRANSFERRED ANY ASSETS TO ANY BUSINESS RELATED TO THE DIP IN ANY WAY?	☐	☑
13. DO YOU HAVE ANY BANK ACCOUNTS OPEN OTHER THAN THE DIP ACCOUNT?	☐	☑

B 25C (Official Form 25C) (12/08) 2

14. HAVE YOU SOLD ANY ASSETS OTHER THAN INVENTORY THIS MONTH?	☐	☑
15. DID ANY INSURANCE COMPANY CANCEL YOUR POLICY THIS MONTH?	☐	☑
16. HAVE YOU BORROWED MONEY FROM ANYONE THIS MONTH?	☐	☑
17. HAS ANYONE MADE AN INVESTMENT IN YOUR BUSINESS THIS MONTH?	☐	☑
18. HAVE YOU PAID ANY BILLS YOU OWED BEFORE YOU FILED BANKRUPTCY?	☐	☑

TAXES

DO YOU HAVE ANY PAST DUE TAX RETURNS OR PAST DUE POST-PETITION TAX OBLIGATIONS? ☐ ☑

IF YES, PLEASE PROVIDE A WRITTEN EXPLANATION INCLUDING WHEN SUCH RETURNS WILL BE FILED, OR WHEN SUCH PAYMENTS WILL BE MADE AND THE SOURCE OF THE FUNDS FOR THE PAYMENT.

(Exhibit A)

INCOME

PLEASE SEPARATELY LIST ALL OF THE INCOME YOU RECEIVED FOR THE MONTH. THE LIST SHOULD INCLUDE ALL INCOME FROM CASH AND CREDIT TRANSACTIONS. *(THE U.S. TRUSTEE MAY WAIVE THIS REQUIREMENT.)*

TOTAL INCOME $ 18,675.46

SUMMARY OF CASH ON HAND

Cash on Hand at Start of Month		$ 17,283.90
Cash on Hand at End on Month		$ 18,556.87
PLEASE PROVIDE THE TOTAL AMOUNT OF CASH CURRENTLY AVAILABLE TO YOU	**TOTAL**	$ 18,556.87

(Exhibit B)

EXPENSES

PLEASE SEPARATELY LIST ALL EXPENSES PAID BY CASH OR BY CHECK FROM YOUR BANK ACCOUNTS THIS MONTH. INCLUDE THE DATE PAID, WHO WAS PAID THE MONEY, THE PURPOSE AND THE AMOUNT. *(THE U.S. TRUSTEE MAY WAIVE THIS REQUIREMENT.)*

TOTAL EXPENSES $ 17,402.49

(Exhibit C)

CASH PROFIT

INCOME FOR THE MONTH *(TOTAL FROM EXHIBIT B)*		$ 18,675.46
EXPENSES FOR THE MONTH *(TOTAL FROM EXHIBIT C)*		$ 17,402.49
(Subtract Line C from Line B)	**CASH PROFIT FOR THE MONTH**	$ 1,272.97

UNPAID BILLS

PLEASE ATTACH A LIST OF ALL DEBTS (INCLUDING TAXES) WHICH YOU HAVE INCURRED SINCE THE DATE YOU FILED BANKRUPTCY BUT HAVE NOT PAID. THE LIST MUST INCLUDE THE DATE THE DEBT WAS INCURRED, WHO IS OWED THE MONEY, THE PURPOSE OF THE DEBT AND WHEN THE DEBT IS DUE. *(THE U.S. TRUSTEE MAY WAIVE THIS REQUIREMENT.)*

TOTAL PAYABLES $ 0.00

(Exhibit D)

MONEY OWED TO YOU

PLEASE ATTACH A LIST OF ALL AMOUNTS OWED TO YOU BY YOUR CUSTOMERS FOR WORK YOU HAVE DONE OR THE MERCHANDISE YOU HAVE SOLD. YOU SHOULD INCLUDE WHO OWES YOU MONEY, HOW MUCH IS OWED AND WHEN PAYMENT IS DUE. *(THE U.S. TRUSTEE MAY WAIVE THIS REQUIREMENT.)*

TOTAL RECEIVABLES $ 11,289.76

(Exhibit E)

BANKING INFORMATION

PLEASE ATTACH A COPY OF YOUR LATEST BANK STATEMENT FOR EVERY ACCOUNT YOU HAVE AS OF THE DATE OF THIS FINANCIAL REPORT OR HAD DURING THE PERIOD COVERED BY THIS REPORT.

(Exhibit F)

EMPLOYEES

NUMBER OF EMPLOYEES WHEN THE CASE WAS FILED? 12

NUMBER OF EMPLOYEES AS OF THE DATE OF THIS MONTHLY REPORT? 12

PROFESSIONAL FEES

BANKRUPTCY RELATED:

PROFESSIONAL FEES RELATING TO THE BANKRUPTCY CASE PAID DURING THIS REPORTING PERIOD? $ 2,876.90

TOTAL PROFESSIONAL FEES RELATING TO THE BANKRUPTCY CASE PAID SINCE THE FILING OF THE CASE? $ 5,169.80

NON-BANKRUPTCY RELATED:

PROFESSIONAL FEES NOT RELATING TO THE BANKRUPTCY CASE PAID DURING THIS REPORTING PERIOD? $ 900.00

TOTAL PROFESSIONAL FEES NOT RELATING TO THE BANKRUPTCY CASE PAID SINCE THE FILING OF THE CASE? $ 1,400.00

B 25C (Official Form 25C) (12/08) 4

PROJECTIONS

COMPARE YOUR ACTUAL INCOME AND EXPENSES TO THE PROJECTIONS FOR THE FIRST 180 DAYS OF YOUR CASE PROVIDED AT THE INITIAL DEBTOR INTERVIEW.

	Projected	Actual	Difference
INCOME	$ 23,000.00	$ 18,675.46	$ -4,324.54
EXPENSES	$ 18,500.00	$ 17,402.49	$ -1,097.51
CASH PROFIT	$ 4,500.00	$ 1,272.97	$ -3,227.03

TOTAL PROJECTED INCOME FOR THE NEXT MONTH:	$ 23,000.00
TOTAL PROJECTED EXPENSES FOR THE NEXT MONTH:	$ 18,500.00
TOTAL PROJECTED CASH PROFIT FOR THE NEXT MONTH:	$ 4,500.00

ADDITIONAL INFORMATION

PLEASE ATTACH ALL FINANCIAL REPORTS INCLUDING AN INCOME STATEMENT AND BALANCE SHEET WHICH YOU PREPARE INTERNALLY.

UNITED STATES BANKRUPTCY COURT
NORTHERN DISTRICT OF INDIANA

IN RE	HARDTIMES SUPPLY CO., INC.,	)	
	an Indiana Corporation,	)	Case No. 16-00019
		)	
	Debtor	)	Chapter 11

OBJECTION TO ALLOWANCE OF CLAIM AND NOTICE OF HEARING

PLEASE TAKE NOTICE that the Debtor, by its attorney, hereby objects to the allowance of the claim of Smith Mercantile, Inc., 240 Main Street, Dyer, Indiana 46311 in the sum of $2,190.00 on the ground that the books of the Debtor do not show an existing liability of the Debtor to the claimant and the Debtor is not indebted to the claimant in that amount, and on the ground that a portion of the said claim is for unmatured interest.

PLEASE TAKE FURTHER NOTICE that a hearing on the above Objection will be held before the Honorable Frances B. Fair, Bankruptcy Judge, in room 200 of The United States Courthouse, 200 Main Street, Gary, Indiana on February 20, 2016 at 11:00 A.M.

Dated January 23, 2016. Reddy, Willing & Able

by ______________________________
Leo E. Lawnoer
Attorneys for Debtor in Possession
1000 First Street
Gary, Indiana 46407

CERTIFICATE OF SERVICE BY MAIL

I hereby certify that I have on the date shown below served, by first class mail, a copy of this document upon the claimant named above at the address shown above for the claimant.

Date: ____________________________ ______________________________

UNITED STATES BANKRUPTCY COURT
NORTHERN DISTRICT OF INDIANA

IN RE	HARDTIMES SUPPLY CO., INC.,	)	
	an Indiana Corporation,	)	Case No. 16-00019
		)	
	Debtor	)	Chapter 11

APPLICATION FOR ALLOWANCE OF ADMINISTRATIVE EXPENSES

The Debtor, by its attorney, represents as follows:

1. The Debtor has filed a voluntary petition under Chapter 11 of the Bankruptcy Code and is operating its roofing supply business as a debtor in possession.

2. The Debtor has incurred the following expenses in the ordinary course of operating its business after the commencement of this case:

Sales tax for the first quarter of 2016 in the amount of $4,126.00

3. The above-listed expenses were incurred by the Debtor in the ordinary course of operating its business as a debtor in possession after the commencement of this case and constitute actual, necessary costs and expenses of preserving the estate and are allowable as administrative expenses under U.S.C. § 507(a)(1).

4. The Debtor has funds available for the payment of the expenses described in this Application, and the expenditure of such funds will not deplete the estate.

WHEREFORE, the Debtor prays for the entry of an order allowing payment of the administrative expenses described above in this Application.

Dated: April 5, 2016

Reddy, Willing & Able

by ______________________________

Leo E. Lawnoer
Attorneys for Debtor in Possession
1000 First Street
Gary, Indiana 46407

CERTIFICATE OF TRANSMITTAL AND SERVICE BY MAIL

The undersigned certifies under penalty of perjury that he or she has, on the date shown below, by first class mail addressed to their respective addresses of record in this case, transmitted and served a true copy of this document to the United States Trustee, and the unsecured creditors' committee, and their respective attorneys of record.

Date: ______________________________ ______________________________

UNITED STATES BANKRUPTCY COURT
NORTHERN DISTRICT OF INDIANA

IN RE	HARDTIMES SUPPLY CO., INC.,	)	
	an Indiana Corporation,	)	Case No. 16-00017
		)	
	Debtor	)	Chapter 11

MOTION FOR APPROVAL OF ASSUMPTION OF EXECUTORY CONTRACT AND NOTICE OF HEARING

The Debtor, by its attorney, represents as follows:

1. The Debtor has filed a voluntary petition under Chapter 11 of the Bankruptcy Code and is operating its business as a debtor in possession.

2. On June 13, 2015 the Debtor entered into a contract with Jones Realty, Inc. of 6700 East Spruce Street, Chicago, Illinois for the purchase of a warehouse located at 4200 Kipling Street, Gary, Indiana for the sum of $95,000, payable in 120 monthly installments of $800, plus interest at 9 percent per annum. A copy of the Purchase Agreement is attached to this Motion and marked as Exhibit A.

3. The present market value of the said warehouse is estimated by the Debtor to exceed $120,000, and the assumption of the contract to purchase the warehouse is in the best interest of the estate.

4. The Debtor is in default under said contract in the amount of $2,400 plus interest at 9 percent per annum, and the Debtor is prepared to cure the default by tendering to the contract seller the sum of $2,510 upon the approval by the court of the assumption of the contract.

5. The contract seller has not incurred any damages as a result of the Debtor's default other than those described above in this motion.

6. The estate has sufficient funds available to promptly cure the above described defaults and to thereafter maintain the payments under the contract.

WHEREFORE, the Debtor prays for the entry of an order approving the assumption of the executory contract described above in this Motion.

Dated: January 22, 2016

Reddy, Willing & Able

by ______________________________

Leo E. Lawnoer
Attorneys for Debtor in Possession
1000 First Street
Gary, Indiana 46407

PLEASE TAKE NOTICE that a hearing on the above Motion For Approval of Assumption of Executory Contract has been scheduled for February 10, 2016 in room 200, United States Courthouse, Gary, Indiana before the Honorable Frances B. Fair, Bankruptcy Judge.

CERTIFICATE OF TRANSMITTAL AND SERVICE BY MAIL

The undersigned certifies under penalty of perjury that he or she has, on the date shown below, by first class mail addressed to their respective addresses of record in this case, transmitted and served a true copy of this document to the United States Trustee and Jones Realty, Inc., 6700 East Spruce Street, Chicago, IL 60624.

Date: ______________________________ ______________________________

UNITED STATES BANKRUPTCY COURT
NORTHERN DISTRICT OF INDIANA

IN RE	HARDTIMES SUPPLY CO., INC.,	)	
	an Indiana Corporation,	)	Case No. 16-00019
		)	
	Debtor	)	Chapter 11

MOTION FOR APPROVAL OF REJECTION OF EXECUTORY CONTRACT AND NOTICE OF HEARING

The Debtor, as a debtor in possession, by its attorney, represents as follows:

1. The Debtor filed a voluntary petition under Chapter 11 of the Bankruptcy Code on January 5, 2016 and since that time has been operating its business as a debtor in possession.

2. On or about August 10, 2015 the Debtor entered into a contract with The Expensive Shingle Co. of 2000 Gold Street, Chicago, Illinois for the purchase of 50,000 gold-plated shingles for the total price of $65,000, payable as follows: $6,500 when the contract was signed and the balance upon delivery of the shingles.

3. The Debtor paid the $6,500 deposit on or about August 10, 2015 and to date has received shipment of only 10,000 of the shingles from the seller. The Debtor has determined that the shingles are not as represented by the seller and that the rejection of the contract to purchase the shingles would be in the best interest of the estate. Further, several of the parties for whom the Debtor purchase the shingles no longer want the shingles and the Debtor has no other method of disposing of the shingles should they be delivered by the seller.

WHEREFORE, the Debtor requests the entry of an order approving the rejection by the Debtor of the executory contract described above in this Motion.

Dated: January 22, 2016

Reddy, Willing & Able

by ______________________________

Leo E. Lawnoer
Attorneys for Debtor in Possession
1000 First Street
Gary, Indiana 46407

PLEASE TAKE NOTICE that a hearing on the above Motion For Approval of Rejection of Executory Contract has been scheduled for February 10, 2016 in room 200, United States Courthouse, Gary, Indiana before the Honorable Frances B. Fair, Bankruptcy Judge.

CERTIFICATE OF TRANSMITTAL AND SERVICE BY MAIL

The undersigned certifies under penalty of perjury that he or she has, on the date shown below, by first class mail addressed to their respective addresses of record in this case, transmitted and served a true copy of this document to the United States Trustee and The Expensive Shingle Co., 2000 Gold Street, Chicago, IL 60638.

Date: ______________________________ ______________________________

UNITED STATES BANKRUPTCY COURT
FOR THE NORTHERN DISTRICT OF INDIANA

In re: HARDTIMES SUPPLY CO., INC. Debtor. Address: P.O. Box 3355 Gary, Indiana Employer's Tax Identification No. 20-33945998	))))))))))))	Bankruptcy Case No. 16-19031-HRT Chapter 11

DEBTOR'S PLAN OF REORGANIZATION, DATED MARCH 15, 2016

ARTICLE I
SUMMARY

This Plan of Reorganization (the "Plan") under chapter 11 of the Bankruptcy Code (the "Code") proposes to pay creditors of Hardtimes Supply Co., Inc. (the "Debtor") from a combination of a cash infusion by the equity holders, the sale of certain assets, and future income of the Debtor.

This Plan provides for one class of secured claims; four classes of unsecured claims; and one class of equity security holders. Unsecured creditors holding allowed claims will receive distributions, which the proponent of this Plan has valued at approximately thirty cents on the dollar. This Plan also provides for the payment of administrative and priority claims in full as of the effective date of this Plan.

All creditors and equity security holders should refer to Articles III through VI of this Plan for information regarding the precise treatment of their claim. A disclosure statement that provides more detailed information regarding this Plan and the rights of creditors and equity security holders has been circulated with this Plan. **Your rights may be affected. You should read these papers carefully and discuss them with your attorney, if you have one. (If you do not have an attorney, you may wish to consult one.)**

ARTICLE II
CLASSIFICATION OF CLAIMS AND INTERESTS

2.01 Class 1. The claim of Big Bank of Boston, to the extent allowed as a secured claim under § 506 of the Code.

2.02 Class 2. The unsecured claims allowed under § 502 of the Code of Ace Shingle Company and Harris Lumber, Inc.

2.03 Class 3. All other unsecured claims allowed under § 502 of the Code.

2.04 Class 4. Equity interests of the Debtor.

ARTICLE III
TREATMENT OF ADMINISTRATIVE EXPENSE CLAIMS, U.S. TRUSTEES FEES, AND PRIORITY TAX CLAIMS

3.01 Unclassified Claims. Under section § 1123(a)(1), administrative expense claims, and priority tax claims are not in classes.

3.02 **Administrative Expense Claims.** Each holder of an administrative expense claim allowed under § 503 of the Code, will be paid in full on the effective date of this Plan (as defined in Article VII), in cash, or upon such other terms as may be agreed upon by the holder of the claim and the Debtor.

3.03 **Priority Tax Claims.** Each holder of a priority tax claim, if one exists, will be paid upon terms consistent with § 1129(a)(9)(C) of the Code.

3.04 **United States Trustee Fees.** All fees required to be paid by 28 U.S.C. § 1930(a)(6) (U.S. Trustee Fees) will accrue and be timely paid until the case is closed, dismissed, or converted to another chapter of the Code. Any U.S. Trustee Fees owed on or before the effective date of this Plan will be paid on the effective date.

ARTICLE IV
TREATMENT OF CLAIMS AND INTERESTS UNDER THE PLAN

4.01 Claims and interests shall be treated as follows under this Plan:

Class	Impairment	Treatment
Class 1 – Secured Claim of Big Bank of Boston	Impaired	The secured claim of Big Bank of Boston will be paid an amount equal to $24,567.00 on the effective date of the Plan to cure defaults in the Debtor's obligations under the secured promissory note dated May 1, 2006. Additionally, on the effective date of the Plan, the Debtor will execute a First Amended Promissory Note and Security Agreement in favor of Big Bank of Boston (in substantially the same form and content as the attached specimen), and will thereafter make 36 equal monthly payments of $3,870.00 to the Class 1 claimant in full satisfaction of the Debtor's obligations under said Note. The Class 1 claimant will be allowed to retain a first position security interest in all of the Debtor's assets during the term of the First Amended Promissory Note.
Class 2 – Unsecured Creditors: Ace Shingle and Harris Lumber	Impaired	The unsecured allowed claims of Ace Shingle and Harris Lumber will be paid 50% of their respective claims on the effective date of the plan, and will be paid two additional payments each equal to 15% of their respective claims on the first and second anniversary of the effective date of the Plan.
Class 3 – General Unsecured Claims	Impaired	All general unsecured claims will be paid an amount equal to 15% of each claimant's respective allowed claim 180 days after the effective date of the Plan.
Class 4 – Equity Security Holders of the Debtor	Impaired	The Bylaws of the Debtor shall be amended as of the effective date of the Plan so as to extinguish any provisions pertaining to annual mandatory dividend payments to shareholders of the Debtor. Additionally, the Debtor will issue an additional 500 shares of common stock to current equity holder John Jones in exchange for his $50,000 capital contribution to the Debtor.

ARTICLE V
ALLOWANCE AND DISALLOWANCE OF CLAIMS

5.01 Disputed Claim. A disputed claim is a claim that has not been allowed or disallowed by a final non-appealable order, and as to which either: (i) a proof of claim has been filed or deemed filed, and the Debtor or another party in interest has filed an objection; or (ii) no proof of claim has been filed, and the Debtor has scheduled such claim as disputed, contingent, or unliquidated.

5.02 Delay of Distribution on a Disputed Claim. No distribution will be made on account of a disputed claim unless such claim is allowed by a final non-appealable order.

5.03 Settlement of Disputed Claims. The Debtor will have the power and authority to settle and compromise a disputed claim with court approval and compliance with Rule 9019 of the Federal Rules of Bankruptcy Procedure.

ARTICLE VI
PROVISIONS FOR EXECUTORY CONTRACTS AND UNEXPIRED LEASES

6.01 Assumed Executory Contracts and Unexpired Leases.

(a) The Debtor assumes the following executory contracts and/or unexpired leases effective upon the effective date of this Plan as provided in Article VII:

Lease No. 10987823 by and between Debtor and Ford Commercial Truck Center of Gary, Inc., for the lease of two F550 Super Duty commercial flat bad trucks, VIN #s 9987876655442347287409 and 9987876655442347287410, dated November 25, 2011 and expiring November 24, 2016.

(b) The Debtor will be conclusively deemed to have rejected all executory contracts and/or unexpired leases not expressly assumed under section 6.01(a) above, or before the date of the order confirming this Plan, upon the effective date of this Plan. A proof of a claim arising from the rejection of an executory contract or unexpired lease under this section must be filed no later than sixty (60) days after the date of the order confirming this Plan.

ARTICLE VII
MEANS FOR IMPLEMENTATION OF THE PLAN

The Plan will be implemented by the restructuring of the Debtor's secured loan with Big Bank of Boston and the cash infusion made by current shareholder John Jones. On the Effective date of the Plan, Mr. Jones will contribute $70,000 to the capital of the Debtor and will receive 500 shares of common stock in the Debtor. Said exchange will make Mr. Jones the majority shareholder of the Debtor, and he will be elected to serve as the President and Chairman of the Board of Directors of the Debtor. The Debtor. The Debtor will reject the remaining term of the lease pertaining to its wholesale operations located at 2345 East Ave., Gary, Indiana, 46407, and consolidate operations at its principal outlet at 667 First Street, Gary, Indiana 46406. The Debtor will reduce its employment staff by 6 as of the effective date of the Plan. The Debtor will also offer for sale 4 delivery trucks currently used at the 2345 East Avenue location.

ARTICLE VIII
GENERAL PROVISIONS

8.01 Definitions and Rules of Construction. The definitions and rules of construction set forth in §§ 101 and 102 of the Code shall apply when terms defined or construed in the Code are used in this Plan.

8.02 Effective Date of Plan. The effective date of this Plan is the 15th business day following the date of the entry of the order of confirmation. But if a stay of the confirmation order is in effect on that date, the effective date will be the first business day after that date on which no stay of the confirmation order is in effect, provided that the confirmation order has not been vacated.

8.03 Severability. If any provision in this Plan is determined to be unenforceable, the determination will in no way limit or affect the enforceability and operative effect of any other provision of this Plan.

8.04 Binding Effect. The rights and obligations of any entity named or referred to in this Plan will be binding upon, and will inure to the benefit of the successors or assigns of such entity.

8.05 Captions. The headings contained in this Plan are for convenience of reference only and do not affect the meaning or interpretation of this Plan.

8.06 Controlling Effect. Unless a rule of law or procedure is supplied by federal law (including the Code or the Federal Rules of Bankruptcy Procedure), the laws of the State of Indiana govern this Plan and any agreements, documents, and instruments executed in connection with this Plan, except as otherwise provided in this Plan.

8.07 Corporate Governance. Pursuant to 11 U.S.C. § 1123(a)(6), the Articles of Incorporation, Charter, and/or Bylaws of the Debtor shall be amended so as to prohibit the issuance of nonvoting stock and to provide, as to classes of stock possessing voting rights, appropriate distribution of voting power among such classes, including, adequate provisions for the election of directors in the event of default in the payment of dividends.

ARTICLE IX
DISCHARGE

9.01 Discharge. On the confirmation date of this Plan, the debtor will be discharged from any debt that arose before confirmation of this Plan, subject to the occurrence of the effective date, to the extent specified in § 1141(d)(1)(A) of the Code, except that the Debtor will not be discharged of any debt: (i) imposed by this Plan; (ii) of a kind specified in § 1141(d)(6)(A) if a timely complaint was filed in accordance with Rule 4007(c) of the Federal Rules of Bankruptcy Procedure; or (iii) of a kind specified in § 1141(d)(6)(B).

ARTICLE X
OTHER PROVISIONS- JURISDICTION

The Court shall retain jurisdiction over the parties to, and the subject matter of, this Plan and all matters related thereto until the Plan has been fully consummated and the case closed, or until the case is dismissed or converted to another chapter of the Code.

Respectfully submitted,

By: ______________________________

The Plan Proponent

By: ______________________________

Attorney for the Plan Proponent

UNITED STATES BANKRUPTCY COURT
FOR THE NORTHERN DISTRICT OF INDIANA

In re:	)	
	)	Bankruptcy Case No.
HARDTIMES SUPPLY CO., INC.	)	16-19031-HRT
	)	Chapter 11
Debtor.	)	
	)	
Address: P.O. Box 3355	)	
Gary, Indiana	)	
	)	
	)	
Employer's Tax Identification	)	
No. 20-33945998	)	

DEBTOR'S DISCLOSURE STATEMENT, DATED MARCH 15, 2016

I. INTRODUCTION

This is the disclosure statement (the "Disclosure Statement") in the small business chapter 11 case of Hardtimes Supply Co., Inc. (the "Debtor"). This Disclosure Statement contains information about the Debtor and describes the Debtor's Plan of Reorganization, dated March 15, 2016 (the "Plan") filed by the Debtor on March 15, 2016. A full copy of the Plan is attached to this Disclosure Statement as Exhibit A. ***Your rights may be affected. You should read the Plan and this Disclosure Statement carefully and discuss them with your attorney. If you do not have an attorney, you may wish to consult one.***

The proposed distributions under the Plan are discussed in Section III of this Disclosure Statement. General unsecured creditors are classified in Class 3, and will receive a distribution of 15% of their allowed claims, to be distributed 180 days after the effective date of the Plan.

A. Purpose of This Document

This Disclosure Statement describes:

- The Debtor and significant events during the bankruptcy case,
- How the Plan proposes to treat claims or equity interests of the type you hold (*i.e.*, what you will receive on your claim or equity interest if the plan is confirmed),
- Who can vote on or object to the Plan,
- What factors the Bankruptcy Court (the "Court") will consider when deciding whether to confirm the Plan,
- Why the Debtor believes the Plan is feasible, and how the treatment of your claim or equity interest under the Plan compares to what you would receive on your claim or equity interest in liquidation, and
- The effect of confirmation of the Plan.

Be sure to read the Plan as well as the Disclosure Statement. This Disclosure Statement describes the Plan, but it is the Plan itself that will, if confirmed, establish your rights.

B. Deadlines for Voting and Objecting; Date of Plan Confirmation Hearing

The Court has not yet confirmed the Plan described in this Disclosure Statement. This section describes the procedures pursuant to which the Plan will or will not be confirmed.

1. *Time and Place of the Hearing to Confirm the plan*

The hearing at which the Court will determine whether to confirm the Plan will take place on May 15, 2016, at 9:30 a.m., in Courtroom 6, at the U.S. Bankruptcy Court, 401 South Michigan Street, South Bend, Indiana 46634.

2. *Deadline For Voting to Accept or Reject the Plan*

If you are entitled to vote to accept or reject the plan, vote on the enclosed ballot and return the ballot in the enclosed envelope to Leo Lawnoer, Esq., 1000 First Street, Gary, Indiana 46407. See section IV.A. below for a discussion of voting eligibility requirements.

Your ballot must be received by May 1, 2016 or it will not be counted.

3. *Deadline For Objecting to the Confirmation of the Plan*

Objections to the confirmation of the Plan must be filed with the Court and served upon Leo Lawnoer, Esq., 1000 First Street, Gary, Indiana 46407 by May 1, 2016.

4. *Identity of Person to Contact for More Information*

If you want additional information about the Plan, you should contact Leo Lawnoer, Esq., 1000 First Street, Gary, Indiana 46407.

C. **Disclaimer**

The Court has approved this Disclosure Statement as containing adequate information to enable parties affected by the Plan to make an informed judgment about its terms. The Court has not yet determined whether the Plan meets the legal requirements for confirmation, and the fact that the Court has approved this Disclosure Statement does not constitute an endorsement of the Plan by the Court, or a recommendation that it be accepted.

II. BACKGROUND

A. **Description and History of the Debtor's Business**

The Debtor is a corporation. Since 1976, the Debtor has been in the business of supplying building materials to general contractors in the Gary, Indiana area. The Debtor specializes in providing supplies to high-end residential contractors.

B. **Insiders of the Debtor**

A detailed list of the names of Debtor's insiders as defined in §101(31) of the United States Bankruptcy Code (the "Code") and their relationship to the Debtor are as follows:

John J. Jones owns 500 shares of common stock and is the President of the Debtor. His compensation for the prior two years has been $60,000 annually. He has received dividends totaling $10,000 annually for the past two years.

Sarah Smith owns 500 shares of common stock and is the Vice President of the Debtor. Her compensation for the prior two years has been $40,000 annually. She has received dividends totaling $10,000 annually for the past two years.

James Smith owns 200 shares of common stock of the Debtor. He is not employed by the Debtor. He has received dividends totaling $4,000 annually for the past two years.

C. **Management of the Debtor Before and During the Bankruptcy**

During the two years prior to the date on which the bankruptcy petition was filed, the officers, directors, managers or other persons in control of the Debtor (collectively the "Managers") were John Jones (President) and Sarah Smith (Vice President).

The Managers of the Debtor during the Debtor's chapter 11 case have been: John Jones (President) and Sarah Smith (Vice President).

After the effective date of the order confirming the Plan, the directors, officers, and voting trustees of the Debtor, any affiliate of the Debtor participating in a joint Plan with the Debtor, or successor of the Debtor under the Plan (collectively the "Post Confirmation Managers"), will be: John Jones (President) and Sarah Smith (Vice President). The responsibilities and compensation of these Post Confirmation Managers are described in section III.D.2 of this Disclosure Statement.

D. **Events Leading to Chapter 11 Filing**

In November of 2013, the Debtor began having difficulty meeting its obligations to creditors as they became due because of the chapter 7 bankruptcy filing of WC Homes, LLC ("WC"). WC was a major client of the Debtor, and at the time of the chapter 7 filing, owed the Debtor $89,167.58. The Debtor has collected nothing on this account. Additionally, the recession has affected builders (and thus their suppliers) quite hard in the Gary, Indiana vicinity.

E. **Significant Events During the Bankruptcy Case**

During the bankruptcy case, the Debtor has sold the materials if was allowed to recapture from the bankruptcy estate of WC to another contractor (Binford Construction) who has taken over 8 of uncompleted homes from WC. Additionally, the Debtor has reached an agreement with Binford Construction to be the sole supplier of materials for a mixed-use project that Binford is currently negotiating with the city of Fort Wayne. A copy of the agreement with Binford is attached to this Disclosure Statement.

The Debtor has retained the law firm of Reddy, Willing & Able, P.C. to represent it in these chapter 11 proceedings. The Debtor has also retained Michael Crouch as its accountant for these proceedings. Copies of their retainer agreements are attached to this Disclosure Statement.

The Debtor has filed a mechanic's lien foreclosure action (14CV1897) post-petition to recover money for materials the Debtor delivered to a jobsite on behalf of Pachello Hardwood Finishes, LLC. The Debtor expects to recover $14,890.00, plus interest and attorneys' fees in this case. Copies of the pertinent documents for this lawsuit are attached to this Disclosure Statement.

The President and Vice-President have taken reduced salaries since the petition date in an effort to improve the Debtor's financial stability. Each has taken a $10,000 annual reduction in pay.

F. **Projected Recovery of Avoidable Transfers**

The Debtor has not yet completed its investigation with regard to prepetition transactions. If you received a payment or other transfer within 90 days of the bankruptcy, or other transfer avoidable under the Code, the Debtor may seek to avoid such transfer.

G. **Claims Objections**

Except to the extent that a claim is already allowed pursuant to a final non-appealable order, the Debtor reserves the right to object to claims. Therefore, even if your claim is allowed for voting purposes, you may not be entitled to a distribution if an objection to your claim is later upheld. The procedures for resolving disputed claims are set forth in Article V of the Plan.

H. **Current and Historical Financial Conditions**

The identity and fair market value of the estate's assets are listed in Exhibit B.

The Debtor's most recent financial statements issued before bankruptcy, each of which was filed with the Court, are set forth in Exhibit C.

The most recent post-petition monthly operating report filed since the commencement of the Debtor's bankruptcy case is set forth in Exhibit D.

III. SUMMARY OF THE PLAN OF REORGANIZATION AND TREATMENT OF CLAIMS AND EQUITY INTERESTS

A. **What is the Purpose of the Plan of Reorganization?**

As required by the Code, the Plan places claims and equity interests in various classes and describes the treatment each class will receive. The Plan also states whether each class of claims or equity interests is impaired or unimpaired. If the Plan is confirmed, your recovery will be limited to the amount provided by the Plan.

B. **Unclassified Claims**

Certain types of claims are automatically entitled to specific treatment under the Code. They are not considered impaired, and holders of such claims do not vote on the Plan. They may, however, object if, in their view, their treatment under the Plan does not comply with that required by the Code. As such, the Plan Proponent has *not* placed the following claims in any class:

1. *Administrative Expenses*

Administrative expenses are costs or expenses of administering the Debtor's chapter 11 case which are allowed under § 507(a)(2) of the Code. Administrative expenses also include the value of any goods sold to the Debtor in the ordinary course of business and received within 20 days before the date of the bankruptcy petition. The Code requires that all administrative expenses be paid on the effective date of the Plan, unless a particular claimant agrees to a different treatment.

The following chart lists the Debtor's estimated administrative expenses, and their proposed treatment under the Plan:

Type	Estimated Amount Owed	Proposed Treatment
Expenses Arising in the Ordinary Course of Business After the Petition Date	$20,000.00	Paid in full on the effective date of the Plan, or according to terms of obligation if later
The Value of Goods Received in the Ordinary Course of Business Within 20 Days Before the Petition Date	$6,890.00	Paid in full on the effective date of the Plan, or according to terms of obligation if later
Professional Fees, as approved by the Court	$12,000.00	Paid in full on the effective date of the Plan, or according to separate written agreement, or according to court order if such fees have not been approved by the Court on the effective date of the Plan
Clerk's Office Fees	-0-	Paid in full on the effective date of the Plan
Other administrative expenses	-0-	Paid in full on the effective date of the Plan or according to separate written agreement
Office of the U.S. Trustee Fees	$1,650.00	Paid in full on the effective date of the Plan
TOTAL	$40,540.00	

2. *Priority Tax Claims*

Priority tax claims are unsecured income, employment, and other taxes described by § 507(a)(8) of the Code. Unless the holder of such a § 507(a)(8) priority tax claim agrees otherwise, it must receive the present value of such claim, in regular installments paid over a period not exceeding 5 years from the order of relief. The Debtor does not have any priority tax claims.

C. **Classes of Claims and Equity Interests**

The following are the classes set forth in the Plan, and the proposed treatment that they will receive under the Plan:

1. *Classes of Secured Claims*

Allowed Secured Claims are claims secured by property of the Debtor's bankruptcy estate (or that are subject to setoff) to the extent allowed as secured claims under § 506 of the Code. If the value of the collateral or setoffs securing the creditor's claim is less than the amount of the creditor's allowed claim, the deficiency will be classified as a general unsecured claim.

The following chart lists all classes containing Debtor's secured prepetition claims and their proposed treatment under the Plan:

Class #	Description	Insider? (Yes or No)	Impairment	Treatment
1	*Secured claim of:* Name = Big Bank of Boston Collateral description = all assets of the Debtor Allowed Secured Amount = $163,887.00 Priority of lien = first Principal owed = $139,320.00 Pre-pet. arrearage = $24,567.00 Total claim = $163,887.00	NO	Impaired	Monthly Pmt = $3,870.00 Pmts begin upon plan effective date Pmts end 36 months after plan effective date [Balloon pmt] = N/A Interest rate % = 6.5% Treatment of Lien = retained during plan Additional payment_ required to cure defaults = $24,567.00

2. *Classes of Priority Unsecured Claims*

Certain priority claims that are referred to in §§ 507(a)(1), (4), (5), (6), and (7) of the Code are required to be placed in classes. The Code requires that each holder of such a claim receive cash on the effective date of the Plan equal to the allowed amount of such claim. However, a class of holders of such claims may vote to accept different treatment. The Debtor has no priority unsecured claims.

3. *Classes of General Unsecured Claims*

General unsecured claims are not secured by property of the estate and are not entitled to priority under § 507(a) of the Code.

The following chart identifies the Plan's proposed treatment of Classes 2 and 3, which contain general unsecured claims against the Debtor:

Class#	Description	Impairment	Treatment
2	Unsecured claims of Ace Shingle Company and Harris Lumber	Impaired	Paid 50% of allowed claim on effective date of plan, and will be paid two additional payments of 15% of each allowed claim on the first and second anniversary of the effective date of the Plan.
3	General Unsecured Class	Impaired	One payment made 180 days after the effective date of the Plan. = Estimated percent of claim paid = 15%

4. *Class of Equity Interest Holders*

Equity interest holders are parties who hold an ownership interest (*i.e.,* equity interest) in the Debtor. In a corporation, entities holding preferred or common stock are equity interest holders. In a partnership, equity interest holders include both general and limited partners. In a limited liability company ("LLC"), the equity interest holders are the members. Finally, with respect to an individual who is a debtor, the Debtor is the equity interest holder.

The following chart sets forth the Plan's proposed treatment of the one class of equity interest holders:

Class#	Description	Impairment	Treatment
4	Equity interest holders	Impaired	Shares diluted by issuance of 500 new shares of common stock to John Jones for capital infusion of $70,000. Mandatory dividend right extinguished.

D. **Means of Implementing the Plan**

1. *Source of Payments*

Payments and distributions under the Plan will be funded by the operations of the Debtor and by a one time cash infusion of $70,000 made by John Jones. Additional funds may come from litigation the debtor is currently pursuing and from the sale of 4 delivery trucks currently owned by the Debtor. Reduction of employment staff by 6 employees and debt re-structuring with Class 1 creditor allows greater monthly income to fund growth strategies.

2. *Post-confirmation Management*

The Post-Confirmation Managers of the Debtor, and their compensation, shall be as follows:

Name	Affiliations	Insider (yes or no)?	Position	Compensation
John Jones	Stockholder	Yes	President	$50,000.00
Sarah Smith	Stockholder	Yes	Vice-President	$30,000.00

E. **Risk Factors**

The proposed Plan has the following risks:

Binford Construction may not obtain approval of its planned unit development in Fort Wayne. The Recession could continue into 2016. The mechanic's lien action may not prevail. The Debtor may not be able to obtain the price it desires for the 4 trucks it is selling.

F. **Executory Contracts and Unexpired Leases**

The Plan, in Exhibit 6.1, lists all executory contracts and unexpired leases that the Debtor will assume under the Plan. Assumption means that the Debtor has elected to continue to perform the obligations under such contracts and unexpired leases, and to cure defaults of the type that must be cured under the Code, if any. Exhibit 6.1 also lists how the Debtor will cure and compensate the other party to such contract or lease for any such defaults.

If you object to the assumption of your unexpired lease or executory contract, the proposed cure of any defaults, or the adequacy of assurance of performance, you must file and serve your objection of the Plan within the deadline for objecting to the confirmation of the Plan, unless the Court has set an earlier time.

All executory contracts and unexpired leases that are not listed in Exhibit 6.1 will be rejected under the Plan. Consult your adviser or attorney for more specific information about particular contracts or leases.

If you object to the rejection of your contract or lease, you must file and serve your objection to the Plan within the deadline for objecting to the confirmation of the Plan.

G. **Tax Consequences of Plan**

Creditors and Equity Interest Holders Concerned with How the Plan May Affect Their Tax Liability Should Consult with Their Own Accountants, Attorneys, and/or Advisors.

The debtor does not anticipate any adverse tax consequences based upon its performance under the Plan.

IV. CONFIRMATION REQUIREMENTS AND PROCEDURES

To be confirmable, the Plan must meet the requirements listed in §§ 1129(a) or (b) of the Code. These include the requirements that: the Plan must be proposed in good faith; at least one impaired class of claims must accept the plan, without counting votes of insiders; the Plan must distribute to each creditor and equity interest holder at least as much as the creditor or equity interest holder would receive in a chapter 7 liquidation case, unless the creditor or equity interest holder votes to accept the Plan; and the Plan must be feasible. These requirements are not the only requirements listed in § 1129, and they are not the only requirements for confirmation.

A. **Who May Vote or Object**

Any party in interest may object to the confirmation of the Plan if the party believes that the requirements for confirmation are not met.

Many parties in interest, however, are not entitled to vote to accept or reject the Plan. A creditor or equity interest holder has a right to vote for or against the Plan only if that creditor or equity interest holder has a claim or equity interest that is both (1) allowed or allowed for voting purposes and (2) impaired.

In this case, the Plan Proponent believes that classes 1, 2, and 3 are impaired and that holders of claims in each of these classes are therefore entitled to vote to accept or reject the Plan. The Plan Proponent believes that class 4 is impaired, however, holders of claims in this class do not have the right to vote to accept or reject the Plan.

1. *What Is an Allowed Claim or an Allowed Equity Interest?*

Only a creditor or equity interest holder with an allowed claim or an allowed equity interest has the right to vote on the Plan. Generally, a claim or equity interest is allowed if either (1) the Debtor has scheduled the claim on the Debtor's schedules, unless the claim has been scheduled as disputed, contingent, or unliquidated, or (2) the creditor has filed a proof of claim or equity interest, unless an objection has been filed to such proof of claim or equity interest. When a claim or equity interest is not allowed, the creditor or equity interest holder holding the claim or equity interest cannot vote unless the Court, after notice and hearing, either overrules the objection or allows the claim or equity interest for voting purposes pursuant to Rule 3018(a) of the Federal Rules of Bankruptcy Procedure.

The deadline for filing a proof of claim in this case is April 25, 2016.

2. *What is an Impaired Claim or Impaired Equity Interest?*

As noted above, the holder of an allowed claim or equity interest has the right to vote only if it is in a class that is *impaired* under the Plan. As provided in § 1124 of the Code, a class is considered impaired if the Plan alters the legal, equitable, or contractual rights of the members of that class.

3. *Who is **Not** Entitled to Vote*

The holders of the following five types of claims and equity interests are *not* entitled to vote:

- holders of claims and equity interests that have been disallowed by an order of the Court;
- holders of other claims or equity interests that are not "allowed claims" or "allowed equity interests" (as discussed above), unless they have been "allowed" for voting purposes.
- holders of claims or equity interests in unimpaired classes;
- holders of claims entitled to priority pursuant to §§ 507(a)(2), (a)(3), and (a)(8) of the Code; and
- holders of claims or equity interests in classes that do not receive or retain any value under the Plan;
- administrative expenses.

Even If You Are Not Entitled to Vote on the Plan, You Have a Right to Object to the Confirmation of the Plan.

4. *Who Can Vote in More Than One Class*

A creditor whose claim has been allowed in part as a secured claim and in part as an unsecured claim, or who otherwise holds claims in multiple classes, is entitled to accept or reject a Plan in each capacity, and should cast one ballot for each claim.

B. **Votes Necessary to Confirm the Plan**

If impaired classes exist, the Court cannot confirm the Plan unless (1) at least one impaired class of creditors has accepted the Plan without counting the votes of any insiders within that class, and (2) all impaired classes have voted to accept the Plan, unless the Plan is eligible to be confirmed by "cram down" on non-accepting classes, as discussed later in Section B.2.

1. *Votes Necessary for a Class to Accept the Plan*

A class of claims accepts the Plan if both of the following occur: (1) the holders of more than one-half (1/2) of the allowed claims in the class, who vote, cast their votes to accept the Plan, and (2) the holders of at least two-thirds (2/3) in dollar amount of the allowed claims in the class, who vote, cast their votes to accept the Plan.

A class of equity interests accepts the Plan if the holders of at least two-thirds (2/3) in amount of the allowed equity interests in the class, who vote, cast their votes to accept the Plan.

2. *Treatment of Nonaccepting Classes*

Even if one or more impaired classes reject the Plan, the Court may nonetheless confirm the Plan if the nonaccepting classes are treated in the manner prescribed by § 1129(b) of the Code. A plan that binds nonaccepting classes is commonly referred to as a "cram down" plan. The Code allows the Plan to bind nonaccepting classes of claims or equity interests if it meets all the requirements for consensual confirmation except the voting requirements of § 1129(a)(8) of the Code, does not "discriminate unfairly," and is "fair and equitable" toward each impaired class that has not voted to accept the Plan.

You should consult your own attorney if a "cramdown" confirmation will affect your claim or equity interest, as the variations on this general rule are numerous and complex.

C. **Liquidation Analysis**

To confirm the Plan, the Court must find that all creditors and equity interest holders who do not accept the Plan will receive at least as much under the Plan as such claim and equity interest holders would receive in a chapter 7 liquidation. A liquidation analysis is attached to this Disclosure Statement as Exhibit E. As the attached liquidation analysis presents, all unsecured creditors would receive nothing under liquidation because the secured claimant in Class 1 would be allowed to repossess all assets of the Debtor in partial satisfaction of its secured claim.

D. **Feasibility**

The Court must find that confirmation of the Plan is not likely to be followed by the liquidation, or the need for further financial reorganization, of the Debtor or any successor to the Debtor, unless such liquidation or reorganization is proposed in the Plan.

1. *Ability to Initially Fund Plan*

The Plan Proponent believes that the Debtor will have enough cash on hand on the effective date of the Plan to pay all the claims and expenses that are entitled to be paid on that date. Tables showing the amount of cash on hand on the effective date of the Plan, and the sources of that cash are attached to this Disclosure Statement as Exhibit F.

2. *Ability to Make Future Plan Payments and Operate Without Further Reorganization*

The Debtor must also show that it will have enough cash over the life of the Plan to make the required Plan payments.

The Debtor has provided projected financial information. Those projections are listed in Exhibit G.

The Debtor's financial projections show that the Debtor will have an aggregate annual average cash flow, after paying operating expenses and post-confirmation taxes, of $100,000- $125,000. The final Plan payment is expected to be paid on June 1, 2016.

You Should Consult with Your Accountant or other Financial Advisor If You Have Any Questions Pertaining to These Projections.

V. **EFFECT OF CONFIRMATION OF PLAN**

A. **DISCHARGE OF DEBTOR**

Discharge. On the effective date of the Plan, the Debtor shall be discharged from any debt that arose before confirmation of the Plan, subject to the occurrence of the effective date, to the extent specified in § 1141(d)(1)(A) of the Code, except that the Debtor shall not be discharged of any debt (i) imposed by the Plan, (ii) of a kind specified in § 1141(d)(6)(A) if a timely complaint was filed in accordance with Rule 4007(c) of the Federal Rules of Bankruptcy Procedure, or (iii) of a kind specified in § 1141(d)(6)(B). After the effective date of the Plan your claims against the Debtor will be limited to the debts described in clauses (i) through (iii) of the preceding sentence.

B. **Modification of Plan**

The Plan Proponent may modify the Plan at any time before confirmation of the Plan. However, the Court may require a new disclosure statement and/or revoting on the Plan. The Plan Proponent may also seek to modify the Plan at any time after confirmation only if (1) the Plan has not been substantially consummated *and* (2) the Court authorizes the proposed modifications after notice and a hearing.

C. **Final Decree**

Once the estate has been fully administered, as provided in Rule 3022 of the Federal Rules of Bankruptcy Procedure, the Plan Proponent, or such other party as the Court shall designate in the Plan Confirmation Order, shall file a motion with the Court to obtain a final decree to close the case. Alternatively, the Court may enter such a final decree on its own motion.

____

[Signature of the Plan Proponent]

____

[Signature of the Attorney for the Plan Proponent]

EXHIBITS

Exhibit A – Copy of Proposed Plan of Reorganization
Exhibit B – Identity and Value of Material Assets of Debtor
Exhibit C – Prepetition Financial Statements
Exhibit D – Most Recently Filed Postpetition Monthly Operating Report
Exhibit E – Liquidation Analysis
Exhibit F – Cash on hand on the effective date of the Plan
Exhibit G – Projections of Cash Flow and Earnings for Post-Confirmation Period

UNITED STATES BANKRUPTCY COURT
NORTHERN DISTRICT OF INDIANA

IN RE	HARDTIMES SUPPLY CO., INC.,	)	
	an Indiana Corporation, aka Hardtimes	)	Case No. 16-00019
	Supply Company	)	
	Debtor	)	Chapter 11
	Employer's Tax Identification No.	)	
	82-0778225	)	

ORDER CONDITIONALLY APPROVING DISCLOSURE STATEMENT, FIXING TIMES FOR FILING ACCEPTANCES OR REJECTIONS OF PLAN, FOR FILING OBJECTIONS TO THE DISCLOSURE STATEMENT, AND FOR FILING OBJECTIONS TO CONFIRMATION OF THE PLAN, AND FIXING DATES FOR HEARING ON FINAL APPROVAL OF DISCLOSURE STATEMENT IF A TIMELY OBJECTION IS FILED AND FOR CONFIRMATION HEARING, COMBINED WITH NOTICE THEREOF

A Disclosure Statement dated March 5, 2016 (the Disclosure Statement) having been filed by Hardtimes Supply Co., Inc., the Debtor herein, on March 10, 2016 referring to a Plan of Reorganization dated March 5, 2016 (the Plan) filed by the said Debtor on March 10, 2016; and

It having been conditionally determined that the Disclosure Statement contains adequate information;

IT IS ORDERED, AND NOTICE IS HEREBY GIVEN THAT:

1. The Disclosure Statement dated March 5, 2016 filed by Hardtimes Supply Co., Inc., the Debtor, is hereby conditionally approved.

2. May 1, 2016 is fixed as the last day for filing written acceptances or rejections of the Plan referred to above.

3. Within seven days after the entry of this order, the Plan, the Disclosure Statement, and a ballot conforming to Official Form 314 shall be mailed to creditors, equity security holders, and other parties in interest, and shall be transmitted to the United States Trustee, as provided in Rules 3017(d) and 3017.1 of the Federal Rules of Bankruptcy Procedure.

4. If acceptances are filed for more than one plan, preferences among the plans so accepted may be indicated.

5. May 10, 2016 at 10:00 A.M. is fixed for the hearing on confirmation of the Plan and for the hearing on final approval of the Disclosure Statement if a timely objection is filed.

6. May 1, 2016 is fixed as the last day for filing and serving written objections to confirmation of the plan pursuant to Federal Rule of Bankruptcy Procedure 3020(b)(1).

7. May 1, 2016 is fixed as the last day for filing and serving objections to the Disclosure Statement pursuant to Rule 3017.1(c)(2) of the Federal Rules of Bankruptcy Procedure.

Dated: March 30, 2016

BY THE COURT

____
United States Bankruptcy Judge

(Cover letter for Rule 3017 or 3017.1 documents)

Hardtimes Supply Company
4455 West 39th Avenue
Gary, Indiana 46404
April 2, 2016

TO: The creditors of Hardtimes Supply Co., Inc.

Subject: Chapter 11 Plan of Reorganization filed by Hardtimes Supply Co., Inc.

Dear Creditor:

As you may be aware, Hardtimes Supply Co., Inc. has filed a proceeding under Chapter 11 of the United States Bankruptcy Code to reorganize the financial aspects of its business under the protection of the bankruptcy court. The recession in the building industry and the financial failure of one of its principal customers are the main reasons that the bankruptcy proceeding was filed.

We are pleased to present for your acceptance and approval a plan for the repayment of as much of our debts as is possible under the circumstances. A copy of our plan is enclosed with this letter. Also enclosed for your information is a copy of a disclosure statement that has been approved by the bankruptcy court and a summary of the court's opinion approving the disclosure statement. The facts and figures supporting our plan are set forth in the disclosure statement. Please take the time to read both the disclosure statement and the plan carefully.

We would like the plan to be accepted by the creditors of every class of impaired claims. A claim that is not paid in full is an impaired claim. To be accepted by a class of claims, the plan must be accepted by more than one-half of the creditors in the class and by creditors holding at least two-thirds of the total dollar amount of claims in the class. Your vote on the acceptance or rejection of our plan is important.

We are enclosing with this letter an official ballot for voting on the acceptance or rejection of our plan. To be counted, this ballot must be properly completed and filed with the clerk of the bankruptcy court, 200 East Court Street, Gary, Indiana, by May 1, 2016. We hope that you will vote to accept our plan.

Once again, please fill out the enclosed ballot and return it to either the undersigned or the clerk of the bankruptcy court in time for the ballot to be counted.

Very truly yours,

____

Joseph P. Jones, President,
Hardtimes Supply Co., Inc.

Enclosures: Plan of Reorganization dated March 5, 2016
Disclosure Statement dated March 5, 2016
Court Order Conditionally Approving Disclosure Statement and Fixing Times and Dates
Ballot For Accepting or Rejecting Plan

UNITED STATES BANKRUPTCY COURT
NORTHERN DISTRICT OF INDIANA

IN RE	HARDTIMES SUPPLY CO., INC.,	)	
	an Indiana Corporation, aka Hardtimes	)	Case No. 16-00019
	Supply Company	)	
	Debtor	)	Chapter 11
	Employer's Tax Identification No.	)	
	82-0778225	)	

(CLASS 7) BALLOT FOR ACCEPTING OR REJECTING PLAN OF REORGANIZATION

Hardtimes Supply Co., Inc., the Debtor, filed a plan of reorganization dated January 5, 2016 (the "Plan") for the Debtor in this case. The Court has conditionally approved a disclosure statement with respect to the Plan (the "Disclosure Statement"). The Disclosure Statement provides information to assist you in deciding how to vote your ballot. If you do not have a Disclosure Statement, you may obtain a copy from Leo E. Lawnoer, Attorney at Law, 1100 First Street, Gary, Indiana, 46407 (telephone: 219-222-1100, fax: 219-222-1101). Court approval of the disclosure statement does not indicate approval of the Plan by the Court.

You should review the Disclosure Statement and the Plan before you vote. You may wish to seek legal advice concerning the Plan and your classification and treatment under the Plan. Your claim has been placed in class 7 under the Plan. If you hold claims or equity interests in more than one class, you will receive a ballot for each class in which you are entitled to vote.

If your ballot is not received by Leo E. Lawnoer, Attorney at Law, at the address shown below on or before May 1, 2016, and if such deadline is not extended, your vote will not count as either an acceptance or a rejection of the Plan.

If the Plan is confirmed by the Bankruptcy Court it will be binding on you whether or not you vote.

ACCEPTANCE OR REJECTION OF THE PLAN

The undersigned, the holder of a Class 7 claim against the Debtor in the amount of Dollars ($)

(Check one box only)

☐ ACCEPTS THE PLAN ☐ REJECTS THE PLAN

Dated: ______________________

Print or type name: ____________________________________

Signature: ____________________________________

Title (if corporation or partnership) ________________________

Address: ____________________________________

____

RETURN THIS BALLOT TO:

Leo E. Lawnoer
Reddy, Willing & Able
Attorneys at Law
1000 First Street, Suite 600
Gary, IN 46407

UNITED STATES BANKRUPTCY COURT
NORTHERN DISTRICT OF INDIANA

IN RE	HARDTIMES SUPPLY CO., INC.,	)	
	an Illinois Corporation,	)	Case No. 16-00019
		)	
	Debtor	)	Chapter 11

OBJECTION TO CONFIRMATION OF PLAN

The Last National Bank of Gary, a secured and unsecured creditor of the Debtor, by its attorneys, objects to confirmation of the Plan dated March 5, 2016 filed and proposed by the Debtor on the grounds that the Plan does not comply with the requirements of Chapter 11 of the Bankruptcy Code or with other requirements of the Bankruptcy Code in the following particulars:

1. The Plan does not properly classify the secured claim of the Last National Bank of Gary in that the claim is impaired by the Plan, is not treated in the Plan as an impaired claim, and the holder of the claim will receive under the plan an amount that is less than what the holder would receive had the debtor been liquidated under Chapter 7 of the Bankruptcy Code on the effective date of the Plan.

2. The Plan was not proposed in good faith by the Debtor in that the primary purpose of the Plan and its proposal is to frustrate creditors and protect secured assets and not to reorganize the Debtor's business.

3. Confirmation of the Plan is likely to be followed by the liquidation or further financial reorganization of the Debtor in that the Plan is not feasible and the Debtor will be unable to make the payments required under the Plan and otherwise comply with the provisions of the Plan.

4. The Last National Bank of Gary, as a secured creditor, has not accepted the Plan.

5. The Plan seeks to modify a residential home mortgage in violation of 11 U.S.C. §1123(b)(5).

WHEREFORE, The Last National Bank of Gary objects to confirmation of the Plan of the debtor dated March 5, 2016 and moves this Honorable Court to deny confirmation of the Plan.

Dated: April 10, 2016

Hornblower & Fogbottom

by ______________________________

Horatio H. Hornblower
Attorneys for Last National Bank
400 Last National Bank Bldg.
Gary, Indiana 46410
Telephone: 219-443-5500

CERTIFICATE OF TRANSMITTAL AND SERVICE BY MAIL

The undersigned certifies under penalty of perjury that he or she has on the date shown below, by first class mail addressed to their respective addresses of record in this case, transmitted and served a true copy of this document to the United States Trustee, the Debtor, the unsecured creditors' committee, and their respective attorneys of record.

Date ______________________________ ______________________________

UNITED STATES BANKRUPTCY COURT
NORTHERN DISTRICT OF INDIANA

IN RE	HARDTIMES SUPPLY CO., INC.,	)	
	an Indiana Corporation, aka Hardtimes	)	Case No. 16-00019
	Supply Company	)	
	Debtor	)	Chapter 11
	Employer's Tax Identification No.	)	
	82-0778225	)	

ORDER CONFIRMING PLAN

Hardtimes Supply Co., the Debtor, filed a Plan of Reorganization Dated March 5, 2016 (the Plan) and a Disclosure Statement Dated March 5, 2016 (the Disclosure Statement) with the Court on March 10, 2016. Copies of the Plan and the Disclosure Statement were transmitted to all holders of claims and interests and to the United States Trustee, and a hearing on confirmation of the Plan was held on May 10, 2016. The Debtor, Big Bank of Boston, Ace Factor Co., and their respective counsel, appeared at the hearing. After considering the Plan and the objections filed thereto, the evidence and testimony, and the arguments of counsel,

THE COURT HEREBY FINDS AND DETERMINES AS FOLLOWS:

1. That every person or entity required to receive notice of the hearing on confirmation of the Plan and of the hearing on the adequacy of the Disclosure Statement receive timely and adequate notice thereof.

2. That the Plan complies with all applicable provisions of the Bankruptcy Code.

3. That the Debtor has complied with all applicable provisions of the Bankruptcy Code.

4. That the Plan has been proposed in good faith and not by any means forbidden by law.

5. That all payments made or to be made by the Debtor in connection with the case, or in connection with the Plan, have been approved by the Court as reasonable, or will be subject to approval by the Court prior to payment.

6. That with respect to each impaired class of claims, each holder of a claim in each impaired class has accepted the Plan, or will receive or retain under the Plan on account of the claim property of a value, as of the effective date of the Plan, that is not less than the amount that the holder would receive or retain if the Debtor was liquidated under Chapter 7 of the Bankruptcy Code on the effective date of the Plan. No holder of a secured claim has made an election under Section 1111(b)(2) of the Bankruptcy Code.

7. That all holders of claims and interests impaired under the Plan have been given adequate opportunity to vote to accept or reject the Plan. The holders of allowed claims in classes 3, 6, and 7 have accepted the Plan within the meaning of Section 1126(c) of the Bankruptcy Code. Classes 1, 4 and 5 are unimpaired within the meaning of Section 1124 of the Bankruptcy Code and are conclusively presumed to have accepted the Plan under Section 1126(f) of the Bankruptcy Code.

8. That except to the extent that the holder of a particular claim has agreed otherwise, the Plan provides that: (a) with respect to a claim of a kind specified in Section 507(a)(1) or (a)(2) of the Bankruptcy Code, on the effective date of the Plan the holder of each claim will receive on account of the claim cash equal to the allowed amount of the claim; and (b) with respect to claims of a kind specified in Section 507(a)(8) of the Bankruptcy Code, the holder of each claim will receive on account of the claim either cash equal to the allowed amount of the claim on or before the effective date of the Plan, or deferred cash payments, over a period not exceeding five (5) years after the date of assessment of the claim, of a value, as of the effective date of the Plan, equal to the allowed amount of the claim.

9. That at least one class of claims of the Debtor that is impaired under the Plan has accepted the Plan, as determined without including the acceptance of the Plan by any insider of the Debtor holding a claim in the class. The classes of impaired claims that have accepted the Plan are classes 3, 6 and 7.

10. That confirmation of the Plan is not likely to be followed by the liquidation or need for further financial reorganization of the Debtor.

11. That all fees payable under 28 U.S.C. §1930, as determined by the Court at the hearing on confirmation of the Plan, have been paid or the Plan provides for the payment of all fees as required by Section 1129(a)(12) of the Bankruptcy Code.

12. That the Disclosure Statement meets the requirements of Section 1125 of the Bankruptcy Code. The Debtor has filed the Disclosure Statement in good faith with reasonable care and diligence, and has not knowingly or negligently included in the Disclosure Statement any materially misleading or erroneous statements or representations.

13. That the solicitation of acceptances of the Plan by the Debtor was in good faith.

14. That the Debtor and all holders of claims and interests are bound by the Plan within the meaning of Section 1141 of the Bankruptcy Code.

15. That the Plan is fair and equitable to all parties-in-interest, including the Debtor, all unsecured creditors, all secured creditors, and all interest holders.

16. That the documents described in the Plan to be executed by the Debtor pursuant to the Plan are each valid, binding, and enforceable against the Debtor, in accordance with their terms, and are entered into for good and valuable consideration.

Based upon the findings and determinations listed above, IT IS HEREBY ORDERED THAT:

1. The Plan, a copy of which is annexed hereto as Exhibit A, be, and hereby is, confirmed.

2. The Debtor is hereby discharged from each debt or claim that arose against the Debtor prior the date of this Order, whether or not a proof of claim based upon the debt or claim is filed or deemed filed in the case, whether or not a claim is allowed, and whether or not the holder of a claim has accepted the Plan; provided that nothing in this Order or in the Plan shall operate as a discharge of the Debtor from claims, obligations, or liabilities to be paid or performed under the Plan or any agreement executed in conjunction with the Plan.

3. The provisions of the Plan, and all documents executed in conjunction with the Plan, and this Confirmation Order are, as of the effective date of the Plan, effective and binding on the Debtor, all creditors of the Debtor, and any other parties-in-interest, as well as their respective heirs, successors, assigns, or other persons claiming through them.

4. The Debtor and its respective agents and attorneys are hereby authorized, empowered, and directed to carry out the provisions of the Plan and to perform the acts and execute and deliver the documents as are necessary or appropriate in connection with the Plan and this Order.

5. The rejection of executory contracts and unexpired leases as provided in the Plan are hereby approved.

6. Except as otherwise expressly provided in the Plan, all payments and other distributions to be made under the Plan shall be timely and proper if mailed by first class mail on or before the date of distribution provided for in the Plan to the address listed in the creditor's proof of claim filed in this case, or, if no proof of claim is filed, to the creditor's last known address.

7. The stay in effect in this case pursuant to Section 362(a) of the Bankruptcy Code is hereby dissolved and is of no force or effect as of the effective date of the Plan.

8. The Court shall retain jurisdiction over this case to the extent provided in the Plan.

Dated: May 10, 2016

BY THE COURT

____

United States Bankruptcy Judge

UNITED STATES BANKRUPTCY COURT
NORTHERN DISTRICT OF INDIANA

IN RE HARDTIMES SUPPLY CO., INC.,	)		
an Indiana Corporation,	)	Case No. 16-00019	
	)		
Debtor	)	Chapter 11	

MOTION TO CONVERT CASE TO CHAPTER 7 UNDER SECTION 1112(a)

The Debtor, by its attorney, represents as follows:

1. The Debtor initiated this case by filing a voluntary petition for relief under Chapter 11 of the Bankruptcy Code on January 10, 2016 and is presently a debtor in possession in this case.

2. A plan has not been confirmed in this Chapter 11 case.

3. The Debtor now wishes to convert this Chapter 11 case to a case under Chapter 7 of the Bankruptcy Code.

4. The Debtor qualifies as a debtor under Chapter 7 of the Bankruptcy Code.

5. The Debtor is entitled to the relief herein requested under the provisions of 11 U.S.C. § 1112(a).

6. Notice and a hearing are not required for the granting of the relief requested by this motion.

7. A copy of this motion has been transmitted to the United States Trustee for this district pursuant to Bankruptcy Rule 9034.

WHEREFORE, the Debtor prays for the entry of an order converting this case to a case under Chapter 7 of the Bankruptcy Code and for relief under Chapter 7.

Dated: March 20, 2016

Reddy, Willing & Able

by ______________________________
Leo E. Lawnoer
Attorneys for Debtor in Possession
1000 First Street
Gary, Indiana 46407

Approved:

Hardtimes Supply Co., Inc.

by ___________________________
Joseph P. Jones, President

CERTIFICATE OF TRANSMITTAL TO UNITED STATES TRUSTEE

The undersigned declares, under penalty of perjury, that he or she has on the date shown below transmitted a true copy of this document to the United States Trustee for this district by first class mail addressed to said trustee's address of record.

Date: ______________________________ ______________________________

UNITED STATES BANKRUPTCY COURT
NORTHERN DISTRICT OF INDIANA

IN RE	HARDTIMES SUPPLY CO., INC.,	)	
	an Indiana Corporation,	)	Case No. 16-00019
		)	
	Debtor	)	Chapter 11

MOTION FOR DISMISSAL OR CONVERSION OF CASE FOR CAUSE UNDER SECTION 1112(b)

The movant, Big State Bank, by its attorney, represents as follows:

1. The Debtor commenced this Chapter 11 case by the filing of a voluntary petition on January 12, 2016, and since then has operated its business and managed its property as a debtor in possession.

2. The movant is a secured creditor in this case and, as such, is a party in interest entitled to file this motion.

3. The Debtor is eligible for relief under Chapter 7 of the Bankruptcy Code and is not a farmer or a corporation that is not a moneyed, business, or commercial corporation.

4. Unusual circumstances establishing that the requested relief is not in the best interests of creditors and the estate do not exist and the requested relief is in the best interest of creditors and the estate.

5. The appointment of a trustee or examiner in this case is not in the best interests of creditors and the estate.

6. Cause exists for the dismissal or conversion of this case under Section 1112(b) of the Bankruptcy Code in the following particulars:

a. The Debtor has failed to file a disclosure statement or plan within the time fixed by the court and the Bankruptcy Code.

b. The Debtor has failed to timely provide information or attend meetings reasonably requested by the United States trustee.

c. The Debtor has failed to file its monthly operating and financial reports with the court and the United States Trustee as required under the Rules of Bankruptcy Procedure and the local rules, and has committed gross mismanagement of the estate.

d. The assets of the estate are decreasing or depreciating in value, the Debtor has incurred new debts since the filing of this case, which has resulted in a continuing diminution of the estate, and there is no reasonable likelihood of rehabilitating the Debtor's business or estate.

WHEREFORE, the movant requests the entry of an order dismissing this Chapter 11 case or converting this case to a case under Chapter 7 of the Bankruptcy Code.

Dated: May 19, 2016

____
Daren D. Doubletree, P.C.
Attorney for Big State Bank
222 East Elm Street
Cedar Lake, IN 46303
Telephone: 554-7766

United States Bankruptcy Court

_______________ District Of _______________

In re ______________________________ Case No. ________________

Debtor

Chapter 11

PERIODIC REPORT REGARDING VALUE, OPERATIONS AND PROFITABILITY OF ENTITIES IN WHICH THE ESTATE OF [NAME OF DEBTOR] HOLDS A SUBSTANTIAL OR CONTROLLING INTEREST

This is the report as of ______________ on the value, operations and profitability of those entities in which the estate holds a substantial or controlling interest, as required by Bankruptcy Rule 2015.3. The estate of [Name of Debtor] holds a substantial or controlling interest in the following entities:

Name of Entity	Interest of the Estate	Tab #

This periodic report (the "Periodic Report") contains separate reports ("Entity Reports") on the value, operations, and profitability of each entity listed above.

Each Entity Report shall consist of three exhibits. Exhibit A contains a valuation estimate for the entity as of a date not more than two years prior to the date of this report. It also contains a description of the valuation method used. Exhibit B contains a balance sheet, a statement of income (loss), a statement of cash flows, and a statement of changes in shareholders' or partners' equity (deficit) for the period covered by the Entity Report, along with summarized footnotes. Exhibit C contains a description of the entity's business operations.

THIS REPORT MUST BE SIGNED BY A REPRESENTATIVE OF THE TRUSTEE OR DEBTOR IN POSSESSION.

The undersigned, having reviewed the above listing of entities in which the estate of [Debtor] holds a substantial or controlling interest, and being familiar with the Debtor's financial affairs, verifies under the penalty of perjury that the listing is complete, accurate and truthful to the best of his/her knowledge.

Date:____________

Signature of Authorized Individual

Name of Authorized Individual

Title of Authorized Individual

Exhibit A
Valuation Estimate for [Name of Entity]

[Provide a statement of the entity's value and the value of the estate's interest in the entity, including a description of the basis for the valuation, the date of the valuation and the valuation method used. This valuation must be no more than two years old. Indicate the source of this information.]

Exhibit B
Financial Statements for [Insert Name of Entity]
As of [date]

Exhibit B-1
Balance Sheet for [Name of Entity]
As of [date]

[Provide a balance sheet dated as of the end of the most recent six-month period of the current fiscal year and as of the end of the preceding fiscal year. Indicate the source of this information.]

Exhibit B-2
Statement of Income (Loss) for [Name of Entity]
Period ending [date]

[Provide a statement of income (loss) for the following periods:
- (i) For the initial report:
  - a. the period between the end of the preceding fiscal year and the end of the most recent six-month period of the current fiscal year; and
  - b. the prior fiscal year.
- (ii) For subsequent reports, since the closing date of the last report.

Indicate the source of this information.]

Exhibit B-3
Statement of Cash Flows for [Name of Entity]
For the Period ending [date]

[Provide a statement of changes in cash flows for the following periods:
- (i) For the initial report:
  - a. the period between the end of the preceding fiscal year and the end of the most recent six-month period of the current fiscal year; and
  - b. the prior fiscal year.
- (ii) For subsequent reports, since the closing date of the last report.

Indicate the source of this information.]

Exhibit B-4
Statement of Changes in Shareholders'/Partners' Equity (Deficit) for [Name of Entity]
Period ending [date]

[Provide a statement of changes in shareholders'/partners' equity (deficit) for the following periods:
- (i) For the initial report:
  - a. the period between the end of the preceding fiscal year and the end of the most recent six-month period of the current fiscal year; and
  - b. the prior fiscal year.
- (ii) For subsequent reports, since the closing date of the last report.

Indicate the source of this information.]

Exhibit C
Description of Operations for [Name of Entity]

[Describe the nature and extent of the estate's interest in the entity. Describe the business conducted and intended to be conducted by the entity, focusing on the entity's dominant business segment(s). Indicate the source of this information.]

CHAPTER FIVE

REPRESENTING A CREDITOR IN A CHAPTER 11 CASE

5.01 Filing and Handling an Involuntary Chapter 11 Case

The most important factor in the filing of an involuntary bankruptcy petition is to be certain that grounds exist to sustain the petition. The filing of an involuntary bankruptcy petition can cause irreparable damage to the reputation of a small business, both in the business community and among its employees. The ability of a small business to continue to function may be severely tested by an unwarranted filing of such a petition. Not surprisingly, then, a small business debtor will often go to extreme measures to contest and defeat an involuntary petition, and may expend much of its financial resources in the process. The Bankruptcy Code recognizes the expenses and damages that may be caused by the improper filing of an involuntary petition by permitting a debtor to recover from the petitioners the costs and expenses of successfully contesting the petition, and, if the petition was filed in bad faith, by permitting the debtor to recover general and punitive damages.

involuntary petition, consequences of filing on debtor

It is a practice of some creditors to use the threat of filing an involuntary bankruptcy petition as a collection device. While it is apparently neither illegal nor unethical to threaten involuntary bankruptcy in attempting to collect a claim, a creditor should carry out such a threat only if grounds for involuntary bankruptcy actually exist and if such a proceeding would be in the creditor's overall best interest. A creditor should be aware that control over an involuntary case passes to the bankruptcy court when the petition is filed, not when the petition is approved by the court. Therefore, even if the petitioner's strategy works and the debtor decides to pay the petitioner's claim in full after the involuntary petition is filed, the case cannot be dismissed without notice to all other creditors, a hearing, and approval by the court.

use of involuntary petition as collection device, consequences

A creditor should also be aware that other creditors are permitted to join in a filed involuntary petition, and are likely to do so when they learn that the claim of a petitioning creditor has been paid. See 11 U.S.C. 303(c). If the petition is not dismissed and is later approved by the court, any payment made to a petitioning creditor on its claim after the petition has been filed is voidable and may be recovered from the creditor by the trustee or debtor in possession. See 11 U.S.C. 549(a). A creditor should also realize that when an involuntary petition is filed the automatic stay goes into effect, precluding collection and related activities against the debtor and, in effect, giving the debtor a moratorium on the payment of its debts. See 11 U.S.C. 362(a). Finally, if an involuntary petition filed as a collection device is contested by the debtor and is later dismissed by the court, a creditor filing such a petition may be liable for the debtor's legal expenses in contesting the petition, and, if the petition is found to have been filed in bad faith, may be liable to the debtor for general or punitive damages. See 11 U.S.C. 303(i), and In re Godroy Wholesale, Inc., 37 B.R. 496 (MA, 1984).

payment to petitioning creditor, consequences

petitioning creditor, liability for damages

The chapter of the Bankruptcy Code under which to seek relief is a matter of obvious concern to a creditor contemplating the filing of an involuntary bankruptcy petition. An involuntary petition may be filed only under Chapter 7 or Chapter 11 of the Bankruptcy Code. See 11 U.S.C. 303(a). Relief under Chapter 7 must be in the form of liquidation, while Chapter 11 relief may be in the form of either reorganization or liquidation. See section 2.04, supra, for a discussion of the relative merits of Chapter 7 and Chapter 11 for small business debtors. Generally, the factors to consider in selecting the appropriate chapter are the debtor's ratio of liabilities to assets, the viability and prospects of the debtor's business, and the integrity and attitude of the debtor's owners or management. It should be noted that the initial proceeding to obtain court approval of an involuntary petition is the same whether relief is sought under Chapter 7 or Chapter 11.

involuntary petition, Chapter 7 vs. Chapter 11

involuntary petition, obtaining reliable information about debtor

To make an informed decision on whether to file an involuntary petition and which chapter to seek relief under, reliable information regarding the debtor, its assets, liabilities, and business practices and prospects must be obtained. Unless a petitioning creditor has a judgment or civil action pending against the debtor wherein the required information may be obtained through discovery proceedings, such information must normally be obtained informally, at least prior to the filing of the petition. Other creditors and disgruntled insiders of the debtor are likely sources of such information. Because of the potential liability of petitioning creditors in involuntary cases, it is important that the information relied on in filing the petition be accurate. Once an involuntary petition has been filed, the petitioners may conduct discovery proceedings to ascertain the condition of the debtor, but this may be too late to avoid liability for a wrongful filing if the information relied on in filing the petition was inaccurate.

involuntary petition, when normally filed

In practice, involuntary bankruptcy petitions are most often filed when one or more of the following circumstances exist:

(1) The creditors believe that the debtor is transferring, concealing, or liquidating its assets for the purpose of avoiding payment to some or all of its creditors.

(2) The creditors believe that the debtor's assets are deteriorating or being dismembered through foreclosures, seizures, or other creditor action.

(3) The creditors believe that the debtor's business is failing and is about to terminate, but would have considerably more value if preserved as a single, going concern, economic unit.

involuntary petition, who may be debtor

Filing requirements. An involuntary petition under Chapter 11 may be filed against any person eligible to file a voluntary petition under Chapter 11, except that an involuntary Chapter 11 petition may not be filed against a farmer, a family farmer, or a non-profit corporation. See 11 U.S.C. 303(a). A farmer is an individual, corporation, or partnership that, during the preceding tax year, received at least 80 percent of its income from a farming operation that it owned or operated. See 11 U.S.C. 101(20). A family farmer is defined in 11 U.S.C. 101(18).

non-profit corporation, what constitutes

A non-profit corporation includes any corporation that is charitable or benevolent in nature, and is not limited to corporations organized under state non-profit corporation laws. If the primary function of a corporation is charitable, it is not subject to an involuntary petition even if it also operates ancillary enterprises that are profit-making. See In re Allen University, 497 F. 2nd 346 (CA 4, 1974). See section 3.02, supra, for further reading on the Chapter 11 eligibility requirements.

involuntary petition, two or more debtors, requirements

A joint petition may not be filed in an involuntary case. See 11 U.S.C. 302. Thus, if an involuntary filing is contemplated against a husband and wife, two separate petitions must be filed and two filing fees paid. See King v. Fidelity National Bank of Baton Rouge, 712 F. 2nd 188 (CA 5, 1983). However, in one case at least, the court permitted an involuntary petition against an individual debtor to be amended so as to include a corporation on the basis that the corporation was the alter ego of the individual debtor. See In re Crabtree, 39 B.R. 718 (ED TN, 1984).

involuntary petition, petitioning creditors, number, amount of claims

An involuntary petition may be filed by three or more creditors, each of which is a holder of a non-contingent claim against the debtor that is not the subject of a bona fide dispute as to liability or amount, provided that the aggregate total of such claims is $15,325* or more than the value of any lien on property of the debtor securing such claims. See 11 U.S.C. 303(b)(1). If there are fewer than 12 such creditors of the debtor, excluding employees and insiders of the debtor and transferees of voidable transfers, an involuntary petition may be filed by one or more of such creditors holding claims totalling $15,325* or more. See 11 U.S.C. 303(b)(2). Thus, if a debtor has fewer than 12 qualifying creditors, an involuntary petition may be filed by a single qualifying creditor with a qualifying claim of $15,325* or more. * Dollar amounts subject to change on April 1, 2016.

Unless they hold other qualifying claims, the holders of fully-secured or contingent claims against the debtor and the holders of claims against the debtor that are the subject of a bona fide dispute as to liability or amount do not qualify as petitioning creditors and are not counted in determining the number of creditors of a debtor. However, the holder of an unliquidated claim against the debtor is a qualifying creditor and may file an involuntary petition. See In re Longhorn 1979-II Drilling Program, 32 B.R. 923 (WD OK, 1983). See section 3.04, supra, for the definition of a contingent claim and an unliquidated claim. See 11 U.S.C. 506(a) and section 4.04, supra, for the definition of a secured claim. An undersecured creditor is a qualified petitioner to the extent that the amount of its claim exceeds the value of its security, and joining in an involuntary petition does not affect the validity of its secured claim. See In re Crabtree, 32 B.R. 837 (ED TN, 1983). A claim is the subject of a bona fide dispute if the debtor has a legitimate factual or legal basis for not paying the claim. See In re Lough, 57 B.R. 993 (ED MI, 1986), and In re Crain, 194 B.R. 663 (SD AL, 1996).

petitioning creditor, qualifications

bona fide dispute, what constitutes

The holders of a joint claim, such as a note payable jointly to two or more persons, constitute but one qualifying creditor, even though there may be two or more payees. See In re Averil, Inc., 33 B.R. 562 (SD FL, 1983). An entity that has transferred or acquired a claim for the purpose of commencing an involuntary case is not a qualified petitioner. See Bankruptcy Rule 1003(a). The holders of small, recurring claims against the debtor, such as charge accounts and utility bills, may join in an involuntary petition and are usually counted as qualifying creditors in determining the number of creditors of the debtor. See In re Rassi, 701 F. 2nd 627, 632 (CA 7, 1983), In re Fox, 162 B.R. 729 (ED VA, 1993), and In re Elsa Designs, Ltd., 155 B.R. 859 (SD NY, 1993).

petitioning creditor, qualifications

One or more (but fewer than all) general partners may file an involuntary petition against their partnership. See 11 U.S.C. 303(b)(3)(A). If bankruptcy relief has been ordered with respect to all of the general partners, then an involuntary petition against the partnership may be filed by any of the general partners, by the trustee of a general partner, or by a creditor of the partnership. See 11 U.S.C. 303(b)(3)(B). Limited partners may not join in an involuntary petition against the partnership unless they are also qualifying creditors of the partnership. After the filing of an involuntary petition against a partnership, the petitioning partners or other petitioners must promptly send to or serve on each general partner who is not a petitioner a copy of the petition and the clerk must promptly issue a summons for service on each general partner who is not a petitioner. See Bankruptcy Rule 1004.

involuntary partnership petition, who may file

An involuntary petition must conform substantially to Official Form 105 (for individual debtors) or 205 (for non-individual debtors). When an involuntary petition is filed with the court, the clerk must forthwith issue a summons, which, together with a copy of the involuntary petition, must be served on the debtor in the manner provided in Bankruptcy Rule 7004(a) or (b). If the debtor cannot be found, service may be made by mailing copies of the summons and petition to the debtor's last known address and by publication in a manner directed by the court. See Bankruptcy Rule 1010, which governs service of process in an involuntary case. A sample Involuntary Petition is set forth in Exhibit 5-A at the end of this chapter.

summons and petition, service of

Grounds for filing. To be approved by the court, an involuntary petition must allege, and the petitioners must prove, one of the following grounds for relief:

involuntary petition, grounds for relief

(1) that the debtor is generally not paying its debts as they become due, unless such debts are the subject of a bona fide dispute as to liability or amount; or

(2) that within 120 days before the date the petition was filed, a custodian was appointed or took possession of substantially all of the debtor's property. See 11 U.S.C. 303(h).

nonpayment of debts, what constitutes

To establish the first ground for relief listed above, which is the ground most frequently alleged, the existence of more than a few unpaid debts must be shown. See In re Dill, 731 F. 2nd 629 (CA 9, 1984). The number of creditors, the total dollar amount of all debts not being paid, and the debt payment practices of the debtor are the factors considered by the court under this ground for relief. See In re B.D. International Discount Corp., 701 F. 2nd 1071 (CA 2, 1983), and In re In re Everett, 178 B.R. 132 (ND OH, 1994). It has been held that a debtor who was paying all of its debts except one, which constituted 97 percent of the total amount of its debts, was not paying its debts as they became due. See In re 7H Land & Cattle Co., 6 B.R. 29 (NV, 1980). If certain debts are not being paid, it does not matter that those creditors are not pressing for payment. See In re Midwest Processing Co., 41 B.R. 90, 101 (ND, 1984). If a debt is the subject of a bona fide dispute as to either liability or amount, it need not be paid to avoid involuntary bankruptcy. See 11 U.S.C. 303(h)(1), and In re Garland Coal & Mining Co., 67 B.R. 514 (WD AR, 1986).

appointment of custodian, what constitutes

The second ground for relief listed above may be established by showing that, within 120 days prior to the date of filing of the petition, a custodian was appointed to take possession of substantially all of the debtor's property. This ground may also be established by showing that the custodian actually took possession of substantially all of the debtor's property within the 120-day period, even if the custodian was appointed at an earlier date. See 11 U.S.C. 303(h)(2). A custodian includes a receiver or trustee appointed in a nonbankruptcy proceeding and an assignee under a general assignment for the benefit of creditors. See 11 U.S.C. 101(11).

debtor's answer to involuntary petition, who may file

The debtor, of course, is permitted to answer and oppose an involuntary petition. If the debtor is a partnership, the petition may be answered by a non-petitioning general partner; otherwise only the debtor is permitted to answer and oppose an involuntary petition. See 11 U.S.C. 303(d) and Bankruptcy Rule 1011(a). Neither limited partners of a partnership nor shareholders of a corporation have standing, in that capacity, to oppose an involuntary petition against the partnership or corporation. Also, non-petitioning creditors of a debtor are not permitted to answer and contest an involuntary petition. See In re Ludlum Enterprises, Inc., 510 F. 2nd 996 (CA 5, 1975).

abstention, dismissal of case for, when granted

While non-petitioning creditors of the debtor may not answer or contest an involuntary petition on the merits, they may join in seeking dismissal of an involuntary case on the grounds of abstention under 11 U.S.C. 305(a). Grounds for dismissal under this statute may be established by showing that a nonbankruptcy proceeding or solution is in the best interests of both the debtor and most of its creditors. See In re E. Egan Co., Inc., 24 B.R. 189 (WD NY, 1982). This remedy may be useful in preventing a few dissenting creditors from upsetting a workout agreement approved by the debtor and most of its creditors. See Matter of Rimpull Corp., 26 B.R. 267 (WD MO, 1982).

debtor's answer, time for filing, failure to file

Defenses and counterclaims. A debtor's defenses to the merits of an involuntary petition must be presented in the form of an answer, which, if no other motions or responsive pleadings are filed, must be filed and served within 21 days after service of the summons. See Bankruptcy Rule 1011(b). If the debtor files a motion or other responsive pleading raising jurisdictional, venue, or procedural issues, the time for filing an answer is extended. See Bankruptcy Rule 1011(c). If an answer or other responsive pleading is not filed within 21 days after service of the summons, the court may enter an order for relief against the debtor as prayed for in the petition. See Bankruptcy Rule 1013(b). It should be noted that in an involuntary case an order for relief may be entered only after a trial on the merits of the petition, unless the petition is not timely controverted. See 11 U.S.C. 303(h). Finally, there is no absolute right to a jury trial on the issues raised in an involuntary petition, as the court may order such issues to be tried without a jury. See 28 U.S.C. 1411(b). A sample Answer to Involuntary Petition and Counterclaim is set forth in Exhibit 5-B, at the end of this chapter.

involuntary petition, defenses of debtor

In responding to an involuntary petition, a debtor may raise a variety of defenses, objections, and protective measures, including the following:

(1) If the debtor is a party to another proceeding or an agreement whereby the interests of most of its creditors are being protected, the debtor may request the court to dismiss or refrain from hearing the case on the grounds of abstention under 11 U.S.C. 305(a).

(2) The debtor may raise defenses challenging the jurisdiction of the court over the debtor, the eligibility of the debtor for the relief prayed for in the petition, or the venue of the proceeding.

(3) The debtor may challenge the standing or qualifications of one or more of the petitioning creditors or general partners. This may be done by showing that one or more of the petitioning creditors fails to meet the statutory requirements for petitioners in an involuntary case. For example, the debtor may show that the claim of a petitioning creditor is secured, contingent, was acquired for the purpose of commencing an involuntary case, or is the subject of a bona fide dispute as to either liability or amount. If the petition was filed by a single creditor, the debtor may show that it has 12 or more qualifying creditors. It should be noted here that if the defense of 12 or more creditors is raised, the debtor is required to file with its answer a list of such creditors and the court must give other creditors a reasonable opportunity to join in the petition prior to holding a hearing. See Bankruptcy Rule 1003(b).

(4) The debtor may challenge the petition on its merits by denying the grounds for relief set forth in the petition and by raising affirmative defenses to the allegations contained in the petition.

(5) The debtor may request the court to require the petitioners to post a bond to indemnify the debtor for any costs, attorney's fees, or damages that it may be allowed in the case. See 11 U.S.C. 303(e).

(6) The debtor may file a counterclaim against the petitioning creditors and seek a judgment against them for the costs, attorney's fees, and other allowable damages incurred by the debtor as a result of the filing of the petition. In addition, the debtor may seek a judgment for general or punitive damages against any petitioner that is found to have filed the petition in bad faith. See 11 U.S.C. 303(i). These matters are discussed below in this section.

If a debtor determines that it has no defenses to an involuntary petition, the debtor may either not contest the involuntary petition, stipulate to the involuntary petition, or file a voluntary petition under the appropriate chapter of the Bankruptcy Code. In this regard, it should be noted that a debtor has an absolute right to convert an involuntary Chapter 7 case to a case under Chapter 11, either before or after the order for relief. See 11 U.S.C. 706(a). Therefore, even if a debtor unsuccessfully contests an involuntary Chapter 7 petition, the debtor may then convert the case to a case under Chapter 11. However, if an involuntary petition seeks relief under Chapter 11, the debtor may not, as of right, convert the case to a case under Chapter 7. See 11 U.S.C. 1112(a)(2). A debtor may convert an involuntary Chapter 11 case to a case under Chapter 7 for cause, however. See 11 U.S.C. 1112(b). See section 4.14, supra, for further reading on the conversion of Chapter 11 cases.

involuntary petition, debtor's right to convert Chapter 7 case to Chapter 11

The court may dismiss an involuntary petition on the motion of a petitioner, on the consent of all petitioners and the debtor, or for want of prosecution, only after notice to all creditors and a hearing. See 11 U.S.C. 303(j). Therefore, should the debtor settle with a petitioning creditor, the case may not be dismissed without first scheduling a hearing and providing notice of the proposed dismissal to all other creditors. Further, before an involuntary case can be dismissed, all other qualifying creditors must be given an opportunity to join in the petition with the same effect as if the joining creditors were petitioning creditors. See 11 U.S.C. 303(c). It is apparent that once an involuntary petition has been filed, it is not easily dismissed.

involuntary petition, dismissal requirements

In an involuntary Chapter 7 case the court may order the appointment of an interim trustee to take possession of the debtor's property and operate the debtor's business pending the order for relief. See 11 U.S.C. 303(g). While statutory authority also exists for the appointment of a trustee prior to the order for relief in an involuntary Chapter 11 case (see 11 U.S.C. 1104(a)), such trustees are seldom appointed. See Matter of Beaucrest Realty Associates, 4 B.R. 164 (ED NY, 1980). If an involuntary Chapter 7 petition is filed and an interim trustee is appointed, the conversion of the case to a case under Chapter 11 by the debtor does not automatically restore the debtor to possession of its property and business. See In re Alpine Lumber & Nursery, 13 B.R. 977 (SD CA, 1981).

involuntary case, appointment of trustee prior to order for relief

Involuntary gap period. The involuntary gap period is the period in an involuntary case between the date the petition is filed and the earlier of the date of the order for relief or the appointment of a trustee in the case. Except to the extent that the court orders otherwise and until an order for relief is entered, the debtor in an involuntary case may continue to operate its business during the involuntary gap period and may continue to use, acquire, or dispose of property as if the case had not been commenced. See 11 U.S.C. 303(f). Whether or not they have notice of the case, persons dealing with the debtor during the involuntary gap period are protected against later having to repay the estate for money or property taken from the debtor during this period to the extent that they gave the debtor new value, including services, after the petition was filed. See 11 U.S.C. 549(b). A prepetition debt, of course, does not constitute new value, and the collection thereof during the involuntary gap period may constitute an avoidable transfer. See 11 U.S.C. 549(a).

involuntary gap, definition

operation of debtor's business, treatment of creditors during gap period

gap claim, priority and treatment

A person who extends unsecured credit to the debtor in the ordinary course of business during the involuntary gap period is given a third priority claim in the ensuing bankruptcy case for the collection of such credit. See 11 U.S.C. 502(f), 507(a)(3). A third priority claim must be paid in full in cash before a Chapter 11 plan may be confirmed. See 11 U.S.C. 1129(a)(9)(A). If unsecured credit not in the ordinary course of business is to be extended during the involuntary gap period, prior court approval must be obtained if the creditor is to be protected. See 11 U.S.C. 364, and section 4.02, supra.

involuntary petition, automatic stay, extent of

The filing of an involuntary petition invokes the automatic stay to the same extent as the filing of a voluntary petition. See 11 U.S.C. 362(a). Thus, the automatic stay operates to protect the debtor during the involuntary gap period when the petition is being contested. While relief from the stay may be applied for during this period, the uncertainty of the case at this point may make such relief difficult to obtain. See 11 U.S.C. 303(f). See section 4.01, supra, for further reading on the effect and extent of the automatic stay.

involuntary case, procedure

Contested petition. The procedure for all proceedings related to a contested involuntary petition, including the trial, are governed by Bankruptcy Rule 1018. Because such proceedings constitute an integral part of a bankruptcy case, they may be heard and determined by the bankruptcy court. See 28 U.S.C. 157(b)(1). Although such proceedings are not adversary proceedings under Bankruptcy Rule 7001, several of the rules in Part VII of the Rules of Bankruptcy Procedure are made applicable to contested involuntary proceedings by Bankruptcy Rule 1018. Such matters as the type of pleadings required, the method of serving and filing pleadings, pre-trial discovery procedures, and the form and method of entering a judgment in the proceeding are governed by the applicable Part VII rules. As indicated above, pre-trial discovery is permitted in a contested involuntary proceeding. Thus, depositions may be taken, written interrogatories may be propounded, documents may ordered produced, and land or other property may be inspected. See Bankruptcy Rules 1018 and 2004.

involuntary case, duties of court, order for relief

The court is required to determine the issues of a contested involuntary petition at the earliest practicable time and to forthwith enter an order for relief, dismiss the petition, or enter other appropriate orders. See Bankruptcy Rule 1013(a). If the debtor prevails at the trial, the court must dismiss the petition and may enter a judgment for the debtor for its costs, attorney's fees, or other damages as provided in 11 U.S.C. 303(i). If the petitioners prevail at the trial, or if the petition is not timely controverted, the court must order relief against the debtor under the chapter of the Bankruptcy Code under which the petition was filed. See 11 U.S.C. 303(h) and Bankruptcy Rule 1013(b).

dismissal of involuntary petition, debtor's right to damages

If the court dismisses an involuntary petition other than upon the consent of all petitioning creditors and the debtor, and if the debtor does not waive its right to such damages, the court may grant the debtor a judgment against the petitioners for any costs or attorney's fees incurred by the debtor in the proceeding or for any damages caused by the taking of possession of the debtor's property by a trustee appointed in the case. See 11 U.S.C. 303(i)(1). In addition, the court may grant the debtor a judgment against a petitioner who is found to have filed the petition in bad faith for any damages proximately caused by the filing of the petition or for punitive damages. See 11 U.S.C. 303(i)(2). Generally, bad faith exists when the filing of an involuntary petition is motivated by malice or bad will. See Camelot, Inc. v. Hayden, 30 B.R. 408 (ED TN, 1983). Bad faith may also be found where the petition was filed primarily to coerce payment of a claim. See In re Advance Press & Lithe, Inc., 46 B.R. 700 (CO, 1985).

bad faith, what constitutes

order for relief, debtor's duties after entry of

Procedure. Within 7 days after the order for relief in an involuntary case, the debtor must file the required schedules, statements and lists. See Bankruptcy Rules 1007(a)(2), 1007(c). The schedules, statements, lists, and other documents required to be filed after the order for relief in an involuntary case are the same as in a voluntary case, and are set forth and discussed in section 3.04, supra. If a list, schedule, or statement is not prepared and filed by the debtor as required, the court may order a petitioning creditor or other party to prepare and file any of these documents within the time fixed by the court. See Bankruptcy Rule 1007(k).

After the order for relief, an involuntary Chapter 11 case proceeds substantially the same as a voluntary case, except that if the debtor is not cooperative, a party other than the debtor is likely to be the plan proponent in the case. If the debtor refuses to cooperate in the case, or if cause otherwise exists, a petitioning creditor or other party in interest may request the court to order the appointment of a trustee or examiner. See section 4.12, supra, for further reading on the appointment of a trustee or examiner.

involuntary case, procedure after order for relief

In an involuntary Chapter 11 case, as in a voluntary case, such matters as preparing a disclosure statement, preparing and filing a plan, obtaining creditor acceptance of the plan, obtaining confirmation of the plan, and implementing and consummating the plan, must be carried out. If the debtor is uncooperative in the case, these functions may have to performed by other parties, often by one or more of the petitioning creditors. If a trustee is appointed in the case, the trustee may assist in carrying out many of these functions. The reader is referred to chapter four of this handbook for further reading on the handling of a Chapter 11 case.

involuntary Chapter 11 case, functions to be performed

5.02 Representing a Secured Creditor in a Chapter 11 Case

secured creditors, attitude toward Chapter 11 cases

Secured creditors generally have little to gain and much to lose in a Chapter 11 case. Given a choice, most secured creditors would prefer the case to be filed under Chapter 7, where they are normally permitted to reclaim their collateral and satisfy their claims under the protection of a trustee. However, unless cause exists for converting the case to Chapter 7, secured creditors are not given a choice, and, like other creditors, must comply with the requirements of Chapter 11. From the viewpoint of a secured creditor, a Chapter 11 case is essentially a conflict between the right of a secured creditor to preserve and protect its collateral and the right of a debtor in possession to use the collateral in the rehabilitation of its business. It is the responsibility of the court to balance these conflicting rights by protecting the interests of secured creditors while according the debtor a reasonable opportunity to rehabilitate its business.

concerns of secured creditors in Chapter 11 case

The aspects of a Chapter 11 case that are of primary concern to most secured creditors are: (1) the effect of the automatic stay and the obtaining of relief therefrom, (2) the ability of the debtor in possession to use or dispose of the creditor's collateral during the course of the case, and (3) the treatment of secured claims under the Chapter 11 plan. Because of its importance in the first two of these aspects, the issue of the adequate protection of a secured creditor's interest in its collateral is an issue of primary concern to most secured creditors in Chapter 11 cases.

fully-secured creditor, definition

undersecured creditor, definition

Undersecured creditors. In practice, there are two types of secured creditors: fully-secured creditors and undersecured creditors. A fully-secured creditor is the holder of an allowed claim against the debtor that is secured by a lien on property of the estate of a value that equals or exceeds the amount of the allowed claim, or that is subject to a setoff that equals or exceeds the amount of the allowed claim. An undersecured creditor is the holder of an allowed claim against the debtor that is secured by a lien on property of the estate of a value that is less than the amount of the allowed claim or subject to a setoff that is less than the amount of the allowed claim. See 11 U.S.C. 506(a).

recourse creditor, definition

non-recourse creditor, definition

Section 1111(b) election, effect of on undersecured creditor

There are two types of undersecured creditors: recourse creditors, and non-recourse creditors. A recourse creditor has rights against both the collateral and the debtor, while a non-recourse creditor has rights only against the collateral and does not have rights or recourse against the debtor separately for payment of its claim. Non-recourse creditors are often referred to as "in rem" creditors. It should be noted, however, that in a Chapter 11 case a non-recourse claim is treated as a recourse claim unless the class of which the claim is a part exercises the Section 1111(b) election or unless the collateral is sold either during the case or under the plan. See 11 U.S.C. 1111(b)(1)(A). If a class of undersecured claims exercises the Section 1111(b) election the claim of each creditor in the class is deemed to be a secured claim to the full extent that the claim is allowed, regardless of the value of the collateral securing the claim. See 11 U.S.C. 1111(b)(2). In other words, by exercising the Section 1111(b) election (i.e., by electing to have subsection 1111(b)(2) apply), a creditor can cause its undersecured claim to be deemed fully secured for purposes of distribution and payment under a plan. The Section 1111(b) election is discussed below in this section and in section 4.09, supra.

undersecured creditor, value of secured claim

An undersecured creditor not exercising the Section 1111(b) election is treated under the Bankruptcy Code as having two separate claims for purposes of both voting and distribution. Such a creditor has a secured claim in an amount equal to the value of its collateral or the amount subject to setoff, and an unsecured claim to the extent that the amount of its allowed claim exceeds the value of its collateral or the amount subject to setoff. See 11 U.S.C. 506(a). The exception to this rule is that if its collateral is sold, either during the case or under the plan, a non-recourse undersecured creditor has only a secured claim in an amount equal to the value of its collateral. See 11 U.S.C. 1111(b)(1)(A)(ii). The valuation of collateral in Chapter 11 cases is discussed in sections 4.01 and 4.04, supra.

As indicated above, a claim that is subject to a right of setoff is treated as a secured claim under the Bankruptcy Code. See 11 U.S.C. 506(a). A right of setoff exists when a creditor owes a debt to the debtor that is unrelated to the claim of the creditor against the debtor. See In re IML Freight, Inc., 65 B.R. 788 (UT, 1986). The automatic stay precludes a creditor from independently exercising a right of setoff after the commencement of the case. See 11 U.S.C. 362(a)(7). If a right of setoff is not exercised, a creditor is likely to lose much of the value of its setoff. If a right of setoff is not exercised, the creditor will most likely have to pay the estate the full amount of the debtor's claim against the creditor. However, unless the plan pays 100 cents on the dollar to the holders of unsecured claims, which is unlikely, the creditor will not collect the full amount of its claim against the debtor. Thus, it is important for a creditor secured by a right of setoff to exercise the right in a manner that will enable the creditor to use as much of its right of setoff as is legally possible. The procedures necessary to effectively exercise a right of setoff in a Chapter 11 case are described in section 4.04, supra, and the reader is referred to that section for further reading.

claim subject to setoff, treatment of, importance of exercising setoff

Effect of automatic stay. The automatic stay comes into effect immediately upon the filing of either a voluntary or involuntary Chapter 11 petition. As applied to secured creditors, the automatic stay precludes any act to obtain possession of or exercise control over property of the estate and any act to create, perfect, or enforce a lien against property of the estate, unless relief from the stay is first obtained from the bankruptcy court. See 11 U.S.C. 362(a)(3),(4),(5). Any creditor who violates the automatic stay may be held in contempt of court and may be liable for damages, and any action taken in violation of the automatic stay is voidable. See section 4.01, supra, for further reading on the extent and effect of the automatic stay. As to what constitutes property of the estate, see section 4.02, supra.

automatic stay, effect of on secured creditor, acts in violation of

A secured creditor may obtain relief from the automatic stay for cause, or upon a showing that the debtor has no equity in the creditor's collateral and that the collateral is not necessary for an effective reorganization of the debtor. See 11 U.S.C. 362(d). The cause most commonly used by secured creditors to obtain relief from the stay is the lack of adequate protection of a creditor's interest in its collateral. See 11 U.S.C. 362(d)(1). When a right to relief from the stay is established on this ground, the court may either grant the creditor relief from the stay or permit the debtor in possession to adequately protect the interest of the creditor in its collateral.

secured creditor, relief from automatic stay, grounds for

A principal function of an attorney representing a secured creditor in a Chapter 11 case is to protect the creditor's interest in its collateral. In so doing it may become necessary to file one or more motions for relief from the automatic stay with respect to the creditor's collateral. A principal issue in most motions of this sort is whether the creditor's interest in its collateral is being adequately protected by the debtor in possession. See section 4.01, supra, for further reading on obtaining relief from the automatic stay and for a discussion of adequate protection. A sample Motion For Relief From Stay of Acts Against Property may be found in Exhibit 4-A, at the end of chapter four, supra.

motion of secured creditor for relief from stay, adequate protection

Protecting collateral. A matter of concern to many secured creditors in Chapter 11 cases is the extent to which the trustee or debtor in possession may use, sell, or lease the creditor's collateral during the course of the case. For purposes of use, sale, or lease, the Bankruptcy Code creates two types of collateral: cash collateral, and all other collateral. Cash collateral includes cash, negotiable instruments, documents of title, securities, deposit accounts, and other cash equivalents, and, if the security agreement so provides, may include both prepetition and postpetition proceeds, products, offspring, rents, or profits of property subject to a security interest. See 11 U.S.C. 363(a), 552(b). Generally, then, cash collateral is cash or property easily converted to cash. Cash collateral is easily used or disposed of, disappears quickly, and is seldom recoverable from the transferee. Therefore, the use, sale, or lease of cash collateral is subject to more stringent rules than is the use, sale, or lease of other collateral.

cash collateral, what constitutes, use of by debtor in possession

use, sale, or lease of secured property by debtor in possession, applicable rules

The rules applicable to the use, sale, or lease of cash and other collateral by a trustee or debtor in possession during a Chapter 11 case may be summarized as follows:

(1) A trustee or debtor in possession must segregate and account for any cash collateral in its possession, custody, or control at any time during the case. See 11 U.S.C. 363(c)(4).

(2) A trustee or debtor in possession may not use, sell, or lease cash collateral unless each creditor with an interest in the collateral consents to the proposed use, sale, or lease, or unless the court, after notice and a hearing, authorizes the proposed use, sale, or lease upon a finding that the interest of any objecting creditor secured thereby is adequately protected. See 11 U.S.C. 363(c)(2), 363(e).

(3) Unless the court orders otherwise, collateral that is not cash collateral may be used, sold, or leased by a trustee or debtor in possession in the ordinary course of operating the debtor's business without notice or a hearing. See 11 U.S.C. 363(c)(1). However, a secured creditor may at any time demand adequate protection of its interest in its collateral as a condition of the continued use, sale, or lease of the collateral by the trustee or debtor in possession. See 11 U.S.C. 363(e).

(4) A trustee or debtor in possession may use, sell, or lease collateral that is not cash collateral other than in the ordinary course of business only after notice and a hearing, and only if the interest of any objecting creditor in the collateral is adequately protected. See 11 U.S.C. 363(b)(1), 363(e). There are special rules dealing with the transfer of personally identifiable information. See U.S.C. 363(b)(1).

(5) If the interest of any creditor secured thereby is adequately protected, a trustee or debtor in possession may, under certain conditions, sell collateral free and clear of the creditor's lien or interest therein. See 11 U.S.C. 363(f).

(6) The trustee or debtor in possession may use, sell or lease estate property only in accordance with applicable nonbankruptcy law governing the transfer of property by nonprofit corporations or trusts and only to the extent that is consistent with any relief from the automatic stay granted by the court. See 11 U.S.C. 363(d).

motion to use cash collateral, response of secured creditor, adequate protection

It is common in Chapter 11 cases for the debtor in possession to file motions for authority to use cash collateral. Such motions are normally filed when cash is needed to meet a payroll or for other expenses of operating the debtor's business, a need that often arises early in the case. When such a motion is filed it is important for any creditor secured by the cash collateral sought to be used to oppose the motion and request the court to either prohibit the proposed use or condition the use so as to provide adequate protection for the creditor's interest in the cash collateral. See 11 U.S.C. 363(e). Even if a creditor has previously consented to the use of cash collateral by the debtor in possession, the consent may be withdrawn and adequate protection requested at any time. See 11 U.S.C. 363(e) and In re Harper Industries, Inc., 18 B.R. 773 (SD OH, 1982). Adequate protection must be requested to be provided, however, as there is no right to adequate protection in the absence of a request. See 11 U.S.C. 363(e). The request should be timely made because the court is not authorized to grant retroactive adequate protection. See In re Broomall Printing Corp., 131 B.R. 32 (MD, 1991). See section 4.02, supra, for further reading on the use of cash collateral.

secured creditor, request for adequate protection, procedure

It is important for a secured creditor to understand that it may at any time during the case request adequate protection of its interest in any property being used, sold, or leased by the debtor in possession. The right to adequate protection is not limited to cash collateral; it applies equally to the use, sale, or lease of any property in which the creditor has an interest. See 11 U.S.C. 363(e). Thus, if, during the course of any use, sale, or lease of a secured creditor's collateral by the debtor in possession, the creditor deems its security interest to be threatened, the creditor may object and request adequate protection as a condition of the continued use, sale, or lease of the property, regardless of whether the use, sale, or lease is in or outside of the ordinary course of business. See In re Aegean Fare, Inc., 34 B.R. 965 (MA, 1983).

use or sale of collateral outside ordinary course of business, adequate protection

If the debtor in possession seeks to use, sell, or lease a creditor's collateral outside the ordinary course of business, the creditor should object to the proposed use, sale, or lease unless adequate protection of its interest in the collateral is provided. When a request is made by a secured creditor for adequate protection, the burden shifts to the trustee or debtor in possession to show that the interest of the creditor is being adequately protected in the transaction. See 11 U.S.C. 363(p)(1). See section 4.01, supra, for further reading on adequate protection. See section 4.02, supra, for further reading on the use, sale, or lease of collateral by a debtor in possession.

The most effective method of raising the issue of adequate protection, especially during the course of any use, sale, or lease of the creditor's collateral by the debtor in possession, is to file a motion for relief from the automatic stay with respect to the collateral on the grounds of lack of adequate protection of an interest in property. See 11 U.S.C. 362(d)(1). Even if the issue of adequate protection can be effectively raised by the creditor during a hearing on a motion by the debtor in possession to use, sell, or lease property, the filing of a motion for relief from the stay may, nevertheless, be advisable. If the creditor files a motion for relief from the stay, a common hearing on the two motions can be scheduled. If, after the hearing, the court determines that adequate protection cannot be provided, it may then grant the creditor relief from the stay and permit it to reclaim or foreclose on its collateral. This procedure, it should be noted, may be employed whenever the debtor in possession seeks to use, sell, or lease collateral of any type, including cash collateral.

motion for relief from stay, adequate protection, importance of

If the debtor in possession sells property that secures an allowed claim, the holder of the secured claim may bid on the property at the sale, unless the court, for cause, orders otherwise. Further, if the secured creditor purchases the property at the sale, it may offset its allowed claim against the purchase price of the property up to the full amount of the claim. See 11 U.S.C. 363(k). This right is particularly important if the debtor in possession proposes to sell secured property at a price that is less than the allowed amount of the creditor's claim. By bidding in the property, a secured creditor can, in effect, pay for the collateral with its claim. Of course, a secured creditor may bid less than the full amount of its claim if that is all that is necessary to purchase the property, in which case the creditor will have an allowed unsecured claim for the unbid balance of its claim. As indicated above, however, the court, for cause, may deny, limit, or condition the right of a secured creditor to bid at the sale of its collateral. See 11 U.S.C. 363(k).

sale of secured property, right of secured creditor to bid on property

Secured creditors that have repossessed, seized, or foreclosed upon property of the debtor prior to the commencement of the case should be aware of the right of the trustee or debtor in possession to compel the turnover of such property. See 11 U.S.C. 542(a). Creditors holding collateral in order to perfect their security interest may also be subject to a turnover proceeding. However, because a secured creditor is normally entitled to adequate protection as a condition to the turnover of property under 11 U.S.C. 542(a), its ultimate right to enforce or collect on its claim should not, in theory at least, be affected by the turnover order. See section 4.02, supra, for further reading on the turnover of property under 11 U.S.C. 542(a).

turnover proceeding, creditors subject to, adequate protection

Amount of secured claim. Most mortgages and other security agreements provide for the assessment of additional interest, late charges, collection costs, attorney's fees, and assorted other charges in the event of default. The question often arises as to whether such charges may be collected by a secured creditor in a Chapter 11 case. The answer to the question depends on the degree to which the creditor's claim is secured and whether the debtor in possession is permitted to recover any costs or expenses incurred in preserving or disposing of the property during the case. See 11 U.S.C. 506(b), (c).

secured claim, interest and fees, when allowable

If a creditor's claim is not fully secured (that is, if the value of its collateral does not exceed the amount of its allowed claim), neither postpetition interest nor any fees or charges may be included in either the secured or unsecured portions of the creditor's claim. See 11 U.S.C. 502(b)(2), 506(b). Because its secured claim is by definition not oversecured, an undersecured creditor exercising the Section 1111(b) election to have its claim treated as fully secured may not include postpetition interest or any fees or charges provided for in the security agreement in determining the amount of its allowed secured claim. See 11 U.S.C. 1111(b)(2).

undersecured creditor, allowance of interest and fees

To the extent that an allowed secured claim is secured by property of a value which, after the recovery of any allowed costs and expenses incurred by the trustee or debtor in possession in preserving or disposing of the property, exceeds the amount of the claim, interest on the claim and any reasonable fees, costs, or charges provided for in the security agreement may be allowed to the holder of the claim. See 11 U.S.C. 506(b). Thus, if a creditor's claim is over-secured, postpetition interest and any reasonable fees, costs, or charges provided for in the security agreement may be included in the creditor's secured claim, but only to the extent that such items do not cause the amount of the claim to exceed the value of the collateral and only after first providing for the payment of any costs and expenses of preserving or disposing of the property to the extent of any benefit to the creditor, including the payment of all ad valorem property taxes with respect to the property. See 11 U.S.C. 506(c).

over-secured creditor, allowance of interest and fees

over-secured creditor, interest and fees, amounts allowable

A higher rate of default or maturity interest may be allowed to an over-secured creditor under 11 U.S.C 506(b), if the security agreement so provides. See In re Berry Estates, Inc., 34 B.R. 612 (SD NY, 1983). Again if the security agreement so provides, an award of attorney's fees may be allowed to an over-secured creditor under 11 U.S.C. 506(b), even if such fees are not recoverable under applicable state law. See In re Carey, 8 B.R. 1000 (SD CA, 1981). If the assessment of late charges is provided for in the security agreement, they may also be allowed and added to the secured claim of an over-secured creditor under 11 U.S.C. 506(b). See Matter of Scarboro, 13 B.R. 439 (MD GA, 1981). However, a $20,000 "termination charge" was not allowed because it was in the nature of a penalty. See In re American Metals Corp., 31 B.R. 229 (KS, 1983).

debtor in possession, surcharge of expenses for preserving or selling secured property

As indicated above, a trustee or debtor in possession may recover from (i.e, surcharge) property securing an allowed secured claim the reasonable and necessary costs and expenses of preserving and disposing of the property, to the extent of any benefit to the holder of the claim, including the payment of all ad valorem property taxes with respect to the property. See 11 U.S.C. 506(c). The costs and expenses recoverable from or chargeable against secured property by the trustee or debtor in possession are payable ahead of any interest, fees, costs, or charges allowed to a secured creditor under 11 U.S.C. 506(b). Further, any costs, expenses or taxes recoverable by the trustee or debtor in possession under 11 U.S.C. 506(c) are recoverable regardless of whether a creditor secured by the property is oversecured or undersecured. See In re Trim-X, Inc., 695 F. 2nd 296 (CA 7, 1982).

surcharge on secured property, burden of proof, consent of creditor

In any proceeding wherein the trustee or debtor in possession attempts to surcharge secured property under 11 U.S.C. 506(c), the burden of proof is on the trustee or debtor in possession to show that the secured creditor received a benefit from the costs, expenses or taxes which are sought to be recovered. See Brookfield Production Credit Ass'n v. Borron, 738 F. 2nd 951 (CA 8, 1984). For a surcharge to be assessed against secured property, the benefit to the secured creditor must be easily discernable and direct, rather than indirect. See Matter of By The Sea Foods, Inc., 30 B.R. 262 (MD FL, 1983), and Matter of Elmwood Farm, Inc., 19 B.R. 338 (SD NY, 1982). If a secured creditor consents to a surcharge against secured property, the charge is normally allowed even if there is no direct benefit to the secured creditor. See In re Hotel Associates, Inc., 6 B.R. 108 (ED PA, 1980). However, the consent to a surcharge must be explicit and will not be inferred. See In re Flagstaff Foodservice Corp., 739 F. 2nd 73 (CA 2, 1984).

secured creditor, allowance of claim, procedure

Filing and allowance of claims. It is obviously important to a secured creditor that its claim be properly filed and allowed. Under Chapter 11, if a claim is listed in the debtor's schedules and is not listed as disputed, contingent, or unliquidated, proof of the claim is deemed filed. See 11 U.S.C. 1111(a) and Bankruptcy Rule 3003(b)(1). If a claim is not listed in the schedules, or is listed as disputed, contingent, or unliquidated, a proof of claim must be filed by the creditor prior to the bar date in order for the claim to be allowed for purposes of both voting and distribution. See Bankruptcy Rule 3003(c)(2). The bar date is the date fixed by the court within which proofs of claims must be filed to be allowed. See Bankruptcy Rule 3003(c)(3). All creditors must be given at least 21 days notice by mail of the bar date. See Bankruptcy Rule 2002(a)(7). If a claim is inaccurately listed in the debtor's schedules as to either amount or status, a proof of claim should be filed to ensure that the claim is allowed in the proper amount and status.

secured creditor, importance of filing proof of claim

A creditor is not normally given notice of either the amount or the status of its claim as it appears in the debtor's schedules of liabilities. It is the creditor's responsibility to determine whether its claim is accurately listed in the debtor's schedules. Unless a secured creditor is generously oversecured, it is likely that its claim will not be listed to the creditor's liking in the debtor's schedules. Therefore, the best practice is for a secured creditor to file a proof of claim on its own behalf. See section 4.04, supra, for further reading on filing proofs of claim. A sample Proof of Claim may be found in Exhibit 5-C at the end of this chapter.

If a proof of a claim is properly filed or deemed filed, the claim is deemed allowed unless a party in interest objects to the allowance of the claim. See 11 U.S.C. 502(a). If an objection to the allowance of a claim is filed, the court, after notice and a hearing, must determine the amount and status of the claim. See 11 U.S.C. 502(b). Generally, the allowability of a secured claim depends on three factors: the allowability of the underlying claim against the debtor, the validity of the creditor's lien or setoff, and the value of the creditor's collateral or the amount of the setoff. An undersecured claim may be allowed in part as a secured claim and in part as an unsecured claim, unless the creditor has exercised the Section 1111(b) election, in which case the full amount of the claim is allowable as a secured claim, regardless of the value of the collateral. See 11 U.S.C. 1111(b)(2). See section 4.04, supra, for further reading on the allowability of secured claims.

allowance of claim, procedure

allowance of secured claim, factors

Accepting or rejecting plan. If a claim is impaired under a proposed plan, it is important that the claim be allowed in time to enable the creditor to vote on the acceptance or rejection of the plan. Only a creditor whose claim is deemed allowed or whose claim has been allowed by the court may vote on the acceptance or rejection of a plan. However, if an objection to the allowance of a claim has been filed, the court, after notice and a hearing, may temporarily allow the claim in an amount deemed proper by the court for the purpose of accepting or rejecting a plan. See Bankruptcy Rule 3018(a). Especially if its claim is undersecured, a secured creditor whose claim has been objected to should either obtain a ruling on the objection prior to the voting deadline or file a motion for the temporary allowance of the claim and obtain a ruling on the motion prior to the voting deadline.

impaired claim, voting on acceptance of plan, requirements

An undersecured creditor whose claim has been allowed in part as a secured claim and in part as an unsecured claim may accept or reject a plan in both capacities if its claim is impaired in both capacities. See Bankruptcy Rule 3018(d). If a class of claims is not impaired under a plan, the class and each creditor in the class are conclusively presumed to have accepted the plan and are not entitled to vote on its acceptance or rejection. See 11 U.S.C. 1126(f). This rule applies separately to the secured and unsecured portions of the claim of an undersecured creditor. Typically, fully-secured claims and the secured portion of undersecured claims are not impaired under the plan, which means that the holders of those claims are deemed to have accepted the plan and are not entitled to vote on the acceptance or rejection of the plan.

undersecured creditor, voting rights

Before being permitted to vote on the acceptance or rejection of a plan, creditors whose claims are impaired under the plan must be provided with information sufficient to enable them to make an informed decision on the matter. The party or person proposing a Chapter 11 plan is required to provide this information in the form of a disclosure statement, which must be approved by the court before it is distributed to creditors. Further, the plan proponent may not solicit the acceptance of its plan until the disclosure statement has been approved or conditionally approved by the court and distributed to creditors. Creditors whose claims are impaired must also be given notice of the disclosure statement hearing and may file objections to any proposed disclosure statement. See 11 U.S.C. 1125. See section 4.07, supra, for further reading on the Chapter 11 disclosure requirements. A sample Disclosure Statement may be found in Exhibit 4-L, at the end of chapter four, supra.

creditors, right to information, disclosure statement

After the court has approved the disclosure statement, a copy of the disclosure statement, a copy or summary of the plan, a ballot for accepting or rejecting the plan, and notice of the voting deadline must be mailed to each creditor whose claim is impaired by the plan. See Bankruptcy Rule 3017(d). Certain other materials and notices may also be mailed to creditors at this time. See section 4.08, supra, for further reading. The solicitation of acceptances or rejections of the plan may begin after these documents have been distributed to creditors. It should be noted that a creditor who opposes the acceptance of a proposed plan may, after court approval and distribution of the disclosure statement, solicit the rejection of the plan by other creditors. An objecting creditor may also appear at the disclosure statement hearing and request the court to order that relevant facts and opinions provided by the creditor be included in the disclosure statement.

voting on plan, documents sent to creditors

creditor opposed to plan, rights of

small business debtor, procedure when debtor elects to be treated as

If the debtor chooses to be treated as a small business debtor in the case, the court may conditionally approve a disclosure statement without a hearing, subject to its final approval at the disclosure statement hearing, which may be combined with the confirmation hearing. In addition, a small business debtor's plan may serve as a disclosure statement if it contains adequate information. Acceptances or rejections of a plan may be solicited based on a conditionally-approved disclosure statement as long as the debtor provides adequate information to each creditor that is solicited. A copy of the conditionally-approved disclosure statement must be mailed to each creditor at least 25 days prior to the confirmation hearing. See 11 U.S.C. 1125(f) and Bankruptcy Rule 3017.1.

acceptance of plan by class of claims, requirements

The ballot accepting or rejecting the plan must be filed by the voting deadline fixed by the court in order to be counted. Under Chapter 11, all voting on the acceptance or rejection of a plan is by class, and each claim (other than certain priority claims) must be placed in a class by the proposed plan. Acceptance of a plan by a class of creditors occurs when the plan is accepted by creditors holding at least two-thirds in dollar amount and more than one-half in number of the allowed claims in the class that actually voted on the plan. See 11 U.S.C. 1126(c). See section 4.08, supra, for further reading on the Chapter 11 voting procedures and requirements.

secured creditors, voting rights and leverage in small business cases

In small business Chapter 11 cases the secured claim of each secured creditor is usually classified separately in a one-creditor class. Typically, fully secured claims and the secured portions of undersecured claims are not impaired under the plan. This means that each secured creditor will be deemed to have accepted the plan in its secured capacity. See 11 U.S.C. 1126(f). Because no portion of their claim is impaired, fully secured creditors (and undersecured creditors who have exercised the Section 1111(b) election) normally do not get to vote on the acceptance or rejection of a plan. On the other hand, because the unsecured portions of their claims are almost always impaired by the plan, undersecured creditors typically do get to vote on the acceptance or rejection of a plan as the holders of impaired unsecured claims, unless a particular unsecured creditor exercises the Section 1111(b) election to have its claim treated as being fully secured. It should be understood that the leverage possessed by an undersecured creditor in a Chapter 11 case is directly proportional to the size of its unsecured claim. Undersecured creditors with large unsecured claims typically have considerable leverage in small business Chapter 11 cases and can often either block confirmation of a plan or, under the rule of absolute priority, prevent the debtor's owners from retaining their ownership interests in the reorganized debtor. See Section 4.09, supra, for further reading on the absolute priority rule.

objection to confirmation, when filed

Objections to plan. Procedurally, a creditor has two methods of opposing a Chapter 11 plan that impairs its claim: it can vote to reject the plan and it can file an objection to confirmation of the plan. An objection to confirmation of a plan may be filed challenging any aspect of confirmation, including the statutory confirmation requirements of 11 U.S.C. 1129(a). An objection to confirmation must be filed within the time fixed by the court for the filing of such objections, and the filing thereof creates a contested matter under Bankruptcy Rule 9014. See Bankruptcy Rule 3020(b). A creditor who is dissatisfied with either the classification of its claim under a proposed plan or the treatment of its claim under the plan, and who has reason to believe that grounds exist for a denial of confirmation, should file an objection to confirmation of the plan.

objections to confirmation, procedure

Unless heard at an earlier date, objections to confirmation are normally heard and ruled upon by the court at the confirmation hearing. It should be noted, however, that even if an objection to confirmation is not filed, a creditor may still oppose confirmation of a plan by appearing at the confirmation hearing and challenging the testimony and other evidence presented by the plan proponent. See section 4.09, supra, for further reading on objections to confirmation. A sample Objection to Confirmation may be found in Exhibit 4-P at the end of chapter four, supra.

impairment of claim, importance of determining

A secured creditor should file an objection to the confirmation of any plan that treats as unimpaired a claim that the creditor deems to be impaired by the plan. The issue of impairment is important because only impaired classes of claims are permitted to vote on the acceptance or rejection of a plan. The holder of an unimpaired secured claim must accept the treatment accorded the claim under the plan, while the holder of an impaired secured claim can usually either prevent confirmation of the plan altogether or force a cramdown, whereunder its claim must be paid in full in deferred cash payments with interest. See 11 U.S.C. 1129(b).

A claim is deemed not impaired by a plan if the plan provides for either of the following methods of treatment with respect to the claim: (1) the rights of the creditor under its claim are unaltered by the plan, or (2) any default by the debtor is cured, the original maturity date is reinstated, the creditor is compensated for any damages incurred as a result of the default, and the rights of the creditor under its claim are thereafter unaltered. See 11 U.S.C. 1124. Impairment disputes most often arise when the debtor has defaulted on a secured obligation containing an acceleration clause, which has been implemented by the debtor's default and has resulted in a foreclosure proceeding being commenced by the creditor. Generally, a default may be cured even if the foreclosure proceeding has gone to judgment, as long as the property has not been transferred to a bona fide purchaser. See section 4.06, supra, for further reading on impairment disputes.

claim, when impaired by plan

impairment disputes, context of

If the holders of one or more classes of impaired claims vote to reject a plan and confirmation is sought under the cramdown provisions of 11 U.S.C. 1129(b), the plan must meet certain requirements with respect to secured claims in order to be confirmed by the court. Generally, to be confirmed under a cramdown a plan must provide for a secured creditor to retain its lien on its collateral and for the creditor to receive deferred cash payments totalling at least the amount of its allowed secured claim and having a present value, as of the effective date of the plan, at least equal to the value of the creditor's interest in its collateral. See 11 U.S.C. 1129(b)(2)(B)(i). For all secured claims except those secured under Section 1111(b), the allowed amount of the claim is, by definition, equal to the creditor's interest in its collateral, thereby entitling the secured creditor to receive deferred cash payments with a present value equal to the amount of its allowed secured claim. The present value of future cash payments is determined by factoring in an appropriate discount or interest rate, usually the current market rate. See section 4.09, supra, for further reading.

secured creditor, cramdown rights

Because of its leverage in the case, an impaired secured creditor should consider what it would be entitled to in a cramdown before accepting or rejecting a proposed plan. Generally, an impaired secured creditor should not accept a plan unless the plan either provides for the surrender of the creditor's collateral or provides for payment in full of its allowed secured claim, either in cash on the effective date of the plan or in deferred cash payments with interest at or above the current market rate. Similarly, an undersecured creditor exercising the Section 1111(b) election should not accept a plan unless the plan provides for deferred cash payments totalling the amount of its allowed secured claim. See infra, this section for further reading on the Section 1111(b) election.

secured creditor, acceptance or rejection of plan, considerations

The Section 1111(b) election. It is important for an undersecured creditor to fully understand the Section 1111(b) election. It should be understood, for example, that in a cramdown the claims of undersecured creditors exercising the Section 1111(b) election are subject to different payment requirements than fully secured claims. Because the allowed secured claim of a creditor exercising the Section 1111(b) election is normally larger than the creditor's interest in its collateral, and because a plan need only provide for deferred cash payments totalling at least the amount of the allowed secured claim, if the total of such payments is greater than the present value of the creditor's interest in its collateral, then that is all that a plan need provide to meet the cramdown requirement of 11 U.S.C. 1129(b)(2)(B)(i)(II). Thus, in a cramdown most undersecured creditors exercising the Section 1111(b) election need only be paid deferred cash payments without interest totalling the amount of the creditor's allowed secured claim after the election without interest. An illustration of this payment requirement is set forth in the third paragraph below.

undersecured creditor exercising Section 1111(b) election, cramdown rights

For undersecured creditors, the decision on whether to exercise the Section 1111(b) election can be a difficult one to make, especially if confirmation is sought under a cramdown. Because a creditor exercising the Section 1111(b) election loses its unsecured claim, the amount paid to the holders of unsecured claims under the plan is an important factor to consider in deciding whether to exercise the election. If the plan proposes to pay unsecured claims in full, then nothing would be gained by exercising the election. However, if, as is more often the case, the plan proposes to pay unsecured creditors only a few cents on the dollar, much could be gained by exercising the election, especially if the unsecured portion of the creditor's claim is large.

exercise of Section 1111(b) election, factors to consider

Section 1111(b) election, amount received if exercised

In making the Section 1111(b) election, a creditor should understand that if the election is made the creditor is only entitled to receive deferred cash payments totalling the greater of the amount of its allowed secured claim after the election or the present value of its interest in its collateral. See 11 U.S.C. 1129(b)(2)(A)(i)(II). Unless the unsecured portion of the creditor's claim is small, the creditor will most likely be entitled to receive deferred cash payments totalling the amount of its allowed secured claim after the election. Further, because an electing creditor is not entitled to receive the present value of its allowed secured claim, interest need not be paid on the claim.

Section 1111(b) election, example

Suppose, for example, that an undersecured creditor has an allowed claim of $10,000, which is secured by collateral valued at $7,000. If the creditor does not exercise the Section 1111(b) election, it will be entitled to receive deferred cash payments with a present value equal to $7,000 on the secured portion of its claim, plus whatever is being paid under the plan to the holders of unsecured claims on the $3,000 unsecured balance of its claim. If the discount rate is 10 percent and if the payments are to be extended over a four-year period, the creditor, by not exercising the election, will receive payments totalling approximately $9,800 on the secured portion of its claim. If the creditor exercises the Section 1111(b) election, it will have an allowed secured claim of $10,000 and no unsecured claim. Because the value of its interest in its collateral is still only $7,000 (the present value of which in deferred cash payments is $9,800), the electing creditor is entitled to receive deferred cash payments totalling $10,000. Therefore, if a dividend of even 10 percent is paid to the holders of unsecured claims, the creditor would be better off not exercising the election.

exercise of Section 1111(b) election, voting considerations

Another factor to consider in making the Section 1111(b) election is the voting power of the creditor's unsecured claim. If its unsecured claim is of sufficient size to enable the creditor to control the vote of the unsecured creditor class of claims, it may not be wise to exercise the election, especially if the creditor is opposed to the plan. If there are no other classes of claims that will accept the plan, the creditor, by voting the unsecured creditor class to reject the plan, may be able to preclude confirmation of the plan, even under a cramdown. If another class of impaired claims votes to accept the plan and confirmation is sought under a cramdown, by voting the unsecured class to reject the plan, the full payment of its unsecured claim may be required under the rule of absolute priority if the ownership interests of the debtor's owners are to survive under the plan. See section 4.09, supra, for further reading on the absolute priority rule.

Section 1111(b) election, when and how to exercise

The Section 1111(b) election may be exercised at any time prior to the conclusion of the hearing on the disclosure statement, or within such later time as the court may fix. If the debtor elected to be treated as a small business in the case and the court conditionally approved the disclosure statement and did not hold a disclosure statement hearing, the Section 1111(b) election may be made not later than the date fixed by the court for filing objections to the disclosure statement or not later than another date fixed by the court. See Bankruptcy Rule 3014, which also provides that unless made at the disclosure statement hearing, the election must be in writing and signed. If there is more than one creditor in the class, the affirmative vote of the holders of at least two-thirds in amount and one-half in number of the allowed claims in the class is required to exercise the election. See 11 U.S.C. 1111(b)(1)(A)(i). It should be noted that the Section 1111(b) election may not be exercised if the interests of the class of claims in the collateral is of inconsequential value or if a claim in the class is a recourse claim and the collateral is sold, either during the case or under a plan. See 11 U.S.C. 1111(b)(1)(B). As a practical matter, the Section 1111(b) election should not be made until all relevant aspects of a proposed plan have been finalized by the plan proponent.

secured creditor, postconfirmation rights

Payment of claims. After confirmation of the plan, a secured creditor should commence receiving its deferred cash payments or other distributions or transfers as provided under the plan. If, after confirmation, the reorganized debtor or other obligor under the plan defaults on an obligation set forth in the plan, a creditor may normally pursue either its bankruptcy or nonbankruptcy remedies. For example, a secured creditor may foreclose on a lien provided for in the plan in a nonbankruptcy forum without first obtaining relief from either the automatic stay or the permanent injunction that accompanies a debtor's discharge. See In re Ernst, 45 B.R. 700 (MN, 1985). If desired, a secured creditor may also be able to obtain relief in the bankruptcy court, especially if the plan or the order of confirmation contains a broad reservation of jurisdiction in the bankruptcy court. See section 4.11, supra, for further reading on postconfirmation remedies.

Another remedy available to an aggrieved creditor is to request revocation of the order of confirmation, if cause exists therefor. However, an order of confirmation may be revoked only upon a showing that the order was procured by fraud and only if the revocation proceeding is commenced within 180 days after the date of the confirmation order. See 11 U.S.C. 1144. See section 4.10, supra, for further reading on revocation of confirmation orders.

revocation of confirmation, requirements

Still another remedy of an aggrieved or dissatisfied Chapter 11 creditor is to seek dismissal of the case or conversion of the case to Chapter 7. A creditor, as a party in interest, may file a motion for the dismissal or conversion of a Chapter 11 case for cause at any time prior to substantial consummation of a plan. See 11 U.S.C. 1112(b), which lists some 16 specific causes for dismissal or conversion. Included in this list are failure to maintain appropriate insurance, unauthorized use of cash collateral, failure to pay taxes, an inability to effectuate substantial consummation of a confirmed plan and a material default with respect to a confirmed plan. See 11 U.S.C. 1112(b)(4). If any of these causes exist, a motion for dismissal or conversion may be in order. See section 4.14, supra, for further reading on the dismissal or conversion of a Chapter 11 case.

dismissal or conversion of case, requirements

If a secured creditor is required under the plan to surrender property, relinquish a lien, or perform any other act as a condition of receiving distribution under the plan, such act must be performed within five years after the date of the order of confirmation in order for the creditor to be entitled to distribution. See 11 U.S.C. 1143. It has been held that if a creditor fails to perform the required act within the five-year period, it is not entitled to distribution under the plan even if it had no notice of the requirement to perform the act. See In re George Rodman, Inc., 50 B.R. 313 (WD OK, 1985).

conditions to distribution, time for performance

5.03 Representing an Unsecured Creditor in a Chapter 11 Case

unsecured creditors, attitude toward Chapter 11 cases

Unsecured creditors generally favor Chapter 11 reorganizations for financially-troubled small business debtors. Most unsecured creditors realize that if the debtor files under Chapter 7, or simply closes its doors, they are likely to receive little or nothing on their claims. Under Chapter 11, not only does an unsecured creditor normally receive payment of at least a portion of its claim, but the debtor remains in business, leaving open the possibility for the creditor to recoup its past losses with future profits.

unsecured creditors, role in Chapter 11 case

Typically, there are two types of unsecured creditors in small business Chapter 11 cases: trade creditors and undersecured institutional creditors. Unsecured trade creditors have little leverage in most small business Chapter 11 cases. In most instances their primary concern is to obtain the allowance of their claims and seek the confirmation of a plan that pays the maximum possible dividend to the holders of general unsecured claims. Depending on the size of the unsecured portion of their claims, undersecured institutional creditors often have considerable leverage in small business cases. See sections 4.09 and 5.02, supra, for further reading on this matter.

creditor, definition

claim, definition

unsecured creditor, definition

A creditor is an entity that has a claim against the debtor that arose, or is treated as having arisen, at the time of or before the order for relief concerning the debtor. See 11 U.S.C. 101(10). A claim is a right to payment or a right to an equitable remedy for breach of performance if such breach gives rise to a right of payment. See 11 U.S.C. 101(5). An unsecured claim is a claim that is not secured by a lien on property of the estate and is not subject to a setoff. See 11 U.S.C. 506(a). An unsecured creditor, then, is the holder of an allowed prepetition unsecured claim against the debtor. The holder of an undersecured claim who does not exercise the Section 1111(b) election is an unsecured creditor to the extent that the amount of its allowed claim exceeds the value of its security or the amount subject to setoff. See 11 U.S.C. 506(a). See sections 4.09 and 5.02, supra, for further reading on the Section 1111(b) election.

unsecured claims, types of, definitions

For purposes of priority of payment, there are four types of unsecured claims under the Bankruptcy Code: (1) superpriority claims, (2) priority claims, (3) nonpriority claims, and (4) subordinated nonpriority claims. Superpriority claims are unsecured claims arising after the commencement of a Chapter 11 case that must be paid ahead of all other unsecured claims, including the expenses of administering the case. Priority claims are unsecured claims that are entitled to payment, in the order of their priority, ahead of all nonpriority unsecured claims. Nonpriority claims are general unsecured claims without priority of payment. Subordinated nonpriority claims are general unsecured claims that have been subordinated, either by agreement or by the court, to all or certain other nonpriority claims for purposes of payment. See section 4.04, supra, for a discussion of the subordination of claims.

claim arising from operation of debtor's business during case, treatment of

Under the Bankruptcy Code there are two superpriority claims and ten classes of priority claims, each of which has a different priority of payment. See 11 U.S.C. 507(a). To avoid confusion, it should be noted here that an unsecured claim against the debtor in possession arising in the ordinary course of operating the debtor's business after the commencement of the case is treated as an administrative expense and constitutes a first priority claim. See 11 U.S.C. 364(a), 503(b). See section 4.04, supra, for further reading on the priority of claims, and for a list showing the priority of payment for all claims in a Chapter 11 case.

classification of claims in plan, requirements

The classification of unsecured claims for purposes of priority of payment should not be confused with the classification of claims in a Chapter 11 plan for purposes of treatment under the plan. A Chapter 11 plan is required to classify all claims except certain priority claims, and, with the exception of small unsecured claims, may place a claim in a particular class only if it is substantially similar to all other claims in the class. See 11 U.S.C. 1122. While the priority of payment to which a claim is entitled is a factor in determining the classification of a claim in a Chapter 11 plan, it is not the only factor. Generally, if a valid reason exists for doing so, a Chapter 11 plan may separate nonpriority unsecured claims into different classes and treat the classes differently under the plan. See section 4.06, supra, for further reading on the classification of unsecured claims in a Chapter 11 plan.

One of the first concerns of an unsecured creditor after the filing of a Chapter 11 case is the effect of the automatic stay. The automatic stay that accompanies the filing of either a voluntary or involuntary petition under Chapter 11 prohibits collection and other activities by unsecured creditors to recover claims against the debtor that arose before the commencement of the case and prohibits the enforcement of judgments obtained before the commencement of the case against either the debtor or property of the estate. See 11 U.S.C. 362(a)(1),(2),(6). Such acts as telephone calls or the sending of letters or bills to the debtor, if for purposes of collecting a prepetition debt, are prohibited by the automatic stay. See section 4.01, supra, for further reading on the effect and extent of the automatic stay.

automatic stay, effect of on unsecured creditor

Unsecured creditors may seek relief from the automatic stay for cause. See 11 U.S.C. 362(d)(1). However, for unsecured creditors cause does not normally include lack of adequate protection of an interest in property. See section 4.01, supra, for further reading on obtaining relief from the automatic stay.

unsecured creditor, relief from stay

A creditor who intentionally violates the automatic stay may be held in contempt of court, fined, or be held liable for damages to the debtor. Any action taken in violation of the automatic stay, either intentionally or unintentionally, is voidable at the request of the trustee or debtor in possession. See section 4.01, supra, for further reading on the automatic stay.

violation of stay, consequences of

Another matter of concern to unsecured creditors early in a Chapter 11 case is the appointment of the unsecured creditors' committee, if one is appointed. If the debtor is treated as a small business debtor in the case, the court may dispense with the appointment of creditors' committees. See 11 U.S.C. 1102(a)(3). If appointed, the unsecured creditors' committee represents the interests of nonpriority unsecured creditors, and may play an important role in representing the interests of general unsecured creditors in Chapter 11 cases. A principal function of the unsecured creditors' committee in many cases is to work with the debtor in formulating a plan that is acceptable to unsecured creditors.

unsecured creditors' committee, appointment of

The unsecured creditors' committee is appointed by the U.S. Trustee and is normally composed of the seven largest unsecured creditors who are willing to serve. If an unsecured creditor wishes to serve on the unsecured creditors' committee but does not hold one of the seven largest unsecured claims against the debtor, the creditor should so inform the U.S. Trustee early in the case. In any event, all unsecured creditors should be aware of the functions performed by the unsecured creditors' committee. A creditors' committee is required to provide access to information for and solicit and receive comments from creditors who hold claims of the kind represented by the committee and are not appointed to the committee. See 11 U.S.C. 1102(b)(3). See section 4.03, supra, for further reading on creditors' committees.

unsecured creditors' committee, composition of

If cause for the appointment of a trustee or examiner exists, an unsecured creditor, as a party in interest, may request the court to order the appointment thereof. See 11 U.S.C. 1104(a), (b). Cause for the appointment of a trustee includes fraud, dishonesty, incompetence, gross mismanagement of the affairs of the debtor by current management, either before or after the commencement of the case, or similar cause. See 11 U.S.C. 1104(a)(1). A trustee may also be appointed if such appointment is in the best interests of creditors, equity security holders, and other interests of the estate or if grounds exist to dismiss or convert the case but the court determines that the appointment of a trustee would better serve the interests of creditors and the estate. See 11 U.S.C. 1104(a)(2), (3). An examiner may be ordered appointed if such appointment is in the best interests of creditors, equity security holders, and the estate. See 11 U.S.C. 1104(b)(1). If an unsecured creditor wishes to request the appointment of a trustee or examiner in the case, the best practice is to bring the matter before the unsecured creditor's committee, if one has been appointed, and request the committee to join in the request. See 11 U.S.C. 1103(c)(4). See section 4.12, supra, for further reading on matters related to the appointment of a trustee or examiner.

trustee, grounds for appointment of

examiner, grounds for appointment of

Executory contracts and unexpired leases. Many actual or potential unsecured creditors are parties to executory contracts or unexpired leases with a Chapter 11 debtor. Such persons should be aware of the rights of a debtor in possession to reject, assume, or assign such contracts or leases. An executory contract or unexpired lease may be rejected, assumed, or assigned by a debtor in possession either as a part of a Chapter 11 plan or by motion during the course of the case. Such a contract or lease may be rejected regardless of when or under what circumstances it was entered into, and the nondebtor party to the contract or lease is usually left with only an unsecured nonpriority claim in the case.

executory contracts, rejection or assumption by debtor in possession

executory contracts, rights of nondebtor party

A nondebtor party to an executory contract or unexpired lease with a Chapter 11 debtor has certain rights under the Bankruptcy Code. These rights include the following:

executory contract breached by debtor, necessity of cure

(1) If an executory contract or unexpired lease has been breached by the debtor either prior to or after the commencement of the case, the contract or lease may be assumed by the debtor only if the default is cured, the nondebtor party is compensated for any losses incurred as a result of the breach, and adequate assurance of future performance under the contract or lease is provided. See 11 U.S.C. 365(b)(1).

assignment of executory contract, necessity of assumption

(2) In order to assign an executory contract or unexpired lease, the debtor must first assume the contract or lease and provide adequate assurance of future performance of the contract or lease by the assignee. See 11 U.S.C. 365(f)(2).

personal service contracts, necessity of consent before assumption

(3) Certain types of contracts or leases may not be assigned by the debtor without the consent of the nondebtor party. Included here are personal service contracts of the debtor wherein the debtor is required to personally perform the services, contracts to make loans or extend credit to the debtor, and leases of nonresidential real property that have been terminated prior to the order for relief in the Chapter 11 case. See 11 U.S.C. 365(c).

rejection of executory contract, claim for damages

(4) If the debtor rejects an executory contract or unexpired lease of the debtor, the nondebtor party to the contract or lease has a claim for damages for breach of contract to the full extent that such damages may be recovered under applicable nonbankruptcy law, except that limitations are placed on damages recoverable from the rejection of a lease of real property, an employment contract, and a contract for the sale of real property where the purchaser is in possession. Damage claims resulting from the rejection of executory contracts or unexpired leases, even though they normally arise after the commencement of the case, are treated as prepetition nonpriority unsecured claims unless the creditor is independently secured by a lien or setoff or is independently entitled to a priority for all or a part of its damage claim. See 11 U.S.C. 365(g).

nondebtor party, right to compel assumption or rejection of executory contract

(5) If the debtor fails or refuses to either assume or reject an executory contract or unexpired lease, the nondebtor party to the contract or lease may request the court to order the debtor to assume or reject the contract or lease within a specified period of time. See 11 U.S.C. 365(d)(2). However, a lease of nonresidential real property under which the debtor is the lessee is deemed rejected and the property must immediately be surrendered if the lease is not assumed or rejected within 120 days after the date of the order for relief, unless the court grants additional time. See 11 U.S.C. 365(d)(4).

rejection of intellectual property contract, licensee's rights

(6) If the debtor rejects an executory contract under which the debtor is a licensor of a right to intellectual property, the licensee may usually either treat the contract as terminated or retain its rights under the contract. See 11 U.S.C. 365(n). See section 4.05, supra, for further reading.

business leases, duties of debtor

(7) The debtor is required to timely perform all obligations that arise after date of the order for relief under an unexpired lease of nonresidential real property until such time as the lease is either assumed or rejected, unless the court extends the time for performance of these obligations. See 11 U.S.C. 365(d)(3).

equipment leases, duties of debtor

(8) The debtor is required to timely perform all obligations that arise 60 days or more after the date of the order for relief under an unexpired lease of equipment or other non-household personal property until such time as the lease is either assumed or rejected, unless the court orders otherwise. See 11 U.S.C. 365(d)(5).

executory contracts, further reading

The treatment of executory contracts and unexpired leases in Chapter 11 cases is discussed at length in section 4.05, supra, and the reader is referred to that section for further reading.

Filing and allowance of claims. It is obviously important for an unsecured creditor to be aware of the claim allowance procedure in a Chapter 11 case. Under Chapter 11, claim allowance plays an important role in establishing the two most significant rights of an unsecured creditor: the right to vote on the acceptance or rejection of a plan, and the right to distribution under the plan. Only a creditor whose claim has been allowed, deemed allowed, or temporarily allowed may vote on the acceptance or rejection of a plan, and only the holder of an allowed claim may participate in distributions under a plan. See 11 U.S.C. 1126(a) and Bankruptcy Rules 3018(a) and 3021.

allowance of claim, importance of

In a Chapter 11 case a proof of claim is deemed filed for any claim that appears in the debtor's schedule of liabilities, unless the claim is listed as disputed, contingent, or unliquidated. See 11 U.S.C. 1111(a) and Bankruptcy Rule 3003(b)(1). If a claim is not listed in the debtor's schedules, or if the claim is listed as a disputed, contingent, or unliquidated claim, a proof of claim must be filed in order for the claim to be allowed. See Bankruptcy Rule 3003(c)(2). If a claim is inaccurately listed in the debtor's schedule of liabilities, a proof of claim must be filed in order for the claim to be allowed in the proper amount and status.

proof of claim, filing procedure

Once a proof of claim has been filed, or deemed filed, the claim is deemed allowed as shown on the proof of claim or schedule unless a party in interest files an objection to the allowance of the claim. See 11 U.S.C. 502(a). Thus, if a claim is listed in the debtor's schedule of liabilities and is not later objected to, the claim will be deemed allowed as it appears in the debtor's schedule. If an objection to the allowance of the claim is filed, the court, after a hearing on notice, must determine the allowance of the claim. See 11 U.S.C. 502(b).

allowance of claim, procedure

In practice, a creditor is not normally given notice of either the amount or the status of its claim as it appears in the debtor's schedules of liabilities. It is the responsibility of a creditor to determine whether its claim is accurately listed in the debtor's schedules and whether it is listed as disputed, contingent, or unliquidated. The safest practice, therefore, is for a creditor to file a proof of claim with the court prior to the bar date, which is the date set by the court after which a proof of claim may not be filed. See section 4.04, supra, for further reading on the allowance of claims. A sample Proof of Claim is set forth in Exhibit 5-C at the end of this chapter.

proof of claim, necessity of filing

If a claim is impaired under a proposed Chapter 11 plan, as most unsecured claims are, it is important that the claim be allowed, or deemed allowed, in time to permit the creditor to vote on the acceptance or rejection of the plan. Only a creditor whose claim is deemed allowed because it has not been objected to, or whose claim has been allowed by the court, may vote on the acceptance or rejection of a plan. However, if an objection to the allowance of a claim has been filed, the court, after notice and a hearing, may temporarily allow the claim in an amount deemed proper for the purpose of accepting or rejecting a plan. See Bankruptcy Rule 3018(a). A creditor whose claim has been objected to should either obtain a ruling on the objection prior to the voting deadline or file a motion for the temporary allowance of its claim and obtain a ruling on the motion prior to the voting deadline. See section 4.08, supra, for further reading on the voting rights of creditors in Chapter 11 cases.

unsecured creditor, right to vote on acceptance of plan, requirements

An objection to the allowance of a claim may be filed at any time, even after the claim has been paid. See Bankruptcy Rule 3007 and the Advisory Committee's Notes thereto. In Chapter 11 cases, objections to the allowance of unsecured claims are often filed after confirmation of the plan when the final list of creditors is prepared, and a common hearing on all such objections is often scheduled. Thus, an unsecured creditor may not know until after confirmation whether its claim will be allowed for purposes of distribution.

objection to allowance of claim, when to file

Acceptance or rejection of plan. Before being permitted to vote on the acceptance or rejection of a plan, creditors must be provided with information sufficient to enable them to make an informed decision on the matter. The party or person proposing a Chapter 11 plan is required to provide this information in the form of a disclosure statement, which must be approved by the court before it is distributed to creditors. Further, the plan proponent may not solicit the acceptance of its plan until the disclosure statement has been approved by the court and distributed to creditors. Creditors must also be given notice of the disclosure statement hearing and may file objections to any proposed disclosure statement. See 11 U.S.C. 1125. See section 4.07, supra, for further reading on the Chapter 11 disclosure requirements. A sample Disclosure Statement may be found in Exhibit 4-L at the end of chapter four, supra.

creditors, right to adequate information, disclosure statement voting on plan, materials supplied to creditors

After the court has approved a disclosure statement, a copy of the disclosure statement, a copy or summary of the plan, a ballot for accepting or rejecting the plan, and notice of the deadline for voting on the plan must be mailed to each creditor. See Bankruptcy Rule 3017(d). Certain other materials and notices may also be mailed to creditors at this time. See section 4.08, supra, for further reading. The solicitation of acceptances or rejections of the plan may begin after these documents have been distributed to creditors. A creditor who opposes a proposed plan may, at this time, solicit rejection of the plan by other creditors.

small business debtor, procedure when debtor elects to be treated as

If the debtor is treated as a small business debtor in the case, the court may conditionally approve a disclosure statement without a hearing, subject to its final approval at the disclosure statement hearing, which may be combined with the confirmation hearing, and the plan may serve as a disclosure statement if it contains adequate information. Acceptances or rejections of a plan may be solicited based on a conditionally-approved disclosure statement as long as the debtor provides adequate information to each creditor that is solicited. A copy of the conditionally-approved disclosure statement must be mailed to each creditor at least 25 days prior to the confirmation hearing. See 11 U.S.C. 1125(f).

acceptance of plan by class of claims, voting requirements

The ballot accepting or rejecting the plan must be filed prior to the voting deadline fixed by the court in order to be counted. Under Chapter 11, all voting on the acceptance or rejection of a plan is by class, and each claim (other than certain priority claims) must be placed in a class by the proposed plan. Acceptance of a plan by a class of creditors occurs when the plan is accepted by creditors holding at least two-thirds in dollar amount and more than one-half in number of the allowed claims in the class that actually voted on the plan. See 11 U.S.C. 1126(c). See section 4.08, supra, for further reading on the Chapter 11 voting procedures and requirements.

obligation to confirmation, grounds for filing

Procedurally, an unsecured creditor in a Chapter 11 case has two methods of opposing a plan that impairs its claim: it can vote to reject the plan, and it can file an objection to confirmation of the plan. An objection to confirmation of a plan may be filed challenging any aspect of confirmation, including the statutory confirmation requirements of 11 U.S.C. 1129(a). An objection to confirmation must be filed within the time fixed by the court for the filing of such objections, and the filing thereof creates a contested matter under Bankruptcy Rule 9014. See Bankruptcy Rule 3020(b). A creditor who is dissatisfied with either the classification of its claim under a proposed plan or the treatment of its claim under the plan, and who has reason to believe that grounds exist for a denial of confirmation, should file an objection to confirmation of the plan.

confirmation hearing, rights of creditors

Unless heard at an earlier date, an objection to confirmation will normally be heard by the court at the confirmation hearing. It should be noted, however, that even if an objection to confirmation is not filed, a creditor may still oppose confirmation of a plan by appearing at the confirmation hearing and challenging the testimony and other evidence presented by the plan proponent. See section 4.09, supra, for further reading on objections to confirmation. A sample Objection to Confirmation may be found in Exhibit 4-P at the end of chapter four, supra.

classification of claims in plan, requirements

In deciding whether to file an objection to confirmation of a plan, an unsecured creditor should check both the classification of its claim in the plan and the treatment accorded its claim under the plan. In classifying claims, a plan may place a claim in a particular class only if the claim is substantially similar to other claims in the class. See 11 U.S.C. 1122(a). For example, priority claims may not be placed in a class with nonpriority claims, and secured claims may not be placed in a class with unsecured claims. However, a separate class of claims may be created consisting of all unsecured claims that are less than or reduced to an amount that the court approves as reasonable and necessary for administrative convenience. See 11 U.S.C. 1122(b). While claims for administrative expenses, gap claims in involuntary cases, and unsecured tax claims may not be classified in a plan, all other claims, secured and unsecured, priority and nonpriority, must be placed in a class under the plan. See 11 U.S.C. 1123(a)(1). A creditor that is not satisfied with the classification of its claim in a plan should either file an objection to confirmation of the plan or file a motion to determine classes of creditors under Bankruptcy Rule 3013. See section 4.06, supra, for further reading on the classification of claims in a plan.

To be confirmed under 11 U.S.C. 1129(a), a Chapter 11 plan need only provide for the holder of an unsecured claim to receive property of a value that is not less than what the holder would receive if the debtor was liquidated under Chapter 7 of the Bankruptcy Code on the effective date of the plan. See 11 U.S.C. 1129(a)(7)(A)(ii). This test is often referred to as the "best interests" test, and is discussed further in section 4.09, supra. An unsecured creditor should vote to reject, and file an objection to the confirmation of, any plan that fails to meet the "best interests" test with respect to the creditor's claim.

unsecured creditor, best interests test

Another matter of concern to unsecured creditors in deciding whether to accept or reject a plan is the rule of absolute priority as it applies to classes of unsecured claims. Under the rule of absolute priority, which applies only when confirmation is sought under the cramdown provisions of 11 U.S.C. 1129(b), a senior class of claims must be paid in full before any distribution can be made to a junior class of claims or interests. See 11 U.S.C. 1129(b)(2)(B). Because unsecured claims are senior to the interests of the debtor's owners, the rule of absolute priority may require unsecured claims to be paid in full if the interests of the debtor's owners are to survive the plan. By voting to reject a plan, a class of unsecured creditors can force a cramdown, wherein the rule of absolute priority must be applied. See section 4.09, supra, for further reading on the rule of absolute priority.

unsecured creditors, rule of absolute priority, requirements

Payment of claims. To be confirmed, a plan must provide for payment in full in cash on the effective date of the plan of all administrative and gap claims, unless the holder of a particular claim agrees otherwise. See 11 U.S.C. 1129(a)(9)(A). Unless the holder of a particular claim agrees otherwise, all other priority claims, except unsecured tax claims, must also be paid in full, either in cash on the effective date of the plan, or, if a class of such claims votes to accept such payments, in deferred cash payments with interest. See 11 U.S.C. 1129(a)(9)(B). Priority unsecured tax claims must be paid in full in regular cash payments with interest within 5 years of the date of the order for relief. See 11 U.S.C. 1129(a)(9)(C). If a plan does not provide for the payment of a priority claim as set forth above in this paragraph, the holder of such a claim should file an objection to confirmation of the plan. See section 4.09, supra, for further reading on the Chapter 11 confirmation requirements.

priority claims, confirmation requirements

After the confirmation of a plan, the debtor will normally prepare a final list of creditors for the purpose of making distributions as provided in the plan. In preparing this list, objections may be filed to the allowance of certain claims, usually nonpriority unsecured claims, and a hearing will be scheduled on the objections. Even if an objection is not filed with respect to its claim, an unsecured creditor should check to ensure that its claim is correctly included in the final list of creditors. See sections 4.04 and 4.11, supra, for further reading.

final list of creditors, preparation procedure

If, after confirmation of a plan, a creditor fails to receive the payments or other distributions called for under the plan, the creditor may normally pursue either its bankruptcy or nonbankruptcy remedies against the reorganized debtor or other obligor under the plan. The nonbankruptcy remedies of an unsecured creditor may include the filing of an action against the reorganized debtor or other obligor under the plan in a state court or other nonbankruptcy forum. An unsecured creditor's bankruptcy remedies may include the filing of an adversary proceeding to revoke the order of confirmation or the filing of a motion to dismiss the case or convert the case to a case under Chapter 7. See section 4.13, supra, for further reading on related litigation. See section 4.10, supra, for further reading on revocation of confirmation. See section 4.14, supra, for further reading on the dismissal or conversion of a Chapter 11 case.

unsecured creditor, postconfirmation rights

Fill in this information to identify the case:

United States Bankruptcy Court for the:
Eastern District of New York (State)

Case number (*If known*): 16-00987 Chapter 11

☐ Check if this is an amended filing

Official Form 205

Involuntary Petition Against a Non-Individual

12/15

Use this form to begin a bankruptcy case against a non-individual you allege to be a debtor subject to an involuntary case. If you want to begin a case against an individual, use the *Involuntary Petition Against an Individual* (Official Form 105). Be as complete and accurate as possible. If more space is needed, attach any additional sheets to this form. On the top of any additional pages, write debtor's name and case number (if known).

Part 1: Identify the Chapter of the Bankruptcy Code Under Which Petition Is Filed

1. **Chapter of the Bankruptcy Code**

   Check one:

   ☐ Chapter 7
   ☒ Chapter 11

Part 2: Identify the Debtor

2. **Debtor's name** Cleaner Image Dry Cleaners, Inc.

3. **Other names you know the debtor has used in the last 8 years** Cleaner Image Laundry Services

   Include any assumed names, trade names, or *doing business as* names.

4. **Debtor's federal Employer Identification Number (EIN)**

   ☐ Unknown

   84-3378966
   EIN

5. **Debtor's address**

   Principal place of business

   6900 Black Forest Avenue
   Number Street

   Buffalo NY 14206
   City State ZIP Code

   Erie
   County

   Mailing address, if different

   P.O. Box 2345
   Number Street

   P.O. Box

   Buffalo NY 14216
   City State ZIP Code

   Location of principal assets, if different from principal place of business

   Number Street

   City State ZIP Code

Debtor Cleaner Image Dry Cleaners, Inc. Case number *(if known)* 16-00987
Name

6. Debtor's website (URL) www.cleanerimage.com

7. Type of debtor

☒ Corporation (including Limited Liability Company (LLC) and Limited Liability Partnership (LLP))
☐ Partnership (excluding LLP)
☐ Other type of debtor. Specify: ______

8. Type of debtor's business

Check one:

☐ Health Care Business (as defined in 11 U.S.C. § 101(27A))
☐ Single Asset Real Estate (as defined in 11 U.S.C. § 101(51B))
☐ Railroad (as defined in 11 U.S.C. § 101(44))
☐ Stockbroker (as defined in 11 U.S.C. § 101(53A))
☐ Commodity Broker (as defined in 11 U.S.C. § 101(6))
☐ Clearing Bank (as defined in 11 U.S.C. § 781(3))
☒ None of the types of business listed.
☐ Unknown type of business.

9. To the best of your knowledge, are any bankruptcy cases pending by or against any partner or affiliate of this debtor?

☒ No
☐ Yes. Debtor ______ Relationship ______
District ______ Date filed ______ MM / DD / YYYY Case number, if known ______

Debtor ______ Relationship ______
District ______ Date filed ______ MM / DD / YYYY Case number, if known ______

Part 3: Report About the Case

10. Venue

Check one:

☒ Over the last 180 days before the filing of this bankruptcy, the debtor had a domicile, principal place of business, or principal assets in this district longer than in any other district.

☐ A bankruptcy case concerning debtor's affiliates, general partner, or partnership is pending in this district.

11. Allegations

Each petitioner is eligible to file this petition under 11 U.S.C. § 303(b).
The debtor may be the subject of an involuntary case under 11 U.S.C. § 303(a).

At least one box must be checked:

☒ The debtor is generally not paying its debts as they become due, unless they are the subject of a bona fide dispute as to liability or amount.

☐ Within 120 days before the filing of this petition, a custodian, other than a trustee, receiver, or an agent appointed or authorized to take charge of less than substantially all of the property of the debtor for the purpose of enforcing a lien against such property, was appointed or took possession.

12. Has there been a transfer of any claim against the debtor by or to any petitioner?

☒ No
☐ Yes. Attach all documents that evidence the transfer and any statements required under Bankruptcy Rule 1003(a).

Debtor Cleaner Image Dry Cleaners, Inc. Case number (if known) 16-00987
Name

13. Each petitioner's claim

Name of petitioner	Nature of petitioner's claim	Amount of the claim above the value of any lien
Allied Laundry Supplies, Inc.	secured note	$ 415,879.90
Erie Real Estate, LLC .	unpaid rent	$ 38,900.00
Dover Laundry Supplies, Inc.	trade account	$ 28,907.69
	Total of petitioners' claims	$ 483,687.59

If more space is needed to list petitioners, attach additional sheets. Write the alleged debtor's name and the case number, if known, at the top of each sheet. Following the format of this form, set out the information required in Parts 3 and 4 of the form for each additional petitioning creditor, the petitioner's claim, the petitioner's representative, and the petitioner's attorney. Include the statement under penalty of perjury set out in Part 4 of the form, followed by each additional petitioner's (or representative's) signature, along with the signature of the petitioner's attorney.

Part 4: Request for Relief

WARNING -- Bankruptcy fraud is a serious crime. Making a false statement in connection with a bankruptcy case can result in fines up to $500,000 or imprisonment for up to 20 years, or both. 18 U.S.C. §§ 152, 1341, 1519, and 3571.

Petitioners request that an order for relief be entered against the debtor under the chapter of 11 U.S.C. specified in this petition. If a petitioning creditor is a corporation, attach the corporate ownership statement required by Bankruptcy Rule 1010(b). If any petitioner is a foreign representative appointed in a foreign proceeding, attach a certified copy of the order of the court granting recognition.

I have examined the information in this document and have a reasonable belief that the information is true and correct.

Petitioners or Petitioners' Representative

Name and mailing address of petitioner

Allied Laundry Supplies, Inc.
Name

2300 South 3rd Avenue
Number Street

Boston MA 02104
City State ZIP Code

Name and mailing address of petitioner's representative, if any

John Smith, President
Name

2300 South 3rd Avenue
Number Street

Boston MA 02104
City State ZIP Code

I declare under penalty of perjury that the foregoing is true and correct.

Executed on 2/25/2016
MM / DD / YYYY

✗ /s/ John Smith, President
Signature of petitioner or representative, including representative's title

Attorneys

James B. Jones, Esq.
Printed name

Applewhite, Jones & Dunnings, P.C.
Firm name, if any

3546 Brisbane Blvd., Ste 1800
Number Street

Boston MA 02108
City State ZIP Code

Contact phone (716) 244-9087 Email jjones@ajdatty.com

Bar number 05-32908

State MA

✗ /s/ James B. Jones, Esq.
Signature of attorney

Date signed 2/25/2016
MM / DD / YYYY

Debtor Cleaner Image Dry Cleaners, Inc. Case number (if known) 16-00987

Name and mailing address of petitioner

Erie Real Estate, LLC
Name

233 State Street
Number Street

Erie NY 14150
City State ZIP Code

Name and mailing address of petitioner's representative, if any

David Davis, Manager
Name

233 State Street
Number Street

Erie NY 14150
City State ZIP Code

I declare under penalty of perjury that the foregoing is true and correct.

Executed on 2/25/2016
MM / DD / YYYY

✗ /s/ David Davis, Manager
Signature of petitioner or representative, including representative's title

William H. Drake
Printed name

The Drake Law Firm, LLC
Firm name, if any

34678 Inverness Court, Ste. 100
Number Street

Erie NY 14156
City State ZIP Code

Contact phone (212) 567-9008 Email whdrake@drakelaw.com

Bar number 10-879327

State NY

✗ /s/ William H. Drake
Signature of attorney

Date signed 2/25/2016
MM / DD / YYYY

Name and mailing address of petitioner

Dover Laundry Supplies, Inc.
Name

4455 East 5th Avenue
Number Street

Newton PA 12334
City State ZIP Code

Name and mailing address of petitioner's representative, if any

Terry Dover, President
Name

4455 East 5th Avenue
Number Street

Newton PA 12334
City State ZIP Code

I declare under penalty of perjury that the foregoing is true and correct.

Executed on 2/25/2016
MM / DD / YYYY

✗ /s/ Terry Dover, President
Signature of petitioner or representative, including representative's title

Richard M. Stevens
Printed name

Stevens & Paschall, LLP
Firm name, if any

3488 East Avenue, Suite 190
Number Street

Philadelphia PA 12573
City State ZIP Code

Contact phone (216) 985-9076 Email rich.stevens@SPLaw.com

Bar number 30398679

State PA

✗ /s/ Richard M. Stevens
Signature of attorney

Date signed 2/25/2016
MM / DD / YYYY

UNITED STATES BANKRUPTCY COURT
WESTERN DISTRICT OF NEW YORK

IN RE	WORST WESTERN HOTEL, INC.	)	
	a Nevada Corporation,	)	Case No. 16-0022
		)	
	Debtor	)	Chapter 11

ANSWER TO INVOLUNTARY PETITION

The Debtor, by its attorney, answers the involuntary petition as follows:

1. Denies the allegations contained in Paragraph No. 11 of the petition.

2. Affirmatively alleges that the Debtor is generally paying its debts as they become due.

3. Affirmatively alleges that the aggregate of the petitioners' unsecured noncontingent claims that are not the subject of a bona fide dispute as to either liability or amount is less than $12,300.

WHEREFORE, the Debtor requests entry of an order dismissing the petition and for such other and further relief as the court finds just.

Dated: March 27, 2016

____
Albert A. Advocate
Attorney for Debtor
200 Main Street
North Tonawanda, NY 14120
Telephone 716-244-5555

COUNTERCLAIM

As a counterclaim against the petitioners, the Debtor, by its attorney, alleges as follows:

1. That the petition was filed by the petitioners in bad faith, that the filing of the petition has caused the Debtor to suffer great damage to its business and reputation, and that the Debtor is entitled to recover general and punitive damages under 11 U.S.C. § 303(i)(2).

2. That the Debtor will incur expenses, attorney's fees, and other damages in establishing and presenting its defenses to the petition and otherwise, and that the Debtor is entitled under 11 U.S.C. § 303(i)(1) to recover these expenses from the petitioners.

3. That, pursuant to 11 U.S.C. § 303(e), the petitioners should be required to post a bond to indemnify the Debtor for the costs, attorney's fees, and damages recoverable by the Debtor in this counterclaim.

WHEREFORE, the Debtor respectfully requests that a judgment for actual and punitive damages be entered against the petitioners, jointly and severally, in an amount to be determined by the court as provided in 11 U.S.C. § 303(i), that the petitioners be required to post a bond to indemnify the Debtor as provided in U.S.C. § 303(e), and for such other and further relief as the court finds just.

Dated: March 27, 2016

____
Albert A. Advocate
Attorney for Debtor
200 Main Street
North Tonawanda, NY 14120
Telephone 716-244-5555

Fill in this information to identify the case:

Debtor 1 Too Big to Fail Builders, Inc.

Debtor 2 (Spouse, if filing) ______

United States Bankruptcy Court for the: Eastern District of New York

Case number SV14-19875-RT

Official Form 410

Proof of Claim

12/15

Read the instructions before filling out this form. This form is for making a claim for payment in a bankruptcy case. Do not use this form to make a request for payment of an administrative expense. Make such a request according to 11 U.S.C. § 503.

Filers must leave out or redact information that is entitled to privacy on this form or on any attached documents. Attach redacted copies of any documents that support the claim, such as promissory notes, purchase orders, invoices, itemized statements of running accounts, contracts, judgments, mortgages, and security agreements. **Do not send original documents;** they may be destroyed after scanning. If the documents are not available, explain in an attachment.

A person who files a fraudulent claim could be fined up to $500,000, imprisoned for up to 5 years, or both. 18 U.S.C. §§ 152, 157, and 3571.

Fill in all the information about the claim as of the date the case was filed. That date is on the notice of bankruptcy (Form 309) **that you received.**

Part 1: Identify the Claim

1. Who is the current creditor?

Becker Mortgages, Inc.
Name of the current creditor (the person or entity to be paid for this claim)

Other names the creditor used with the debtor Becker Mortgage Company

2. Has this claim been acquired from someone else?

☑ No
☐ Yes. From whom? ______

3. Where should notices and payments to the creditor be sent?

Federal Rule of Bankruptcy Procedure (FRBP) 2002(g)

	Where should notices to the creditor be sent?	**Where should payments to the creditor be sent?** (if different)
Name	Steve Smith, Esq.	
Number Street	12345 E. 17th Street, Suite 100A	
City / State / ZIP Code	Los Angeles CA 90012	
Contact phone	213-348-9087	
Contact email	ssmith@smithlaw.com	

Uniform claim identifier for electronic payments in chapter 13 (if you use one):

_ _

4. Does this claim amend one already filed?

☑ No
☐ Yes. Claim number on court claims registry (if known) ______ Filed on ______ MM / DD / YYYY

5. Do you know if anyone else has filed a proof of claim for this claim?

☑ No
☐ Yes. Who made the earlier filing? ______

Part 2: Give Information About the Claim as of the Date the Case Was Filed

6. Do you have any number you use to identify the debtor?

☐ No
☑ Yes. Last 4 digits of the debtor's account or any number you use to identify the debtor: 6 7 8 9

7. How much is the claim?

$ 186,980.56. **Does this amount include interest or other charges?**

☑ No
☐ Yes. Attach statement itemizing interest, fees, expenses, or other charges required by Bankruptcy Rule 3001(c)(2)(A).

8. What is the basis of the claim?

Examples: Goods sold, money loaned, lease, services performed, personal injury or wrongful death, or credit card.

Attach redacted copies of any documents supporting the claim required by Bankruptcy Rule 3001(c).

Limit disclosing information that is entitled to privacy, such as health care information.

First Mortgage on Real Property (34 1st Ave., Alameda, CA)

9. Is all or part of the claim secured?

☐ No
☑ Yes. The claim is secured by a lien on property.

Nature of property:

☑ Real estate. If the claim is secured by the debtor's principal residence, file a *Mortgage Proof of Claim Attachment* (Official Form 410-A) with this *Proof of Claim*.
☐ Motor vehicle
☐ Other. Describe: ____________________

Basis for perfection: Mortgage recorded at Document No. 9874209

Attach redacted copies of documents, if any, that show evidence of perfection of a security interest (for example, a mortgage, lien, certificate of title, financing statement, or other document that shows the lien has been filed or recorded.)

Value of property: $ 250,000.00

Amount of the claim that is secured: $ 186,980.56

Amount of the claim that is unsecured: $ 0.00 (The sum of the secured and unsecured amounts should match the amount in line 7.)

Amount necessary to cure any default as of the date of the petition: $ 3,980.56

Annual Interest Rate (when case was filed) 4.13 %

☑ Fixed
☐ Variable

10. Is this claim based on a lease?

☑ No
☐ Yes. **Amount necessary to cure any default as of the date of the petition.** $____________

11. Is this claim subject to a right of setoff?

☑ No
☐ Yes. Identify the property: ____________________

12. Is all or part of the claim entitled to priority under 11 U.S.C. § 507(a)?

A claim may be partly priority and partly nonpriority. For example, in some categories, the law limits the amount entitled to priority.

☑ No

☐ Yes. *Check all that apply:*

	Amount entitled to priority
☐ Domestic support obligations (including alimony and child support) under 11 U.S.C. § 507(a)(1)(A) or (a)(1)(B).	$________
☐ Up to $2,775* of deposits toward purchase, lease, or rental of property or services for personal, family, or household use. 11 U.S.C. § 507(a)(7).	$________
☐ Wages, salaries, or commissions (up to $12,475*) earned within 180 days before the bankruptcy petition is filed or the debtor's business ends, whichever is earlier. 11 U.S.C. § 507(a)(4).	$________
☐ Taxes or penalties owed to governmental units. 11 U.S.C. § 507(a)(8).	$________
☐ Contributions to an employee benefit plan. 11 U.S.C. § 507(a)(5).	$________
☐ Other. Specify subsection of 11 U.S.C. § 507(a)(__) that applies.	$________

* Amounts are subject to adjustment on 4/01/16 and every 3 years after that for cases begun on or after the date of adjustment.

Part 3: Sign Below

The person completing this proof of claim must sign and date it. FRBP 9011(b).

If you file this claim electronically, FRBP 5005(a)(2) authorizes courts to establish local rules specifying what a signature is.

A person who files a fraudulent claim could be fined up to $500,000, imprisoned for up to 5 years, or both. 18 U.S.C. §§ 152, 157, and 3571.

Check the appropriate box:

☐ I am the creditor.

☑ I am the creditor's attorney or authorized agent.

☐ I am the trustee, or the debtor, or their authorized agent. Bankruptcy Rule 3004.

☐ I am a guarantor, surety, endorser, or other codebtor. Bankruptcy Rule 3005.

I understand that an authorized signature on this *Proof of Claim* serves as an acknowledgment that when calculating the amount of the claim, the creditor gave the debtor credit for any payments received toward the debt.

I have examined the information in this *Proof of Claim* and have a reasonable belief that the information is true and correct.

I declare under penalty of perjury that the foregoing is true and correct.

Executed on date 01/15/2016
MM / DD / YYYY

/s/ Steve Smith, Esq.
Signature

Print the name of the person who is completing and signing this claim:

Name: Steve Smith, Esq.
First name / Middle name / Last name

Title: Attorney for Creditor

Company: The Smith Law Firm
Identify the corporate servicer as the company if the authorized agent is a servicer.

Address: 12345 E. 17th Street, Suite 100A
Number Street

Los Angeles CA 90012
City State ZIP Code

Contact phone: 213-348-9087 Email: ssmith@smithlaw.com

Print | Save As... | Add Attachment | Reset

Mortgage Proof of Claim Attachment

(12/15)

If you file a claim secured by a security interest in the debtor's principal residence, you must use this form as an attachment to your proof of claim. See separate instructions.

Part 1: Mortgage and Case Information

Case number: ____________

Debtor 1: ____________

Debtor 2: ____________

Last 4 digits to identify: __ __ __ __

Creditor: ____________

Servicer: ____________

Fixed accrual/daily simple interest/other: ____________

Part 2: Total Debt Calculation

Principal balance: ________

Interest due: ________

Fees, costs due: ________

Escrow deficiency for funds advanced: ________

Less total funds on hand: – ________

Total debt: ________

Part 3: Arrearage as of Date of the Petition

Principal & interest due: ________

Prepetition fees due: ________

Escrow deficiency for funds advanced: ________

Projected escrow shortage: ________

Less funds on hand: – ________

Total prepetition arrearage: ________

Part 4: Monthly Mortgage Payment

Principal & interest: ________

Monthly escrow: ________

Private mortgage insurance: ________

Total monthly payment: ________

Part 5 : Loan Payment History from First Date of Default

	Account Activity						How Funds Were Applied/Amount Incurred					Balance After Amount Received or Incurred				
A.	**B.**	**C.**	**D.**	**E.**	**F.**	**G.**	**H.**	**I.**	**J.**	**K.**	**L.**	**M.**	**N.**	**O.**	**P.**	**Q.**
Date	Contractual payment amount	Funds received	Amount incurred	Description	Contractual due date	Prin, int & esc past due balance	Amount to principal	Amount to interest	Amount to escrow	Amount to fees or charges	Unapplied funds	Principal balance	Accrued interest balance	Escrow balance	Fees / Charges balance	Unapplied funds balance

APPENDIX I

UNITED STATES BANKRUPTCY CODE

(TITLE 11 UNITED STATES CODE)

(Current to January 1, 2016)

CONTENTS

Note: Chapters 7, 9, 12, 13 and 15 of the Bankruptcy Code are irrelevant to small business Chapter 11 cases and are therefore omitted.

Chapter 1 - General Provisions

Sec.
101. Definitions
102. Rules of construction
103. Applicability of chapters
104. Adjustment of dollar amounts
105. Power of court
106. Waiver of sovereign immunity
107. Public access to papers
108. Extension of time
109. Who may be a debtor
110. Penalty for persons who negligently or fraudulently prepare bankruptcy petitions.
111. Nonprofit budget and credit counseling agencies; financial management instructional courses.
112. Prohibition on disclosure of name of minor children.

101. Definitions

In this title the following definitions shall apply:

(1) The term "accountant" means accountant authorized under applicable law to practice public accounting, and includes professional accounting association, corporation, or partnership, if so authorized.

(2) The term "affiliate" means -

(A) entity that directly or indirectly owns, controls, or holds with power to vote, 20 percent or more of the outstanding voting securities of the debtor, other than an entity that holds such securities -

(i) in a fiduciary or agency capacity without sole discretionary power to vote such securities; or

(ii) solely to secure a debt, if such entity has not in fact exercised such power to vote;

(B) corporation 20 percent or more of whose outstanding voting securities are directly or indirectly owned, controlled, or held with power to vote, by the debtor, or by an entity that directly or indirectly owns, controls, or holds with power to vote, 20 percent or more of the outstanding voting securities of the debtor, other than an entity that holds such securities -

(i) in a fiduciary or agency capacity without sole discretionary power to vote such securities; or

(ii) solely to secure a debt, if such entity has not in fact exercised such power to vote;

(C) person whose business is operated under a lease or operating agreement by a debtor, or person substantially all of whose property is operated under an operating agreement with the debtor; or

(D) entity that operates the business or substantially all of the property of the debtor under a lease or operating agreement.

(3) The term "assisted person" means any person whose debts consist primarily of consumer debts and the value of whose nonexempt property is less than $186,825.

(4) The term "attorney" means attorney, professional law association, corporation, or partnership, authorized under applicable law to practice law.

(4A) The term "bankruptcy assistance" means any goods or services sold or otherwise provided to an assisted person with the express or implied purpose of providing information, advice, counsel, document preparation, or filing, or attendance at a creditors' meeting or appearing in a case or proceeding on behalf of another or providing legal representation with respect to a case or proceeding under this title.

(5) The term "claim" means -

(A) right to payment, whether or not such right is reduced to judgment, liquidated, unliquidated, fixed, contingent, matured, unmatured, disputed, undisputed, legal, equitable, secured, or unsecured; or

(B) right to an equitable remedy for breach of performance if such breach gives rise to a right to payment, whether or not such right to an equitable remedy is reduced to judgment, fixed, contingent, matured, unmatured, disputed, undisputed, secured, or unsecured.

(6) The term "commodity broker" means futures commission merchant, foreign futures commission merchant, clearing organization, leverage transaction merchant, or commodity options dealer, as defined in section 761 of this title, with respect to which there is a customer, as defined in section 761 of this title.

(7) The term "community claim" means claim that arose before the commencement of the case concerning the debtor for which property of the kind specified in section 541(a)(2) of this title is liable, whether or not there is any such property at the time of the commencement of the case.

(7A) The term "commercial fishing operation" means -

(A) the catching or harvesting of fish, shrimp, lobsters, urchins, seaweed, shellfish, or other aquatic species or products of such species; or

(B) for purposes of section 109 and chapter 12, aquaculture activities consisting of raising for market any species or product described in subparagraph (A).

(7B) The term "commercial fishing vessel" means a vessel used by a family fisherman to carry out a commercial fishing operation.

(8) The term "consumer debt" means debt incurred by an individual primarily for a personal, family, or household purpose.

(9) The term "corporation" -

(A) includes -

(i) association having a power or privilege that a private corporation, but not an individual or a partnership, possesses;

(ii) partnership association organized under a law that makes only the capital subscribed responsible for the debts of such association;

(iii) joint-stock company;

(iv) unincorporated company or association; or

(v) business trust; but

(B) does not include limited partnership.

(10) The term "creditor" means -

(A) entity that has a claim against the debtor that arose at the time of or before the order for relief concerning the debtor;

(B) entity that has a claim against the estate of a kind specified in section 348(d), 502(f), 502(g), 502(h), or 502(i) of this title; or

(C) entity that has a community claim.

(10A) The term "current monthly income" -

(A) means the average monthly income from all sources that the debtor receives (or in a joint case the debtor and the debtor's spouse receive) without regard to whether such income is taxable income, derived during the 6-month period ending on –

(i) the last day of the calendar month immediately preceding the date of the commencement of the case if the debtor files the schedule of current income required by section 521(a)(1)(B)(ii); or

(ii) the date on which current income is determined by the court for purposes of this title if the debtor does not file the schedule of current income required by section 521(a)(1)(B)(ii); and

(B) includes any amount paid by any entity other than the debtor (or in a joint case the debtor and the debtor's spouse), on a regular basis for the household expenses of the debtor or the debtor's dependents (and in a joint case the debtor's spouse if not otherwise a dependent), but excludes benefits received under the Social Security Act, payments to victims of war crimes or crimes against humanity on account of their status as victims of such crimes, and payments to victims of international terrorism (as defined in section 2331 of title 18) or domestic terrorism (as defined in section 2331 of title 18) on account of their status as victims of such terrorism

(11) The term "custodian" means -

(A) receiver or trustee of any of the property of the debtor, appointed in a case or proceeding not under this title;

(B) assignee under a general assignment for the benefit of the debtor's creditors; or

(C) trustee, receiver, or agent under applicable law, or under a contract, that is appointed or authorized to take charge of property of the debtor for the purpose of enforcing a lien against such property, or for the purpose of general administration of such property for the benefit of the debtor's creditors.

(12) The term "debt" means liability on a claim.

(12A) The term "debt relief agency" means any person who provides any bankruptcy assistance to an assisted person in return for the payment of money or other valuable consideration, or who is a bankruptcy petition preparer under section 110, but does not include –

(A) any person who is an officer, director, employee, or agent of a person who provides such assistance or of the bankruptcy petition preparer;

(B) a nonprofit organization that is exempt from taxation under section 501(c)(3) of the Internal Revenue Code of 1986;

(C) a creditor of such assisted person, to the extent that the creditor is assisting such assisted person to restructure any debt owed by such assisted person to the creditor;

(D) a depository institution (as defined in section 3 of the Federal Deposit Insurance Act) or any Federal credit union or State credit union (as those terms are defined in section 101 of the Federal Credit Union Act), or any affiliate or subsidiary of such depository institution or credit union; or

(E) an author, publisher, distributor, or seller of works subject to copyright protection under title 17, when acting in such capacity.

(13) The term "debtor" means person or municipality concerning which a case under this title has been commenced.

(13A) The term "debtor's principal residence" –

(A) means a residential structure if used as the principal residence by the debtor, including incidental property, without regard to whether that structure is attached to real property; and

(B) includes an individual condominium or cooperative unit, a mobile or manufactured home, or trailer if used as the principal residence by the debtor.

(14) The term "disinterested person" means a person that –

(A) is not a creditor, an equity security holder, or an insider;

(B) is not and was not, within 2 years before the date of the filing of the petition, a director, officer, or employee of the debtor; and

(C) does not have an interest materially adverse to the interest of the estate or of any class of creditors or equity security holders, by reason of any direct or indirect relationship to, connection with, or interest in, the debtor, or for any other reason.

(14A) The term "domestic support obligation" means a debt that accrues before, on, or after the date of the order for relief in a case under this title, including interest that accrues on that debt as provided under applicable nonbankruptcy law notwithstanding any other provision of this title, that is –

(A) owed to or recoverable by –

(i) a spouse, former spouse, or child of the debtor or such child's parent, legal guardian, or responsible relative; or

(ii) a governmental unit;

(B) in the nature of alimony, maintenance, or support (including assistance provided by a governmental unit) of such spouse, former spouse, or child of the debtor or such child's parent, without regard to whether such debt is expressly so designated;

(C) established or subject to establishment before, on, or after the date of the order for relief in a case under this title, by reason of applicable provisions of –

(i) a separation agreement, divorce decree, or property settlement agreement;

(ii) an order of a court of record; or

(iii) a determination made in accordance with applicable nonbankruptcy law by a governmental unit; and

(D) not assigned to a nongovernmental entity, unless that obligation is assigned voluntarily by the spouse, former spouse, child of the debtor, or such child's parent, legal guardian, or responsible relative for the purpose of collecting the debt.

(15) The term "entity" includes person, estate, trust, governmental unit, and United States trustee.

(16) The term "equity security" means -

(A) share in a corporation, whether or not transferable or denominated "stock", or similar security;

(B) interest of a limited partner in a limited partnership; or

(C) warrant or right, other than a right to convert, to purchase, sell, or subscribe to a share, security, or interest of a kind specified in subparagraph (A) or (B) of this paragraph.

(17) The term "equity security holder" means holder of an equity security of the debtor.

(18) The term "family farmer" means -

(A) individual or individual and spouse engaged in a farming operation whose aggregate debts do not exceed $4,031,575 and not less than 50 percent of whose aggregate noncontingent, liquidated debts (excluding a debt for the principal residence of such individual or such individual and spouse unless such debt arises out of a farming operation), on the date the case is filed, arise out of a farming operation owned or operated by such individual or such individual and spouse, and such individual or such individual and spouse receive from such farming operation more than 50 percent of such individual's or such individual and spouse's gross income for –

(i) the taxable year preceding; or

(ii) each of the 2d and 3d taxable years preceding;

the taxable year in which the case concerning such individual or such individual and spouse was filed; or

(B) corporation or partnership in which more than 50 percent of the outstanding stock or equity is held by one family, or by one family and the relatives of the members of such family, and such family or such relatives conduct the farming operation, and

(i) more than 80 percent of the value of its assets consists of assets related to the farming operation;

(ii) its aggregate debts do not exceed $4,031,575 and not less than 50 percent of its aggregate noncontingent, liquidated debts (excluding a debt for one dwelling which is owned by such corporation or partnership and which a shareholder or partner maintains as a principal residence, unless such debt arises out of a farming operation), on the date the case is filed, arise out of the farming operation owned or operated by such corporation or such partnership; and

(iii) if such corporation issues stock, such stock is not publicly traded.

(19) The term "family farmer with regular annual income" means family farmer whose annual income is sufficiently stable and regular to enable such family farmer to make payments under a plan under chapter 12 of this title.

(19A) The term "family fisherman" means –

(A) an individual or individual and spouse engaged in a commercial fishing operation –

(i) whose aggregate debts do not exceed $1,868,200 and not less than 80 percent of whose aggregate noncontingent, liquidated debts (excluding a debt for the principal residence of such individual or such individual and spouse, unless such debt arises out of a commercial fishing operation), on the date the case is filed, arise out of a commercial fishing operation owned or operated by such individual or such individual and spouse; and

(ii) who receive from such commercial fishing operation more than 50 percent of such individual's or such individual's and spouse's gross income for the taxable year preceding the taxable year in which the case concerning such individual or such individual and spouse was filed; or

(B) a corporation or partnership –

(i) in which more than 50 percent of the outstanding stock or equity is held by –

(I) 1 family that conducts the commercial fishing operation; or

(II) 1 family and the relatives of the members of such family, and such family or such relatives conduct the commercial fishing operation; and

(ii)(I) more than 80 percent of the value of its assets consists of assets related to the commercial fishing operation;

(II) its aggregate debts do not exceed $1,868,200 and not less than 80 percent of its aggregate noncontingent, liquidated debts (excluding a debt for 1 dwelling which is owned by such corporation or partnership and which a shareholder or partner maintains as a principal residence, unless such debt arises out of a commercial fishing operation), on the date the case is filed, arise out of a commercial fishing operation owned or operated by such corporation or such partnership; and

(III) if such corporation issues stock, such stock is not publicly traded.

(19B) The term "family fisherman with regular annual income" means a family fisherman whose annual income is sufficiently stable and regular to enable such family fisherman to make payments under a plan under chapter 12 of this title.

(20) The term "farmer" means (except when such term appears in the term "family farmer") person that received more than 80 percent of such person's gross income during the taxable year of such person immediately preceding the taxable year of such person during which the case under this title concerning such person was commenced from a farming operation owned or operated by such person.

(21) The term "farming operation" includes farming, tillage of the soil, dairy farming, ranching, production or raising of crops, poultry, or livestock, and production of poultry or livestock products in an unmanufactured state.

(21A) The term "farmout agreement" means a written agreement in which-

(A) the owner of a right to drill, produce, or operate liquid or gaseous hydrocarbons on property agrees or has agreed to transfer or assign all or a part of such right to another entity; and

(B) such other entity (either directly or through its agents or its assigns), as consideration, agrees to perform drilling, reworking, recompleting, testing, or similar or related operations, to develop or produce liquid or gaseous hydrocarbons on the property.

(21B) The term "Federal depository institutions regulatory agency" means-

(A) with respect to an insured depository institution (as defined in section 3(c)(2) of the Federal Deposit Insurance Act) for which no conservator or receiver has been appointed, the appropriate Federal banking agency (as defined in section 3(q) of such Act);

(B) with respect to an insured credit union (including an insured credit union for which the National Credit Union Administration has been appointed conservator or liquidating agent), the National Credit Union Administration;

(C) with respect to any insured depository institution for which the Resolution Trust Corporation has been appointed conservator or receiver, the Resolution Trust Corporation; and

(D) with respect to any insured depository institution for which the Federal Deposit Insurance Corporation has been appointed conservator or receiver, the Federal Deposit Insurance Corporation.

(22) The term "financial institution" means –

(A) a Federal reserve bank, or an entity that is a commercial or savings bank, industrial savings bank, savings and loan association, trust company, federally-insured credit union, or receiver, liquidating agent, or conservator for such entity and, when any such Federal reserve bank, receiver, liquidating agent, conservator or entity is acting as agent or custodian for a customer (whether or not a 'customer', as defined in section 741) in connection with a securities contract (as defined in section 741) such customer; or

(B) in connection with a securities contract (as defined in section 741) an investment company registered under the Investment Company Act of 1940.

(22A) The term "financial participant" means –

(A) an entity that, at the time it enters into a securities contract, commodity contract, swap agreement, repurchase agreement, or forward contract, or at the time of the date of the filing of the petition, has one or more agreements or transactions described in paragraph (1), (2), (3), (4), (5), or (6) of section 561(a) with the debtor or any other entity (other than an affiliate) of a total gross dollar value of not less than $1,000,000,000 in notional or actual principal amount outstanding (aggregated across counterparties) at such time or on any day during the 15-month period preceding the date of the filing of the petition, or has gross mark-to-market positions of not less than $100,000,000 (aggregated across counterparties) in one or more such agreements or transactions with the debtor or any other entity (other than an affiliate) at such time or on any day during the 15-month period preceding the date of the filing of the petition; or

(B) a clearing organization (as defined in section 402 of the Federal Deposit Insurance Corporation Improvement Act of 1991).

(23) The term "foreign proceeding" means a collective judicial or administrative proceeding in a foreign country, including an interim proceeding, under a law relating to insolvency or adjustment of debt in which proceeding the assets and affairs of the debtor are subject to control or supervision by a foreign court, for the purpose of reorganization or liquidation.

(24) The term "foreign representative" means a person or body, including a person or body appointed on an interim basis, authorized in a foreign proceeding to administer the reorganization or the liquidation of the debtor's assets or affairs or to act as a representative of such foreign proceeding.

(25) The term "forward contract" means –

(A) a contract (other than a commodity contract, as defined in section 761) for the purchase, sale, or transfer of a commodity, as defined in section 761(8) of this title, or any similar good, article, service, right, or interest which is presently or in the future becomes the subject of dealing in the forward contract trade, or product or byproduct thereof, with a maturity date more than two days after the date the contract is entered into, including, but not limited to, a repurchase or reverse repurchase transaction (whether or not such repurchase or reverse repurchase transaction is a 'repurchase agreement', as defined in this section), consignment, lease, swap, hedge transaction, deposit, loan, option, allocated transaction, unallocated transaction, or any other similar agreement;

(B) any combination of agreements or transactions referred to in subparagraphs (A) and (C);

(C) any option to enter into an agreement or transaction referred to in subparagraph (A) or (B);

(D) a master agreement that provides for an agreement or transaction referred to in subparagraph (A), (B), or (C), together with all supplements to any such master agreement, without regard to whether such master agreement provides for an agreement or transaction that is not a forward contract under this paragraph, except that such master agreement shall be considered to be a forward contract under this paragraph only with respect to each agreement or transaction under such master agreement that is referred to in subparagraph (A), (B), or (C); or

(E) any security agreement or arrangement, or other credit enhancement related to any agreement or transaction referred to in subparagraph (A), (B), (C), or (D), including any guarantee or reimbursement obligation by or to a forward contract merchant or financial participant in connection with any agreement or transaction referred to in any such subparagraph, but not to exceed the damages in connection with any such agreement or transaction, measured in accordance with section 562.

(26) The term "forward contract merchant" means a Federal reserve bank, or an entity the business of which consists in whole or in part of entering into forward contracts as or with merchants in a commodity (as defined in section 761) or any similar good, article, service, right, or interest which is presently or in the future becomes the subject of dealing in the forward contract trade.

(27) The term "governmental unit" means United States; State; Commonwealth; District; Territory; municipality; foreign state; department, agency, or instrumentality of the United States (but not a United States trustee while serving as a trustee in a case under this title), a State, a Commonwealth, a District, a Territory, a municipality, or a foreign state; or other foreign or domestic government.

(27A) The term "health care business" –

(A) means any public or private entity (without regard to whether that entity is organized for profit or not for profit) that is primarily engaged in offering to the general public facilities and services for –

(i) the diagnosis or treatment of injury, deformity, or disease; and

(ii) surgical, drug treatment, psychiatric, or obstetric care; and

(B) includes –

(i) any –

(I) general or specialized hospital; (II) ancillary ambulatory, emergency, or surgical treatment facility;

(III) hospice;

(IV) home health agency; and

(V) other health care institution that is similar to an entity referred to in subclause (I), (II), (III), or (IV); and

(ii) any long-term care facility, including any –

(I) skilled nursing facility;

(II) intermediate care facility;

(III) assisted living facility;

(IV) home for the aged;

(V) domiciliary care facility; and

(VI) health care institution that is related to a facility referred to in subclause (I), (II), (III), (IV), or (V), if that institution is primarily engaged in offering room, board, laundry, or personal assistance with activities of daily living and incidentals to activities of daily living.

(27B) The term "incidental property" means, with respect to a debtor's principal residence –

(A) property commonly conveyed with a principal residence in the area where the real property is located;

(B) all easements, rights, appurtenances, fixtures, rents, royalties, mineral rights, oil or gas rights or profits, water rights, escrow funds, or insurance proceeds; and

(C) all replacements or additions.

(28) The term "indenture" means mortgage, deed of trust, or indenture, under which there is outstanding a security, other than a voting-trust certificate, constituting a claim against the debtor, a claim secured by a lien on any of the debtor's property, or an equity security of the debtor.

(29) The term "indenture trustee" means trustee under an indenture.

(30) The term "individual with regular income" means individual whose income is sufficiently stable and regular to enable such individual to make payments under a plan under chapter 13 of this title, other than a stockbroker or a commodity broker.

(31) The term "insider" includes -

(A) if the debtor is an individual -

(i) relative of the debtor or of a general partner of the debtor ;

(ii) partnership in which the debtor is a general partner;

(iii) general partner of the debtor; or

(iv) corporation of which the debtor is a director, officer, or person in control;

(B) if the debtor is a corporation -

(i) director of the debtor;

(ii) officer of the debtor;

(iii) person in control of the debtor;

(iv) partnership in which the debtor is a general partner;

(v) general partner of the debtor; or

(vi) relative of a general partner, director, officer, or person in control of the debtor;

(C) if the debtor is a partnership -

(i) general partner in the debtor;

(ii) relative of a general partner in, general partner of, or person in control of the debtor;

(iii) partnership in which the debtor is a general partner;

(iv) general partner of the debtor; or

(v) person in control of the debtor;

(D) if the debtor is a municipality, elected official of the debtor or relative of an elected official of the debtor;

(E) affiliate, or insider of an affiliate as if such affiliate were the debtor; and

(F) managing agent of the debtor.

(32) The term "insolvent" means -

(A) with reference to an entity other than a partnership and a municipality, financial condition such that the sum of such entity's debts is greater than all of such entity's property, at a fair valuation, exclusive of -

(i) property transferred, concealed, or removed with intent to hinder, delay, or defraud such entity's creditors; and

(ii) property that may be exempted from property of the estate under section 522 of this title;

(B) with reference to a partnership, financial condition such that the sum of such partnership's debts is greater than the aggregate of, at fair valuation -

(i) all of such partnership's property, exclusive of property of the kind specified in subparagraph (A)(i) of this paragraph; and

(ii) the sum of the excess of the value of each general partner's nonpartnership property, exclusive of property of the kind specified in subparagraph (A) of this paragraph, over such partner's nonpartnership debts; and

(C) with reference to a municipality, financial condition such that the municipality is -

(i) generally not paying its debts as they become due unless such debts are the subject of a bona fide dispute; or

(ii) unable to pay its debts as they become due.

(33) The term "institution-affiliated party"-

(A) with respect to an insured depository institution (as defined in section 3(c)(2) of the Federal Deposit Insurance Act), has the meaning given it in section 3(u) of the Federal Deposit Insurance Act; and

(B) with respect to an insured credit union, has the meaning given it in section 206(r) of the Federal Credit Union Act.

(34) The term "insured credit union" has the meaning given it in section 101(7) of the Federal Credit Union Act.

(35) The term "insured depository institution"-

(A) has the meaning given it in section 3(c)(2) of the Federal Deposit Insurance Act; and

(B) includes an insured credit union (except in the case of paragraphs (21B) and (33)(A) of this subsection).

(35A) The term "intellectual property" means -

(A) trade secret;

(B) invention, process, design, or plant protected under title 35;

(C) patent application;

(D) plant variety;

(E) work of authorship protected under title 17; or

(F) mask work protected under chapter 9 of title 17; to the extent protected by applicable nonbankruptcy law.

(36) The term "judicial lien" means lien obtained by judgment, levy, sequestration, or other legal or equitable process or proceeding.

(37) The term "lien" means charge against or interest in property to secure payment of a debt or performance of an obligation.

(38) The term "margin payment" means, for purposes of the forward contract provisions of this title, payment or deposit of cash, a security or other property, that is commonly known in the forward contract trade as original margin, initial margin, maintenance margin, or variation margin, including mark-to-market payments, or variation payments.

(38A) The term "master netting agreement" –

(A) means an agreement providing for the exercise of rights, including rights of netting, setoff, liquidation, termination, acceleration, or close out, under or in connection with one or more contracts that are described in any one or more of paragraphs (1) through (5) of section 561(a), or any security agreement or arrangement or other credit enhancement related to one or more of the foregoing, including any guarantee or reimbursement obligation related to 1 or more of the foregoing; and

(B) if the agreement contains provisions relating to agreements or transactions that are not contracts described in paragraphs (1) through (5) of section 561(a), shall be deemed to be a master netting agreement only with respect to those agreements or transactions that are described in any one or more of paragraphs (1) through (5) of section 561(a).

(38B) The term "master netting agreement participant" means an entity that, at any time before the date of the filing of the petition, is a party to an outstanding master netting agreement with the debtor.

(39) The term "mask work" has the meaning given it in section 901(a)(2) of title 17;

(39A) The term "median family income" means for any year –

(A) the median family income both calculated and reported by the Bureau of the Census in the then most recent year; and

(B) if not so calculated and reported in the then current year, adjusted annually after such most recent year until the next year in which median family income is both calculated and reported by the Bureau of the Census, to reflect the percentage change in the Consumer Price Index for All Urban Consumers during the period of years occurring after such most recent year and before such current year.

(40) The term "municipality" means political subdivision or public agency or instrumentality of a State.

(40A) The term "patient" means any individual who obtains or receives services from a health care business.

(40B) The term "patient records" means any record relating to a patient, including a written document or a record recorded in a magnetic, optical, or other form of electronic medium.

(41) The term"person" includes individual, partnership, and corporation, but does not include governmental unit, except that a governmental unit that -

(A) acquires an asset from a person -

(i) as a result of the operation of a loan guarantee agreement; or

(ii) as receiver or liquidating agent of a person;

(B) is a guarantor of a pension benefit payable by or on behalf of the debtor or an affiliate of the debtor; or

(C) is the legal or beneficial owner of an asset of -

(i) an employee pension benefit plan that is a governmental plan, as defined in section 414(d) of the Internal Revenue Code of 1986; or

(ii) an eligible deferred compensation plan, as defined in section 457(b) of the Internal Revenue Code of 1986;

shall be considered, for purposes of section 1102 of this title, to be a person with respect to such asset or such benefit.

(41A) The term "personally identifiable information" means –

(A) if provided by an individual to the debtor in connection with obtaining a product or a service from the debtor primarily for personal, family, or household purposes –

(i) the first name (or initial) and last name of such individual, whether given at birth or time of adoption, or resulting from a lawful change of name;

(ii) the geographical address of a physical place of residence of such individual;

(iii) an electronic address (including an e-mail address) of such individual;

(iv) a telephone number dedicated to contacting such individual at such physical place of residence;

(v) a social security account number issued to such individual; or

(vi) the account number of a credit card issued to such individual; or

(B) if identified in connection with 1 or more of the items of information specified in subparagraph (A) –

(i) a birth date, the number of a certificate of birth or adoption, or a place of birth; or

(ii) any other information concerning an identified individual that, if disclosed, will result in contacting or identifying such individual physically or electronically.

(42) The term "petition" means petition filed under section 301, 302, 303 and 1504 of this title, as the case may be, commencing a case under this title.

(42A) The term "production payment" means a term overriding royalty satisfiable in cash or in kind -

(A) contingent on the production of a liquid or gaseous hydrocarbon from particular real property; and

(B) from a specified volume, or a specified value, from the liquid or gaseous hydrocarbon produced from such property, and determined without regard to production costs.

(43) The term "purchaser" means transferee of a voluntary transfer, and includes immediate or mediate transferee of such a transferee.

(44) The term "railroad" means common carrier by railroad engaged in the transportation of individuals or property or owner of trackage facilities leased by such a common carrier.

(45) The term "relative" means individual related by affinity or consanguinity within the third degree as determined by the common law, or individual in a step or adoptive relationship within such third degree.

(46) The term "repo participant" means an entity that, at any time before the filing of the petition, has an outstanding repurchase agreement with the debtor.

(47) The term "repurchase agreement" (which definition also applies to a reverse repurchase agreement) –

(A) means –

(i) an agreement, including related terms, which provides for the transfer of one or more certificates of deposit, mortgage related securities (as defined in section 3 of the Securities Exchange Act of 1934), mortgage loans, interests in mortgage related securities or mortgage loans, eligible bankers' acceptances, qualified foreign government securities (defined as a security that is a direct obligation of, or that is fully guaranteed by, the central government of a member of the Organization for Economic Cooperation and Development), or securities that are direct obligations of, or that are fully guaranteed by, the United States or any agency of the United States against the transfer of funds by the transferee of such certificates of deposit, eligible bankers' acceptances, securities, mortgage loans, or interests, with a simultaneous agreement by such transferee to transfer to the transferor thereof certificates of deposit, eligible bankers' acceptance, securities, mortgage loans, or interests of the kind described in this clause, at a date certain not later than 1 year after such transfer or on demand, against the transfer of funds;

(ii) any combination of agreements or transactions referred to in clauses (i) and (iii);

(iii) an option to enter into an agreement or transaction referred to in clause (i) or (ii);

(iv) a master agreement that provides for an agreement or transaction referred to in clause (i), (ii), or (iii), together with all supplements to any such master agreement, without regard to whether such master agreement provides for an agreement or transaction that is not a repurchase agreement under this paragraph, except that such master agreement shall be considered to be a repurchase agreement under this paragraph only with respect to each agreement or transaction under the master agreement that is referred to in clause (i), (ii), or (iii); or

(v) any security agreement or arrangement or other credit enhancement related to any agreement or transaction referred to in clause (i), (ii), (iii), or (iv), including any guarantee or reimbursement obligation by or to a repo participant or financial participant in connection with any agreement or transaction referred to in any such clause, but not to exceed the damages in connection with any such agreement or transaction, measured in accordance with section 562 of this title; and

(B) does not include a repurchase obligation under a participation in a commercial mortgage loan.

(48) The term "securities clearing agency" means person that is registered as a clearing agency under section 17A of the Securities Exchange Act of 1934, or exempt from such registration under such section pursuant to an order of the Securities and Exchange Commission, or whose business is confined to the performance of functions of a clearing agency with respect to exempted securities, as defined in section 3 (a)(12) of such Act for the purposes of such section 17A.

(48A) The term "securities self regulatory organization" means either a securities association registered with the Securities and Exchange Commission under section 15A of the Securities Exchange Act of 1934 or a national securities exchange registered with the Securities and Exchange Commission under section 6 of the Securities Exchange Act of 1934.

(49) The term "security" -

(A) includes -

(i) note;

(ii) stock;

(iii) treasury stock;

(iv) bond;

(v) debenture;

(vi) collateral trust certificate;

(vii) pre-organization certificate or subscription;

(viii) transferable share;

(ix) voting-trust certificate;

(x) certificate of deposit;

(xi) certificate of deposit for security;

(xii) investment contract or certificate of interest or participation in a profit-sharing agreement or in an oil, gas, or mineral royalty or lease, if such contract or interest is required to be the subject of a registration statement filed with the Securities and Exchange Commission under the provisions of the Securities Act of 1933, or is exempt under section 3(b) of such Act from the requirement to file such a statement;

(xiii) interest of a limited partner in a limited partnership;

(xiv) other claim or interest commonly known as "security"; and

(xv) certificate of interest or participation in, temporary or interim certificate for, receipt for, or warrant or right to subscribe to or purchase or sell, a security; but

(B) does not include -

(i) currency, check, draft, bill of exchange, or bank letter of credit;

(ii) leverage transaction, as defined in section 761 of this title;

(iii) commodity futures contract or forward contract;

(iv) option, warrant, or right to subscribe to or purchase or sell a commodity futures contract;

(v) option to purchase or sell a commodity;

(vi) contract or certificate of a kind specified in subparagraph (A)(xii) of this paragraph that is not required to be the subject of a registration statement filed with the Securities and Exchange Commission and is not exempt under section 3(b) of the Securities Act of 1933 from the requirement to file such a statement; or

(vii) debt or evidence of indebtedness for goods sold and delivered or services rendered.

(50) The term "security agreement" means agreement that creates or provides for a security interest.

(51) The term "security interest" means lien created by an agreement.

(51A) The term "settlement payment" means, for purposes of the forward contract provisions of this title, a preliminary settlement payment, a partial settlement payment, an interim settlement payment, a settlement payment on account, a final settlement payment, a net settlement payment, or any other similar payment commonly used in the forward contract trade.

(51B) The term "single asset real estate" means real property constituting a single property or project, other than residential real property with fewer than 4 residential units, which generates substantially all of the gross income of a debtor who is not a family farmer and on which no substantial business is being conducted by a debtor other than the business of operating the real property and activities incidental thereto.

(51C) The term "small business case" means a case filed under chapter 11 of this title in which the debtor is a small business debtor.

(51D) The term "small business debtor" –

(A) subject to subparagraph (B), means a person engaged in commercial or business activities (including any affiliate of such person that is also a debtor under this title and excluding a person whose primary activity is the business of owning or operating real property or activities incidental thereto) that has aggregate noncontingent liquidated secured and unsecured debts as of the date of the filing of the petition or the date of the order for relief in an amount not more than $2,490,925 (excluding debts owed to 1 or more affiliates or insiders) for a case in which the United States trustee has not appointed under section 1102(a)(1) a committee of unsecured creditors or where the court has determined that the committee of unsecured creditors is not sufficiently active and representative to provide effective oversight of the debtor; and

(B) does not include any member of a group of affiliated debtors that has aggregate noncontingent liquidated secured and unsecured debts in an amount greater than $2,490,925 (excluding debt owed to 1 or more affiliates or insiders).

(52) The term "State" includes the District of Columbia and Puerto Rico, except for the purpose of defining who may be a debtor under chapter 9 of this title.

(53) The term "statutory lien" means lien arising solely by force of a statute on specified circumstances or conditions, or lien of distress for rent, whether or not statutory, but does not include security interest or judicial lien, whether or not such interest or lien is provided by or is dependent on a statute and whether or not such interest or lien is made fully effective by statute.

(53A) The term "stockbroker" means person -

(A) with respect to which there is a customer, as defined in section 741 of this title; and

(B) that is engaged in the business of effecting transactions in securities-

(i) for the account of others; or

(ii) with members of the general public, from or for such person's own account.

(53B) The term "swap agreement" –

(A) means –

(i) any agreement, including the terms and conditions incorporated by reference in such agreement, which is –

(I) an interest rate swap, option, future, or forward agreement, including a rate floor, rate cap, rate collar, cross-currency rate swap, and basis swap;

(II) a spot, same day-tomorrow, tomorrow-next, forward, or other foreign exchange, precious metals, or other commodity agreement;

(III) a currency swap, option, future, or forward agreement;

(IV) an equity index or equity swap, option, future, or forward agreement;

(V) a debt index or debt swap, option, future, or forward agreement;

(VI) a total return, credit spread or credit swap, option, future, or forward agreement;

(VII) a commodity index or a commodity swap, option, future, or forward agreement;

(VIII) a weather swap, option, future, or forward agreement;

(IX) an emissions swap, option, future, or forward agreement; or

(X) an inflation swap, option, future, or forward agreement;

(ii) any agreement or transaction that is similar to any other agreement or transaction referred to in this paragraph and that –

(I) is of a type that has been, is presently, or in the future becomes, the subject of recurrent dealings in the swap or other derivatives markets (including terms and conditions incorporated by reference therein); and

(II) is a forward, swap, future, option, or spot transaction on one or more rates, currencies, commodities, equity securities, or other equity instruments, debt securities or other debt instruments, quantitative measures associated with an occurrence, extent of an occurrence, or contingency associated with a financial, commercial, or economic consequence, or economic or financial indices or measures of economic or financial risk or value;

(iii) any combination of agreements or transactions referred to in this subparagraph;

(iv) any option to enter into an agreement or transaction referred to in this subparagraph;

(v) a master agreement that provides for an agreement or transaction referred to in clause (i), (ii), (iii), or (iv), together with all supplements to any such master agreement, and without regard to whether the master agreement contains an agreement or transaction that is not a swap agreement under this paragraph, except that the master agreement shall be considered to be a swap agreement under this paragraph only with respect to each agreement or transaction under the master agreement that is referred to in clause (i), (ii), (iii), or (iv); or

(vi) any security agreement or arrangement or other credit enhancement related to any agreements or transactions referred to in clause (i) through (v), including any guarantee or reimbursement obligation by or to a swap participant or financial participant in connection with any agreement or transaction referred to in any such clause, but not to exceed the damages in connection with any such agreement or transaction, measured in accordance with section 562; and

(B) is applicable for purposes of this title only, and shall not be construed or applied so as to challenge or affect the characterization, definition, or treatment of any swap agreement under any other statute, regulation, or rule, including the Gramm-Leach-Bliley Act, the Legal Certainty for Bank Products Act of 2000, the securities laws (as such term is defined in section 3(a)(47) of the Securities Exchange Act of 1934) and the Commodity Exchange Act.

(53C) The term "swap participant" means an entity that, at any time before the filing of the petition, has an outstanding swap agreement with the debtor.

(53D) The term "timeshare plan" means and shall include that interest purchased in any arrangement, plan, scheme, or similar device, but not including exchange programs, whether by membership, agreement, tenancy in common, sale, lease, deed, rental agreement, license, right to use agreement, or by any other means, whereby a purchaser, in exchange for consideration, receives a right to use accommodations, facilities, or recreational sites, whether improved or unimproved, for a specific period of time less than a full year during any given year, but not necessarily for consecutive years, and which extends for a period of more than three years. A "timeshare interest" is that interest purchased in a timeshare plan which grants the purchaser the right to use and occupy accommodations, facilities, or recreational sites, whether improved or unimproved, pursuant to a timeshare plan.

(54) The term "transfer" means –

(A) the creation of a lien;

(B) the retention of title as a security interest;

(C) the foreclosure of a debtor's equity of redemption; or

(D) each mode, direct or indirect, absolute or conditional, voluntary or involuntary, of disposing of or parting with –

(i) property; or

(ii) an interest in property.

(54A) The term "uninsured State member bank" means a State member bank (as defined in section 3 of the Federal Deposit Insurance Act) the deposits of which are not insured by the Federal Deposit Insurance Corporation.

(55) The term "United States", when used in a geographical sense, includes all locations where the judicial jurisdiction of the United States extends, including territories and possessions of the United States.

(56A) The term "term overriding royalty" means an interest in liquid or gaseous hydrocarbons in place or to be produced from particular real property that entitles the owner thereof to a share of production, or the value thereof, for a term limited by time, quantity, or value realized.

102. Rules of construction

In this title -

(1) "after notice and a hearing", or a similar phrase -

(A) means after such notice as is appropriate in the particular circumstances, and such opportunity for a hearing as is appropriate in the particular circumstances; but

(B) authorizes an act without an actual hearing if such notice is given properly and if -

(i) such a hearing is not requested timely by a party in interest; or

(ii) there is insufficient time for a hearing to be commenced before such act must be done, and the court authorizes such act;

(2) "claim against the debtor" includes claim against property of the debtor;

(3) "includes" and "including" are not limiting;

(4) "may not" is prohibitive, and not permissive;

(5) "or" is not exclusive;

(6) "order for relief" means entry of an order for relief;

(7) the singular includes the plural;

(8) a definition, contained in a section of this title that refers to another section of this title, does not, for the purpose of such reference, affect the meaning of a term used in such other section; and

(9) "United States trustee" includes a designee of the United States trustee.

103. Applicability of chapters

(a) Except as provided in section 1161 of this title, chapters 1, 3, and 5 of this title apply in a case under chapter 7, 11, 12, or 13 of this title, and this chapter, sections 307, 362(o), 555 through 557, and 559 through 562 apply in a case under chapter 15.

(b) Subchapters I and II of chapter 7 of this title apply only in a case under such chapter.

(c) Subchapter III of chapter 7 of this title applies only in a case under such chapter concerning a stockbroker.

(d) Subchapter IV of chapter 7 of this title applies only in a case under such chapter concerning a commodity broker.

(e) SCOPE OF APPLICATION. – Subchapter V of chapter 7 of this title shall apply only in a case under such chapter concerning the liquidation of an uninsured State member bank, or a corporation organized under section 25A of the Federal Reserve Act, which operates, or operates as, a multilateral clearing organization pursuant to section 409 of the Federal Deposit Insurance Corporation Improvement Act of 1991.

(f) Except as provided in section 901 of this title, only chapters 1 and 9 of this title apply in a case under such chapter 9.

(g) Except as provided in section 901 of this title, subchapters I, II, and III of chapter 11 of this title apply only in a case under such chapter.

(h) Subchapter IV of chapter 11 of this title applies only in a case under such chapter concerning a railroad.

(i) Chapter 13 of this title applies only in a case under such chapter.

(j) Chapter 12 of this title applies only in a case under such chapter.

(k) Chapter 15 applies only in a case under such chapter, except that –

(1) sections 1505, 1513, and 1514 apply in all cases under this title; and

(2) section 1509 applies whether or not a case under this title is pending.

104. Adjustment of dollar amounts

(a) On April 1, 1998, and at each 3-year interval ending on April 1 thereafter, each dollar amount in effect under sections 101(3), 101(18), 101(19A), 101(51D), 109(e), 303(b), 507(a), 522(d), 522(f)(3) and 522(f)(4), 522(n), 522(p), 522(q), 523(a)(2)(C), 541(b), 547(c)(9), 707(b), 1322(d), 1325(b), and 1326(b)(3) of this title and section 1409(b) of title 28 immediately before such April 1 shall be adjusted –

(1) to reflect the change in the Consumer Price Index for All Urban Consumers, published by the Department of Labor, for the most recent 3-year period ending immediately before January 1 preceding such April 1, and

(2) to round to the nearest $25 the dollar amount that represents such change.

(b) Not later than March 1, 1998, and at each 3-year interval ending on March 1 thereafter, the Judicial Conference of the United States shall publish in the Federal Register the dollar amounts that will become effective on such April 1 under sections 101(3), 101(18), 101(19A), 101(51D), 109(e), 303(b), 507(a), 522(d), 522(f)(3) and 522(f)(4), 522(n), 522(p), 522(q), 523(a)(2)(C), 541(b), 547(c)(9), 707(b), 1322(d), 1325(b), and 1326(b)(3) of this title and section 1409(b) of title 28.

(c) Adjustments made in accordance with subsection (a) shall not apply with respect to cases commenced before the date of such adjustments.

105. Power of court

(a) The court may issue any order, process, or judgment that is necessary or appropriate to carry out the provisions of this title. No provision of this title providing for the raising of an issue by a party in interest shall be construed to preclude the court from, sua sponte, taking any action or making any determination necessary or appropriate to enforce or implement court orders or rules, or to prevent an abuse of process.

(b) Notwithstanding subsection (a) of this section, a court may not appoint a receiver in a case under this title.

(c) The ability of any district judge or other officer or employee of a district court to exercise any of the authority or responsibilities conferred upon the court under this title shall be determined by reference to the provisions relating to such judge, officer, or employee set forth in title 28. This subsection shall not be interpreted to exclude bankruptcy judges and other officers or employees appointed pursuant to chapter 6 of title 28 from its operation.

(d) The court, on its own motion or on the request of a party in interest -

(1) shall hold such status conferences as are necessary to further the expeditious and economical resolution of the case; and

(2) unless inconsistent with another provision of this title or with applicable Federal Rules of Bankruptcy Procedure, may issue an order at any such conference prescribing such limitations and conditions as the court deems appropriate to ensure that the case is handled expeditiously and economically, including an order that -

(A) sets the date by which the trustee must assume or reject an executory contract or unexpired lease; or

(B) in a case under chapter 11 of this title -

(i) sets a date by which the debtor, or trustee if one has been appointed, shall file a disclosure statement and plan;

(ii) sets a date by which the debtor, or trustee if one has been appointed, shall solicit acceptances of a plan;

(iii) sets the date by which a party in interest other than a debtor may file a plan;

(iv) sets a date by which a proponent of a plan, other than the debtor, shall solicit acceptances of such plan;

(v) fixes the scope and format of the notice to be provided regarding the hearing on approval of the disclosure statement; or

(vi) provides that the hearing on approval of the disclosure statement may be combined with the hearing on confirmation of the plan.

106. Waiver of sovereign immunity

(a) Notwithstanding an assertion of sovereign immunity, sovereign immunity is abrogated as to a governmental unit to the extent set forth in this section with respect to the following:

(1) Sections 105, 106, 107, 108, 303, 346, 362, 363, 364, 365, 366, 502, 503, 505, 506, 510, 522, 523, 524, 525, 542, 543, 544, 545, 546, 547, 548, 549, 550, 551, 552, 553, 722, 724, 726, 744, 749, 764, 901, 922, 926, 928, 929, 944, 1107, 1141, 1142, 1143, 1146, 1201, 1203, 1205, 1206, 1227, 1231, 1301, 1303, 1305, and 1327 of this title.

(2) The court may hear and determine any issue arising with respect to the application of such sections to governmental units.

(3) The court may issue against a governmental unit an order, process, or judgment under such sections or the Federal Rules of Bankruptcy Procedure, including an order or judgment awarding a money recovery, but not including an award of punitive damages. Such order or judgment for costs or fees under this title or the Federal Rules of Bankruptcy Procedure against any governmental unit shall be consistent with the provisions and limitations of section 2412(d)(2)(A) of title 28.

(4) The enforcement of any such order, process, or judgment against any governmental unit shall be consistent with appropriate nonbankruptcy law applicable to such governmental unit and, in the case of a money judgment against the United States, shall be paid as if it is a judgment rendered by a district court of the United States.

(5) Nothing in this section shall create any substantive claim for relief or cause of action not otherwise existing under this title, the Federal Rules of Bankruptcy Procedure, or nonbankruptcy law.

(b) A governmental unit that has filed a proof of claim in the case is deemed to have waived sovereign immunity with respect to a claim against such governmental unit that is property of the estate and that arose out of the same transaction or occurrence out of which the claim of such governmental unit arose.

(c) Notwithstanding any assertion of sovereign immunity by a governmental unit, there shall be offset against a claim or interest of a governmental unit any claim against such governmental unit that is property of the estate.

107. Public access to papers

(a) Except as provided in subsections (b) and (c) and subject to section 112, a paper filed in a case under this title and the dockets of a bankruptcy court are public records and open to examination by an entity at reasonable times without charge.

(b) On request of a party in interest, the bankruptcy court shall, and on the bankruptcy court's own motion, the bankruptcy court may -

(1) protect an entity with respect to a trade secret or confidential research, development, or commercial information; or

(2) protect a person with respect to scandalous or defamatory matter contained in a paper filed in a case under this title.

(c)(1) The bankruptcy court, for cause, may protect an individual, with respect to the following types of information to the extent the court finds that disclosure of such information would create undue risk of identity theft or other unlawful injury to the individual or the individual's property:

(A) Any means of identification (as defined in section 1028(d) of title 18) contained in a paper filed, or to be filed, in a case under this title.

(B) Other information contained in a paper described in subparagraph (A).

(2) Upon ex parte application demonstrating cause, the court shall provide access to information protected pursuant to paragraph (1) to an entity acting pursuant to the police or regulatory power of a domestic governmental unit.

(3) The United States trustee, bankruptcy administrator, trustee, and any auditor serving under section 586(f) of title 28 –

(A) shall have full access to all information contained in any paper filed or submitted in a case under this title; and

(B) shall not disclose information specifically protected by the court under this title.

108. Extension of time

(a) If applicable nonbankruptcy law, an order entered in a nonbankruptcy proceeding, or an agreement fixes a period within which the debtor may commence an action, and such period has not expired before the date of the filing of the petition, the trustee may commence such action only before the later of -

(1) the end of such period, including any suspension of such period occurring on or after the commencement of the case; or

(2) two years after the order for relief.

(b) Except as provided in subsection (a) of this section, if applicable nonbankruptcy law, an order entered in a nonbankruptcy proceeding, or an agreement fixes a period within which the debtor or an individual protected under section 1201 or 1301 of this title may file any pleading, demand, notice, or proof of claim or loss, cure a default, or perform any other similar act, and such period has not expired before the date of the filing of the petition, the trustee may only file, cure, or perform, as the case may be, before the later of

(1) the end of such period, including any suspension of such period occurring on or after the commencement of the case; or

(2) 60 days after the order for relief.

(c) Except as provided in section 524 of this title, if applicable nonbankruptcy law, an order entered in a nonbankruptcy proceeding, or an agreement fixes a period for commencing or continuing a civil action in a court other than a bankruptcy court on a claim against the debtor, or against an individual with respect to which such individual is protected under section 1201 or 1301 of this title, and such period has not expired before the date of the filing of the petition, then such period does not expire until the later of -

(1) the end of such period, including any suspension of such period occurring on or after the commencement of the case; or

(2) 30 days after notice of the termination or expiration of the stay under section 362, 922, 1201, or 1301 of this title, as the case may be, with respect to such claim.

109. Who may be a debtor

(a) Notwithstanding any other provision of this section, only a person that resides or has a domicile, a place of business, or property in the United States, or a municipality, may be a debtor under this title.

(b) A person may be a debtor under chapter 7 of this title only if such person is not -

(1) a railroad;

(2) a domestic insurance company, bank, savings bank, cooperative bank, savings and loan association, building and loan association, homestead association a New Markets Venture Capital company as defined in section 351 of the Small Business Investment Act of 1958, a small business investment company licensed by the Small Business Administration under section 301 of the Small Business Investment Act of 1958, credit union, or industrial bank or similar institution which is an insured bank as defined in section 3(h) of the Federal Deposit Insurance Act, except that an uninsured State member bank, or a corporation organized under section 25A of the Federal Reserve Act, which operates, or operates as, a multilateral clearing organization pursuant to section 409 of the Federal Deposit Insurance Corporation Improvement Act of 1991 may be a debtor if a petition is filed at the direction of the Board of Governors of the Federal Reserve System; or

(3)(A) a foreign insurance company, engaged in such business in the United States; or

(B) a foreign bank, savings bank, cooperative bank, savings and loan association, building and loan association, or credit union, that has a branch or agency (as defined in section 1(b) of the International Banking Act of 1978) in the United States.

(c) An entity may be a debtor under chapter 9 of this title if and only if such entity -

(1) is a municipality;

(2) is specifically authorized in its capacity as a municipality or by name, to be a debtor under such chapter by State law, or by a governmental officer or organization empowered by State law to authorize such entity to be a debtor under such chapter;

(3) is insolvent;

(4) desires to effect a plan to adjust such debts; and

(5)(A) has obtained the agreement of creditors holding at least a majority in amount of the claims of each class that such entity intends to impair under a plan in a case under such chapter;

(B) has negotiated in good faith with creditors and has failed to obtain the agreement of creditors holding at least a majority in amount of the claims of each class that such entity intends to impair under a plan in a case under such chapter;

(C) is unable to negotiate with creditors because such negotiation is impracticable; or

(D) reasonably believes that a creditor may attempt to obtain a transfer that is avoidable under section 547 of this title.

(d) Only a railroad, a person that may be a debtor under chapter 7 of this title (except a stockbroker or a commodity broker), and an uninsured State member bank, or a corporation organized under section 25A of the Federal Reserve Act, which operates, or operates as, a multilateral clearing organization pursuant to section 409 of the Federal Deposit Insurance Corporation Improvement Act of 1991 may be a debtor under chapter 11 of this title.

(e) Only an individual with regular income that owes, on the date of the filing of the petition, noncontingent, liquidated, unsecured debts of less than $383,175 and noncontingent, liquidated, secured debts of less than $1,149,525, or an individual with regular income and such individual's spouse, except a stockbroker or a commodity broker, that owe, on the date of the filing of the petition, noncontingent, liquidated, unsecured debts that aggregate less than $383,175 and noncontingent, liquidated, secured debts of less than $1,149,525 may be a debtor under chapter 13 of this title.

(f) Only a family farmer or family fisherman with regular annual income may be a debtor under chapter 12 of this title.

(g) Notwithstanding any other provision of this section, no individual or family farmer may be a debtor under this title who has been a debtor in a case pending under this title at any time in the preceding 180 days if -

(1) the case was dismissed by the court for willful failure of the debtor to abide by orders of the court, or to appear before the court in proper prosecution of the case; or

(2) the debtor requested and obtained the voluntary dismissal of the case following the filing of a request for relief from the automatic stay provided by section 362 of this title.

(h)(1) Subject to paragraphs (2) and (3), and notwithstanding any other provision of this section other than paragraph (4) of this subsection, an individual may not be a debtor under this title unless such individual has, during the 180-day period ending on the date of filing of the petition by such individual, received from an approved nonprofit budget and credit counseling agency described in section 111(a) an individual or group briefing (including a briefing conducted by telephone or on the Internet) that outlined the opportunities for available credit counseling and assisted such individual in performing a related budget analysis.

(2)(A) Paragraph (1) shall not apply with respect to a debtor who resides in a district for which the United States trustee (or the bankruptcy administrator, if any) determines that the approved nonprofit budget and credit counseling agencies for such district are not reasonably able to provide adequate services to the additional individuals who would otherwise seek credit counseling from such agencies by reason of the requirements of paragraph (1).

(B) The United States trustee (or the bankruptcy administrator, if any) who makes a determination described in subparagraph (A) shall review such determination not later than 1 year after the date of such determination, and not less frequently than annually thereafter. Notwithstanding the preceding sentence, a nonprofit budget and credit counseling agency may be disapproved by the United States trustee (or the bankruptcy administrator, if any) at any time.

(3)(A) Subject to subparagraph (B), the requirements of paragraph (1) shall not apply with respect to a debtor who submits to the court a certification that –

(i) describes exigent circumstances that merit a waiver of the requirements of paragraph (1);

(ii) states that the debtor requested credit counseling services from an approved nonprofit budget and credit counseling agency, but was unable to obtain the services referred to in paragraph (1) during the 7-day period beginning on the date on which the debtor made that request; and

(iii) is satisfactory to the court.

(B) With respect to a debtor, an exemption under subparagraph (A) shall cease to apply to that debtor on the date on which the debtor meets the requirements of paragraph (1), but in no case may the exemption apply to that debtor after the date that is 30 days after the debtor files a petition, except that the court, for cause, may order an additional 15 days.

(4) The requirements of paragraph (1) shall not apply with respect to a debtor whom the court determines, after notice and hearing, is unable to complete those requirements because of incapacity, disability, or active military duty in a military combat zone. For the purposes of this paragraph, incapacity means that the debtor is impaired by reason of mental illness or mental deficiency so that he is incapable of realizing and making rational decisions with respect to his financial responsibilities; and "disability" means that the debtor is so physically impaired as to be unable, after reasonable effort, to participate in an in person, telephone, or Internet briefing required under paragraph (1).

110. Penalty for persons who negligently or fraudulently prepare bankruptcy petitions

(a) In this section -

(1) "bankruptcy petition preparer" means a person, other than an attorney for the debtor or an employee of such attorney under the direct supervision of such attorney, who prepares for compensation a document for filing; and

(2) "document for filing" means a petition or any other document prepared for filing by a debtor in a United States bankruptcy court or a United States district court in connection with a case under this title.

(b)(1) A bankruptcy petition preparer who prepares a document for filing shall sign the document and print on the document the preparer's name and address. If a bankruptcy petition preparer is not an individual, then an officer, principal, responsible person, or partner of the bankruptcy petition preparer shall be required to –

(A) sign the document for filing; and

(B) print on the document the name and address of that officer, principal, responsible person, or partner.

(2)(A) Before preparing any document for filing or accepting any fees from or on behalf of a debtor, the bankruptcy petition preparer shall provide to the debtor a written notice which shall be on an official form prescribed by the Judicial Conference of the United States in accordance with rule 9009 of the Federal Rules of Bankruptcy Procedure.

(B) The notice under the subparagraph (A) –

(i) shall inform the debtor in simple language that a bankruptcy petition preparer is not an attorney and may not practice law or give legal advice;

(ii) may contain a description of examples of legal advice that a bankruptcy petition preparer is not authorized to give, in addition to any advice that the preparer may not give by reason of subsection (e)(2); and

(iii) shall –

(I) be signed by the debtor and, under penalty of perjury, by the bankruptcy petition preparer; and

(II) be filed with any document for filing.

(c)(1) A bankruptcy petition preparer who prepares a document for filing shall place on the document, after the preparer's signature, an identifying number that identifies individuals who prepared the document.

(2)(A) Subject to subparagraph (B), for purposes of this section, the identifying number of a bankruptcy petition preparer shall be the Social Security account number of each individual who prepared the document or assisted in its preparation.

(B) If a bankruptcy petition preparer is not an individual, the identifying number of the bankruptcy petition preparer shall be the Social Security account number of the officer, principal, responsible person, or partner of the bankruptcy petition preparer.

(d) A bankruptcy petition preparer shall, not later than the time at which a document for filing is presented for the debtor's signature, furnish to the debtor a copy of the document.

(e)(1) A bankruptcy petition preparer shall not execute any document on behalf of a debtor.

(2)(A) A bankruptcy petition preparer may not offer a potential bankruptcy debtor any legal advice, including any legal advice described in subparagraph (B).

(B) The legal advice referred to in subparagraph (A) includes advising the debtor –

(i) whether –

(I) to file a petition under this title; or

(II) commencing a case under chapter 7, 11, 12, or 13 is appropriate;

(ii) whether the debtor's debts will be discharged in a case under this title;

(iii) whether the debtor will be able to retain the debtor's home, car, or other property after commencing a case under this title;

(iv) concerning –

(I) the tax consequences of a case brought under this title; or

(II) the dischargeability of tax claims;

(v) whether the debtor may or should promise to repay debts to a creditor or enter into a reaffirmation agreement with a creditor to reaffirm a debt;

(vi) concerning how to characterize the nature of the debtor's interests in property or the debtor's debts; or

(vii) concerning bankruptcy procedures and rights.

(f) A bankruptcy petition preparer shall not use the word "legal" or any similar term in any advertisements, or advertise under any category that includes the word "legal" or any similar term.

(g) A bankruptcy petition preparer shall not collect or receive any payment from the debtor or on behalf of the debtor for the court fees in connection with filing the petition.

(h)(1) The Supreme Court may promulgate rules under section 2075 of title 28, or the Judicial Conference of the United States may prescribe guidelines, for setting a maximum allowable fee chargeable by a bankruptcy petition preparer. A bankruptcy petition preparer shall notify the debtor of any such maximum amount before preparing any document for filing for the debtor or accepting any fee from or on behalf of the debtor.

(2) A declaration under penalty of perjury by the bankruptcy petition preparer shall be filed together with the petition, disclosing any fee received from or on behalf of the debtor within 12 months immediately prior to the filing of the case, and any unpaid fee charged to the debtor. If rules or guidelines setting a maximum fee for services have been promulgated or prescribed under paragraph (1), the declaration under this paragraph shall include a certification that the bankruptcy petition preparer complied with the notification requirement under paragraph (1).

(3)(A) The court shall disallow and order the immediate turnover to the bankruptcy trustee any fee referred to in paragraph (2) –

(i) found to be in excess of the value of any services rendered by the bankruptcy petition preparer during the 12-month period immediately preceding the date of the filing of the petition; or

(ii) found to be in violation of any rule or guideline promulgated or prescribed under paragraph (1).

(B) All fees charged by a bankruptcy petition preparer may be forfeited in any case in which the bankruptcy petition preparer fails to comply with this subsection or subsection (b), (c), (d), (e), (f), or (g).

(C) An individual may exempt any funds recovered under this paragraph under section 522(b).

(4) The debtor, the trustee, a creditor, the United States trustee (or the bankruptcy administrator, if any) or the court, on the initiative of the court, may file a motion for an order under paragraph (3).

(5) A bankruptcy petition preparer shall be fined not more than $500 for each failure to comply with a court order to turn over funds within 30 days of service of such order.

(i)(1) If a bankruptcy petition preparer violates this section or commits any act that the court finds to be fraudulent, unfair, or deceptive, on the motion of the debtor, trustee, United States trustee (or the bankruptcy administrator, if any), and after notice and a hearing, the court shall order the bankruptcy petition preparer to pay to the debtor –

(A) the debtor's actual damages;

(B) the greater of -

(i) $2,000; or

(ii) twice the amount paid by the debtor to the bankruptcy petition preparer for the preparer's services; and

(C) reasonable attorneys' fees and costs in moving for damages under this subsection.

(2) If the trustee or creditor moves for damages on behalf of the debtor under this subsection, the bankruptcy petition preparer shall be ordered to pay the movant the additional amount of $1,000 plus reasonable attorneys' fees and costs incurred.

(j)(1) A debtor for whom a bankruptcy petition preparer has prepared a document for filing, the trustee, a creditor, or the United States trustee in the district in which the bankruptcy petition preparer resides, has conducted business, or the United States trustee in any other district in which the debtor resides may bring a civil action to enjoin a bankruptcy petition preparer from engaging in any conduct in violation of this section or from further acting as a bankruptcy petition preparer.

(2)(A) In an action under paragraph (1), if the court finds that -

(i) a bankruptcy petition preparer has -

(I) engaged in conduct in violation of this section or of any provision of this title;

(II) misrepresented the preparer's experience or education as a bankruptcy petition preparer; or

(III) engaged in any other fraudulent, unfair, or deceptive conduct; and

(ii) injunctive relief is appropriate to prevent the recurrence of such conduct,

the court may enjoin the bankruptcy petition preparer from engaging in such conduct.

(B) If the court finds that a bankruptcy petition preparer has continually engaged in conduct described in subclause (I), (II), or (III) of clause (i) and that an injunction prohibiting such conduct would not be sufficient to prevent such person's interference with the proper administration of this title, has not paid a penalty imposed under this section, or failed to disgorge all fees ordered by the court, the court may enjoin the person from acting as a bankruptcy petition preparer.

(3) The court, as part of its contempt power, may enjoin a bankruptcy petition preparer that has failed to comply with a previous order issued under this section. The injunction under this paragraph may be issued on the motion of the court, the trustee, or the United States trustee (or the bankruptcy administrator, if any).

(4) The court shall award to a debtor, trustee, or creditor that brings a successful action under this subsection reasonable attorneys' fees and costs of the action, to be paid by the bankruptcy petition preparer.

(k) Nothing in this section shall be construed to permit activities that are otherwise prohibited by law, including rules and laws that prohibit the unauthorized practice of law.

(l)(1) A bankruptcy petition preparer who fails to comply with any provision of subsection (b), (c), (d), (e), (f), (g), or (h) may be fined not more than $500 for each such failure.

(2) The court shall triple the amount of a fine assessed under paragraph (1) in any case in which the court finds that a bankruptcy petition preparer –

(A) advised the debtor to exclude assets or income that should have been included on applicable schedules;

(B) advised the debtor to use a false Social Security account number;

(C) failed to inform the debtor that the debtor was filing for relief under this title; or

(D) prepared a document for filing in a manner that failed to disclose the identity of the bankruptcy petition preparer.

(3) A debtor, trustee, creditor, or United States trustee (or the bankruptcy administrator, if any) may file a motion for an order imposing a fine on the bankruptcy petition preparer for any violation of this section.

(4)(A) Fines imposed under this subsection in judicial districts served by United States trustees shall be paid to the United States trustees, who shall deposit an amount equal to such fines in the United States Trustee Fund.

(B) Fines imposed under this subsection in judicial districts served by bankruptcy administrators shall be deposited as offsetting receipts to the fund established under section 1931 of title 28, and shall remain available until expended to reimburse any appropriation for the amount paid out of such appropriation for expenses of the operation and maintenance of the courts of the United States.

111. Nonprofit budget and credit counseling agencies; financial management instructional courses

(a) The clerk shall maintain a publicly available list of –

(1) nonprofit budget and credit counseling agencies that provide 1 or more services described in section 109(h) currently approved by the United States trustee (or the bankruptcy administrator, if any); and

(2) instructional courses concerning personal financial management currently approved by the United States trustee (or the bankruptcy administrator, if any), as applicable.

(b) The United States trustee (or bankruptcy administrator, if any) shall only approve a nonprofit budget and credit counseling agency or an instructional course concerning personal financial management as follows:

(1) The United States trustee (or bankruptcy administrator, if any) shall have thoroughly reviewed the qualifications of the nonprofit budget and credit counseling agency or of the provider of the instructional course under the standards set forth in this section, and the services or instructional courses that will be offered by such agency or such provider, and may require such agency or such provider that has sought approval to provide information with respect to such review.

(2) The United States trustee (or bankruptcy administrator, if any) shall have determined that such agency or such instructional course fully satisfies the applicable standards set forth in this section.

(3) If a nonprofit budget and credit counseling agency or instructional course did not appear on the approved list for the district under subsection (a) immediately before approval under this section, approval under this subsection of such agency or such instructional course shall be for a probationary period not to exceed 6 months.

(4) At the conclusion of the applicable probationary period under paragraph (3), the United States trustee (or bankruptcy administrator, if any) may only approve for an additional 1-year period, and for successive 1-year periods thereafter, an agency or instructional course that has demonstrated during the probationary or applicable subsequent period of approval that such agency or instructional course –

(A) has met the standards set forth under this section during such period; and

(B) can satisfy such standards in the future.

(5) Not later than 30 days after any final decision under paragraph (4), an interested person may seek judicial review of such decision in the appropriate district court of the United States.

(c)(1) The United States trustee (or the bankruptcy administrator, if any) shall only approve a nonprofit budget and credit counseling agency that demonstrates that it will provide qualified counselors, maintain adequate provision for safekeeping and payment of client funds, provide adequate counseling with respect to client credit problems, and deal responsibly and effectively with other matters relating to the quality, effectiveness, and financial security of the services it provides.

(2) To be approved by the United States trustee (or the bankruptcy administrator, if any), a nonprofit budget and credit counseling agency shall, at a minimum –

(A) have a board of directors the majority of which –

(i) are not employed by such agency; and

(ii) will not directly or indirectly benefit financially from the outcome of the counseling services provided by such agency;

(B) if a fee is charged for counseling services, charge a reasonable fee, and provide services without regard to ability to pay the fee;

(C) provide for safekeeping and payment of client funds, including an annual audit of the trust accounts and appropriate employee bonding;

(D) provide full disclosures to a client, including funding sources, counselor qualifications, possible impact on credit reports, and any costs of such program that will be paid by such client and how such costs will be paid;

(E) provide adequate counseling with respect to a client's credit problems that includes an analysis of such client's current financial condition, factors that caused such financial condition, and how such client can develop a plan to respond to the problems without incurring negative amortization of debt;

(F) provide trained counselors who receive no commissions or bonuses based on the outcome of the counseling services provided by such agency, and who have adequate experience, and have been adequately trained to provide counseling services to individuals in financial difficulty, including the matters described in subparagraph (E);

(G) demonstrate adequate experience and background in providing credit counseling; and

(H) have adequate financial resources to provide continuing support services for budgeting plans over the life of any repayment plan.

(d) The United States trustee (or the bankruptcy administrator, if any) shall only approve an instructional course concerning personal financial management –

(1) for an initial probationary period under subsection (b)(3) if the course will provide at a minimum –

(A) trained personnel with adequate experience and training in providing effective instruction and services;

(B) learning materials and teaching methodologies designed to assist debtors in understanding personal financial management and that are consistent with stated objectives directly related to the goals of such instructional course;

(C) adequate facilities situated in reasonably convenient locations at which such instructional course is offered, except that such facilities may include the provision of such instructional course by telephone or through the Internet, if such instructional course is effective;

(D) the preparation and retention of reasonable records (which shall include the debtor's bankruptcy case number) to permit evaluation of the effectiveness of such instructional course, including any evaluation of satisfaction of instructional course requirements for each debtor attending such instructional course, which shall be available for inspection and evaluation by the Executive Office for United States Trustees, the United States trustee (or the bankruptcy administrator, if any), or the chief bankruptcy judge for the district in which such instructional course is offered; and

(E) if a fee is charged for the instructional course, charge a reasonable fee, and provide services without regard to ability to pay the fee; and

(2) for any 1-year period if the provider thereof has demonstrated that the course meets the standards of paragraph (1) and, in addition –

(A) has been effective in assisting a substantial number of debtors to understand personal financial management; and

(B) is otherwise likely to increase substantially the debtor's understanding of personal financial management.

(e) The district court may, at any time, investigate the qualifications of a nonprofit budget and credit counseling agency referred to in subsection (a), and request production of documents to ensure the integrity and effectiveness of such agency. The district court may, at any time, remove from the approved list under subsection (a) a nonprofit budget and credit counseling agency upon finding such agency does not meet the qualifications of subsection (b).

(f) The United States trustee (or the bankruptcy administrator, if any) shall notify the clerk that a nonprofit budget and credit counseling agency or an instructional course is no longer approved, in which case the clerk shall remove it from the list maintained under subsection (a).

(g)(1) No nonprofit budget and credit counseling agency may provide to a credit reporting agency information concerning whether a debtor has received or sought instruction concerning personal financial management from such agency.

(2) A nonprofit budget and credit counseling agency that willfully or negligently fails to comply with any requirement under this title with respect to a debtor shall be liable for damages in an amount equal to the sum of –

(A) any actual damages sustained by the debtor as a result of the violation; and

(B) any court costs or reasonable attorneys' fees (as determined by the court) incurred in an action to recover those damages.

112. Prohibition on disclosure of name of minor children

The debtor may be required to provide information regarding a minor child involved in matters under this title but may not be required to disclose in the public records in the case the name of such minor child. The debtor may be required to disclose the name of such minor child in a nonpublic record that is maintained by the court and made available by the court for examination by the United States trustee, the trustee, and the auditor (if any) serving under section 586(f) of title 28, in the case. The court, the United States trustee, the trustee, and such auditor shall not disclose the name of such minor child maintained in such nonpublic record.

Chapter 3 - Case Administration

Subchapter I - Commencement of a Case

Subchapter II - Officers

Subchapter III - Administration

Subchapter IV - Administrative Powers

SUBCHAPTER I - COMMENCEMENT OF A CASE

301. Voluntary cases

(a) A voluntary case under a chapter of this title is commenced by the filing with the bankruptcy court of a petition under such chapter by an entity that may be a debtor under such chapter.

(b) The commencement of a voluntary case under a chapter of this title constitutes an order for relief under such chapter.

302. Joint cases

(a) A joint case under a chapter of this title is commenced by the filing with the bankruptcy court of a single petition under such chapter by an individual that may be a debtor under such chapter and such individual's spouse. The commencement of a joint case under a chapter of this title constitutes an order for relief under such chapter.

(b) After the commencement of a joint case, the court shall determine the extent, if any, to which the debtors' estates shall be consolidated.

303. Involuntary cases

(a) An involuntary case may be commenced only under chapter 7 or 11 of this title, and only against a person, except a farmer, family farmer, or a corporation that is not a moneyed, business, or commercial corporation, that may be a debtor under the chapter under which such case is commenced.

(b) An involuntary case against a person is commenced by the filing with the bankruptcy court of a petition under chapter 7 or 11 of this title-

(1) by three or more entities, each of which is either a holder of a claim against such person that is not contingent as to liability or the subject of a bona fide dispute as to liability or amount, or an indenture trustee representing such a holder, if such noncontingent, undisputed claims aggregate at least $15,325 more than the value of any lien on property of the debtor securing such claims held by the holders of such claims;

(2) if there are fewer than 12 such holders, excluding any employee or insider of such person and any transferee of a transfer that is voidable under section 544, 545, 547, 548, 549, or 724(a) of this title, by one or more of such holders that hold in the aggregate at least $15,325 of such claims;

(3) if such person is a partnership-

(A) by fewer than all of the general partners in such partnership; or

(B) if relief has been ordered under this title with respect to all of the general partners in such partnership, by a general partner in such partnership, the trustee of such a general partner, or a holder of a claim against such partnership; or

(4) by a foreign representative of the estate in a foreign proceeding concerning such person.

(c) After the filing of a petition under this section but before the case is dismissed or relief is ordered, a creditor holding an unsecured claim that is not contingent, other than a creditor filing under subsection (b) of this section, may join in the petition with the same effect as if such joining creditor were a petitioning creditor under subsection (b) of this section.

(d) The debtor, or a general partner in a partnership debtor that did not join in the petition, may file an answer to a petition under this section.

(e) After notice and a hearing, and for cause, the court may require the petitioners under this section to file a bond to indemnify the debtor for such amounts as the court may later allow under subsection (i) of this section.

(f) Notwithstanding section 363 of this title, except to the extent that the court orders otherwise, and until an order for relief in the case, any business of the debtor may continue to operate, and the debtor may continue to use, acquire, or dispose of property as if an involuntary case concerning the debtor had not been commenced.

(g) At any time after the commencement of an involuntary case under chapter 7 of this title but before an order for relief in the case, the court, on request of a party in interest, after notice to the debtor and a hearing, and if necessary to preserve the property of the estate or to prevent loss to the estate, may order the United States trustee to appoint an interim trustee under section 701 of this title to take possession of the property of the estate and to operate any business of the debtor. Before an order for relief, the debtor may regain possession of property in the possession of a trustee ordered appointed under this subsection if the debtor files such bond as the court requires, conditioned on the debtor's accounting for and delivering to the trustee, if there is an order for relief in the case, such property, or the value, as of the date the debtor regains possession, of such property.

(h) If the petition is not timely controverted, the court shall order relief against the debtor in an involuntary case under the chapter under which the petition was filed. Otherwise, after trial, the court shall order relief against the debtor in an involuntary case under the chapter under which the petition was filed, only if-

(1) the debtor is generally not paying such debtor's debts as such debts become due unless such debts are the subject of a bona fide dispute as to liability or amount; or

(2) within 120 days before the date of the filing of the petition, a custodian, other than a trustee, receiver, or agent appointed or authorized to take charge of less than substantially all of the property of the debtor for the purpose of enforcing a lien against such property, was appointed or took possession.

(i) If the court dismisses a petition under this section other than on consent of all petitioners and the debtor, and if the debtor does not waive the right to judgment under this subsection, the court may grant judgment-

(1) against the petitioners and in favor of the debtor for-

(A) costs; or

(B) a reasonable attorney's fee; or

(2) against any petitioner that filed the petition in bad faith, for-

(A) any damages proximately caused by such filing; or

(B) punitive damages.

(j) Only after notice to all creditors and a hearing may the court dismiss a petition filed under this section-

(1) on the motion of a petitioner;

(2) on consent of all petitioners and the debtor; or

(3) for want of prosecution.

(k)(1) If –

(A) the petition under this section is false or contains any materially false, fictitious, or fraudulent statement;

(B) the debtor is an individual; and

(C) the court dismisses such petition,

the court, upon the motion of the debtor, shall seal all the records of the court relating to such petition, and all references to such petition.

(2) If the debtor is an individual and the court dismisses a petition under this section, the court may enter an order prohibiting all consumer reporting agencies (as defined in section 603(f) of the Fair Credit Reporting Act (15 U.S.C. 1681a(f))) from making any consumer report (as defined in section 603(d) of that Act) that contains any information relating to such petition or to the case commenced by the filing of such petition.

(3) Upon the expiration of the statute of limitations described in section 3282 of title 18, for a violation of section 152 or 157 of such title, the court, upon the motion of the debtor and for good cause, may expunge any records relating to a petition filed under this section.

305. Abstention

(a) The court, after notice and a hearing, may dismiss a case under this title, or may suspend all proceedings in a case under this title, at any time if -

(1) the interests of creditors and the debtor would be better served by such dismissal or suspension; or

(2)(A) a petition under section 1515 for recognition of a foreign proceeding has been granted; and

(B) the purposes of chapter 15 of this title would be best served by such dismissal or suspension.

(b) A foreign representative may seek dismissal or suspension under subsection(a)(2) of this section.

(c) An order under subsection (a) of this section dismissing a case or suspending all proceedings in a case, or a decision not so to dismiss or suspend, is not reviewable by appeal or otherwise by the court of appeals under section 158(d), 1291, or 1292 of title 28 or by the Supreme Court of the United States under section 1254 of title 28.

306. Limited appearance

An appearance in a bankruptcy court by a foreign representative in connection with a petition or request under section 303 or 305 of this title does not submit such foreign representative to the jurisdiction of any court in the United States for any other purpose, but the bankruptcy court may condition any order under section 303 or 305 of this title on compliance by such foreign representative with the orders of such bankruptcy court.

307. United States trustee

The United States trustee may raise and may appear and be heard on any issue in any case or proceeding under this title but may not file a plan pursuant to section 1121(c) of this title.

308. Debtor reporting requirements

(a) For purposes of this section, the term "profitability" means, with respect to a debtor, the amount of money that the debtor has earned or lost during current and recent fiscal periods.

(b) A debtor in a small business case shall file periodic financial and other reports containing information including –

(1) the debtor's profitability;

(2) reasonable approximations of the debtor's projected cash receipts and cash disbursements over a reasonable period;

(3) comparisons of actual cash receipts and disbursements with projections in prior reports;

(4) whether the debtor is –

(A) in compliance in all material respects with postpetition requirements imposed by this title and the Federal Rules of Bankruptcy Procedure; and

(B) timely filing tax returns and other required government filings and paying taxes and other administrative expenses when due;

(5) if the debtor is not in compliance with the requirements referred to in paragraph (4)(A) or filing tax returns and other required government filings and making the payments referred to in paragraph (4)(B), what the failures are and how, at what cost, and when the debtor intends to remedy such failures; and

(6) such other matters as are in the best interests of the debtor and creditors, and in the public interest in fair and efficient procedures under chapter 11 of this title.

SUBCHAPTER II - OFFICERS

321. Eligibility to serve as trustee

(a) A person may serve as trustee in a case under this title only if such person is-

(1) an individual that is competent to perform the duties of trustee and, in a case under chapter 7, 12, or 13 of this title, resides or has an office in the judicial district within which the case is pending, or in any judicial district adjacent to such district; or

(2) a corporation authorized by such corporation's charter or bylaws to act as trustee, and, in a case under chapter 7, 12, or 13 of this title, having an office in at least one of such districts.

(b) A person that has served as an examiner in the case may not serve as trustee in the case.

(c) The United States trustee for the judicial district in which the case is pending is eligible to serve as trustee in the case if necessary.

322. Qualification of trustee

(a) Except as provided in subsection (b)(1), a person selected under section 701, 702, 703, 1104, 1163, 1202, or 1302 of this title to serve as trustee in a case under this title qualifies if before seven days after such selection, and before beginning official duties, such person has filed with the court a bond in favor of the United States conditioned on the faithful performance of such official duties.

(b)(1) The United States trustee qualifies wherever such trustee serves as trustee in a case under this title.

(2) The United States trustee shall determine -

(A) the amount of a bond required to be filed under subsection (a) of this section; and

(B) the sufficiency of the surety on such bond.

(c) A trustee is not liable personally or on such trustee's bond in favor of the United States for any penalty or forfeiture incurred by the debtor.

(d) A proceeding on a trustee's bond may not be commenced after two years after the date on which such trustee was discharged.

323. Role and capacity of trustee

(a) The trustee in a case under this title is the representative of the estate.

(b) The trustee in a case under this title has capacity to sue and be sued.

324. Removal of trustee or examiner

(a) The court, after notice and a hearing, may remove a trustee, other than the United States trustee, or an examiner, for cause.

(b) Whenever the court removes a trustee or examiner under subsection (a) in a case under this title, such trustee or examiner shall thereby be removed in all other cases under this title in which such trustee or examiner is then serving unless the court orders otherwise.

325. Effect of vacancy

A vacancy in the office of trustee during a case does not abate any pending action or proceeding, and the successor trustee shall be substituted as a party in such action or proceeding.

326. Limitation on compensation of trustee

(a) In a case under chapter 7 or 11, the court may allow reasonable compensation under section 330 of this title of the trustee for the trustee's services, payable after the trustee renders such services, not to exceed 25 percent on the first $5,000 or less, 10 percent on any amount in excess of $5,000 but not in excess of $50,000, 5 percent on any amount in excess of $50,000 but not in excess of $1,000,000, and reasonable compensation not to exceed 3 percent of such moneys in excess of $1,000,000, upon all moneys disbursed or turned over in the case by the trustee to parties in interest, excluding the debtor, but including holders of secured claims.

(b) In a case under chapter 12 or 13 of this title, the court may not allow compensation for services or reimbursement of expenses of the United States trustee or of a standing trustee appointed under section 586(b) of title 28, but may allow reasonable compensation under section 330 of this title of a trustee appointed under section 1202(a) or 1302(a) of this title for the trustee's services, payable after the trustee renders such services, not to exceed five percent upon all payments under the plan.

(c) If more than one person serves as trustee in the case, the aggregate compensation of such persons for such service may not exceed the maximum compensation prescribed for a single trustee by subsection (a) or (b) of this section, as the case may be.

(d) The court may deny allowance of compensation for services or reimbursement of expenses of the trustee if the trustee failed to make diligent inquiry into facts that would permit denial of allowance under section 328(c) of this title or, with knowledge of such facts, employed a professional person under section 327 of this title.

327. Employment of professional persons

(a) Except as otherwise provided in this section, the trustee, with the court's approval, may employ one or more attorneys, accountants, appraisers, auctioneers, or other professional persons, that do not hold or represent an interest adverse to the estate, and that are disinterested persons, to represent or assist the trustee in carrying out the trustee's duties under this title.

(b) If the trustee is authorized to operate the business of the debtor under section 721, 1202, or 1108 of this title, and if the debtor has regularly employed attorneys, accountants, or other professional persons on salary, the trustee may retain or replace such professional persons if necessary in the operation of such business.

(c) In a case under chapter 7, 12, or 11 of this title, a person is not disqualified for employment under this section solely because of such person's employment by or representation of a creditor, unless there is objection by another creditor or the United States trustee, in which case the court shall disapprove such employment if there is an actual conflict of interest.

(d) The court may authorize the trustee to act as attorney or accountant for the estate if such authorization is in the best interest of the estate.

(e) The trustee, with the court's approval, may employ, for a specified special purpose, other than to represent the trustee in conducting the case, an attorney that has represented the debtor, if in the best interest of the estate, and if such attorney does not represent or hold any interest adverse to the debtor or to the estate with respect to the matter on which such attorney is to be employed.

(f) The trustee may not employ a person that has served as an examiner in the case.

328. Limitation on compensation of professional persons

(a) The trustee, or a committee appointed under section 1102 of this title, with the court's approval, may employ or authorize the employment of a professional person under section 327 or 1103 of this title, as the case may be, on any reasonable terms and conditions of employment, including on a retainer, on an hourly basis, on a fixed or percentage fee basis, or on a contingent fee basis. Notwithstanding such terms and conditions, the court may allow compensation different from the compensation provided under such terms and conditions after the conclusion of such employment, if such terms and conditions prove to have been improvident in light of developments not capable of being anticipated at the time of the fixing of such terms and conditions.

(b) If the court has authorized a trustee to serve as an attorney or accountant for the estate under section 327(d) of this title, the court may allow compensation for the trustee's services as such attorney or accountant only to the extent that the trustee performed services as attorney or accountant for the estate and not for performance of any of the trustee's duties that are generally performed by a trustee without the assistance of an attorney or accountant for the estate.

(c) Except as provided in section 327(c), 327(e), or 1107(b) of this title, the court may deny allowance of compensation for services and reimbursement of expenses of a professional person employed under section 327 or 1103 of this title if, at any time during such professional person's employment under section 327 or 1103 of this title, such professional person is not a disinterested person, or represents or holds an interest adverse to the interest of the estate with respect to the matter on which such professional person is employed.

329. Debtor's transactions with attorneys

(a) Any attorney representing a debtor in a case under this title, or in connection with such a case, whether or not such attorney applies for compensation under this title, shall file with the court a statement of the compensation paid or agreed to be paid, if such payment or agreement was made after one year before the date of the filing of the petition, for services rendered or to be rendered in contemplation of or in connection with the case by such attorney, and the source of such compensation.

(b) If such compensation exceeds the reasonable value of any such services, the court may cancel any such agreement, or order the return of any such payment, to the extent excessive, to -

(1) the estate, if the property transferred -

(A) would have been property of the estate; or

(B) was to be paid by or on behalf of the debtor under a plan under chapter 11, 12, or 13 of this title; or

(2) the entity that made such payment.

330. Compensation of officers

(a)(1) After notice to the parties in interest and the United States Trustee and a hearing, and subject to sections 326, 328, and 329, the court may award to a trustee, a consumer privacy ombudsman appointed under section 332, an examiner, an ombudsman appointed under section 333, or a professional person employed under section 327 or 1103 -

(A) reasonable compensation for actual, necessary services rendered by the trustee, examiner, ombudsman, professional person, or attorney and by any paraprofessional person employed by any such person; and

(B) reimbursement for actual, necessary expenses.

(2) The court may, on its own motion or on the motion of the United States Trustee, the United States Trustee for the District or Region, the trustee for the estate, or any other party in interest, award compensation that is less than the amount of compensation that is requested.

(3) In determining the amount of reasonable compensation to be awarded to an examiner, trustee under chapter 11, or professional person, the court shall consider the nature, the extent, and the value of such services, taking into account all relevant factors, including -

(A) the time spent on such services;

(B) the rates charged for such services;

(C) whether the services were necessary to the administration of, or beneficial at the time at which the service was rendered toward the completion of, a case under this title;

(D) whether the services were performed within a reasonable amount of time commensurate with the complexity, importance, and nature of the problem, issue, or task addressed;

(E) with respect to a professional person, whether the person is board certified or otherwise has demonstrated skill and experience in the bankruptcy field; and

(F) whether the compensation is reasonable based on the customary compensation charged by comparably skilled practitioners in cases other than cases under this title.

(4)(A) Except as provided in subparagraph (B), the court shall not allow compensation for -

(i) unnecessary duplication of services; or

(ii) services that were not -

(I) reasonably likely to benefit the debtor's estate; or

(II) necessary to the administration of the case.

(B) In a chapter 12 or chapter 13 case in which the debtor is an individual, the court may allow reasonable compensation to the debtor's attorney for representing the interests of the debtor in connection with the bankruptcy case based on a consideration of the benefit and necessity of such services to the debtor and the other factors set forth in this section.

(5) The court shall reduce the amount of compensation awarded under this section by the amount of any interim compensation awarded under section 331, and, if the amount of such interim compensation exceeds the amount of compensation awarded under this section, may order the return of the excess to the estate.

(6) Any compensation awarded for the preparation of a fee application shall be based on the level and skill reasonably required to prepare the application.

(7) In determining the amount of reasonable compensation to be awarded to a trustee, the court shall treat such compensation as a commission, based on section 326.

(b)(1) There shall be paid from the filing fee in a case under chapter 7 of this title $45 to the trustee serving in such case, after such trustee's services are rendered.

(2) The Judicial Conference of the United States -

(A) shall prescribe additional fees of the same kind as prescribed under section 1914(b) of title 28; and

(B) may prescribe notice of appearance fees and fees charged against distributions in cases under this title;

to pay $15 to trustees serving in cases after such trustees' services are rendered. Beginning 1 year after the date of the enactment of the Bankruptcy Reform Act of 1994, such $15 shall be paid in addition to the amount paid under paragraph (1).

(c) Unless the court orders otherwise, in a case under chapter 12 or 13 of this title the compensation paid to the trustee serving in the case shall not be less than $5 per month from any distribution under the plan during the administration of the plan.

(d) In a case in which the United States trustee serves as trustee, the compensation of the trustee under this section shall be paid to the clerk of the bankruptcy court and deposited by the clerk into the United States Trustee System Fund established by section 589a of title 28.

331. Interim compensation

A trustee, an examiner, a debtor's attorney, or any professional person employed under section 327 or 1103 of this title may apply to the court not more than once every 120 days after an order for relief in a case under this title, or more often if the court permits, for such compensation for services rendered before the date of such an application or reimbursement for expenses incurred before such date as is provided under section 330 of this title. After notice and a hearing, the court may allow and disburse to such applicant such compensation or reimbursement.

332. Consumer privacy ombudsman

(a) If a hearing is required under section 363(b)(1)(B), the court shall order the United States trustee to appoint, not later than 7 days before the commencement of the hearing, 1 disinterested person (other than the United States trustee) to serve as the consumer privacy ombudsman in the case and shall require that notice of such hearing be timely given to such ombudsman.

(b) The consumer privacy ombudsman may appear and be heard at such hearing and shall provide to the court information to assist the court in its consideration of the facts, circumstances, and conditions of the proposed sale or lease of personally identifiable information under section 363(b)(1)(B). Such information may include presentation of –

(1) the debtor's privacy policy;

(2) the potential losses or gains of privacy to consumers if such sale or such lease is approved by the court;

(3) the potential costs or benefits to consumers if such sale or such lease is approved by the court; and

(4) the potential alternatives that would mitigate potential privacy losses or potential costs to consumers.

(c) A consumer privacy ombudsman shall not disclose any personally identifiable information obtained by the ombudsman under this title.

333. Appointment of patient care ombudsman

(a)(1) If the debtor in a case under chapter 7, 9, or 11 is a health care business, the court shall order, not later than 30 days after the commencement of the case, the appointment of an ombudsman to monitor the quality of patient care and to represent the interests of the patients of the health care business unless the court finds that the appointment of such ombudsman is not necessary for the protection of patients under the specific facts of the case.

(2)(A) If the court orders the appointment of an ombudsman under paragraph(1), the United States trustee shall appoint 1 disinterested person (other than the United States trustee) to serve as such ombudsman.

(B) If the debtor is a health care business that provides long-term care, then the United States trustee may appoint the State Long-Term Care Ombudsman appointed under the Older Americans Act of 1965 for the State in which the case is pending to serve as the ombudsman required by paragraph (1).

(C) If the United States trustee does not appoint a State Long-Term Care Ombudsman under subparagraph (B), the court shall notify the State Long-Term Care Ombudsman appointed under the Older Americans Act of 1965 for the State in which the case is pending, of the name and address of the person who is appointed under subparagraph (A).

(b) An ombudsman appointed under subsection (a) shall –

(1) monitor the quality of patient care provided to patients of the debtor, to the extent necessary under the circumstances, including interviewing patients and physicians;

(2) not later than 60 days after the date of appointment, and not less frequently than at 60-day intervals thereafter, report to the court after notice to the parties in interest, at a hearing or in writing, regarding the quality of patient care provided to patients of the debtor; and

(3) if such ombudsman determines that the quality of patient care provided to patients of the debtor is declining significantly or is otherwise being materially compromised, file with the court a motion or a written report, with notice to the parties in interest immediately upon making such determination.

(c)(1) An ombudsman appointed under subsection (a) shall maintain any information obtained by such ombudsman under this section that relates to patients (including information relating to patient records) as confidential information. Such ombudsman may not review confidential patient records unless the court approves such review in advance and imposes restrictions on such ombudsman to protect the confidentiality of such records.

(2) An ombudsman appointed under subsection (a)(2)(B) shall have access to patient records consistent with authority of such ombudsman under the Older Americans Act of 1965 and under non-Federal laws governing the State Long-Term Care Ombudsman program.

SUBCHAPTER III - ADMINISTRATION

341. Meetings of creditors and equity security holders

(a) Within a reasonable time after the order for relief in a case under this title, the United States trustee shall convene and preside at a meeting of creditors.

(b) The United States trustee may convene a meeting of any equity security holders.

(c) The court may not preside at, and may not attend, any meeting under this section including any final meeting of creditors. Notwithstanding any local court rule, provision of a State constitution, any otherwise applicable nonbankruptcy law, or any other requirement that representation at the meeting of creditors under subsection (a) be by an attorney, a creditor holding a consumer debt or any representative of the creditor (which may include an entity or an employee of an entity and may be a representative for more than 1 creditor) shall be permitted to appear at and participate in the meeting of creditors in a case under chapter 7 or 13, either alone or in conjunction with an attorney for the creditor. Nothing in this subsection shall be construed to require any creditor to be represented by an attorney at any meeting of creditors.

(d) Prior to the conclusion of the meeting of creditors or equity security holders, the trustee shall orally examine the debtor to ensure that the debtor in a case under chapter 7 of this title is aware of –

(1) the potential consequences of seeking a discharge in bankruptcy, including the effects on credit history;

(2) the debtor's ability to file a petition under a different chapter of this title;

(3) the effect of receiving a discharge of debts under this title; and

(4) the effect of reaffirming a debt, including the debtor's knowledge of the provisions of section 524(d) of this title.

(e) Notwithstanding subsections (a) and (b), the court, on the request of a party in interest and after notice and a hearing, for cause may order that the United States trustee not convene a meeting of creditors or equity security holders if the debtor has filed a plan as to which the debtor solicited acceptances prior to the commencement of the case.

342. Notice

(a) There shall be given such notice as is appropriate, including notice to any holder of a community claim, of an order for relief in a case under this title.

(b) Before the commencement of a case under this title by an individual whose debts are primarily consumer debts, the clerk shall give to such individual written notice containing –

(1) a brief description of –

(A) chapters 7, 11, 12, and 13 and the general purpose, benefits, and costs of proceeding under each of those chapters; and

(B) the types of services available from credit counseling agencies; and

(2) statements specifying that –

(A) a person who knowingly and fraudulently conceals assets or makes a false oath or statement under penalty of perjury in connection with a case under this title shall be subject to fine, imprisonment, or both; and

(B) all information supplied by a debtor in connection with a case under this title is subject to examination by the Attorney General.

(c)(1) If notice is required to be given by the debtor to a creditor under this title, any rule, any applicable law, or any order of the court, such notice shall contain the name, address, and last 4 digits of the taxpayer identification number of the debtor. If the notice concerns an amendment that adds a creditor to the schedules of assets and liabilities, the debtor shall include the full taxpayer identification number in the notice sent to that creditor, but the debtor shall include only the last 4 digits of the taxpayer identification number in the copy of the notice filed with the court.

(2)(A) If, within the 90 days before the commencement of a voluntary case, a creditor supplies the debtor in at least 2 communications sent to the debtor with the current account number of the debtor and the address at which such creditor requests to receive correspondence, then any notice required by this title to be sent by the debtor to such creditor shall be sent to such address and shall include such account number.

(B) If a creditor would be in violation of applicable nonbankruptcy law by sending any such communication within such 90-day period and if such creditor supplies the debtor in the last 2 communications with the current account number of the debtor and the address at which such creditor requests to receive correspondence, then any notice required by this title to be sent by the debtor to such creditor shall be sent to such address and shall include such account number.

(d) In a case under chapter 7 of this title in which the debtor is an individual and in which the presumption of abuse arises under section 707(b), the clerk shall give written notice to all creditors not later than 10 days after the date of the filing of the petition that the presumption of abuse has arisen.

(e)(1) In a case under chapter 7 or 13 of this title of a debtor who is an individual, a creditor at any time may both file with the court and serve on the debtor a notice of address to be used to provide notice in such case to such creditor.

(2) Any notice in such case required to be provided to such creditor by the debtor or the court later than 7 days after the court and the debtor receive such creditor's notice of address, shall be provided to such address.

(f)(1) An entity may file with any bankruptcy court a notice of address to be used by all the bankruptcy courts or by particular bankruptcy courts, as so specified by such entity at the time such notice is filed, to provide notice to such entity in all cases under chapters 7 and 13 pending in the courts with respect to which such notice is filed, in which such entity is a creditor.

(2) In any case filed under chapter 7 or 13, any notice required to be provided by a court with respect to which a notice is filed under paragraph (1), to such entity later than 30 days after the filing of such notice under paragraph (1) shall be provided to such address unless with respect to a particular case a different address is specified in a notice filed and served in accordance with subsection (e).

(3) A notice filed under paragraph (1) may be withdrawn by such entity.

(g)(1) Notice provided to a creditor by the debtor or the court other than in accordance with this section (excluding this subsection) shall not be effective notice until such notice is brought to the attention of such creditor. If such creditor designates a person or an organizational subdivision of such creditor to be responsible for receiving notices under this title and establishes reasonable procedures so that such notices receivable by such creditor are to be delivered to such person or such subdivision, then a notice provided to such creditor other than in accordance with this section (excluding this subsection) shall not be considered to have been brought to the attention of such creditor until such notice is received by such person or such subdivision.

(2) A monetary penalty may not be imposed on a creditor for a violation of a stay in effect under section 362(a) (including a monetary penalty imposed under section 362(k)) or for failure to comply with section 542 or 543 unless the conduct that is the basis of such violation or of such failure occurs after such creditor receives notice effective under this section of the order for relief.

343. Examination of the debtor

The debtor shall appear and submit to examination under oath at the meeting of creditors under section 341(a) of this title. Creditors, any indenture trustee, any trustee or examiner in the case, or the United States trustee may examine the debtor. The United States trustee may administer the oath required under this section.

344. Self-incrimination; immunity

Immunity for persons required to submit to examination, to testify, or to provide information in a case under this title may be granted under part V of title 18.

345. Money of estates

(a) A trustee in a case under this title may make such deposit or investment of the money of the estate for which such trustee serves as will yield the maximum reasonable net return on such money, taking into account the safety of such deposit or investment.

(b) Except with respect to a deposit or investment that is insured or guaranteed by the United States or by a department, agency, or instrumentality of the United States or backed by the full faith and credit of the United States, the trustee shall require from an entity with which such money is deposited or invested -

(1) a bond-

(A) in favor of the United States;

(B) secured by the undertaking of a corporate surety approved by the United States trustee for the district in which the case is pending; and

(C) conditioned on -

(i) a proper accounting for all money so deposited or invested and for any return on such money;

(ii) prompt repayment of such money and return; and

(iii) faithful performance of duties as a depository; or

(2) the deposit of securities of the kind specified in section 9303 of title 31; unless the court for cause orders otherwise.

(c) An entity with which such moneys are deposited or invested is authorized to deposit or invest such moneys as may be required under this section.

346. Special provisions related to the treatment of State and local taxes

(a) Whenever the Internal Revenue Code of 1986 provides that a separate taxable estate or entity is created in a case concerning a debtor under this title, and the income, gain, loss, deductions, and credits of such estate shall be taxed to or claimed by the estate, a separate taxable estate is also created for purposes of any State and local law imposing a tax on or measured by income and such income, gain, loss, deductions, and credits shall be taxed to or claimed by the estate and may not be taxed to or claimed by the debtor. The preceding sentence shall not apply if the case is dismissed. The trustee shall make tax returns of income required under any such State or local law.

(b) Whenever the Internal Revenue Code of 1986 provides that no separate taxable estate shall be created in a case concerning a debtor under this title, and the income, gain, loss, deductions, and credits of an estate shall be taxed to or claimed by the debtor, such income, gain, loss, deductions, and credits shall be taxed to or claimed by the debtor under a State or local law imposing a tax on or measured by income and may not be taxed to or claimed by the estate. The trustee shall make such tax returns of income of corporations and of partnerships as are required under any State or local law, but with respect to partnerships, shall make such returns only to the extent such returns are also required to be made under such Code. The estate shall be liable for any tax imposed on such corporation or partnership, but not for any tax imposed on partners or members.(c) With respect to a partnership or any entity treated as a partnership under a State or local law imposing a tax on or measured by income that is a debtor in a case under this title, any gain or loss resulting from a distribution of property from such partnership, or any distributive share of any income, gain, loss, deduction, or credit of a partner or member that is distributed, or considered distributed, from such partnership, after the commencement of the case, is gain, loss, income, deduction, or credit, as the case may be, of the partner or member, and if such partner or member is a debtor in a case under this title, shall be subject to tax in accordance with subsection (a) or (b).

(d) For purposes of any State or local law imposing a tax on or measured by income, the taxable period of a debtor in a case under this title shall terminate only if and to the extent that the taxable period of such debtor terminates under the Internal Revenue Code of 1986.

(e) The estate in any case described in subsection (a) shall use the same accounting method as the debtor used immediately before the commencement of the case, if such method of accounting complies with applicable nonbankruptcy tax law.

(f) For purposes of any State or local law imposing a tax on or measured by income, a transfer of property from the debtor to the estate or from the estate to the debtor shall not be treated as a disposition for purposes of any provision assigning tax consequences to a disposition, except to the extent that such transfer is treated as a disposition under the Internal Revenue Code of 1986.

(g) Whenever a tax is imposed pursuant to a State or local law imposing a tax on or measured by income pursuant to subsection (a) or (b), such tax shall be imposed at rates generally applicable to the same types of entities under such State or local law.

(h) The trustee shall withhold from any payment of claims for wages, salaries, commissions, dividends, interest, or other payments, or collect, any amount required to be withheld or collected under applicable State or local tax law, and shall pay such withheld or collected amount to the appropriate governmental unit at the time and in the manner required by such tax law, and with the same priority as the claim from which such amount was withheld or collected was paid.

(i)(1) To the extent that any State or local law imposing a tax on or measured by income provides for the carryover of any tax attribute from one taxable period to a subsequent taxable period, the estate shall succeed to such tax attribute in any case in which such estate is subject to tax under subsection (a).

(2) After such a case is closed or dismissed, the debtor shall succeed to any tax attribute to which the estate succeeded under paragraph (1) to the extent consistent with the Internal Revenue Code of 1986.

(3) The estate may carry back any loss or tax attribute to a taxable period of the debtor that ended before the date of the order for relief under this title to the extent that –

(A) applicable State or local tax law provides for a carryback in the case of the debtor; and

(B) the same or a similar tax attribute may be carried back by the estate to such a taxable period of the debtor under the Internal Revenue Code of 1986.

(j)(1) For purposes of any State or local law imposing a tax on or measured by income, income is not realized by the estate, the debtor, or a successor to the debtor by reason of discharge of indebtedness in a case under this title, except to the extent, if any, that such income is subject to tax under the Internal Revenue Code of 1986.

(2) Whenever the Internal Revenue Code of 1986 provides that the amount excluded from gross income in respect of the discharge of indebtedness in a case under this title shall be applied to reduce the tax attributes of the debtor or the estate, a similar reduction shall be made under any State or local law imposing a tax on or measured by income to the extent such State or local law recognizes such attributes. Such State or local law may also provide for the reduction of other attributes to the extent that the full amount of income from the discharge of indebtedness has not been applied.

(k)(1) Except as provided in this section and section 505, the time and manner of filing tax returns and the items of income, gain, loss, deduction, and credit of any taxpayer shall be determined under applicable nonbankruptcy law.

(2) For Federal tax purposes, the provisions of this section are subject to the Internal Revenue Code of 1986 and other applicable Federal nonbankruptcy law.

347. Unclaimed property

(a) Ninety days after the final distribution under section 726, 1226, or 1326 of this title in a case under chapter 7, 12, or 13 of this title, as the case may be, the trustee shall stop payment on any check remaining unpaid, and any remaining property of the estate shall be paid into the court and disposed of under chapter 129 of title 28.

(b) Any security, money, or other property remaining unclaimed at the expiration of the time allowed in a case under chapter 9, 11, or 12 of this title for the presentation of a security or the performance of any other act as a condition to participation in the distribution under any plan confirmed under section 943(b), 1129, 1173, or 1225 of this title, as the case may be, becomes the property of the debtor or of the entity acquiring the assets of the debtor under the plan, as the case may be.

348. Effect of conversion

(a) Conversion of a case from a case under one chapter of this title to a case under another chapter of this title constitutes an order for relief under the chapter to which the case is converted, but, except as provided in subsections (b) and (c) of this section, does not effect a change in the date of the filing of the petition, the commencement of the case, or the order for relief.

(b) Unless the court for cause orders otherwise, in sections 701(a), 727(a)(10), 727(b), 1102(a), 1110(a)(1), 1121(b), 1121(c), 1141(d)(4), 1201(a), 1221, 1228(a), 1301(a), and 1305(a) of this title, "the order for relief under this chapter" in a chapter to which a case has been converted under section 706, 1112, 1208, or 1307 of this title means the conversion of such case to such chapter.

(c) Sections 342 and 365(d) of this title apply in a case that has been converted under section 706, 1112, 1208, or 1307 of this title, as if the conversion order were the order for relief.

(d) A claim against the estate or the debtor that arises after the order for relief but before conversion in a case that is converted under section 1112, 1208, or 1307 of this title, other than a claim specified in section 503(b) of this title, shall be treated for all purposes as if such claim had arisen immediately before the date of the filing of the petition.

(e) Conversion of a case under section 706, 1112, 1208, or 1307 of this title terminates the service of any trustee or examiner that is serving in the case before such conversion.

(f)(1) Except as provided in paragraph (2), when a case under chapter 13 of this title is converted to a case under another chapter under this title -

(A) property of the estate in the converted case shall consist of property of the estate, as of the date of filing of the petition, that remains in the possession of or is under the control of the debtor on the date of conversion;

(B) valuations of property and of allowed secured claims in the chapter 13 case shall apply only in a case converted to a case under chapter 11 or 12, but not in a case converted to a case under chapter 7, with allowed secured claims in cases under chapters 11 and 12 reduced to the extent that they have been paid in accordance with the chapter 13 plan; and

(C) with respect to cases converted from chapter 13 –

(i) the claim of any creditor holding security as of the date of the filing of the petition shall continue to be secured by that security unless the full amount of such claim determined under applicable nonbankruptcy law has been paid in full as of the date of conversion, notwithstanding any valuation or determination of the amount of an allowed secured claim made for the purposes of the case under chapter 13; and

(ii) unless a prebankruptcy default has been fully cured under the plan at the time of conversion, in any proceeding under this title or otherwise, the default shall have the effect given under applicable nonbankruptcy law.

(2) If the debtor converts a case under chapter 13 of this title to a case under another chapter under this title in bad faith, the property of the estate in the converted case shall consist of the property of the estate as of the date of conversion.

349. Effect of dismissal

(a) Unless the court, for cause, orders otherwise, the dismissal of a case under this title does not bar the discharge, in a later case under this title, of debts that were dischargeable in the case dismissed; nor does the dismissal of a case under this title prejudice the debtor with regard to the filing of a subsequent petition under this title, except as provided in section 109(g) of this title.

(b) Unless the court, for cause, orders otherwise, a dismissal of a case other than under section 742 of this title -

(1) reinstates -

(A) any proceeding or custodianship superseded under section 543 of this title;

(B) any transfer avoided under section 522, 544, 545, 547, 548, 549, or 724(a) of this title, or preserved under section 510(c)(2), 522(i)(2), or 551 of this title; and

(C) any lien voided under section 506(d) of this title;

(2) vacates any order, judgment, or transfer ordered, under section 522(i)(1), 542, 550, or 553 of this title; and

(3) revests the property of the estate in the entity in which such property was vested immediately before the commencement of the case under this title.

350. Closing and reopening cases

(a) After an estate is fully administered and the court has discharged the trustee, the court shall close the case.

(b) A case may be reopened in the court in which such case was closed to administer assets, to accord relief to the debtor, or for other cause.

351. Disposal of patient records

If a health care business commences a case under chapter 7, 9, or 11, and the trustee does not have a sufficient amount of funds to pay for the storage of patient records in the manner required under applicable Federal or State law, the following requirements shall apply:

(1) The trustee shall –

(A) promptly publish notice, in 1 or more appropriate newspapers, that if patient records are not claimed by the patient or an insurance provider (if applicable law permits the insurance provider to make that claim) by the date that is 365 days after the date of that notification, the trustee will destroy the patient records; and

(B) during the first 180 days of the 365-day period described in subparagraph (A), promptly attempt to notify directly each patient that is the subject of the patient records and appropriate insurance carrier concerning the patient records by mailing to the most recent known address of that patient, or a family member or contact person for that patient, and to the appropriate insurance carrier an appropriate notice regarding the claiming or disposing of patient records.

(2) If, after providing the notification under paragraph (1), patient records are not claimed during the 365-day period described under that paragraph, the trustee shall mail, by certified mail, at the end of such 365-day period a written request to each appropriate Federal agency to request permission from that agency to deposit the patient records with that agency, except that no Federal agency is required to accept patient records under this paragraph.

(3) If, following the 365-day period described in paragraph (2) and after providing the notification under paragraph (1), patient records are not claimed by a patient or insurance provider, or request is not granted by a Federal agency to deposit such records with that agency, the trustee shall destroy those records by –

(A) if the records are written, shredding or burning the records; or

(B) if the records are magnetic, optical, or other electronic records, by otherwise destroying those records so that those records cannot be retrieved.

SUBCHAPTER IV - ADMINISTRATIVE POWERS

361. Adequate protection

When adequate protection is required under section 362, 363, or 364 of this title of an interest of an entity in property, such adequate protection may be provided by -

(1) requiring the trustee to make a cash payment or periodic cash payments to such entity, to the extent that the stay under section 362 of this title, use, sale, or lease under section 363 of this title, or any grant of a lien under section 364 of this title results in a decrease in the value of such entity's interest in such property;

(2) providing to such entity an additional or replacement lien to the extent that such stay, use, sale, lease, or grant results in a decrease in the value

of such entity's interest in such property; or

(3) granting such other relief, other than entitling such entity to compensation allowable under section 503(b)(1) of this title as an administrative expense, as will result in the realization by such entity of the indubitable equivalent of such entity's interest in such property.

362. Automatic stay

(a) Except as provided in subsection (b) of this section, a petition filed under section 301, 302, or 303 of this title, or an application filed under section 5(a)(3) of the Securities Investor Protection Act of 1970, operates as a stay, applicable to all entities, of -

(1) the commencement or continuation, including the issuance or employment of process, of a judicial, administrative, or other action or proceeding against the debtor that was or could have been commenced before the commencement of the case under this title, or to recover a claim against the debtor that arose before the commencement of the case under this title;

(2) the enforcement, against the debtor or against property of the estate, of a judgment obtained before the commencement of the case under this title;

(3) any act to obtain possession of property of the estate or of property from the estate or to exercise control over property of the estate;

(4) any act to create, perfect, or enforce any lien against property of the estate;

(5) any act to create, perfect, or enforce against property of the debtor any lien to the extent that such lien secures a claim that arose before the commencement of the case under this title;

(6) any act to collect, assess, or recover a claim against the debtor that arose before the commencement of the case under this title;

(7) the setoff of any debt owing to the debtor that arose before the commencement of the case under this title against any claim against the debtor; and

(8) the commencement or continuation of a proceeding before the United States Tax Court concerning a tax liability of a debtor that is a corporation for a taxable period the bankruptcy court may determine or concerning the tax liability of a debtor who is an individual for a taxable period ending before the date of the order for relief under this title.

(b) The filing of a petition under section 301, 302, or 303 of this title, or of an application under section 5(a)(3) of the Securities Investor Protection Act of 1970, does not operate as a stay -

(1) under subsection (a) of this section, of the commencement or continuation of a criminal action or proceeding against the debtor;

(2) under subsection (a) –

(A) of the commencement or continuation of a civil action or proceeding –

(i) for the establishment of paternity;

(ii) for the establishment or modification of an order for domestic support obligations;

(iii) concerning child custody or visitation;

(iv) for the dissolution of a marriage, except to the extent that such proceeding seeks to determine the division of property that is property of the estate; or

(v) regarding domestic violence;

(B) of the collection of a domestic support obligation from property that is not property of the estate;

(C) with respect to the withholding of income that is property of the estate or property of the debtor for payment of a domestic support obligation under a judicial or administrative order or a statute;

(D) of the withholding, suspension, or restriction of a driver's license, a professional or occupational license, or a recreational license, under State law, as specified in section 466(a)(16) of the Social Security Act;

(E) of the reporting of overdue support owed by a parent to any consumer reporting agency as specified in section 466(a)(7) of the Social Security Act;

(F) of the interception of a tax refund, as specified in sections 464 and 466(a)(3) of the Social Security Act or under an analogous State law; or

(G) of the enforcement of a medical obligation, as specified under title IV of the Social Security Act;

(3) under subsection (a) of this section, of any act to perfect, or to maintain or continue the perfection of, an interest in property to the extent that the trustee's rights and powers are subject to such perfection under section 546(b) of this title or to the extent that such act is accomplished within the period provided under section 547(e)(2)(A) of this title;

(4) under paragraph (1), (2), (3), or (6) of subsection (a) of this section, of the commencement or continuation of an action or proceeding by a governmental unit or any organization exercising authority under the Convention on the Prohibition of the Development, Production, Stockpiling and Use of Chemical Weapons and on Their Destruction, opened for signature on January 13, 1993, to enforce such governmental unit's or organization's police and regulatory power, including the enforcement of a judgment other than a money judgment, obtained in an action or proceeding by the governmental unit to enforce such governmental unit's or organization's police or regulatory power;

(5) [Repealed Oct. 21, 1998; 112 Stat. 2681-886].

(6) under subsection (a) of this section, of the exercise by a commodity broker, forward contract merchant, stockbroker, financial institution, financial participant, or securities clearing agency of any contractual right (as defined in section 555 or 556) under any security agreement or arrangement or other credit enhancement forming a part of or related to any commodity contract, forward contract or securities contract, or of any contractual right (as defined in section 555 or 556) to offset or net out any termination value, payment amount, or other transfer obligation arising under or in connection with 1 or more such contracts, including any master agreement for such contracts;

(7) under subsection (a) of this section, of the exercise by a repo participant or financial participant of any contractual right (as defined in section 559) under any security agreement or arrangement or other credit enhancement forming a part of or related to any repurchase agreement, or of any contractual right (as defined in section 559) to offset or net out any termination value, payment amount, or other transfer obligation arising under or in connection with 1 or more such agreements, including any master agreement for such agreements;

(8) under subsection (a) of this section, of the commencement of any action by the Secretary of Housing and Urban Development to foreclose a mortgage or deed of trust in any case in which the mortgage or deed of trust held by the Secretary is insured or was formerly insured under the National Housing Act and covers property, or combinations of property, consisting of five or more living units;

(9) under subsection (a), of -

(A) an audit by a governmental unit to determine tax liability;

(B) the issuance to the debtor by a governmental unit of a notice of tax deficiency;

(C) a demand for tax returns; or

(D) the making of an assessment for any tax and issuance of a notice and demand for payment of such an assessment (but any tax lien that would otherwise attach to property of the estate by reason of such an assessment shall not take effect unless such tax is a debt of the debtor that will not be discharged in the case and such property or its proceeds are transferred out of the estate to, or otherwise revested in, the debtor).

(10) under subsection (a) of this section, of any act by a lessor to the debtor under a lease of nonresidential real property that has terminated by the expiration of the stated term of the lease before the commencement of or during a case under this title to obtain possession of such property;

(11) under subsection (a) of this section, of the presentment of a negotiable instrument and the giving of notice of and protesting dishonor of such an instrument;

(12) under subsection (a) of this section, after the date which is 90 days after the filing of such petition, of the commencement or continuation, and conclusion to the entry of final judgment, of an action which involves a debtor subject to reorganization pursuant to chapter 11 of this title and which was brought by the Secretary of Transportation under section 31325 of title 46 (including distribution of any proceeds of sale) to foreclose a preferred ship or fleet mortgage, or a security interest in or relating to a vessel or vessel under construction, held by the Secretary of Transportation under chapter 537 of title 46 or section 109(h) of title 49, or under applicable State law;

(13) under subsection (a) of this section, after the date which is 90 days after the filing of such petition, of the commencement or continuation, and conclusion to the entry of final judgment, of an action which involves a debtor subject to reorganization pursuant to chapter 11 of this title and which was brought by the Secretary of Commerce under section 31325 of title 46 (including distribution of any proceeds of sale) to foreclose a preferred ship or fleet mortgage in a vessel or a mortgage, deed of trust, or other security interest in a fishing facility held by the Secretary of Commerce under chapter 537 of title 46;

(14) under subsection (a) of this section, of any action by an accrediting

agency regarding the accreditation status of the debtor as an educational institution;

(15) under subsection (a) of this section, of any action by a State licensing body regarding the licensure of the debtor as an educational institution;

(16) under subsection (a) of this section, of any action by a guaranty agency, as defined in section 435(j) of the Higher Education Act of 1965 or the Secretary of Education regarding the eligibility of the debtor to participate in programs authorized under such Act;

(17) under subsection (a) of this section, of the exercise by a swap participant or financial participant of any contractual right (as defined in section 560) under any security agreement or arrangement or other credit enhancement forming a part of or related to any swap agreement, or of any contractual right (as defined in section 560) to offset or net out any termination value, payment amount, or other transfer obligation arising under or in connection with 1 or more such agreements, including any master agreement for such agreements;

(18) under subsection (a) of the creation or perfection of a statutory lien for an ad valorem property tax, or a special tax or special assessment on real property whether or not ad valorem, imposed by a governmental unit, if such tax or assessment comes due after the date of the filing of the petition;

(19) under subsection (a), of withholding of income from a debtor's wages and collection of amounts withheld, under the debtor's agreement authorizing that withholding and collection for the benefit of a pension, profit-sharing, stock bonus, or other plan established under section 401, 403, 408, 408A, 414, 457, or 501(c) of the Internal Revenue Code of 1986, that is sponsored by the employer of the debtor, or an affiliate, successor, or predecessor of such employer –

(A) to the extent that the amounts withheld and collected are used solely for payments relating to a loan from a plan under section 408(b)(1) of the Employee Retirement Income Security Act of 1974 or is subject to section 72(p) of the Internal Revenue Code of 1986; or

(B) a loan from a thrift savings plan permitted under subchapter III of chapter 84 of title 5, that satisfies the requirements of section 8433(g) of such title;

but nothing in this paragraph may be construed to provide that any loan made under a governmental plan under section 414(d), or a contract or account under section 403(b), of the Internal Revenue Code of 1986 constitutes a claim or a debt under this title;

(20) under subsection (a), of any act to enforce any lien against or security interest in real property following entry of the order under subsection (d)(4) as to such real property in any prior case under this title, for a period of 2 years after the date of the entry of such an order, except that the debtor, in a subsequent case under this title, may move for relief from such order based upon changed circumstances or for other good cause shown, after notice and a hearing;

(21) under subsection (a), of any act to enforce any lien against or security interest in real property –

(A) if the debtor is ineligible under section 109(g) to be a debtor in a case under this title; or

(B) if the case under this title was filed in violation of a bankruptcy court order in a prior case under this title prohibiting the debtor from being a debtor in another case under this title;

(22) subject to subsection (l), under subsection (a)(3), of the continuation of any eviction, unlawful detainer action, or similar proceeding by a lessor against a debtor involving residential property in which the debtor resides as a tenant under a lease or rental agreement and with respect to which the lessor has obtained before the date of the filing of the bankruptcy petition, a judgment for possession of such property against the debtor;

(23) subject to subsection (m), under subsection (a)(3), of an eviction action that seeks possession of the residential property in which the debtor resides as a tenant under a lease or rental agreement based on endangerment of such property or the illegal use of controlled substances on such property, but only if the lessor files with the court, and serves upon the debtor, a certification under penalty of perjury that such an eviction action has been filed, or that the debtor, during the 30-day period preceding the date of the filing of the certification, has endangered property or illegally used or allowed to be used a controlled substance on the property;

(24) under subsection (a), of any transfer that is not avoidable under section 544 and that is not avoidable under section 549;

(25) under subsection (a), of –

(A) the commencement or continuation of an investigation or action by a securities self regulatory organization to enforce such organization's regulatory power;

(B) the enforcement of an order or decision, other than for monetary sanctions, obtained in an action by such securities self regulatory organization to enforce such organization's regulatory power; or

(C) any act taken by such securities self regulatory organization to delist, delete, or refuse to permit quotation of any stock that does not meet applicable regulatory requirements;

(26) under subsection (a), of the setoff under applicable nonbankruptcy law of an income tax refund, by a governmental unit, with respect to a taxable period that ended before the date of the order for relief against an income tax liability for a taxable period that also ended before the date of the order for relief, except that in any case in which the setoff of an income tax refund is not permitted under applicable nonbankruptcy law because of a pending action to determine the amount or legality of a tax liability, the governmental unit may hold the refund pending the resolution of the action, unless the court, on the motion of the trustee and after notice and a hearing, grants the taxing authority adequate protection (within the meaning of section 361) for the secured claim of such authority in the setoff under section 506(a);

(27) under subsection (a) of this section, of the exercise by a master netting agreement participant of any contractual right (as defined in section 555, 556, 559, or 560) under any security agreement or arrangement or other credit enhancement forming a part of or related to any master netting agreement, or of any contractual right (as defined in section 555, 556, 559, or 560) to offset or net out any termination value, payment amount, or other transfer obligation arising under or in connection with 1 or more such master netting agreements to the extent that such participant is eligible to exercise such rights under paragraph (6), (7), or (17) for each individual contract covered by the master netting agreement in issue; and

(28) under subsection (a), of the exclusion by the Secretary of Health and Human Services of the debtor from participation in the medicare program or any other Federal health care program (as defined in section 1128B(f) of the Social Security Act pursuant to title XI or XVIII of such Act).

The provisions of paragraphs (12) and (13) of this subsection shall apply with respect to any such petition filed on or before December 31, 1989.

(c) Except as provided in subsections (d), (e), (f), and (h) of this section -

(1) the stay of an act against property of the estate under subsection (a) of this section continues until such property is no longer property of the estate;

(2) the stay of any other act under subsection (a) of this section continues until the earliest of -

(A) the time the case is closed;

(B) the time the case is dismissed; or

(C) if the case is a case under chapter 7 of this title concerning an individual or a case under chapter 9, 11, 12, or 13 of this title, the time a discharge is granted or denied;

(3) if a single or joint case is filed by or against a debtor who is an individual in a case under chapter 7, 11, or 13, and if a single or joint case of the debtor was pending within the preceding 1-year period but was dismissed, other than a case refiled under a chapter other than chapter 7 after dismissal under section 707(b) –

(A) the stay under subsection (a) with respect to any action taken with respect to a debt or property securing such debt or with respect to any lease shall terminate with respect to the debtor on the 30th day after the filing of the later case;

(B) on the motion of a party in interest for continuation of the automatic stay and upon notice and a hearing, the court may extend the stay in particular cases as to any or all creditors (subject to such conditions or limitations as the court may then impose) after notice and a hearing completed before the expiration of the 30-day period only if the party in interest demonstrates that the filing of the later case is in good faith as to the creditors to be stayed; and

(C) for purposes of subparagraph (B), a case is presumptively filed not in good faith (but such presumption may be rebutted by clear and convincing evidence to the contrary)-

(i) as to all creditors, if –

(I) more than 1 previous case under any of chapters 7, 11, and 13 in which the individual was a debtor was pending within the preceding 1-year period;

(II) a previous case under any of chapters 7, 11, and 13 in which the individual was a debtor was dismissed within such 1-year period, after the debtor failed to –

(aa) file or amend the petition or other documents as required by this title or the court without substantial excuse (but mere inadvertence or negligence shall not be a substantial excuse unless the dismissal was caused by the negligence of the debtor's attorney);

(bb) provide adequate protection as ordered by the court; or

(cc) perform the terms of a plan confirmed by the court, or

(III) there has not been a substantial change in the financial or personal affairs of the debtor since the dismissal of the next most previous case under chapter 7, 11, or 13 or any other reason to conclude that the later case will be concluded –

(aa) if a case under chapter 7, with a discharge; or

(bb) if a case under chapter 11 or 13, with a confirmed plan that will be fully performed; and

(ii) as to any creditor that commenced an action under subsection (d) in a previous case in which the individual was a debtor if, as of the date of dismissal of such case, that action was still pending or had been resolved by terminating, conditioning, or limiting the stay as to actions of such creditor; and

(4)(A)(i) if a single or joint case is filed by or against a debtor who is an individual under this title, and if 2 or more single or joint cases of the debtor were pending within the previous year but were dismissed, other than a case refiled under a chapter other than chapter 7 after dismissal under section 707(b), the stay under subsection (a) shall not go into effect upon the filing of the later case; and

(ii) on request of a party in interest, the court shall promptly enter an order confirming that no stay is in effect;

(B) if, within 30 days after the filing of the later case, a party in interest requests the court may order the stay to take effect in the case as to any or all creditors (subject to such conditions or limitations as the court may impose), after notice and a hearing, only if the party in interest demonstrates that the filing of the later case is in good faith as to the creditors to be stayed;

(C) a stay imposed under subparagraph (B) shall be effective on the date of the entry of the order allowing the stay to go into effect; and

(D) for purposes of subparagraph (B), a case is presumptively filed not in good faith (but such presumption may be rebutted by clear and convincing evidence to the contrary) –

(i) as to all creditors if –

(I) 2 or more previous cases under this title in which the individual was a debtor were pending within the 1-year period;

(II) a previous case under this title in which the individual was a debtor was dismissed within the time period stated in this paragraph after the debtor failed to file or amend the petition or other documents as required by this title or the court without substantial excuse (but mere inadvertence or negligence shall not be substantial excuse unless the dismissal was caused by the negligence of the debtor's attorney), failed to provide adequate protection as ordered by the court, or failed to perform the terms of a plan confirmed by the court; or

(III) there has not been a substantial change in the financial or personal affairs of the debtor since the dismissal of the next most previous case under this title, or any other reason to conclude that the later case will not be concluded, if a case under chapter 7, with a discharge, and if a case under chapter 11 or 13, with a confirmed plan that will be fully performed; or

(ii) as to any creditor that commenced an action under subsection (d) in a previous case in which the individual was a debtor if, as of the date of dismissal of such case, such action was still pending or had been resolved by terminating, conditioning, or limiting the stay as to such action of such creditor.

(d) On request of a party in interest and after notice and a hearing, the court shall grant relief from the stay provided under subsection (a) of this section, such as by terminating, annulling, modifying, or conditioning such stay-

(1) for cause, including the lack of adequate protection of an interest in property of such party in interest;

(2) with respect to a stay of an act against property under subsection (a) of this section, if -

(A) the debtor does not have an equity in such property; and

(B) such property is not necessary to an effective reorganization;

(3) with respect to a stay of an act against single asset real estate under subsection (a), by a creditor whose claim is secured by an interest in such real estate, unless, not later than the date that is 90 days after the entry of the order for relief (or such later date as the court may determine for cause by order entered within that 90-day period) or 30 days after the court determines that the debtor is subject to this paragraph, whichever is later –

(A) the debtor has filed a plan of reorganization that has a reasonable possibility of being confirmed within a reasonable time; or

(B) the debtor has commenced monthly payments that –

(i) may, in the debtor's sole discretion, notwithstanding section 363(c)(2), be made from rents or other income generated before, on, or after the date of the commencement of the case by or from the property to each creditor whose claim is secured by such real estate (other than a claim secured by a judgment lien or by an unmatured statutory lien); and

(ii) are in an amount equal to interest at the then applicable nondefault contract rate of interest on the value of the creditor's interest in the real estate; or

(4) with respect to a stay of an act against real property under subsection (a), by a creditor whose claim is secured by an interest in such real property, if the court finds that the filing of the petition was part of a scheme to delay, hinder, or defraud creditors that involved either –

(A) transfer of all or part ownership of, or other interest in, such real property without the consent of the secured creditor or court approval; or

(B) multiple bankruptcy filings affecting such real property.

If recorded in compliance with applicable State laws governing notices of interests or liens in real property, an order entered under paragraph (4) shall be binding in any other case under this title purporting to affect such real property filed not later than 2 years after the date of the entry of such order by the court, except that a debtor in a subsequent case under this title may move for relief from such order based upon changed circumstances or for good cause shown, after notice and a hearing. Any Federal, State, or local governmental unit that accepts notices of interests or liens in real property shall accept any certified copy of an order described in this subsection for indexing and recording.

(e)(1) Thirty days after a request under subsection (d) of this section for relief from the stay of any act against property of the estate under subsection (a) of this section, such stay is terminated with respect to the party in interest making such request, unless the court, after notice and a hearing, orders such stay continued in effect pending the conclusion of, or as a result of, a final hearing and determination under subsection (d) of this section. A hearing under this subsection may be a preliminary hearing, or may be consolidated with the final hearing under subsection (d) of this section. The court shall order such stay continued in effect pending the conclusion of the final hearing under subsection (d) of this section if there is a reasonable likelihood that the party opposing relief from such stay will prevail at the conclusion of such final hearing. If the hearing under this subsection is a preliminary hearing, then such final hearing shall be concluded not later than thirty days after the conclusion of such preliminary hearing, unless the 30-day period is extended with the consent of the parties in interest or for a specific time which the court finds is required by compelling circumstances.

(2) Notwithstanding paragraph (1), in a case under chapter 7, 11, or 13 in which the debtor is an individual, the stay under subsection (a) shall terminate on the date that is 60 days after a request is made by a party in interest under subsection (d), unless –

(A) a final decision is rendered by the court during the 60-day period beginning on the date of the request; or

(B) such 60-day period is extended –

(i) by agreement of all parties in interest; or

(ii) by the court for such specific period of time as the court finds is required for good cause, as described in findings made by the court.

(f) Upon request of a party in interest, the court, with or without a hearing, shall grant such relief from the stay provided under subsection (a) of this section as is necessary to prevent irreparable damage to the interest of an entity in property, if such interest will suffer such damage before there is an opportunity for notice and a hearing under subsection (d) or (e) of this section.

(g) In any hearing under subsection (d) or (e) of this section concerning relief from the stay of any act under subsection (a) of this section -

(1) the party requesting such relief has the burden of proof on the issue of the debtor's equity in property; and

(2) the party opposing such relief has the burden of proof on all other issues.

(h)(1) In a case in which the debtor is an individual, the stay provided by subsection (a) is terminated with respect to personal property of the estate or of the debtor securing in whole or in part a claim, or subject to an unexpired lease, and such personal property shall no longer be property of the estate if the debtor fails within the applicable time set by section 521(a)(2) –

(A) to file timely any statement of intention required under section

521(a)(2) with respect to such personal property or to indicate in such statement that the debtor will either surrender such personal property or retain it and, if retaining such personal property, either redeem such personal property pursuant to section 722, enter into an agreement of the kind specified in section 524(c) applicable to the debt secured by such personal property, or assume such unexpired lease pursuant to section 365(p) if the trustee does not do so, as applicable; and

(B) to take timely the action specified in such statement, as it may be amended before expiration of the period for taking action, unless such statement specifies the debtor's intention to reaffirm such debt on the original contract terms and the creditor refuses to agree to the reaffirmation on such terms.

(2) Paragraph (1) does not apply if the court determines, on the motion of the trustee filed before the expiration of the applicable time set by section 521(a)(2), after notice and a hearing, that such personal property is of consequential value or benefit to the estate, and orders appropriate adequate protection of the creditor's interest, and orders the debtor to deliver any collateral in the debtor's possession to the trustee. If the court does not so determine, the stay provided by subsection (a) shall terminate upon the conclusion of the hearing on the motion.

(i) If a case commenced under chapter 7, 11, or 13 is dismissed due to the creation of a debt repayment plan, for purposes of subsection (c)(3), any subsequent case commenced by the debtor under any such chapter shall not be presumed to be filed not in good faith.

(j) On request of a party in interest, the court shall issue an order under subsection (c) confirming that the automatic stay has been terminated.

(k)(1) Except as provided in paragraph (2), an individual injured by any willful violation of a stay provided by this section shall recover actual damages, including costs and attorneys' fees, and, in appropriate circumstances, may recover punitive damages.

(2) If such violation is based on an action taken by an entity in the good faith belief that subsection (h) applies to the debtor, the recovery under paragraph (1) of this subsection against such entity shall be limited to actual damages.

(l)(1) Except as otherwise provided in this subsection, subsection (b)(22) shall apply on the date that is 30 days after the date on which the bankruptcy petition is filed, if the debtor files with the petition and serves upon the lessor a certification under penalty of perjury that –

(A) under nonbankruptcy law applicable in the jurisdiction, there are circumstances under which the debtor would be permitted to cure the entire monetary default that gave rise to the judgment for possession, after that judgment for possession was entered; and

(B) the debtor (or an adult dependent of the debtor) has deposited with the clerk of the court, any rent that would become due during the 30-day period after the filing of the bankruptcy petition.

(2) If, within the 30-day period after the filing of the bankruptcy petition, the debtor (or an adult dependent of the debtor) complies with paragraph (1) and files with the court and serves upon the lessor a further certification under penalty of perjury that the debtor (or an adult dependent of the debtor) has cured, under nonbankruptcy law applicable in the jurisdiction, the entire monetary default that gave rise to the judgment under which possession is sought by the lessor, subsection (b)(22) shall not apply, unless ordered to apply by the court under paragraph (3).

(3)(A) If the lessor files an objection to any certification filed by the debtor under paragraph (1) or (2), and serves such objection upon the debtor, the court shall hold a hearing within 10 days after the filing and service of such objection to determine if the certification filed by the debtor under paragraph (1) or (2) is true.

(B) If the court upholds the objection of the lessor filed under subparagraph (A) –

(i) subsection (b)(22) shall apply immediately and relief from the stay provided under subsection (a)(3) shall not be required to enable the lessor to complete the process to recover full possession of the property; and

(ii) the clerk of the court shall immediately serve upon the lessor and the debtor a certified copy of the court's order upholding the lessor's objection.

(4) If a debtor, in accordance with paragraph (5), indicates on the petition that there was a judgment for possession of the residential rental property in which the debtor resides and does not file a certification under paragraph (1) or (2) –

(A) subsection (b)(22) shall apply immediately upon failure to file such certification, and relief from the stay provided under subsection (a)(3) shall not be required to enable the lessor to complete the process to recover full possession of the property; and

(B) the clerk of the court shall immediately serve upon the lessor and the debtor a certified copy of the docket indicating the absence of a filed certification and the applicability of the exception to the stay under subsection (b)(22).

(5)(A) Where a judgment for possession of residential property in which the debtor resides as a tenant under a lease or rental agreement has been obtained by the lessor, the debtor shall so indicate on the bankruptcy petition and shall provide the name and address of the lessor that obtained that pre-petition judgment on the petition and on any certification filed under this subsection.

(B) The form of certification filed with the petition, as specified in this subsection, shall provide for the debtor to certify, and the debtor shall certify –

(i) whether a judgment for possession of residential rental housing in which the debtor resides has been obtained against the debtor before the date of the filing of the petition; and

(ii) whether the debtor is claiming under paragraph (1) that under nonbankruptcy law applicable in the jurisdiction, there are circumstances under which the debtor would be permitted to cure the entire monetary default that gave rise to the judgment for possession, after that judgment of possession was entered, and has made the appropriate deposit with the court.

(C) The standard forms (electronic and otherwise) used in a bankruptcy proceeding shall be amended to reflect the requirements of this subsection.

(D) The clerk of the court shall arrange for the prompt transmittal of the rent deposited in accordance with paragraph (1)(B) to the lessor.

(m)(1) Except as otherwise provided in this subsection, subsection (b)(23) shall apply on the date that is 15 days after the date on which the lessor files and serves a certification described in subsection (b)(23).

(2)(A) If the debtor files with the court an objection to the truth or legal sufficiency of the certification described in subsection (b)(23) and serves such objection upon the lessor, subsection (b)(23) shall not apply, unless ordered to apply by the court under this subsection.

(B) If the debtor files and serves the objection under subparagraph (A), the court shall hold a hearing within 10 days after the filing and service of such objection to determine if the situation giving rise to the lessor's certification under paragraph (1) existed or has been remedied.

(C) If the debtor can demonstrate to the satisfaction of the court that the situation giving rise to the lessor's certification under paragraph (1) did not exist or has been remedied, the stay provided under subsection (a)(3) shall remain in effect until the termination of the stay under this section.

(D) If the debtor cannot demonstrate to the satisfaction of the court that the situation giving rise to the lessor's certification under paragraph (1) did not exist or has been remedied –

(i) relief from the stay provided under subsection (a)(3) shall not be required to enable the lessor to proceed with the eviction; and

(ii) the clerk of the court shall immediately serve upon the lessor and the debtor a certified copy of the court's order upholding the lessor's certification.

(3) If the debtor fails to file, within 15 days, an objection under paragraph (2)(A) –

(A) subsection (b)(23) shall apply immediately upon such failure and relief from the stay provided under subsection (a)(3) shall not be required to enable the lessor to complete the process to recover full possession of the property; and

(B) the clerk of the court shall immediately serve upon the lessor and the debtor a certified copy of the docket indicating such failure.

(n)(1) Except as provided in paragraph (2), subsection (a) does not apply in a case in which the debtor –

(A) is a debtor in a small business case pending at the time the petition is filed;

(B) was a debtor in a small business case that was dismissed for any reason by an order that became final in the 2-year period ending on the date of the order for relief entered with respect to the petition;

(C) was a debtor in a small business case in which a plan was confirmed in the 2-year period ending on the date of the order for relief entered with respect to the petition; or

(D) is an entity that has acquired substantially all of the assets or business of a small business debtor described in subparagraph (A), (B), or (C), unless such entity establishes by a preponderance of the evidence that such entity acquired substantially all of the assets or business of such small business debtor in good faith and not for the purpose of evading this paragraph.

(2) Paragraph (1) does not apply –

(A) to an involuntary case involving no collusion by the debtor with creditors; or

(B) to the filing of a petition if –

(i) the debtor proves by a preponderance of the evidence that the filing of the petition resulted from circumstances beyond the control of the debtor not foreseeable at the time the case then pending was filed; and

(ii) it is more likely than not that the court will confirm a feasible plan, but not a liquidating plan, within a reasonable period of time.

(o) The exercise of rights not subject to the stay arising under subsection (a) pursuant to paragraph (6), (7), (17), or (27) of subsection (b) shall not be stayed by any order of a court or administrative agency in any proceeding under this title.

363. Use, sale, or lease of property

(a) In this section, "cash collateral" means cash, negotiable instruments, documents of title, securities, deposit accounts, or other cash equivalents whenever acquired in which the estate and an entity other than the estate have an interest and includes the proceeds, products, offspring, rents, or profits of property and the fees, charges, accounts or other payments for the use or occupancy of rooms and other public facilities in hotels, motels, or other lodging properties subject to a security interest as provided in section 552(b) of this title, whether existing before or after the commencement of a case under this title.

(b)(1) The trustee, after notice and a hearing, may use, sell, or lease, other than in the ordinary course of business, property of the estate, except that if the debtor in connection with offering a product or a service discloses to an individual a policy prohibiting the transfer of personally identifiable information about individuals to persons that are not affiliated with the debtor and if such policy is in effect on the date of the commencement of the case, then the trustee may not sell or lease personally identifiable information to any person unless –

(A) such sale or such lease is consistent with such policy; or

(B) after appointment of a consumer privacy ombudsman in accordance with section 332, and after notice and a hearing, the court approves such sale or such lease –

(i) giving due consideration to the facts, circumstances, and conditions of such sale or such lease; and

(ii) finding that no showing was made that such sale or such lease would violate applicable nonbankruptcy law.

(2) If notification is required under subsection (a) of section 7A of the Clayton Act in the case of a transaction under this subsection, then -

(A) notwithstanding subsection (a) of such section, the notification required by such subsection to be given by the debtor shall be given by the trustee; and

(B) notwithstanding subsection (b) of such section, the required waiting period shall end on the 15th day after the date of the receipt, by the Federal Trade Commission and the Assistant Attorney General in charge of the Antitrust Division of the Department of Justice, of the notification required under such subsection (a), unless such waiting period is extended-

(i) pursuant to subsection (e)(2) of such section, in the same manner as such subsection (e)(2) applies to a cash tender offer;

(ii) pursuant to subsection (g)(2) of such section; or

(iii) by the court after notice and a hearing.

(c)(1) If the business of the debtor is authorized to be operated under section 721, 1108, 1203, 1204, or 1304 of this title and unless the court orders otherwise, the trustee may enter into transactions, including the sale or lease of property of the estate, in the ordinary course of business, without notice or a hearing, and may use property of the estate in the ordinary course of business without notice or a hearing.

(2) The trustee may not use, sell, or lease cash collateral under paragraph (1) of this subsection unless -

(A) each entity that has an interest in such cash collateral consents; or

(B) the court, after notice and a hearing, authorizes such use, sale, or lease in accordance with the provisions of this section.

(3) Any hearing under paragraph (2)(B) of this subsection may be a preliminary hearing or may be consolidated with a hearing under subsection (e) of this section, but shall be scheduled in accordance with the needs of the debtor. If the hearing under paragraph (2)(B) of this subsection is a preliminary hearing, the court may authorize such use, sale, or lease only if there is a reasonable likelihood that the trustee will prevail at the final hearing under subsection (e) of this section. The court shall act promptly on any request for authorization under paragraph (2)(B) of this subsection.

(4) Except as provided in paragraph (2) of this subsection, the trustee shall segregate and account for any cash collateral in the trustee's possession, custody, or control.

(d) The trustee may use, sell, or lease property under subsection (b) or (c) of this section –

(1) in the case of a debtor that is a corporation or trust that is not a moneyed business, commercial corporation, or trust, only in accordance with nonbankruptcy law applicable to the transfer of property by a debtor that is such a corporation or trust; and

(2) only to the extent not inconsistent with any relief granted under subsection (c), (d), (e), or (f) of section 362.

(e) Notwithstanding any other provision of this section, at any time, on request of an entity that has an interest in property used, sold, or leased, or proposed to be used, sold, or leased, by the trustee, the court, with or without a hearing, shall prohibit or condition such use, sale, or lease as is necessary to provide adequate protection of such interest. This subsection also applies to property that is subject to any unexpired lease of personal property (to the exclusion of such property being subject to an order to grant relief from the stay under section 362).

(f) The trustee may sell property under subsection (b) or (c) of this section free and clear of any interest in such property of an entity other than the estate, only if -

(1) applicable nonbankruptcy law permits sale of such property free and clear of such interest;

(2) such entity consents;

(3) such interest is a lien and the price at which such property is to be sold is greater than the aggregate value of all liens on such property;

(4) such interest is in bona fide dispute; or

(5) such entity could be compelled, in a legal or equitable proceeding, to accept a money satisfaction of such interest.

(g) Notwithstanding subsection (f) of this section, the trustee may sell property under subsection (b) or (c) of this section free and clear of any vested or contingent right in the nature of dower or curtesy.

(h) Notwithstanding subsection (f) of this section, the trustee may sell both the estate's interest, under subsection (b) or (c) of this section, and the interest of any co-owner in property in which the debtor had, at the time of the commencement of the case, an undivided interest as a tenant in common, joint tenant, or tenant by the entirety, only if -

(1) partition in kind of such property among the estate and such co-owners is impracticable;

(2) sale of the estate's undivided interest in such property would realize significantly less for the estate than sale of such property free of the interests of such co-owners;

(3) the benefit to the estate of a sale of such property free of the interests of co-owners outweighs the detriment, if any, to such co-owners; and

(4) such property is not used in the production, transmission, or distribution, for sale, of electric energy or of natural or synthetic gas for heat, light, or power.

(i) Before the consummation of a sale of property to which subsection (g) or (h) of this section applies, or of property of the estate that was community property of the debtor and the debtor's spouse immediately before the commencement of the case, the debtor's spouse, or a co-owner of such property, as the case may be, may purchase such property at the price at which such sale is to be consummated.

(j) After a sale of property to which subsection (g) or (h) of this section applies, the trustee shall distribute to the debtor's spouse or the co-owners of such property, as the case may be, and to the estate, the proceeds of such sale, less the costs and expenses, not including any compensation of the trustee, of such sale, according to the interests of such spouse or co-owners, and of the estate.

(k) At a sale under subsection (b) of this section of property that is subject to a lien that secures an allowed claim, unless the court for cause orders otherwise the holder of such claim may bid at such sale, and, if the holder of such claim purchases such property, such holder may offset such claim against the purchase price of such property.

(l) Subject to the provisions of section 365, the trustee may use, sell, or lease property under subsection (b) or (c) of this section, or a plan under chapter 11, 12, or 13 of this title may provide for the use, sale, or lease of property, notwithstanding any provision in a contract, a lease, or applicable law that is conditioned on the insolvency or financial condition of the debtor, on the commencement of a case under this title concerning the debtor, or on the appointment of or the taking possession by a trustee in a case under this title or a custodian, and that effects, or gives an option to effect, a forfeiture, modification, or termination of the debtor's interest in such property.

(m) The reversal or modification on appeal of an authorization under subsection (b) or (c) of this section of a sale or lease of property does not affect the validity of a sale or lease under such authorization to an entity that purchased or leased such property in good faith, whether or not such entity knew of the pendency of the appeal, unless such authorization and such sale or lease were stayed pending appeal.

(n) The trustee may avoid a sale under this section if the sale price was controlled by an agreement among potential bidders at such sale, or may recover from a party to such agreement any amount by which the value of the property sold exceeds the price at which such sale was consummated, and may recover any costs, attorneys' fees, or expenses incurred in avoiding such sale or recovering such amount. In addition to any recovery under the preceding sentence, the court may grant judgment for punitive damages in favor of the estate and against any such party that entered into such an agreement in willful disregard of this subsection.

(o) Notwithstanding subsection (f), if a person purchases any interest in a consumer credit transaction that is subject to the Truth in Lending Act or any interest in a consumer credit contract (as defined in section 433.1 of title 16 of the Code of Federal Regulations (January 1, 2004), as amended from time to time), and if such interest is purchased through a sale under this section, then such person shall remain subject to all claims and defenses that are related to such consumer credit transaction or such consumer credit contract, to the same extent as such person would be subject to such claims and defenses of the consumer had such interest been purchased at a sale not under this section.

(p) In any hearing under this section -

(1) the trustee has the burden of proof on the issue of adequate protection; and

(2) the entity asserting an interest in property has the burden of proof on the issue of the validity, priority, or extent of such interest.

364. Obtaining credit

(a) If the trustee is authorized to operate the business of the debtor under section 721, 1108, 1203, 1204, or 1304 of this title, unless the court orders otherwise, the trustee may obtain unsecured credit and incur unsecured debt in the ordinary course of business allowable under section 503(b)(1) of this title as an administrative expense.

(b) The court, after notice and a hearing, may authorize the trustee to obtain unsecured credit or to incur unsecured debt other than under subsection (a) of this section, allowable under section 503(b)(1) of this title as an administrative expense.

(c) If the trustee is unable to obtain unsecured credit allowable under section 503(b)(1) of this title as an administrative expense, the court, after notice and a hearing, may authorize the obtaining of credit or the incurring of debt -

(1) with priority over any or all administrative expenses of the kind specified in section 503(b) or 507(b) of this title;

(2) secured by a lien on property of the estate that is not otherwise subject to a lien; or

(3) secured by a junior lien on property of the estate that is subject to a lien.

(d)(1) The court, after notice and a hearing, may authorize the obtaining of credit or the incurring of debt secured by a senior or equal lien on property of the estate that is subject to a lien only if -

(A) the trustee is unable to obtain such credit otherwise; and(B) there is adequate protection of the interest of the holder of the lien on the property of the estate on which such senior or equal lien is proposed to be granted.

(2) In any hearing under this subsection, the trustee has the burden of proof on the issue of adequate protection.

(e) The reversal or modification on appeal of an authorization under this section to obtain credit or incur debt, or of a grant under this section of a priority or a lien, does not affect the validity of any debt so incurred, or any priority or lien so granted, to an entity that extended such credit in good faith, whether or not such entity knew of the pendency of the appeal, unless such authorization and the incurring of such debt, or the granting of such priority or lien, were stayed pending appeal.

(f) Except with respect to an entity that is an underwriter as defined in section 1145(b) of this title, section 5 of the Securities Act of 1933, the Trust Indenture Act of 1939, and any State or local law requiring registration for offer or sale of a security or registration or licensing of an issuer of, underwriter of, or broker or dealer in, a security does not apply to the offer or sale under this section of a security that is not an equity security.

365. Executory contracts and unexpired leases

(a) Except as provided in sections 765 and 766 of this title and in subsections (b), (c), and (d) of this section, the trustee, subject to the court's approval, may assume or reject any executory contract or unexpired lease of the debtor.

(b)(1) If there has been a default in an executory contract or unexpired lease of the debtor, the trustee may not assume such contract or lease unless, at the time of assumption of such contract or lease, the trustee -

(A) cures, or provides adequate assurance that the trustee will promptly cure, such default other than a default that is a breach of a provision relating to the satisfaction of any provision (other than a penalty rate or penalty provision) relating to a default arising from any failure to perform nonmonetary obligations under an unexpired lease of real property, if it is impossible for the trustee to cure such default by performing nonmonetary acts at and after the time of assumption, except that if such default arises from a failure to operate in accordance with a nonresidential real property lease, then such default shall be cured by performance at and after the time of assumption in accordance with such lease, and pecuniary losses resulting from such default shall be compensated in accordance with the provisions of this paragraph;

(B) compensates, or provides adequate assurance that the trustee will promptly compensate, a party other than the debtor to such contract or lease, for any actual pecuniary loss to such party resulting from such default; and

(C) provides adequate assurance of future performance under such contract or lease.

(2) Paragraph (1) of this subsection does not apply to a default that is a breach of a provision relating to -

(A) the insolvency or financial condition of the debtor at any time before the closing of the case;

(B) the commencement of a case under this title;

(C) the appointment of or taking possession by a trustee in a case under this title or a custodian before such commencement; or

(D) the satisfaction of any penalty rate or penalty provision relating to a default arising from any failure by the debtor to perform nonmonetary obligations under the executory contract or unexpired lease.

(3) For the purposes of paragraph (1) of this subsection and paragraph (2)(B) of subsection (f), adequate assurance of future performance of a lease of real property in a shopping center includes adequate assurance -

(A) of the source of rent and other consideration due under such lease, and in the case of an assignment, that the financial condition and operating performance of the proposed assignee and its guarantors, if any, shall be similar to the financial condition and operating performance of the debtor and its guarantors, if any, as of the time the debtor became the lessee under the lease;

(B) that any percentage rent due under such lease will not decline substantially;

(C) that assumption or assignment of such lease is subject to all the provisions thereof, including (but not limited to) provisions such as a radius, location, use, or exclusivity provision, and will not breach any such provision contained in any other lease, financing agreement, or master agreement relating to such shopping center; and

(D) that assumption or assignment of such lease will not disrupt any tenant mix or balance in such shopping center.

(4) Notwithstanding any other provision of this section, if there has been a default in an unexpired lease of the debtor, other than a default of a kind specified in paragraph (2) of this subsection, the trustee may not require a lessor to provide services or supplies incidental to such lease before assumption of such lease unless the lessor is compensated under the terms of such lease for any services and supplies provided under such lease before assumption of such lease.

(c) The trustee may not assume or assign any executory contract or unexpired lease of the debtor, whether or not such contract or lease prohibits or restricts assignment of rights or delegation of duties, if -

(1)(A) applicable law excuses a party, other than the debtor, to such contract or lease from accepting performance from or rendering performance to an entity other than the debtor or the debtor in possession whether or not such contract or lease prohibits or restricts assignment of rights or delegation of duties; and

(B) such party does not consent to such assumption or assignment; or

(2) such contract is a contract to make a loan, or extend other debt financing or financial accommodations, to or for the benefit of the debtor, or to issue a security of the debtor; or

(3) such lease is of nonresidential real property and has been terminated under applicable nonbankruptcy law prior to the order for relief.

(4) [Repealed April 20, 2005; 119 Stat. 100].

(d)(1) In a case under chapter 7 of this title, if the trustee does not assume or reject an executory contract or unexpired lease of residential real property or of personal property of the debtor within 60 days after the order for relief, or within such additional time as the court, for cause, within such 60-day period, fixes, then such contract or lease is deemed rejected.

(2) In a case under chapter 9, 11, 12, or 13 of this title, the trustee may assume or reject an executory contract or unexpired lease of residential real property or of personal property of the debtor at any time before the confirmation of a plan but the court, on the request of any party to such contract or lease, may order the trustee to determine within a specified period of time whether to assume or reject such contract or lease.

(3) The trustee shall timely perform all the obligations of the debtor, except those specified in section 365(b)(2), arising from and after the order for relief under any unexpired lease of nonresidential real property, until such lease is assumed or rejected, notwithstanding section 503(b)(1) of this title. The court may extend, for cause, the time for performance of any such obligation that arises within 60 days after the date of the order for relief, but the time for performance shall not be extended beyond such 60-day period. This subsection shall not be deemed to affect the trustee's obligations under the provisions of subsection (b) or (f) of this section. Acceptance of any such performance does not constitute waiver or relinquishment of the lessor's rights under such lease or under this title.

(4)(A) Subject to subparagraph (B), an unexpired lease of nonresidential real property under which the debtor is the lessee shall be deemed rejected, and the trustee shall immediately surrender that nonresidential real property to the lessor, if the trustee does not assume or reject the unexpired lease by the earlier of –

(i) the date that is 120 days after the date of the order for relief; or

(ii) the date of the entry of an order confirming a plan.

(B)(i) The court may extend the period determined under subparagraph (A), prior to the expiration of the 120-day period, for 90 days on the motion of the trustee or lessor for cause.

(ii) If the court grants an extension under clause (i), the court may grant a subsequent extension only upon prior written consent of the lessor in each instance.

(5) The trustee shall timely perform all of the obligations of the debtor, except those specified in section 365(b)(2), first arising from or after 60 days after the order for relief in a case under chapter 11 of this title under an unexpired lease of personal property (other than personal property leased to an individual primarily for personal, family, or household purposes), until such lease is assumed or rejected notwithstanding section 503(b)(1) of this title, unless the court, after notice and a hearing and based on the equities of the case, orders otherwise with respect to the obligations or timely performance thereof. This subsection shall not be deemed to affect the trustee's obligations under the provisions of subsection (b) or (f). Acceptance of any such performance does not constitute waiver or relinquishment of the lessor's rights under such lease or under this title.

(6)-(9) [Repealed April 20, 2005; 119 Stat. 100. (10) redesignated to (5)].

(e)(1) Notwithstanding a provision in an executory contract or unexpired lease, or in applicable law, an executory contract or unexpired lease of the debtor may not be terminated or modified, and any right or obligation under such contract or lease may not be terminated or modified, at any time after the commencement of the case solely because of a provision in such contract or lease that is conditioned on -

(A) the insolvency or financial condition of the debtor at any time before the closing of the case;

(B) the commencement of a case under this title; or

(C) the appointment of or taking possession by a trustee in a case under this title or a custodian before such commencement.

(2) Paragraph (1) of this subsection does not apply to an executory contract or unexpired lease of the debtor, whether or not such contract or lease prohibits or restricts assignment of rights or delegation of duties, if -

(A)(i) applicable law excuses a party, other than the debtor, to such contract or lease from accepting performance from or rendering performance to the trustee or to an assignee of such contract or lease, whether or not such contract or lease prohibits or restricts assignment of rights or delegation of duties; and

(ii) such party does not consent to such assumption or assignment; or

(B) such contract is a contract to make a loan, or extend other debt financing or financial accommodations, to or for the benefit of the debtor, or to issue a security of the debtor.

(f)(1) Except as provided in subsections (b) and (c) of this section, notwithstanding a provision in an executory contract or unexpired lease of the debtor, or in applicable law, that prohibits, restricts, or conditions the assignment of such contract or lease, the trustee may assign such contract or lease under paragraph (2) of this subsection.

(2) The trustee may assign an executory contract or unexpired lease of the debtor only if -

(A) the trustee assumes such contract or lease in accordance with the provisions of this section; and

(B) adequate assurance of future performance by the assignee of such contract or lease is provided, whether or not there has been a default in such contract or lease.

(3) Notwithstanding a provision in an executory contract or unexpired lease of the debtor, or in applicable law that terminates or modifies, or permits a party other than the debtor to terminate or modify, such contract or lease or a right or obligation under such contract or lease on account of an assignment of such contract or lease, such contract, lease, right, or obligation may not be terminated or modified under such provision because of the assumption or assignment of such contract or lease by the trustee.

(g) Except as provided in subsections (h)(2) and (i)(2) of this section, the rejection of an executory contract or unexpired lease of the debtor constitutes a breach of such contract or lease -

(1) if such contract or lease has not been assumed under this section or under a plan confirmed under chapter 9, 11, 12, or 13 of this title, immediately before the date of the filing of the petition; or

(2) if such contract or lease has been assumed under this section or under a plan confirmed under chapter 9, 11, 12, or 13 of this title -

(A) if before such rejection the case has not been converted under section 1112, 1208, or 1307 of this title, at the time of such rejection; or

(B) if before such rejection the case has been converted under section 1112, 1208, or 1307 of this title -

(i) immediately before the date of such conversion, if such contract or lease was assumed before such conversion; or

(ii) at the time of such rejection, if such contract or lease was assumed after such conversion.

(h)(1)(A) If the trustee rejects an unexpired lease of real property under which the debtor is the lessor and -

(i) if the rejection by the trustee amounts to such a breach as would entitle the lessee to treat such lease as terminated by virtue of its terms, applicable nonbankruptcy law, or any agreement made by the lessee, then the lessee under such lease may treat such lease as terminated by the rejection; or

(ii) if the term of such lease has commenced, the lessee may retain its rights under such lease (including rights such as those relating to the amount and timing of payment of rent and other amounts payable by the lessee and any right of use, possession, quiet enjoyment, subletting, assignment, or hypothecation) that are in or appurtenant to the real property for the balance of the term of such lease and for any renewal or extension of such rights to the extent that such rights are enforceable under applicable nonbankruptcy law.

(B) If the lessee retains its rights under subparagraph (A)(ii), the lessee may offset against the rent reserved under such lease for the balance of the term after the date of the rejection of such lease and for the term of any renewal or extension of such lease, the value of any damage caused by the nonperformance after the date of such rejection, of any obligation of the debtor under such lease, but the lessee shall not have any other right against the estate or the debtor on account of any damage occurring after such date caused by such nonperformance.

(C) The rejection of a lease of real property in a shopping center with respect to which the lessee elects to retain its rights under subparagraph (A)(ii) does not affect the enforceability under applicable nonbankruptcy law of any provision in the lease pertaining to radius, location, use, exclusivity, or tenant mix or balance.

(D) In this paragraph, "lessee" includes any successor, assign, or mortgagee permitted under the terms of such lease.

(2)(A) If the trustee rejects a timeshare interest under a timeshare plan under which the debtor is the timeshare interest seller and -

(i) if the rejection amounts to such a breach as would entitle the timeshare interest purchaser to treat the timeshare plan as terminated under its terms, applicable nonbankruptcy law, or any agreement made by timeshare interest purchaser, the timeshare interest purchaser under the timeshare plan may treat the timeshare plan as terminated by such rejection; or

(ii) if the term of such timeshare interest has commenced, then the timeshare interest purchaser may retain its rights in such timeshare interest for the balance of such term and for any term of renewal or extension of such timeshare interest to the extent that such rights are enforceable under applicable nonbankruptcy law.

(B) If the timeshare interest purchaser retains its rights under subparagraph (A), such timeshare interest purchaser may offset against the moneys due for such timeshare interest for the balance of the term after the date of the rejection of such timeshare interest, and the term of any renewal or extension of such timeshare interest, the value of any damage caused by the nonperformance after the date of such rejection, of any obligation of the debtor under such timeshare plan, but the timeshare interest purchaser shall not have any right against the estate or the debtor on account of any damage occurring after such date caused by such nonperformance.

(i)(1) If the trustee rejects an executory contract of the debtor for the sale of real property or for the sale of a timeshare interest under a timeshare plan, under which the purchaser is in possession, such purchaser may treat such contract as terminated, or, in the alternative, may remain in possession of such real property or timeshare interest.

(2) If such purchaser remains in possession -

(A) such purchaser shall continue to make all payments due under such contract, but may, offset against such payments any damages occurring after the date of the rejection of such contract caused by the nonperformance of any obligation of the debtor after such date, but such purchaser does not have any rights against the estate on account of any damages arising after such date from such rejection, other than such offset; and

(B) the trustee shall deliver title to such purchaser in accordance with the provisions of such contract, but is relieved of all other obligations to perform under such contract.

(j) A purchaser that treats an executory contract as terminated under subsection (i) of this section, or a party whose executory contract to purchase real property from the debtor is rejected and under which such party is not in possession, has a lien on the interest of the debtor in such property for the recovery of any portion of the purchase price that such purchaser or party has paid.

(k) Assignment by the trustee to an entity of a contract or lease assumed under this section relieves the trustee and the estate from any liability for any breach of such contract or lease occurring after such assignment.

(l) If an unexpired lease under which the debtor is the lessee is assigned pursuant to this section, the lessor of the property may require a deposit or other security for the performance of the debtor's obligations under the lease substantially the same as would have been required by the landlord upon the initial leasing to a similar tenant.

(m) For purposes of this section 365 and sections 541(b)(2) and 362(b)(10), leases of real property shall include any rental agreement to use real property.

(n)(1) If the trustee rejects an executory contract under which the debtor is a licensor of a right to intellectual property, the licensee under such contract may elect -

(A) to treat such contract as terminated by such rejection if such rejection by the trustee amounts to such a breach as would entitle the licensee to treat such contract as terminated by virtue of its own terms, applicable nonbankruptcy law, or an agreement made by the licensee with another entity; or

(B) to retain its rights (including a right to enforce any exclusivity provision of such contract, but excluding any other right under applicable nonbankruptcy law to specific performance of such contract) under such contract and under any agreement supplementary to such contract, to such intellectual property (including any embodiment of such intellectual property to the extent protected by applicable nonbankruptcy law), as such rights existed immediately before the case commenced, for -

(i) the duration of such contract; and

(ii) any period for which such contract may be extended by the licensee as of right under applicable nonbankruptcy law.

(2) If the licensee elects to retain its rights, as described in paragraph (1)(B) of this subsection, under such contract -

(A) the trustee shall allow the licensee to exercise such rights;

(B) the licensee shall make all royalty payments due under such contract for the duration of such contract and for any period described in paragraph (1)(B) of this subsection for which the licensee extends such contract; and

(C) the licensee shall be deemed to waive -

(i) any right of setoff it may have with respect to such contract under this title or applicable nonbankruptcy law; and

(ii) any claim allowable under section 503(b) of this title arising from the performance of such contract.

(3) If the licensee elects to retain its rights, as described in paragraph (1) (B) of this subsection, then on the written request of the licensee the trustee shall -

(A) to the extent provided in such contract, or any agreement supplementary to such contract, provide to the licensee any intellectual property (including such embodiment) held by the trustee; and

(B) not interfere with the rights of the licensee as provided in such contract, or any agreement supplementary to such contract, to such intellectual property (including such embodiment) including any right to obtain such intellectual property (or such embodiment) from another entity.

(4) Unless and until the trustee rejects such contract, on the written request of the licensee the trustee shall -

(A) to the extent provided in such contract or any agreement supplementary to such contract -

(i) perform such contract; or

(ii) provide to the licensee such intellectual property (including any embodiment of such intellectual property to the extent protected by applicable nonbankruptcy law) held by the trustee; and

(B) not interfere with the rights of the licensee as provided in such contract, or any agreement supplementary to such contract, to such intellectual property (including such embodiment), including any right to obtain such intellectual property (or such embodiment) from another entity.

(o) In a case under chapter 11 of this title, the trustee shall be deemed to have assumed (consistent with the debtor's other obligations under section 507), and shall immediately cure any deficit under, any commitment by the debtor to a Federal depository institutions regulatory agency (or predecessor to such agency) to maintain the capital of an insured depository institution, and any claim for a subsequent breach of the obligations thereunder shall be entitled to priority under section 507. This subsection shall not extend any commitment that would otherwise be terminated by any act of such an agency.

(p)(1) If a lease of personal property is rejected or not timely assumed by the trustee under subsection (d), the leased property is no longer property of the estate and the stay under section 362(a) is automatically terminated.

(2)(A) If the debtor in a case under chapter 7 is an individual, the debtor may notify the creditor in writing that the debtor desires to assume the lease. Upon being so notified, the creditor may, at its option, notify the debtor that it is willing to have the lease assumed by the debtor and may condition such assumption on cure of any outstanding default on terms set by the contract.

(B) If, not later than 30 days after notice is provided under subparagraph (A), the debtor notifies the lessor in writing that the lease is assumed, the liability under the lease will be assumed by the debtor and not by the estate.

(C) The stay under section 362 and the injunction under section 524(a)(2) shall not be violated by notification of the debtor and negotiation of cure under this subsection.

(3) In a case under chapter 11 in which the debtor is an individual and in a case under chapter 13, if the debtor is the lessee with respect to personal property and the lease is not assumed in the plan confirmed by the court, the lease is deemed rejected as of the conclusion of the hearing on confirmation. If the lease is rejected, the stay under section 362 and any stay under section 1301 is automatically terminated with respect to the property subject to the lease.

366. Utility service

(a) Except as provided in subsections (b) and (c) of this section, a utility may not alter, refuse, or discontinue service to, or discriminate against, the trustee or the debtor solely on the basis of the commencement of a case under this title or that a debt owed by the debtor to such utility for service rendered before the order for relief was not paid when due.

(b) Such utility may alter, refuse, or discontinue service if neither the trustee nor the debtor, within 20 days after the date of the order for relief, furnishes adequate assurance of payment, in the form of a deposit or other security, for service after such date. On request of a party in interest and after notice and a hearing, the court may order reasonable modification of the amount of the deposit or other security necessary to provide adequate assurance of payment.

(c)(1)(A) For purposes of this subsection, the term "assurance of payment" means –

(i) a cash deposit;

(ii) a letter of credit;

(iii) a certificate of deposit;

(iv) a surety bond;

(v) a prepayment of utility consumption; or

(vi) another form of security that is mutually agreed on between the utility and the debtor or the trustee.

(B) For purposes of this subsection an administrative expense priority shall not constitute an assurance of payment.

(2) Subject to paragraphs (3) and (4), with respect to a case filed under chapter 11, a utility referred to in subsection (a) may alter, refuse, or discontinue utility service, if during the 30-day period beginning on the date of the filing of the petition, the utility does not receive from the debtor or the trustee adequate assurance of payment for utility service that is satisfactory to the utility.

(3)(A) On request of a party in interest and after notice and a hearing, the court may order modification of the amount of an assurance of payment under paragraph (2).

(B) In making a determination under this paragraph whether an assurance of payment is adequate, the court may not consider –

(i) the absence of security before the date of the filing of the petition;

(ii) the payment by the debtor of charges for utility service in a timely manner before the date of the filing of the petition; or

(iii) the availability of an administrative expense priority.

(4) Notwithstanding any other provision of law, with respect to a case subject to this subsection, a utility may recover or set off against a security deposit provided to the utility by the debtor before the date of the filing of the petition without notice or order of the court.

Chapter 5 - Creditors, the Debtor, and the Estate

Subchapter I - Creditors and Claims

SUBCHAPTER I - CREDITORS AND CLAIMS

501. Filing of proofs of claims or interests

(a) A creditor or an indenture trustee may file a proof of claim. An equity security holder may file a proof of interest.

(b) If a creditor does not timely file a proof of such creditor's claim, an entity that is liable to such creditor with the debtor, or that has secured such creditor, may file a proof of such claim.

(c) If a creditor does not timely file a proof of such creditor's claim, the debtor or the trustee may file a proof of such claim.

(d) A claim of a kind specified in section 502(e)(2), 502(f), 502(g), 502(h) or 502(i) of this title may be filed under subsection (a), (b), or (c) of this section the same as if such claim were a claim against the debtor and had arisen before the date of the filing of the petition.

(e) A claim arising from the liability of a debtor for fuel use tax assessed consistent with the requirements of section 31705 of title 49 may be filed by the base jurisdiction designated pursuant to the International Fuel Tax Agreement (as defined in section 31701 of title 49) and, if so filed, shall be allowed as a single claim.

502. Allowance of claims or interests

(a) A claim or interest, proof of which is filed under section 501 of this title, is deemed allowed, unless a party in interest, including a creditor of a general partner in a partnership that is a debtor in a case under chapter 7 of this title, objects.

(b) Except as provided in subsections (e)(2), (f), (g), (h) and (i) of this section, if such objection to a claim is made, the court, after notice and a hearing, shall determine the amount of such claim in lawful currency of the United States as of the date of the filing of the petition, and shall allow such claim in such amount, except to the extent that -

(1) such claim is unenforceable against the debtor and property of the debtor, under any agreement or applicable law for a reason other than because such claim is contingent or unmatured;

(2) such claim is for unmatured interest;

(3) if such claim is for a tax assessed against property of the estate, such claim exceeds the value of the interest of the estate in such property;

(4) if such claim is for services of an insider or attorney of the debtor, such claim exceeds the reasonable value of such services;

(5) such claim is for a debt that is unmatured on the date of the filing of the petition and that is excepted from discharge under section 523(a)(5) of this title;

(6) if such claim is the claim of a lessor for damages resulting from the termination of a lease of real property, such claim exceeds -

(A) the rent reserved by such lease, without acceleration, for the greater of one year, or 15 percent, not to exceed three years, of the remaining term of such lease, following the earlier of -

(i) the date of the filing of the petition; and

(ii) the date on which such lessor repossessed, or the lessee surrendered, the leased property; plus

(B) any unpaid rent due under such lease, without acceleration, on the earlier of such dates;

(7) if such claim is the claim of an employee for damages resulting from the termination of an employment contract, such claim exceeds -

(A) the compensation provided by such contract, without acceleration, for one year following the earlier of -

(i) the date of the filing of the petition; or

(ii) the date on which the employer directed the employee to terminate, or such employee terminated, performance under such contract; plus

(B) any unpaid compensation due under such contract, without acceleration, on the earlier of such dates;

(8) such claim results from a reduction, due to late payment, in the amount of an otherwise applicable credit available to the debtor in connection with an employment tax on wages, salaries, or commissions earned from the debtor; or

(9) proof of such claim is not timely filed, except to the extent tardily filed as permitted under paragraph (1), (2), or (3) of section 726(a) of this title or under the Federal Rules of Bankruptcy Procedure, except that a claim of a governmental unit shall be timely filed if it is filed before 180 days after the date of the order for relief or such later time as the Federal Rules of Bankruptcy Procedure may provide, and except that in a case under chapter 13, a claim of a governmental unit for a tax with respect to a return filed under section 1308 shall be timely if the claim is filed on or before the date that is 60 days after the date on which such return was filed as required.

(c) There shall be estimated for purpose of allowance under this section -

(1) any contingent or unliquidated claim, the fixing or liquidation of which, as the case may be, would unduly delay the administration of the case; or

(2) any right to payment arising from a right to an equitable remedy for breach of performance.

(d) Notwithstanding subsections (a) and (b) of this section, the court shall disallow any claim of any entity from which property is recoverable under section 542, 543, 550, or 553 of this title or that is a transferee of a transfer avoidable under section 522(f), 522(h), 544, 545, 547, 548, 549, or 724(a) of this title, unless such entity or transferee has paid the amount, or turned over any such property, for which such entity or transferee is liable under section 522(i), 542, 543, 550, or 553 of this title.

(e)(1) Notwithstanding subsections (a), (b), and (c) of this section and paragraph (2) of this subsection, the court shall disallow any claim for reimbursement or contribution of an entity that is liable with the debtor on or has secured the claim of a creditor, to the extent that -

(A) such creditor's claim against the estate is disallowed;

(B) such claim for reimbursement or contribution is contingent as of the time of allowance or disallowance of such claim for reimbursement or contribution; or

(C) such entity asserts a right of subrogation to the rights of such creditor under section 509 of this title.

(2) A claim for reimbursement or contribution of such an entity that becomes fixed after the commencement of the case shall be determined, and shall be allowed under subsection (a), (b), or (c) of this section, or disallowed under subsection (d) of this section, the same as if such claim had become fixed before the date of the filing of the petition.

(f) In an involuntary case, a claim arising in the ordinary course of the debtor's business or financial affairs after the commencement of the case but before the earlier of the appointment of a trustee and the order for relief shall be determined as of the date such claim arises, and shall be allowed under subsection (a), (b), or (c) of this section or disallowed under subsection (d) or (e) of this section, the same as if such claim had arisen before the date of the filing of the petition.

(g)(1) A claim arising from the rejection, under section 365 of this title or under a plan under chapter 9, 11, 12, or 13 of this title, of an executory contract or unexpired lease of the debtor that has not been assumed shall be determined, and shall be allowed under subsection (a), (b), or (c) of this section or disallowed under subsection (d) or (e) of this section, the same as if such claim had arisen before the date of the filing of the petition.

(2) A claim for damages calculated in accordance with section 562 shall be allowed under subsection (a), (b), or (c), or disallowed under subsection (d) or (e), as if such claim had arisen before the date of the filing of the petition.

(h) A claim arising from the recovery of property under section 522, 550, or 553 of this title shall be determined, and shall be allowed under subsection (a), (b), or (c) of this section, or disallowed under subsection (d) or (e) of this section, the same as if such claim had arisen before the date of the filing of the petition.

(i) A claim that does not arise until after the commencement of the case for a tax entitled to priority under section 507(a)(8) of this title shall be determined, and shall be allowed under subsection (a), (b), or (c) of this section, or disallowed under subsection (d) or (e) of this section, the same as if such claim had arisen before the date of the filing of the petition.

(j) A claim that has been allowed or disallowed may be reconsidered for cause. A reconsidered claim may be allowed or disallowed according to the equities of the case. Reconsideration of a claim under this subsection does not affect the validity of any payment or transfer from the estate made to a holder of an allowed claim on account of such allowed claim that is not reconsidered, but if a reconsidered claim is allowed and is of the same class as such holder's claim, such holder may not receive any additional payment or transfer from the estate on account of such holder's allowed claim until the holder of such reconsidered and allowed claim receives payment on account of such claim proportionate in value to that already received by such other holder. This subsection does not alter or modify the trustee's right to recover from a creditor any excess payment or transfer made to such creditor.

(k)(1) The court, on the motion of the debtor and after a hearing, may reduce a claim filed under this section based in whole on an unsecured consumer debt by not more than 20 percent of the claim, if –

(A) the claim was filed by a creditor who unreasonably refused to negotiate a reasonable alternative repayment schedule proposed on behalf of the debtor by an approved nonprofit budget and credit counseling agency described in section 111;

(B) the offer of the debtor under subparagraph (A) –

(i) was made at least 60 days before the date of the filing of the petition; and

(ii) provided for payment of at least 60 percent of the amount of the debt over a period not to exceed the repayment period of the loan, or a reasonable extension thereof; and

(C) no part of the debt under the alternative repayment schedule is nondischargeable.

(2) The debtor shall have the burden of proving, by clear and convincing evidence, that –

(A) the creditor unreasonably refused to consider the debtor's proposal; and

(B) the proposed alternative repayment schedule was made prior to expiration of the 60-day period specified in paragraph (1)(B)(i).

503. Allowance of administrative expenses

(a) An entity may timely file a request for payment of an administrative expense, or may tardily file such request if permitted by the court for cause.

(b) After notice and a hearing, there shall be allowed administrative expenses, other than claims allowed under section 502(f) of this title, including-

(1)(A) the actual, necessary costs and expenses of preserving the estate including –

(i) wages, salaries, and commissions for services rendered after the commencement of the case; and

(ii) wages and benefits awarded pursuant to a judicial proceeding or a proceeding of the National Labor Relations Board as back pay attributable to any period of time occurring after commencement of the case under this title, as a result of a violation of Federal or State law by the debtor, without regard to the time of the occurrence of unlawful conduct on which such award is based or to whether any services were rendered, if the court determines that payment of wages and benefits by reason of the operation of this clause will not substantially increase the probability of layoff or termination of current employees, or of nonpayment of domestic support obligations, during the case under this title;

(B) any tax -

(i) incurred by the estate, whether secured or unsecured, including property taxes for which liability is in rem, in personam, or both, except a tax of a kind specified in section 507(a)(8) of this title; or

(ii) attributable to an excessive allowance of a tentative carryback adjustment that the estate received, whether the taxable year to which such adjustment relates ended before or after the commencement of the case;

(C) any fine, penalty, or reduction in credit relating to a tax of a kind specified in subparagraph (B) of this paragraph; and

(D) notwithstanding the requirements of subsection (a), a governmental unit shall not be required to file a request for the payment of an expense described in subparagraph (B) or (C), as a condition of its being an allowed administrative expense;

(2) compensation and reimbursement awarded under section 330(a) of this title;

(3) the actual, necessary expenses, other than compensation and reimbursement specified in paragraph (4) of this subsection, incurred by -

(A) a creditor that files a petition under section 303 of this title;

(B) a creditor that recovers, after the court's approval, for the benefit of the estate any property transferred or concealed by the debtor;

(C) a creditor in connection with the prosecution of a criminal offense relating to the case or to the business or property of the debtor;

(D) a creditor, an indenture trustee, an equity security holder, or a committee representing creditors or equity security holders other than a committee appointed under section 1102 of this title, in making a substantial contribution in a case under chapter 9 or 11 of this title;

(E) a custodian superseded under section 543 of this title, and compensation for the services of such custodian; or

(F) a member of a committee appointed under section 1102 of this title, if such expenses are incurred in the performance of the duties of such committee;

(4) reasonable compensation for professional services rendered by an attorney or an accountant of an entity whose expense is allowable under subparagraph (A), (B), (C), (D), or (E) of paragraph (3) of this subsection, based on the time, the nature, the extent, and the value of such services, and the cost of comparable services other than in a case under this title, and reimbursement for actual, necessary expenses incurred by such attorney or accountant;

(5) reasonable compensation for services rendered by an indenture trustee in making a substantial contribution in a case under chapter 9 or 11 of this title, based on the time, the nature, the extent, and the value of such services, and the cost of comparable services other than in a case under this title;

(6) the fees and mileage payable under chapter 119 of title 28;

(7) with respect to a nonresidential real property lease previously assumed under section 365, and subsequently rejected, a sum equal to all monetary obligations due, excluding those arising from or relating to a failure to operate or a penalty provision, for the period of 2 years following the later of the rejection date or the date of actual turnover of the premises, without reduction or setoff for any reason whatsoever except for sums actually received or to be received from an entity other than the debtor, and the claim for remaining sums due for the balance of the term of the lease shall be a claim under section 502(b)(6);

(8) the actual, necessary costs and expenses of closing a health care business incurred by a trustee or by a Federal agency (as defined in section 551(1) of title 5) or a department or agency of a State or political subdivision thereof, including any cost or expense incurred –

(A) in disposing of patient records in accordance with section 351; or

(B) in connection with transferring patients from the health care business that is in the process of being closed to another health care business; and

(9) the value of any goods received by the debtor within 20 days before the date of commencement of a case under this title in which the goods have been sold to the debtor in the ordinary course of such debtor's business.

(c) Notwithstanding subsection (b), there shall neither be allowed, nor paid –

(1) a transfer made to, or an obligation incurred for the benefit of, an insider of the debtor for the purpose of inducing such person to remain with the debtor's business, absent a finding by the court based on evidence in the record that –

(A) the transfer or obligation is essential to retention of the person because the individual has a bona fide job offer from another business at the same or greater rate of compensation;

(B) the services provided by the person are essential to the survival of the business; and

(C) either –

(i) the amount of the transfer made to, or obligation incurred for the benefit of, the person is not greater than an amount equal to 10 times the amount of the mean transfer or obligation of a similar kind given to nonmanagement employees for any purpose during the calendar year in which the transfer is made or the obligation is incurred; or

(ii) if no such similar transfers were made to, or obligations were incurred for the benefit of, such nonmanagement employees during such calendar year, the amount of the transfer or obligation is not greater than an amount equal to 25 percent of the amount of any similar transfer or obligation made to or incurred for the benefit of such insider for any purpose during the calendar year before the year in which such transfer is made or obligation is incurred;

(2) a severance payment to an insider of the debtor, unless –

(A) the payment is part of a program that is generally applicable to all full-time employees; and

(B) the amount of the payment is not greater than 10 times the amount of the mean severance pay given to nonmanagement employees during the calendar year in which the payment is made; or

(3) other transfers or obligations that are outside the ordinary course of business and not justified by the facts and circumstances of the case, including transfers made to, or obligations incurred for the benefit of, officers, managers, or consultants hired after the date of the filing of the petition.

504. Sharing of compensation

(a) Except as provided in subsection (b) of this section, a person receiving compensation or reimbursement under section 503(b)(2) or 503(b)(4) of this title may not share or agree to share -

(1) any such compensation or reimbursement with another person; or

(2) any compensation or reimbursement received by another person under such sections.

(b)(1) A member, partner, or regular associate in a professional association, corporation, or partnership may share compensation or reimbursement received under section 503(b)(2) or 503(b)(4) of this title with another member, partner, or regular associate in such association, corporation, or partnership, and may share in any compensation or reimbursement received under such sections by another member, partner, or regular associate in such association, corporation, or partnership.

(2) An attorney for a creditor that files a petition under section 303 of this title may share compensation and reimbursement received under section 503(b)(4) of this title with any other attorney contributing to the services rendered or expenses incurred by such creditor's attorney.

(c) This section shall not apply with respect to sharing, or agreeing to share, compensation with a bona fide public service attorney referral program that operates in accordance with non-Federal law regulating attorney referral services and with rules of professional responsibility applicable to attorney acceptance of referrals.

505. Determination of tax liability

(a)(1) Except as provided in paragraph (2) of this subsection, the court may determine the amount or legality of any tax, any fine or penalty relating to a tax, or any addition to tax, whether or not previously assessed, whether or not paid, and whether or not contested before and adjudicated by a judicial or administrative tribunal of competent jurisdiction.

(2) The court may not so determine-

(A) the amount or legality of a tax, fine, penalty, or addition to tax if such amount or legality was contested before and adjudicated by a judicial or administrative tribunal of competent jurisdiction before the commencement of the case under this title;

(B) any right of the estate to a tax refund, before the earlier of –

(i) 120 days after the trustee properly requests such refund from the governmental unit from which such refund is claimed; or

(ii) a determination by such governmental unit of such request; or

(C) the amount or legality of any amount arising in connection with an ad valorem tax on real or personal property of the estate, if the applicable period for contesting or redetermining that amount under applicable nonbankruptcy law has expired.

(b)(1)(A) The clerk shall maintain a list under which a Federal, State, or local governmental unit responsible for the collection of taxes within the district may –

(i) designate an address for service of requests under this subsection; and

(ii) describe where further information concerning additional requirements for filing such requests may be found.

(B) If such governmental unit does not designate an address and provide such address to the clerk under subparagraph (A), any request made under this subsection may be served at the address for the filing of a tax return or protest with the appropriate taxing authority of such governmental unit.

(2) A trustee may request a determination of any unpaid liability of the estate for any tax incurred during the administration of the case by submitting a tax return for such tax and a request for such a determination to the governmental unit charged with responsibility for collection or determination of such tax at the address and in the manner designated in paragraph (1). Unless such return is fraudulent, or contains a material misrepresentation, the estate, the trustee, the debtor, and any successor to the debtor are discharged from any liability for such tax-

(A) upon payment of the tax shown on such return, if-

(i) such governmental unit does not notify the trustee, within 60 days after such request, that such return has been selected for examination; or

(ii) such governmental unit does not complete such an examination and notify the trustee of any tax due, within 180 days after such request or within such additional time as the court, for cause, permits;

(B) upon payment of the tax determined by the court, after notice and a hearing, after completion by such governmental unit of such examination; or

(C) upon payment of the tax determined by such governmental unit to be due.

(c) Notwithstanding section 362 of this title, after determination by the court of a tax under this section, the governmental unit charged with responsibility for collection of such tax may assess such tax against the estate, the debtor, or a successor to the debtor, as the case may be, subject to any otherwise applicable law.

506. Determination of secured status

(a)(1) An allowed claim of a creditor secured by a lien on property in which the estate has an interest, or that is subject to setoff under section 553 of this title, is a secured claim to the extent of the value of such creditor's interest in the estate's interest in such property, or to the extent of the amount subject to setoff, as the case may be, and is an unsecured claim to the extent that the value of such creditor's interest or the amount so subject to setoff is less than the amount of such allowed claim. Such value shall be determined in light of the purpose of the valuation and of the proposed disposition or use of such property, and in conjunction with any hearing on such disposition or use or on a plan affecting such creditor's interest.

(2) If the debtor is an individual in a case under chapter 7 or 13, such value with respect to personal property securing an allowed claim shall be determined based on the replacement value of such property as of the date of the filing of the petition without deduction for costs of sale or marketing. With respect to property acquired for personal, family, or household purposes, replacement value shall mean the price a retail merchant would charge for property of that kind considering the age and condition of the property at the time value is determined.

(b) To the extent that an allowed secured claim is secured by property the value of which, after any recovery under subsection (c) of this section, is greater than the amount of such claim, there shall be allowed to the holder of such claim, interest on such claim, and any reasonable fees, costs, or charges provided for under the agreement or State statute under which such claim arose.

(c) The trustee may recover from property securing an allowed secured claim the reasonable, necessary costs and expenses of preserving, or disposing of, such property to the extent of any benefit to the holder of such claim, including the payment of all ad valorem property taxes with respect to the property.

(d) To the extent that a lien secures a claim against the debtor that is not an allowed secured claim, such lien is void, unless -

(1) such claim was disallowed only under section 502(b)(5) or 502(e) of this title; or

(2) such claim is not an allowed secured claim due only to the failure of any entity to file a proof of such claim under section 501 of this title.

507. Priorities

(a) The following expenses and claims have priority in the following order:

(1) First:

(A) Allowed unsecured claims for domestic support obligations that, as of the date of the filing of the petition in a case under this title, are owed to or recoverable by a spouse, former spouse, or child of the debtor, or such child's parent, legal guardian, or responsible relative, without regard to whether the claim is filed by such person or is filed by a governmental unit on behalf of such person, on the condition that funds received under this paragraph by a governmental unit under this title after the date of the filing of the petition shall be applied and distributed in accordance with applicable nonbankruptcy law.

(B) Subject to claims under subparagraph (A), allowed unsecured claims for domestic support obligations that, as of the date of the filing of the petition, are assigned by a spouse, former spouse, child of the debtor, or such child's parent, legal guardian, or responsible relative to a governmental unit (unless such obligation is assigned voluntarily by the spouse, former spouse, child, parent, legal guardian, or responsible relative of the child for the purpose of collecting the debt) or are owed directly to or recoverable by a governmental unit under applicable nonbankruptcy law, on the condition that funds received under this paragraph by a governmental unit under this title after the date of the filing of the petition be applied and distributed in accordance with applicable nonbankruptcy law.

(C) If a trustee is appointed or elected under section 701, 702, 703, 1104, 1202, or 1302, the administrative expenses of the trustee allowed under paragraphs (1)(A), (2), and (6) of section 503(b) shall be paid before payment of claims under subparagraphs (A) and (B), to the extent that the trustee administers assets that are otherwise available for the payment of such claims.

(2) Second, administrative expenses allowed under section 503(b) of this title, unsecured claims of any federal reserve bank related to loans made through programs or facilities authorized under Section 13(3) of the Federal Reserve Act (12 U.S.C. 343), and any fees and charges assessed against the estate under chapter 123 of title 28.

(3) Third, unsecured claims allowed under section 502(f) of this title.

(4) Fourth, allowed unsecured claims, but only to the extent of $12,475 for each individual or corporation, as the case may be, earned within 180 days before the date of the filing of the petition or the date of the cessation of the debtor's business, whichever occurs first, for -

(A) wages, salaries, or commissions, including vacation, severance, and sick leave pay earned by an individual; or

(B) sales commissions earned by an individual or by a corporation with only 1 employee, acting as an independent contractor in the sale of goods or services for the debtor in the ordinary course of the debtor's business if, and only if, during the 12 months preceding that date, at least 75 percent of the amount that the individual or corporation earned by acting as an independent contractor in the sale of goods or services was earned from the debtor.

(5) Fifth, allowed unsecured claims for contributions to an employee benefit plan -

(A) arising from services rendered within 180 days before the date of the filing of the petition or the date of the cessation of the debtor's business, whichever occurs first; but only

(B) for each such plan, to the extent of -

(i) the number of employees covered by each such plan multiplied by $12,475; less

(ii) the aggregate amount paid to such employees under paragraph (4) of this subsection, plus the aggregate amount paid by the estate on behalf of such employees to any other employee benefit plan.

(6) Sixth, allowed unsecured claims of persons -

(A) engaged in the production or raising of grain, as defined in section 557(b) of this title, against a debtor who owns or operates a grain storage facility, as defined in section 557(b) of this title, for grain or the proceeds of grain, or

(B) engaged as a United States fisherman against a debtor who has acquired fish or fish produce from a fisherman through a sale or conversion, and who is engaged in operating a fish produce storage or processing facility -

but only to the extent of $6,150 for each such individual.

(7) Seventh, allowed unsecured claims of individuals, to the extent of $2,775 for each such individual, arising from the deposit, before the commencement of the case, of money in connection with the purchase, lease, or rental of property, or the purchase of services, for the personal, family, or household use of such individuals, that were not delivered or provided.

(8) Eighth, allowed unsecured claims of governmental units, only to the extent that such claims are for -

(A) a tax on or measured by income or gross receipts for a taxable year ending on or before the date of the filing of the petition -

(i) for which a return, if required, is last due, including extensions, after three years before the date of the filing of the petition;

(ii) assessed within 240 days before the date of the filing of the petition, exclusive of –

(I) any time during which an offer in compromise with respect to that tax was pending or in effect during that 240-day period, plus 30 days; and

(II) any time during which a stay of proceedings against collections was in effect in a prior case under this title during that 240-day period, plus 90 days; or

(iii) other than a tax of a kind specified in section 523(a)(1)(B) or 523(a)(1)(C) of this title, not assessed before, but assessable, under applicable law or by agreement, after, the commencement of the case;

(B) a property tax incurred before the commencement of the case and last payable without penalty after one year before the date of the filing of the petition;

(C) a tax required to be collected or withheld and for which the debtor is liable in whatever capacity;

(D) an employment tax on a wage, salary, or commission of a kind specified in paragraph (4) of this subsection earned from the debtor before the date of the filing of the petition, whether or not actually paid before such date, for which a return is last due, under applicable law or under any extension, after three years before the date of the filing of the petition;

(E) an excise tax on -

(i) a transaction occurring before the date of the filing of the petition for which a return, if required, is last due, under applicable law or under any extension, after three years before the date of the filing of the petition; or

(ii) if a return is not required, a transaction occurring during the three years immediately preceding the date of the filing of the petition;

(F) a customs duty arising out of the importation of merchandise-

(i) entered for consumption within one year before the date of the filing of the petition;

(ii) covered by an entry liquidated or reliquidated within one year before the date of the filing of the petition; or

(iii) entered for consumption within four years before the date of the filing of the petition but unliquidated on such date, if the Secretary of the Treasury certifies that failure to liquidate such entry was due to an investigation pending on such date into assessment of antidumping or countervailing duties or fraud, or if information needed for the proper appraisement or classification of such merchandise was not available to the appropriate customs officer before such date;

or

(G) a penalty related to a claim of a kind specified in this paragraph and in compensation for actual pecuniary loss.

An otherwise applicable time period specified in this paragraph shall be suspended for any period during which a governmental unit is prohibited under applicable nonbankruptcy law from collecting a tax as a result of a request by the debtor for a hearing and an appeal of any collection action taken or proposed against the debtor, plus 90 days; plus any time during which the stay of proceedings was in effect in a prior case under this title or during which collection was precluded by the existence of 1 or more confirmed plans under this title, plus 90 days.

(9) Ninth, allowed unsecured claims based upon any commitment by the debtor to a Federal depository institutions regulatory agency (or predecessor to such agency) to maintain the capital of an insured depository institution.

(10) Tenth, allowed claims for death or personal injury resulting from the operation of a motor vehicle or vessel if such operation was unlawful because the debtor was intoxicated from using alcohol, a drug, or another substance.

(b) If the trustee, under section 362, 363, or 364 of this title, provides adequate protection of the interest of a holder of a claim secured by a lien on property of the debtor and if, notwithstanding such protection, such creditor has a claim allowable under subsection (a)(2) of this section arising from the stay of action against such property under section 362 of this title, from the use, sale, or lease of such property under section 363 of this title, or from the granting of a lien under section 364(d) of this title, then such creditor's claim under such subsection shall have priority over every other claim allowable under such subsection.

(c) For the purpose of subsection (a) of this section, a claim of a governmental unit arising from an erroneous refund or credit of a tax has the same priority as a claim for the tax to which such refund or credit relates.

(d) An entity that is subrogated to the rights of a holder of a claim of a kind specified in subsection (a)(1), (a)(4), (a)(5), (a)(6), (a)(7), (a)(8), or (a)(9) of this section is not subrogated to the right of the holder of such claim to priority under such subsection.

508. Effect of distribution other than under this title

If a creditor of a partnership debtor receives, from a general partner that is not a debtor in a case under chapter 7 of this title, payment of, or a transfer of property on account of, a claim that is allowed under this title and that is not secured by a lien on property of such partner, such creditor may not receive any payment under this title on account of such claim until each of the other holders of claims on account of which such holders are entitled to share equally with such creditor under this title has received payment under this title equal in value to the consideration received by such creditor from such general partner.

509. Claims of codebtors

(a) Except as provided in subsection (b) or (c) of this section, an entity that is liable with the debtor on, or that has secured, a claim of a creditor against the debtor, and that pays such claim, is subrogated to the rights of such creditor to the extent of such payment.

(b) Such entity is not subrogated to the rights of such creditor to the extent that -

(1) a claim of such entity for reimbursement or contribution on account of such payment of such creditor's claim is -

(A) allowed under section 502 of this title;

(B) disallowed other than under section 502(e) of this title; or

(C) subordinated under section 510 of this title; or

(2) as between the debtor and such entity, such entity received the consideration for the claim held by such creditor.

(c) The court shall subordinate to the claim of a creditor and for the benefit of such creditor an allowed claim, by way of subrogation under this section, or for reimbursement or contribution, of an entity that is liable with the debtor on, or that has secured, such creditor's claim, until such creditor's claim is paid in full, either through payments under this title or otherwise.

510. Subordination

(a) A subordination agreement is enforceable in a case under this title to the same extent that such agreement is enforceable under applicable nonbankruptcy law.

(b) For the purpose of distribution under this title, a claim arising from rescission of a purchase or sale of a security of the debtor or of an affiliate of the debtor, for damages arising from the purchase or sale of such a security, or for reimbursement or contribution allowed under section 502 on account of such a claim, shall be subordinated to all claims or interests that are senior to or equal the claim or interest represented by such security, except that if such security is common stock, such claim has the same priority as common stock.

(c) Notwithstanding subsections (a) and (b) of this section, after notice and a hearing, the court may -

(1) under principles of equitable subordination, subordinate for purposes of distribution all or part of an allowed claim to all or part of another allowed claim or all or part of an allowed interest to all or part of another allowed interest; or

(2) order that any lien securing such a subordinated claim be transferred to the estate.

511. Rate of interest on tax claims

(a) If any provision of this title requires the payment of interest on a tax claim or on an administrative expense tax, or the payment of interest to enable a creditor to receive the present value of the allowed amount of a tax claim, the rate of interest shall be the rate determined under applicable nonbankruptcy law.

(b) In the case of taxes paid under a confirmed plan under this title, the rate of interest shall be determined as of the calendar month in which the plan is confirmed.

SUBCHAPTER II - DEBTOR'S DUTIES AND BENEFITS

521. Debtor's duties

(a) The debtor shall -

(1) file –

(A) a list of creditors; and

(B) unless the court orders otherwise –

(i) a schedule of assets and liabilities;

(ii) a schedule of current income and current expenditures;

(iii) a statement of the debtor's financial affairs and, if section 342(b) applies, a certificate –

(I) of an attorney whose name is indicated on the petition as the attorney for the debtor, or a bankruptcy petition preparer signing the petition under section 110(b)(1), indicating that such attorney or the bankruptcy petition preparer delivered to the debtor the notice required by section 342(b); or

(II) if no attorney is so indicated, and no bankruptcy petition preparer signed the petition, of the debtor that such notice was received and read by the debtor;

(iv) copies of all payment advices or other evidence of payment received within 60 days before the date of the filing of the petition, by the debtor from any employer of the debtor;

(v) a statement of the amount of monthly net income, itemized to show how the amount is calculated; and

(vi) a statement disclosing any reasonably anticipated increase in income or expenditures over the 12-month period following the date of the filing of the petition;

(2) if an individual debtor's schedule of assets and liabilities includes

debts which are secured by property of the estate -

(A) within thirty days after the date of the filing of a petition under chapter 7 of this title or on or before the date of the meeting of creditors, whichever is earlier, or within such additional time as the court, for cause, within such period fixes, file with the clerk a statement of his intention with respect to the retention or surrender of such property and, if applicable, specifying that such property is claimed as exempt, that the debtor intends to redeem such property, or that the debtor intends to reaffirm debts secured by such property; and

(B) within 30 days after the first date set for the meeting of creditors under section 341(a), or within such additional time as the court, for cause, within such 30-day period fixes, perform his intention with respect to such property, as specified by subparagraph (A) of this paragraph;except that nothing in subparagraphs (A) and (B) of this paragraph shall alter the debtor's or the trustee's rights with regard to such property under this title, except as provided in section 362(h);

(3) if a trustee is serving in the case or an auditor is serving under section 586(f) of title 28, cooperate with the trustee as necessary to enable the trustee to perform the trustee's duties under this title;

(4) if a trustee is serving in the case or an auditor is serving under section 586(f) of title 28, surrender to the trustee all property of the estate and any recorded information, including books, documents, records, and papers, relating to property of the estate, whether or not immunity is granted under section 344 of this title;

(5) appear at the hearing required under section 524(d) of this title;

(6) in a case under chapter 7 of this title in which the debtor is an individual, not retain possession of personal property as to which a creditor has an allowed claim for the purchase price secured in whole or in part by an interest in such personal property unless the debtor, not later than 45 days after the first meeting of creditors under section 341(a), either –

(A) enters into an agreement with the creditor pursuant to section 524(c) with respect to the claim secured by such property; or

(B) redeems such property from the security interest pursuant to section 722; and

(7) unless a trustee is serving in the case, continue to perform the obligations required of the administrator (as defined in section 3 of the Employee Retirement Income Security Act of 1974) of an employee benefit plan if at the time of the commencement of the case the debtor (or any entity designated by the debtor) served as such administrator.

If the debtor fails to so act within the 45-day period referred to in paragraph (6), the stay under section 362(a) is terminated with respect to the personal property of the estate or of the debtor which is affected, such property shall no longer be property of the estate, and the creditor may take whatever action as to such property as is permitted by applicable nonbankruptcy law, unless the court determines on the motion of the trustee filed before the expiration of such 45-day period, and after notice and a hearing, that such property is of consequential value or benefit to the estate, orders appropriate adequate protection of the creditor's interest, and orders the debtor to deliver any collateral in the debtor's possession to the trustee.

(b) In addition to the requirements under subsection (a), a debtor who is an individual shall file with the court –

(1) a certificate from the approved nonprofit budget and credit counseling agency that provided the debtor services under section 109(h) describing the services provided to the debtor; and

(2) a copy of the debt repayment plan, if any, developed under section 109(h) through the approved nonprofit budget and credit counseling agency referred to in paragraph (1).

(c) In addition to meeting the requirements under subsection (a), a debtor shall file with the court a record of any interest that a debtor has in an education individual retirement account (as defined in section 530(b)(1) of the Internal Revenue Code of 1986) or under a qualified State tuition program (as defined in section 529(b)(1) of such Code).

(d) If the debtor fails timely to take the action specified in subsection (a)(6) of this section, or in paragraphs (1) and (2) of section 362(h), with respect to property which a lessor or bailor owns and has leased, rented, or bailed to the debtor or as to which a creditor holds a security interest not otherwise voidable under section 522(f), 544, 545, 547, 548, or 549, nothing in this title shall prevent or limit the operation of a provision in the underlying lease or agreement that has the effect of placing the debtor in default under such lease or agreement by reason of the occurrence, pendency, or existence of a proceeding under this title or the insolvency of the debtor. Nothing in this subsection shall be deemed to justify limiting such a provision in any other circumstance.

(e)(1) If the debtor in a case under chapter 7 or 13 is an individual and if a creditor files with the court at any time a request to receive a copy of the petition, schedules, and statement of financial affairs filed by the debtor, then the court shall make such petition, such schedules, and such statement available to such creditor.

(2)(A) The debtor shall provide –

(i) not later than 7 days before the date first set for the first meeting of creditors, to the trustee a copy of the Federal income tax return required under applicable law (or at the election of the debtor, a transcript of such return) for the most recent tax year ending immediately before the commencement of the case and for which a Federal income tax return was filed; and

(ii) at the same time the debtor complies with clause (i), a copy of such return (or if elected under clause (i), such transcript) to any creditor that timely requests such copy.

(B) If the debtor fails to comply with clause (i) or (ii) of subparagraph (A), the court shall dismiss the case unless the debtor demonstrates that the failure to so comply is due to circumstances beyond the control of the debtor.

(C) If a creditor requests a copy of such tax return or such transcript and if the debtor fails to provide a copy of such tax return or such transcript to such creditor at the time the debtor provides such tax return or such transcript to the trustee, then the court shall dismiss the case unless the debtor demonstrates that the failure to provide a copy of such tax return or such transcript is due to circumstances beyond the control of the debtor.

(3) If a creditor in a case under chapter 13 files with the court at any time a request to receive a copy of the plan filed by the debtor, then the court shall make available to such creditor a copy of the plan –

(A) at a reasonable cost; and

(B) not later than 7 days after such request is filed.

(f) At the request of the court, the United States trustee, or any party in interest in a case under chapter 7, 11, or 13, a debtor who is an individual shall file with the court –

(1) at the same time filed with the taxing authority, a copy of each Federal income tax return required under applicable law (or at the election of the debtor, a transcript of such tax return) with respect to each tax year of the debtor ending while the case is pending under such chapter;

(2) at the same time filed with the taxing authority, each Federal income tax return required under applicable law (or at the election of the debtor, a transcript of such tax return) that had not been filed with such authority as of the date of the commencement of the case and that was subsequently filed for any tax year of the debtor ending in the 3-year period ending on the date of the commencement of the case;

(3) a copy of each amendment to any Federal income tax return or transcript filed with the court under paragraph (1) or (2); and

(4) in a case under chapter 13 –

(A) on the date that is either 90 days after the end of such tax year or 1 year after the date of the commencement of the case, whichever is later, if a plan is not confirmed before such later date; and

(B) annually after the plan is confirmed and until the case is closed, not later than the date that is 45 days before the anniversary of the confirmation of the plan;

a statement, under penalty of perjury, of the income and expenditures of the debtor during the tax year of the debtor most recently concluded before such statement is filed under this paragraph, and of the monthly income of the debtor, that shows how income, expenditures, and monthly income are calculated.

(g)(1) A statement referred to in subsection (f)(4) shall disclose –

(A) the amount and sources of the income of the debtor;

(B) the identity of any person responsible with the debtor for the support of any dependent of the debtor; and

(C) the identity of any person who contributed, and the amount contributed, to the household in which the debtor resides.

(2) The tax returns, amendments, and statement of income and expenditures described in subsections (e)(2)(A) and (f) shall be available to the United States trustee (or the bankruptcy administrator, if any), the trustee, and any party in interest for inspection and copying, subject to the requirements of section 315(c) of the Bankruptcy Abuse Prevention and Consumer Protection Act of 2005.

(h) If requested by the United States trustee or by the trustee, the debtor shall provide –

(1) a document that establishes the identity of the debtor, including a driver's license, passport, or other document that contains a photograph of the debtor; or

(2) such other personal identifying information relating to the debtor that establishes the identity of the debtor.

(i)(1) Subject to paragraphs (2) and (4) and notwithstanding section 707(a), if an individual debtor in a voluntary case under chapter 7 or 13 fails to file all of the information required under subsection (a)(1) within 45 days after the date of the filing of the petition, the case shall be automatically dismissed effective on the 46th day after the date of the filing of the petition.

(2) Subject to paragraph (4) and with respect to a case described in paragraph (1), any party in interest may request the court to enter an order dismissing the case. If requested, the court shall enter an order of dismissal not later than 7 days after such request.

(3) Subject to paragraph (4) and upon request of the debtor made within 45 days after the date of the filing of the petition described in paragraph (1), the court may allow the debtor an additional period of not to exceed 45 days to file the information required under subsection (a)(1) if the court finds justification for extending the period for the filing.

(4) Notwithstanding any other provision of this subsection, on the motion of the trustee filed before the expiration of the applicable period of time specified in paragraph (1), (2), or (3), and after notice and a hearing, the court may decline to dismiss the case if the court finds that the debtor attempted in good faith to file all the information required by subsection (a)(1)(B)(iv) and that the best interests of creditors would be served by administration of the case.

(j)(1) Notwithstanding any other provision of this title, if the debtor fails to file a tax return that becomes due after the commencement of the case or to properly obtain an extension of the due date for filing such return, the taxing authority may request that the court enter an order converting or dismissing the case.

(2) If the debtor does not file the required return or obtain the extension referred to in paragraph (1) within 90 days after a request is filed by the taxing authority under that paragraph, the court shall convert or dismiss the case, whichever is in the best interests of creditors and the estate.

522. Exemptions

(a) In this section -

(1) "dependent" includes spouse, whether or not actually dependent; and

(2) "value" means fair market value as of the date of the filing of the petition or, with respect to property that becomes property of the estate after such date, as of the date such property becomes property of the estate.

(b)(1) Notwithstanding section 541 of this title, an individual debtor may exempt from property of the estate the property listed in either paragraph (2) or, in the alternative, paragraph (3) of this subsection. In joint cases filed under section 302 of this title and individual cases filed under section 301 or 303 of this title by or against debtors who are husband and wife, and whose estates are ordered to be jointly administered under Rule 1015(b) of the Federal Rules of Bankruptcy Procedure, one debtor may not elect to exempt property listed in paragraph (2) and the other debtor elect to exempt property listed in paragraph (3) of this subsection. If the parties cannot agree on the alternative to be elected, they shall be deemed to elect paragraph (2), where such election is permitted under the law of the jurisdiction where the case is filed.

(2) Property listed in this paragraph is property that is specified under subsection (d), unless the State law that is applicable to the debtor under paragraph (3)(A) specifically does not so authorize.

(3) Property listed in this paragraph is –

(A) subject to subsections (o) and (p), any property that is exempt under Federal law, other than subsection (d) of this section, or State or local law that is applicable on the date of the filing of the petition to the place in which the debtor's domicile has been located for the 730 days immediately preceding the date of the filing of the petition or if the debtor's domicile has not been located in a single State for such 730-day period, the place in which the debtor's domicile was located for 180 days immediately preceding the 730-day period or for a longer portion of such 180-day period than in any other place;

(B) any interest in property in which the debtor had, immediately before the commencement of the case, an interest as a tenant by the entirety or joint tenant to the extent that such interest as a tenant by the entirety or joint tenant is exempt from process under applicable nonbankruptcy law; and

(C) retirement funds to the extent that those funds are in a fund or account that is exempt from taxation under section 401, 403, 408, 408A, 414, 457, or 501(a) of the Internal Revenue Code of 1986.

If the effect of the domiciliary requirement under subparagraph (A) is to render the debtor ineligible for any exemption, the debtor may elect to exempt property that is specified under subsection (d).

(4) For purposes of paragraph (3)(C) and subsection (d)(12), the following shall apply:

(A) If the retirement funds are in a retirement fund that has received a favorable determination under section 7805 of the Internal Revenue Code of 1986, and that determination is in effect as of the date of the filing of the petition in a case under this title, those funds shall be presumed to be exempt from the estate.

(B) If the retirement funds are in a retirement fund that has not received a favorable determination under such section 7805, those funds are exempt from the estate if the debtor demonstrates that –

(i) no prior determination to the contrary has been made by a court or the Internal Revenue Service; and

(ii)(I) the retirement fund is in substantial compliance with the applicable requirements of the Internal Revenue Code of 1986; or

(II) the retirement fund fails to be in substantial compliance with the applicable requirements of the Internal Revenue Code of 1986 and the debtor is not materially responsible for that failure.

(C) A direct transfer of retirement funds from 1 fund or account that is exempt from taxation under section 401, 403, 408, 408A, 414, 457, or 501(a) of the Internal Revenue Code of 1986, under section 401(a)(31) of the Internal Revenue Code of 1986, or otherwise, shall not cease to qualify for exemption under paragraph (3)(C) or subsection (d)(12) by reason of such direct transfer.

(D)(i) Any distribution that qualifies as an eligible rollover distribution within the meaning of section 402(c) of the Internal Revenue Code of 1986 or that is described in clause (ii) shall not cease to qualify for exemption under paragraph (3)(C) or subsection (d)(12) by reason of such distribution.

(ii) A distribution described in this clause is an amount that –

(I) has been distributed from a fund or account that is exempt from taxation under section 401, 403, 408, 408A, 414, 457, or 501(a) of the Internal Revenue Code of 1986; and

(II) to the extent allowed by law, is deposited in such a fund or account not later than 60 days after the distribution of such amount.

(c) Unless the case is dismissed, property exempted under this section is not liable during or after the case for any debt of the debtor that arose, or that is determined under section 502 of this title as if such debt had arisen, before the commencement of the case, except -

(1) a debt of a kind specified in paragraph (1) or (5) of section 523(a) (in which case, notwithstanding any provision of applicable nonbankruptcy law to the contrary, such property shall be liable for a debt of a kind specified in such paragraph);

(2) a debt secured by a lien that is -

(A)(i) not avoided under subsection (f) or (g) of this section or under section 544, 545, 547, 548, 549, or 724(a) of this title; and

(ii) not void under section 506(d) of this title; or

(B) a tax lien, notice of which is properly filed;

(3) a debt of a kind specified in section 523(a)(4) or 523(a)(6) of this title owed by an institution-affiliated party of an insured depository institution to a Federal depository institutions regulatory agency acting in its capacity as conservator, receiver, or liquidating agent for such institution; or

(4) a debt in connection with fraud in the obtaining or providing of any scholarship, grant, loan, tuition, discount, award, or other financial assistance for purposes of financing an education at an institution of higher education (as that term is defined in section 101 of the Higher Education Act of 1965 (20 U.S.C. 1001)).

(d) The following property may be exempted under subsection (b)(2) of this section:

(1) The debtor's aggregate interest, not to exceed $22,975 in value, in real property or personal property that the debtor or a dependent of the debtor uses as a residence, in a cooperative that owns property that the debtor or a dependent of the debtor uses as a residence, or in a burial plot for the debtor or a dependent of the debtor.

(2) The debtor's interest, not to exceed $3,675 in value, in one motor vehicle.

(3) The debtor's interest, not to exceed $575 in value in any particular item or $12,250 in aggregate value, in household furnishings, household goods, wearing apparel, appliances, books, animals, crops, or musical instruments, that are held primarily for the personal, family, or household use of the debtor or a dependent of the debtor.

(4) The debtor's aggregate interest, not to exceed $1,550 in value, in jewelry held primarily for the personal, family, or household use of the debtor or a dependent of the debtor.

(5) The debtor's aggregate interest in any property, not to exceed in value $1,225 plus up to $11,500 of any unused amount of the exemption provided under paragraph (1) of this subsection.

(6) The debtor's aggregate interest, not to exceed $2,300 in value, in any implements, professional books, or tools, of the trade of the debtor or the trade of a dependent of the debtor.

(7) Any unmatured life insurance contract owned by the debtor, other than a credit life insurance contract.

(8) The debtor's aggregate interest, not to exceed in value $12,250 less any amount of property of the estate transferred in the manner specified in section 542(d) of this title, in any accrued dividend or interest under, or loan value of, any unmatured life insurance contract owned by the debtor under which the insured is the debtor or an individual of whom the debtor is a dependent.

(9) Professionally prescribed health aids for the debtor or a dependent of the debtor.

(10) The debtor's right to receive -

(A) a social security benefit, unemployment compensation, or a local public assistance benefit;

(B) a veterans' benefit;

(C) a disability, illness, or unemployment benefit;

(D) alimony, support, or separate maintenance, to the extent reasonably necessary for the support of the debtor and any dependent of the debtor;

(E) a payment under a stock bonus, pension, profitsharing, annuity, or similar plan or contract on account of illness, disability, death, age, or length of service, to the extent reasonably necessary for the support of the debtor and any dependent of the debtor, unless -

(i) such plan or contract was established by or under the auspices of an insider that employed the debtor at the time the debtor's rights under such plan or contract arose;

(ii) such payment is on account of age or length of service; and

(iii) such plan or contract does not qualify under section 401(a), 403(a), 403(b), or 408 of the Internal Revenue Code of 1986.

(11) The debtor's right to receive, or property that is traceable to -

(A) an award under a crime victim's reparation law;

(B) a payment on account of the wrongful death of an individual of whom the debtor was a dependent, to the extent reasonably necessary for the support of the debtor and any dependent of the debtor;

(C) a payment under a life insurance contract that insured the life of an individual of whom the debtor was a dependent on the date of such individual's death, to the extent reasonably necessary for the support of the debtor and any dependent of the debtor;

(D) a payment, not to exceed $22,975, on account of personal bodily injury, not including pain and suffering or compensation for actual pecuniary loss, of the debtor or an individual of whom the debtor is a dependent; or

(E) a payment in compensation of loss of future earnings of the debtor or an individual of whom the debtor is or was a dependent, to the extent reasonably necessary for the support of the debtor and any dependent of the debtor.

(12) Retirement funds to the extent that those funds are in a fund or account that is exempt from taxation under section 401, 403, 408, 408A, 414, 457, or 501(a) of the Internal Revenue Code of 1986.

(e) A waiver of an exemption executed in favor of a creditor that holds an unsecured claim against the debtor is unenforceable in a case under this title with respect to such claim against property that the debtor may exempt under subsection (b) of this section. A waiver by the debtor of a power under subsection (f) or (h) of this section to avoid a transfer, under subsection (g) or (i) of this section to exempt property, or under subsection (i) of this section to recover property or to preserve a transfer, is unenforceable in a case under this title

(f)(1) Notwithstanding any waiver of exemptions but subject to paragraph (3), the debtor may avoid the fixing of a lien on an interest of the debtor in property to the extent that such lien impairs an exemption to which the debtor would have been entitled under subsection (b) of this section, if such lien is -

(A) a judicial lien, other than a judicial lien that secures a debt of a kind that is specified in section 523(a)(5); or

(B) a nonpossessory, nonpurchase-money security interest in any -

(i) household furnishings, household goods, wearing apparel, appliances, books, animals, crops, musical instruments, or jewelry that are held primarily for the personal, family, or household use of the debtor or a dependent of the debtor;

(ii) implements, professional books, or tools, of the trade of the debtor or the trade of a dependent of the debtor; or

(iii) professionally prescribed health aids for the debtor or a dependent of the debtor.

(2)(A) For the purposes of this subsection, a lien shall be considered to impair an exemption to the extent that the sum of -

(i) the lien;

(ii) all other liens on the property; and

(iii) the amount of the exemption that the debtor could claim if there were no liens on the property;

exceeds the value that the debtor's interest in the property would have in the absence of any liens.

(B) In the case of a property subject to more than 1 lien, a lien that has been avoided shall not be considered in making the calculation under subparagraph (A) with respect to other liens.

(C) This paragraph shall not apply with respect to a judgment arising out of a mortgage foreclosure.

(3) In a case in which State law that is applicable to the debtor -

(A) permits a person to voluntarily waive a right to claim exemptions under subsection (d) or prohibits a debtor from claiming exemptions under subsection (d); and

(B) either permits the debtor to claim exemptions under State law without limitation in amount, except to the extent that the debtor has permitted the fixing of a consensual lien on any property or prohibits avoidance of a consensual lien on property otherwise eligible to be claimed as exempt property;

the debtor may not avoid the fixing of a lien on an interest of the debtor or a dependent of the debtor in property if the lien is a nonpossessory, nonpurchase-money security interest in implements, professional books, or tools of the trade of the debtor or a dependent of the debtor or farm animals or crops of the debtor or a dependent of the debtor to the extent the value of such implements, professional books, tools of the trade, animals, and crops exceeds $6,225.

(4)(A) Subject to subparagraph (B), for purposes of paragraph (1)(B), the term "household goods" means –

(i) clothing;

(ii) furniture;

(iii) appliances;

(iv) 1 radio;

(v) 1 television;

(vi) 1 VCR;

(vii) linens;

(viii) china;

(ix) crockery;

(x) kitchenware;

(xi) educational materials and educational equipment primarily for the use of minor dependent children of the debtor;

(xii) medical equipment and supplies;

(xiii) furniture exclusively for the use of minor children, or elderly or disabled dependents of the debtor;

(xiv) personal effects (including the toys and hobby equipment of minor dependent children and wedding rings) of the debtor and the dependents of the debtor; and

(xv) 1 personal computer and related equipment.

(B) The term "household goods" does not include –

(i) works of art (unless by or of the debtor, or any relative of the debtor);

(ii) electronic entertainment equipment with a fair market value of more than $650 in the aggregate (except 1 television, 1 radio, and 1 VCR);

(iii) items acquired as antiques with a fair market value of more than $650 in the aggregate;

(iv) jewelry with a fair market value of more than $650 in the aggregate (except wedding rings); and

(v) a computer (except as otherwise provided for in this section), motor vehicle (including a tractor or lawn tractor), boat, or a motorized recreational device, conveyance, vehicle, watercraft, or aircraft.

(g) Notwithstanding sections 550 and 551 of this title, the debtor may exempt under subsection (b) of this section property that the trustee recovers under section 510(c)(2), 542, 543, 550, 551, or 553 of this title, to the extent that the debtor could have exempted such property under subsection (b) of this section if such property had not been transferred, if -

(1)(A) such transfer was not a voluntary transfer of such property by the debtor; and

(B) the debtor did not conceal such property ; or

(2) the debtor could have avoided such transfer under subsection (f)(1)(B) of this section.

(h) The debtor may avoid a transfer of property of the debtor or recover a setoff to the extent that the debtor could have exempted such property under subsection (g)(1) of this section if the trustee had avoided such transfer, if -

(1) such transfer is avoidable by the trustee under section 544, 545, 547, 548, 549, or 724(a) of this title or recoverable by the trustee under section 553 of this title; and

(2) the trustee does not attempt to avoid such transfer.

(i)(1) If the debtor avoids a transfer or recovers a setoff under subsection (f) or (h) of this section, the debtor may recover in the manner prescribed by, and subject to the limitations of, section 550 of this title, the same as if the trustee had avoided such transfer, and may exempt any property so recovered under subsection (b) of this section.

(2) Notwithstanding section 551 of this title, a transfer avoided under section 544, 545, 547, 548, 549, or 724(a) of this title, under subsection (f) or (h) of this section, or property recovered under section 553 of this title, may be preserved for the benefit of the debtor to the extent that the debtor may exempt such property under subsection (g) of this section or paragraph (1) of this subsection.

(j) Notwithstanding subsections (g) and (i) of this section, the debtor may exempt a particular kind of property under subsections (g) and (i) of this section only to the extent that the debtor has exempted less property in value of such kind than that to which the debtor is entitled under subsection (b) of this section.

(k) Property that the debtor exempts under this section is not liable for payment of any administrative expense except -

(1) the aliquot share of the costs and expenses of avoiding a transfer of property that the debtor exempts under subsection (g) of this section, or of recovery of such property, that is attributable to the value of the portion of such property exempted in relation to the value of the property recovered; and

(2) any costs and expenses of avoiding a transfer under subsection (f) or (h) of this section, or of recovery of property under subsection (i)(1) of this section, that the debtor has not paid.

(l) The debtor shall file a list of property that the debtor claims as exempt under subsection (b) of this section. If the debtor does not file such a list, a dependent of the debtor may file such a list, or may claim property as exempt from property of the estate on behalf of the debtor. Unless a party in interest objects, the property claimed as exempt on such list is exempt.

(m) Subject to the limitation in subsection (b), this section shall apply separately with respect to each debtor in a joint case.

(n) For assets in individual retirement accounts described in section 408 or 408A of the Internal Revenue Code of 1986, other than a simplified employee pension under section 408(k) of such Code or a simple retirement account under section 408(p) of such Code, the aggregate value of such assets exempted under this section, without regard to amounts attributable to rollover contributions under section 402(c), 402(e)(6), 403(a)(4), 403(a)(5), and 403(b)(8) of the Internal Revenue Code of 1986, and earnings thereon, shall not exceed $1,245,475 in a case filed by a debtor who is an individual, except that such amount may be increased if the interests of justice so require.

(o) For purposes of subsection (b)(3)(A), and notwithstanding subsection (a), the value of an interest in –

(1) real or personal property that the debtor or a dependent of the debtor uses as a residence;

(2) a cooperative that owns property that the debtor or a dependent of the debtor uses as a residence;

(3) a burial plot for the debtor or a dependent of the debtor; or

(4) real or personal property that the debtor or a dependent of the debtor claims as a homestead;

shall be reduced to the extent that such value is attributable to any portion of any property that the debtor disposed of in the 10-year period ending on the date of the filing of the petition with the intent to hinder, delay, or defraud a creditor and that the debtor could not exempt, or that portion that the debtor could not exempt, under subsection (b), if on such date the debtor had held the property so disposed of.

(p)(1) Except as provided in paragraph (2) of this subsection and sections 544 and 548, as a result of electing under subsection (b)(3)(A) to exempt property under State or local law, a debtor may not exempt any amount of interest that was acquired by the debtor during the 1215-day period preceding the date of the filing of the petition that exceeds in the aggregate $155,675 in value in –

(A) real or personal property that the debtor or a dependent of the debtor uses as a residence;

(B) a cooperative that owns property that the debtor or a dependent of the debtor uses as a residence;

(C) a burial plot for the debtor or a dependent of the debtor; or

(D) real or personal property that the debtor or dependent of the debtor claims as a homestead.

(2)(A) The limitation under paragraph (1) shall not apply to an exemption claimed under subsection (b)(3)(A) by a family farmer for the principal residence of such farmer.

(B) For purposes of paragraph (1), any amount of such interest does not include any interest transferred from a debtor's previous principal residence (which was acquired prior to the beginning of such 1215-day period) into the debtor's current principal residence, if the debtor's previous and current residences are located in the same State.

(q)(1) As a result of electing under subsection (b)(3)(A) to exempt property under State or local law, a debtor may not exempt any amount of an interest in property described in subparagraphs (A), (B), (C), and (D) of subsection (p)(1) which exceeds in the aggregate $155,675 if –

(A) the court determines, after notice and a hearing, that the debtor has been convicted of a felony (as defined in section 3156 of title 18), which under the circumstances, demonstrates that the filing of the case was an abuse of the provisions of this title; or

(B) the debtor owes a debt arising from –

(i) any violation of the Federal securities laws (as defined in section 3(a)(47) of the Securities Exchange Act of 1934), any State securities laws, or any regulation or order issued under Federal securities laws or State securities laws;

(ii) fraud, deceit, or manipulation in a fiduciary capacity or in connection with the purchase or sale of any security registered under section 12 or 15(d) of the Securities Exchange Act of 1934 or under section 6 of the Securities Act of 1933;

(iii) any civil remedy under section 1964 of title 18; or

(iv) any criminal act, intentional tort, or willful or reckless misconduct that caused serious physical injury or death to another individual in the preceding 5 years.

(2) Paragraph (1) shall not apply to the extent the amount of an interest in property described in subparagraphs (A), (B), (C), and (D) of subsection (p)(1) is reasonably necessary for the support of the debtor and any dependent of the debtor.

523. Exceptions to discharge

(a) A discharge under section 727, 1141, 1228(a), 1228(b), or 1328(b) of this title does not discharge an individual debtor from any debt -

(1) for a tax or a customs duty -

(A) of the kind and for the periods specified in section 507(a)(3) or 507(a)(8) of this title, whether or not a claim for such tax was filed or allowed;

(B) with respect to which a return, or equivalent report or notice, if required -

(i) was not filed or given; or

(ii) was filed or given after the date on which such return, report, or notice was last due, under applicable law or under any extension, and after two years before the date of the filing of the petition; or

(C) with respect to which the debtor made a fraudulent return or willfully attempted in any manner to evade or defeat such tax;

(2) for money, property, services, or an extension, renewal, or refinancing of credit, to the extent obtained by -

(A) false pretenses, a false representation, or actual fraud, other than a statement respecting the debtor's or an insider's financial condition;

(B) use of a statement in writing -

(i) that is materially false;

(ii) respecting the debtor's or an insider's financial condition;

(iii) on which the creditor to whom the debtor is liable for such money, property, services, or credit reasonably relied; and

(iv) that the debtor caused to be made or published with intent to deceive; or

(C)(i) for purposes of subparagraph (A) –

(I) consumer debts owed to a single creditor and aggregating more than $650 for luxury goods or services incurred by an individual debtor on or within 90 days before the order for relief under this title are presumed to be nondischargeable; and

(II) cash advances aggregating more than $925 that are extensions of consumer credit under an open end credit plan obtained by an individual debtor on or within 70 days before the order for relief under this title, are presumed to be nondischargeable; and

(ii) for purposes of this subparagraph –

(I) the terms "consumer", "credit", and "open end credit plan" have the same meanings as in section 103 of the Truth in Lending Act; and

(II) the term "luxury goods or services" does not include goods or services reasonably necessary for the support or maintenance of the debtor or a dependent of the debtor;

(3) neither listed nor scheduled under section 521(a)(1) of this title, with the name, if known to the debtor, of the creditor to whom such debt is owed, in time to permit -

(A) if such debt is not of a kind specified in paragraph (2), (4), or (6) of this subsection, timely filing of a proof of claim, unless such creditor had notice or actual knowledge of the case in time for such timely filing; or

(B) if such debt is of a kind specified in paragraph (2), (4), or (6) of this subsection, timely filing of a proof of claim and timely request for a determination of dischargeability of such debt under one of such paragraphs, unless such creditor had notice or actual knowledge of the case in time for such timely filing and request;

(4) for fraud or defalcation while acting in a fiduciary capacity, embezzlement, or larceny;

(5) for a domestic support obligation;

(6) for willful and malicious injury by the debtor to another entity or to the property of another entity;

(7) to the extent such debt is for a fine, penalty, or forfeiture payable to and for the benefit of a governmental unit, and is not compensation for actual pecuniary loss, other than a tax penalty -

(A) relating to a tax of a kind not specified in paragraph (1) of this subsection; or

(B) imposed with respect to a transaction or event that occurred before three years before the date of the filing of the petition;

(8) unless excepting such debt from discharge under this paragraph would impose an undue hardship on the debtor and the debtor's dependents, for –

(A)(i) an educational benefit overpayment or loan made, insured, or guaranteed by a governmental unit, or made under any program funded in whole or in part by a governmental unit or nonprofit institution; or

(ii) an obligation to repay funds received as an educational benefit, scholarship, or stipend; or

(B) any other educational loan that is a qualified education loan, as defined in section 221(d)(1) of the Internal Revenue Code of 1986, incurred by a debtor who is an individual;

(9) for death or personal injury caused by the debtor's operation of a motor vehicle, vessel, or aircraft if such operation was unlawful because the debtor was intoxicated from using alcohol, a drug, or another substance;

(10) that was or could have been listed or scheduled by the debtor in a prior case concerning the debtor under this title or under the Bankruptcy Act in which the debtor waived discharge, or was denied a discharge under section 727(a)(2), (3), (4), (5), (6), or (7) of this title, or under section 14c(1), (2), (3), (4), (6), or (7) of such Act;

(11) provided in any final judgment, unreviewable order, or consent order or decree entered in any court of the United States or of any State, issued by a Federal depository institutions regulatory agency, or contained in any settlement agreement entered into by the debtor, arising from any act of fraud or defalcation while acting in a fiduciary capacity committed with respect to any depository institution or insured credit union;

(12) for malicious or reckless failure to fulfill any commitment by the debtor to a Federal depository institutions regulatory agency to maintain the capital of an insured depository institution, except that this paragraph shall not extend any such commitment which would otherwise be terminated due to any act of such agency;

(13) for any payment of an order of restitution issued under title 18, United States Code;

(14) incurred to pay a tax to the United States that would be nondischargeable pursuant to paragraph (1);

(14A) incurred to pay a tax to a governmental unit, other than the United States, that would be nondischargeable under paragraph (1);

(14B) incurred to pay fines or penalties imposed under Federal election law;

(15) to a spouse, former spouse, or child of the debtor and not of the kind described in paragraph (5) that is incurred by the debtor in the course of a divorce or separation or in connection with a separation agreement, divorce decree or other order of a court of record, or a determination made in accordance with State or territorial law by a governmental unit;

(16) for a fee or assessment that becomes due and payable after the order for relief to a membership association with respect to the debtor's interest in a unit that has condominium ownership, in a share of a cooperative corporation, or a lot in a homeowners association, for as long as the debtor or the trustee has a legal, equitable, or possessory ownership interest in such unit, such corporation, or such lot, but nothing in this paragraph shall except from discharge the debt of a debtor for a membership association fee or assessment for a period arising before entry of the order for relief in a pending or subsequent bankruptcy case;

(17) for a fee imposed on a prisoner by any court for the filing of a case, motion, complaint, or appeal, or for other costs and expenses assessed with respect to such filing, regardless of an assertion of poverty by the debtor under subsection (b) or (f)(2) of section 1915 of title 28 (or a similar non-Federal law), or the debtor's status as a prisoner, as defined in section 1915(h) of title 28 (or a similar non-Federal law);

(18) owed to a pension, profit-sharing, stock bonus, or other plan established under section 401, 403, 408, 408A, 414, 457, or 501(c) of the Internal Revenue Code of 1986, under –

(A) a loan permitted under section 408(b)(1) of the Employee Retirement Income Security Act of 1974, or subject to section 72(p) of the Internal Revenue Code of 1986; or

(B) a loan from a thrift savings plan permitted under subchapter III of chapter 84 of title 5, that satisfies the requirements of section 8433(g) of such title;

but nothing in this paragraph may be construed to provide that any loan made under a governmental plan under section 414(d), or a contract or account under section 403(b), of the Internal Revenue Code of 1986 constitutes a claim or a debt under this title; or

(19) that -

(A) is for –

(i) the violation of any of the Federal securities laws (as that term is defined in section 3(a)(47) of the Securities Exchange Act of 1934 [15 USC § 78c(a)(47)]), any of the State securities laws, or any regulation or order issued under such Federal or State securities laws; or

(ii) common law fraud, deceit, or manipulation in connection with the purchase or sale of any security; and

(B) results, before, on, or after the date on which the petition was filed, from -

(i) any judgment, order, consent order, or decree entered in any Federal or State judicial or administrative proceeding;

(ii) any settlement agreement entered into by the debtor; or

(iii) any court or administrative order for any damages, fine, penalty, citation, restitutionary payment, disgorgement payment, attorney fee, cost, or other payment owed by the debtor.

For purposes of this subsection, the term "return" means a return that satisfies the requirements of applicable nonbankruptcy law (including applicable filing requirements). Such term includes a return prepared pursuant to section 6020(a) of the Internal Revenue Code of 1986, or similar State or local law, or a written stipulation to a judgment or a final order entered by a nonbankruptcy tribunal, but does not include a return made pursuant to section 6020(b) of the Internal Revenue Code of 1986, or a similar State or local law.

(b) Notwithstanding subsection (a) of this section, a debt that was excepted from discharge under subsection (a)(1), (a)(3), or (a)(8) of this section, under section 17a(1), 17a(3), or 17a(5) of the Bankruptcy Act, under section 439A of the Higher Education Act of 1965, or under section 733(g) of the Public Health Service Act in a prior case concerning the debtor under this title, or under the Bankruptcy Act, is dischargeable in a case under this title unless, by the terms of subsection (a) of this section, such debt is not dischargeable in the case under this title.

(c)(1) Except as provided in subsection (a)(3)(B) of this section, the debtor shall be discharged from a debt of a kind specified in paragraph (2), (4), or (6) of subsection (a) of this section, unless, on request of the creditor to whom such debt is owed, and after notice and a hearing, the court determines such debt to be excepted from discharge under paragraph (2), (4), or (6), as the case may be, of subsection (a) of this section.

(2) Paragraph (1) shall not apply in the case of a Federal depository institutions regulatory agency seeking, in its capacity as conservator, receiver, or liquidating agent for an insured depository institution, to recover a debt described in subsection (a)(2), (a)(4), (a)(6), or (a)(11) owed to such institution by an institution-affiliated party unless the receiver, conservator, or liquidating agent was appointed in time to reasonably comply, or for a Federal depository institutions regulatory agency acting in its corporate capacity as a successor

to such receiver, conservator, or liquidating agent to reasonably comply, with subsection (a)(3)(B) as a creditor of such institution-affiliated party with respect to such debt.

(d) If a creditor requests a determination of dischargeability of a consumer debt under subsection (a)(2) of this section, and such debt is discharged, the court shall grant judgment in favor of the debtor for the costs of, and a reasonable attorney's fee for, the proceeding if the court finds that the position of the creditor was not substantially justified, except that the court shall not award such costs and fees if special circumstances would make the award unjust.

(e) Any institution-affiliated party of an insured depository institution shall be considered to be acting in a fiduciary capacity with respect to the purposes of subsection (a) (4) or (11).

524. Effect of discharge

(a) A discharge in a case under this title -

(1) voids any judgment at any time obtained, to the extent that such judgment is a determination of the personal liability of the debtor with respect to any debt discharged under section 727, 944, 1141, 1228 or 1328 of this title, whether or not discharge of such debt is waived;

(2) operates as an injunction against the commencement or continuation of an action, the employment of process, or an act, to collect, recover or offset any such debt as a personal liability of the debtor, whether or not discharge of such debt is waived; and

(3) operates as an injunction against the commencement or continuation of an action, the employment of process, or an act, to collect or recover from, or offset against, property of the debtor of the kind specified in section 541(a)(2) of this title that is acquired after the commencement of the case, on account of any allowable community claim, except a community claim that is excepted from discharge under section 523, 1228(a)(1), or 1328(a)(1), or that would be so excepted, determined in accordance with the provisions of sections 523(c) and 523(d) of this title, in a case concerning the debtor's spouse commenced on the date of the filing of the petition in the case concerning the debtor, whether or not discharge of the debt based on such community claim is waived.

(b) Subsection (a)(3) of this section does not apply if –

(1)(A) the debtor's spouse is a debtor in a case under this title, or a bankrupt or a debtor in a case under the Bankruptcy Act, commenced within six years of the date of the filing of the petition in the case concerning the debtor; and

(B) the court does not grant the debtor's spouse a discharge in such case concerning the debtor's spouse; or

(2)(A) the court would not grant the debtor's spouse a discharge in a case under chapter 7 of this title concerning such spouse commenced on the date of the filing of the petition in the case concerning the debtor; and

(B) a determination that the court would not so grant such discharge is made by the bankruptcy court within the time and in the manner provided for a determination under section 727 of this title of whether a debtor is granted a discharge.

(c) An agreement between a holder of a claim and the debtor, the consideration for which, in whole or in part, is based on a debt that is dischargeable in a case under this title is enforceable only to any extent enforceable under applicable nonbankruptcy law, whether or not discharge of such debt is waived, only if –

(1) such agreement was made before the granting of the discharge under section 727, 1141, 1228, or 1328 of this title;

(2) the debtor received the disclosures described in subsection (k) at or before the time at which the debtor signed the agreement;

(3) such agreement has been filed with the court and, if applicable, accompanied by a declaration or an affidavit of the attorney that represented the debtor during the course of negotiating an agreement under this subsection, which states that –

(A) such agreement represents a fully informed and voluntary agreement by the debtor;

(B) such agreement does not impose an undue hardship on the debtor or a dependent of the debtor; and

(C) the attorney fully advised the debtor of the legal effect and consequences of –

(i) an agreement of the kind specified in this subsection; and

(ii) any default under such an agreement;

(4) the debtor has not rescinded such agreement at any time prior to discharge or within sixty days after such agreement is filed with the court, whichever occurs later, by giving notice of rescission to the holder of such claim;

(5) the provisions of subsection (d) of this section have been complied with; and

(6)(A) in a case concerning an individual who was not represented by an attorney during the course of negotiating an agreement under this subsection, the court approves such agreement as –

(i) not imposing an undue hardship on the debtor or a dependent of the debtor; and

(ii) in the best interest of the debtor.

(B) Subparagraph (A) shall not apply to the extent that such debt is a consumer debt secured by real property.

(d) In a case concerning an individual, when the court has determined whether to grant or not to grant a discharge under section 727, 1141, 1228, or 1328 of this title, the court may hold a hearing at which the debtor shall appear in person. At any such hearing, the court shall inform the debtor that a discharge has been granted or the reason why a discharge has not been granted. If a discharge has been granted and if the debtor desires to make an agreement of the kind specified in subsection (c) of this section and was not represented by an attorney during the course of negotiating such agreement, then the court shall hold a hearing at which the debtor shall appear in person and at such hearing the court shall –

(1) inform the debtor –

(A) that such an agreement is not required under this title, under nonbankruptcy law, or under any agreement not made in accordance with the provisions of subsection (c) of this section; and

(B) of the legal effect and consequences of –

(i) an agreement of the kind specified in subsection (c) of this section; and

(ii) a default under such an agreement; and

(2) determine whether the agreement that the debtor desires to make complies with the requirements of subsection (c)(6) of this section, if the consideration for such agreement is based in whole or in part on a consumer debt that is not secured by real property of the debtor.

(e) Except as provided in subsection (a)(3) of this section, discharge of a debt of the debtor does not affect the liability of any other entity on, or the property of any other entity for, such debt.

(f) Nothing contained in subsection (c) or (d) of this section prevents a debtor from voluntarily repaying any debt.

(g)(1)(A) After notice and hearing, a court that enters an order confirming a plan of reorganization under chapter 11 may issue, in connection with such order, an injunction in accordance with this subsection to supplement the injunctive effect of a discharge under this section.

(B) An injunction may be issued under subparagraph (A) to enjoin entities from taking legal action for the purpose of directly or indirectly collecting, recovering, or receiving payment or recovery with respect to any claim or demand that, under a plan of reorganization, is to be paid in whole or in part by a trust described in paragraph (2)(B)(i), except such legal actions as are expressly allowed by the injunction, the confirmation order, or the plan of reorganization.

(2)(A) Subject to subsection (h), if the requirements of subparagraph (B) are met at the time an injunction described in paragraph (1) is entered, then after entry of such injunction, any proceeding that involves the validity, application, construction, or modification of such injunction, or of this subsection with respect to such injunction, may be commenced only in the district court in which such injunction was entered, and such court shall have exclusive jurisdiction over any such proceeding without regard to the amount in controversy.

(B) The requirements of this subparagraph are that –

(i) the injunction is to be implemented in connection with a trust that, pursuant to the plan of reorganization –

(I) is to assume the liabilities of a debtor which at the time of entry of the order for relief has been named as a defendant in personal injury, wrongful death, or property-damage actions seeking recovery for damages allegedly caused by the presence of, or exposure to, asbestos or asbestos-containing products;

(II) is to be funded in whole or in part by the securities of 1 or more debtors involved in such plan and by the obligation of such debtor or debtors to make future payments, including dividends;

(III) is to own, or by the exercise of rights granted under such plan would be entitled to own if specified contingencies occur, a majority of the voting shares of –

(aa) each such debtor;

(bb) the parent corporation of each such debtor; or

(cc) a subsidiary of each such debtor that is also a debtor; and

(IV) is to use its assets or income to pay claims and demands; and

(ii) subject to subsection (h), the court determines that –

(I) the debtor is likely to be subject to substantial future demands for payment arising out of the same or similar conduct or events that gave rise to the claims that are addressed by the injunction;

(II) the actual amounts, numbers, and timing of such future demands cannot be determined;

(III) pursuit of such demands outside the procedures prescribed by such plan is likely to threaten the plan's purpose to deal equitably with claims and future demands;

(IV) as part of the process of seeking confirmation of such plan-

(aa) the terms of the injunction proposed to be issued under paragraph (1)(A), including any provisions barring actions against third parties pursuant to paragraph (4)(A), are set out in such plan and in any disclosure statement supporting the plan; and

(bb) a separate class or classes of the claimants whose claims are to be addressed by a trust described in clause (i) is established and votes, by at least 75 percent of those voting, in favor of the plan; and

(V) subject to subsection (h), pursuant to court orders or otherwise, the trust will operate through mechanisms such as structured, periodic, or supplemental payments, pro rata distributions, matrices, or periodic review of estimates of the numbers and values of present claims and future demands, or other comparable mechanisms, that provide reasonable assurance that the trust will value, and be in a financial position to pay, present claims and future demands that involve similar claims in substantially the same manner.

(3)(A) If the requirements of paragraph (2)(B) are met and the order confirming the plan of reorganization was issued or affirmed by the district court that has jurisdiction over the reorganization case, then after the time for appeal of the order that issues or affirms the plan –

(i) the injunction shall be valid and enforceable and may not be revoked or modified by any court except through appeal in accordance with paragraph (6);

(ii) no entity that pursuant to such plan or thereafter becomes a direct or indirect transferee of, or successor to any assets of, a debtor or trust that is the subject of the injunction shall be liable with respect to any claim or demand made against such entity by reason of its becoming such a transferee or successor; and

(iii) no entity that pursuant to such plan or thereafter makes a loan to such a debtor or trust or to such a successor or transferee shall, by reason of making the loan, be liable with respect to any claim or demand made against such entity, nor shall any pledge of assets made in connection with such a loan be upset or impaired for that reason;

(B) Subparagraph (A) shall not be construed to –

(i) imply that an entity described in subparagraph (A)(ii) or (iii) would, if this paragraph were not applicable, necessarily be liable to any entity by reason of any of the acts described in subparagraph (A);

(ii) relieve any such entity of the duty to comply with, or of liability under, any Federal or State law regarding the making of a fraudulent conveyance in a transaction described in subparagraph (A)(ii) or (iii); or

(iii) relieve a debtor of the debtor's obligation to comply with the terms of the plan of reorganization, or affect the power of the court to exercise its authority under sections 1141 and 1142 to compel the debtor to do so.

(4)(A)(i) Subject to subparagraph (B), an injunction described in paragraph (1) shall be valid and enforceable against all entities that it addresses.

(ii) Notwithstanding the provisions of section 524(e), such an injunction may bar any action directed against a third party who is identifiable from the terms of such injunction (by name or as part of an identifiable group) and is alleged to be directly or indirectly liable for the conduct of, claims against, or demands on the debtor to the extent such alleged liability of such third party arises by reason of –

(I) the third party's ownership of a financial interest in the debtor, a past or present affiliate of the debtor, or a predecessor in interest of the debtor;

(II) the third party's involvement in the management of the debtor or a predecessor in interest of the debtor, or service as an officer, director or employee of the debtor or a related party;

(III) the third party's provision of insurance to the debtor or a related party; or

(IV) the third party's involvement in a transaction changing the corporate structure, or in a loan or other financial transaction affecting the financial condition, of the debtor or a related party, including but not limited to –

(aa) involvement in providing financing (debt or equity), or advice to an entity involved in such a transaction; or

(bb) acquiring or selling a financial interest in an entity as part of such a transaction.

(iii) As used in this subparagraph, the term "related party" means –

(I) a past or present affiliate of the debtor;

(II) a predecessor in interest of the debtor; or

(III) any entity that owned a financial interest in –

(aa) the debtor;

(bb) a past or present affiliate of the debtor, or

(cc) a predecessor in interest of the debtor.

(B) Subject to subsection (h), if, under a plan of reorganization, a kind of demand described in such plan is to be paid in whole or in part by a trust described in paragraph (2)(B)(i) in connection with which an injunction described in paragraph (1) is to be implemented, then such injunction shall be valid and enforceable with respect to a demand of such kind made, after such plan is confirmed against the debtor or debtors involved, or against a third party described in subparagraph (A)(ii), if –

(i) as part of the proceedings leading to issuance of such injunction, the court appoints a legal representative for the purpose of protecting the rights of persons that might subsequently assert demands of such kind, and

(ii) the court determines, before entering the order confirming such plan, that identifying such debtor or debtors, or such third party (by name or as part of an identifiable group), in such injunction with respect to such demands for purposes of this subparagraph is fair and equitable with respect to the persons that might subsequently assert such demands, in light of the benefits provided, or to be provided, to such trust on behalf of such debtor or debtors or such third party.

(5) In this subsection, the term "demand" means a demand for payment, present or future, that –

(A) was not a claim during the proceedings leading to the confirmation of a plan of reorganization;

(B) arises out of the same or similar conduct or events that gave rise to the claims addressed by the injunction issued under paragraph (1); and

(C) pursuant to the plan, is to be paid by a trust described in paragraph (2)(B)(i).

(6) Paragraph (3)(A)(i) does not bar an action taken by or at the direction of an appellate court on appeal of an injunction issued under paragraph (1) or of the order of confirmation that relates to the injunction.

(7) This subsection does not affect the operation of section 1144 or the power of the district court to refer a proceeding under section 157 of title 28 or any reference of a proceeding made prior to the date of the enactment of this subsection.

(h) Application to Existing Injunctions.- For purposes of subsection (g)-

(1) subject to paragraph (2), if an injunction of the kind described in subsection (g)(1)(B) was issued before the date of the enactment of this Act, as part of a plan of reorganization confirmed by an order entered before such date, then the injunction shall be considered to meet the requirements of subsection (g)(2)(B) for purposes of subsection (g)(2)(A), and to satisfy subsection (g)(4)(A)(ii), if –

(A) the court determined at the time the plan was confirmed that the plan was fair and equitable in accordance with the requirements of section 1129(b);

(B) as part of the proceedings leading to issuance of such injunction and confirmation of such plan, the court had appointed a legal representative for the purpose of protecting the rights of persons that might subsequently assert demands described in subsection (g)(4)(B) with respect to such plan; and

(C) such legal representative did not object to confirmation of such plan or issuance of such injunction; and

(2) for purposes of paragraph (1), if a trust described in subsection (g)(2)(B)(i) is subject to a court order on the date of the enactment of this Act staying such trust from settling or paying further claims –

(A) the requirements of subsection (g)(2)(B)(ii)(V) shall not apply with respect to such trust until such stay is lifted or dissolved; and

(B) if such trust meets such requirements on the date such stay is lifted or dissolved, such trust shall be considered to have met such requirements continuously from the date of the enactment of this Act.

(i) The willful failure of a creditor to credit payments received under a plan confirmed under this title, unless the order confirming the plan is revoked, the plan is in default, or the creditor has not received payments required to be made under the plan in the manner required by the plan (including crediting the amounts required under the plan), shall constitute a violation of an injunction under subsection (a)(2) if the act of the creditor to collect and failure to credit payments in the manner required by the plan caused material injury to the debtor.

(j) Subsection (a)(2) does not operate as an injunction against an act by a creditor that is the holder of a secured claim, if –

(1) such creditor retains a security interest in real property that is the principal residence of the debtor;

(2) such act is in the ordinary course of business between the creditor and the debtor; and

(3) such act is limited to seeking or obtaining periodic payments associated with a valid security interest in lieu of pursuit of in rem relief to enforce the lien.

(k)(1) The disclosures required under subsection (c)(2) shall consist of the disclosure statement described in paragraph (3), completed as required in that paragraph, together with the agreement specified in subsection (c), statement, declaration, motion and order described, respectively, in paragraphs (4) through (8), and shall be the only disclosures required in connection with entering into such agreement.

(2) Disclosures made under paragraph (1) shall be made clearly and conspicuously and in writing. The terms "Amount Reaffirmed" and "Annual Percentage Rate" shall be disclosed more conspicuously than other terms, data or information provided in connection with this disclosure, except that the phrases "Before agreeing to reaffirm a debt, review these important disclosures" and "Summary of Reaffirmation Agreement" may be equally conspicuous. Disclosures may be made in a different order and may use terminology different from that set forth in paragraphs (2) through (8), except that the terms "Amount Reaffirmed" and "Annual Percentage Rate" must be used where indicated.

(3) The disclosure statement required under this paragraph shall consist of the following:

(A) The statement: "Part A: Before agreeing to reaffirm a debt, review these important disclosures:";

(B) Under the heading "Summary of Reaffirmation Agreement", the statement: "This Summary is made pursuant to the requirements of the Bankruptcy Code";

(C) The "Amount Reaffirmed", using that term, which shall be –

(i) the total amount of debt that the debtor agrees to reaffirm by entering into an agreement of the kind specified in subsection (c), and

(ii) the total of any fees and costs accrued as of the date of the disclosure statement, related to such total amount.

(D) In conjunction with the disclosure of the "Amount Reaffirmed", the statements –

(i) "The amount of debt you have agreed to reaffirm"; and

(ii) "Your credit agreement may obligate you to pay additional amounts which may come due after the date of this disclosure. Consult your credit agreement.".

(E) The "Annual Percentage Rate", using that term, which shall be disclosed as –

(i) if, at the time the petition is filed, the debt is an extension of credit under an open end credit plan, as the terms "credit" and "open end credit plan" are defined in section 103 of the Truth in Lending Act, then –

(I) the annual percentage rate determined under paragraphs (5) and (6) of section 127(b) of the Truth in Lending Act, as applicable, as disclosed to the debtor in the most recent periodic statement prior to entering into an agreement of the kind specified in subsection (c) or, if no such periodic statement has been given to the debtor during the prior 6 months, the annual percentage rate as it would have been so disclosed at the time the disclosure statement is given to the debtor, or to the extent this annual percentage rate is not readily available or not applicable, then

(II) the simple interest rate applicable to the amount reaffirmed as of the date the disclosure statement is given to the debtor, or if different simple interest rates apply to different balances, the simple interest rate applicable to each such balance, identifying the amount of each such balance included in the amount reaffirmed, or

(III) if the entity making the disclosure elects, to disclose the annual percentage rate under subclause (I) and the simple interest rate under subclause (II); or

(ii) if, at the time the petition is filed, the debt is an extension of credit other than under an open end credit plan, as the terms "credit" and "open end credit plan" are defined in section 103 of the Truth in Lending Act, then –

(I) the annual percentage rate under section 128(a)(4) of the Truth in Lending Act, as disclosed to the debtor in the most recent disclosure statement given to the debtor prior to the entering into an agreement of the kind specified in subsection (c) with respect to the debt, or, if no such disclosure statement was given to the debtor, the annual percentage rate as it would have been so disclosed at the time the disclosure statement is given to the debtor, or to the extent this annual percentage rate is not readily available or not applicable, then

(II) the simple interest rate applicable to the amount reaffirmed as of the date the disclosure statement is given to the debtor, or if different simple interest rates apply to different balances, the simple interest rate applicable to each such balance, identifying the amount of such balance included in the amount reaffirmed, or

(III) if the entity making the disclosure elects, to disclose the annual percentage rate under (I) and the simple interest rate under (II).

(F) If the underlying debt transaction was disclosed as a variable rate transaction on the most recent disclosure given under the Truth in Lending Act, by stating "The interest rate on your loan may be a variable interest rate which changes from time to time, so that the annual percentage rate disclosed here may be higher or lower.".

(G) If the debt is secured by a security interest which has not been waived in whole or in part or determined to be void by a final order of the court at the time of the disclosure, by disclosing that a security interest or lien in goods or property is asserted over some or all of the debts the debtor is reaffirming and listing the items and their original purchase price that are subject to the asserted security interest, or if not a purchase-money security interest then listing by items or types and the original amount of the loan.

(H) At the election of the creditor, a statement of the repayment schedule using 1 or a combination of the following –

(i) by making the statement: "Your first payment in the amount of $XXX is due on XXX but the future payment amount may be different. Consult your reaffirmation agreement or credit agreement, as applicable.", and stating the amount of the first payment and the due date of that payment in the places provided;

(ii) by making the statement: "Your payment schedule will be:", and describing the repayment schedule with the number, amount, and due dates or period of payments scheduled to repay the debts reaffirmed to the extent then known by the disclosing party; or

(iii) by describing the debtor's repayment obligations with reasonable specificity to the extent then known by the disclosing party.

(I) The following statement: "Note: When this disclosure refers to what a creditor "may" do, it does not use the word "may" to give the creditor specific permission. The word "may" is used to tell you what might occur if the law permits the creditor to take the action. If you have questions about your reaffirming a debt or what the law requires, consult with the attorney who helped you negotiate this agreement reaffirming a debt. If you don't have an attorney helping you, the judge will explain the effect of your reaffirming a debt when the hearing on the reaffirmation agreement is held.".

(J)(i) The following additional statements:

"Reaffirming a debt is a serious financial decision. The law requires you to take certain steps to make sure the decision is in your best interest. If these steps are not completed, the reaffirmation agreement is not effective, even though you have signed it.

"1. Read the disclosures in this Part A carefully. Consider the decision to reaffirm carefully. Then, if you want to reaffirm, sign the reaffirmation agreement in Part B (or you may use a separate agreement you and your creditor agree on).

"2. Complete and sign Part D and be sure you can afford to make the payments you are agreeing to make and have received a copy of the disclosure statement and a completed and signed reaffirmation agreement.

"3. If you were represented by an attorney during the negotiation of your reaffirmation agreement, the attorney must have signed the certification in Part C.

"4. If you were not represented by an attorney during the negotiation of your reaffirmation agreement, you must have completed and signed Part E.

"5. The original of this disclosure must be filed with the court by you or your creditor. If a separate reaffirmation agreement (other than the one in Part B) has been signed, it must be attached.

"6. If you were represented by an attorney during the negotiation of your reaffirmation agreement, your reaffirmation agreement becomes effective upon filing with the court unless the reaffirmation is presumed to be an undue hardship as explained in Part D.

"7. If you were not represented by an attorney during the negotiation of your reaffirmation agreement, it will not be effective unless the court approves it. The court will notify you of the hearing on your reaffirmation agreement. You must attend this hearing in bankruptcy court where the judge will review your reaffirmation agreement. The bankruptcy court must approve your reaffirmation agreement as consistent with your best interests, except that no court approval is required if your reaffirmation agreement is for a consumer debt secured by a mortgage, deed of trust, security deed, or other lien on your real property, like your home.

"Your right to rescind (cancel) your reaffirmation agreement. You may rescind (cancel) your reaffirmation agreement at any time before the bankruptcy court enters a discharge order, or before the expiration of the 60-day period that begins on the date your reaffirmation agreement is filed with the court, whichever occurs later. To rescind (cancel) your reaffirmation agreement, you must notify the creditor that your reaffirmation agreement is rescinded (or canceled).

"What are your obligations if you reaffirm the debt? A reaffirmed debt remains your personal legal obligation. It is not discharged in your bankruptcy case. That means that if you default on your reaffirmed debt after your bankruptcy case is over, your creditor may be able to take your property or your wages. Otherwise, your obligations will be determined by the reaffirmation agreement which may have changed the terms of the original agreement. For example, if you are reaffirming an open end credit agreement, the creditor may be permitted by that agreement or applicable law to change the terms of that agreement in the future under certain conditions.

"Are you required to enter into a reaffirmation agreement by any law? No, you are not required to reaffirm a debt by any law. Only agree to reaffirm a debt if it is in your best interest. Be sure you can afford the payments you agree to make.

"What if your creditor has a security interest or lien? Your bankruptcy discharge does not eliminate any lien on your property. A "lien" is often referred to as a security interest, deed of trust, mortgage or security deed. Even if you do not reaffirm and your personal liability on the debt is discharged, because of the lien your creditor may still have the right to take the property securing the lien if you do not pay the debt or default on it. If the lien is on an item of personal property that is exempt under your State's law or that the trustee has abandoned, you may be able to redeem the item rather than reaffirm the debt. To redeem, you must make a single payment to the creditor equal to the amount of the allowed secured claim, as agreed by the parties or determined by the court.".

(ii) In the case of a reaffirmation under subsection (m)(2), numbered paragraph 6 in the disclosures required by clause (i) of this subparagraph shall read as follows:

"6. If you were represented by an attorney during the negotiation of your reaffirmation agreement, your reaffirmation agreement becomes effective upon filing with the court.".

(4) The form of such agreement required under this paragraph shall consist of the following:

"Part B: Reaffirmation Agreement. I (we) agree to reaffirm the debts arising under the credit agreement described below.

"Brief description of credit agreement:

"Description of any changes to the credit agreement made as part of this reaffirmation agreement:

"Signature: Date:

"Borrower:

"Co-borrower, if also reaffirming these debts:

"Accepted by creditor:

"Date of creditor acceptance:".

(5) The declaration shall consist of the following:

(A) The following certification:

"Part C: Certification by Debtor's Attorney (If Any).

"I hereby certify that (1) this agreement represents a fully informed and voluntary agreement by the debtor; (2) this agreement does not impose an undue hardship on the debtor or any dependent of the debtor; and (3) I have fully advised the debtor of the legal effect and consequences of this agreement and any default under this agreement.

"Signature of Debtor's Attorney: Date:".

(B) If a presumption of undue hardship has been established with respect to such agreement, such certification shall state that, in the opinion of the attorney, the debtor is able to make the payment.

(C) In the case of a reaffirmation agreement under subsection (m)(2), subparagraph (B) is not applicable.

(6)(A) The statement in support of such agreement, which the debtor shall sign and date prior to filing with the court, shall consist of the following:

"Part D: Debtor's Statement in Support of Reaffirmation Agreement.

"1. I believe this reaffirmation agreement will not impose an undue hardship on my dependents or me. I can afford to make the payments on the reaffirmed debt because my monthly income (take home pay plus any other income received) is $XXX, and my actual current monthly expenses including monthly payments on post-bankruptcy debt and other reaffirmation agreements total $XXX, leaving $XXX to make the required payments on this reaffirmed debt. I understand that if my income less my monthly expenses does not leave enough to make the payments, this reaffirmation agreement is presumed to be an undue hardship on me and must be reviewed by the court. However, this presumption may be overcome if I explain to the satisfaction of the court how I can afford to make the payments here: XXX.

"2. I received a copy of the Reaffirmation Disclosure Statement in Part A and a completed and signed reaffirmation agreement.".

(B) Where the debtor is represented by an attorney and is reaffirming a debt owed to a creditor defined in section 19(b)(1)(A)(iv) of the Federal Reserve Act, the statement of support of the reaffirmation agreement, which the debtor shall sign and date prior to filing with the court, shall consist of the following:

"I believe this reaffirmation agreement is in my financial interest. I can afford to make the payments on the reaffirmed debt. I received a copy of the Reaffirmation Disclosure Statement in Part A and a completed and signed reaffirmation agreement.".

(7) The motion that may be used if approval of such agreement by the court is required in order for it to be effective, shall be signed and dated by the movant and shall consist of the following:

"Part E: Motion for Court Approval (To be completed only if the debtor is not represented by an attorney.). I (we), the debtor(s), affirm the following to be true and correct:

"I am not represented by an attorney in connection with this reaffirmation agreement.

"I believe this reaffirmation agreement is in my best interest based on the income and expenses I have disclosed in my Statement in Support of this reaffirmation agreement, and because (provide any additional relevant reasons the court should consider):

"Therefore, I ask the court for an order approving this reaffirmation agreement.".

(8) The court order, which may be used to approve such agreement, shall consist of the following:

"Court Order: The court grants the debtor's motion and approves the reaffirmation agreement described above.".

(l) Notwithstanding any other provision of this title the following shall apply:

(1) A creditor may accept payments from a debtor before and after the filing of an agreement of the kind specified in subsection (c) with the court.

(2) A creditor may accept payments from a debtor under such agreement that the creditor believes in good faith to be effective.

(3) The requirements of subsections (c)(2) and (k) shall be satisfied if disclosures required under those subsections are given in good faith.

(m)(1) Until 60 days after an agreement of the kind specified in subsection (c) is filed with the court (or such additional period as the court, after notice and a hearing and for cause, orders before the expiration of such period), it shall be presumed that such agreement is an undue hardship on the debtor if the debtor's monthly income less the debtor's monthly expenses as shown on the debtor's completed and signed statement in support of such agreement required under subsection (k)(6)(A) is less than the scheduled payments on the reaffirmed debt. This presumption shall be reviewed by the court. The presumption may be rebutted in writing by the debtor if the statement includes an explanation that identifies additional sources of funds to make the payments as agreed upon under the terms of such agreement. If the presumption is not rebutted to the satisfaction of the court, the court may disapprove such agreement. No agreement shall be disapproved without notice and a hearing to the debtor and creditor, and such hearing shall be concluded before the entry of the debtor's discharge.

(2) This subsection does not apply to reaffirmation agreements where the creditor is a credit union, as defined in section 19(b)(1)(A)(iv) of the Federal Reserve Act.

525. Protection against discriminatory treatment

(a) Except as provided in the Perishable Agricultural Commodities Act, 1930, the Packers and Stockyards Act, 1921, and section 1 of the Act entitled "An Act making appropriations for the Department of Agriculture for the fiscal year ending June 30, 1944, and for other purposes," approved July 12, 1943, a governmental unit may not deny, revoke, suspend, or refuse to renew a license, permit, charter, franchise, or other similar grant to, condition such a grant to, discriminate with respect to such a grant against, deny employment to, terminate the employment of, or discriminate with respect to employment against, a person that is or has been a debtor under this title or a bankrupt or a debtor under the

Bankruptcy Act, or another person with whom such bankrupt or debtor has been associated, solely because such bankrupt or debtor is or has been a debtor under this title or a bankrupt or debtor under the Bankruptcy Act, has been insolvent before the commencement of the case under this title, or during the case but before the debtor is granted or denied a discharge, or has not paid a debt that is dischargeable in the case under this title or that was discharged under the Bankruptcy Act.

(b) No private employer may terminate the employment of, or discriminate with respect to employment against, an individual who is or has been a debtor under this title, a debtor or bankrupt under the Bankruptcy Act, or an individual associated with such debtor or bankrupt, solely because such debtor or bankrupt -

(1) is or has been a debtor under this title or a debtor or bankrupt under the Bankruptcy Act;

(2) has been insolvent before the commencement of a case under this title or during the case but before the grant or denial of a discharge; or

(3) has not paid a debt that is dischargeable in a case under this title or that was discharged under the Bankruptcy Act.

(c)(1) A governmental unit that operates a student grant or loan program and a person engaged in a business that includes the making of loans guaranteed or insured under a student loan program may not deny a student grant, loan, loan guarantee, or loan insurance to a person that is or has been a debtor under this title or a bankrupt or debtor under the Bankruptcy Act, or another person with whom the debtor or bankrupt has been associated, because the debtor or bankrupt is or has been a debtor under this title or a bankrupt or debtor under the Bankruptcy Act, has been insolvent before the commencement of a case under this title or during the pendency of the case but before the debtor is granted or denied a discharge, or has not paid a debt that is dischargeable in the case under this title or that was discharged under the Bankruptcy Act.

(2) In this section, "student loan program" means any program operated under title IV of the Higher Education Act of 1965 or a similar program operated under State or local law.

526. Restrictions on debt relief agencies

(a) A debt relief agency shall not –

(1) fail to perform any service that such agency informed an assisted person or prospective assisted person it would provide in connection with a case or proceeding under this title;

(2) make any statement, or counsel or advise any assisted person or prospective assisted person to make a statement in a document filed in a case or proceeding under this title, that is untrue or misleading, or that upon the exercise of reasonable care, should have been known by such agency to be untrue or misleading;

(3) misrepresent to any assisted person or prospective assisted person, directly or indirectly, affirmatively or by material omission, with respect to –

(A) the services that such agency will provide to such person; or

(B) the benefits and risks that may result if such person becomes a debtor in a case under this title; or

(4) advise an assisted person or prospective assisted person to incur more debt in contemplation of such person filing a case under this title or to pay an attorney or bankruptcy petition preparer a fee or charge for services performed as part of preparing for or representing a debtor in a case under this title.

(b) Any waiver by any assisted person of any protection or right provided under this section shall not be enforceable against the debtor by any Federal or State court or any other person, but may be enforced against a debt relief agency.

(c)(1) Any contract for bankruptcy assistance between a debt relief agency and an assisted person that does not comply with the material requirements of this section, section 527, or section 528 shall be void and may not be enforced by any Federal or State court or by any other person, other than such assisted person.

(2) Any debt relief agency shall be liable to an assisted person in the amount of any fees or charges in connection with providing bankruptcy assistance to such person that such debt relief agency has received, for actual damages, and for reasonable attorneys' fees and costs if such agency is found, after notice and a hearing, to have –

(A) intentionally or negligently failed to comply with any provision of this section, section 527, or section 528 with respect to a case or proceeding under this title for such assisted person;

(B) provided bankruptcy assistance to an assisted person in a case or proceeding under this title that is dismissed or converted to a case under another chapter of this title because of such agency's intentional or negligent failure to file any required document including those specified in section 521; or

(C) intentionally or negligently disregarded the material requirements of this title or the Federal Rules of Bankruptcy Procedure applicable to such agency.

(3) In addition to such other remedies as are provided under State law, whenever the chief law enforcement officer of a State, or an official or agency designated by a State, has reason to believe that any person has violated or is violating this section, the State –

(A) may bring an action to enjoin such violation;

(B) may bring an action on behalf of its residents to recover the actual damages of assisted persons arising from such violation, including any liability under paragraph (2); and

(C) in the case of any successful action under subparagraph (A) or (B), shall be awarded the costs of the action and reasonable attorneys' fees as determined by the court.

(4) The district courts of the United States for districts located in the State shall have concurrent jurisdiction of any action under subparagraph (A) or (B) of paragraph (3).

(5) Notwithstanding any other provision of Federal law and in addition to any other remedy provided under Federal or State law, if the court, on its own motion or on the motion of the United States trustee or the debtor, finds that a person intentionally violated this section, or engaged in a clear and consistent pattern or practice of violating this section, the court may –

(A) enjoin the violation of such section; or

(B) impose an appropriate civil penalty against such person.

(d) No provision of this section, section 527, or section 528 shall –

(1) annul, alter, affect, or exempt any person subject to such sections from complying with any law of any State except to the extent that such law is inconsistent with those sections, and then only to the extent of the inconsistency; or

(2) be deemed to limit or curtail the authority or ability –

(A) of a State or subdivision or instrumentality thereof, to determine and enforce qualifications for the practice of law under the laws of that State; or

(B) of a Federal court to determine and enforce the qualifications for the practice of law before that court.

527. Disclosures

(a) A debt relief agency providing bankruptcy assistance to an assisted person shall provide –

(1) the written notice required under section 342(b)(1); and

(2) to the extent not covered in the written notice described in paragraph (1), and not later than 3 business days after the first date on which a debt relief agency first offers to provide any bankruptcy assistance services to an assisted person, a clear and conspicuous written notice advising assisted persons that –

(A) all information that the assisted person is required to provide with a petition and thereafter during a case under this title is required to be complete, accurate, and truthful;

(B) all assets and all liabilities are required to be completely and accurately disclosed in the documents filed to commence the case, and the replacement value of each asset as defined in section 506 must be stated in those documents where requested after reasonable inquiry to establish such value;

(C) current monthly income, the amounts specified in section 707(b)(2), and, in a case under chapter 13 of this title, disposable income (determined in accordance with section 707(b)(2)), are required to be stated after reasonable inquiry; and

(D) information that an assisted person provides during their case may be audited pursuant to this title, and that failure to provide such information may result in dismissal of the case under this title or other sanction, including a criminal sanction.

(b) A debt relief agency providing bankruptcy assistance to an assisted person shall provide each assisted person at the same time as the notices required under subsection (a)(1) the following statement, to the extent applicable, or one substantially similar. The statement shall be clear and conspicuous and shall be in a single document separate from other documents or notices provided to the assisted person:

"IMPORTANT INFORMATION ABOUT BANKRUPTCY ASSISTANCE SERVICES FROM AN ATTORNEY OR BANKRUPTCY PETITION PREPARER.

"If you decide to seek bankruptcy relief, you can represent yourself, you can hire an attorney to represent you, or you can get help in some localities from a bankruptcy petition preparer who is not an attorney. THE LAW REQUIRES AN ATTORNEY OR BANKRUPTCY PETITION PREPARER TO GIVE YOU A WRITTEN CONTRACT SPECIFYING WHAT THE ATTORNEY OR BANKRUPTCY PETITION PREPARER WILL DO FOR YOU AND HOW MUCH IT WILL COST. Ask to see the contract before you hire anyone.

"The following information helps you understand what must be done in a routine bankruptcy case to help you evaluate how much service you need. Although bankruptcy can be complex, many cases are routine.

"Before filing a bankruptcy case, either you or your attorney should analyze your eligibility for different forms of debt relief available under the Bankruptcy Code and which form of relief is most likely to be beneficial for you. Be sure you understand the relief you can obtain and its limitations. To file a bankruptcy case, documents called a Petition, Schedules, and Statement of Financial Affairs, and in some cases a Statement of Intention, need to be prepared correctly and filed with the bankruptcy court. You will have to pay a filing fee to the bankruptcy court. Once your case starts, you will have to attend the required first meeting of creditors where you may be questioned by a court official called a "trustee" and by creditors.

"If you choose to file a chapter 7 case, you may be asked by a creditor to reaffirm a debt. You may want help deciding whether to do so. A creditor is not permitted to coerce you into reaffirming your debts.

"If you choose to file a chapter 13 case in which you repay your creditors what you can afford over 3 to 5 years, you may also want help with preparing your chapter 13 plan and with the confirmation hearing on your plan which will be before a bankruptcy judge.

"If you select another type of relief under the Bankruptcy Code other than chapter 7 or chapter 13, you will want to find out what should be done from someone familiar with that type of relief.

"Your bankruptcy case may also involve litigation. You are generally permitted to represent yourself in litigation in bankruptcy court, but only attorneys, not bankruptcy petition preparers, can give you legal advice.".

(c) Except to the extent the debt relief agency provides the required information itself after reasonably diligent inquiry of the assisted person or others so as to obtain such information reasonably accurately for inclusion on the petition, schedules or statement of financial affairs, a debt relief agency providing bankruptcy assistance to an assisted person, to the extent permitted by nonbankruptcy law, shall provide each assisted person at the time required for the notice required under subsection (a)(1) reasonably sufficient information (which shall be provided in a clear and conspicuous writing) to the assisted person on how to provide all the information the assisted person is required to provide under this title pursuant to section 521, including –

(1) how to value assets at replacement value, determine current monthly income, the amounts specified in section 707(b)(2) and, in a chapter 13 case, how to determine disposable income in accordance with section 707(b)(2) and related calculations;

(2) how to complete the list of creditors, including how to determine what amount is owed and what address for the creditor should be shown; and

(3) how to determine what property is exempt and how to value exempt property at replacement value as defined in section 506.

(d) A debt relief agency shall maintain a copy of the notices required under subsection (a) of this section for 2 years after the date on which the notice is given the assisted person.

528. Requirements for debt relief agencies

(a) A debt relief agency shall –

(1) not later than 5 business days after the first date on which such agency provides any bankruptcy assistance services to an assisted person, but prior to such assisted person's petition under this title being filed, execute a written contract with such assisted person that explains clearly and conspicuously –

(A) the services such agency will provide to such assisted person; and

(B) the fees or charges for such services, and the terms of payment;

(2) provide the assisted person with a copy of the fully executed and completed contract;

(3) clearly and conspicuously disclose in any advertisement of bankruptcy assistance services or of the benefits of bankruptcy directed to the general public (whether in general media, seminars or specific mailings, telephonic or electronic messages, or otherwise) that the services or benefits are with respect to bankruptcy relief under this title; and

(4) clearly and conspicuously use the following statement in such advertisement: "We are a debt relief agency. We help people file for bankruptcy relief under the Bankruptcy Code." or a substantially similar statement.

(b)(1) An advertisement of bankruptcy assistance services or of the benefits of bankruptcy directed to the general public includes –

(A) descriptions of bankruptcy assistance in connection with a chapter 13 plan whether or not chapter 13 is specifically mentioned in such advertisement; and

(B) statements such as "federally supervised repayment plan" or "Federal debt restructuring help" or other similar statements that could lead a reasonable consumer to believe that debt counseling was being offered when in fact the services were directed to providing bankruptcy assistance with a chapter 13 plan or other form of bankruptcy relief under this title.

(2) An advertisement, directed to the general public, indicating that the debt relief agency provides assistance with respect to credit defaults, mortgage foreclosures, eviction proceedings, excessive debt, debt collection pressure, or inability to pay any consumer debt shall –

(A) disclose clearly and conspicuously in such advertisement that the assistance may involve bankruptcy relief under this title; and

(B) include the following statement: "We are a debt relief agency. We help people file for bankruptcy relief under the Bankruptcy Code." or a substantially similar statement.

SUBCHAPTER III - THE ESTATE

541. Property of the estate

(a) The commencement of a case under section 301, 302, or 303 of this title creates an estate. Such estate is comprised of all the following property, wherever located and by whomever held:

(1) Except as provided in subsections (b) and (c)(2) of this section, all legal or equitable interests of the debtor in property as of the commencement of the case.

(2) All interests of the debtor and the debtor's spouse in community property as of the commencement of the case that is -

(A) under the sole, equal, or joint management and control of the debtor; or

(B) liable for an allowable claim against the debtor, or for both an allowable claim against the debtor and an allowable claim against the debtor's spouse, to the extent that such interest is so liable.

(3) Any interest in property that the trustee recovers under section 329(b), 363(n), 543, 550, 553, or 723 of this title.

(4) Any interest in property preserved for the benefit of or ordered transferred to the estate under section 510(c) or 551 of this title.

(5) Any interest in property that would have been property of the estate if such interest had been an interest of the debtor on the date of the filing of the petition, and that the debtor acquires or becomes entitled to acquire within 180 days after such date -

(A) by bequest, devise, or inheritance;

(B) as a result of a property settlement agreement with the debtor's spouse, or of an interlocutory or final divorce decree; or

(C) as a beneficiary of a life insurance policy or of a death benefit plan.

(6) Proceeds, product, offspring, rents, or profits of or from property of the estate, except such as are earnings from services performed by an individual debtor after the commencement of the case.

(7) Any interest in property that the estate acquires after the commencement of the case.

(b) Property of the estate does not include -

(1) any power that the debtor may exercise solely for the benefit of an entity other than the debtor;

(2) any interest of the debtor as a lessee under a lease of nonresidential real property that has terminated at the expiration of the stated term of such lease before the commencement of the case under this title, and ceases to include any interest of the debtor as a lessee under a lease of nonresidential real property that has terminated at the expiration of the stated term of such lease during the case;

(3) any eligibility of the debtor to participate in programs authorized under the Higher Education Act of 1965 (20 U.S.C. 1001 et seq.; 42 U.S.C. 2751 et seq.), or any accreditation status or State licensure of the debtor as an educational institution;

(4) any interest of the debtor in liquid or gaseous hydrocarbons to the extent that -

(A)(i) the debtor has transferred or has agreed to transfer such interest pursuant to a farmout agreement or any written agreement directly related to a farmout agreement; and

(ii) but for the operation of this paragraph, the estate could include the interest referred to in clause (i) only by virtue of section 365 or 544(a)(3) of this title; or

(B)(i) the debtor has transferred such interest pursuant to a written conveyance of a production payment to an entity that does not participate in the operation of the property from which such production payment is transferred; and

(ii) but for the operation of this paragraph, the estate could include the interest referred to in clause (i) only by virtue of section 365 or 542 of this title;

(5) funds placed in an education individual retirement account (as defined in section 530(b)(1) of the Internal Revenue Code of 1986) not later than 365 days before the date of the filing of the petition in a case under this title, but –

(A) only if the designated beneficiary of such account was a child, stepchild, grandchild, or stepgrandchild of the debtor for the taxable year for which funds were placed in such account;

(B) only to the extent that such funds –

(i) are not pledged or promised to any entity in connection with any extension of credit; and

(ii) are not excess contributions (as described in section 4973(e) of the Internal Revenue Code of 1986); and

(C) in the case of funds placed in all such accounts having the same designated beneficiary not earlier than 720 days nor later than 365 days before such date, only so much of such funds as does not exceed $6,225;

(6) funds used to purchase a tuition credit or certificate or contributed to an account in accordance with section 529(b)(1)(A) of the Internal Revenue Code of 1986 under a qualified State tuition program (as defined in section 529(b)(1) of such Code) not later than 365 days before the date of the filing of the petition in a case under this title, but –

(A) only if the designated beneficiary of the amounts paid or contributed to such tuition program was a child, stepchild, grandchild, or stepgrandchild of the debtor for the taxable year for which funds were paid or contributed;

(B) with respect to the aggregate amount paid or contributed to such program having the same designated beneficiary, only so much of such amount as does not exceed the total contributions permitted under section 529(b)(6) of such Code with respect to such beneficiary, as adjusted beginning on the date of the filing of the petition in a case under this title by the annual increase or decrease (rounded to the nearest tenth of 1 percent) in the education expenditure category of the Consumer Price Index prepared by the Department of Labor; and

(C) in the case of funds paid or contributed to such program having the same designated beneficiary not earlier than 720 days nor later than 365 days before such date, only so much of such funds as does not exceed $6,225;

(7) any amount –

(A) withheld by an employer from the wages of employees for payment as contributions –

(i) to –

(I) an employee benefit plan that is subject to title I of the Employee Retirement Income Security Act of 1974 or under an employee benefit plan which is a governmental plan under section 414(d) of the Internal Revenue Code of 1986;

(II) a deferred compensation plan under section 457 of the Internal Revenue Code of 1986; or

(III) a tax-deferred annuity under section 403(b) of the Internal Revenue Code of 1986;

except that such amount under this subparagraph shall not constitute disposable income as defined in section 1325(b)(2); or

(ii) to a health insurance plan regulated by State law whether or not subject to such title; or

(B) received by an employer from employees for payment as contributions –

(i) to –

(I) an employee benefit plan that is subject to title I of the Employee Retirement Income Security Act of 1974 or under an employee benefit plan which is a governmental plan under section 414(d) of the Internal Revenue Code of 1986;

(II) a deferred compensation plan under section 457 of the Internal Revenue Code of 1986; or

(III) a tax-deferred annuity under section 403(b) of the Internal Revenue Code of 1986;

except that such amount under this subparagraph shall not constitute disposable income, as defined in section 1325(b)(2); or

(ii) to a health insurance plan regulated by State law whether or not subject to such title;

(8) subject to subchapter III of chapter 5, any interest of the debtor in property where the debtor pledged or sold tangible personal property (other than securities or written or printed evidences of indebtedness or title) as collateral for a loan or advance of money given by a person licensed under law to make such loans or advances, where –

(A) the tangible personal property is in the possession of the pledgee or transferee;

(B) the debtor has no obligation to repay the money, redeem the collateral, or buy back the property at a stipulated price; and

(C) neither the debtor nor the trustee have exercised any right to redeem provided under the contract or State law, in a timely manner as provided under State law and section 108(b); or

(9) any interest in cash or cash equivalents that constitute proceeds of a sale by the debtor of a money order that is made -

(A) on or after the date that is 14 days prior to the date on which the petition is filed; and

(B) under an agreement with a money order issuer that prohibits the commingling of such proceeds with property of the debtor (notwithstanding that, contrary to the agreement, the proceeds may have been commingled with property of the debtor),

unless the money order issuer had not taken action, prior to the filing of the petition, to require compliance with the prohibition.

Paragraph (4) shall not be construed to exclude from the estate any consideration the debtor retains, receives, or is entitled to receive for transferring an interest in liquid or gaseous hydrocarbons pursuant to a farmout agreement.

(c)(1) Except as provided in paragraph (2) of this subsection, an interest of the debtor in property becomes property of the estate under subsection (a)(1), (a)(2), or (a)(5) of this section notwithstanding any provision in an agreement, transfer instrument, or applicable nonbankruptcy law -

(A) that restricts or conditions transfer of such interest by the debtor; or

(B) that is conditioned on the insolvency or financial condition of the debtor, on the commencement of a case under this title, or on the appointment of or taking possession by a trustee in a case under this title or a custodian before such commencement, and that effects or gives an option to effect a forfeiture, modification, or termination of the debtor's interest in property.

(2) A restriction on the transfer of a beneficial interest of the debtor in a trust that is enforceable under applicable nonbankruptcy law is enforceable in a case under this title.

(d) Property in which the debtor holds, as of the commencement of the case, only legal title and not an equitable interest, such as a mortgage secured by real property, or an interest in such a mortgage, sold by the debtor but as to which the debtor retains legal title to service or supervise the servicing of such mortgage or interest, becomes property of the estate under subsection (a)(1) or (2) of this section only to the extent of the debtor's legal title to such property, but not to the extent of any equitable interest in such property that the debtor does not hold.

(e) In determining whether any of the relationships specified in paragraph(5)(A) or (6)(A) of subsection (b) exists, a legally adopted child of an individual (and a child who is a member of an individual's household, if placed with such individual by an authorized placement agency for legal adoption by such individual), or a foster child of an individual (if such child has as the child's principal place of abode the home of the debtor and is a member of the debtor's household) shall be treated as a child of such individual by blood.

(f) Notwithstanding any other provision of this title, property that is held by a debtor that is a corporation described in section 501(c)(3) of the Internal Revenue Code of 1986 and exempt from tax under section 501(a) of such Code may be transferred to an entity that is not such a corporation, but only under the same conditions as would apply if the debtor had not filed a case under this title.

542. Turnover of property to the estate

(a) Except as provided in subsection (c) or (d) of this section, an entity, other than a custodian, in possession, custody, or control, during the case, of property that the trustee may use, sell, or lease under section 363 of this title, or that the debtor may exempt under section 522 of this title, shall deliver to the trustee, and account for, such property or the value of such property, unless such property is of inconsequential value or benefit to the estate.

(b) Except as provided in subsection (c) or (d) of this section, an entity that owes a debt that is property of the estate and that is matured, payable on demand, or payable on order, shall pay such debt to, or on the order of, the trustee, except to the extent that such debt may be offset under section 553 of this title against a claim against the debtor.

(c) Except as provided in section 362(a)(7) of this title, an entity that has neither actual notice nor actual knowledge of the commencement of the case concerning the debtor may transfer property of the estate, or pay a debt owing to the debtor, in good faith and other than in the manner specified in subsection

(d) of this section, to an entity other than the trustee, with the same effect as to the entity making such transfer or payment as if the case under this title concerning the debtor had not been commenced.

(d) A life insurance company may transfer property of the estate or property of the debtor to such company in good faith, with the same effect with respect to such company as if the case under this title concerning the debtor had not been commenced, if such transfer is to pay a premium or to carry out a nonforfeiture insurance option, and is required to be made automatically, under a life insurance contract with such company that was entered into before the date of the filing of the petition and that is property of the estate.

(e) Subject to any applicable privilege, after notice and a hearing, the court may order an attorney, accountant, or other person that holds recorded information, including books, documents, records, and papers, relating to the debtor's property or financial affairs, to turn over or disclose such recorded information to the trustee.

543. Turnover of property by a custodian

(a) A custodian with knowledge of the commencement of a case under this title concerning the debtor may not make any disbursement from, or take any action in the administration of, property of the debtor, proceeds, product, offspring, rents, or profits of such property, or property of the estate, in the possession, custody, or control of such custodian, except such action as is necessary to preserve such property.

(b) A custodian shall -

(1) deliver to the trustee any property of the debtor held by or transferred to such custodian, or proceeds, product, offspring, rents, or profits of such property, that is in such custodian's possession, custody, or control on the date that such custodian acquires knowledge of the commencement of the case; and

(2) file an accounting of any property of the debtor, or proceeds, product, offspring, rents, or profits of such property, that, at any time, came into the possession, custody, or control of such custodian.

(c) The court, after notice and a hearing, shall -

(1) protect all entities to which a custodian has become obligated with respect to such property or proceeds, product, offspring, rents, or profits of such property;

(2) provide for the payment of reasonable compensation for services rendered and costs and expenses incurred by such custodian; and

(3) surcharge such custodian, other than an assignee for the benefit of the debtor's creditors that was appointed or took possession more than 120 days before the date of the filing of the petition, for any improper or excessive disbursement, other than a disbursement that has been made in accordance with applicable law or that has been approved, after notice and a hearing, by a court of competent jurisdiction before the commencement of the case under this title.

(d) After notice and hearing, the bankruptcy court -

(1) may excuse compliance with subsection (a), (b), or (c) of this section if the interests of creditors and, if the debtor is not insolvent, of equity security holders would be better served by permitting a custodian to continue in possession, custody, or control of such property, and

(2) shall excuse compliance with subsections (a) and (b)(1) of this section if the custodian is an assignee for the benefit of the debtor's creditors that was appointed or took possession more than 120 days before the date of the filing of the petition, unless compliance with such subsections is necessary to prevent fraud or injustice.

544. Trustee as lien creditor and as successor to certain creditors and purchasers

(a) The trustee shall have, as of the commencement of the case, and without regard to any knowledge of the trustee or of any creditor, the rights and powers of, or may avoid any transfer of property of the debtor or any obligation incurred by the debtor that is voidable by -

(1) a creditor that extends credit to the debtor at the time of the commencement of the case, and that obtains, at such time and with respect to such credit, a judicial lien on all property on which a creditor on a simple contract could have obtained such a judicial lien, whether or not such a creditor exists;

(2) a creditor that extends credit to the debtor at the time of the commencement of the case, and obtains, at such time and with respect to such credit, an execution against the debtor that is returned unsatisfied at such time, whether or not such a creditor exists; or

(3) a bona fide purchaser of real property, other than fixtures, from the debtor, against whom applicable law permits such transfer to be perfected, that obtains the status of a bona fide purchaser and has perfected such transfer at the time of the commencement of the case, whether or not such a purchaser exists.

(b)(1) Except as provided in paragraph (2), the trustee may avoid any transfer of an interest of the debtor in property or any obligation incurred by the debtor that is voidable under applicable law by a creditor holding an unsecured claim that is allowable under section 502 of this title or that is not allowable only under section 502(e) of this title.

(2) Paragraph (1) shall not apply to a transfer of a charitable contribution (as that term is defined in section 548(d)(3)) that is not covered under section 548(a)(1)(B), by reason of section 548(a)(2). Any claim by any person to recover a transferred contribution described in the preceding sentence under Federal or State law in a Federal or State court shall be preempted by the commencement of the case.

545. Statutory liens

The trustee may avoid the fixing of a statutory lien on property of the debtor to the extent that such lien -

(1) first becomes effective against the debtor -

(A) when a case under this title concerning the debtor is commenced;

(B) when an insolvency proceeding other than under this title concerning the debtor is commenced;

(C) when a custodian is appointed or authorized to take or takes possession;

(D) when the debtor becomes insolvent;

(E) when the debtor's financial condition fails to meet a specified standard; or

(F) at the time of an execution against property of the debtor levied at the instance of an entity other than the holder of such statutory lien;

(2) is not perfected or enforceable at the time of the commencement of the case against a bona fide purchaser that purchases such property at the time of the commencement of the case, whether or not such a purchaser exists, except in any case in which a purchaser is a purchaser described in section 6323 of the Internal Revenue Code of 1986, or in any other similar provision of State or local law;

(3) is for rent; or

(4) is a lien of distress for rent.

546. Limitations on avoiding powers

(a) An action or proceeding under section 544, 545, 547, 548, or 553 of this title may not be commenced after the earlier of -

(1) the later of -

(A) 2 years after the entry of the order for relief; or

(B) 1 year after the appointment or election of the first trustee under section 702, 1104, 1163, 1202, or 1302 of this title if such appointment or such election occurs before the expiration of the period specified in subparagraph (A); or

(2) the time the case is closed or dismissed.

(b)(1) The rights and powers of a trustee under sections 544, 545, and 549 of this title are subject to any generally applicable law that -

(A) permits perfection of an interest in property to be effective against an entity that acquires rights in such property before the date of perfection; or

(B) provides for the maintenance or continuation of perfection of an interest in property to be effective against an entity that acquires rights in such property before the date on which action is taken to effect such maintenance or continuation.

(2) If -

(A) a law described in paragraph (1) requires seizure of such property or commencement of an action to accomplish such perfection, or maintenance or continuation of perfection of an interest in property; and

(B) such property has not been seized or such an action has not been commenced before the date of the filing of the petition;

such interest in such property shall be perfected, or perfection of such interest shall be maintained or continued, by giving notice within the time fixed by such law for such seizure or such commencement.

(c)(1) Except as provided in subsection (d) of this section and in section 507(c), and subject to the prior rights of a holder of a security interest in such goods or the proceeds thereof, the rights and powers of the trustee under sections 544(a), 545, 547, and 549 are subject to the right of a seller of goods that has sold goods to the debtor, in the ordinary course of such seller's business, to reclaim such goods if the debtor has received such goods while insolvent, within 45 days before the date of the commencement of a case under this title, but such seller may not reclaim such goods unless such seller demands in writing reclamation of such goods –

(A) not later than 45 days after the date of receipt of such goods by the debtor; or

(B) not later than 20 days after the date of commencement of the case, if the 45-day period expires after the commencement of the case.

(2) If a seller of goods fails to provide notice in the manner described in paragraph (1), the seller still may assert the rights contained in section 503(b)(9).

(d) In the case of a seller who is a producer of grain sold to a grain storage facility, owned or operated by the debtor, in the ordinary course of such seller's business (as such terms are defined in section 557 of this title) or in the case of a United States fisherman who has caught fish sold to a fish processing facility owned or operated by the debtor in the ordinary course of such fisherman's business, the rights and powers of the trustee under sections 544(a), 545, 547, and 549 of this title are subject to any statutory or common law right of such producer or fisherman to reclaim such grain or fish if the debtor has received such grain or fish while insolvent, but -

(1) such producer or fisherman may not reclaim any grain or fish unless such producer or fisherman demands, in writing, reclamation of such grain or fish before ten days after receipt thereof by the debtor; and

(2) the court may deny reclamation to such a producer or fisherman with a right of reclamation that has made such a demand only if the court secures such claim by a lien.

(e) Notwithstanding sections 544, 545, 547, 548(a)(1)(B), and 548(b) of this title, the trustee may not avoid a transfer that is a margin payment, as defined in section 101, 741 or 761 of this title, or settlement payment, as defined in section 101 or 741 of this title, made by or to (or for the benefit of) a commodity broker, forward contract merchant, stockbroker, financial institution, financial participant, or securities clearing agency, or that is a transfer made by or to (or for the benefit of) a commodity broker, forward contract merchant, stockbroker, financial institution, financial participant, or securities clearing agency, in connection with a securities contract, as defined in section 741(7), commodity contract, as defined in section 761(4), or forward contract, that is made before the commencement of the case, except under section 548(a)(1)(A) of this title.

(f) Notwithstanding sections 544, 545, 547, 548(a)(1)(B), and 548(b) of this title, the trustee may not avoid a transfer made by or to (or for the benefit of) a repo participant or financial participant, in connection with a repurchase agreement and that is made before the commencement of the case, except under section 548(a)(1)(A) of this title.

(g) Notwithstanding sections 544, 545, 547, 548(a)(1)(B) and 548(b) of this title, the trustee may not avoid a transfer, made by or to (or for the benefit of) a swap participant or financial participant, under or in connection with any swap agreement and that is made before the commencement of the case, except under section 548(a)(1)(A) of this title.

(h) Notwithstanding the rights and powers of a trustee under sections 544(a), 545, 547, 549, and 553, if the court determines on a motion by the trustee made not later than 120 days after the date of the order for relief in a case under chapter 11 of this title and after notice and a hearing, that a return is in the best interests of the estate, the debtor, with the consent of a creditor and subject to the prior rights of holders of security interests in such goods or the proceeds of such goods, may return goods shipped to the debtor by the creditor before the commencement of the case, and the creditor may offset the purchase price of such goods against any claim of the creditor against the debtor that arose before the commencement of the case.

(i)(1) Notwithstanding paragraphs (2) and (3) of section 545, the trustee may not avoid a warehouseman's lien for storage, transportation, or other costs incidental to the storage and handling of goods.

(2) The prohibition under paragraph (1) shall be applied in a manner consistent with any State statute applicable to such lien that is similar to section 7-209 of the Uniform Commercial Code, as in effect on the date of enactment of the Bankruptcy Abuse Prevention and Consumer Protection Act of 2005, or any successor to such section 7-209.

(j) Notwithstanding sections 544, 545, 547, 548(a)(1)(B), and 548(b) the trustee may not avoid a transfer made by or to (or for the benefit of) a master netting agreement participant under or in connection with any master netting agreement or any individual contract covered thereby that is made before the commencement of the case, except under section 548(a)(1)(A) and except to the extent that the trustee could otherwise avoid such a transfer made under an individual contract covered by such master netting agreement.

547. Preferences

(a) In this section -

(1) "inventory" means personal property leased or furnished, held for sale or lease, or to be furnished under a contract for service, raw materials, work in process, or materials used or consumed in a business, including farm products such as crops or livestock, held for sale or lease;

(2) "new value" means money or money's worth in goods, services, or new credit, or release by a transferee of property previously transferred to such transferee in a transaction that is neither void nor voidable by the debtor or the trustee under any applicable law, including proceeds of such property, but does not include an obligation substituted for an existing obligation;

(3) "receivable" means right to payment, whether or not such right has been earned by performance; and

(4) a debt for a tax is incurred on the day when such tax is last payable without penalty, including any extension.

(b) Except as provided in subsections (c) and (i) of this section, the trustee may avoid any transfer of an interest of the debtor in property -

(1) to or for the benefit of a creditor;

(2) for or on account of an antecedent debt owed by the debtor before such transfer was made;

(3) made while the debtor was insolvent;

(4) made -

(A) on or within 90 days before the date of the filing of the petition; or

(B) between ninety days and one year before the date of the filing of the petition, if such creditor at the time of such transfer was an insider; and

(5) that enables such creditor to receive more than such creditor would receive if -

(A) the case were a case under chapter 7 of this title;

(B) the transfer had not been made; and

(C) such creditor received payment of such debt to the extent provided by the provisions of this title.

(c) The trustee may not avoid under this section a transfer -

(1) to the extent that such transfer was -

(A) intended by the debtor and the creditor to or for whose benefit such transfer was made to be a contemporaneous exchange for new value given to the debtor; and

(B) in fact a substantially contemporaneous exchange;

(2) to the extent that such transfer was in payment of a debt incurred by the debtor in the ordinary course of business or financial affairs of the debtor and the transferee, and such transfer was –

(A) made in the ordinary course of business or financial affairs of the debtor and the transferee; or

(B) made according to ordinary business terms;

(3) that creates a security interest in property acquired by the debtor-

(A) to the extent such security interest secures new value that was -

(i) given at or after the signing of a security agreement that contains a description of such property as collateral;

(ii) given by or on behalf of the secured party under such agreement;

(iii) given to enable the debtor to acquire such property; and

(iv) in fact used by the debtor to acquire such property; and

(B) that is perfected on or before 30 days after the debtor receives possession of such property;

(4) to or for the benefit of a creditor, to the extent that, after such transfer, such creditor gave new value to or for the benefit of the debtor -

(A) not secured by an otherwise unavoidable security interest; and

(B) on account of which new value the debtor did not make an otherwise unavoidable transfer to or for the benefit of such creditor;

(5) that creates a perfected security interest in inventory or a receivable or the proceeds of either, except to the extent that the aggregate of all such transfers to the transferee caused a reduction, as of the date of the filing of the petition and to the prejudice of other creditors holding unsecured claims, of any amount by which the debt secured by such security interest exceeded the value of all security interests for such debt on the later of -

(A)(i) with respect to a transfer to which subsection (b)(4)(A) of this section applies, 90 days before the date of the filing of the petition; or

(ii) with respect to a transfer to which subsection (b)(4)(B) of this section applies, one year before the date of the filing of the petition; or

(B) the date on which new value was first given under the security agreement creating such security interest;

(6) that is the fixing of a statutory lien that is not avoidable under section 545 of this title;

(7) to the extent such transfer was a bona fide payment of a debt for a domestic support obligation;

(8) if, in a case filed by an individual debtor whose debts are primarily consumer debts, the aggregate value of all property that constitutes or is affected by such transfer is less than $600; or

(9) if, in a case filed by a debtor whose debts are not primarily consumer debts, the aggregate value of all property that constitutes or is affected by such transfer is less than $6,225.

(d) The trustee may avoid a transfer of an interest in property of the debtor transferred to or for the benefit of a surety to secure reimbursement of such a surety that furnished a bond or other obligation to dissolve a judicial lien that would have been avoidable by the trustee under subsection (b) of this section. The liability of such surety under such bond or obligation shall be discharged to the extent of the value of such property recovered by the trustee or the amount paid to the trustee.

(e)(1) For the purposes of this section -

(A) a transfer of real property other than fixtures, but including the interest of a seller or purchaser under a contract for the sale of real property, is perfected when a bona fide purchaser of such property from the debtor against whom applicable law permits such transfer to be perfected cannot acquire an interest that is superior to the interest of the transferee; and

(B) a transfer of a fixture or property other than real property is perfected when a creditor on a simple contract cannot acquire a judicial lien that is superior to the interest of the transferee.

(2) For the purposes of this section, except as provided in paragraph (3) of this subsection, a transfer is made -

(A) at the time such transfer takes effect between the transferor and the transferee, if such transfer is perfected at, or within 30 days after, such time, except as provided in subsection (c)(3)(B);

(B) at the time such transfer is perfected, if such transfer is perfected after such 30 days; or

(C) immediately before the date of the filing of the petition, if such transfer is not perfected at the later of -

(i) the commencement of the case; or

(ii) 30 days after such transfer takes effect between the transferor and the transferee.

(3) For the purposes of this section, a transfer is not made until the debtor has acquired rights in the property transferred.

(f) For the purposes of this section, the debtor is presumed to have been insolvent on and during the 90 days immediately preceding the date of the filing of the petition.

(g) For the purposes of this section, the trustee has the burden of proving the avoidability of a transfer under subsection (b) of this section, and the creditor or party in interest against whom recovery or avoidance is sought has the burden of proving the nonavoidability of a transfer under subsection (c) of this section.

(h) The trustee may not avoid a transfer if such transfer was made as a part of an alternative repayment schedule between the debtor and any creditor of the debtor created by an approved nonprofit budget and credit counseling agency.

(i) If the trustee avoids under subsection (b) a transfer made between 90 days and 1 year before the date of the filing of the petition, by the debtor to an entity that is not an insider for the benefit of a creditor that is an insider, such transfer shall be considered to be avoided under this section only with respect to the creditor that is an insider.

548. Fraudulent transfers and obligations

(a)(1) The trustee may avoid any transfer (including any transfer to or for the benefit of an insider under an employment contract) of an interest of the debtor in property, or any obligation (including any obligation to or for the benefit of an insider under an employment contract) incurred by the debtor, that was made or incurred on or within 2 years before the date of the filing of the petition, if the debtor voluntarily or involuntarily -

(A) made such transfer or incurred such obligation with actual intent to hinder, delay, or defraud any entity to which the debtor was or became, on or after the date that such transfer was made or such obligation was incurred, indebted; or

(B)(i) received less than a reasonably equivalent value in exchange for such transfer or obligation; and

(ii)(I) was insolvent on the date that such transfer was made or such obligation was incurred, or became insolvent as a result of such transfer or obligation;

(II) was engaged in business or a transaction, or was about to engage in business or a transaction, for which any property remaining with the debtor was an unreasonably small capital;

(III) intended to incur, or believed that the debtor would incur, debts that would be beyond the debtor's ability to pay as such debts matured; or

(IV) made such transfer to or for the benefit of an insider, or incurred such obligation to or for the benefit of an insider, under an employment contract and not in the ordinary course of business.

(2) A transfer of a charitable contribution to a qualified religious or charitable entity or organization shall not be considered to be a transfer covered under paragraph (1)(B) in any case in which -

(A) the amount of that contribution does not exceed 15 percent of the gross annual income of the debtor for the year in which the transfer of the contribution is made; or

(B) the contribution made by a debtor exceeded the percentage amount of gross annual income specified in subparagraph (A), if the transfer was consistent with the practices of the debtor in making charitable contributions.

(b) The trustee of a partnership debtor may avoid any transfer of an interest of the debtor in property, or any obligation incurred by the debtor, that was made or incurred on or within 2 years before the date of the filing of the petition, to a general partner in the debtor, if the debtor was insolvent on the date such transfer was made or such obligation was incurred, or became insolvent as a result of such transfer or obligation.

(c) Except to the extent that a transfer or obligation voidable under this section is voidable under section 544, 545, or 547 of this title, a transferee or obligee of such a transfer or obligation that takes for value and in good faith has a lien on or may retain any interest transferred or may enforce any obligation incurred, as the case may be, to the extent that such transferee or obligee gave value to the debtor in exchange for such transfer or obligation.

(d)(1) For the purposes of this section, a transfer is made when such transfer is so perfected that a bona fide purchaser from the debtor against whom applicable law permits such transfer to be perfected cannot acquire an interest in the property transferred that is superior to the interest in such property of the transferee, but if such transfer is not so perfected before the commencement of the case, such transfer is made immediately before the date of the filing of the petition.

(2) In this section -

(A) "value" means property, or satisfaction or securing of a present or antecedent debt of the debtor, but does not include an unperformed promise to furnish support to the debtor or to a relative of the debtor;

(B) a commodity broker, forward contract merchant, stockbroker, financial institution, financial participant, or securities clearing agency that receives a margin payment, as defined in section 101, 741 or 761 of this title, or settlement payment, as defined in section 101 or 741 of this title, takes for value to the extent of such payment;

(C) a repo participant or financial participant that receives a margin payment, as defined in section 741 or 761 of this title, or settlement payment, as defined in section 741 of this title, in connection with a repurchase agreement, takes for value to the extent of such payment;

(D) a swap participant or financial participant that receives a transfer in connection with a swap agreement takes for value to the extent of such transfer; and

(E) a master netting agreement participant that receives a transfer in connection with a master netting agreement or any individual contract covered thereby takes for value to the extent of such transfer, except that, with respect to a transfer under any individual contract covered thereby, to the extent that such master netting agreement participant otherwise did not take (or is otherwise not deemed to have taken) such transfer for value.

(3) In this section, the term "charitable contribution" means a charitable contribution, as that term is defined in section 170(c) of the Internal Revenue Code of 1986, if that contribution -

(A) is made by a natural person; and

(B) consists of -

(i) a financial instrument (as that term is defined in section 731(c) (2)(C) of the Internal Revenue Code of 1986); or

(ii) cash.

(4) In this section, the term "qualified religious or charitable entity or organization" means -

(A) an entity described in section 170(c)(1) of the Internal Revenue Code of 1986; or

(B) an entity or organization described in section 170(c)(2) of the Internal Revenue Code of 1986.

(e)(1) In addition to any transfer that the trustee may otherwise avoid, the trustee may avoid any transfer of an interest of the debtor in property that was made on or within 10 years before the date of the filing of the petition, if –

(A) such transfer was made to a self-settled trust or similar device;

(B) such transfer was by the debtor;

(C) the debtor is a beneficiary of such trust or similar device; and

(D) the debtor made such transfer with actual intent to hinder, delay, or defraud any entity to which the debtor was or became, on or after the date that such transfer was made, indebted.

(2) For the purposes of this subsection, a transfer includes a transfer made in anticipation of any money judgment, settlement, civil penalty, equitable order, or criminal fine incurred by, or which the debtor believed would be incurred by –

(A) any violation of the securities laws (as defined in section 3(a)(47) of the Securities Exchange Act of 1934 (15 U.S.C. 78c(a)(47))), any State securities laws, or any regulation or order issued under Federal securities laws or State securities laws; or

(B) fraud, deceit, or manipulation in a fiduciary capacity or in connection with the purchase or sale of any security registered under section 12 or 15(d) of the Securities Exchange Act of 1934 (15 U.S.C. 78l and 78o(d)) or under section 6 of the Securities Act of 1933 (15 U.S.C. 77f).

549. Postpetition transactions

(a) Except as provided in subsection (b) or (c) of this section, the trustee may avoid a transfer of property of the estate -

(1) that occurs after the commencement of the case; and

(2)(A) that is authorized only under section 303(f) or 542(c) of this title; or

(B) that is not authorized under this title or by the court.

(b) In an involuntary case, the trustee may not avoid under subsection (a) of this section a transfer made after the commencement of such case but before the order for relief to the extent any value, including services, but not including satisfaction or securing of a debt that arose before the commencement of the case, is given after the commencement of the case in exchange for such transfer, notwithstanding any notice or knowledge of the case that the transferee has.

(c) The trustee may not avoid under subsection (a) of this section a transfer of an interest in real property to a good faith purchaser without knowledge of the commencement of the case and for present fair equivalent value unless a copy or notice of the petition was filed, where a transfer of an interest in such real property may be recorded to perfect such transfer, before such transfer is so perfected that a bona fide purchaser of such real property, against whom applicable law permits such transfer to be perfected, could not acquire an interest that is superior to such interest of such good faith purchaser. A good faith purchaser without knowledge of the commencement of the case and for less than present fair equivalent value has a lien on the property transferred to the extent of any present value given, unless a copy or notice of the petition was so filed before such transfer was so perfected.

(d) An action or proceeding under this section may not be commenced after the earlier of -

(1) two years after the date of the transfer sought to be avoided; or

(2) the time the case is closed or dismissed.

550. Liability of transferee of avoided transfer

(a) Except as otherwise provided in this section, to the extent that a transfer is avoided under section 544, 545, 547, 548, 549, 553(b), or 724(a) of this title, the trustee may recover, for the benefit of the estate, the property transferred, or, if the court so orders, the value of such property, from -

(1) the initial transferee of such transfer or the entity for whose benefit such transfer was made; or

(2) any immediate or mediate transferee of such initial transferee.

(b) The trustee may not recover under section (a)(2) of this section from-

(1) a transferee that takes for value, including satisfaction or securing of a present or antecedent debt, in good faith, and without knowledge of the voidability of the transfer avoided; or

(2) any immediate or mediate good faith transferee of such transferee.

(c) If a transfer made between 90 days and one year before the filing of the petition -

(1) is avoided under section 547(b) of this title; and

(2) was made for the benefit of a creditor that at the time of such transfer was an insider; the trustee may not recover under subsection (a) from a transferee that is not an insider.

(d) The trustee is entitled to only a single satisfaction under subsection (a) of this section.

(e)(1) A good faith transferee from whom the trustee may recover under subsection (a) of this section has a lien on the property recovered to secure the lesser of -

(A) the cost, to such transferee, of any improvement made after the transfer, less the amount of any profit realized by or accruing to such transferee from such property; and

(B) any increase in the value of such property as a result of such improvement, of the property transferred.

(2) In this subsection, "improvement" includes -

(A) physical additions or changes to the property transferred;

(B) repairs to such property;

(C) payment of any tax on such property;

(D) payment of any debt secured by a lien on such property that is superior or equal to the rights of the trustee; and

(E) preservation of such property.

(f) An action or proceeding under this section may not be commenced after the earlier of -

(1) one year after the avoidance of the transfer on account of which recovery under this section is sought; or

(2) the time the case is closed or dismissed.

551. Automatic preservation of avoided transfer

Any transfer avoided under section 522, 544, 545, 547, 548, 549, or 724(a) of this title, or any lien void under section 506(d) of this title, is preserved for the benefit of the estate but only with respect to property of the estate.

552. Postpetition effect of security interest

(a) Except as provided in subsection (b) of this section, property acquired by the estate or by the debtor after the commencement of the case is not subject to any lien resulting from any security agreement entered into by the debtor before the commencement of the case.

(b)(1) Except as provided in sections 363, 506(c), 522, 544, 545, 547, and 548 of this title, if the debtor and an entity entered into a security agreement before the commencement of the case and if the security interest created by such security agreement extends to property of the debtor acquired before the commencement of the case and to proceeds, products, offspring, or profits of such property, then such security interest extends to such proceeds, products, offspring, or profits acquired by the estate after the commencement of the case to the extent provided by such security agreement and by applicable nonbankruptcy law, except to any extent that the court, after notice and a hearing and based on the equities of the case, orders otherwise.

(2) Except as provided in sections 363, 506(c), 522, 544, 545, 547, and 548 of this title, and notwithstanding section 546(b) of this title, if the debtor and an entity entered into a security agreement before the commencement of the case and if the security interest created by such security agreement extends to property of the debtor acquired before the commencement of the case and to amounts paid as rents of such property or the fees, charges, accounts, or other payments for the use or occupancy of rooms and other public facilities in hotels, motels, or other lodging properties, then such security interest extends to such rents and such fees, charges, accounts, or other payments acquired by the estate after the commencement of the case to the extent provided in such security agreement, except to any extent that the court, after notice and a hearing and based on the equities of the case, orders otherwise.

553. Setoff

(a) Except as otherwise provided in this section and in sections 362 and 363 of this title, this title does not affect any right of a creditor to offset a mutual debt owing by such creditor to the debtor that arose before the commencement of the case under this title against a claim of such creditor against the debtor that arose before the commencement of the case, except to the extent that -

(1) the claim of such creditor against the debtor is disallowed;

(2) such claim was transferred, by an entity other than the debtor, to such creditor -

(A) after the commencement of the case; or

(B)(i) after 90 days before the date of the filing of the petition; and

(ii) while the debtor was insolvent (except for a setoff of a kind described in section 362(b)(6), 362(b)(7), 362(b)(17), 362(b)(27), 555, 556, 559, 560, or 561); or

(3) the debt owed to the debtor by such creditor was incurred by such creditor -

(A) after 90 days before the date of the filing of the petition;

(B) while the debtor was insolvent; and

(C) for the purpose of obtaining a right of setoff against the debtor (except for a setoff of a kind described in section 362(b)(6), 362(b)(7), 362(b)(17), 362(b)(27), 555, 556, 559, 560, or 561).

(b)(1) Except with respect to a setoff of a kind described in section 362(b)(6), 362(b)(7), 362(b)(17), 362(b)(27), 555, 556, 559, 560, 561, 365(h), 546(h), or 365(i)(2) of this title, if a creditor offsets a mutual debt owing to the debtor against a claim against the debtor on or within 90 days before the date of the filing of the petition, then the trustee may recover from such creditor the amount so offset to the extent that any insufficiency on the date of such setoff is less than the insufficiency on the later of -

(A) 90 days before the date of the filing of the petition; and

(B) the first date during the 90 days immediately preceding the date of the filing of the petition on which there is an insufficiency.

(2) In this subsection, "insufficiency" means amount, if any, by which a claim against the debtor exceeds a mutual debt owing to the debtor by the holder of such claim.

(c) For the purposes of this section, the debtor is presumed to have been insolvent on and during the 90 days immediately preceding the date of the filing of the petition.

554. Abandonment of property of the estate

(a) After notice and a hearing, the trustee may abandon any property of the estate that is burdensome to the estate or that is of inconsequential value and benefit to the estate.

(b) On request of a party in interest and after notice and a hearing, the court may order the trustee to abandon any property of the estate that is burdensome to the estate or that is of inconsequential value and benefit to the estate.

(c) Unless the court orders otherwise, any property scheduled under section 521(a)(1) of this title not otherwise administered at the time of the closing of a case is abandoned to the debtor and administered for purposes of section 350 of this title.

(d) Unless the court orders otherwise, property of the estate that is not abandoned under this section and that is not administered in the case remains property of the estate.

555. Contractual right to liquidate, terminate, or accelerate a securities contract

The exercise of a contractual right of a stockbroker, financial institution, financial participant, or securities clearing agency to cause the liquidation, termination, or acceleration of a securities contract, as defined in section 741 of this title, because of a condition of the kind specified in section 365(e)(1) of this title shall not be stayed, avoided, or otherwise limited by operation of any provision of this title or by order of a court or administrative agency in any proceeding under this title unless such order is authorized under the provisions of the Securities Investor Protection Act of 1970 or any statute administered by the Securities and Exchange Commission. As used in this section, the term "contractual right" includes a right set forth in a rule or bylaw of a derivatives clearing organization (as defined in the Commodity Exchange Act), a multilateral clearing organization (as defined in the Federal Deposit Insurance Corporation Improvement Act of 1991), a national securities exchange, a national securities association, a securities clearing agency, a contract market designated under the Commodity Exchange Act, a derivatives transaction execution facility registered under the Commodity Exchange Act, or a board of trade (as defined in the Commodity Exchange Act), or in a resolution of the governing board thereof, and a right, whether or not in writing, arising under common law, under law merchant, or by reason of normal business practice.

556. Contractual right to liquidate, terminate, or accelerate a commodities contract or forward contract

The contractual right of a commodity broker, financial participant, or forward contract merchant to cause the liquidation, termination, or acceleration of a commodity contract, as defined in section 761 of this title, or forward contract because of a condition of the kind specified in section 365(e)(1) of this title, and the right to a variation or maintenance margin payment received from a trustee with respect to open commodity contracts or forward contracts, shall not be stayed, avoided, or otherwise limited by operation of any provision of this title or by the order of a court in any proceeding under this title. As used in this section, the term "contractual right" includes a right set forth in a rule or bylaw of a derivatives clearing organization (as defined in the Commodity Exchange Act), a multilateral clearing organization (as defined in the Federal Deposit Insurance Corporation Improvement Act of 1991), a national securities exchange, a national securities association, a securities clearing agency, a contract market designated under the Commodity Exchange Act, a derivatives transaction execution facility registered under the Commodity Exchange Act, or a board of trade (as defined in the Commodity Exchange Act) or in a resolution of the governing board thereof and a right, whether or not evidenced in writing, arising under common law, under law merchant or by reason of normal business practice.

557. Expedited determination of interests in, and abandonment or other disposition of grain assets

(a) This section applies only in a case concerning a debtor that owns or operates a grain storage facility and only with respect to grain and the proceeds of grain. This section does not affect the application of any other section of this title to property other than grain and proceeds of grain.

(b) In this section-

(1) "grain" means wheat, corn, flaxseed, grain sorghum, barley, oats, rye, soybeans, other dry edible beans, or rice;

(2) "grain storage facility" means a site or physical structure regularly used to store grain for producers, or to store grain acquired from producers for resale; and

(3) "producer" means an entity which engages in the growing of grain.

(c)(1) Notwithstanding sections 362, 363, 365, and 554 of this title, on the court's own motion the court may, and on the request of the trustee or an entity that claims an interest in grain or the proceeds of grain the court shall, expedite the procedures for the determination of interests in and the disposition of grain and the proceeds of grain, by shortening to the greatest extent feasible such time periods as are otherwise applicable for such procedures and by establishing, by order, a timetable having a duration of not to exceed 120 days for the completion of the applicable procedure specified in subsection (d) of this section. Such time periods and such timetable may be modified by the court, for cause, in accordance with subsection (f) of this section.

(2) The court shall determine the extent to which such time periods shall be shortened, based upon-

(A) any need of an entity claiming an interest in such grain or the proceeds of grain for a prompt determination of such interest;

(B) any need of such entity for a prompt disposition of such grain;

(C) the market for such grain;

(D) the conditions under which such grain is stored;

(E) the costs of continued storage or disposition of such grain;

(F) the orderly administration of the estate;

(G) the appropriate opportunity for an entity to assert an interest in such grain; and

(H) such other considerations as are relevant to the need to expedite such procedures in the case.

(d) The procedures that may be expedited under subsection (c) of this section include-

(1) the filing of and response to-

(A) a claim of ownership;

(B) a proof of claim;

(C) a request for abandonment;

(D) a request for relief from the stay of action against property under section 362(a) of this title;

(E) a request for determination of secured status;

(F) a request for determination of whether such grain or the proceeds of grain-

(i) is property of the estate;

(ii) must be turned over to the estate; or

(iii) may be used, sold, or leased; and

(G) any other request for determination of an interest in such grain or the proceeds of grain;

(2) the disposition of such grain or the proceeds of grain, before or after determination of interests in such grain or the proceeds of grain, by way of-

(A) sale of such grain;

(B) abandonment;

(C) distribution; or

(D) such other method as is equitable in the case;

(3) subject to sections 701, 702, 703, 1104, 1202, and 1302 of this title; the appointment of a trustee or examiner and the retention and compensation of any professional person required to assist with respect to matters relevant to the determination of interests in or disposition of such grain or the proceeds of grain; and

(4) the determination of any dispute concerning a matter specified in paragraph (1), (2), or (3) of this subsection.

(e)(1) Any governmental unit that has regulatory jurisdiction over the operation or liquidation of the debtor or the debtor's business shall be given notice of any request made or order entered under subsection (c) of this section.

(2) Any such governmental unit may raise, and may appear and be heard on, any issue relating to grain or the proceeds of grain in a case in which a request is made, or an order is entered, under subsection (c) of this section.

(3) The trustee shall consult with such governmental unit before taking any action relating to the disposition of grain in the possession, custody, or control of the debtor or the estate.

(f) The court may extend the period for final disposition of grain or the proceeds of grain under this section beyond 120 days if the court finds that-

(1) the interests of justice so require in light of the complexity of the case; and

(2) the interests of those claimants entitled to distribution of grain or the proceeds of grain will not be materially injured by such additional delay.

(g) Unless an order establishing an expedited procedure under subsection (c) of this section, or determining any interest in or approving any disposition of grain or the proceeds of grain, is stayed pending appeal-

(1) the reversal or modification of such order on appeal does not affect the validity of any procedure, determination, or disposition that occurs before such reversal or modification, whether or not any entity knew of the pendency of the appeal; and

(2) neither the court nor the trustee may delay, due to the appeal of such order, any proceeding in the case in which such order is issued.

(h)(1) The trustee may recover from grain and the proceeds of grain the reasonable and necessary costs and expenses allowable under section 503(b) of this title attributable to preserving or disposing of grain or the proceeds of grain, but may not recover from such grain or the proceeds of grain any other costs or expenses.

(2) Notwithstanding section 326(a) of this title, the dollar amounts of money specified in such section include the value, as of the date of disposition, of any grain that the trustee distributes in kind.

(i) In all cases where the quantity of a specific type of grain held by a debtor operating a grain storage facility exceeds ten thousand bushels, such grain shall be sold by the trustee and the assets thereof distributed in accordance with the provisions of this section.

558. Defenses of the estate

The estate shall have the benefit of any defense available to the debtor as against any entity other than the estate, including statutes of limitation, statutes of frauds, usury, and other personal defenses. A waiver of any such defense by the debtor after the commencement of the case does not bind the estate.

559. Contractual right to liquidate, terminate, or accelerate a repurchase agreement

The exercise of a contractual right of a repo participant or financial participant to cause the liquidation, termination, or acceleration of a repurchase agreement because of a condition of the kind specified in section 365(e)(1) of this title shall not be stayed, avoided, or otherwise limited by operation of any provision of this title or by order of a court or administrative agency in any proceeding under this title, unless, where the debtor is a stockbroker or securities clearing agency, such order is authorized under the provisions of the Securities Investor Protection Act of 1970 or any statute administered by the Securities and Exchange Commission. In the event that a repo participant or financial participant liquidates one or more repurchase agreements with a debtor and under the terms of one or more such agreements has agreed to deliver assets subject to repurchase agreements to the debtor, any excess of the market prices received on liquidation of such assets (or if any such assets are not disposed of on the date of liquidation of such repurchase agreements, at the prices available at the time of liquidation of such repurchase agreements from a generally recognized source or the most recent closing bid quotation from such a source) over the sum of the stated repurchase prices and all expenses in connection with the liquidation of such repurchase agreements shall be deemed property of the estate, subject to the available rights of setoff. As used in this section, the term "contractual right" includes a right set forth in a rule or bylaw, of a derivatives clearing organization (as defined in the Commodity Exchange Act), a multilateral clearing organization (as defined in the Federal Deposit Insurance Corporation Improvement Act of 1991), a national securities exchange, a national securities association, a securities clearing agency, a contract market designated under the Commodity Exchange Act, a derivatives transaction execution facility registered under the Commodity Exchange Act, or a board of trade (as defined in the Commodity Exchange Act) or in a resolution of the governing board thereof and a right, whether or not evidenced in writing, arising under common law, under law merchant or by reason of normal business practice.

560. Contractual right to liquidate, terminate, or accelerate a swap agreement

The exercise of any contractual right of any swap participant or financial participant to cause the liquidation, termination, or acceleration of one or more swap agreements because of a condition of the kind specified in section 365(e)(1) of this title or to offset or net out any termination values or payment amounts arising under or in connection with the termination, liquidation, or acceleration of one or more swap agreements shall not be stayed, avoided, or otherwise limited by operation of any provision of this title or by order of a court or administrative agency in any proceeding under this title. As used in this section, the term "contractual right" includes a right set forth in a rule or bylaw of a derivatives clearing organization (as defined in the Commodity Exchange Act), a multilateral clearing organization (as defined in the Federal Deposit Insurance Corporation Improvement Act of 1991), a national securities exchange, a national securities association, a securities clearing agency, a contract market designated under the Commodity Exchange Act, a derivatives transaction execution facility registered under the Commodity Exchange Act, or a board of trade (as defined in the Commodity Exchange Act) or in a resolution of the governing board thereof and a right, whether or not evidenced in writing, arising under common law, under law merchant, or by reason of normal business practice.

561. Contractual right to terminate, liquidate, accelerate, or offset under a master netting agreement and across contracts; proceedings under chapter 15

(a) Subject to subsection (b), the exercise of any contractual right, because of a condition of the kind specified in section 365(e)(1), to cause the termination, liquidation, or acceleration of or to offset or net termination values, payment amounts, or other transfer obligations arising under or in connection with one or more (or the termination, liquidation, or acceleration of one or more) –

(1) securities contracts, as defined in section 741(7);

(2) commodity contracts, as defined in section 761(4);

(3) forward contracts;

(4) repurchase agreements;

(5) swap agreements; or

(6) master netting agreements

shall not be stayed, avoided, or otherwise limited by operation of any provision of this title or by any order of a court or administrative agency in any proceeding under this title.

(b)(1) A party may exercise a contractual right described in subsection (a) to terminate, liquidate, or accelerate only to the extent that such party could exercise such a right under section 555, 556, 559, or 560 for each individual contract covered by the master netting agreement in issue.

(2) If a debtor is a commodity broker subject to subchapter IV of chapter 7 –

(A) a party may not net or offset an obligation to the debtor arising under, or in connection with, a commodity contract traded on or subject to the rules of a contract market designated under the Commodity Exchange Act or a derivatives transaction execution facility registered under the Commodity Exchange Act against any claim arising under, or in connection with, other instruments, contracts, or agreements listed in subsection (a) except to the extent that the party has positive net equity in the commodity accounts at the debtor, as calculated under such subchapter; and

(B) another commodity broker may not net or offset an obligation to the debtor arising under, or in connection with, a commodity contract entered into or held on behalf of a customer of the debtor and traded on or subject to the rules of a contract market designated under the Commodity Exchange Act or a derivatives transaction execution facility registered under the Commodity Exchange Act against any claim arising under, or in connection with, other instruments, contracts, or agreements listed in subsection (a).

(3) No provision of subparagraph (A) or (B) of paragraph (2) shall prohibit the offset of claims and obligations that arise under –

(A) a cross-margining agreement or similar arrangement that has been approved by the Commodity Futures Trading Commission or submitted to the Commodity Futures Trading Commission under paragraph (1) or (2) of section 5c(c) of the Commodity Exchange Act and has not been abrogated or rendered ineffective by the Commodity Futures Trading Commission; or

(B) any other netting agreement between a clearing organization (as defined in section 761) and another entity that has been approved by the Commodity Futures Trading Commission.

(c) As used in this section, the term "contractual right" includes a right set forth in a rule or bylaw of a derivatives clearing organization (as defined in the Commodity Exchange Act), a multilateral clearing organization (as defined in the Federal Deposit Insurance Corporation Improvement Act of 1991), a national securities exchange, a national securities association, a securities clearing agency, a contract market designated under the Commodity Exchange Act, a derivatives transaction execution facility registered under the Commodity Exchange Act, or a board of trade (as defined in the Commodity Exchange Act) or in a resolution of the governing board thereof, and a right, whether or not evidenced in writing, arising under common law, under law merchant, or by reason of normal business practice.

(d) Any provisions of this title relating to securities contracts, commodity contracts, forward contracts, repurchase agreements, swap agreements, or master netting agreements shall apply in a case under chapter 15, so that enforcement of contractual provisions of such contracts and agreements in accordance with their terms will not be stayed or otherwise limited by operation of any provision of this title or by order of a court in any case under this title, and to limit avoidance powers to the same extent as in a proceeding under chapter 7 or 11 of this title (such enforcement not to be limited based on the presence or absence of assets of the debtor in the United States).

562. Timing of damage measurement in connection with swap agreements, securities contracts, forward contracts, commodity contracts, repurchase agreements, and master netting agreements

(a) If the trustee rejects a swap agreement, securities contract (as defined in section 741), forward contract, commodity contract (as defined in section 761), repurchase agreement, or master netting agreement pursuant to section 365(a), or if a forward contract merchant, stockbroker, financial institution, securities clearing agency, repo participant, financial participant, master netting agreement participant, or swap participant liquidates, terminates, or accelerates such contract or agreement, damages shall be measured as of the earlier of –

(1) the date of such rejection; or

(2) the date or dates of such liquidation, termination, or acceleration.

(b) If there are not any commercially reasonable determinants of value as of any date referred to in paragraph (1) or (2) of subsection (a), damages shall be measured as of the earliest subsequent date or dates on which there are commercially reasonable determinants of value.

(c) For the purposes of subsection (b), if damages are not measured as of the date or dates of rejection, liquidation, termination, or acceleration, and the forward contract merchant, stockbroker, financial institution, securities clearing agency, repo participant, financial participant, master netting agreement participant, or swap participant or the trustee objects to the timing of the measurement of damages –

(1) the trustee, in the case of an objection by a forward contract merchant, stockbroker, financial institution, securities clearing agency, repo participant, financial participant, master netting agreement participant, or swap participant; or

(2) the forward contract merchant, stockbroker, financial institution, securities clearing agency, repo participant, financial participant, master netting agreement participant, or swap participant, in the case of an objection by the trustee,

has the burden of proving that there were no commercially reasonable determinants of value as of such date or dates.

CHAPTER 11 - REORGANIZATION

SUBCHAPTER I - OFFICERS AND ADMINISTRATION

Sec.

SUBCHAPTER II - THE PLAN

SUBCHAPTER III - POSTCONFIRMATION MATTERS

SUBCHAPTER IV - RAILROAD REORGANIZATIONS
(omitted)

SUBCHAPTER I - OFFICERS AND ADMINISTRATION

1101. Definitions for this chapter

In this chapter -

(1) "debtor in possession" means debtor except when a person that has qualified under section 322 of this title is serving as trustee in the case;

(2) "substantial consummation" means-

(A) transfer of all or substantially all of the property proposed by the plan to be transferred;

(B) assumption by the debtor or by the successor to the debtor under the plan of the business or of the management of all or substantially all of the property dealt with by the plan; and

(C) commencement of distribution under the plan.

1102. Creditors' and equity security holders' committees

(a)(1) Except as provided in paragraph (3), as soon as practicable after the order for relief under chapter 11 of this title, the United States trustee shall appoint a committee of creditors holding unsecured claims and may appoint additional committees of creditors or of equity security holders as the United States trustee deems appropriate.

(2) On request of a party in interest, the court may order the appointment of additional committees of creditors or of equity security holders if necessary to assure adequate representation of creditors or of equity security holders. The United States trustee shall appoint any such committee.

(3) On request of a party in interest in a case in which the debtor is a small business debtor and for cause, the court may order that a committee of creditors not be appointed.

(4) On request of a party in interest and after notice and a hearing, the court may order the United States trustee to change the membership of a committee appointed under this subsection, if the court determines that the change is necessary to ensure adequate representation of creditors or equity security holders. The court may order the United States trustee to increase the number of members of a committee to include a creditor that is a small business concern (as described in section 3(a)(1) of the Small Business Act), if the court determines that the creditor holds claims (of the kind represented by the committee) the aggregate amount of which, in comparison to the annual gross revenue of that creditor, is disproportionately large.

(b)(1) A committee of creditors appointed under subsection (a) of this section shall ordinarily consist of the persons, willing to serve, that hold the seven largest claims against the debtor of the kinds represented on such committee, or of the members of a committee organized by creditors before the commencement of the case under this chapter, if such committee was fairly chosen and is representative of the different kinds of claims to be represented.

(2) A committee of equity security holders appointed under subsection (a)(2) of this section shall ordinarily consist of the persons, willing to serve, that hold the seven largest amounts of equity securities of the debtor of the kinds represented on such committee.

(3) A committee appointed under subsection (a) shall –

(A) provide access to information for creditors who –

(i) hold claims of the kind represented by that committee; and

(ii) are not appointed to the committee;

(B) solicit and receive comments from the creditors described in subparagraph (A); and

(C) be subject to a court order that compels any additional report or disclosure to be made to the creditors described in subparagraph (A).

1103. Powers and duties of committees

(a) At a scheduled meeting of a committee appointed under section 1102 of this title, at which a majority of the members of such committee are present, and with the court's approval, such committee may select and authorize the employment by such committee of one or more attorneys, accountants, or other agents, to represent or perform services for such committee.

(b) An attorney or accountant employed to represent a committee appointed under section 1102 of this title may not, while employed by such committee, represent any other entity having an adverse interest in connection with the case. Representation of one or more creditors of the same class as represented by the committee shall not per se constitute the representation of an adverse interest.

(c) A committee appointed under section 1102 of this title may-

(1) consult with the trustee or debtor in possession concerning the administration of the case;

(2) investigate the acts, conduct, assets, liabilities, and financial condition of the debtor, the operation of the debtor's business and the desirability of the continuance of such business, and any other matter relevant to the case or to the formulation of a plan;

(3) participate in the formulation of a plan, advise those represented by such committee of such committee's determinations as to any plan formulated, and collect and file with the court acceptances or rejections of a plan;

(4) request the appointment of a trustee or examiner under section 1104 of this title; and

(5) perform such other services as are in the interest of those represented.

(d) As soon as practicable after the appointment of a committee under section 1102 of this title, the trustee shall meet with such committee to transact such business as may be necessary and proper.

1104. Appointment of trustee or examiner

(a) At any time after the commencement of the case but before confirmation of a plan, on request of a party in interest or the United States trustee, and after notice and a hearing, the court shall order the appointment of a trustee-

(1) for cause, including fraud, dishonesty, incompetence, or gross mismanagement of the affairs of the debtor by current management, either before or after the commencement of the case, or similar cause, but not including the number of holders of securities of the debtor or the amount of assets or liabilities of the debtor or;

(2) if such appointment is in the interests of creditors, any equity security holders, and other interests of the estate, without regard to the number of holders of securities of the debtor or the amount of assets or liabilities of the debtor; or

(3) [Repealed by Pub. L. 111-327 (2010)]

(b)(1) Except as provided in section 1163 of this title, on the request of a party in interest made not later than 30 days after the court orders the appointment of a trustee under subsection (a), the United States trustee shall convene a meeting of creditors for the purpose of electing one disinterested person to serve as trustee in the case. The election of a trustee shall be conducted in the manner provided in subsections (a), (b), and (c) of section 702 of this title.

(2)(A) If an eligible, disinterested trustee is elected at a meeting of creditors under paragraph (1), the United States trustee shall file a report certifying that election.

(B) Upon the filing of a report under subparagraph (A) –

(i) the trustee elected under paragraph (1) shall be considered to have been selected and appointed for purposes of this section; and

(ii) the service of any trustee appointed under subsection (a) shall terminate.

(C) The court shall resolve any dispute arising out of an election described in subparagraph (A).

(c) If the court does not order the appointment of a trustee under this section, then at any time before the confirmation of a plan, on request of a party in interest or the United States trustee, and after notice and a hearing, the court shall order the appointment of an examiner to conduct such an investigation of the debtor as is appropriate, including an investigation of any allegations of fraud, dishonesty, incompetence, misconduct, mismanagement, or irregularity in the management of the affairs of the debtor of or by current or former management of the debtor, if-

(1) such appointment is in the interests of creditors, any equity security holders, and other interests of the estate; or

(2) the debtor's fixed, liquidated, unsecured debts, other than debts for goods, services, or taxes, or owing to an insider, exceed $5,000,000.

(d) If the court orders the appointment of a trustee or an examiner, if a trustee or an examiner dies or resigns during the case or is removed under section 324 of this title, or if a trustee fails to qualify under section 322 of this title, then the United States trustee, after consultation with parties in interest, shall appoint, subject to the court's approval, one disinterested person other than the United States trustee to serve as trustee or examiner, as the case may be, in the case

(e) The United States trustee shall move for the appointment of a trustee under subsection (a) if there are reasonable grounds to suspect that current members of the governing body of the debtor, the debtor's chief executive or chief financial officer, or members of the governing body who selected the debtor's chief executive or chief financial officer, participated in actual fraud, dishonesty, or criminal conduct in the management of the debtor or the debtor's public financial reporting.

1105. Termination of trustee's appointment

At any time before confirmation of a plan, on request of a party in interest or the United States trustee, and after notice and a hearing, the court may terminate the trustee's appointment and restore the debtor to possession and management of the property of the estate and of the operation of the debtor's business.

1106. Duties of trustee and examiner

(a) A trustee shall-

(1) perform the duties of the trustee, as specified in paragraphs (2), (5), (7), (8), (9), (10), (11), and (12) of section 704(a);

(2) if the debtor has not done so, file the list, schedule, and statement required under section 521(a)(1) of this title;

(3) except to the extent that the court orders otherwise, investigate the acts, conduct, assets, liabilities, and financial condition of the debtor, the operation of the debtor's business and the desirability of the continuance of such business, and any other matter relevant to the case or to the formulation of a plan;

(4) as soon as practicable-

(A) file a statement of any investigation conducted under paragraph (3) of this subsection, including any fact ascertained pertaining to fraud, dishonesty, incompetence, misconduct, mismanagement, or irregularity in the management of the affairs of the debtor, or to a cause of action available to the estate; and

(B) transmit a copy or a summary of any such statement to any creditors' committee or equity security holders' committee, to any indenture trustee, and to such other entity as the court designates;

(5) as soon as practicable, file a plan under section 1121 of this title, file a report of why the trustee will not file a plan, or recommend conversion of the case to a case under chapter 7, 12, or 13 of this title or dismissal of the case;

(6) for any year for which the debtor has not filed a tax return required by law, furnish, without personal liability, such information as may be required by the governmental unit with which such tax return was to be filed, in light of the condition of the debtor's books and records and the availability of such information;

(7) after confirmation of a plan, file such reports as are necessary or as the court orders; and

(8) if with respect to the debtor there is a claim for a domestic support obligation, provide the applicable notice specified in subsection (c).

(b) An examiner appointed under section 1104(d) of this title shall perform the duties specified in paragraphs (3) and (4) of subsection (a) of this section, and, except to the extent that the court orders otherwise, any other duties of the trustee that the court orders the debtor in possession not to perform.

(c)(1) In a case described in subsection (a)(8) to which subsection (a)(8) applies, the trustee shall –

(A)(i) provide written notice to the holder of the claim described in subsection (a)(8) of such claim and of the right of such holder to use the services of the State child support enforcement agency established under sections 464 and 466 of the Social Security Act for the State in which such holder resides, for assistance in collecting child support during and after the case under this title; and

(ii) include in the notice required by clause (i) the address and telephone number of such State child support enforcement agency;

(B)(i) provide written notice to such State child support enforcement agency of such claim; and

(ii) include in the notice required by clause (i) the name, address, and telephone number of such holder; and

(C) at such time as the debtor is granted a discharge under section 1141, provide written notice to such holder and to such State child support enforcement agency of –

(i) the granting of the discharge;

(ii) the last recent known address of the debtor;

(iii) the last recent known name and address of the debtor's employer; and

(iv) the name of each creditor that holds a claim that –

(I) is not discharged under paragraph (2), (4), or (14A) of section 523(a); or

(II) was reaffirmed by the debtor under section 524(c).

(2)(A) The holder of a claim described in subsection (a)(8) or the State child enforcement support agency of the State in which such holder resides may request from a creditor described in paragraph (1)(C)(iv) the last known address of the debtor.

(B) Notwithstanding any other provision of law, a creditor that makes a disclosure of a last known address of a debtor in connection with a request made under subparagraph (A) shall not be liable by reason of making such disclosure.

1107. Rights, powers, and duties of debtor in possession

(a) Subject to any limitations on a trustee serving in a case under this chapter, and to such limitations or conditions as the court prescribes, a debtor in possession shall have all the rights, other than the right to compensation under section 330 of this title, and powers, and shall perform all the functions and duties, except the duties specified in sections 1106(a)(2), (3), and (4) of this title, of a trustee serving in a case under this chapter.

(b) Notwithstanding section 327(a) of this title, a person is not disqualified for employment under section 327 of this title by a debtor in possession solely because of such person's employment by or representation of the debtor before the commencement of the case.

1108. Authorization to operate business

Unless the court, on request of a party in interest and after notice and a hearing, orders otherwise, the trustee may operate the debtor's business.

1109. Right to be heard

(a) The Securities and Exchange Commission may raise and may appear and be heard on any issue in a case under this chapter, but the Securities and Exchange Commission may not appeal from any judgment, order, or decree entered in the case.

(b) A party in interest, including the debtor, the trustee, a creditors' committee, an equity security holders' committee, a creditor, an equity security holder, or any indenture trustee, may raise and may appear and be heard on any issue in a case under this chapter.

1110. Aircraft equipment and vessels

This section is not applicable to small business cases and is therefore omitted.

1111. Claims and interests

(a) A proof of claim or interest is deemed filed under section 501 of this title for any claim or interest that appears in the schedules filed under section 521(a)(1) or 1106(a)(2) of this title, except a claim or interest that is scheduled as disputed, contingent, or unliquidated.

(b)(1)(A) A claim secured by a lien on property of the estate shall be allowed or disallowed under section 502 of this title the same as if the holder of such claim had recourse against the debtor on account of such claim, whether or not such holder has such recourse, unless-

(i) the class of which such claim is a part elects, by at least two-thirds in amount and more than half in number of allowed claims of such class, application of paragraph (2) of this subsection; or

(ii) such holder does not have such recourse and such property is sold under section 363 of this title or is to be sold under the plan.

(B) A class of claims may not elect application of paragraph (2) of this subsection if-

(i) the interest on account of such claims of the holders of such claims in such property is of inconsequential value; or

(ii) the holder of a claim of such class has recourse against the debtor on account of such claim and such property is sold under section 363 of this title or is to be sold under the plan.

(2) If such an election is made, then notwithstanding section 506(a) of this title, such claim is a secured claim to the extent that such claim is allowed.

1112. Conversion or dismissal

(a) The debtor may convert a case under this chapter to a case under chapter 7 of this title unless-

(1) the debtor is not a debtor in possession;

(2) the case originally was commenced as an involuntary case under this chapter; or

(3) the case was converted to a case under this chapter other than on the debtor's request.

(b)(1) Except as provided in paragraph (2) and subsection (c), on request of a party in interest, and after notice and a hearing, the court shall convert a case under this chapter to a case under chapter 7 or dismiss a case under this chapter, whichever is in the best interests of creditors and the estate, for cause unless the court determines that the appointment under section 1104(a) of a trustee or an examiner is in the best interests of creditors and the estate.

(2) The court may not convert a case under this chapter to a case under chapter 7 or dismiss a case under this chapter if the court finds and specifically identifies unusual circumstances establishing that converting or dismissing the case is not in the best interests of creditors and the estate, and the debtor or any other party in interest establishes that –

(A) there is a reasonable likelihood that a plan will be confirmed within the timeframes established in sections 1121(e) and 1129(e) of this title, or if such sections do not apply, within a reasonable period of time; and

(B) the grounds for converting or dismissing the case include an act or omission of the debtor other than under paragraph (4)(A) –

(i) for which there exists a reasonable justification for the act or omission; and

(ii) that will be cured within a reasonable period of time fixed by the court.

(3) The court shall commence the hearing on a motion under this subsection not later than 30 days after filing of the motion, and shall decide the motion not later than 15 days after commencement of such hearing, unless the movant expressly consents to a continuance for a specific period of time or compelling circumstances prevent the court from meeting the time limits established by this paragraph.

(4) For purposes of this subsection, the term "cause" includes –

(A) substantial or continuing loss to or diminution of the estate and the absence of a reasonable likelihood of rehabilitation;

(B) gross mismanagement of the estate;

(C) failure to maintain appropriate insurance that poses a risk to the estate or to the public;

(D) unauthorized use of cash collateral substantially harmful to 1 or more creditors;

(E) failure to comply with an order of the court;

(F) unexcused failure to satisfy timely any filing or reporting requirement established by this title or by any rule applicable to a case under this chapter;

(G) failure to attend the meeting of creditors convened under section 341(a) or an examination ordered under rule 2004 of the Federal Rules of Bankruptcy Procedure without good cause shown by the debtor;

(H) failure timely to provide information or attend meetings reasonably requested by the United States trustee (or the bankruptcy administrator, if any);

(I) failure timely to pay taxes owed after the date of the order for relief or to file tax returns due after the date of the order for relief;

(J) failure to file a disclosure statement, or to file or confirm a plan, within the time fixed by this title or by order of the court;

(K) failure to pay any fees or charges required under chapter 123 of title 28;

(L) revocation of an order of confirmation under section 1144;

(M) inability to effectuate substantial consummation of a confirmed plan;

(N) material default by the debtor with respect to a confirmed plan;

(O) termination of a confirmed plan by reason of the occurrence of a condition specified in the plan; and

(P) failure of the debtor to pay any domestic support obligation that first becomes payable after the date of the filing of the petition.

(c) The court may not convert a case under this chapter to a case under chapter 7 of this title if the debtor is a farmer or a corporation that is not a moneyed, business, or commercial corporation, unless the debtor requests such conversion.

(d) The court may convert a case under this chapter to a case under chapter 12 or 13 of this title only if-

(1) the debtor requests such conversion;

(2) the debtor has not been discharged under section 1141(d) of this title; and

(3) if the debtor requests conversion to chapter 12 of this title, such conversion is equitable.

(e) Except as provided in subsections (c) and (f), the court, on request of the United States trustee, may convert a case under this chapter to a case under chapter 7 of this title or may dismiss a case under this chapter, whichever is in the best interest of creditors and the estate if the debtor in a voluntary case fails to file, within fifteen days after the filing of the petition commencing such case or such additional time as the court may allow, the information required by paragraph (1) of section 521(a), including a list containing the names and addresses of the holders of the twenty largest unsecured claims (or of all unsecured claims if there are fewer than twenty unsecured claims), and the approximate dollar amounts of each of such claims.

(f) Notwithstanding any other provision of this section, a case may not be converted to a case under another chapter of this title unless the debtor may be a debtor under such chapter.

1113. Rejection of collective bargaining agreements

(a) The debtor in possession, or the trustee if one has been appointed under the provisions of this chapter, other than a trustee in a case covered by subchapter IV of this chapter and by title I of the Railway Labor Act, may assume or reject a collective bargaining agreement only in accordance with the provisions of this section.

(b)(1) Subsequent to filing a petition and prior to filing an application seeking rejection of a collective bargaining agreement, the debtor in possession or trustee (hereinafter in this section "trustee" shall include a debtor in possession), shall-

(A) make a proposal to the authorized representative of the employees covered by such agreement, based on the most complete and reliable information available at the time of such proposal, which provides for those necessary modifications in the employees benefits and protections that are necessary to permit the reorganization of the debtor and assures that all creditors, the debtor and all of the affected parties are treated fairly and equitably; and

(B) provide, subject to subsection (d)(3), the representative of the employees with such relevant information as is necessary to evaluate the proposal.

(2) During the period beginning on the date of the making of a proposal provided for in paragraph (1) and ending on the date of the hearing provided for in subsection (d)(1), the trustee shall meet, at reasonable times, with the authorized representative to confer in good faith in attempting to reach mutually satisfactory modifications of such agreement.

(c) The court shall approve an application for rejection of a collective bargaining agreement only if the court finds that-

(1) the trustee has, prior to the hearing, made a proposal that fulfills the requirements of subsection (b)(1);

(2) the authorized representative of the employees has refused to accept such proposal without good cause; and

(3) the balance of the equities clearly favors rejection of such agreement.

(d)(1) Upon the filing of an application for rejection the court shall schedule a hearing to be held not later than fourteen days after the date of the filing of such application. All interested parties may appear and be heard at such hearing. Adequate notice shall be provided to such parties at least ten days before the date of such hearing. The court may extend the time for the commencement of such hearing for a period not exceeding seven days where the circumstances of the case, and the interests of justice require such extension, or for additional periods of time to which the trustee and representative agree.

(2) The court shall rule on such application for rejection within thirty days after the date of the commencement of the hearing. In the interests of justice, the court may extend such time for ruling for such additional period as the trustee and the employees' representative may agree to. If the court does not rule on such application within thirty days after the date of the commencement of the hearing, or within such additional time as the trustee and the employees' representative may agree to, the trustee may terminate or alter any provisions of the collective bargaining agreement pending the ruling of the court on such application.

(3) The court may enter such protective orders, consistent with the need of the authorized representative of the employee to evaluate the trustee's proposal and the application for rejection, as may be necessary to prevent disclosure of information provided to such representative where such disclosure could compromise the position of the debtor with respect to its competitors in the industry in which it is engaged.

(e) If during a period when the collective bargaining agreement continues in effect, and if essential to the continuation of the debtor's business, or in order to avoid irreparable damage to the estate, the court, after notice and a hearing, may authorize the trustee to implement interim changes in the terms, conditions, wages, benefits, or work rules provided by a collective bargaining agreement. Any hearing under this paragraph shall be scheduled in accordance with the needs of the trustee. The implementation of such interim changes shall not render the application for rejection moot.

(f) No provision of this title shall be construed to permit a trustee to unilaterally terminate or alter any provisions of a collective bargaining agreement prior to compliance with the provisions of this section.

1114. Payment of insurance benefits to retired employees.

(a) For purposes of this section, the term "retiree benefits" means payments to any entity or person for the purpose of providing or reimbursing payments for retired employees and their spouses and dependents, for medical, surgical, or hospital care benefits, or benefits in the event of sickness, accident, disability, or death under any plan, fund, or program (through the purchase of insurance or otherwise) maintained or established in whole or in part by the debtor prior to filing a petition commencing a case under this title.

(b)(1) For purposes of this section, the term "authorized representative" means the authorized representative designated pursuant to subsection (c) for persons receiving any retiree benefits covered by a collective bargaining agreement or subsection (d) in the case of persons receiving retiree benefits not covered by such an agreement.

(2) Committees of retired employees appointed by the court pursuant to this section shall have the same rights, powers, and duties as committees appointed under sections 1102 and 1103 of this title for the purpose of carrying out the purposes of sections 1114 and 1129(a)(13) and, as permitted by the court, shall have the power to enforce the rights of persons under this title as they relate to retiree benefits.

(c)(1) A labor organization shall be, for purposes of this section, the authorized representative of those persons receiving any retiree benefits covered by any collective bargaining agreement to which that labor organization is signatory, unless (A) such labor organization elects not to serve as the authorized representative of such persons, or (B) the court, upon a motion by any party in interest, after notice and hearing, determines that different representation of such persons is appropriate.

(2) In cases where the labor organization referred to in paragraph (1) elects not to serve as the authorized representative of those persons receiving any retiree benefits covered by any collective bargaining agreement to which that labor organization is signatory, or in cases where the court, pursuant to paragraph (1) finds different representation of such persons appropriate, the court, upon a motion by any party in interest, and after notice and a hearing, shall appoint a committee of retired employees if the debtor seeks to modify or not pay the retiree benefits or if the court otherwise determines that it is appropriate, from among such persons, to serve as the authorized representative of such persons under this section.

(d) The court, upon a motion by any party in interest, and after notice and a hearing, shall order the appointment of a committee of retired employees if the debtor seeks to modify or not pay the retiree benefits or if the court otherwise determines that it is appropriate, to serve as the authorized representative, under this section, of those persons receiving any retiree benefits not covered by a collective bargaining agreement. The United States trustee shall appoint any such committee.

(e)(1) Notwithstanding any other provision of this title, the debtor in possession, or the trustee if one has been appointed under the provisions of this chapter (hereinafter in this section "trustee" shall include a debtor in possession), shall timely pay and shall not modify any retiree benefits, except that-

(A) the court, on motion of the trustee or authorized representative, and after notice and a hearing, may order modification of such payments, pursuant to the provisions of subsections (g) and (h) of this section, or

(B) the trustee and the authorized representative of the recipients of those benefits may agree to modification of such payments, after which such benefits as modified shall continue to be paid by the trustee.

(2) Any payment for retiree benefits required to be made before a plan confirmed under section 1129 of this title is effective has the status of an allowed administrative expense as provided in section 503 of this title.

(f)(1) Subsequent to filing a petition and prior to filing an application seeking modification of the retiree benefits, the trustee shall-

(A) make a proposal to the authorized representative of the retirees, based on the most complete and reliable information available at the time of such proposal, which provides for those necessary modifications in the retiree benefits that are necessary to permit the reorganization of the debtor and assures that all creditors, the debtor and all of the affected parties are treated fairly and equitably; and

(B) provide, subject to subsection (k)(3), the representative of the retirees with such relevant information as is necessary to evaluate the proposal.

(2) During the period beginning on the date of the making of a proposal provided for in paragraph (1), and ending on the date of the hearing provided for in subsection (k)(1), the trustee shall meet, at reasonable times, with the authorized representative to confer in good faith in attempting to reach mutually satisfactory modifications of such retiree benefits.

(g) The court shall enter an order providing for modification in the payment of retiree benefits if the court finds that-

(1) the trustee has, prior to the hearing, made a proposal that fulfills the requirements of subsection (f);

(2) the authorized representative of the retirees has refused to accept such proposal without good cause; and

(3) such modification is necessary to permit the reorganization of the debtor and assures that all creditors, the debtor, and all of the affected parties are treated fairly and equitably, and is clearly favored by the balance of the equities; except that in no case shall the court enter an order providing for such modification which provides for a modification to a level lower than that proposed by the trustee in the proposal found by the court to have complied with the requirements of this subsection and subsection (f): Provided, however, That at any time after an order is entered providing for modification in the payment of retiree benefits, or at any time after an agreement modifying such benefits is made between the trustee and the authorized representative of the recipients of such benefits, the authorized representative may apply to the court for an order increasing those benefits which order shall be granted if the increase in retiree benefits sought is consistent with the standard set forth in paragraph (3): Provided further, That neither the trustee nor the authorized representative is precluded from making more than one motion for a modification order governed by this subsection.

(h)(1) Prior to a court issuing a final order under subsection (g) of this section, if essential to the continuation of the debtor's business, or in order to avoid irreparable damage to the estate, the court, after notice and a hearing, may authorize the trustee to implement interim modifications in retiree benefits.

(2) Any hearing under this subsection shall be scheduled in accordance with the needs of the trustee.

(3) The implementation of such interim changes does not render the motion for modification moot.

(i) No retiree benefits paid between the filing of the petition and the time a plan confirmed under section 1129 of this title becomes effective shall be deducted or offset from the amounts allowed as claims for any benefits which remain unpaid, or from the amounts to be paid under the plan with respect to such claims for unpaid benefits, whether such claims for unpaid benefits are based upon or arise from a right to future unpaid benefits or from any benefits not paid as a result of modifications allowed pursuant to this section.

(j) No claim for retiree benefits shall be limited by section 502(b)(7) of this title.

(k)(1) Upon the filing of an application for modifying retiree benefits, the court shall schedule a hearing to be held not later than fourteen days after the date of the filing of such application. All interested parties may appear and be heard at such hearing. Adequate notice shall be provided to such parties at least ten days before the date of such hearing. The court may extend the time for the commencement of such hearing for a period not exceeding seven days where the circumstances of the case, and the interests of justice require such extension, or for additional periods of time to which the trustee and the authorized representative agree.

(2) The court shall rule on such application for modification within ninety days after the date of the commencement of the hearing. In the interests of justice, the court may extend such time for ruling for such additional period as the trustee and the authorized representative may agree to. If the court does not rule on such application within ninety days after the date of the commencement of the hearing, or within such additional time as the trustee and the authorized representative may agree to, the trustee may implement the proposed modifications pending the ruling of the court on such application.

(3) The court may enter such protective orders, consistent with the need of the authorized representative of the retirees to evaluate the trustee's proposal and the application for modification, as may be necessary to prevent disclosure of information provided to such representative where such disclosure could compromise the position of the debtor with respect to its competitors in the industry in which it is engaged.

(l) If the debtor, during the 180-day period ending on the date of the filing of the petition –

(1) modified retiree benefits; and

(2) was insolvent on the date such benefits were modified;

the court, on motion of a party in interest, and after notice and a hearing, shall issue an order reinstating as of the date the modification was made, such benefits as in effect immediately before such date unless the court finds that the balance of the equities clearly favors such modification.

(m) This section shall not apply to any retiree, or the spouse or dependents of such retiree, if such retiree's gross income for the twelve months preceding the filing of the bankruptcy petition equals or exceeds $250,000, unless such retiree can demonstrate to the satisfaction of the court that he is unable to obtain health, medical, life, and disability coverage for himself, his spouse, and his dependents who would otherwise be covered by the employer's insurance plan, comparable to the coverage provided by the employer on the day before the filing of a petition under this title.

1115. Property of the estate

(a) In a case in which the debtor is an individual, property of the estate includes, in addition to the property specified in section 541 –

(1) all property of the kind specified in section 541 that the debtor acquires after the commencement of the case but before the case is closed, dismissed, or converted to a case under chapter 7, 12, or 13, whichever occurs first; and

(2) earnings from services performed by the debtor after the commencement of the case but before the case is closed, dismissed, or converted to a case under chapter 7, 12, or 13, whichever occurs first.

(b) Except as provided in section 1104 or a confirmed plan or order confirming a plan, the debtor shall remain in possession of all property of the estate.

1116. Duties of trustee or debtor in possession in small business cases

In a small business case, a trustee or the debtor in possession, in addition to the duties provided in this title and as otherwise required by law, shall –

(1) append to the voluntary petition or, in an involuntary case, file not later than 7 days after the date of the order for relief –

(A) its most recent balance sheet, statement of operations, cash-flow statement, and Federal income tax return; or

(B) a statement made under penalty of perjury that no balance sheet, statement of operations, or cash-flow statement has been prepared and no Federal tax return has been filed;

(2) attend, through its senior management personnel and counsel, meetings scheduled by the court or the United States trustee, including initial debtor interviews, scheduling conferences, and meetings of creditors convened under section 341 unless the court, after notice and a hearing, waives that requirement upon a finding of extraordinary and compelling circumstances;

(3) timely file all schedules and statements of financial affairs, unless the court, after notice and a hearing, grants an extension, which shall not extend such time period to a date later than 30 days after the date of the order for relief, absent extraordinary and compelling circumstances;

(4) file all postpetition financial and other reports required by the Federal Rules of Bankruptcy Procedure or by local rule of the district court;

(5) subject to section 363(c)(2), maintain insurance customary and appropriate to the industry;

(6)(A) timely file tax returns and other required government filings; and

(B) subject to section 363(c)(2), timely pay all taxes entitled to administrative expense priority except those being contested by appropriate proceedings being diligently prosecuted; and

(7) allow the United States trustee, or a designated representative of the United States trustee, to inspect the debtor's business premises, books, and records at reasonable times, after reasonable prior written notice, unless notice is waived by the debtor.

SUBCHAPTER II - THE PLAN

1121. Who may file a plan

(a) The debtor may file a plan with a petition commencing a voluntary case, or at any time in a voluntary case or an involuntary case.

(b) Except as otherwise provided in this section, only the debtor may file a plan until after 120 days after the date of the order for relief under this chapter.

(c) Any party in interest, including the debtor, the trustee, a creditors' committee, an equity security holders' committee, a creditor, an equity security holder, or any indenture trustee, may file a plan if and only if-

(1) a trustee has been appointed under this chapter;

(2) the debtor has not filed a plan before 120 days after the date of the order for relief under this chapter; or

(3) the debtor has not filed a plan that has been accepted, before 180 days after the date of the order for relief under this chapter, by each class of claims or interests that is impaired under the plan.

(d)(1) Subject to paragraph (2) on request of a party in interest made within the respective periods specified in subsections (b) and (c) of this section and after notice and a hearing, the court may for cause reduce or increase the 120-day period or the 180-day period referred to in this section.

(2)(A) The 120-day period specified in paragraph (1) may not be extended beyond a date that is 18 months after the date of the order for relief under this chapter.

(B) The 180-day period specified in paragraph (1) may not be extended beyond a date that is 20 months after the date of the order for relief under this chapter.

(e) In a small business case –

(1) only the debtor may file a plan until after 180 days after the date of the order for relief, unless that period is –

(A) extended as provided by this subsection, after notice and a hearing; or

(B) the court, for cause, orders otherwise;

(2) the plan and a disclosure statement (if any) shall be filed not later than 300 days after the date of the order for relief; and

(3) the time periods specified in paragraphs (1) and (2), and the time fixed in section 1129(e) within which the plan shall be confirmed, may be extended only if –

(A) the debtor, after providing notice to parties in interest (including the United States trustee), demonstrates by a preponderance of the evidence that it is more likely than not that the court will confirm a plan within a reasonable period of time;

(B) a new deadline is imposed at the time the extension is granted; and

(C) the order extending time is signed before the existing deadline has expired.

1122. Classification of claims or interests

(a) Except as provided in subsection (b) of this section, a plan may place a claim or an interest in a particular class only if such claim or interest is substantially similar to the other claims or interests of such class.

(b) A plan may designate a separate class of claims consisting only of every unsecured claim that is less than or reduced to an amount that the court approves as reasonable and necessary for administrative convenience.

1123. Contents of plan

(a) Notwithstanding any otherwise applicable nonbankruptcy law, a plan shall-

(1) designate, subject to section 1122 of this title, classes of claims, other than claims of a kind specified in section 507(a)(2), 507(a)(3), or 507(a)(8) of this title, and classes of interests;

(2) specify any class of claims or interests that is not impaired under the plan;

(3) specify the treatment of any class of claims or interests that is impaired under the plan;

(4) provide the same treatment for each claim or interest of a particular class, unless the holder of a particular claim or interest agrees to a less favorable treatment of such particular claim or interest;

(5) provide adequate means for the plan's implementation, such as-

(A) retention by the debtor of all or any part of the property of the estate;

(B) transfer of all or any part of the property of the estate to one or more entities, whether organized before or after the confirmation of such plan;

(C) merger or consolidation of the debtor with one or more persons;

(D) sale of all or any part of the property of the estate, either subject to or free of any lien, or the distribution of all or any part of the property of the estate among those having an interest in such property of the estate;

(E) satisfaction or modification of any lien;

(F) cancellation or modification of any indenture or similar instrument;

(G) curing or waiving of any default;

(H) extension of a maturity date or a change in an interest rate

or other term of outstanding securities;

(I) amendment of the debtor's charter; or

(J) issuance of securities of the debtor, or of any entity referred to in subparagraph (B) or (C) of this paragraph, for cash, for property, for existing securities, or in exchange for claims or interests, or for any other appropriate purpose;

(6) provide for the inclusion in the charter of the debtor, if the debtor is a corporation, or of any corporation referred to in paragraph (5)(B) or (5)(C) of this subsection, of a provision prohibiting the issuance of nonvoting equity securities, and providing, as to the several classes of securities possessing voting power, an appropriate distribution of such power among such classes, including, in the case of any class of equity securities having a preference over another class of equity securities with respect to dividends, adequate provisions for the election of directors representing such preferred class in the event of default in the payment of such dividends;

(7) contain only provisions that are consistent with the interests of creditors and equity security holders and with public policy with respect to the manner of selection of any officer, director, or trustee under the plan and any successor to such officer, director, or trustee; and

(8) in a case in which the debtor is an individual, provide for the payment to creditors under the plan of all or such portion of earnings from personal services performed by the debtor after the commencement of the case or other future income of the debtor as is necessary for the execution of the plan.

(b) Subject to subsection (a) of this section, a plan may -

(1) impair or leave unimpaired any class of claims, secured or unsecured, or of interests;

(2) subject to section 365 of this title, provide for the assumption, rejection, or assignment of any executory contract or unexpired lease of the debtor not previously rejected under such section;

(3) provide for -

(A) the settlement or adjustment of any claim or interest belonging to the debtor or to the estate; or

(B) the retention and enforcement by the debtor, by the trustee, or by a representative of the estate appointed for such purpose, of any such claim or interest;

(4) provide for the sale of all or substantially all of the property of the estate, and the distribution of the proceeds of such sale among holders of claims or interests;

(5) modify the rights of holders of secured claims, other than a claim secured only by a security interest in real property that is the debtor's principal residence, or of holders of unsecured claims, or leave unaffected the rights of holders of any class of claims; and

(6) include any other appropriate provision not inconsistent with the applicable provisions of this title.

(c) In a case concerning an individual, a plan proposed by an entity other than the debtor may not provide for the use, sale, or lease of property exempted under section 522 of this title, unless the debtor consents to such use, sale, or lease.

(d) Notwithstanding subsection (a) of this section and sections 506(b), 1129(a)(7), and 1129(b) of this title, if it is proposed in a plan to cure a default the amount necessary to cure the default shall be determined in accordance with the underlying agreement and applicable nonbankruptcy law.

1124. Impairment of claims or interests

Except as provided in section 1123(a)(4) of this title, a class of claims or interests is impaired under a plan unless, with respect to each claim or interest of such class, the plan -

(1) leaves unaltered the legal, equitable, and contractual rights to which such claim or interest entitles the holder of such claim or interest; or

(2) notwithstanding any contractual provision or applicable law that entitles the holder of such claim or interest to demand or receive accelerated payment of such claim or interest after the occurrence of a default -

(A) cures any such default that occurred before or after the commencement of the case under this title, other than a default of a kind specified in section 365(b)(2) of this title or of a kind that section 365(b)(2) expressly does not require to be cured;

(B) reinstates the maturity of such claim or interest as such maturity existed before such default;

(C) compensates the holder of such claim or interest for any damages incurred as a result of any reasonable reliance by such holder on such contractual provision or such applicable law;

(D) if such claim or such interest arises from any failure to perform a nonmonetary obligation, other than a default arising from failure to operate a nonresidential real property lease subject to section 365(b)(1)(A), compensates the holder of such claim or such interest (other than the debtor or an insider) for any actual pecuniary loss incurred by such holder as a result of such failure; and

(E) does not otherwise alter the legal, equitable, or contractual rights to which such claim or interest entitles the holder of such claim or interest.

1125. Postpetition disclosure and solicitation

(a) In this section-

(1) "adequate information" means information of a kind, and in sufficient detail, as far as is reasonably practicable in light of the nature and history of the debtor and the condition of the debtor's books and records, including a discussion of the potential material Federal tax consequences of the plan to the debtor, any successor to the debtor, and a hypothetical investor typical of the holders of claims or interests in the case, that would enable such a hypothetical investor of the relevant class to make an informed judgment about the plan, but adequate information need not include such information about any other possible or proposed plan and in determining whether a disclosure statement provides adequate information, the court shall consider the complexity of the case, the benefit of additional information to creditors and other parties in interest, and the cost of providing additional information; and

(2) "investor typical of holders of claims or interests of the relevant class" means investor having-

(A) a claim or interest of the relevant class;

(B) such a relationship with the debtor as the holders of other claims or interests of such class generally have; and

(C) such ability to obtain such information from sources other than the disclosure required by this section as holders of claims or interests in such class generally have.

(b) An acceptance or rejection of a plan may not be solicited after the commencement of the case under this title from a holder of a claim or interest with respect to such claim or interest, unless, at the time of or before such solicitation, there is transmitted to such holder the plan or a summary of the plan, and a written disclosure statement approved, after notice and a hearing, by the court as containing adequate information. The court may approve a disclosure statement without a valuation of the debtor or an appraisal of the debtor's assets.

(c) The same disclosure statement shall be transmitted to each holder of a claim or interest of a particular class, but there may be transmitted different disclosure statements, differing in amount, detail, or kind of information, as between classes.

(d) Whether a disclosure statement required under subsection (b) of this section contains adequate information is not governed by any otherwise applicable nonbankruptcy law, rule, or regulation, but an agency or official whose duty is to administer or enforce such a law, rule, or regulation may be heard on the issue of whether a disclosure statement contains adequate information. Such an agency or official may not appeal from, or otherwise seek review of, an order approving a disclosure statement.

(e) A person that solicits acceptance or rejection of a plan, in good faith and in compliance with the applicable provisions of this title, or that participates, in good faith and in compliance with the applicable provisions of this title, in the offer, issuance, sale, or purchase of a security, offered or sold under the plan, of the debtor, of an affiliate participating in a joint plan with the debtor, or of a newly organized successor to the debtor under the plan, is not liable, on account of such solicitation or participation, for violation of any applicable law, rule, or regulation governing solicitation of acceptance or rejection of a plan or the offer, issuance, sale, or purchase of securities.

(f) Notwithstanding subsection (b), in a small business case –

(1) the court may determine that the plan itself provides adequate information and that a separate disclosure statement is not necessary;

(2) the court may approve a disclosure statement submitted on standard forms approved by the court or adopted under section 2075 of title 28; and

(3)(A) the court may conditionally approve a disclosure statement subject to final approval after notice and a hearing;

(B) acceptances and rejections of a plan may be solicited based on a conditionally approved disclosure statement if the debtor provides adequate information to each holder of a claim or interest that is solicited, but a conditionally approved disclosure statement shall be mailed not later than 25 days before the date of the hearing on confirmation of the plan; and

(C) the hearing on the disclosure statement may be combined with the hearing on confirmation of a plan.

(g) Notwithstanding subsection (b), an acceptance or rejection of the plan may be solicited from a holder of a claim or interest if such solicitation complies with applicable nonbankruptcy law and if such holder was solicited before the commencement of the case in a manner complying with applicable nonbankruptcy law.

1126. Acceptance of plan

(a) The holder of a claim or interest allowed under section 502 of this title may accept or reject a plan. If the United States is a creditor or equity security holder, the Secretary of the Treasury may accept or reject the plan on behalf of the United States.

(b) For the purposes of subsections (c) and (d) of this section, a holder of a claim or interest that has accepted or rejected the plan before the commencement of the case under this title is deemed to have accepted or rejected such plan, as the case may be, if-

(1) the solicitation of such acceptance or rejection was in compliance with any applicable nonbankruptcy law, rule, or regulation governing the adequacy of disclosure in connection with such solicitation; or

(2) if there is not any such law, rule, or regulation, such acceptance or rejection was solicited after disclosure to such holder of adequate information, as defined in section 1125(a) of this title.

(c) A class of claims has accepted a plan if such plan has been accepted by creditors, other than any entity designated under subsection (e) of this section, that hold at least two-thirds in amount and more than one-half in number of the allowed claims of such class held by creditors, other than any entity designated under subsection (e) of this section, that have accepted or rejected such plan.

(d) A class of interests has accepted a plan if such plan has been accepted by holders of such interests, other than any entity designated under subsection (e) of this section, that hold at least two-thirds in amount of the allowed interests of such class held by holders of such interests, other than any entity designated under subsection (e) of this section, that have accepted or rejected such plan.

(e) On request of a party in interest, and after notice and a hearing, the court may designate any entity whose acceptance or rejection of such plan was not in good faith, or was not solicited or procured in good faith or in accordance with the provisions of this title.

(f) Notwithstanding any other provision of this section, a class that is not impaired under a plan, and each holder of a claim or interest of such class, are conclusively presumed to have accepted the plan, and solicitation of acceptances with respect to such class from the holders of claims or interests of such class is not required.

(g) Notwithstanding any other provision of this section, a class is deemed not to have accepted a plan if such plan provides that the claims or interests of such class do not entitle the holders of such claims or interests to receive or retain any property under the plan on account of such claims or interests.

1127. Modification of plan

(a) The proponent of a plan may modify such plan at any time before confirmation, but may not modify such plan so that such plan as modified fails to meet the requirements of sections 1122 and 1123 of this title. After the proponent of a plan files a modification of such plan with the court, the plan as modified becomes the plan.

(b) The proponent of a plan or the reorganized debtor may modify such plan at any time after confirmation of such plan and before substantial consummation of such plan, but may not modify such plan so that such plan as modified fails to meet the requirements of sections 1122 and 1123 of this title. Such plan as modified under this subsection becomes the plan only if circumstances warrant such modification and the court, after notice and a hearing, confirms such plan as modified, under section 1129 of this title.

(c) The proponent of a modification shall comply with section 1125 of this title with respect to the plan as modified.

(d) Any holder of a claim or interest that has accepted or rejected a plan is deemed to have accepted or rejected, as the case may be, such plan as modified, unless, within the time fixed by the court, such holder changes such holder's previous acceptance or rejection.

(e) If the debtor is an individual, the plan may be modified at any time after confirmation of the plan but before the completion of payments under the plan, whether or not the plan has been substantially consummated, upon request of the debtor, the trustee, the United States trustee, or the holder of an allowed unsecured claim, to –

(1) increase or reduce the amount of payments on claims of a particular class provided for by the plan;

(2) extend or reduce the time period for such payments; or

(3) alter the amount of the distribution to a creditor whose claim is provided for by the plan to the extent necessary to take account of any payment of such claim made other than under the plan.

(f)(1) Sections 1121 through 1128 and the requirements of section 1129 apply to any modification under subsection (e).

(2) The plan, as modified, shall become the plan only after there has been disclosure under section 1125 as the court may direct, notice and a hearing, and such modification is approved.

1128. Confirmation hearing

(a) After notice, the court shall hold a hearing on confirmation of a plan.

(b) A party in interest may object to confirmation of a plan.

1129. Confirmation of plan

(a) The court shall confirm a plan only if all of the following requirements are met:

(1) The plan complies with the applicable provisions of this title.

(2) The proponent of the plan complies with the applicable provisions of this title.

(3) The plan has been proposed in good faith and not by any means forbidden by law.

(4) Any payment made or to be made by the proponent, by the debtor, or by a person issuing securities or acquiring property under the plan, for services or for costs and expenses in or in connection with the case, or in connection with the plan and incident to the case, has been approved by, or is subject to the approval of, the court as reasonable.

(5)(A)(i) The proponent of the plan has disclosed the identity and affiliations of any individual proposed to serve, after confirmation of the plan, as a director, officer, or voting trustee of the debtor, an affiliate of the debtor participating in a joint plan with the debtor, or a successor to the debtor under the plan; and

(ii) the appointment to, or continuance in, such office of such individual, is consistent with the interests of creditors and equity security holders and with public policy; and

(B) the proponent of the plan has disclosed the identity of any insider that will be employed or retained by the reorganized debtor, and the nature of any compensation for such insider.

(6) Any governmental regulatory commission with jurisdiction, after confirmation of the plan, over the rates of the debtor has approved any rate change provided for in the plan, or such rate change is expressly conditioned on such approval.

(7) With respect to each impaired class of claims or interests-

(A) each holder of a claim or interest of such class-

(i) has accepted the plan; or

(ii) will receive or retain under the plan on account of such claim or interest property of a value, as of the effective date of the plan, that is not less than the amount that such holder would so receive or retain if the debtor were liquidated under chapter 7 of this title on such date; or

(B) if section 1111(b)(2) of this title applies to the claims of such class, each holder of a claim of such class will receive or retain under the plan on account of such claim property of a value, as of the effective date of the plan, that is not less than the value of such holder's interest in the estate's interest in the property that secures such claims.

(8) With respect to each class of claims or interests-

(A) such class has accepted the plan; or

(B) such class is not impaired under the plan.

(9) Except to the extent that the holder of a particular claim has agreed to a different treatment of such claim, the plan provides that-

(A) with respect to a claim of a kind specified in section 507(a)(2) or 507(a)(3) of this title, on the effective date of the plan, the holder of such claim will receive on account of such claim cash equal to the allowed amount of such claim;

(B) with respect to a class of claims of a kind specified in section 507(a)(1), 507(a)(4), 507(a)(5), 507(a)(6), or 507(a)(7) of this title, each holder of a claim of such class will receive-

(i) if such class has accepted the plan, deferred cash payments of a value, as of the effective date of the plan, equal to the allowed amount of such claim; or

(ii) if such class has not accepted the plan, cash on the effective date of the plan equal to the allowed amount of such claim;

(C) with respect to a claim of a kind specified in section 507(a)(8) of this title, the holder of such claim will receive on account of such claim regular installment payments in cash –

(i) of a total value, as of the effective date of the plan, equal to the allowed amount of such claim;

(ii) over a period ending not later than 5 years after the date of the order for relief under section 301, 302, or 303; and

(iii) in a manner not less favorable than the most favored nonpriority unsecured claim provided for by the plan (other than cash payments made to a class of creditors under section 1122(b)); and

(D) with respect to a secured claim which would otherwise meet the description of an unsecured claim of a governmental unit under section 507(a)(8), but for the secured status of that claim, the holder of that claim will receive on account of that claim, cash payments, in the same manner and over the same period, as prescribed in subparagraph (C).

(10) If a class of claims is impaired under the plan, at least one class of claims that is impaired under the plan has accepted the plan, determined without including any acceptance of the plan by any insider.

(11) Confirmation of the plan is not likely to be followed by the liquidation, or the need for further financial reorganization, of the debtor or any successor to the debtor under the plan, unless such liquidation or reorganization is proposed in the plan.

(12) All fees payable under section 1930 of title 28, as determined by the court at the hearing on confirmation of the plan, have been paid or the plan provides for the payment of all such fees on the effective date of the plan.

(13) The plan provides for the continuation after its effective date of payment of all retiree benefits, as that term is defined in section 1114 of this title, at the level established pursuant to subsection (e)(1)(B) or (g) of section 1114 of this title, at any time prior to confirmation of the plan, for the duration of the period the debtor has obligated itself to provide such benefits.

(14) If the debtor is required by a judicial or administrative order, or by statute, to pay a domestic support obligation, the debtor has paid all amounts payable under such order or such statute for such obligation that first become payable after the date of the filing of the petition.

(15) In a case in which the debtor is an individual and in which the holder of an allowed unsecured claim objects to the confirmation of the plan –

(A) the value, as of the effective date of the plan, of the property to be distributed under the plan on account of such claim is not less than the amount of such claim; or

(B) the value of the property to be distributed under the plan is not less than the projected disposable income of the debtor (as defined in section 1325(b)(2)) to be received during the 5-year period beginning on the date that the first payment is due under the plan, or during the period for which the plan provides payments, whichever is longer.

(16) All transfers of property under the plan shall be made in accordance with any applicable provisions of nonbankruptcy law that govern the transfer of property by a corporation or trust that is not a moneyed, business, or commercial corporation or trust.

(b)(1) Notwithstanding section 510(a) of this title, if all of the applicable requirements of subsection (a) of this section other than paragraph (8) are met with respect to a plan, the court, on request of the proponent of the plan, shall confirm the plan notwithstanding the requirements of such paragraph if the plan does not discriminate unfairly, and is fair and equitable, with respect to each class of claims or interests that is impaired under, and has not accepted, the plan.

(2) For the purpose of this subsection, the condition that a plan be fair and equitable with respect to a class includes the following requirements:

(A) With respect to a class of secured claims, the plan provides-

(i)(I) that the holders of such claims retain the liens securing such claims, whether the property subject to such liens is retained by the debtor or transferred to another entity, to the extent of the allowed amount of such claims; and

(II) that each holder of a claim of such class receive on account of such claim deferred cash payments totaling at least the allowed amount of such claim, of a value, as of the effective date of the plan, of at least the value of such holder's interest in the estate's interest in such property;

(ii) for the sale, subject to section 363(k) of this title, of any property that is subject to the liens securing such claims, free and clear of such liens, with such liens to attach to the proceeds of such sale, and the treatment of such liens on proceeds under clause (i) or (iii) of this subparagraph; or

(iii) for the realization by such holders of the indubitable equivalent of such claims.

(B) With respect to a class of unsecured claims-

(i) the plan provides that each holder of a claim of such class receive or retain on account of such claim property of a value, as of the effective date of the plan, equal to the allowed amount of such claim; or

(ii) the holder of any claim or interest that is junior to the claims of such class will not receive or retain under the plan on account of such junior claim or interest any property, except that in a case in which the debtor is an individual, the debtor may retain property included in the estate under section 1115, subject to the requirements of subsection (a)(14) of this section.

(C) With respect to a class of interests-

(i) the plan provides that each holder of an interest of such class receive or retain on account of such interest property of a value, as of the effective date of the plan, equal to the greatest of the allowed amount of any fixed liquidation preference to which such holder is entitled, any fixed redemption price to which such holder is entitled, or the value of such interest; or

(ii) the holder of any interest that is junior to the interests of such class will not receive or retain under the plan on account of such junior interest any property.

(c) Notwithstanding subsections (a) and (b) of this section and except as provided in section 1127(b) of this title, the court may confirm only one plan, unless the order of confirmation in the case has been revoked under section 1144 of this title. If the requirements of subsections (a) and (b) of this section are met with respect to more than one plan, the court shall consider the preferences of creditors and equity security holders in determining which plan to confirm.(d) Notwithstanding any other provision of this section, on request of a party in interest that is a governmental unit, the court may not confirm a plan if the principal purpose of the plan is the avoidance of taxes or the avoidance of the application of section 5 of the Securities Act of 1933. In any hearing under this subsection, the governmental unit has the burden of proof on the issue of avoidance.

(e) In a small business case, the court shall confirm a plan that complies with the applicable provisions of this title and that is filed in accordance with section 1121(e) not later than 45 days after the plan is filed unless the time for confirmation is extended in accordance with section 1121(e)(3).

SUBCHAPTER III - POSTCONFIRMATION MATTERS

1141. Effect of confirmation

(a) Except as provided in subsections (d)(2) and (d)(3) of this section, the provisions of a confirmed plan bind the debtor, any entity issuing securities under the plan, any entity acquiring property under the plan, and any creditor, equity security holder, or general partner in the debtor, whether or not the claim or interest of such creditor, equity security holder, or general partner is impaired under the plan and whether or not such creditor, equity security holder, or general partner has accepted the plan.

(b) Except as otherwise provided in the plan or the order confirming the plan, the confirmation of a plan vests all of the property of the estate in the debtor.

(c) Except as provided in subsections (d)(2) and (d)(3) of this section and except as otherwise provided in the plan or in the order confirming the plan, after confirmation of a plan, the property dealt with by the plan is free and clear of all claims and interests of creditors, equity security holders, and of general partners in the debtor.

(d)(1) Except as otherwise provided in this subsection, in the plan, or in the order confirming the plan, the confirmation of a plan-

(A) discharges the debtor from any debt that arose before the date

of such confirmation, and any debt of a kind specified in section 502(g), 502(h), or 502(i) of this title, whether or not-

(i) a proof of the claim based on such debt is filed or deemed filed under section 501 of this title;

(ii) such claim is allowed under section 502 of this title; or

(iii) the holder of such claim has accepted the plan; and

(B) terminates all rights and interests of equity security holders and general partners provided for by the plan.

(2) A discharge under this chapter does not discharge a debtor who is an individual from any debt excepted from discharge under section 523 of this title.

(3) The confirmation of a plan does not discharge a debtor if-

(A) the plan provides for the liquidation of all or substantially all of the property of the estate;

(B) the debtor does not engage in business after consummation of the plan; and

(C) the debtor would be denied a discharge under section 727(a) of this title if the case were a case under chapter 7 of this title.

(4) The court may approve a written waiver of discharge executed by the debtor after the order for relief under this chapter.

(5) In a case in which the debtor is an individual –

(A) unless after notice and a hearing the court orders otherwise for cause, confirmation of the plan does not discharge any debt provided for in the plan until the court grants a discharge on completion of all payments under the plan;

(B) at any time after the confirmation of the plan, and after notice and a hearing, the court may grant a discharge to the debtor who has not completed payments under the plan if –

(i) the value, as of the effective date of the plan, of property actually distributed under the plan on account of each allowed unsecured claim is not less than the amount that would have been paid on such claim if the estate of the debtor had been liquidated under chapter 7 on such date;

(ii) modification of the plan under section 1127 is not practicable; and

(iii) subparagraph (C) permits the court to grant a discharge; and

(C) the court may grant a discharge if, after notice and a hearing held not more than 10 days before the date of the entry of the order granting the discharge, the court finds that there is no reasonable cause to believe that –

(i) section 522(q)(1) may be applicable to the debtor, and

(ii) there is pending any proceeding in which the debtor may be found guilty of a felony of the kind described in section 522(q)(1)(A) or liable for a debt of the kind described in section 522(q)(1)(B);

and if the requirements of subparagraph (A) or (B) are met.

(6) Notwithstanding paragraph (1), the confirmation of a plan does not discharge a debtor that is a corporation from any debt –

(A) of a kind specified in paragraph (2)(A) or (2)(B) of section 523(a) that is owed to a domestic governmental unit, or owed to a person as the result of an action filed under subchapter III of chapter 37 of title 31 or any similar State statute; or

(B) for a tax or customs duty with respect to which the debtor –

(i) made a fraudulent return; or

(ii) willfully attempted in any manner to evade or to defeat such tax or such customs duty.

1142. Implementation of plan

(a) Notwithstanding any otherwise applicable nonbankruptcy law, rule, or regulation relating to financial condition, the debtor and any entity organized or to be organized for the purpose of carrying out the plan shall carry out the plan and shall comply with any orders of the court.

(b) The court may direct the debtor and any other necessary party to execute or deliver or to join in the execution or delivery of any instrument required to effect a transfer of property dealt with by a confirmed plan, and to perform any other act, including the satisfaction of any lien, that is necessary for the consummation of the plan.

1143. Distribution

If a plan requires presentment or surrender of a security or the performance of any other act as a condition to participation in distribution under the plan, such action shall be taken not later than five years after the date of the entry of the order of confirmation. Any entity that has not within such time presented or surrendered such entity's security or taken any such other action that the plan requires may not participate in distribution under the plan.

1144. Revocation of an order of confirmation

On request of a party in interest at any time before 180 days after the date of the entry of the order of confirmation, and after notice and a hearing, the court may revoke such order if and only if such order was procured by fraud. An order under this section revoking an order of confirmation shall-

(1) contain such provisions as are necessary to protect any entity acquiring rights in good faith reliance on the order of confirmation; and

(2) revoke the discharge of the debtor.

1145. Exemption from securities laws

(a) Except with respect to an entity that is an underwriter as defined in subsection (b) of this section, section 5 of the Securities Act of 1933 and any State or local law requiring registration for offer or sale of a security or registration or licensing of an issuer of, underwriter of, or broker or dealer in, a security do not apply to-

(1) the offer or sale under a plan of a security of the debtor, of an affiliate participating in a joint plan with the debtor, or of a successor to the debtor under the plan-

(A) in exchange for a claim against, an interest in, or a claim for an administrative expense in the case concerning, the debtor or such affiliate; or

(B) principally in such exchange and partly for cash or property;

(2) the offer of a security through any warrant, option, right to subscribe, or conversion privilege that was sold in the manner specified in paragraph (1) of this subsection, or the sale of a security upon the exercise of such a warrant, option, right, or privilege;

(3) the offer or sale, other than under a plan, of a security of an issuer other than the debtor or an affiliate, if-

(A) such security was owned by the debtor on the date of the filing of the petition;

(B) the issuer of such security is-

(i) required to file reports under section 13 or 15(d) of the Securities Exchange Act of 1934; and

(ii) in compliance with the disclosure and reporting provision of such applicable section; and

(C) such offer or sale is of securities that do not exceed-

(i) during the two-year period immediately following the date of the filing of the petition, four percent of the securities of such class outstanding on such date; and

(ii) during any 180-day period following such two-year period, one percent of the securities outstanding at the beginning of such 180-day period; or

(4) a transaction by a stockbroker in a security that is executed after a transaction of a kind specified in paragraph (1) or (2) of this subsection in such security and before the expiration of 40 days after the first date on which such security was bona fide offered to the public by the issuer or by or through an underwriter, if such stockbroker provides, at the time of or before such transaction by such stockbroker, a disclosure statement approved under section 1125 of this title, and, if the court orders, information supplementing such disclosure statement.

(b)(1) Except as provided in paragraph (2) of this subsection and except with respect to ordinary trading transactions of an entity that is not an issuer, an entity is an underwriter under section 2(a)(11) of the Securities Act of 1933, if such entity-

(A) purchases a claim against, interest in, or claim for an administrative expense in the case concerning, the debtor, if such purchase is with a view to distribution of any security received or to be received in exchange for such a claim or interest:

(B) offers to sell securities offered or sold under the plan for the holders of such securities;

(C) offers to buy securities offered or sold under the plan from the holders of such securities, if such offer to buy is-

(i) with a view to distribution of such securities; and

(ii) under an agreement made in connection with the plan, with the consummation of the plan, or with the offer or sale of securities under the plan; or

(D) is an issuer, as used in such section 2(a)(11), with respect to such securities.

(2) An entity is not an underwriter under section 2(a)(11) of the Securities Act of 1933 or under paragraph (1) of this subsection with respect to an agreement that provides only for-

(A)(i) the matching or combining of fractional interests in securities offered or sold under the plan into whole interests; or

(ii) the purchase or sale of such fractional interests from or to entities receiving such fractional interests under the plan; or

(B) the purchase or sale for such entities of such fractional or whole interests as are necessary to adjust for any remaining fractional interests after such matching.

(3) An entity other than an entity of the kind specified in paragraph (1) of this subsection is not an underwriter under section 2(a)(11) of the Securities Act of 1933 with respect to any securities offered or sold to such entity in the manner specified in subsection (a)(1) of this section.

(c) An offer or sale of securities of the kind and in the manner specified under subsection (a)(1) of this section is deemed to be a public offering.

(d) The Trust Indenture Act of 1939 does not apply to a note issued under the plan that matures not later than one year after the effective date of the plan.

1146. Special tax provisions

(a) The issuance, transfer, or exchange of a security, or the making or delivery of an instrument of transfer under a plan confirmed under section 1129 of this title, may not be taxed under any law imposing a stamp tax or similar tax.

(b) The court may authorize the proponent of a plan to request a determination, limited to questions of law, by a State or local governmental unit charged with responsibility for collection or determination of a tax on or measured by income, of the tax effects, under section 346 of this title and under the law imposing such tax, of the plan. In the event of an actual controversy, the court may declare such effects after the earlier of-

(1) the date on which such governmental unit responds to the request under this subsection; or

(2) 270 days after such request.

MISCELLANEOUS STATUTES

28 U.S.C. 157. Procedures

(a) Each district court may provide that any or all cases under title 11 and any or all proceedings arising under title 11 or arising in or related to a case under title 11 shall be referred to the bankruptcy judges for the district.

(b)(1) Bankruptcy judges may hear and determine all cases under title 11 and all core proceedings arising under title 11, or arising in a case under title 11, referred under subsection (a) of this section, and may enter appropriate orders and judgments, subject to review under section 158 of this title.

(2) Core proceedings include, but are not limited to -

(A) matters concerning the administration of the estate;

(B) allowance or disallowance of claims against the estate or exemptions from property of the estate, and estimation of claims or interests for the purposes of confirming a plan under chapter 11, 12, or 13 of title 11 but not the liquidation or estimation of contingent or unliquidated personal injury tort or wrongful death claims against the estate for purposes of distribution in a case under title 11;

(C) counterclaims by the estate against persons filing claims against the estate;

(D) orders in respect to obtaining credit;

(E) orders to turn over property of the estate;

(F) proceedings to determine, avoid, or recover preferences;

(G) motions to terminate, annul, or modify the automatic stay;

(H) proceedings to determine, avoid, or recover fraudulent conveyances;

(I) determinations as to the dischargeability of particular debts;

(J) objections to discharges;

(K) determinations of the validity, extent, or priority of liens;

(L) confirmations of plans;

(M) orders approving the use or lease of property, including the use of cash collateral;

(N) orders approving the sale of property other than property resulting from claims brought by the estate against persons who have not filed claims against the estate;

(O) other proceedings affecting the liquidation of the assets of the estate or the adjustment of the debtor-creditor or the equity security holder relationship, except personal injury tort or wrongful death claims; and

(P) recognition of foreign proceedings and other matters under chapter 15 of title 11.

(3) The bankruptcy judge shall determine, on the judge's own motion or on timely motion of a party, whether a proceeding is a core proceeding under this subsection or is a proceeding that is otherwise related to a case under title 11. A determination that a proceeding is not a core proceeding shall not be made solely on the basis that its resolution may be affected by State law.

(4) Non-core proceedings under section 157(b)(2)(B) of title 28, United States Code, shall not be subject to the mandatory abstention provisions of section 1334(c)(2).

(5) The district court shall order that personal injury tort and wrongful death claims shall be tried in the district court in which the bankruptcy case is pending, or in the district court in the district in which the claim arose, as determined by the district court in which the bankruptcy case is pending.

(c)(1) A bankruptcy judge may hear a proceeding that is not a core proceeding but that is otherwise related to a case under title 11. In such proceeding, the bankruptcy judge shall submit proposed findings of fact and conclusions of law to the district court, and any final order or judgment shall be entered by the district judge after considering the bankruptcy judge's proposed findings and conclusions and after reviewing de novo those matters to which any party has timely and specifically objected.

(2) Notwithstanding the provisions of paragraph (1) of this subsection, the district court, with the consent of all the parties to the proceeding, may refer a proceeding related to a case under title 11 to a bankruptcy judge to hear and determine and to enter appropriate orders and judgments, subject to review under section 158 of this title.

(d) The district court may withdraw, in whole or in part, any case or proceeding referred under this section, on its own motion or on timely motion of any party, for cause shown. The district court shall, on timely motion of a party, so withdraw a proceeding if the court determines that resolution of the proceeding requires consideration of both title 11 and other laws of the United States regulating organizations or activities affecting interstate commerce.

(e) If the right to a jury trial applies in a proceeding that may be heard under this section by a bankruptcy judge, the bankruptcy judge may conduct the jury trial if specially designated to exercise such jurisdiction by the district court and with the express consent of all the parties.

28 U.S.C. 158. Appeals

(a) The district courts of the United States shall have jurisdiction to hear appeals

(1) from final judgments, orders, and decrees;

(2) from interlocutory orders and decrees issued under section 1121(d) of title 11 increasing or reducing the time periods referred to in section 1121 of such title; and

(3) with leave of the court, from other interlocutory orders and decrees; and, with leave of the court, from interlocutory orders and decrees, of bankruptcy judges entered in cases and proceedings referred to the bankruptcy judges under section 157 of this title. An appeal under this subsection shall be taken only to the district court for the judicial district in which the bankruptcy judge is serving.

(b)(1) The judicial council of a circuit shall establish a bankruptcy appellate panel service composed of bankruptcy judges of the districts in the circuit who are appointed by the judicial council in accordance with paragraph (3), to hear and determine, with the consent of all the parties, appeals under subsection (a) unless the judicial council finds that -

(A) there are insufficient judicial resources available in the circuit; or

(B) establishment of such service would result in undue delay or increased cost to parties in cases under title 11.

Not later than 90 days after making the finding, the judicial council shall submit to the Judicial Conference of the United States a report containing the factual basis of such finding.

(2)(A) A judicial council may reconsider, at any time, the finding described in paragraph (1).

(B) On the request of a majority of the district judges in a circuit for which a bankruptcy appellate panel service is established under paragraph (1), made after the expiration of the 1-year period beginning on the date such service is established, the judicial council of the circuit shall determine whether a circumstance specified in subparagraph (A) or (B) of such paragraph exists.

(C) On its own motion, after the expiration of the 3-year period beginning on the date a bankruptcy appellate panel service is established under paragraph

(1), the judicial council of the circuit may determine whether a circumstance specified in subparagraph (A) or (B) of such paragraph exists.

(D) If the judicial council finds that either of such circumstances exists, the judicial council may provide for the completion of the appeals then pending before such service and the orderly termination of such service.

(3) Bankruptcy judges appointed under paragraph (1) shall be appointed and may be reappointed under such paragraph.

(4) If authorized by the Judicial Conference of the United States, the judicial councils of 2 or more circuits may establish a joint bankruptcy appellate panel comprised of bankruptcy judges from the districts within the circuits for which such panel is established, to hear and determine, upon the consent of all the parties, appeals under subsection (a) of this section.

(5) An appeal to be heard under this subsection shall be heard by a panel of 3 members of the bankruptcy appellate panel service, except that a member of such service may not hear an appeal originating in the district for which such member is appointed or designated under section 152 of this title.

(6) Appeals may not be heard under this subsection by a panel of the bankruptcy appellate panel service unless the district judges for the district in which the appeals occur, by majority vote, have authorized such service to hear and determine appeals originating in such district.

(c)(1) Subject to subsections (b), and (d)(2), each appeal under subsection (a) shall be heard by a 3-judge panel of the bankruptcy appellate panel service established under subsection (b)(1) unless -

(A) the appellant elects at the time of filing the appeal; or

(B) any other party elects, not later than 30 days after service of notice of the appeal;

to have such appeal heard by the district court.

(2) An appeal under subsections (a) and (b) of this section shall be taken in the same manner as appeals in civil proceedings generally are taken to the courts of appeals from the district courts and in the time provided by Rule 8002 of the Bankruptcy Rules.

(d)(1) The courts of appeals shall have jurisdiction of appeals from all final decisions, judgments, orders, and decrees entered under subsections (a) and (b) of this section.

(2)(A) The appropriate court of appeals shall have jurisdiction of appeals described in the first sentence of subsection (a) if the bankruptcy court, the district court, or the bankruptcy appellate panel involved, acting on its own motion or on the request of a party to the judgment, order, or decree described in such first sentence, or all the appellants and appellees (if any) acting jointly, certify that –

(i) the judgment, order, or decree involves a question of law as to which there is no controlling decision of the court of appeals for the circuit or of the Supreme Court of the United States, or involves a matter of public importance;

(ii) the judgment, order, or decree involves a question of law requiring resolution of conflicting decisions; or

(iii) an immediate appeal from the judgment, order, or decree may materially advance the progress of the case or proceeding in which the appeal is taken; and if the court of appeals authorizes the direct appeal of the judgment, order, or decree.

(B) If the bankruptcy court, the district court, or the bankruptcy appellate panel –

(i) on its own motion or on the request of a party, determines that a circumstance specified in clause (i), (ii), or (iii) of subparagraph (A) exists; or

(ii) receives a request made by a majority of the appellants and a majority of appellees (if any) to make the certification described in subparagraph (A);

then the bankruptcy court, the district court, or the bankruptcy appellate panel shall make the certification described in subparagraph (A).

(C) The parties may supplement the certification with a short statement of the basis for the certification.

(D) An appeal under this paragraph does not stay any proceeding of the bankruptcy court, the district court, or the bankruptcy appellate panel from which the appeal is taken, unless the respective bankruptcy court, district court, or bankruptcy appellate panel, or the court of appeals in which the appeal is pending, issues a stay of such proceeding pending the appeal.

(E) Any request under subparagraph (B) for certification shall be made not later than 60 days after the entry of the judgment, order, or decree.

APPENDIX II

RULES OF PRACTICE AND PROCEDURE IN BANKRUPTCY

(THE FEDERAL RULES OF BANKRUPTCY PROCEDURE)

(Current to January 1, 2016)

CONTENTS

CONTENTS

RULE

RULES OF PRACTICE AND PROCEDURE IN BANKRUPTCY

Rule 1001. Scope of Rules and Forms; Short Title

The Bankruptcy Rules and Forms govern procedure in cases under title 11 of the United States Code. The rules shall be cited as the Federal Rules of Bankruptcy Procedure and the forms as the Official Bankruptcy Forms. These rules shall be construed to secure the just, speedy, and inexpensive determination of every case and proceeding.

PART I

COMMENCEMENT OF CASE; PROCEEDINGS RELATING TO PETITION AND ORDER FOR RELIEF

Rule 1002. Commencement of Case

(a) PETITION. A petition commencing a case under the Code shall be filed with the clerk.

(b) TRANSMISSION TO UNITED STATES TRUSTEE. The clerk shall forthwith transmit to the United States trustee a copy of the petition filed pursuant to subdivision (a) of this rule.

Rule 1003. Involuntary Petition

(a) TRANSFEROR OR TRANSFEREE OF CLAIM. A transferor or transferee of a claim shall annex to the original and each copy of the petition a copy of all documents evidencing the transfer, whether transferred unconditionally, for security, or otherwise, and a signed statement that the claim was not transferred for the purpose of commencing the case and setting forth the consideration for and terms of the transfer. An entity that has transferred or acquired a claim for the purpose of commencing a case for liquidation under chapter 7 or for reorganization under chapter 11 shall not be a qualified petitioner.

(b) JOINDER OF PETITIONERS AFTER FILING. If the answer to an involuntary petition filed by fewer than three creditors avers the existence of 12 or more creditors, the debtor shall file with the answer a list of all creditors with their addresses, a brief statement of the nature of their claims, and the amounts thereof. If it appears that there are 12 or more creditors as provided in Section 303(b) of the Code, the court shall afford a reasonable opportunity for other creditors to join in the petition before a hearing is held thereon.

Rule 1004. Involuntary Petition Against a Partnership

After filing of an involuntary petition under § 303(b)(3) of the Code, (1) the petitioning partners or other petitioners shall promptly send to or serve on each general partner who is not a petitioner a copy of the petition; and (2) the clerk shall promptly issue a summons for service on each general partner who is not a petitioner. Rule 1010 applies to the form and service of the summons.

Rule 1004.1. Petition for an Infant or Incompetent Person

If an infant or incompetent person has a representative, including a general guardian, committee, conservator, or similar fiduciary, the representative may file a voluntary petition on behalf of the infant or incompetent person. An infant or incompetent person who does not have a duly appointed representative may file a voluntary petition by next friend or guardian ad litem. The court shall appoint a guardian ad litem for an infant or incompetent person who is a debtor and is not otherwise represented or shall make any other order to protect the infant or incompetent debtor.

Rule 1004.2 Petition in Chapter 15 Cases

(a) DESIGNATING CENTER OF MAIN INTERESTS. A petition for recognition of a foreign proceeding under chapter 15 of the Code shall state the country where the debtor has its center of main interests. The petition shall also identify each country in which a foreign proceeding by, regarding, or against the debtor is pending.

(b) CHALLENGING DESIGNATION. The United States trustee or a party in interest may file a motion for a determination that the debtor's center of main interests is other than as stated in the petition for recognition commencing the chapter 15 case. Unless the court orders otherwise, the motion shall be filed no later than seven days before the date set for the hearing on the petition. The motion shall be transmitted to the United States trustee and served on the debtor, all persons or bodies authorized to administer foreign proceedings of the debtor, all entities against whom provisional relief is being sought under §1519 of the Code, all parties to litigation pending in the United States in which the debtor was a party as of the time the petition was filed, and such other entities as the court may direct.

Rule 1005. Caption of Petition

The caption of a petition commencing a case under the Code shall contain the name of the court, the title of the case, and the docket number. The title of the case shall include the following information about the debtor: name, employer identification number, last four digits of the social-security number or individual debtor's taxpayer-identification number, any other federal taxpayer-identification number, and all other names used within eight years before filing the petition. If the petition is not filed by the debtor, it shall include all names used by the debtor which are known to the petitioners.

Rule 1006. Filing Fee

(a) GENERAL REQUIREMENT. Every petition shall be accompanied by the filing fee except as provided in subdivisions (b) and (c) of this rule. For the purpose of this rule, "filing fee" means the filing fee prescribed by 28 U.S.C. § 1930(a)(1)-(a)(5) and any other fee prescribed by the Judicial Conference of the United States under 28 U.S.C. § 1930(b) that is payable to the clerk upon the commencement of a case under the Code.

(b) PAYMENT OF FILING FEE IN INSTALLMENTS.

(1) Application to Pay Filing Fee in Installments. A voluntary petition by an individual shall be accepted for filing if accompanied by the debtor's signed application, prepared as prescribed by the appropriate Official Form, stating that the debtor is unable to pay the filing fee except in installments.

(2) Action on Application. Prior to the meeting of creditors, the court may order the filing fee paid to the clerk or grant leave to pay in installments and fix the number, amount and dates of payment. The number of installments shall not exceed four, and the final installment shall be payable not later than

120 days after filing the petition. For cause shown, the court may extend the time of any installment, provided the last installment is paid not later than 180 days after filing the petition.

(3) Postponement of Attorney's Fees. All installments of the filing fee must be paid in full before the debtor or chapter 13 trustee may make further payments to an attorney or any other person who renders services to the debtor in connection with the case.

(c) WAIVER OF FILING FEE. A voluntary chapter 7 petition filed by an individual shall be accepted for filing if accompanied by the debtor's application requesting a waiver under 28 U.S.C. § 1930(f), prepared as prescribed by the appropriate Official Form.

Rule 1007. Lists, Schedules, Statements, and Other Documents; Time Limits

(a) CORPORATE OWNERSHIP STATEMENT, LIST OF CREDITORS AND EQUITY SECURITY HOLDERS, AND OTHER LISTS.

(1) Voluntary Case. In a voluntary case, the debtor shall file with the petition a list containing the name and address of each entity included or to be included on Schedules D, E, F, G, and H as prescribed by the Official Forms. If the debtor is a corporation, other than a governmental unit, the debtor shall file with the petition a corporate ownership statement containing the information described in Rule 7007.1. The debtor shall file a supplemental statement promptly upon any change in circumstances that renders the corporate ownership statement inaccurate.

(2) Involuntary Case. In an involuntary case, the debtor shall file within seven days after entry of the order for relief, a list containing the name and address of each entity included or to be included on Schedules D, E, F, G, and H as prescribed by the Official Forms.

(3) Equity Security Holders. In a chapter 11 reorganization case, unless the court orders otherwise, the debtor shall file within 14 days after entry of the order for relief a list of the debtor's equity security holders of each class showing the number and kind of interests registered in the name of each holder, and the last known address or place of business of each holder.

(4) Chapter 15 Case. In addition to the documents required under § 1515 of the Code, a foreign representative filing a petition for recognition under chapter 15 shall file with the petition: (A) a corporate ownership statement containing the information described in Rule 7007.1; and (B) unless the court orders otherwise, a list containing the names and addresses of all persons or bodies authorized to administer foreign proceedings of the debtor, all parties to litigation pending in the United States in which the debtor is a party at the time of the filing of the petition, and all entities against whom provisional relief is being sought under § 1519 of the Code.

(5) Extension of Time. Any extension of time for the filing of the lists required by this subdivision may be granted only on motion for cause shown and on notice to the United States trustee and to any trustee, committee elected under § 705 or appointed under § 1102 of the Code, or other party as the court may direct.

(b) SCHEDULES, STATEMENTS, AND OTHER DOCUMENTS REQUIRED.

(1) Except in a chapter 9 municipality case, the debtor, unless the court orders otherwise, shall file the following schedules, statements, and other documents, prepared as prescribed by the appropriate Official Forms, if any:

(A) schedules of assets and liabilities;

(B) a schedule of current income and expenditures;

(C) a schedule of executory contracts and unexpired leases;

(D) a statement of financial affairs;

(E) copies of all payment advices or other evidence of payment, if any, received by the debtor from an employer within 60 days before the filing of the petition, with redaction of all but the last four digits of the debtor's social-security number or individual taxpayer-identification number; and

(F) a record of any interest that the debtor has in an account or program of the type specified in § 521(c) of the Code.

(2) An individual debtor in a chapter 7 case shall file a statement of intention as required by § 521(a) of the Code, prepared as prescribed by the appropriate Official Form. A copy of the statement of intention shall be served on the trustee and the creditors named in the statement on or before the filing of the statement.

(3) Unless the United States trustee has determined that the credit counseling requirement of § 109(h) does not apply in the district, an individual debtor must file a statement of compliance with the credit counseling requirement, prepared as prescribed by the appropriate Official Form which must include one of the following:

(A) an attached certificate and debt repayment plan, if any, required by § 521(b);

(B) a statement that the debtor has received the credit counseling briefing required by § 109(h)(1) but does not have the certificate required by § 521(b);

(C) a certification under § 109(h)(3); or

(D) a request for a determination by the court under § 109(h)(4).

(4) Unless § 707(b)(2)(D) applies, an individual debtor in a chapter 7 case shall file a statement of current monthly income prepared as prescribed by the appropriate Official Form, and, if the current monthly income exceeds the median family income for the applicable state and household size, the information, including calculations, required by § 707(b), prepared as prescribed by the appropriate Official Form.

(5) An individual debtor in a chapter 11 case shall file a statement of current monthly income, prepared as prescribed by the appropriate Official Form.

(6) A debtor in a chapter 13 case shall file a statement of current monthly income, prepared as prescribed by the appropriate Official Form, and, if the current monthly income exceeds the median family income for the applicable state and household size, a calculation of disposable income made in accordance with § 1325(b)(3), prepared as prescribed by the appropriate Official Form.

(7) Unless an approved provider of an instructional course concerning personal financial management has notified the court that a debtor has completed the course after filing the petition:

(A) An individual debtor in a chapter 7 or chapter 13 case shall file a statement of completion of the course, prepared as prescribed by the appropriate Official Form; and

(B) An individual debtor in a chapter 11 case shall file the statement if § 1141(d)(3) applies.

(8) If an individual debtor in a chapter 11, 12, or 13 case has claimed an exemption under § 522(b)(3)(A) in property of the kind described in § 522(p)(1) with a value in excess of the amount set out in § 522(q)(1), the debtor shall file a statement as to whether there is any proceeding pending in which the debtor may be found guilty of a felony of a kind described in § 522(q)(1)(A) or found liable for a debt of the kind described in § 522(q)(1)(B).

(c) TIME LIMITS. In a voluntary case, the schedules, statements, and other documents required by subdivision (b)(1), (4), (5), and (6) shall be filed with the petition or within 14 days thereafter, except as otherwise provided in subdivisions(d), (e), (f), and (h) of this rule. In an involuntary case, the schedules, statements, and other documents required by subdivision (b)(1) shall be filed by the debtor within 14 days after the entry of the order for relief. In a voluntary case, the documents required by paragraphs (A), (C), and (D) of subdivision (b)(3) shall be filed with the petition. Unless the court orders otherwise, a debtor who has filed a statement under subdivision (b)(3)(B), shall file the documents required by subdivision (b)(3)(A) within 14 days of the order for relief. In a chapter 7 case, the debtor shall file the statement required by subdivision (b)(7) within 60 days after the first date set for the meeting of creditors under § 341 of the Code, and in a chapter 11 or 13 case no later than the date when the last payment was made by the debtor as required by the plan or the filing of a motion for a discharge under § 1141(d)(5)(B) or § 1328(b) of the Code. The court may, at any time and in its discretion, enlarge the time to file the statement required by subdivision (b)(7). The debtor shall file the statement required by subdivision (b)(8) no earlier than the date of the last payment made under the plan or the date of the filing of a motion for a discharge under §§ 1141(d)(5)(B), 1228(b), or 1328(b) of the Code. Lists, schedules, statements, and other documents filed prior to the conversion of a case to another chapter shall be deemed filed in the converted case unless the court directs otherwise. Except as provided in § 1116(3), any extension of time to file schedules, statements, and other documents required under this rule may be granted only on motion for cause shown and on notice to the United States trustee, any committee elected under § 705 or appointed under § 1102 of the Code, trustee, examiner, or other party as the court may direct. Notice of an extension shall be given to the United States trustee and to any committee, trustee, or other party as the court may direct.

(d) LIST OF 20 LARGEST CREDITORS IN CHAPTER 9 MUNICIPALITY CASE OR CHAPTER 11 REORGANIZATION CASE. In addition to the list required by subdivision (a) of this rule, a debtor in a chapter 9 municipality case or a debtor in a voluntary chapter 11 reorganization case shall file with the petition a list containing the name, address and claim of the creditors that hold the 20 largest unsecured claims, excluding insiders, as prescribed by the appropriate Official Form. In an involuntary chapter 11 reorganization case, such list shall be filed by the debtor within 2 days after entry of the order for relief under Section 303(h) of the Code.

(e) LIST IN CHAPTER 9 MUNICIPALITY CASES. The list required by subdivision (a) of this rule shall be filed by the debtor in a chapter 9 municipality case within such time as the court shall fix. If a proposed plan requires a revision of assessments so that the proportion of special assessments or special taxes to be assessed against some real property will be different from the proportion in effect at the date the petition is filed, the debtor shall also file a list showing the name and address of each known holder of title, legal or equitable, to real property adversely affected. On motion for cause shown, the court may modify the requirements of this subdivision and subdivision (a) of this rule.

(f) STATEMENT OF SOCIAL SECURITY NUMBER. An individual debtor shall submit a verified statement that sets out the debtor's social security number, or states that the debtor does not have a social security number. In a voluntary case, the debtor shall submit the statement with the petition. In an involuntary case, the debtor shall submit the statement within 14 days after the entry of the order for relief.

(g) PARTNERSHIP AND PARTNERS. The general partners of a debtor partnership shall prepare and file the list required under subdivision (a), the schedules of the assets and liabilities, schedule of current income and expenditures, schedule of executory contracts and unexpired leases, and statement of financial affairs of the partnership. The court may order any general partner to file a statement of personal assets and liabilities within such time as the court may fix.

(h) INTERESTS ACQUIRED OR ARISING AFTER PETITION. If, as provided by Section 541(a)(5) of the Code, the debtor acquires or becomes entitled to acquire any interest in property, the debtor shall within 14 days after the information comes to the debtor's knowledge or within such further time the court may allow, file a supplemental schedule in the chapter 7 liquidation case, chapter 11 reorganization case, chapter 12 family farmer's debt adjustment case, or chapter 13 individual debt adjustment case. If any of the property required to be reported under this subdivision is claimed by the debtor as exempt, the debtor shall claim the exemptions in the supplemental schedule. The duty to file a supplemental schedule in accordance with this subdivision continues notwithstanding the closing of the case, except that the schedule need not be filed in a chapter 11, chapter 12, or chapter 13 case with respect to property acquired after entry of the order confirming a chapter 11 plan or discharging the debtor in a chapter 12 or chapter 13 case.

(i) DISCLOSURE OF LIST OF SECURITY HOLDERS. After notice and hearing and for cause shown, the court may direct an entity other than the debtor or trustee to disclose any list of security holders of the debtor in its possession or under its control, indicating the name, address and security held by any of them. The entity possessing this list may be required either to produce the list or a true copy thereof, or permit inspection or copying, or otherwise disclose the information contained on the list.

(j) IMPOUNDING OF LISTS. On motion of a party in interest and for cause shown the court may direct the impounding of the lists filed under this rule, and may refuse to permit inspection by any entity. The court may permit inspection or use of the lists, however, by any party in interest on terms prescribed by the court.

(k) PREPARATION OF LIST, SCHEDULES, OR STATEMENTS ON DEFAULT OF DEBTOR. If a list, schedule, or statement, other than a statement of intention, is not prepared and filed as required by this rule, the court may order the trustee, a petitioning creditor, committee, or other party to prepare and file any of these papers within a time fixed by the court. The court may approve reimbursement of the cost incurred in complying with such an order as an administrative expense.

(l) TRANSMISSION TO UNITED STATES TRUSTEE. The clerk shall forthwith transmit to the United States trustee a copy of every list, schedule, and statement filed pursuant to subdivision (a)(1), (a)(2), (b), (d), or (h) of this rule.

(m) INFANTS AND INCOMPETENT PERSONS. If the debtor knows that a person on the list of creditors or schedules is an infant or incompetent person, the debtor also shall include the name, address, and legal relationship of any person upon whom process would be served in an adversary proceeding against the infant or incompetent person in accordance with Rule 7004(b)(2).

Rule 1008. Verification of Petitions and Accompanying Papers

All petitions, lists, schedules, statements and amendments thereto shall be verified or contain an unsworn declaration as provided in 28 U.S.C. Section 1746.

Rule 1009. Amendments of Voluntary Petitions, Lists, Schedules and Statements

(a) GENERAL RIGHT TO AMEND. A voluntary petition, list, schedule, or statement may be amended by the debtor as a matter of course at any time before the case is closed. The debtor shall give notice of the amendment to the trustee and to any entity affected thereby. On motion of a party in interest, after notice and a hearing, the court may order any voluntary petition, list, schedule, or statement to be amended and the clerk shall give notice of the amendment to entities designated by the court.

(b) STATEMENT OF INTENTION. The statement of intention may be amended by the debtor at any time before the expiration of the period provided in § 521(a) of the Code. The debtor shall give notice of the amendment to the trustee and to any entity affected thereby.

(c) STATEMENT OF SOCIAL SECURITY NUMBER. If a debtor becomes aware that the statement of social security number submitted under Rule 1007(f) is incorrect, the debtor shall promptly submit an amended verified statement setting forth the correct social security number. The debtor shall give notice of the amendment to all of the entities required to be included on the list filed under Rule 1007(a)(1) or (a)(2).

(d) TRANSMISSION TO UNITED STATES TRUSTEE. The clerk shall promptly transmit to the United States trustee a copy of every amendment filed or submitted under subdivision (a), (b) or (c) of this rule.

Rule 1010. Service of Involuntary Petition and Summons; Petition For Recognition of a Foreign Nonmain Proceeding

(a) SERVICE OF INVOLUNTARY PETITION AND SUMMONS; SERVICE OF PETITION FOR RECOGNITION OF FOREIGN NONMAIN PROCEEDING. On the filing of an involuntary petition or a petition for recognition of a foreign nonmain proceeding, the clerk shall forthwith issue a summons for service. When an involuntary petition is filed, service shall be made on the debtor. When a petition for recognition of a foreign nonmain proceeding is filed, service shall be made on the debtor, any entity against whom provisional relief is sought under § 1519 of the Code, and on any other party as the court may direct. The summons shall be served with a copy of the petition in the manner provided for service of a summons and complaint by Rule 7004(a) or (b). If service cannot be so made, the court may order that the summons and petition be served by mailing copies to the party's last known address, and by at least one publication in a manner and form directed by the court. The summons and petition may be served on the party anywhere. Rule 7004(e) and Rule 4(l) F.R.Civ.P. apply when service is made or attempted under this rule.

(b) CORPORATE OWNERSHIP STATEMENT. Each petitioner that is a corporation shall file with the involuntary petition a corporate ownership statement containing the information described in Rule 7007.1.

Rule 1011. Responsive Pleading or Motion in Involuntary and Cross-Border Cases

(a) WHO MAY CONTEST PETITION. The debtor named in an involuntary petition, or a party in interest to a petition for recognition of a foreign proceeding, may contest the petition. In the case of a petition against a partnership under Rule 1004, a nonpetitioning general partner, or a person who is alleged to be a general partner but denies the allegation, may contest the petition.

(b) DEFENSES AND OBJECTIONS; WHEN PRESENTED. Defenses and objections to the petition shall be presented in the manner prescribed by Rule 12 F. R. Civ. P. and shall be filed and served within 21 days after service of the summons, except that if service is made by publication on a party or partner not residing or found within the state in which the court sits, the court shall prescribe the time for filing and serving the response.

(c) EFFECT OF MOTION. Service of a motion under Rule 12(b) F. R. Civ. P. shall extend the time for filing and serving a responsive pleading as permitted by Rule 12(a) F. R. Civ. P.

(d) CLAIMS AGAINST PETITIONERS. A claim against a petitioning creditor may not be asserted in the answer except for the purpose of defeating the petition.

(e) OTHER PLEADINGS. No other pleadings shall be permitted, except that the court may order a reply to an answer and prescribe the time for filing and service.

(f) CORPORATE OWNERSHIP STATEMENT. If the entity responding to the involuntary petition or the petition for recognition of a foreign proceeding is a corporation, the entity shall file with its first appearance, pleading, motion, response, or other request addressed to the court a corporate ownership statement containing the information described in Rule 7007.1.

Rule 1012. [Abrogated]

Rule 1013. Hearing and Disposition of Petition in Involuntary Cases

(a) CONTESTED PETITION. The court shall determine the issues of a contested petition at the earliest practicable time and forthwith enter an order for relief, dismiss the petition, or enter any other appropriate order.

(b) DEFAULT. If no pleading or other defense to a petition is filed within the time provided by Rule 1011, the court, on the next day, or as soon thereafter as practicable, shall enter an order for the relief requested in the petition

Rule 1014. Dismissal and Change of Venue

(a) DISMISSAL AND TRANSFER OF CASES.

(1) Cases Filed in Proper District. If a petition is filed in the proper district, the court, on the timely motion of a party in interest or on its own motion, and after hearing on notice to the petitioners, the United States trustee, and other entities as directed by the court, may transfer the case to any other district if the court determines that the transfer is in the interest of justice or for the convenience of the parties.

(2) Cases Filed in Improper District. If a petition is filed in an improper district, the court, on the timely motion of a party in interest or on its own motion, and after hearing on notice to the petitioners, the United States trustee, and other entities as directed by the court, may dismiss the case or transfer it to any other district if the court determines that transfer is in the interest of justice or for the convenience of the parties.

(b) PROCEDURE WHEN PETITIONS INVOLVING THE SAME DEBTOR OR RELATED DEBTORS ARE FILED IN DIFFERENT COURTS. If petitions commencing cases under the Code or seeking recognition under chapter 15 are filed in different districts by, regarding, or against (1) the same debtor, (2) a partnership and one or more of its general partners, (3) two or more general partners, or (4) a debtor and an affiliate, the court in the district in which the first-filed petition is pending may determine, in the interest of justice or for the convenience of the parties, the district or districts in which any of the cases should proceed. The court may so determine on motion and after a hearing, with notice to the following entities in the affected cases: the United States trustee, entities entitled to notice under Rule 2002(a), and other entities as the court directs. The court may order the parties to the later-filed cases not to proceed further until it makes the determination.

Rule 1015. Consolidation or Joint Administration of Cases Pending in Same Court

(a) CASES INVOLVING SAME DEBTOR. If two or more petitions by, regarding, or against the same debtor are pending in the same court, the court may order consolidation of the cases.

(b) CASES INVOLVING TWO OR MORE RELATED DEBTORS. If a joint petition or two or more petitions are pending in the same court by or against (1) a husband and wife, or (2) a partnership and one or more of its general partners, or (3) two or more general partners, or (4) a debtor and an affiliate, the court may order a joint administration of the estates. Prior to entering an order the court shall give consideration to protecting creditors of different estates against potential conflicts of interest. An order directing joint administration of individual cases of a husband and wife shall, if one spouse has elected the exemptions under § 522(b)(2) of the Code and the other has elected the exemptions under § 522(b)(3), fix a reasonable time within which either may amend the election so that both shall have elected the same exemptions. The order shall notify the debtors that unless they elect the same exemptions within the time fixed by the court, they will be deemed to have elected the exemptions provided by § 522(b)(2).

(c) EXPEDITING AND PROTECTIVE ORDERS. When an order for consolidation or joint administration of a joint case or two or more cases is entered pursuant to this rule, while protecting the rights of the parties under the Code, the court may enter orders as may tend to avoid unnecessary costs and delay.

Rule 1016. Death or Incompetency of Debtor

Death or incompetency of the debtor shall not abate a liquidation case under chapter 7 of the Code. In such event the estate shall be administered and the case concluded in the same manner, so far as possible, as though the death or incompetency had not occurred. If a reorganization, family farmer's debt adjustment, or individual's debt adjustment case is pending under chapter 11, chapter 12, or chapter 13, the case may be dismissed; or if further administration is possible and in the best interest of the parties, the case may proceed and be concluded in the same manner, so far as possible, as though the death or incompetency had not occurred.

Rule 1017. Dismissal or Conversion of Case; Suspension

(a) VOLUNTARY DISMISSAL; DISMISSAL FOR WANT OF PROSECUTION OR OTHER CAUSE. Except as provided in §§707(a)(3), 707(b), 1208(b), and 1307(b) of the Code, and in Rule 1017(b), (c), and (e), a case shall not be dismissed on motion of the petitioner, for want of prosecution or other cause, or by consent of the parties, before a hearing on notice as provided in Rule 2002. For the purpose of the notice, the debtor shall file a list of creditors with their addresses within the time fixed by the court unless the list was previously filed. If the debtor fails to file the list, the court may order the debtor or another entity to prepare and file it.

(b) DISMISSAL FOR FAILURE TO PAY FILING FEE.

(1) If any installment of the filing fee has not been paid, the court may, after a hearing on notice to the debtor and the trustee, dismiss the case.

(2) If the case is dismissed or closed without full payment of the filing fee, the installments collected shall be distributed in the same manner and proportions as if the filing fee had been paid in full.

(c) DISMISSAL OF VOLUNTARY CHAPTER 7 OR CHAPTER 13 CASE FOR FAILURE TO TIMELY FILE LIST OF CREDITORS, SCHEDULES, AND STATEMENT OF FINANCIAL AFFAIRS. The court may dismiss a voluntary chapter 7 or chapter 13 case under §707(a)(3) or §1307(c)(9) after a hearing on notice served by the United States trustee on the debtor, the trustee, and any other entities as the court directs.

(d) SUSPENSION. The court shall not dismiss a case or suspend proceedings under §305 before a hearing on notice as provided in Rule 2002(a).

(e) DISMISSAL OF AN INDIVIDUAL DEBTOR'S CHAPTER 7 CASE, OR CONVERSION TO A CASE UNDER CHAPTER 11 OR 13, FOR ABUSE. The court may dismiss or, with the debtor's consent, convert an individual debtor's case for abuse under § 707(b) only on motion and after a hearing on notice to the debtor, the trustee, the United States trustee, and any other entity as the court directs.

(1) Except as otherwise provided in § 704(b)(2), a motion to dismiss a case for abuse under § 707(b) or (c) may be filed only within 60 days after the first date set for the meeting of creditors under § 341(a), unless, on request filed before the time has expired, the court for cause extends the time for filing the motion to dismiss. The party filing the motion shall set forth in the motion all matters to be considered at the hearing. In addition, a motion to dismiss under § 707(b)(1) and (3) shall state with particularity the circumstances alleged to constitute abuse.

(2) If the hearing is set on the court's own motion, notice of the hearing shall be served on the debtor no later than 60 days after the first date set for the meeting of creditors under §341(a). The notice shall set forth all matters to be considered by the court at the hearing.

(f) PROCEDURE FOR DISMISSAL, CONVERSION OR SUSPENSION.

(1) Rule 9014 governs a proceeding to dismiss or suspend a case, or to convert a case to another chapter, except under §§706(a), 1112(a), 1208(a) or (b), or 1307(a) or (b),

(2) Conversion or dismissal under §§706(a), 1112(a), 1208(b), or 1307(b) shall be on motion filed and served as required by Rule 9013.

(3) A chapter 12 or chapter 13 case shall be converted without court order when the debtor files a notice of conversion under §§1208(a) or 1307(a). The filing date of the notice becomes the date of the conversion order for the purposes of applying §348(c) and Rule 1019. The clerk shall promptly transmit a copy of the notice to the United States trustee.

Rule 1018. Contested Involuntary Petitions; Contested Petitions Commencing Chapter 15 Cases; Proceedings to Vacate Order for Relief; Applicability of Rules in Part VII Governing Adversary Proceedings

Unless the court otherwise directs and except as otherwise prescribed in Part 1 of these rules, the following rules in Part VII apply to all proceedings contesting an involuntary petition or a chapter 15 petition for recognition, and to all proceedings to vacate an order for relief: Rules 7005, 7008-7010, 7015, 7016, 7024-7026, 7028-7037, 7052, 7054, 7056, and 7062. The court may direct that other rules in Part VII shall also apply. For the purposes of this rule a reference in the Part VII rules to adversary proceedings shall be read as a reference to proceedings contesting an involuntary petition or a chapter 15 petition for recognition, or proceedings to vacate an order for relief. Reference in the Federal Rules of Civil Procedure to the complaint shall be read as a reference to the petition.

Rule 1019. Conversion of Chapter 11 Reorganization Case, Chapter 12 Family Farmer's Debt Adjustment Case, or Chapter 13 Individual's Debt Adjustment Case to Chapter 7 Liquidation Case

When a chapter 11, chapter 12, or chapter 13 case has been converted or reconverted to a chapter 7 case:

(1) Filing of Lists, Inventories, Schedules, Statements.

(A) Lists, inventories, schedules, and statements of financial affairs theretofore filed shall be deemed to be filed in the chapter 7 case, unless the court directs otherwise. If they have not been previously filed, the debtor shall comply with Rule 1007 as if an order for relief had been entered on an involuntary petition on the date of the entry of the order directing that the case continue under chapter 7.

(B) If a statement of intention is required, it shall be filed within 30 days after entry of the order of conversion or before the first date set for the meeting of creditors, whichever is earlier. The court may grant an extension of time for cause only on written motion filed, or oral request made during a hearing, before the time has expired. Notice of an extension shall be given to the United States trustee and to any committee, trustee, or other party as the court may direct.

(2) New Filing Periods.

(A) A new time period for filing a motion under § 707(b) or (c), a claim, a complaint objecting to discharge, or a complaint to obtain a determination of dischargeability of any debt shall commence under Rules 1017, 3002, 4004, or 4007, but a new time period shall not commence if a chapter 7 case had been converted to a chapter 11, 12, or 13 case and thereafter reconverted to a chapter 7 case and the time for filing a motion under § 707(b) or (c), a claim, a complaint objecting to discharge, or a complaint to obtain a determination of the dischargeability of any debt, or any extension thereof, expired in the original chapter 7 case.

(B) A new time period for filing an objection to a claim of exemptions shall commence under Rule 4003(b) after conversion of a case to chapter 7 unless:

(i) the case was converted to chapter 7 more than one year after the entry of the first order confirming a plan under chapter 11, 12, or 13; or

(ii) the case was previously pending in chapter 7 and the time to object to a claimed exemption had expired in the original chapter 7 case.

(3) Claims Filed Before Conversion. All claims actually filed by a creditor before conversion of the case are deemed filed in the chapter 7 case.

(4) Turnover of Records And Property. After qualification of, or assumption of duties by the chapter 7 trustee, any debtor in possession or trustee previously acting in the chapter 11, 12, or 13 case shall, forthwith, unless otherwise ordered, turn over to the chapter 7 trustee all records and property of the estate in the possession or control of the debtor in possession or trustee.

(5) Filing Final Report and Schedule of Postpetition Debts.

(A) Conversion of Chapter 11 or Chapter 12 Case. Unless the court directs otherwise, if a chapter 11 or chapter 12 case is converted to chapter 7, the debtor in possession or, if the debtor is not a debtor in possession, the trustee serving at the time of conversion, shall:

(i) not later than 14 days after conversion of the case, file a schedule of unpaid debts incurred after the filing of the petition and before conversion of the case, including the name and address of each holder of a claim; and

(ii) not later than 30 days after conversion of the case, file and transmit to the United States trustee a final report and account;

(B) Conversion of Chapter 13 Case. Unless the court directs otherwise, if a chapter 13 case is converted to chapter 7,

(i) the debtor, not later than 14 days after conversion of the case, shall file a schedule of unpaid debts incurred after the filing of the petition and before conversion of the case, including the name and address of each holder of a claim; and

(ii) the trustee, not later than 30 days after conversion of the case, shall file and transmit to the United States trustee a final report and account;

(C) Conversion After Confirmation of a Plan. Unless the court orders otherwise, if a chapter 11, chapter 12, or chapter 13 case is converted to chapter 7 after confirmation of a plan, the debtor shall file:

(i) a schedule of property not listed in the final report and account acquired after the filing of the petition but before conversion, except if the case is converted from chapter 13 to chapter 7 and §348(f)(2) does not apply;

(ii) a schedule of unpaid debts not listed in the final report and account incurred after confirmation but before the conversion; and

(iii) a schedule of executory contracts and unexpired leases entered into or assumed after the filing of the petition but before conversion.

(D) Transmission to United States Trustee. The clerk shall forthwith transmit to the United States trustee a copy of every schedule filed pursuant to Rule 1019(5).

(6) Postpetition claims; preconversion administrative expenses; notice. A request for payment of an administrative expense incurred before conversion of the case is timely filed under §503(a) of the Code if it is filed before conversion or a time fixed by the court. If the request is filed by a governmental unit, it is timely if it is filed before conversion or within the later of a time fixed by the court or 180 days after the date of the conversion. A claim of a kind specified in §348(d) may be filed in accordance with Rules 3001(a)-(d) and 3002. Upon the filing of the schedule of unpaid debts incurred after commencement of the case and before conversion, the clerk, or some other person as the court may direct, shall give notice to those entities listed on the schedule of the time for filing a request for payment of an administrative expense and, unless a notice of insufficient assets to pay a dividend is mailed in accordance with Rule 2002(e), the time for filing a claim of a kind specified in §348(d).

Rule 1020. Small Business Chapter 11 Reorganization Case

(a) SMALL BUSINESS DEBTOR DESIGNATION. In a voluntary chapter 11 case, the debtor shall state in the petition whether the debtor is a small business debtor. In an involuntary chapter 11 case, the debtor shall file within 14 days after entry of the order for relief a statement as to whether the debtor is a small business debtor. Except as provided in subdivision (c), the status of the case as a small business case shall be in accordance with the debtor's statement under this subdivision, unless and until the court enters an order finding that the debtor's statement is incorrect.

(b) OBJECTING TO DESIGNATION. Except as provided in subdivision (c), the United States trustee or a party in interest may file an objection to the debtor's statement under subdivision (a) no later than 30 days after the conclusion of the meeting of creditors held under § 341(a) of the Code, or within 30 days after any amendment to the statement, whichever is later.

(c) APPOINTMENT OF COMMITTEE OF UNSECURED CREDITORS. If a committee of unsecured creditors has been appointed under § 1102(a)(1), the case shall proceed as a small business case only if, and from the time when, the court enters an order determining that the committee has not been sufficiently active and representative to provide effective oversight of the debtor and that the debtor satisfies all the other requirements for being a small business. A request for a determination under this subdivision may be filed by the United States trustee or a party in interest only within a reasonable time after the failure of the committee to be sufficiently active and representative. The debtor may file a request for a determination at any time as to whether the committee has been sufficiently active and representative.

(d) PROCEDURE FOR OBJECTION OR DETERMINATION. Any objection or request for a determination under this rule shall be governed by Rule 9014 and served on: the debtor; the debtor's attorney; the United States trustee; the trustee; any committee appointed under § 1102 or its authorized agent, or, if no committee of unsecured creditors has been appointed under § 1102, the creditors included on the list filed under Rule 1007(d); and any other entity as the court directs.

Rule 1021. Health Care Business Case

(a) HEALTH CARE BUSINESS DESIGNATION. Unless the court orders otherwise, if a petition in a case under chapter 7, chapter 9, or chapter 11 states that the debtor is a health care business, the case shall proceed as a case in which the debtor is a health care business.

(b) MOTION. The United States trustee or a party in interest may file a motion to determine whether the debtor is a health care business. The motion shall be transmitted to the United States trustee and served on: the debtor; the trustee; any committee elected under § 705 or appointed under § 1102 of the Code or its authorized agent, or, if the case is a chapter 9 municipality case or a chapter 11 reorganization case and no committee of unsecured creditors has been appointed under § 1102, the creditors included on the list filed under Rule 1007(d); and any other entity as the court directs. The motion shall be governed by Rule 9014.

PART II

OFFICERS AND ADMINISTRATION; NOTICES; MEETINGS; EXAMINATIONS; ELECTIONS; ATTORNEYS AND ACCOUNTANTS

Rule 2001. Appointment of Interim Trustee Before Order for Relief in a Chapter 7 Liquidation Case

(a) APPOINTMENT. At any time following the commencement of an involuntary liquidation case and before an order for relief, the court on written motion of a party in interest may order the appointment of an interim trustee under Section 303(g) of the Code. The motion shall set forth the necessity for the appointment and may be granted only after hearing on notice to the debtor, the petitioning creditors, the United States trustee, and other parties in interest as the court may designate.

(b) BOND OF MOVANT. An interim trustee may not be appointed under this rule unless the movant furnishes a bond in an amount approved by the court, conditioned to indemnify the debtor for costs, attorney's fee, expenses, and damages allowable under Section 303(i) of the Code.

(c) ORDER OF APPOINTMENT. The order directing the appointment of an interim trustee shall state the reason the appointment is necessary and shall specify the trustee's duties.

(d) TURNOVER AND REPORT. Following qualification of the trustee selected under Section 702 of the Code, the interim trustee, unless otherwise ordered, shall (1) forthwith deliver to the trustee all the records and property of the estate in possession or subject to control of the interim trustee and, (2) within 30 days thereafter file a final report and account.

Rule 2002. Notices to Creditors, Equity Security Holders, Administrators in Foreign Proceedings, Persons Against Whom Provisional Relief is Sought in Ancillary and Other Cross-Border Cases, United States, and United States Trustee

(a) TWENTY-ONE-DAY NOTICES TO PARTIES IN INTEREST. Except as provided in subdivisions (h), (i), (l), (p), and (q) of this rule, the clerk, or some other person as the court may direct, shall give the debtor, the trustee, all creditors and indenture trustees at least 21 days' notice by mail of:

(1) the meeting of creditors under §341 or §1104(b) of the Code; which notice, unless the court orders otherwise, shall include the debtor's employer identification number, social security number, and any other federal taxpayer identification number.

(2) a proposed use, sale, or lease of property of the estate other than in the ordinary course of business, unless the court for cause shown shortens the time or directs another method of giving notice;

(3) the hearing on approval of a compromise or settlement of a controversy other than approval of an agreement pursuant to Rule 4001(d), unless the court for cause shown directs that notice not be sent;

(4) in a chapter 7 liquidation, a chapter 11 reorganization case, or a chapter 12 family farmer debt adjustment case, the hearing on the dismissal of the case or the conversion of the case to another chapter, unless the hearing is under §707(a)(3) or §707(b) or is on dismissal of the case for failure to pay the filing fee;

(5) the time fixed to accept or reject a proposed modification of a plan;

(6) a hearing on any entity's request for compensation or reimbursement of expenses if the request exceeds $1,000;

(7) the time fixed for filing proofs of claims pursuant to Rule 3003(c); and

(8) the time fixed for filing objections and the hearing to consider confirmation of a chapter 12 plan.

(b) TWENTY-EIGHT-DAY NOTICES TO PARTIES IN INTEREST. Except as provided in subdivision (l) of this rule, the clerk, or some other person as the court may direct, shall give the debtor, the trustee, all creditors and indenture trustees not less than 28 days' notice by mail of the time fixed (1) for filing objections and the hearing to consider approval of a disclosure statement or, under § 1125(f), to make a final determination whether the plan provides adequate information so that a separate disclosure statement is not necessary; and (2) for filing objections and the hearing to consider confirmation of a chapter 9, chapter 11, or chapter 13 plan.

(c) CONTENT OF NOTICE.

(1) Proposed Use, Sale, or Lease of Property. Subject to Rule 6004, the notice of a proposed use, sale, or lease of property required by subdivision (a)(2) of this rule shall include the time and place of any public sale, the terms and conditions of any private sale and the time fixed for filing objections. The notice of a proposed use, sale, or lease of property, including real estate, is sufficient if it generally describes the property. The notice of a proposed sale or lease of personally identifiable information under § 363(b)(1) of the Code shall state whether the sale is consistent with any policy prohibiting the transfer of the information.

(2) Notice of Hearing on Compensation. The notice of a hearing on an application for compensation or reimbursement of expenses required by subdivision (a)(6) of this rule shall identify the applicant and the amounts requested.

(3) Notice of Hearing on Confirmation When Plan Provides for an Injunction. If a plan provides for an injunction against conduct not otherwise enjoined under the Code, the notice required under Rule 2002(b)(2) shall:

(A) include in conspicuous language (bold, italic, or underlined text) a statement that the plan proposes an injunction;

(B) describe briefly the nature of the injunction; and

(C) identify the entities that would be subject to the injunction.

(d) NOTICE TO EQUITY SECURITY HOLDERS. In a chapter 11 reorganization case, unless otherwise ordered by the court, the clerk, or some other person as the court may direct, shall in the manner and form directed by the court give notice to all equity security holders of (1) the order for relief; (2) any meeting of equity security holders held pursuant to Section 341 of the Code; (3) the hearing on the proposed sale of all or substantially all of the debtor's assets; (4) the hearing on the dismissal or conversion of a case to another chapter; (5) the time fixed for filing objections to and the hearing to consider approval of a disclosure statement; (6) the time fixed for filing objections to and the hearing to consider confirmation of a plan; and (7) the time fixed to accept or reject a proposed modification of a plan.

(e) NOTICE OF NO DIVIDEND. In a chapter 7 liquidation case, if it appears from the schedules that there are no assets from which a dividend can be paid, the notice of the meeting of creditors may include a statement to that effect; that it is unnecessary to file claims; and that if sufficient assets become available for the payment of a dividend, further notice will be given for the filing of claims.

(f) OTHER NOTICES. Except as provided in subdivision (l) of this rule, the clerk, or some other person as the court may direct, shall give the debtor, all creditors, and indenture trustees notice by mail of:

(1) the order for relief;

(2) the dismissal or the conversion of the case to another chapter, or the suspension of proceedings under § 305;

(3) the time allowed for filing claims pursuant to Rule 3002;

(4) the time fixed for filing a complaint objecting to the debtor's discharge pursuant to § 727 of the Code as provided in Rule 4004;

(5) the time fixed for filing a complaint to determine the dischargeability of a debt pursuant to § 523 of the Code as provided in Rule 4007;

(6) the waiver, denial, or revocation of a discharge as provided in Rule 4006;

(7) entry of an order confirming a chapter 9, 11, or 12 plan;

(8) a summary of the trustee's final report in a chapter 7 case if the net proceeds realized exceed $1,500;

(9) a notice under Rule 5008 regarding the presumption of abuse;

(10) a statement under § 704(b)(1) as to whether the debtor's case would be presumed to be an abuse under § 707(b); and

(11) the time to request a delay in the entry of the discharge under §§ 1141(d)(5)(C), 1228(f), and 1328(h). Notice of the time fixed for accepting or rejecting a plan pursuant to Rule 3017(c) shall be given in accordance with Rule 3017(d).

(g) ADDRESSING NOTICES.

(1) Notices required to be mailed under Rule 2002 to a creditor, indenture trustee, or equity security holder shall be addressed as such entity or an authorized agent has directed in its last request filed in the particular case. For the purposes of this subdivision –

(A) a proof of claim filed by a creditor or indenture trustee that designates a mailing address constitutes a filed request to mail notices to that address, unless a notice of no dividend has been given under Rule 2002(e) and a later notice of possible dividend under Rule 3002(c)(5) has not been given; and

(B) a proof of interest filed by an equity security holder that designates a mailing address constitutes a filed request to mail notices to that address.

(2) Except as provided in § 342(f) of the Code, if a creditor or indenture trustee has not filed a request designating a mailing address under Rule 2002(g)(1) or Rule 5003(e), the notices shall be mailed to the address

shown on the list of creditors or schedule of liabilities, whichever is filed later. If an equity security holder has not filed a request designating a mailing address under Rule 2002(g)(1) or Rule 5003(e), the notices shall be mailed to the address shown on the list of equity security holders.

(3) If a list or schedule filed under Rule 1007 includes the name and address of a legal representative of an infant or incompetent person, and a person other than that representative files a request or proof of claim designating a name and mailing address that differs from the name and address of the representative included in the list or schedule, unless the court orders otherwise, notices under Rule 2002 shall be mailed to the representative included in the list or schedules and to the name and address designated in the request or proof of claim.

(4) Notwithstanding Rule 2002(g)(1)-(3), an entity and a notice provider may agree that when the notice provider is directed by the court to give a notice, the notice provider shall give the notice to the entity in the manner agreed to and at the address or addresses the entity supplies to the notice provider. That address is conclusively presumed to be a proper address for the notice. The notice provider's failure to use the supplied address does not invalidate any notice that is otherwise effective under applicable law.

(5) A creditor may treat a notice as not having been brought to the creditor's attention under § 342(g)(1) only if, prior to issuance of the notice, the creditor has filed a statement that designates the name and address of the person or organizational subdivision of the creditor responsible for receiving notices under the Code, and that describes the procedures established by the creditor to cause such notices to be delivered to the designated person or subdivision.

(h) NOTICES TO CREDITORS WHOSE CLAIMS ARE FILED. In a chapter 7 case, after 90 days following the first date set for the meeting of creditors under Section 341 of the Code, the court may direct that all notices required by subdivision (a) of this rule be mailed only to the debtor, the trustee, all indenture trustees, creditors that hold claims for which proofs of claim have been filed, and creditors, if any, that are still permitted to file claims by reason of an extension granted pursuant to Rule 3002(c)(1) or (c)(2). In a case where notice of insufficient assets to pay a dividend has been given to creditors pursuant to subdivision (e) of this rule, after 90 days following the mailing of a notice of the time for filing claims pursuant to Rule 3002(c)(5), the court may direct that notices be mailed only to the entities specified in the preceding sentence.

(i) NOTICES TO COMMITTEES. Copies of all notices required to be mailed pursuant to this rule shall be mailed to the committees elected under Section 705 or appointed under Section 1102 of the Code or to their authorized agents. Notwithstanding the foregoing subdivisions, the court may order that notices required by subdivision (a)(2), (3) and (6) of this rule be transmitted to the United States trustee and be mailed only to the committees elected under Section 705 or appointed under Section 1102 of the Code or to their authorized agents and to the creditors and equity security holders who serve on the trustee or debtor in possession and file a request that all notices be mailed to them. A committee appointed under Section 1114 shall receive copies of all notices required by subdivisions (a)(1), (a)(5), (b), (f)(2), and (f)(7), and such other notices as the court may direct.

(j) NOTICES TO THE UNITED STATES. Copies of notices required to be mailed to all creditors under this rule shall be mailed (1) in a chapter 11 reorganization case to the Securities and Exchange Commission at any place the Commission designates, if the Commission has filed either a notice of appearance in the case or a written request to receive notices; (2) in a commodity broker case, to the Commodity Futures Trading Commission at Washington, D.C.; (3) in a chapter 11 case to the Internal Revenue Service at its address set out in the register maintained under Rule 5003(e) for the district in which the case is pending; (4) if the papers in the case disclose a debt to the United States other than for taxes, to the United States attorney for the district in which the case is pending and to the department, agency, or instrumentality of the United States through which the debtor became indebted; or if the filed papers disclose a stock interest of the United States, to the Secretary of the Treasury at Washington, D.C.

(k) NOTICES TO UNITED STATES TRUSTEE. Unless the case is a chapter 9 municipality case or unless the United States trustee requests otherwise, the clerk, or some other person as the court may direct, shall transmit to the United States trustee notice of the matters described in subdivisions (a)(2), (a)(3), (a)(4), (a)(8), (b), (f)(1), (f)(2), (f)(4), (f)(6), (f)(7), (f)(8), and (q) of this rule and notice of hearings on all applications for compensation or reimbursement of expenses. Notices to the United States trustee shall be transmitted within the time prescribed in subdivision (a) or (b) of this rule. The United States trustee shall also receive notice of any other matter if such notice is requested by the United States trustee or ordered by the court. Nothing in these rules requires the clerk or any other person to transmit to the United States trustee any notice, schedule, report, application or other document in a case under the Securities Investor Protection Act, 15 U.S.C. § 78aaa et. seq.

(l) NOTICE BY PUBLICATION. The court may order notice by publication if it finds that notice by mail is impracticable or that it is desirable to supplement the notice.

(m) ORDERS DESIGNATING MATTER OF NOTICES. The court may from time to time enter orders designating the matters in respect to which, the entity to whom, and the form and manner in which notices shall be sent except as otherwise provided by these rules.

(n) CAPTION. The caption of every notice given under this rule shall comply with Rule 1005. The caption of every notice required to be given by the debtor to a creditor shall include the information required to be in the notice by §342(c) of the Code.

(o) NOTICE OF ORDER FOR RELIEF IN CONSUMER CASE. In a voluntary case commenced by an individual debtor whose debts are primarily consumer debts, the clerk or some other person as the court may direct shall give the trustee and all creditors notice by mail of the order for relief within 21 days from the date thereof.

(p) NOTICE TO A CREDITOR WITH A FOREIGN ADDRESS.

(1) If, at the request of the United States trustee or a party in interest, or on its own initiative, the court finds that a notice mailed within the time prescribed by these rules would not be sufficient to give a creditor with a foreign address to which notices under these rules are mailed reasonable notice under the circumstances, the court may order that the notice be supplemented with notice by other means or that the time prescribed for the notice by mail be enlarged.

(2) Unless the court for cause orders otherwise, a creditor with a foreign address to which notices under this rule are mailed shall be given at least 30 days' notice of the time fixed for filing a proof of claim under Rule 3002(c) or Rule 3003(c).

(3) Unless the court for cause orders otherwise, the mailing address of a creditor with a foreign address shall be determined under Rule 2002(g).

(q) NOTICE OF PETITION FOR RECOGNITION OF FOREIGN PROCEEDING AND OF COURT'S INTENTION TO COMMUNICATE WITH FOREIGN COURTS AND FOREIGN REPRESENTATIVES.

(1) Notice of Petition for Recognition. The clerk, or some other person as the court may direct, shall forthwith give the debtor, all persons or bodies authorized to administer foreign proceedings of the debtor, all entities against whom provisional relief is being sought under § 1519 of the Code, all parties to litigation pending in the United States in which the debtor is a party at the time of the filing of the petition, and such other entities as the court may direct, at least 21 days' notice by mail of the hearing on the petition for recognition of a foreign proceeding. The notice shall state whether the petition seeks recognition as a foreign main proceeding or foreign nonmain proceeding.

(2) Notice of Court's Intention to Communicate with Foreign Courts and Foreign Representatives. The clerk, or some other person as the court may direct, shall give the debtor, all persons or bodies authorized to administer foreign proceedings of the debtor, all entities against whom provisional relief is being sought under § 1519 of the Code, all parties to litigation pending in the United States in which the debtor is a party at the time of the filing of the petition, and such other entities as the court may direct, notice by mail of the court's intention to communicate with a foreign court or foreign representative.

Rule 2003. Meeting of Creditors or Equity Security Holders

(a) DATE AND PLACE. Except as otherwise provided in § 341(e) of the Code, in a chapter 7 liquidation or a chapter 11 reorganization case, the United States trustee shall call a meeting of creditors to be held no fewer than 21 and no more than 40 days after the order for relief. In a chapter 12 family farmer debt adjustment case, the United States trustee shall call a meeting of creditors to be held no fewer than 21 and no more than 35 days after the order for relief. In a chapter 13 individual's debt adjustment case, the United States trustee shall call a meeting of creditors to be held no fewer than 21 and no more than 50 days after the order for relief. If there is an appeal from or a motion to vacate the order for relief, or if there is a motion to dismiss the case, the United States trustee may set a later date for the meeting. The meeting may be held at a regular place for holding court or at any other place designated by the United States trustee within the district convenient for the parties in interest. If the United States trustee designates a place for the meeting which is not regularly staffed by the United States trustee or an assistant who may preside at the meeting, the meeting may be held not more than 60 days after the order for relief.

(b) ORDER OF MEETING.

(1) Meeting of Creditors. The United States trustee shall preside at the meeting of creditors. The business of the meeting shall include the examination of the debtor under oath and, in a chapter 7 liquidation case, may include the election of a creditors' committee and, if the case is not under subchapter V of Chapter 7, the election of a trustee. The presiding officer shall have the authority to administer oaths.

(2) Meeting of Equity Security Holders. If the United States trustee convenes a meeting of equity security holders pursuant to Section 341(b) of the Code, the United States trustee shall fix a date for the meeting and shall preside.

(3) Right to Vote. In a chapter 7 liquidation case, a creditor is entitled to vote at a meeting if, at or before the meeting, the creditor has filed a proof of claim or a writing setting forth facts evidencing a right to vote pursuant to Section 702(a) of the Code unless objection is made to the claim or the proof of claim is insufficient on its face. A creditor of a partnership may file a proof of claim or writing evidencing a right to vote for the trustee for the estate of a general partner notwithstanding that a trustee for the estate of the partnership has previously qualified. In the event of an objection to the amount or allowability of a claim for the purpose of voting, unless the court orders otherwise, the United States trustee shall tabulate the votes for each alternative presented by the dispute and, if resolution of such dispute is necessary to determine the result of the election, the tabulations for each alternative shall be reported to the court.

(c) RECORD OF MEETING. Any examination under oath at the meeting of creditors held pursuant to Section 341(a) of the Code shall be recorded verbatim by the United States trustee using electronic sound recording equipment or other means of recording, and such record shall be preserved by the United States trustee and available for public access until two years after the conclusion of the meeting of creditors. Upon request of any entity, the United States trustee shall certify and provide a copy or transcript of such recording at the entity's expense.

(d) REPORT OF ELECTION AND RESOLUTION OF DISPUTES IN A CHAPTER 7 CASE.

(1) Report of undisputed election. In a chapter 7 case, if the election of a trustee or a member of a creditors' committee is not disputed, the United States trustee shall promptly file a report of the election, including the name and address of the person or entity elected and a statement that the election is undisputed.

(2) Disputed election. If the election is disputed, the United States trustee shall promptly file a report stating that the election is disputed, informing the court of the nature of the dispute, and listing the name and address of any candidate elected under any alternative presented by the dispute. No later than the date on which the report is filed, the United States trustee shall mail a copy of the report to any party in interest that has made a request to receive a copy of the report. Pending disposition by the court of a disputed election for trustee, the interim trustee shall continue in office. Unless a motion for the resolution of the dispute is filed no later than 14 days after the United States trustee files a report of disputed election for trustee, the interim trustee shall serve as trustee in the case.

(e) ADJOURNMENT. The meeting may be adjourned from time to time by announcement at the meeting of the adjourned date and time. The presiding official shall promptly file a statement specifying the date and time to which the meeting is adjourned.

(f) SPECIAL MEETINGS. The United States trustee may call a special meeting of creditors on request of a party in interest or on the United States trustee's own initiative.

(g) FINAL MEETING. If the United States trustee calls a final meeting of creditors in a case in which the net proceeds realized exceed $1,500, the clerk shall mail a summary of the trustee's final account to the creditors with a notice of the meeting, together with a statement of the amount of the claims allowed. The trustee shall attend the final meeting and shall, if requested, report on the administration of the estate.

Rule 2004. Examination

(a) EXAMINATION ON MOTION. On motion of any party in interest, the court may order the examination of any entity.

(b) SCOPE OF EXAMINATION. The examination of an entity under this rule or of the debtor under Section 343 of the Code may relate only to the acts, conduct, or property or to the liabilities and financial condition of the debtor, or to any matter which may affect the administration of the debtor's estate, or to the debtor's right to a discharge. In a family farmer's debt adjustment case under chapter 12, an individual's debt adjustment case under chapter 13, or a reorganization case under chapter 11 of the Code, other than for the reorganization of a railroad, the examination may also relate to the operation of any business and the desirability of its continuance, the source of any money or property acquired or to be acquired by the debtor for purposes of consummating a plan and the consideration given or offered therefor, and any other matter relevant to the case or to the formulation of a plan.

(c) COMPELLING ATTENDANCE AND PRODUCTION OF DOCUMENTS. The attendance of an entity for examination and for the production of documents, whether the examination is to be conducted within or without the district in which the case is pending, may be compelled as provided in Rule 9016 for the attendance of a witness at a hearing or trial. As an officer of the court, an attorney may issue and sign a subpoena on behalf of the court for the district in which the examination is to be held if the attorney is admitted to practice in that court or in the court in which the case is pending.

(d) TIME AND PLACE OF EXAMINATION OF DEBTOR. The court may for cause shown and on terms as it may impose order the debtor to be examined under this rule at any time or place it designates, whether within or without the district wherein the case is pending.

(e) MILEAGE. An entity other than a debtor shall not be required to attend as a witness unless lawful mileage and witness fee for one day's attendance shall be first tendered. If the debtor resides more than 100 miles from the place of examination when required to appear for an examination under this rule, the mileage allowed by law to a witness shall be tendered for any distance more than 100 miles from the debtor's residence at the date of the filing of the first petition commencing a case under the Code or the residence at the time the debtor is required to appear for the examination, whichever is the lesser.

Rule 2005. Apprehension and Removal of Debtor to Compel Attendance for Examination

(a) ORDER TO COMPEL ATTENDANCE FOR EXAMINATION. On motion of any party in interest supported by an affidavit alleging (1) that the examination of the debtor is necessary for the proper administration of the estate and that there is reasonable cause to believe that the debtor is about to leave or has left the debtor's residence or principal place of business to avoid examination, or (2) that the debtor has evaded service of a subpoena or of an order to attend for examination, or (3) that the debtor has willfully disobeyed a subpoena or order to attend for examination, duly served, the court may issue to the marshal, or some other officer authorized by law, an order directing the officer to bring the debtor before the court without unnecessary delay. If, after hearing, the court finds the allegations to be true, the court shall thereupon cause the debtor to be examined forthwith. If necessary, the court shall fix conditions for further examination and for the debtor's obedience to all orders made in reference thereto.

(b) REMOVAL. Whenever any order to bring the debtor before the court is issued under this rule and the debtor is found in a district other than that of the court issuing the order, the debtor may be taken into custody under the order and removed in accordance with the following rules:

(1) If the debtor is taken into custody under the order at a place less than 100 miles from the place of issue of the order, the debtor shall be brought forthwith before the court that issued the order.

(2) If the debtor is taken into custody under the order at a place 100 miles or more from the place of issue of the order, the debtor shall be brought without unnecessary delay before the nearest available United States magistrate judge, bankruptcy judge, or district judge. If, after hearing, the magistrate judge, bankruptcy judge, or district judge finds that an order has issued under this rule and that the person in custody is the debtor, or if the person in custody waives a hearing, the magistrate judge, bankruptcy judge, or district judge shall order removal, and the person in custody shall be released on conditions ensuring prompt appearance before the court that issued the order to compel the attendance.

(c) CONDITIONS OF RELEASE. In determining what conditions will reasonably assure attendance or obedience under subdivision (a) of this rule or appearance under subdivision (b) of this rule, the court shall be governed by the provisions and policies of title 18, U. S. C., Section 3146(a) and (b).

Rule 2006. Solicitation and Voting of Proxies in Chapter 7 Liquidation Cases

(a) APPLICABILITY. This rule applies only in a liquidation case pending under chapter 7 of the Code.

(b) DEFINITIONS.

(1) Proxy. A proxy is a written power of attorney authorizing any

entity to vote the claim or otherwise act as the owner's attorney in fact in connection with the administration of the estate.

(2) Solicitation of Proxy. The solicitation of a proxy is any communication, other than one from an attorney to a regular client who owns a claim or from an attorney to the owner of a claim who has requested the attorney to represent the owner, by which a creditor is asked, directly or indirectly, to give a proxy after or in contemplation of the filing of a petition by or against the debtor.

(c) AUTHORIZED SOLICITATION.

(1) A proxy may be solicited only by (A) a creditor owning an allowable unsecured claim against the estate on the date of the filing of the petition; (B) a committee elected pursuant to Section 705 of the Code; (C) a committee of creditors selected by a majority in number and amount of claims of creditors (i) whose claims are not contingent or unliquidated, (ii) who are not disqualified from voting under Section 702(a) of the Code and (iii) who were present or represented at a meeting of which all creditors having claims of over $500 or the 100 creditors having the largest claims had at least seven days notice in writing and of which meeting written minutes were kept and are available reporting the names of the creditors present or represented and voting and the amounts of their claims; or (D) a bona fide trade or credit association, but such association may solicit only creditors who were its members or subscribers in good standing and had allowable unsecured claims on the date of the filing of the petition.

(2) A proxy may be solicited only in writing.

(d) SOLICITATION NOT AUTHORIZED. This rule does not permit solicitation (1) in any interest other than that of general creditors; (2) by or on behalf of any custodian; (3) by the interim trustee or by or on behalf of any entity not qualified to vote under Section 702(a) of the Code; (4) by or on behalf of an attorney at law; or (5) by or on behalf of a transferee of a claim for collection only.

(e) DATA REQUIRED FROM HOLDERS OF MULTIPLE PROXIES. At any time before the voting commences at any meeting of creditors pursuant to Section 341(a) of the Code, or at any other time as the court may direct, a holder of two or more proxies shall file and transmit to the United States trustee a verified list of the proxies to be voted and a verified statement of the pertinent facts and circumstances in connection with the execution and delivery of each proxy, including:

(1) a copy of the solicitation;

(2) identification of the solicitor, the forwarder, if the forwarder is neither the solicitor nor the owner of the claim, and the proxyholder, including their connections with the debtor and with each other. If the solicitor, forwarder, or proxyholder is an association, there shall also be included a statement that the creditors whose claims have been solicited and the creditors whose claims are to be voted were members or subscribers in good standing and had allowable unsecured claims on the date of the filing of the petition. If the solicitor, forwarder, or proxyholder is a committee of creditors, the statement shall also set forth the date and place the committee was organized, that the committee was organized in accordance with clause (B) or (C) of paragraph (c)(1) of this rule, the members of the committee, the amounts of their claims, when the claims were acquired, the amounts paid therefor, and the extent to which the claims of the committee members are secured or entitled to priority;

(3) a statement that no consideration has been paid or promised by the proxyholder for the proxy;

(4) a statement as to whether there is any agreement and, if so, the particulars thereof, between the proxyholder and any other entity for the payment of any consideration in connection with voting the proxy, or for the sharing of compensation with any entity, other than a member or regular associate of the proxyholder's law firm, which may be allowed the trustee or any entity for services rendered in the case, or for the employment of any person as attorney, accountant, appraiser, auctioneer, or other employee for the estate;

(5) if the proxy was solicited by an entity other than the proxyholder, or forwarded to the holder by an entity who is neither a solicitor of the proxy nor the owner of the claim, a statement signed and verified by the solicitor or forwarder that no consideration has been paid or promised for the proxy, and whether there is any agreement, and, if so, the particulars thereof, between the solicitor or forwarder and any other entity for the payment of any consideration in connection with voting the proxy, or for sharing compensation with any entity other than a member or regular associate of the solicitor's or forwarder's law firm which may be allowed the trustee or any entity for services rendered in the case, or for the employment of any person as attorney, accountant, appraiser, auctioneer, or other employee for the estate;

(6) if the solicitor, forwarder, or proxyholder is a committee, a statement signed and verified by each member as to the amount and source of any consideration paid or to be paid to such member in connection with the case other than by way of dividend on the member's claim.

(f) ENFORCEMENT OF RESTRICTIONS ON SOLICITATION. On motion of any party in interest or on its own initiative, the court may determine whether there has been a failure to comply with the provisions of this rule or any other impropriety in connection with the solicitation or voting of a proxy. After notice and a hearing the court may reject any proxy for cause, vacate any order entered in consequence of the voting of any proxy which should have been rejected, or take any other appropriate action.

Rule 2007. Review of Appointment of Creditors' Committee Organized Before Commencement of the Case

(a) MOTION TO REVIEW APPOINTMENT. If a committee appointed by the United States trustee pursuant to Section 1102(a) of the Code consists of the members of a committee organized by creditors before the commencement of a chapter 9 or chapter 11 case, on motion of a party in interest and after a hearing on notice to the United States trustee and other entities as the court may direct, the court may determine whether the appointment of the committee satisfies the requirements of Section 1102(b)(1) of the Code.

(b) SELECTION OF MEMBERS OF COMMITTEE. The court may find that a committee organized by unsecured creditors before the commencement of a chapter 9 or chapter 11 case was fairly chosen if:

(1) it was selected by a majority in number and amount of claims of unsecured creditors who may vote under Section 702(a) of the Code and were present in person or represented at a meeting of which all creditors having unsecured claims of over $1,000 or the 100 unsecured creditors having the largest claims had at least seven days' notice in writing, and of which meeting written minutes reporting the names of the creditors present or represented and voting and the amounts of their claims were kept and are available for inspection;

(2) all proxies voted at the meeting for the elected committee were solicited pursuant to Rule 2006 and the lists and statements required by subdivision (e) thereof have been transmitted to the United States trustee; and

(3) the organization of the committee was in all other respects fair and proper.

(c) FAILURE TO COMPLY WITH REQUIREMENTS FOR APPOINTMENT. After a hearing on notice pursuant to subdivision (a) of this rule, the court shall direct the United States trustee to vacate the appointment of the committee and may order other appropriate action if the court finds that such appointment failed to satisfy the requirements of Section 1102(b)(1) of the Code.

Rule 2007.1. Appointment of Trustee or Examiner in a Chapter 11 Reorganization Case

(a) ORDER TO APPOINT TRUSTEE OR EXAMINER. In a chapter 11 reorganization case, a motion for an order to appoint a trustee or an exam-iner under Section 1104(a) or Section 1104(c) of the Code shall be made in accordance with Rule 9014.

(b) ELECTION OF TRUSTEE.

(1) Request for an Election. A request to convene a meeting of creditors for the purpose of electing a trustee in a chapter 11 reorganization case shall be filed and transmitted to the United States trustee in accordance with Rule 5005 within the time prescribed by §1104(b) of the Code. Pending court approval of the person elected, any person appointed by the United States trustee under §1104(d) and approved in accordance with subdivision (c) of this rule shall serve as trustee.

(2) Manner of Election and Notice. An election of a trustee under §1104(b) of the Code shall be conducted in the manner provided in Rules 2003(b)(3) and 2006. Notice of the meeting of creditors convened under §1104(b) shall be given as provided in Rule 2002. The United States trustee shall preside at the meeting. A proxy for the purpose of voting in the election may be solicited only by a committee of creditors appointed under § 1102 of the Code or by any other party entitled to solicit a proxy pursuant to Rule 2006.

(3) Report of Election and Resolution of Disputes.

(A) Report of Undisputed Election. If no dispute arises out of the election, the United States trustee shall promptly file a report certifying the election, including the name and address of the person elected and a statement that the election is undisputed. The report shall be accompanied by a verified statement of the person elected setting forth that person's connections with the debtor, creditors, any other party in interest, their respective attorneys and accountants, the United States trustee, or any person employed in the office of the United States trustee.

(B) Dispute Arising Out of an Election. If a dispute arises out of an election, the United States trustee shall promptly file a report stating that the election is disputed, informing the court of the nature of the dispute, and listing the name and address of any candidate elected under any alternative presented by the dispute. The report shall be accompanied by a verified statement by each candidate elected under each alternative presented by the dispute, setting forth the person's connections with the debtor, creditors, any other party in interest, their respective attorneys and accountants, the United States trustee, or any person employed in the office of the United States trustee. Not later than the date on which the report of the disputed election is filed, the United States trustee shall mail a copy of the report and each verified statement to any party in interest that has made a request to convene a meeting under § 1104(b) or to receive a copy of the report, and to any committee appointed under § 1102 of the Code.

(c) APPROVAL OF APPOINTMENT. An order approving the appointment of a trustee or an examiner under §1104(d) of the Code shall be made on application of the United States trustee. The application shall state the name of the person appointed and, to the best of the applicant's knowledge, all the person's connections with the debtor, creditors, any other parties in interest, their respective attorneys and accountants, the United States trustee, or persons employed in the office of the United States trustee. The application shall state the names of the parties in interest with whom the United States trustee consulted regarding the appointment. The application shall be accompanied by a verified statement of the person appointed setting forth the person's connections with the debtor, creditors, any other party in interest, their respective attorneys and accountants, the United States trustee, or any person employed in the office of the United States trustee.

Rule 2007.2. Appointment of Patient Care Ombudsman in a Health Care Business Case

(a) ORDER TO APPOINT PATIENT CARE OMBUDSMAN. In a chapter 7, chapter 9, or chapter 11 case in which the debtor is a health care business, the court shall order the appointment of a patient care ombudsman under § 333 of the Code, unless the court, on motion of the United States trustee or a party in interest filed no later than 21 days after the commencement of the case or within another time fixed by the court, finds that the appointment of a patient care ombudsman is not necessary under the specific circumstances of the case for the protection of patients.

(b) MOTION FOR ORDER TO APPOINT OMBUDSMAN. If the court has found that the appointment of an ombudsman is not necessary, or has terminated the appointment, the court, on motion of the United States trustee or a party in interest, may order the appointment at a later time if it finds that the appointment has become necessary to protect patients.

(c) NOTICE OF APPOINTMENT. If a patient care ombudsman is appointed under § 333, the United States trustee shall promptly file a notice of the appointment, including the name and address of the person appointed. Unless the person appointed is a State Long-Term Care Ombudsman, the notice shall be accompanied by a verified statement of the person appointed setting forth the person's connections with the debtor, creditors, patients, any other party in interest, their respective attorneys and accountants, the United States trustee, and any person employed in the office of the United States trustee.

(d) TERMINATION OF APPOINTMENT. On motion of the United States trustee or a party in interest, the court may terminate the appointment of a patient care ombudsman if the court finds that the appointment is not necessary to protect patients.

(e) MOTION. A motion under this rule shall be governed by Rule 9014. The motion shall be transmitted to the United States trustee and served on: the debtor; the trustee; any committee elected under § 705 or appointed under § 1102 of the Code or its authorized agent, or, if the case is a chapter 9 municipality case or a chapter 11 reorganization case and no committee of unsecured creditors has been appointed under § 1102, on the creditors included on the list filed under Rule 1007(d); and such other entities as the court may direct.

Rule 2008. Notice to Trustee of Selection

The United States trustee shall immediately notify the person selected as trustee how to qualify and, if applicable, the amount of the trustee's bond. A trustee that has filed a blanket bond pursuant to Rule 2010 and has been selected as trustee in a chapter 7, chapter 12, or chapter 13 case that does not notify the court and the United States trustee in writing of rejection of the office within seven days after receipt of notice of selection shall be deemed to have accepted the office. Any other person selected as trustee shall notify the court and the United States trustee in writing of acceptance of the office within seven days after receipt of notice of selection or shall be deemed to have rejected the office.

Rule 2009. Trustee for Estates When Joint Administration Ordered

(a) ELECTION OF SINGLE TRUSTEE FOR ESTATES BEING JOINTLY ADMINISTERED. If the court orders a joint administration of two or more estates under Rule 1015(b), creditors may elect a single trustee for the estates being jointly administered, unless the case is under subchapter V of chapter 7 of the Code.

(b) RIGHT OF CREDITORS TO ELECT SEPARATE TRUSTEE. Notwithstanding entry of an order for joint administration under Rule 1015(b), the creditors of any debtor may elect a separate trustee for the estate of the debtor as provided in Section 702 of the Code, unless the case is under subchapter V of chapter 7 of the Code.

(c) APPOINTMENT OF TRUSTEES FOR ESTATES BEING JOINTLY ADMINISTERED.

(1) Chapter 7 Liquidation Cases. Except in a case governed by subchapter V of chapter 7, the United States trustee may appoint one or more interim trustees for estates being jointly administered in chapter 7 cases.

(2) Chapter 11 Reorganization Cases. If the appointment of a trustee is ordered, the United States trustee may appoint one or more trustees for estates being jointly administered in chapter 11 cases.

(3) Chapter 12 Family Farmer's Debt Adjustment Cases. The United States trustee may appoint one or more trustees for estates being jointly administered in chapter 12 cases.

(4) Chapter 13 Individual's Debt Adjustment Cases. The United States trustee may appoint one or more trustees for estates being jointly administered in chapter 13 cases.

(d) POTENTIAL CONFLICTS OF INTEREST. On a showing that creditors or equity security holders of the different estates will be prejudiced by conflicts of interest of a common trustee who has been elected or appointed, the court shall order the selection of separate trustees for estates being jointly administered.

(e) SEPARATE ACCOUNTS. The trustee or trustees of estates being jointly administered shall keep separate accounts of the property and distribution of each estate.

Rule 2010. Qualification by Trustee; Proceeding on Bond

(a) BLANKET BOND. The United States trustee may authorize a blanket bond in favor of the United States conditioned on the faithful performance of official duties by the trustee or trustees to cover (1) a person who qualifies as trustee in a number of cases, and (2) a number of trustees each of whom qualifies in a different case.

(b) PROCEEDING ON BOND. A proceeding on the trustee's bond may be brought by any party in interest in the name of the United States for the use of the entity injured by the breach of the condition.

Rule 2011. Evidence of Debtor in Possession or Qualification of Trustee

(a) Whenever evidence is required that a debtor is a debtor in possession or that a trustee has qualified, the clerk may so certify and the certificate shall constitute conclusive evidence of that fact.

(b) If a person elected or appointed as trustee does not qualify within the time prescribed by Section 322(a) of the Code, the clerk shall so notify the court and the United States trustee.

Rule 2012. Substitution of Trustee or Successor Trustee; Accounting

(a) TRUSTEE. If a trustee is appointed in a chapter 11 case or the debtor is removed as debtor in possession in a chapter 12 case, the trustee is substituted automatically for the debtor in possession as a party in any pending action, proceeding, or matter.

(b) SUCCESSOR TRUSTEE. When a trustee dies, resigns, is removed, or otherwise ceases to hold office during the pendency of a case under the Code (1) the successor is automatically substituted as a party in any pending action, proceeding, or matter; and (2) the successor trustee shall prepare, file, and transmit to the United States trustee an accounting of the prior administration of the estate.

Rule 2013. Public Record of Compensation Awarded to Trustees, Examiners, and Professionals

(a) RECORD TO BE KEPT. The clerk shall maintain a public record listing fees awarded by the court (1) to trustees and attorneys, accountants, appraisers, auctioneers and other professionals employed by trustees, and (2) to examiners. The record shall include the name and docket number of the case, the name of the individual or firm receiving the fee and the amount of the fee awarded. The record shall be maintained chronologically and shall be kept current and open to examination by the public without charge. "Trustees," as used in this rule, does not include debtors in possession.

(b) SUMMARY OF RECORD. At the close of each annual period, the clerk shall prepare a summary of the public record by individual or firm name, to reflect total fees awarded during the preceding year. The summary shall be open to examination by the public without charge. The clerk shall transmit a copy of the summary to the United States trustee.

Rule 2014. Employment of Professional Persons

(a) APPLICATION FOR AN ORDER OF EMPLOYMENT. An order approving the employment of attorneys, accountants, appraisers, auctioneers, agents, or other professionals pursuant to Section 327, Section 1103, or Section 1114 of the Code shall be made only on application of the trustee or committee. The application shall be filed and, unless the case is a chapter 9 municipality case, a copy of the application shall be transmitted by the applicant to the United States trustee. The application shall state the specific facts showing the necessity for the employment, the name of the person to be employed, the reasons for the selection, the professional services to be rendered, any proposed arrangement for compensation, and, to the best of the applicant's knowledge, all of the person's connections with the debtor, creditors, any other party in interest, their respective attorneys and accountants, the United States trustee, or any person employed in the office of the United States trustee. The application shall be accompanied by a verified statement of the person to be employed setting forth the person's connections with the debtor, creditors, any other party in interest, their respective attorneys and accountants, the United States trustee, or any person employed in the office of the United States trustee.

(b) SERVICES RENDERED BY MEMBER OR ASSOCIATE OF FIRM OF ATTORNEYS OR ACCOUNTANTS. If, under the Code and this rule, a law partnership or corporation is employed as an attorney, or an accounting partnership or corporation is employed as an accountant, or if a named attorney or accountant is employed, any partner, member, or regular associate of the partnership, corporation or individual may act as attorney or accountant so employed, without further order of the court.

Rule 2015. Duty to Keep Records, Make Reports, and Give Notice of Case or Change of Status

(a) TRUSTEE OR DEBTOR IN POSSESSION. A trustee or debtor in possession shall:

(1) in a chapter 7 liquidation case and, if the court directs, in a chapter 11 reorganization case file and transmit to the United States trustee a complete inventory of the property of the debtor within 30 days after qualifying as a trustee or debtor in possession, unless such an inventory has already been filed;

(2) keep a record of receipts and the disposition of money and property received;

(3) file the reports and summaries required by § 704(a)(8) of the Code which shall include a statement, if payments are made to employees, of the amounts of deductions for all taxes required to be withheld or paid for and in behalf of employees and the place where these amounts are deposited;

(4) as soon as possible after the commencement of the case, give notice of the case to every entity known to be holding money or property subject to withdrawal or order of the debtor, including every bank, savings or building and loan association, public utility company, and landlord with whom the debtor has a deposit, and to every insurance company which has issued a policy having a cash surrender value payable to the debtor, except that notice need not be given to any entity who has knowledge or has previously been notified of the case;

(5) in a chapter 11 reorganization case, on or before the last day of the month after each calendar quarter during which there is a duty to pay fees under 28 U.S.C. § 1930(a)(6), file and transmit to the United States trustee a statement of any disbursements made during that quarter and of any fees payable under 28 U.S.C. § 1930(a)(6) for that quarter; and

(6) in a chapter 11 small business case, unless the court, for cause, sets another reporting interval, file and transmit to the United States trustee for each calendar month after the order for relief, on the appropriate Official Form, the report required by § 308. If the order for relief is within the first 15 days of a calendar month, a report shall be filed for the portion of the month that follows the order for relief. If the order for relief is after the 15th day of a calendar month, the period for the remainder of the month shall be included in the report for the next calendar month. Each report shall be filed no later than 21 days after the last day of the calendar month following the month covered by the report. The obligation to file reports under this subparagraph terminates on the effective date of the plan, or conversion or dismissal of the case.

(b) CHAPTER 12 TRUSTEE AND DEBTOR IN POSSESSION. In a chapter 12 family farmer's debt adjustment case, the debtor in possession shall perform the duties prescribed in clauses (2)-(4) of subdivision (a) of this rule and, if the court directs, shall file and transmit to the United States trustee a complete inventory of the property of the debtor within the time fixed by the court. If the debtor is removed as debtor in possession, the trustee shall perform the duties of the debtor in possession prescribed in this paragraph.

(c) CHAPTER 13 TRUSTEE AND DEBTOR.

(1) Business Cases. In a chapter 13 individual's debt adjustment case, when the debtor is engaged in business, the debtor shall perform the duties prescribed by clauses (2)-(4) of subdivision (a) of this rule and, if the court directs, shall file and transmit to the United States trustee a complete inventory of the property of the debtor within the time fixed by the court.

(2) Nonbusiness Cases. In a chapter 13 individual's debt adjustment case, when the debtor is not engaged in business, the trustee shall perform the duties prescribed by clause (2) of subdivision (a) of this rule.

(d) FOREIGN REPRESENTATIVE. In a case in which the court has granted recognition of a foreign proceeding under chapter 15, the foreign representative shall file any notice required under § 1518 of the Code within 14 days after the date when the representative becomes aware of the subsequent information.

(e) TRANSMISSION OF REPORTS. In a chapter 11 case the court may direct that copies or summaries of annual reports and copies or summaries of other reports shall be mailed to the creditors, equity security holders, and indenture trustees. The court may also direct the publication of summaries of any such reports. A copy of every report or summary mailed or published pursuant to this subdivision shall be transmitted to the United States trustee.

Rule 2015.1. Patient Care Ombudsman

(a) REPORTS. A patient care ombudsman, at least 14 days before making a report under § 333(b)(2) of the Code, shall give notice that the report will be made to the court, unless the court orders otherwise. The notice shall be transmitted to the United States trustee, posted conspicuously at the health care facility that is the subject of the report, and served on: the debtor; the trustee; all patients; and any committee elected under § 705 or appointed under § 1102 of the Code or its authorized agent, or, if the case is a chapter 9 municipality case or a chapter 11 reorganization case and no committee of unsecured creditors has been appointed under § 1102, on the creditors included on the list filed under Rule 1007(d); and such other entities as the court may direct. The notice shall state the date and time when the report will be made, the manner in which the report will be made, and, if the report is in writing, the name, address, telephone number, email address, and website, if any, of the person from whom a copy of the report may be obtained at the debtor's expense.

(b) AUTHORIZATION TO REVIEW CONFIDENTIAL PATIENT RECORDS. A motion by a patient care ombudsman under § 333(c) to review confidential patient records shall be governed by Rule 9014, served on the patient and any family member or other contact person whose name and address have been given to the trustee or the debtor for the purpose of providing information regarding the patient's health care, and transmitted to the United States trustee subject to applicable nonbankruptcy law relating to patient privacy. Unless the court orders otherwise, a hearing on the motion may not be commenced earlier than 14 days after service of the motion.

Rule 2015.2. Transfer of Patient in Health Care Business Case

Unless the court orders otherwise, if the debtor is a health care business, the trustee may not transfer a patient to another health care business under § 704(a)(12) of the Code unless the trustee gives at least 14 days' notice of the transfer to the patient care ombudsman, if any, the patient, and any family member or other contact person whose name and address has been given to the trustee or the debtor for the purpose of providing information regarding the patient's health care. The notice is subject to applicable nonbankruptcy law relating to patient privacy.

Rule 2015.3. Reports of Financial Information on Entities in Which a Chapter 11 Estate Holds a Controlling or Substantial Interest

(a) REPORTING REQUIREMENT. In a chapter 11 case, the trustee or debtor in possession shall file periodic financial reports of the value, operations, and profitability of each entity that is not a publicly traded corporation or a debtor in a case under title 11, and in which the estate holds a substantial or controlling interest. The reports shall be prepared as prescribed by the appropriate Official Form, and shall be based upon the most recent information reasonably available to the trustee or debtor in possession.

(b) TIME FOR FILING; SERVICE. The first report required by this rule shall be filed no later than seven days before the first date set for the meeting of creditors under § 341 of the Code. Subsequent reports shall be filed no less frequently than every six months thereafter, until the effective date of a plan or the case is dismissed or converted. Copies of the report shall be served on the United States trustee, any committee appointed under § 1102 of the Code, and any other party in interest that has filed a request therefor.

(c) PRESUMPTION OF SUBSTANTIAL OR CONTROLLING INTEREST; JUDICIAL DETERMINATION. For purposes of this rule, an entity of which the estate controls or owns at least a 20 percent interest, shall be presumed to be an entity in which the estate has a substantial or controlling interest. An entity in which the estate controls or owns less than a 20 percent interest shall be presumed not to be an entity in which the estate has a substantial or controlling interest. Upon motion, the entity, any holder of an interest therein, the United States trustee, or any other party in interest may seek to rebut either presumption, and the court shall, after notice and a hearing, determine whether the estate's interest in the entity is substantial or controlling.

(d) MODIFICATION OF REPORTING REQUIREMENT. The court may, after notice and a hearing, vary the reporting requirement established by subdivision (a) of this rule for cause, including that the trustee or debtor in possession is not able, after a good faith effort, to comply with those reporting requirements, or that the information required by subdivision (a) is publicly available.

(e) NOTICE AND PROTECTIVE ORDERS. No later than 14 days before filing the first report required by this rule, the trustee or debtor in possession shall send notice to the entity in which the estate has a substantial or controlling interest, and to all holders – known to the trustee or debtor in possession – of an interest in that entity, that the trustee or debtor in possession expects to file and serve financial information relating to the entity in accordance with this rule. The entity in which the estate has a substantial or controlling interest, or a person holding an interest in that entity, may request protection of the information under § 107 of the Code.

(f) EFFECT OF REQUEST. Unless the court orders otherwise, the pendency of a request under subdivisions (c), (d), or (e) of this rule shall not alter or stay the requirements of subdivision (a).

Rule 2016. Compensation for Services Rendered and Reimbursement of Expenses

(a) APPLICATION FOR COMPENSATION OR REIMBURSEMENT. An entity seeking interim or final compensation for services, or reimbursement of necessary expenses, from the estate shall file an application setting forth a detailed statement of (1) the services rendered, time expended and expenses incurred, and (2) the amounts requested. An application for compensation shall include a statement as to what payments have theretofore been made or promised to the applicant for services rendered or to be rendered in any capacity whatsoever in connection with the case, the source of the compensation so paid or promised, whether any compensation previously received has been shared and whether an agreement or understanding exists between the applicant and any other entity for the sharing of compensation received or to be received for services rendered in or in connection with the case, and the particulars of any sharing of compensation or agreement or understanding therefor, except that details of any agreement by the applicant for the sharing of compensation as a member or regular associate of a firm of lawyers or accountants shall not be required. The requirements of this subdivision shall apply to an application for compensation for services rendered by an attorney or accountant even though the application is filed by a creditor or other entity. Unless the case is a chapter 9 municipality case, the applicant shall transmit to the United States trustee a copy of the application.

(b) DISCLOSURE OF COMPENSATION PAID OR PROMISED TO ATTORNEY FOR DEBTOR. Every attorney for a debtor, whether or not the attorney applies for compensation, shall file and transmit to the United States trustee within 14 days after the order for relief, or at another time as the court may direct, the statement required by Section 329 of the Code including whether the attorney has shared or agreed to share the compensation with any other entity. The statement shall include the particulars of any such sharing or agreement to share by the attorney, but the details of any agreement for the sharing of the compensation with a member or regular associate of the attorney's law firm shall not be required. A supplemental statement shall be filed and transmitted to the United States trustee within 14 days after any payment or agreement not previously disclosed.

(c) DISCLOSURE OF COMPENSATION PAID OR PROMISED TO BANKRUPTCY PETITION PREPARER. Before a petition is filed, every bankruptcy petition preparer for a debtor shall deliver to the debtor, the declaration under penalty of perjury required by § 110(h)(2). The declaration shall disclose any fee, and the source of any fee, received from or on behalf of the debtor within 12 months of the filing of the case and all unpaid fees charged to the debtor. The declaration shall also describe the services performed and documents prepared or caused to be prepared by the bankruptcy petition preparer. The declaration shall be filed with the petition. The petition preparer shall file a supplemental statement within 14 days after any payment or agreement not previously disclosed.

Rule 2017. Examination of Debtor's Transactions with Debtor's Attorney

(a) PAYMENT OR TRANSFER TO ATTORNEY BEFORE ORDER FOR RELIEF. On motion by any party in interest or on the court's own initiative, the court after notice and a hearing may determine whether any payment of money or any transfer of property by the debtor, made directly or indirectly and in contemplation of the filing of a petition under the Code by or against the debtor or before entry of the order for relief in an involuntary case, to an attorney for services rendered or to be rendered is excessive.

(b) PAYMENT OR TRANSFER TO ATTORNEY AFTER ORDER FOR RELIEF. On motion by the debtor, the United States trustee, or on the court's own initiative, the court after notice and a hearing may determine whether any payment of money or any transfer of property, or any agreement therefor, by the debtor to an attorney after entry of an order for relief in a case under the Code is excessive, whether the payment or transfer is made or is to be made directly or indirectly, if the payment, transfer, or agreement therefor is for services in any way related to the case.

Rule 2018. Intervention; Right to be Heard

(a) PERMISSIVE INTERVENTION. In a case under the Code, after hearing on such notice as the court directs and for cause shown, the court may permit any interested entity to intervene generally or with respect to any specified matter.

(b) INTERVENTION BY ATTORNEY GENERAL OF A STATE. In a chapter 7, 11, 12, or 13 case, the Attorney General of a State may appear and be heard on behalf of consumer creditors if the court determines the appearance is in the public interest, but the Attorney General may not appeal from any judgment, order, or decree in the case.

(c) CHAPTER 9 MUNICIPALITY CASE. The Secretary of the Treasury of the United States may, or if requested by the court shall, intervene in a chapter 9 case. Representatives of the state in which the debtor is located may intervene in a chapter 9 case with respect to matters specified by the court.

(d) LABOR UNIONS. In a chapter 9, 11, or 12 case, a labor union or employees' association, representative of employees of the debtor, shall have the right to be heard on the economic soundness of a plan affecting the interests of the employees. A labor union or employees' association which exercises its right to be heard under this subdivision shall not be entitled to appeal any judgment, order, or decree relating to the plan, unless otherwise permitted by law.

(e) SERVICE ON ENTITIES COVERED BY THIS RULE. The court may enter orders governing the service of notice and papers on entities permitted to intervene or be heard pursuant to this rule

Rule 2019. Disclosure Regarding Creditors and Equity Security Holders in Chapter 9 and Chapter 11 Cases

(a) DEFINITIONS. In this rule the following terms have the meanings indicated:

(1) "Disclosable economic interest" means any claim, interest, pledge, lien, option, participation, derivative instrument, or any other right or derivative right granting the holder an economic interest that is affected

by the value, acquisition, or disposition of a claim or interest.

(2)"Represent" or "represents" means to take a position before the court or to solicit votes regarding the confirmation of a plan on behalf of another.

(b) DISCLOSURE BY GROUPS, COMMITTEES, AND ENTITIES.

(1) In a chapter 9 or 11 case, a verified statement setting forth the information specified in subdivision (c) of this rule shall be filed by every group or committee that consists of or represents, and every entity that represents, multiple creditors or equity security holders that are (A) acting in concert to advance their common interests, and (B) not composed entirely of affiliates or insiders of one another.

(2) Unless the court orders otherwise, an entity is not required to file the verified statement described in paragraph (1) of this subdivision solely because of its status as:

(A) an indenture trustee;

(B) an agent for one or more other entities under an agreement for the extension of credit;

(C) a class action representative; or

(D) a governmental unit that is not a person.

(c) INFORMATION REQUIRED. The verified statement shall include:

(1) the pertinent facts and circumstances concerning:

(A) with respect to a group or committee, other than a committee appointed under § 1102 or § 1114 of the Code, the formation of the group or committee, including the name of each entity at whose instance the group or committee was formed or for whom the group or committee has agreed to act; or

(B) with respect to an entity, the employment of the entity, including the name of each creditor or equity security holder at whose instance the employment was arranged;

(2) if not disclosed under subdivision (c)(1), with respect to an entity, and with respect to each member of a group or committee;

(A) name and address

(B) the nature and amount of each disclosable economic interest held in relation to the debtor as of the date the entity was employed or the group or committee was formed; and

(C) with respect to each member of a group or committee that claims to represent any entity in addition to the members of the group or committee, other than a committee appointed under § 1102 or § 1114 of the Code, the date of acquisition by quarter and year of each disclosable economic interest, unless acquired more than one year before the petition was filed;

(3) if not disclosed under subdivision (c)(1) or (c)(2), with respect to each creditor or equity security holder represented by an entity, group, or committee, other than a committee appointed under § 1102 or § 1114 of the Code;

(A) name and address; and

(B) the nature and amount of each disclosable economic interest held in relation to the debtor as of the date of the statement; and

(4) a copy of the instrument, if any, authorizing the entity, group, or committee to act on behalf of creditors or equity security holders.

(d) SUPPLEMENTAL STATEMENTS. If any fact disclosed in its most recently filed statement has changed materially, an entity, group, or committee shall file a verified supplemental statement whenever it takes a position before the court or solicits votes on the confirmation of a plan. The supplemental statement shall set forth the material changes in the facts required by subdivision (c) to be disclosed.

(e) DETERMINATION OF FAILURE TO COMPLY; SANCTIONS.

(1) On motion of any party in interest , or on its own motion, the court may determine whether there has been a failure to comply with any provision of this rule.

(2) If the court finds such a failure to comply, it may:

(A) refuse to permit the entity, group, or committee to be heard or to intervene in the case;

(B) hold invalid any authority, acceptance, rejection, or objection given, procured, or received by the entity, group, or committee; or

(C) grant other appropriate relief.

Rule 2020. Review of Acts by United States Trustee

A proceeding to contest any act or failure to act by the United States trustee is governed by Rule 9014.

PART III

CLAIMS AND DISTRIBUTION TO CREDITORS AND EQUITY INTEREST HOLDERS; PLANS

Rule 3001. Proof of Claim.

(a) FORM AND CONTENT. A proof of claim is a written statement setting forth a creditor's claim. A proof of claim shall conform substantially to the appropriate Official Form.

(b) WHO MAY EXECUTE. A proof of claim shall be executed by the creditor or the creditor's authorized agent except as provided in Rules 3004 and 3005.

(c) SUPPORTING INFORMATION.

(1) Claim Based on a Writing. Except for a claim governed by paragraph (3) of this subdivision, when a claim, or an interest in property of the debtor securing the claim, is based on a writing, a copy of the writing shall be filed with the proof of claim. If the writing has been lost or destroyed, a statement of the circumstances of the loss or destruction shall be filed with the claim.

(2) Additional Requirements in an Individual Debtor Case; Sanctions for Failure to Comply. In a case in which the debtor is an individual:

(A) If, in addition to its principal amount, a claim includes interest, fees, expenses, or other charges incurred before the petition was filed, an itemized statement of the interest, fees, expenses, or charges shall be filed with the proof of claim.

(B) If a security interest is claimed in the debtor's property, a statement of the amount necessary to cure any default as of the date of the petition shall be filed with the proof of claim.

(C) If a security interest is claimed in property that is the debtor's principal residence, the attachment prescribed by the appropriate Official Form shall be filed with the proof of claim. If an escrow account has been established in connection with the claim, an escrow account statement prepared as of the date the petition was filed and in a form consistent with applicable nonbankruptcy law shall be filed with the attachment to the proof of claim.

(D) If the holder of a claim fails to provide any information required by this subdivision (c), the court may, after notice and hearing, take either or both of the following actions:

(i) preclude the holder from presenting the omitted information, in any form, as evidence in any contested matter or adversary proceeding in the case, unless the court determines that the failure was substantially justified or is harmless, or

(ii) award other appropriate relief, including reasonable expenses and attorney's fees caused by the failure.

(3) **Claim based on an open-end or revolving consumer credit agreement.**

(A) When a claim is based on an open-end or revolving consumer credit agreement--except one for which a security interest is claimed in the debtor's real property--a statement shall be filed with the proof of claim, including all of the following information that applies to the account:

(i) the name of the entity from whom the creditor purchased the account;

(ii) the name of the entity to whom the debt was owed at the time of an account holder's last transaction on the account;

(iii) the date of an account holder's last transaction;

(iv) the date of the last payment on the account; and

(v) the date on which the account was charged to profit and loss.

(B) On written request by a party in interest, the holder of a claim based on an open-end or revolving consumer credit agreement shall, within 30 days after the request is sent, provide the requesting party a copy of the writing specified in paragraph (1) of this subdivision.

(d) EVIDENCE OF PERFECTION OF SECURITY INTEREST. If a security interest in property of the debtor is claimed, the proof of claim shall be accompanied by evidence that the security interest has been perfected.

(e) TRANSFERRED CLAIM.

(1) Transfer of Claim Other Than for Security Before Proof Filed. If a claim has been transferred other than for security before proof of the claim has been filed, the proof of claim may be filed only by the transferee or an indenture trustee.

(2) Transfer of Claim Other Than for Security After Proof Filed. If

a claim other than one based on a publicly traded note, bond, or debenture has been transferred other than for security after the proof of claim has been filed, evidence of the transfer shall be filed by the transferee. The clerk shall immediately notify the alleged transferor by mail of the filing of the evidence of transfer and that objection thereto, if any, must be filed within 21 days of the mailing of the notice or within any additional time allowed by the court. If the alleged transferor files a timely objection and the court finds, after notice and a hearing, that the claim has been transferred other than for security, it shall enter an order substituting the transferee for the transferor. If a timely objection is not filed by the alleged transferor, the transferee shall be substituted for the transferor.

(3) Transfer of Claim for Security Before Proof Filed. If a claim other than one based on a publicly traded note, bond, or debenture has been transferred for security before proof of the claim has been filed, the transferor or transferee or both may file a proof of claim for the full amount. The proof shall be supported by a statement setting forth the terms of the transfer. If either the transferor or the transferee files a proof of claim, the clerk shall immediately notify the other by mail of the right to join in the filed claim. If both transferor and transferee file proofs of the same claim, the proofs shall be consolidated. If the transferor or transferee does not file an agreement regarding its relative rights respecting voting of the claim, payment of dividends thereon, or participation in the administration of the estate, on motion by a party in interest and after notice and a hearing, the court shall enter such orders respecting these matters as may be appropriate.

(4) Transfer of Claim for Security After Proof Filed. If a claim other than one based on a publicly traded note, bond, or debenture has been transferred for security after the proof of claim has been filed, evidence of the terms of the transfer shall be filed by the transferee. The clerk shall immediately notify the alleged transferor by mail of the filing of the evidence of transfer and that objection thereto, if any, must be filed within 21 days of the mailing of the notice or within any additional time allowed by the court. If a timely objection is filed by the alleged transferor, the court, after notice and a hearing, shall determine whether the claim has been transferred for security. If the transferor or transferee does not file an agreement regarding its relative rights respecting voting of the claim, payment of dividends thereon, or participation in the administration of the estate, on motion by a party in interest and after notice and a hearing, the court shall enter such orders respecting these matters as may be appropriate.

(5) Service of Objection or Motion; Notice of Hearing. A copy of an objection filed pursuant to paragraph (2) or (4) or a motion filed pursuant to paragraph (3) or (4) of this subdivision together with a notice of a hearing shall be mailed or otherwise delivered to the transferor or transferee, whichever is appropriate, at least 30 days prior to the hearing.

(f) EVIDENTIARY EFFECT. A proof of claim executed and filed in accordance with these rules shall constitute prima facie evidence of the validity and amount of the claim.

(g) To the extent not inconsistent with the United States Warehouse Act or applicable State law, a warehouse receipt, scale ticket, or similar document of the type routinely issued as evidence of title by a grain storage facility, as defined in Section 557 of title 11, shall constitute prima facie evidence of the validity and amount of a claim of ownership of a quantity of grain.

Rule 3002. Filing Proof of Claim or Interest

(a) NECESSITY FOR FILING. An unsecured creditor or an equity security holder must file a proof of claim or interest for the claim or interest to be allowed, except as provided in Rules 1019(3), 3003, 3004 and 3005.

(b) PLACE OF FILING. A proof of claim or interest shall be filed in accordance with Rule 5005.

(c) TIME FOR FILING. In a chapter 7 liquidation, chapter 12 family farmer's debt adjustment, or chapter 13 individual's debt adjustment case, a proof of claim is timely filed if it is filed not later than 90 days after the first date set for the meeting of creditors called under § 341(a) of the Code, except as follows:

(1) A proof of claim filed by a governmental unit, other than for a claim resulting from a tax return filed under § 1308, is timely filed if it is filed not later than 180 days after the date of the order for relief. A proof of claim filed by a governmental unit for a claim resulting from a tax return filed under § 1308 is timely filed if it is filed no later than 180 days after the date of the order for relief or 60 days after the date of the filing of the tax return. The court may, for cause, enlarge the time for a governmental unit to file a proof of claim only upon motion of the governmental unit made before expiration of the period for filing a timely proof of claim.

(2) In the interest of justice and if it will not unduly delay the administration of the case, the court may extend the time for filing a proof of claim by an infant or incompetent person or the representative of either.

(3) An unsecured claim which arises in favor of an entity or becomes allowable as a result of a judgment may be filed within 30 days after the judgment becomes final if the judgment is for the recovery of money or property from that entity or denies or avoids the entity's interest in property. If the judgment imposes a liability which is not satisfied, or a duty which is not performed within such period or such further time as the court may permit, the claim shall not be allowed.

(4) A claim arising from the rejection of an executory contract or unexpired lease of the debtor may be filed within such time as the court may direct.

(5) If notice of insufficient assets to pay a dividend was given to creditors under Rule 2002(e), and subsequently the trustee notifies the court that payment of a dividend appears possible, the clerk shall give at least 90 days' notice by mail to creditors of that fact and of the date by which proofs of claim must be filed.

(6) If notice of the time to file a proof of claim has been mailed to a creditor at a foreign address, on motion filed by the creditor before or after the expiration of the time, the court may extend the time by not more than 60 days if the court finds that the notice was insufficient under the circumstances to give the creditor a reasonable time to file a proof of claim.

Rule 3002.1 Notice Relating to Claims Secured by Security Interest in the Debtor's Principal Residence

(a) IN GENERAL. This rule applies in a chapter 13 case to claims that are (1) secured by a security interest in the debtor's principal residence, and (2) provided for under § 1322(b)(5) of the Code in the debtor's plan.

(b) NOTICE OF PAYMENT CHANGES. The holder of the claim shall file and serve on the debtor, debtor's counsel, and the trustee a notice of any change in the payment amount, including any change that results from an interest rate or escrow account adjustment, no later than 21 days before a payment in the new amount is due.

(c) NOTICE OF FEES, EXPENSES, AND CHARGES. The holder of the claim shall file and serve on the debtor, debtor's counsel, and the trustee a notice itemizing all fees, expenses, or charges (1) that were incurred in connection with the claim after the bankruptcy case was filed, and (2) that the holder asserts are recoverable against the debtor or against the debtor's principal residence. The notice shall be served within 180 days after the date on which the fees, expenses, or charges are incurred.

(d) FORM AND CONTENT. A notice filed and served under subdivision (b) or (c) of this rule shall be prepared as prescribed by the appropriate Official Form, and filed as a supplement to the holder's proof of claim. The notice is not subject to Rule 3001 (f).

(e) DETERMINATION OF FEES, EXPENSES, OR CHARGES. On motion of the debtor or trustee filed within one year after sevice of a notice under subdivision (c) of this rule, the court shall, after notice and hearing, determine whether payment of any claimed fee, expense, or charge is required by the underlying agreement and applicable nonbankruptcy law to cure a default or maintain payments in accordance with § 1322(b)(5) of the Code.

(f) NOTICE OF FINAL CURE PAYMENT. Within 30 days after the debtor completes all payments under the plan, the trustee shall file and serve on the holder of the claim, the debtor, and debtor's counsel a notice stating that the debtor has paid in full the amount required to cure any default on the claim. The notice shall also inform the holder of its obligation to file and serve a response under subdivision (g). If the debtor contends that final cure payment has been made and all plan payments have been completed, and the trustee does not timely file and serve the notice required by this subdivision, the debtor may file and serve the notice.

(g) RESPONSE TO NOTICE OF FINAL CURE PAYMENT. Within 21 days after service of the notice under subdivision (f) of this rule, the holder shall file and serve on the debtor, debtor's counsel, and the trustee a statement indicating (1) whether it agrees that the debtor has paid in full the amount required to cure the default on the claim, and (2) whether the debtor is otherwise current on all payments consistent with § 1322(b)(5) of the Code.

The statement shall itemize the required cure or postpetition amounts, if any, that the holder contends remain unpaid as of the date of the statement. The statement shall be filed as a supplement to the holder's proof of claim and is not subject to Rule 3001(f).

(h) DETERMINATION OF FINAL CURE AND PAYMENT. On motion of the debtor or trustee filed within 21 days after service of the statement under subdivision (g) of this rule, the court shall, after notice and hearing, determine whether the debtor has cured the default and paid all required postpetition amounts.

(i) FAILURE TO NOTIFY. If the holder of a claim fails to provide any information as required by subdivision (b),(c), or (g) of this rule, the court may, after notice and hearing, take either or both of the following actions:

(1) preclude the holder from presenting the omitted information, in any form, as evidence in any contested matter or adversary proceeding in the case, unless the court determines that the failure was substantially justified or is harmless; or

(2) award other appropriate relief, including reasonable expenses and attorney's fees caused by the failure.

Rule 3003. Filing Proof of Claim or Equity Security Interest in Chapter 9 Municipality or Chapter 11 Reorganization Cases

(a) APPLICABILITY OF RULE. This rule applies in chapter 9 and 11 cases.

(b) SCHEDULE OF LIABILITIES AND LIST OF EQUITY SECURITY HOLDERS.

(1) Schedule of Liabilities. The schedule of liabilities filed pursuant to Section 521(1) of the Code shall constitute prima facie evidence of the validity and amount of the claims of creditors, unless they are scheduled as disputed, contingent, or unliquidated. It shall not be necessary for a creditor or equity security holder to file a proof of claim or interest except as provided in subdivision (c)(2) of this rule.

(2) List of Equity Security Holders. The list of equity security holders filed pursuant to Rule 1007(a)(3) shall constitute prima facie evidence of the validity and amount of the equity security interests and it shall not be necessary for the holders of such interests to file a proof of interest.

(c) FILING PROOF OF CLAIM.

(1) Who May File. Any creditor or indenture trustee may file a proof of claim within the time prescribed by subdivision (c)(3) of this rule.

(2) Who Must File. Any creditor or equity security holder whose claim or interest is not scheduled or scheduled as disputed, contingent, or unliquidated shall file a proof of claim or interest within the time prescribed by subdivision (c)(3) of this rule; any creditor who fails to do so shall not be treated as a creditor with respect to such claim for the purposes of voting and distribution.

(3) Time for Filing. The court shall fix and for cause shown may extend the time within which proofs of claim or interest may be filed. Notwithstanding the expiration of such time, a proof of claim may be filed to the extent and under the conditions stated in Rule 3002(c)(2), (c)(3), (c)(4), and (c)(6).

(4) Effect of Filing Claim or Interest. A proof of claim or interest executed and filed in accordance with this subdivision shall supersede any scheduling of that claim or interest pursuant to § 521(a)(1) of the Code.

(5) Filing by Indenture Trustee. An indenture trustee may file a claim on behalf of all known or unknown holders of securities issued pursuant to the trust instrument under which it is trustee.

(d) PROOF OF RIGHT TO RECORD STATUS. For the purposes of Rules 3017, 3018 and 3021 and for receiving notices, an entity who is not the record holder of a security may file a statement setting forth facts which entitle that entity to be treated as the record holder. An objection to the statement may be filed by any party in interest.

Rule 3004. Filing of Claims by Debtor or Trustee

If a creditor does not timely file a proof of claim under Rule 3002(c) or 3003(c), the debtor or trustee may file a proof of the claim within 30 days after the expiration of the time for filing claims prescribed by Rule 3002(c) or 3003(c), whichever is applicable. The clerk shall forthwith give notice of the filing to the creditor, the debtor and the trustee.

Rule 3005. Filing of Claim, Acceptance, or Rejection by Guarantor, Surety, Indorser, or Other Codebtor

(a) FILING OF CLAIM. If a creditor does not timely file a proof of claim under Rule 3002(c) or 3003(c), any entity that is or may be liable with the debtor to that creditor, or who has secured that creditor, may file a proof of the claim within 30 days after the expiration of the time for filing claims prescribed by Rule 3002(c) or Rule 3003(c) whichever is applicable. No distribution shall be made on the claim except on satisfactory proof that the original debt will be diminished by the amount of distribution.

(b) FILING OF ACCEPTANCE OR REJECTION; SUBSTITUTION OF CREDITOR. An entity which has filed a claim pursuant to the first sentence of subdivision (a) of this rule may file an acceptance or rejection of a plan in the name of the creditor, if known, or if unknown, in the entity's own name but if the creditor files a proof of claim within the time permitted by Rule 3003(c) or files a notice prior to confirmation of a plan of the creditor's intention to act in the creditor's own behalf, the creditor shall be substituted for the obligor with respect to that claim.

Rule 3006. Withdrawal of Claim; Effect on Acceptance or Rejection of Plan

A creditor may withdraw a claim as of right by filing a notice of withdrawal, except as provided in this rule. If after a creditor has filed a proof of claim an objection is filed thereto or a complaint is filed against that creditor in an adversary proceeding, or the creditor has accepted or rejected the plan or otherwise has participated significantly in the case, the creditor may not withdraw the claim except on order of the court after a hearing on notice to the trustee or debtor in possession, and any creditors' committee elected pursuant to Section 705(a) or appointed pursuant to Section 1102 of the Code. The order of the court shall contain such terms and conditions as the court deems proper. Unless the court orders otherwise, an authorized withdrawal of a claim shall constitute withdrawal of any related acceptance or rejection of a plan.

Rule 3007. Objections to Claims

(a) OBJECTIONS TO CLAIMS. An objection to the allowance of a claim shall be in writing and filed. A copy of the objection with notice of the hearing thereon shall be mailed or otherwise delivered to the claimant, the debtor or debtor in possession, and the trustee at least 30 days prior to the hearing.

(b) DEMAND FOR RELIEF REQUIRING AN ADVERSARY PROCEEDING. A party in interest shall not include a demand for relief of a kind specified in Rule 7001 in an objection to the allowance of a claim, but may include the objection in an adversary proceeding.

(c) LIMITATION ON JOINDER OF CLAIMS OBJECTIONS. Unless otherwise ordered by the court, or permitted by subdivision (d), objections to more than one claim shall not be joined in a single objection.

(d) OMNIBUS OBJECTION. Subject to subdivision (e), objections to more than one claim may be joined in an omnibus objection if all the claims were filed by the same entity, or the objections are based solely on the grounds that the claims should be disallowed, in whole or in part, because:

(1) they duplicate other claims;

(2) they have been filed in the wrong case;

(3) they have been amended by subsequently filed proofs of claim;

(4) they were not timely filed;

(5) they have been satisfied or released during the case in accordance with the Code, applicable rules, or a court order;

(6) they were presented in a form that does not comply with applicable rules, and the objection states that the objector is unable to determine the validity of the claim because of the noncompliance;

(7) they are interests, rather than claims; or

(8) they assert priority in an amount that exceeds the maximum amount under § 507 of the Code.

(e) REQUIREMENTS FOR OMNIBUS OBJECTION. An omnibus objection shall:

(1) state in a conspicuous place that claimants receiving the objection should locate their names and claims in the objection;

(2) list claimants alphabetically, provide a cross-reference to claim numbers, and, if appropriate, list claimants by category of claims;

(3) state the grounds of the objection to each claim and provide a cross-reference to the pages in the omnibus objection pertinent to the stated grounds;

(4) state in the title the identity of the objector and the grounds for the objections;

(5) be numbered consecutively with other omnibus objections filed by the same objector; and

(6) contain objections to no more than 100 claims.

(f) FINALITY OF OBJECTION. The finality of any order regarding a claim objection included in an omnibus objection shall be determined as though the claim had been subject to an individual objection.

Rule 3008. Reconsideration of Claims

A party in interest may move for reconsideration of an order allowing or disallowing a claim against the estate. The court after a hearing on notice shall enter an appropriate order.

Rule 3009. Declaration and Payment of Dividends in a Chapter 7 Liquidation Case

In chapter 7 cases, dividends to creditors shall be paid as promptly as practicable. Dividend checks shall be made payable to and mailed to each creditor whose claim has been allowed, unless a power of attorney authorizing another entity to receive dividends has been executed and filed in accordance with Rule 9010. In that event, dividend checks shall be made payable to the creditor and to the other entity and shall be mailed to the other entity.

Rule 3010. Small Dividends and Payments in Chapter 7 Liquidation, Chapter 12 Family Farmer's Debt Adjustment, and Chapter 13 Individual's Debt Adjustment Cases

(a) CHAPTER 7 CASES. In a chapter 7 case no dividend in an amount less than $5 shall be distributed by the trustee to any creditor unless authorized by local rule or order of the court. Any dividend not distributed to a creditor shall be treated in the same manner as unclaimed funds as provided in Section 347 of the Code.

(b) CHAPTER 12 AND CHAPTER 13 CASES. In a chapter 12 or chapter 13 case no payment in an amount less than $15 shall be distributed by the trustee to any creditor unless authorized by local rule or order of the court. Funds not distributed because of this subdivision shall accumulate and shall be paid whenever the accumulation aggregates $15. Any funds remaining shall be distributed with the final payment.

Rule 3011. Unclaimed Funds in Chapter 7 Liquidation, Chapter 12 Family Farmer's Debt Adjustment, and Chapter 13 Individual's Debt Adjustment Cases

The trustee shall file a list of all known names and addresses of the entities and the amounts which they are entitled to be paid from remaining property of the estate that is paid into court pursuant to Section 347(a) of the Code.

Rule 3012. Valuation of Security

The court may determine the value of a claim secured by a lien on property in which the estate has an interest on motion of any party in interest and after a hearing on notice to the holder of the secured claim and any other entity as the court may direct.

Rule 3013. Classification of Claims and Interests

For the purposes of the plan and its acceptance, the court may, on motion after hearing on notice as the court may direct, determine classes of creditors and equity security holders pursuant to Sections 1122, 1222(b)(1), and 1322(b)(1) of the Code.

Rule 3014. Election Pursuant to Section 1111(b) by Secured Creditor in Chapter 9 Municipality and Chapter 11 Reorganization Case

An election of application of §1111(b)(2) of the Code by a class of secured creditors in a chapter 9 or 11 case may be made at any time prior to the conclusion of the hearing on the disclosure statement or within such later time as the court may fix. If the disclosure statement is conditionally approved pursuant to Rule 3017.1, and a final hearing on the disclosure statement is not held, the election of application of 1111(b)(2) may be made not later than the date fixed pursuant to Rule 3017.1(a)(2) or another date the court may fix. The election shall be in writing and signed unless made at the hearing on the disclosure statement. The election, if made by the majorities required by §1111(b)(1)(A)(i), shall be binding on all members of the class with respect to the plan.

Rule 3015. Filing, Objection to Confirmation, and Modification of a Plan in a Chapter 12 Family Farmer's Debt Adjustment or a Chapter 13 Individual's Debt Adjustment Case

(a) CHAPTER 12 PLAN. The debtor may file a chapter 12 plan with the petition. If a plan is not filed with the petition, it shall be filed within the time prescribed by Section 1221 of the Code.

(b) CHAPTER 13 PLAN. The debtor may file a chapter 13 plan with the petition. If a plan is not filed with the petition, it shall be filed within 14 days thereafter, and such time may not be further extended except for cause shown and on notice as the court may direct. If a case is converted to chapter 13, a plan shall be filed within 14 days thereafter, and such time may not be further extended except for cause shown and on notice as the court may direct.

(c) DATING. Every proposed plan and any modification thereof shall be dated.

(d) NOTICE AND COPIES. The plan or a summary of the plan shall be included with each notice of the hearing on confirmation mailed pursuant to Rule 2002. If required by the court, the debtor shall furnish a sufficient number of copies to enable the clerk to include a copy of the plan with the notice of the hearing.

(e) TRANSMISSION TO UNITED STATES TRUSTEE. The clerk shall forthwith transmit to the United States trustee a copy of the plan and any modification thereof filed pursuant to subdivision (a) or (b) of this rule.

(f) OBJECTION TO CONFIRMATION; DETERMINATION OF GOOD FAITH IN THE ABSENCE OF AN OBJECTION. An objection to confirmation of a plan shall be filed and served on the debtor, the trustee, and any other entity designated by the court, and shall be transmitted to the United States trustee, before confirmation of the plan. An objection to confirmation is governed by Rule 9014. If no objection is timely filed, the court may determine that the plan has been proposed in good faith and not by any means forbidden by law without receiving evidence on such issues.

(g) MODIFICATION OF PLAN AFTER CONFIRMATION. A request to modify a plan pursuant to Section 1229 or Section 1329 of the Code shall identify the proponent and shall be filed together with the proposed modification. The clerk, or some other person as the court may direct, shall give the debtor, the trustee, and all creditors not less than 21 days' notice by mail of the time fixed for filing objections and, if an objection is filed, the hearing to consider the proposed modification, unless the court orders otherwise with respect to creditors who are not affected by the proposed modification. A copy of the notice shall be transmitted to the United States trustee. A copy of the proposed modification, or a summary thereof, shall be included with the notice. If required by the court, the proponent shall furnish a sufficient number of copies of the proposed modification, or a summary thereof, to enable the clerk to include a copy with each notice. Any objection to the proposed modification shall be filed and served on the debtor, the trustee, and any other entity designated by the court, and shall be transmitted to the United States trustee. An objection to a proposed modification is governed by Rule 9014.

Rule 3016. Filing of Plan and Disclosure Statement in a Chapter 9 Municipality or Chapter 11 Reorganization Case

(a) IDENTIFICATION OF PLAN. Every proposed plan and any modification thereof shall be dated and, in a chapter 11 case, identified with the name of the entity or entities submitting or filing it.

(b) DISCLOSURE STATEMENT. In a chapter 9 or 11 case, a disclosure statement under § 1125 of the Code or evidence showing compliance with § 1126(b) shall be filed with the plan or within a time fixed by the court, unless the plan is intended to provide adequate information under § 1125(f)(1). If the plan is intended to provide adequate information under § 1125(f)(1), it shall be so designated and Rule 3017.1 shall apply as if the plan is a disclosure statement.

(c) INJUNCTION UNDER A PLAN. If a plan provides for an injunction against conduct not otherwise enjoined under the Code, the plan and disclosure statement shall describe in specific and conspicuous language (bold, italic, or underlined text) all acts to be enjoined and identify the entities that would be subject to the injunction.

(d) STANDARD FORM SMALL BUSINESS DISCLOSURE STATEMENT AND PLAN. In a small business case, the court may approve a disclosure statement and may confirm a plan that conform substantially to the appropriate Official Forms or other standard forms approved by the court.

Rule 3017. Court Consideration of Disclosure Statement in a Chapter 9 Municipality or Chapter 11 Reorganization Case

(a) HEARING ON DISCLOSURE STATEMENT AND OBJECTIONS. Except as provided in Rule 3017.1, after a disclosure statement is filed in accordance with Rule 3016(b), the court shall hold a hearing on at least 28 days' notice to the debtor, creditors, equity security holders and other parties in interest as provided in Rule 2002 to consider the disclosure statement and any objections or modifications thereto. The plan and the disclosure statement shall be mailed with the notice of the hearing only to the debtor, any trustee or committee appointed under the Code, the Securities and Exchange Commission, and any party in interest who requests in writing a copy of the statement or plan. Objections to the disclosure statement shall be filed and served on the debtor, the trustee, any committee appointed under the Code, and any other entity designated by the court, at any time before the disclosure statement is approved or by an earlier date as the court may fix. In a chapter 11 reorganization case, every notice, plan, disclosure statement, and objection required to be served or mailed pursuant to this subdivision shall be transmitted to the United States trustee within the time provided in this subdivision.

(b) DETERMINATION ON DISCLOSURE STATEMENT. Following the hearing the court shall determine whether the disclosure statement should be approved.

(c) DATES FIXED FOR VOTING ON PLAN AND CONFIRMATION. On or before approval of the disclosure statement, the court shall fix a time within which the holders of claims and interests may accept or reject the plan and may fix a date for the hearing on confirmation.

(d) TRANSMISSION AND NOTICE TO UNITED STATES TRUSTEE, CREDITORS AND EQUITY SECURITY HOLDERS. Upon approval of a disclosure statement, - except to the extent that the court orders otherwise with respect to one or more unimpaired classes of creditors or equity security holders - the debtor in possession, trustee, proponent of the plan, or clerk as the court orders shall mail to all creditors and equity security holders, and in a chapter 11 reorganization case shall transmit to the United States trustee:

(1) the plan or a court-approved summary of the plan;

(2) the disclosure statement approved by the court;

(3) notice of the time within which acceptances and rejections of the plan may be filed; and

(4) any other information as the court may direct, including any court opinion approving the disclosure statement or a court-approved summary of the opinion.

In addition, notice of the time fixed for filing objections and the hearing on confirmation shall be mailed to all creditors and equity security holders in accordance with Rule 2002(b), and a form of ballot conforming to the appropriate Official Form shall be mailed to creditors and equity security holders entitle to vote on the plan. If the court opinion is not transmitted or only a summary of the plan is transmitted, the court opinion or the plan shall be provided on request of a party in interest at the plan proponent's expense. If the court orders that the disclosure statement and the plan or a summary of the plan shall not be mailed to any unimpaired class, notice that the class is designated in the plan as unimpaired and notice of the name and address of the person from whom the plan or summary of the plan and disclosure statement may be obtained upon request and at the plan proponent's expense, shall be mailed to members of the unimpaired class together with the notice of the time fixed for filing objections to and the hearing on confirmation. For the purposes of this subdivision, creditors and equity security holders shall include holders of stock, bonds, debentures, notes, and other securities of record on the date the order approving the disclosure statement is entered or another date fixed by the court, for cause, after notice and a hearing.

(e) TRANSMISSION TO BENEFICIAL HOLDERS OF SECURITIES. At the hearing held pursuant to subdivision (a) of this rule, the court shall consider the procedures for transmitting the documents and information required by subdivision (d) of this rule to beneficial holders of stock, bonds, debentures, notes, and other securities, determine the adequacy of the procedures, and enter any orders the court deems appropriate.

(f) NOTICE AND TRANSMISSION OF DOCUMENTS TO ENTITIES SUBJECT TO AN INJUNCTION UNDER A PLAN. If a plan provides for an injunction against conduct not otherwise enjoined under the Code and an entity that would be subject to the injunction is not a creditor or equity security holder, at the hearing held under Rule 3017(a), the court shall consider procedures for providing the entity with:

(1) at least 28 days' notice of the time fixed for filing objections and the hearing on confirmation of the plan containing the information described in Rule 2002(c)(3); and

(2) to the extent feasible, a copy of the plan and disclosure statement.

Rule 3017.1. Court Consideration of Disclosure Statement in a Small Business Case

(a) CONDITIONAL APPROVAL OF DISCLOSURE STATEMENT. In a small business case, the court may, on application of the plan proponent or on its own initiative, conditionally approve a disclosure statement filed in accordance with Rule 3016. On or before conditional approval of the disclosure statement, the court shall:

(1) fix a time within which the holders of claims and interests may accept or reject the plan;

(2) fix a time for filing objections to the disclosure statement;

(3) fix a date for the hearing on final approval of the disclosure statement to be held if a timely objection is filed; and

(4) fix a date for the hearing on confirmation.

(b) APPLICATION OF RULE 3017. Rule 3017(a), (b), (c), and (e) do not apply to a conditionally approved disclosure statement. Rule 3017(d) applies to a conditionally approved disclosure statement, except that conditional approval is considered approval of the disclosure statement for the purpose of applying Rule 3017(d).

(c) FINAL APPROVAL

(1) Notice. Notice of the time fixed for filing objections and the hearing to consider final approval of the disclosure statement shall be given in accordance with Rule 2002 and may be combined with notice of the hearing on confirmation of the plan.

(2) Objections. Objections to the disclosure statement shall be filed, transmitted to the United States trustee, and served on the debtor, the trustee, any committee appointed under the Code and any other entity designated by the court at any time before final approval of the disclosure statement or by an earlier date as the court may fix.

(3) Hearing. If a timely objection to the disclosure statement is filed, the court shall hold a hearing to consider final approval before or combined with the hearing on confirmation of the plan.

Rule 3018. Acceptance or Rejection of Plan in a Chapter 9 Municipality or a Chapter 11 Reorganization Case

(a) ENTITIES ENTITLED TO ACCEPT OR REJECT PLAN; TIME FOR ACCEPTANCE OR REJECTION. A plan may be accepted or rejected in accordance with Section 1126 of the Code within the time fixed by the court pursuant to Rule 3017. Subject to subdivision (b) of this rule, an equity security holder or creditor whose claim is based on a security of record shall not be entitled to accept or reject a plan unless the equity security holder or creditor is the holder of record of the security on the date the order approving the disclosure statement is entered or on another date fixed by the court, for cause, after notice and a hearing. For cause shown, the court after notice and hearing may permit a creditor or equity security holder to change or withdraw an acceptance or rejection. Notwithstanding objection to a claim or interest, the court after notice and hearing may temporarily allow the claim or interest in an amount which the court deems proper for the purpose of accepting or rejecting a plan.

(b) ACCEPTANCES OR REJECTIONS OBTAINED BEFORE PETITION. An equity security holder or creditor whose claim is based on a security of record who accepted or rejected the plan before the commencement of the case shall not be deemed to have accepted or rejected the plan pursuant to Section 1126(b) of the Code unless the equity security holder or creditor was the holder of record of the security on the date specified in the solicitation of such acceptance or rejection for the purposes of such solicitation. A holder of a claim or interest who has accepted or rejected a plan before the commencement of the case under the Code shall not be deemed to have accepted or rejected the plan if the court finds after notice and hearing that the plan was not transmitted to substantially all creditors and equity security holders of the same class, that an unreasonably short time was prescribed for such creditors and equity security holders to accept or reject the plan, or that the solicitation was not in compliance with Section 1126(b) of the Code.

(c) FORM OF ACCEPTANCE OR REJECTION. An acceptance or rejection shall be in writing, identify the plan or plans accepted or rejected, be signed by the creditor or equity security holder or an authorized agent, and conform to the appropriate Official Form. If more than one plan is transmitted pursuant to Rule 3017, an acceptance or rejection may be filed by each creditor or equity security holder for any number of plans transmitted and if acceptances are filed for more than one plan, the creditor or equity security holder may indicate a preference or preferences among the plans so accepted.

(d) ACCEPTANCE OR REJECTION BY PARTIALLY SECURED CREDITOR. A creditor whose claim has been allowed in part as a secured claim and in part as an unsecured claim shall be entitled to accept or reject a plan in both capacities.

Rule 3019. Modification of Accepted Plan in a Chapter 9 Municipality or a Chapter 11 Reorganization Case

(a) MODIFICATION OF PLAN BEFORE CONFIRMATION. In a

chapter 9 or chapter 11 case, after a plan has been accepted and before its confirmation, the proponent may file a modification of the plan. If the court finds after hearing on notice to the trustee, any committee appointed under the Code, and any other entity designated by the court that the proposed modification does not adversely change the treatment of the claim of any creditor or the interest of any equity security holder who has not accepted in writing the modification, it shall be deemed accepted by all creditors and equity security holders who have previously accepted the plan.

(b) MODIFICATION OF PLAN AFTER CONFIRMATION IN INDIVIDUAL DEBTOR CASE. If the debtor is an individual, a request to modify the plan under § 1127(e) of the Code is governed by Rule 9014. The request shall identify the proponent and shall be filed together with the proposed modification. The clerk, or some other person as the court may direct, shall give the debtor, the trustee, and all creditors not less than 21 days' notice by mail of the time fixed to file objections and, if an objection is filed, the hearing to consider the proposed modification, unless the court orders otherwise with respect to creditors who are not affected by the proposed modification. A copy of the notice shall be transmitted to the United States trustee, together with a copy of the proposed modification. Any objection to the proposed modification shall be filed and served on the debtor, the proponent of the modification, the trustee, and any other entity designated by the court, and shall be transmitted to the United States trustee.

Rule 3020. Deposit; Confirmation of Plan in a Chapter 9 Municipality or Chapter 11 Reorganization Case

(a) DEPOSIT. In a chapter 11 case, prior to entry of the order confirming the plan, the court may order the deposit with the trustee or debtor in possession of the consideration required by the plan to be distributed on confirmation. Any money deposited shall be kept in a special account established for the exclusive purpose of making the distribution.

(b) OBJECTIONS TO AND HEARING ON CONFIRMATION IN A CHAPTER 9 OR CHAPTER 11 CASE.

(1) Objection. An objection to confirmation of the plan shall be filed and served on the debtor, the trustee, the proponent of the plan, any committee appointed under the Code and on any other entity designated by the court, within a time fixed by the court. Unless the case is a chapter 9 municipality case, a copy of every objection to confirmation shall be transmitted by the objecting party to the United States trustee within the time fixed for the filing of objections. An objection to confirmation is governed by Rule 9014.

(2) Hearing. The court shall rule on confirmation of the plan after notice and hearing as provided in Rule 2002. If no objection is timely filed, the court may determine that the plan has been proposed in good faith and not by any means forbidden by law without receiving evidence on such issues.

(c) ORDER OF CONFIRMATION.

(1) The order of confirmation shall conform to the appropriate Official Form. If the plan provides for an injunction against conduct not otherwise enjoined under the Code, the order of confirmation shall (1) describe in reasonable detail all acts enjoined; (2) be specific in its terms regarding the injunction; and (3) identify the entities subject to the injunction.

(2)Notice of entry of the order of confirmation shall be mailed promptly to the debtor, the trustee, creditors, equity security holders, other parties in interest, and, if known, to any identified entity subject to an injunction provided for in the plan against conduct not otherwise enjoined under the Code.

(3) Except in a chapter 9 municipality case, notice of entry of the order of confirmation shall be transmitted to the United States trustee as provided in Rule 2002(k).

(d) RETAINED POWER. Notwithstanding the entry of the order of confirmation, the court may issue any other order necessary to administer the estate.

(e) STAY OF CONFIRMATION ORDER. An order confirming a plan is stayed until the expiration of 14 days after the entry of the order, unless the court orders otherwise.

Rule 3021. Distribution Under Plan

Except as provided in Rule 3020(e), after a plan is confirmed, distribution shall be made to creditors whose claims have been allowed, to interest holders whose interests have not been disallowed, and to indenture trustees who have filed claims under Rule 3003(c)(5) that have been allowed. For purposes of this rule, creditors include holders of bonds, debentures, notes, and other debt securities, and interest holders include the holders of stock and other equity securities, of record at the time of commencement of distribution, unless a different time is fixed by the plan or the order confirming the plan.

Rule 3022. Final Decree in Chapter 11 Reorganization Case

After an estate is fully administered in a chapter 11 reorganization case, the court, on its own motion or on motion of a party in interest, shall enter a final decree closing the case.

PART IV

THE DEBTOR: DUTIES AND BENEFITS

Rule 4001. Relief from Automatic Stay; Prohibiting or Conditioning the Use, Sale, or Lease of Property; Use of Cash Collateral; Obtaining Credit; Agreements

(a) RELIEF FROM STAY; PROHIBITING OR CONDITIONING THE USE, SALE, OR LEASE OF PROPERTY.

(1) Motion. A motion for relief from an automatic stay provided by the Code or a motion to prohibit or condition the use, sale, or lease of property pursuant to Section 363(e) shall be made in accordance with Rule 9014 and shall be served on any committee elected pursuant to Section 705 or appointed pursuant to Section 1102 of the Code or its authorized agent, or, if the case is a chapter 9 municipality case or a chapter 11 reorganization case and no committee of unsecured creditors has been appointed pursuant to Section 1102, on the creditors included on the list filed pursuant to Rule 1007(d), and on such other entities as the court may direct.

(2) Ex Parte Relief. Relief from a stay under Section 362(a) or a request to prohibit or condition the use, sale, or lease of property pursuant to Section 363(e) may be granted without prior notice only if (A) it clearly appears from specific facts shown by affidavit or by a verified motion that immediate and irreparable injury, loss, or damage will result to the movant before the adverse party or the attorney for the adverse party can be heard in opposition, and (B) the movant's attorney certifies to the court in writing the efforts, if any, which have been made to give notice and the reasons why notice should not be required. The party obtaining relief under this subdivision and Section 362(f) or Section 363(e) shall immediately give oral notice thereof to the trustee or debtor in possession and to the debtor and forthwith mail or otherwise transmit to such adverse party or parties a copy of the order granting relief. On two days notice to the party who obtained relief from the stay without notice or on shorter notice to that party as the court may prescribe, the adverse party may appear and move reinstatement of the stay or reconsideration of the order prohibiting or conditioning the use, sale, or lease of property. In that event, the court shall proceed expeditiously to hear and determine the motion.

(3) Stay of Order. An order granting a motion for relief from an automatic stay made in accordance with Rule 4001(a)(1) is stayed until the expiration of 14 days after the entry of the order, unless the court orders otherwise.

(b) USE OF CASH COLLATERAL.

(1) Motion; Service.

(A) Motion. A motion for authority to use cash collateral shall be made in accordance with Rule 9014 and shall be accompanied by a proposed form of order.

(B) Contents. The motion shall consist of or (if the motion is more than five pages in length) begin with a concise statement of the relief requested, not to exceed five pages, that lists or summarizes, and sets out the location within the relevant documents of, all material provisions, including:

(i) the name of each entity with an interest in the cash collateral;

(ii) the purposes for the use of the cash collateral;

(iii) the material terms, including duration, of the use of the cash collateral; and

(iv) any liens, cash payments, or other adequate protection that will be provided to each entity with an interest in the cash collateral or, if no additional adequate protection is proposed, an explanation of why each entity's interest is adequately protected.

(C) Service. The motion shall be served on: (1) any entity with an interest in the cash collateral; (2) any committee elected under § 705 or appointed under § 1102 of the Code, or its authorized agent, or, if the case is a chapter 9 municipality case or a chapter 11 reorganization case and no committee of unsecured creditors has been appointed under § 1102, the creditors included on the list filed under Rule 1007(d); and (3) any other entity that the court directs.

(2) Hearing. The court may commence a final hearing on a motion for authorization to use cash collateral no earlier than 14 days after service of the motion. If the motion so requests, the court may conduct a preliminary hearing before such 14 day period expires, but the court may authorize the use of only that amount of cash collateral as is necessary to avoid immediate and irreparable harm to the estate pending a final hearing.

(3) Notice. Notice of hearing pursuant to this subdivision shall be given to the parties on whom service of the motion is required by paragraph (1) of this subdivision and to such other entities as the court may direct.

(c) OBTAINING CREDIT.

(1) Motion; Service.

(A) Motion. A motion for authority to obtain credit shall be made in accordance with Rule 9014 and shall be accompanied by a copy of the credit agreement and a proposed form of order.

(B) Contents. The motion shall consist of or (if the motion is more than five pages in length) begin with a concise statement of the relief requested, not to exceed five pages, that lists or summarizes, and sets out the location within the relevant documents of, all material provisions of the proposed credit agreement and form of order, including interest rate, maturity, events of default, liens, borrowing limits, and borrowing conditions. If the proposed credit agreement or form of order includes any of the provisions listed below, the concise statement shall also: briefly list or summarize each one; identify its specific location in the proposed agreement and form of order; and identify any such provision that is proposed to remain in effect if interim approval is granted, but final relief is denied, as provided under Rule 4001(c)(2). In addition, the motion shall describe the nature and extent of each provision listed below:

(i) a grant of priority or a lien on property of the estate under § 364(c) or (d);

(ii) the providing of adequate protection or priority for a claim that arose before the commencement of the case, including the granting of a lien on property of the estate to secure the claim, or the use of property of the estate or credit obtained under § 364 to make cash payments on account of the claim;

(iii) a determination of the validity, enforceability, priority, or amount of a claim that arose before the commencement of the case, or of any lien securing the claim;

(iv) a waiver or modification of Code provisions or applicable rules relating to the automatic stay;

(v) a waiver or modification of any entity's authority or right to file a plan, seek an extension of time in which the debtor has the exclusive right to file a plan, request the use of cash collateral under § 363(c), or request authority to obtain credit under § 364;

(vi) the establishment of deadlines for filing a plan of reorganization, for approval of a disclosure statement, for a hearing on confirmation, or for entry of a confirmation order;

(vii) a waiver or modification of the applicability of nonbankruptcy law relating to the perfection of a lien on property of the estate, or on the foreclosure or other enforcement of the lien;

(viii) a release, waiver, or limitation on any claim or other cause of action belonging to the estate or the trustee, including any modification of the statute of limitations or other deadline to commence an action;

(ix) the indemnification of any entity;

(x) a release, waiver, or limitation of any right under § 506(c); or

(xi) the granting of a lien on any claim or cause of action arising under §§ 544, 545, 547, 548, 549, 553(b), 723(a), or 724(a).

(C) Service. The motion shall be served on: (1) any committee elected under § 705 or appointed under § 1102 of the Code, or its authorized agent, or, if the case is a chapter 9 municipality case or a chapter 11 reorganization case and no committee of unsecured creditors has been appointed under § 1102, on the creditors included on the list filed under Rule 1007(d); and (2) on any other entity that the court directs.

(2) Hearing. The court may commence a final hearing on a motion for authority to obtain credit no earlier than 14 days after service of the motion. If the motion so requests, the court may conduct a hearing before such 14 day period expires, but the court may authorize the obtaining of credit only to the extent necessary to avoid immediate and irreparable harm to the estate pending a final hearing.

(3) Notice. Notice of hearing pursuant to this subdivision shall be given to the parties on whom service of the motion is required by paragraph (1) of this subdivision and to such other entities as the court may direct.

(d) AGREEMENT RELATING TO RELIEF FROM THE AUTOMATIC STAY, PROHIBITING OR CONDITIONING THE USE, SALE, OR LEASE OF PROPERTY, PROVIDING ADEQUATE PROTECTION, USE OF CASH COLLATERAL, AND OBTAINING CREDIT.

(1) Motion; Service.

(A) Motion. A motion for approval of any of the following shall be accompanied by a copy of the agreement and a proposed form of order:

(i) an agreement to provide adequate protection;

(ii) an agreement to prohibit or condition the use, sale, or lease of property;

(iii) an agreement to modify or terminate the stay provided for in § 362;

(iv) an agreement to use cash collateral; or

(v) an agreement between the debtor and an entity that has a lien or interest in property of the estate pursuant to which the entity consents to the creation of a lien senior or equal to the entity's lien or interest in such property.

(B) Contents. The motion shall consist of or (if the motion is more than five pages in length) begin with a concise statement of the relief requested, not to exceed five pages, that lists or summarizes, and sets out the location within the relevant documents of, all material provisions of the agreement. In addition, the concise statement shall briefly list or summarize, and identify the specific location of, each provision in the proposed form of order, agreement, or other document of the type listed in subdivision (c)(1)(B). The motion shall also describe the nature and extent of each such provision.

(C) Service. The motion shall be served on: (1) any committee elected under § 705 or appointed under § 1102 of the Code, or its authorized agent, or, if the case is a chapter 9 municipality case or a chapter 11 reorganization case and no committee of unsecured creditors has been appointed under § 1102, on the creditors included on the list filed under Rule 1007(d); and (2) on any other entity the court directs.

(2) Objection. Notice of the motion and the time within which objections may be filed and served on the debtor in possession or trustee shall be mailed to the parties on whom service is required by paragraph (1) of this subdivision and to such other entities as the court may direct. Unless the court fixes a different time, objections may be filed within 14 days of the mailing of the notice.

(3) Disposition; Hearing. If no objection is filed, the court may enter an order approving or disapproving the agreement without conducting a hearing. If an objection is filed or if the court determines a hearing is appropriate, the court shall hold a hearing on no less than seven days' notice to the objector, the movant, the parties on whom service is required by paragraph (1) of this subdivision and such other entities as the court may direct.

(4) Agreement in Settlement of Motion. The court may direct that the procedures prescribed in paragraphs (1), (2), and (3) of this subdivision shall not apply and the agreement may be approved without further notice if the court determines that a motion made pursuant to subdivisions (a), (b), or (c) of this rule was sufficient to afford reasonable notice of the material provisions of the agreement and opportunity for a hearing.

Rule 4002. Duties of Debtor

(a) IN GENERAL. In addition to performing other duties prescribed by the Code and rules, the debtor shall:

(1) attend and submit to an examination at the times ordered by the court;

(2) attend the hearing on a complaint objecting to discharge and testify, if called as a witness;

(3) inform the trustee immediately in writing as to the location of real property in which the debtor has an interest and the name and address of every person holding money or property subject to the debtor's withdrawal or order if a schedule of property has not yet been filed pursuant to Rule 1007;

(4) cooperate with the trustee in the preparation of an inventory, the

examination of proofs of claim, and the administration of the estate; and

(5) file a statement of any change of the debtor's address.

(b) INDIVIDUAL DEBTOR'S DUTY TO PROVIDE DOCUMENTATION.

(1) Personal Identification. Every individual debtor shall bring to the meeting of creditors under § 341:

(A) a picture identification issued by a governmental unit, or other personal identifying information that establishes the debtor's identity; and

(B) evidence of social-security number(s), or a written statement that such documentation does not exist.

(2) Financial Information. Every individual debtor shall bring to the meeting of creditors under § 341, and make available to the trustee, the following documents or copies of them, or provide a written statement that the documentation does not exist or is not in the debtor's possession:

(A) evidence of current income such as the most recent payment advice;

(B) unless the trustee or the United States trustee instructs otherwise, statements for each of the debtor's depository and investment accounts, including checking, savings, and money market accounts, mutual funds and brokerage accounts for the time period that includes the date of the filing of the petition; and

(C) documentation of monthly expenses claimed by the debtor if required by § 707(b)(2)(A) or (B).

(3) Tax Return. At least 7 days before the first date set for the meeting of creditors under § 341, the debtor shall provide to the trustee a copy of the debtor's federal income tax return for the most recent tax year ending immediately before the commencement of the case and for which a return was filed, including any attachments, or a transcript of the tax return, or provide a written statement that the documentation does not exist.

(4) Tax Returns Provided to Creditors. If a creditor, at least 14 days before the first date set for the meeting of creditors under § 341, requests a copy of the debtor's tax return that is to be provided to the trustee under subdivision (b)(3), the debtor, at least 7 days before the first date set for the meeting of creditors under § 341, shall provide to the requesting creditor a copy of the return, including any attachments, or a transcript of the tax return, or provide a written statement that the documentation does not exist.

(5) Confidentiality of Tax Information. The debtor's obligation to provide tax returns under Rule 4002(b)(3) and (b)(4) is subject to procedures for safeguarding the confidentiality of tax information established by the Director of the Administrative Office of the United States Courts.

Rule 4003. Exemptions

(a) CLAIM OF EXEMPTIONS. A debtor shall list the property claimed as exempt under Section 522 of the Code on the schedule of assets required to be filed by Rule 1007. If the debtor fails to claim exemptions or file the schedule within the time specified in Rule 1007, a dependent of the debtor may file the list within 30 days thereafter.

(b) OBJECTING TO A CLAIM OF EXEMPTIONS.

(1) Except as provided in paragraphs (2) and (3), a party in interest may file an objection to the list of property claimed as exempt within 30 days after the meeting of creditors held under § 341(a) is concluded or within 30 days after any amendment to the list or supplemental schedules is filed, whichever is later. The court may, for cause, extend the time for filing objections if, before the time to object expires, a party in interest files a request for an extension.

(2) The trustee may file an objection to a claim of exemption at any time prior to one year after the closing of the case if the debtor fraudulently asserted the claim of exemption. The trustee shall deliver or mail the objection to the debtor and the debtor's attorney, and to any person filing the list of exempt property and that person's attorney.

(3) An objection to a claim of exemption based on § 522(q) shall be filed before the closing of the case. If an exemption is first claimed after a case is reopened, an objection shall be filed before the reopened case is closed.

(4) A copy of any objection shall be delivered or mailed to the trustee, the debtor and the debtor's attorney, and the person filing the list and that person's attorney.

(c) BURDEN OF PROOF. In any hearing under this rule, the objecting party has the burden of proving that the exemptions are not properly claimed. After hearing on notice, the court shall determine the issues presented by the objections.

(d) AVOIDANCE BY DEBTOR OF TRANSFERS OF EXEMPT PROPERTY. A proceeding by the debtor to avoid a lien or other transfer of property exempt under § 522(f) of the Code shall be by motion in accordance with Rule 9014. Notwithstanding the provisions of subdivision (b), a creditor may object to a motion filed under § 522(f) by challenging the validity of the exemption asserted to be impaired by the lien.

Rule 4004. Grant Or Denial of Discharge

(a) TIME FOR OBJECTING TO DISCHARGE; NOTICE OF TIME FIXED. In a chapter 7 case, a complaint, or a motion under § 727(a)(8) or (a)(9) of the Code, objecting to the debtor's discharge shall be filed no later than 60 days after the first date set for the meeting of creditors under Section 341(a). In a chapter 11 case, the complaint shall be filed no later than the first date set for the hearing on confirmation. In a Chapter 13 case, a motion objecting to the debtor's discharge under § 1328(f) shall be filed no later than 60 days after the first date set for the meeting of creditors under § 341(a). At least 28 days' notice of the time so fixed shall be given to the United States trustee and all creditors as provided in Rule 2002(f) and (k), and to the trustee and the trustee's attorney.

(b) EXTENSION OF TIME.

(1) On motion of any party in interest, after notice and hearing, the court may for cause extend the time to object to discharge. Except as provided in subdivision (b)(2), the motion shall be filed before the time has expired.

(2) A motion to extend the time to object to discharge may be filed after the time for objection has expired and before discharge is granted if (A) the objection is based on facts that, if learned after the discharge, would provide a basis for revocation under § 727 (d) of the Code, and (B) the movant did not have knowledge of those facts in time to permit an objection. The motion shall be filed promptly after the movant discovers the facts on which the objection is based.

(c) GRANT OF DISCHARGE.

(1) In a chapter 7 case, on expiration of the times fixed for objecting to discharge and for filing a motion to dismiss the case under Rule 1017(e), the court shall forthwith grant the discharge, except that the court shall not grant the discharge if:

(A) the debtor is not an individual;

(B) a complaint, or a motion under § 727(a)(8) or (a)(9), objecting to the discharge has been filed and not decided in the debtor's favor;

(C) the debtor has filed a waiver under § 727(a)(10);

(D) a motion to dismiss the case under § 707 is pending;

(E) a motion to extend the time for filing a complaint objecting to the discharge is pending;

(F) a motion to extend the time for filing a motion to dismiss the case under Rule 1017(e)(1) is pending;

(G) the debtor has not paid in full the filing fee prescribed by 28 U.S.C. § 1930(a) and any other fee prescribed by the Judicial Conference of the United States under 28 U.S.C. § 1930(b) that is payable to the clerk upon the commencement of a case under the Code, unless the court has waived the fees under 28 U.S.C. § 1930(f);

(H) the debtor has not filed with the court a statement of completion of a course concerning personal financial management if required by Rule 1007(b)(7);

(I) a motion to delay or postpone discharge under § 727(a)(12) is pending;

(J) a motion to enlarge the time to file a reaffirmation agreement under Rule 4008(a) is pending;

(K) a presumption is in effect under § 524(m) that a reaffirmation agreement is an undue hardship and the court has not concluded a hearing on the presumption; or

(L) a motion is pending to delay discharge because the debtor has not filed with the court all tax documents required to be filed under § 521(f).

(2) Notwithstanding Rule 4004(c)(1), on motion of the debtor, the court may defer the entry of an order granting a discharge for 30 days and, on motion within that period, the court may defer entry of the order to a date certain.

(3) If the debtor is required to file a statement under Rule 1007(b)(8), the court shall not grant a discharge earlier than 30 days after the statement is filed.

(4) In a chapter 11 case in which the debtor is an individual, or a chapter 13 case, the court shall not grant a discharge if the debtor has not filed any statement required by Rule 1007(b)(7).

(d) APPLICABILITY OF RULES IN PART VII AND RULE 9014. An

objection to discharge is governed by Part VII of these rules, except that an objection to discharge under §§ 727(a)(8), (a)(9), or 1328(f) is commenced by motion and governed by Rule 9014.

(e) ORDER OF DISCHARGE. An order of discharge shall conform to the appropriate Official Form.

(f) REGISTRATION IN OTHER DISTRICTS. An order of discharge that has become final may be registered in any other district by filing a certified copy of the order in the office of the clerk of that district. When so registered the order of discharge shall have the same effect as an order of the court of the district where registered.

(g) NOTICE OF DISCHARGE. The clerk shall promptly mail a copy of the final order of discharge to those specified in subdivision (a) of this rule.

Rule 4005. Burden of Proof in Objecting to Discharge

At the trial on a complaint objecting to a discharge, the plaintiff has the burden of proving the objection.

Rule 4006. Notice of No Discharge

If an order is entered: denying a discharge; revoking a discharge; approving a waiver of discharge; or, in the case of an individual debtor, closing the case without the entry of a discharge, the clerk shall promptly notify all parties in interest in the manner provided by Rule 2002.

Rule 4007. Determination of Dischargeability of a Debt

(a) PERSONS ENTITLED TO FILE COMPLAINT. A debtor or any creditor may file a complaint to obtain a determination of the dischargeability of any debt.

(b) TIME FOR COMMENCING PROCEEDING OTHER THAN UNDER SECTION 523(c) OF THE CODE. A complaint other than under Section 523(c) may be filed at any time. A case may be reopened without payment of an additional filing fee for the purpose of filing a complaint to obtain a determination under this rule.

(c) TIME FOR FILING COMPLAINT UNDER § 523(c) IN A CHAPTER 7 LIQUIDATION, CHAPTER 11 REORGANIZATION, CHAPTER 12 FAMILY FARMER'S DEBT ADJUSTMENT CASE, OR CHAPTER 13 INDIVIDUAL'S DEBT ADJUSTMENT CASE; NOTICE OF TIME FIXED. Except as otherwise provided in subdivision (d), a complaint to determine the dischargeability of a debt under § 523(c) shall be filed no later than 60 days after the first date set for the meeting of creditors under § 341(a). The court shall give all creditors no less than 30 days' notice of the time so fixed in the manner provided in Rule 2002. On motion of a party in interest, after hearing on notice, the court may for cause extend the time fixed under this subdivision. The motion shall be filed before the time has expired.

(d) TIME FOR FILING COMPLAINT UNDER § 523(a)(6) IN A CHAPTER 13 INDIVIDUAL'S DEBT ADJUSTMENT CASE; NOTICE OF TIME FIXED. On motion by a debtor for a discharge under § 1328(b), the court shall enter an order fixing the time to file a complaint to determine the dischargeability of any debt under § 523(a)(6) and shall give no less than 30 days' notice of the time fixed to all creditors in the manner provided in Rule 2002. On motion of any party in interest, after hearing on notice, the court may for cause extend the time fixed under this subdivision. The motion shall be filed before the time has expired.

(e) APPLICABILITY OF RULES IN PART VII. A proceeding commenced by a complaint filed under this rule is governed by Part VII of these rules.

Rule 4008. Filing of Reaffirmation Agreement; Statement in Support of Reaffirmation Agreement

(a) FILING OF REAFFIRMATION AGREEMENT. A reaffirmation agreement shall be filed no later than 60 days after the first date set for the meeting of creditors under § 341(a) of the Code. The reaffirmation agreement shall be accompanied by a cover sheet, prepared as prescribed by the appropriate Official Form. The court may, at any time and in its discretion, enlarge the time to file a reaffirmation agreement.

(b) STATEMENT IN SUPPORT OF REAFFIRMATION AGREEMENT. The debtor's statement required under § 524(k)(6)(A) of the Code shall be accompanied by a statement of the total income and expenses stated on schedules I and J. If there is a difference between the total income and expenses stated on those schedules and the statement required under § 524(k)(6)(A), the statement required by this subdivision shall include an explanation of the difference.

PART V

COURTS AND CLERKS

Rule 5001. Courts and Clerks' Offices

(a) COURTS ALWAYS OPEN. The courts shall be deemed always open for the purpose of filing any pleading or other proper paper, issuing and returning process, and filing, making, or entering motions, orders and rules.

(b) TRIALS AND HEARINGS; ORDERS IN CHAMBERS. All trials and hearings shall be conducted in open court and so far as convenient in a regular court room. Except as otherwise provided in 28 U.S.C. § 152(c), all other acts or proceedings may be done or conducted by a judge in chambers and at any place either within or without the district; but no hearing, other than one ex parte, shall be conducted outside the district without the consent of all parties affected thereby.

(c) CLERK'S OFFICE. The clerk's office with the clerk or a deputy in attendance shall be open during business hours on all days except Saturdays, Sundays and the legal holidays listed in Rule 9006(a).

Rule 5002. Restrictions on Approval of Appointments

(a) APPROVAL OF APPOINTMENT OF RELATIVES PROHIBITED. The appointment of an individual as a trustee or examiner pursuant to Section 1104 of the Code shall not be approved by the court if the individual is a relative of the bankruptcy judge approving the appointment or the United States trustee in the region in which the case is pending. The employment of an individual as attorney, accountant, appraiser, auctioneer, or other professional person pursuant to Sections 327, 1103, or 1114 shall not be approved by the court if the individual is a relative of the bankruptcy judge approving the employment. The employment of an individual as attorney, accountant, appraiser, auctioneer, or other professional person pursuant to Sections 327, 1103, or 1114 may be approved by the court if the individual is a relative of the United States trustee in the region in which the case is pending, unless the court finds that the relationship with the United States trustee renders the employment improper under the circumstances of the case. Whenever under this subdivision an individual may not be approved for appointment or employment, the individual's firm, partnership, corporation, or any other form of business association or relationship, and all members, associates and professional employees thereof also may not be approved for appointment or employment.

(b) JUDICIAL DETERMINATION THAT APPROVAL OF APPOINTMENT OR EMPLOYMENT IS IMPROPER. A bankruptcy judge may not approve the appointment of a person as a trustee or examiner pursuant to Section 1104 of the Code or approve the employment of a person as an attorney, accountant, appraiser, auctioneer, or other professional person pursuant to Sections 327, 1103, or 1114 of the Code if that person is or has been so connected with such judge or the United States trustee as to render the appointment or employment improper.

Rule 5003. Records Kept By the Clerk

(a) BANKRUPTCY DOCKETS. The clerk shall keep a docket in each case under the Code and shall enter thereon each judgment, order, and activity in that case as prescribed by the Director of the Administrative Office of the United States Courts. The entry of a judgment or order in a docket shall show the date the entry is made.

(b) CLAIMS REGISTER. The clerk shall keep in a claims register a list of claims filed in a case when it appears that there will be a distribution to unsecured creditors.

(c) JUDGMENTS AND ORDERS. The clerk shall keep, in the form and manner as the Director of the Administrative Office of the United States Courts may prescribe, a correct copy of every final judgment or order affecting title to or lien on real property or for the recovery of money or property, and any other order which the court may direct to be kept. On request of the prevailing party, a correct copy of every judgment or order affecting title to or lien upon real or personal property or for the recovery of money or property shall be kept and indexed with the civil judgments of the district court.

(d) INDEX OF CASES; CERTIFICATE OF SEARCH. The clerk shall keep indices of all cases and adversary proceedings as prescribed by the Director of the Administrative Office of the United States Courts. On request, the clerk shall make a search of any index and papers in the clerk's custody and certify whether a case or proceeding has been filed in or transferred to the court or if a discharge has been entered in its records.

(e) REGISTER OF MAILING ADDRESSES OF FEDERAL AND STATE GOVERNMENTAL UNITS AND CERTAIN TAXING AUTHORITIES. The United States or the state or territory in which the court is located may file a statement designating its mailing address. The United States, state, territory, or local governmental unit responsible for collecting taxes within the district in which the case is pending may also file a statement designating an address for service of requests under § 505(b) of the Code, and the designation shall describe where further information concerning additional requirements for filing such requests may be found. The clerk shall keep, in the form and manner as the Director of the Administrative Office of the United States Courts may prescribe, a register that includes the mailing addresses designated under the first sentence of this subdivision, and a separate register of the addresses designated for the service of requests under § 505(b)
of the Code. The clerk is not required to include in any single register more than one mailing address for each department, agency, or instrumentality of the United States or the state or territory. If more than one address for a department, agency, or instrumentality is included in the register, the clerk shall also include information that would enable a user of the register to determine the circumstances when each address is applicable, and mailing notice to only one applicable address is sufficient to provide effective notice. The clerk shall update the register annually, effective January 2 of each year. The mailing address in the register is conclusively presumed to be a proper address for the governmental unit, but the failure to use that mailing address does not invalidate any notice that is otherwise effective under applicable law.

(f) OTHER BOOKS AND RECORDS OF THE CLERK. The clerk shall keep any other books and records required by the Director of the Administrative Office of the United States Courts.

Rule 5004. Disqualification

(a) DISQUALIFICATION OF JUDGE. A bankruptcy judge shall be governed by 28 U. S. C. Section 455, and disqualified from presiding over the proceeding or contested matter in which the disqualifying circumstance arises or, if appropriate, shall be disqualified from presiding over the case.

(b) DISQUALIFICATION OF JUDGE FROM ALLOWING COMPENSATION. A bankruptcy judge shall be disqualified from allowing compensation to a person who is a relative of the bankruptcy judge or with whom the judge is so connected as to render it improper for the judge to authorize such compensation.

Rule 5005. Filing and Transmittal of Papers

(a) FILING.

(1) Place of Filing. The lists, schedules, statements, proofs of claim or interest, complaints, motions, applications, objections and other papers required to be filed by these rules, except as provided in 28 U.S.C. §1409, shall be filed with the clerk in the district where the case under the Code is pending. The judge of that court may permit the papers to be filed with the judge, in which event the filing date shall be noted thereon, and they shall be forthwith transmitted to the clerk. The clerk shall not refuse to accept for filing any petition or other paper presented for the purpose of filing solely because it is not presented in proper form as required by these rules or any local rules or practices.

(2) Filing by Electronic Means. A court may by local rule permit or require documents to be filed, signed, or verified by electronic means that are consistent with technical standards, if any, that the Judicial Conference of the United States establishes. A local rule may require filing by electronic means only if reasonable exceptions are allowed. A document filed by electronic means in compliance with a local rule constitutes a written paper for the purpose of applying these rules, the Federal Rules of Civil Procedure made applicable by these rules, and §107 of the Code.

(b) TRANSMITTAL TO THE UNITED STATES TRUSTEE.

(1) The complaints, motions, applications, objections and other papers required to be transmitted to the United States trustee by these rules shall be mailed or delivered to an office of the United States trustee, or to another place designated by the United States trustee, in the district where the case under the Code is pending.

(2) The entity, other than the clerk, transmitting a paper to the United States trustee shall promptly file as proof of such transmittal a verified statement identifying the paper and stating the date on which it was transmitted to the United States trustee.

(3) Nothing in these rules shall require the clerk to transmit any paper to the United States trustee if the United States trustee requests in writing that the paper not be transmitted.

(c) ERROR IN FILING OR TRANSMITTAL. A paper intended to be filed with the clerk but erroneously delivered to the United States trustee, the trustee, the attorney for the trustee, a bankruptcy judge, a district judge, the clerk of the bankruptcy appellate panel, or the clerk of the district court shall, after the date of its receipt has been noted thereon, be transmitted forthwith to the clerk of the bankruptcy court. A paper intended to be transmitted to the United States trustee but erroneously delivered to the clerk, the trustee, the attorney for the trustee, a bankruptcy judge, a district judge, the clerk of the bankruptcy appellate panel, or the clerk of the district court shall, after the date of its receipt has been noted thereon, be transmitted forthwith to the United States trustee. In the interest of justice, the court may order that a paper erroneously delivered shall be deemed filed with the clerk or transmitted to the United States trustee as of the date of its original delivery.

Rule 5006. Certification of Copies of Papers

The clerk shall issue a certified copy of the record of any proceeding in a case under the Code or of any paper filed with the clerk on payment of any prescribed fee.

Rule 5007. Record of Proceedings and Transcripts

(a) FILING OF RECORD OR TRANSCRIPT. The reporter or operator of a recording device shall certify the original notes of testimony, tape recording, or other original record of the proceeding and promptly file them with the clerk. The person preparing any transcript shall promptly file a certified copy.

(b) TRANSCRIPT FEES. The fees for copies of transcripts shall be charged at rates prescribed by the Judicial Conference of the United States. No fee may be charged for the certified copy filed with the clerk.

(c) ADMISSIBILITY OF RECORD IN EVIDENCE. A certified sound recording or a transcript of a proceeding shall be admissible as prima facie evidence to establish the record.

Rule 5008. Notice Regarding Presumption of Abuse in Chapter 7 Cases of Individual Debtors

If a presumption of abuse has arisen under § 707(b) in a chapter 7 case of an individual with primarily consumer debts, the clerk shall within 10 days after the date of the filing of the petition notify creditors of the presumption of abuse in accordance with Rule 2002. If the debtor has not filed a statement indicating whether a presumption of abuse has arisen, the clerk shall within 10 days after the date of the filing of the petition notify creditors that the debtor has not filed the statement and that further notice will be given if a later filed statement indicates that a presumption of abuse has arisen. If a debtor later files a statement indicating that a presumption of abuse has arisen, the clerk shall notify creditors of the presumption of abuse as promptly as practicable.

Rule 5009. Closing Chapter 7 Liquidation, Chapter 12 Family Farmer's Debt Adjustment, Chapter 13 Individual's Debt Adjustment, and Chapter 15 Ancillary and Cross-Border Cases

(a) CASES UNDER CHAPTERS 7, 12, AND 13. If in a chapter 7, chapter 12, or chapter 13 case the trustee has filed a final report and final account and has certified that the estate has been fully administered, and if within 30 days no objection has been filed by the United States trustee or a party in interest, there shall be a presumption that the estate has been fully administered.

(b) NOTICE OF FAILURE TO FILE RULE 1007(b)(7) STATEMENT. If an individual debtor in a chapter 7 or 13 case is required to file a statement under Rule 1007(b)(7) and fails to do so within 45 days after the first date set for the meeting of creditors under § 341(a) of the Code, the clerk shall promptly notify the debtor that the case will be closed without entry of a discharge unless the required statement is filed within the applicable time limit under Rule 1007(c).

(c) CASES UNDER CHAPTER 15. A foreign representative in a proceeding recognized under § 1517 of the Code shall file a final report when the purpose of the representative's appearance in the court is completed. The report shall describe the nature and results of the representative's activities in the court. The foreign representative shall transmit the report to the United States trustee, and give notice of its filing to the debtor, all persons or bodies authorized to administer foreign proceedings of the debtor, all parties to litigation pending in the United States in which the debtor was a party at the time of the filing of the petition, and such other entities as the court may direct. The foreign representative shall file a certificate with the court that notice has been given. If no objection has been filed by the United States trustee or a party in interest within 30 days after the certificate is filed, there shall be a presumption that the case has been fully administered.

Rule 5010. Reopening Cases

A case may be reopened on motion of the debtor or other party in interest pursuant to Section 350(b) of the Code. In a chapter 7, 12, or 13 case a trustee shall not be appointed by the United States trustee unless the court determines that a trustee is necessary to protect the interests of creditors and the debtor or to insure efficient administration of the case.

Rule 5011. Withdrawal and Abstention from Hearing a Proceeding

(a) WITHDRAWAL. A motion for withdrawal of a case or proceeding shall be heard by a district judge.

(b) ABSTENTION FROM HEARING A PROCEEDING. A motion for abstention pursuant to 28 U. S. C. Section 1334(c) shall be governed by Rule 9014 and shall be served on the parties to the proceeding.

(c) EFFECT OF FILING OF MOTION FOR WITHDRAWAL OR ABSTENTION. The filing of a motion for withdrawal of a case or proceeding or for abstention pursuant to 28 U. S. C. Section 1334(c) shall not stay the administration of the case or any proceeding therein before the bankruptcy judge except that the bankruptcy judge may stay, on such terms and conditions as are proper, proceedings pending disposition of the motion. A motion for a stay ordinarily shall be presented first to the bankruptcy judge. A motion for a stay or relief from a stay filed in the district court shall state why it has not been presented to or obtained from the bankruptcy judge. Relief granted by the district judge shall be on such terms and conditions as the judge deems proper.

Rule 5012. Agreements Concerning Coordination of Proceedings in Chapter 15 Cases

Approval of an agreement under § 1527(4) of the Code shall be sought by motion. The movant shall attach to the motion a copy of the proposed agreement or protocol and, unless the court directs otherwise, give at least 30 days' notice of any hearing on the motion by transmitting the motion to the United States trustee, and serving it on the debtor, all persons or bodies authorized to administer foreign proceedings of the debtor, all entities against whom provisional relief is being sought under § 1519, all parties to litigation pending in the United States in which the debtor was a party at the time of the filing of the petition, and such other entities as the court may direct.

PART VI

COLLECTION AND LIQUIDATION OF THE ESTATE

Rule 6001. Burden of Proof As to Validity of Postpetition Transfer

Any entity asserting the validity of a transfer under Section 549 of the Code shall have the burden of proof.

Rule 6002. Accounting by Prior Custodian of Property of the Estate

(a) ACCOUNTING REQUIRED. Any custodian required by the Code to deliver property in the custodian's possession or control to the trustee shall promptly file and transmit to the United States trustee a report and account with respect to the property of the estate and the administration thereof.

(b) EXAMINATION OF ADMINISTRATION. On the filing and transmittal of the report and account required by subdivision (a) of this rule and after an examination has been made into the superseded administration, after notice and a hearing, the court shall determine the propriety of the administration, including the reasonableness of all disbursements.

Rule 6003. Interim and Final Relief Immediately Following the Commencement of the Case – Applications for Employment; Motions for Use, Sale, or Lease of Property; and Motions for Assumption or Assignment of Executory Contracts

Except to the extent that relief is necessary to avoid immediate and irreparable harm, the court shall not, within 21 days after the filing of the petition, issue an order granting the following:

(a) an application under Rule 2014;

(b) a motion to use, sell, lease, or otherwise incur an obligation regarding property of the estate, including a motion to pay all or part of a claim that arose before the filing of the petition, but not a motion under Rule 4001; or

(c) a motion to assume or assign an executory contract or unexpired lease in accordance with § 365.

Rule 6004. Use, Sale, or Lease of Property

(a) NOTICE OF PROPOSED USE, SALE, OR LEASE OF PROPERTY. Notice of a proposed use, sale, or lease of property, other than cash collateral, not in the ordinary course of business shall be given pursuant to Rule 2002(a)(2), (c)(1), (i), and (k) and, if applicable, in accordance with Section 363(b)(2) of the Code.

(b) OBJECTION TO PROPOSAL. Except as provided in subdivisions (c) and (d) of this rule, an objection to a proposed use, sale, or lease of property shall be filed and served not less than seven days before the date set for the proposed action or within the time fixed by the court. An objection to the proposed use, sale, or lease of property is governed by Rule 9014.

(c) SALE FREE AND CLEAR OF LIENS AND OTHER INTERESTS. A motion for authority to sell property free and clear of liens or other interests shall be made in accordance with Rule 9014 and shall be served on the parties who have liens or other interests in the property to be sold. The notice required by subdivision (a) of this rule shall include the date of the hearing on the motion and the time within which objections may be filed and served on the debtor in possession or trustee.

(d) SALE OF PROPERTY UNDER $2,500. Notwithstanding subdivision (a) of this rule, when all of the nonexempt property of the estate has an aggregate gross value less than $2,500, it shall be sufficient to give a general notice of intent to sell such property other than in the ordinary course of business to all creditors, indenture trustees, committees appointed or elected pursuant to the Code, the United States trustee and other persons as the court may direct. An objection to any such sale may be filed and served by a party in interest within 14 days of the mailing of the notice, or within the time fixed by the court. An objection is governed by Rule 9014.

(e) HEARING. If a timely objection is made pursuant to subdivision (b) or (d) of this rule, the date of the hearing thereon may be set in the notice given pursuant to subdivision (a) of this rule.

(f) CONDUCT OF SALE NOT IN THE ORDINARY COURSE OF BUSINESS.

(1) Public or Private Sale. All sales not in the ordinary course of business may be by private sale or by public auction. Unless it is impracticable, an itemized statement of the property sold, the name of each purchaser, and the price received for each item or lot or for the property as a whole if sold in bulk shall be filed on completion of a sale. If the property is sold by an auctioneer, the auctioneer shall file the statement, transmit a copy thereof to the United States trustee, and furnish a copy to the trustee, debtor in possession, or chapter 13 debtor. If the property is not sold by an auctioneer, the trustee, debtor in possession, or chapter 13 debtor shall file the statement and transmit a copy thereof to the United States trustee.

(2) Execution of Instruments. After a sale in accordance with this rule the debtor, the trustee, or debtor in possession, as the case may be, shall execute any instrument necessary or ordered by the court to effectuate the transfer to the purchaser.

(g) SALE OF PERSONALLY IDENTIFIABLE INFORMATION.

(1) Motion. A motion for authority to sell or lease personally identifiable information under § 363(b)(1)(B) shall include a request for an order directing the United States trustee to appoint a consumer privacy ombudsman under § 332. Rule 9014 governs the motion which shall be served on: any committee elected under § 705 or appointed under § 1102 of the Code, or if the case is a chapter 11 reorganization case and no committee of unsecured creditors has been appointed under § 1102, on the creditors included on the list of creditors filed under Rule 1007(d); and on such other entities as the court may direct. The motion shall be transmitted to the United States trustee.

(2) Appointment. If a consumer privacy ombudsman is appointed under § 332, no later than seven days before the hearing on the motion under § 363(b)(1)(B), the United States trustee shall file a notice of the appointment, including the name and address of the person appointed. The United States trustee's notice shall be accompanied by a verified statement of the person appointed setting forth the person's connections with the debtor, creditors, any other party in interest, their respective attorneys and accountants, the

United States trustee, or any person employed in the office of the United States trustee.

(h) STAY OF ORDER AUTHORIZING USE, SALE, OR LEASE OF PROPERTY. An order authorizing the use, sale, or lease of property other than cash collateral is stayed until the expiration of 14 days after entry of the order, unless the court orders otherwise.

Rule 6005. Appraisers and Auctioneers

The order of the court approving the employment of an appraiser or auctioneer shall fix the amount or rate of compensation. No officer or employee of the Judicial Branch of the United States or the United States Department of Justice shall be eligible to act as appraiser or auctioneer. No residence or licensing requirement shall disqualify an appraiser or auctioneer from employment.

Rule 6006. Assumption, Rejection or Assignment of an Executory Contract or Unexpired Lease

(a) PROCEEDING TO ASSUME, REJECT OR ASSIGN. A proceeding to assume, reject, or assign an executory contract or unexpired lease, other than as part of a plan, is governed by Rule 9014.

(b) PROCEEDING TO REQUIRE TRUSTEE TO ACT. A proceeding by a party to an executory contract or unexpired lease in a chapter 9 municipality case, chapter 11 reorganization case, chapter 12 family farmer's debt adjustment case, or chapter 13 individual's debt adjustment case, to require the trustee, debtor in possession, or debtor to determine whether to assume or reject the contract or lease is governed by Rule 9014.

(c) NOTICE. Notice of a motion made pursuant to subdivision (a) or (b) of this rule shall be given to the other party to the contract or lease, to other parties in interest as the court may direct, and, except in a chapter 9 municipality case, to the United States trustee.

(d) STAY OF ORDER AUTHORIZING ASSIGNMENT. An order authorizing the trustee to assign an executory contract or unexpired lease under §365(f) is stayed until the expiration of 14 days after the entry of the order, unless the court orders otherwise.

(e) LIMITATIONS. The trustee shall not seek authority to assume or assign multiple executory contracts or unexpired leases in one motion unless: (1) all executory contracts or unexpired leases to be assumed or assigned are between the same parties or are to be assigned to the same assignee; (2) the trustee seeks to assume, but not assign to more than one assignee, unexpired leases of real property; or (3) the court otherwise authorizes the motion to be filed. Subject to subdivision (f), the trustee may join requests for authority to reject multiple executory contracts or unexpired leases in one motion.

(f) OMNIBUS MOTIONS. A motion to reject or, if permitted under subdivision (e), a motion to assume or assign multiple executory contracts or unexpired leases that are not between the same parties shall:

(1) state in a conspicuous place that parties receiving the omnibus motion should locate their names and their contracts or leases listed in the motion;

(2) list parties alphabetically and identify the corresponding contract or lease;

(3) specify the terms, including the curing of defaults, for each requested assumption or assignment;

(4) specify the terms, including the identity of each assignee and the adequate assurance of future performance by each assignee, for each requested assignment;

(5) be numbered consecutively with other omnibus motions to assume, assign, or reject executory contracts or unexpired leases; and

(6) be limited to no more than 100 executory contracts or unexpired leases.

(g) FINALITY OF DETERMINATION. The finality of any order respecting an executory contract or unexpired lease included in an omnibus motion shall be determined as though such contract or lease had been the subject of a separate motion.

Rule 6007. Abandonment or Disposition of Property

(a) NOTICE OF PROPOSED ABANDONMENT OR DISPOSITION; OBJECTIONS; HEARING. Unless otherwise directed by the court, the trustee or debtor in possession shall give notice of a proposed abandonment or disposition of property to the United States trustee, all creditors, indenture trustees, and committees elected pursuant to Section 705 or appointed pursuant to Section 1102 of the Code. A party in interest may file and serve an objection within 14 days of the mailing of the notice, or within the time fixed by the court. If a timely objection is made, the court shall set a hearing on notice to the United States trustee and to other entities as the court may direct.

(b) MOTION BY PARTY IN INTEREST. A party in interest may file and serve a motion requiring the trustee or debtor in possession to abandon property of the estate.

Rule 6008. Redemption of Property from Lien or Sale

On motion by the debtor, trustee, or debtor in possession and after hearing on notice as the court may direct, the court may authorize the redemption of property from a lien or from a sale to enforce a lien in accordance with applicable law.

Rule 6009. Prosecution and Defense of Proceedings by Trustee or Debtor in Possession

With or without court approval, the trustee or debtor in possession may prosecute or may enter an appearance and defend any pending action or proceeding by or against the debtor, or commence and prosecute any action or proceeding in behalf of the estate before any tribunal.

Rule 6010. Proceeding to Avoid Indemnifying Lien or Transfer to Surety

If a lien voidable under Section 547 of the Code has been dissolved by the furnishing of a bond or other obligation and the surety thereon has been indemnified by the transfer of, or the creation of a lien upon, nonexempt property of the debtor, the surety shall be joined as a defendant in any proceeding to avoid the indemnifying transfer or lien. Such proceeding is governed by the rules in Part VII.

Rule 6011. Disposal of Patient Records in Health Care Business Case

(a) NOTICE BY PUBLICATION UNDER § 351(1)(A). A notice regarding the claiming or disposing of patient records under § 351(1)(A) shall not identify any patient by name or other identifying information, but shall:

(1) identify with particularity the health care facility whose patient records the trustee proposes to destroy;

(2) state the name, address, telephone number, email address, and website, if any, of a person from whom information about the patient records may be obtained;

(3) state how to claim the patient records; and

(4) state the date by which patient records must be claimed, and that if they are not so claimed the records will be destroyed.

(b) NOTICE BY MAIL UNDER § 351(1)(B). Subject to applicable nonbankruptcy law relating to patient privacy, a notice regarding the claiming or disposing of patient records under § 351(1)(B) shall, in addition to including the information in subdivision (a), direct that a patient's family member or other representative who receives the notice inform the patient of the notice. Any notice under this subdivision shall be mailed to the patient and any family member or other contact person whose name and address have been given to the trustee or the debtor for the purpose of providing information regarding the patient's health care, to the Attorney General of the State where the health care facility is located, and to any insurance company known to have provided health care insurance to the patient.

(c) PROOF OF COMPLIANCE WITH NOTICE REQUIREMENT. Unless the court orders the trustee to file proof of compliance with § 351(1)(B) under seal, the trustee shall not file, but shall maintain, the proof of compliance for a reasonable time.

(d) REPORT OF DESTRUCTION OF RECORDS. The trustee shall file, no later than 30 days after the destruction of patient records under § 351(3), a report certifying that the unclaimed records have been destroyed and explaining the method used to effect the destruction. The report shall not identify any patient by name or other identifying information.

PART VII

ADVERSARY PROCEEDINGS

Rule 7001. Scope of Rules of Part VII

An adversary proceeding is governed by the rules of this Part VII. The following are adversary proceedings:

(1) a proceeding to recover money or property, other than a proceeding to compel the debtor to deliver property to the trustee, or a proceeding under §554(b) or §725 of the Code, Rule 2017, or Rule 6002;

(2) a proceeding to determine the validity, priority, or extent of a lien or other interest in property, other than a proceeding under Rule 4003(d);

(3) a proceeding to obtain approval under §363(h) for the sale of both the interest of the estate and of a co-owner in property;

(4) a proceeding to object to or revoke a discharge, other than an objection to discharge under §§ 727(a)(8), (a)(9), or 1328(f);

(5) a proceeding to revoke an order of confirmation of a chapter 11, chapter 12, or chapter 13 plan;

(6) a proceeding to determine the dischargeability of a debt;

(7) a proceeding to obtain an injunction or other equitable relief, except when a chapter 9, chapter 11, chapter 12, or chapter 13 plan provides for the relief;

(8) a proceeding to subordinate any allowed claim or interest, except when a chapter 9, chapter 11, chapter 12, or chapter 13 plan provides for subordination;

(9) a proceeding to obtain a declaratory judgment relating to any of the foregoing; or

(10) a proceeding to determine a claim or cause of action removed under 28 U.S.C. §1452.

Rule 7002. References to Federal Rules of Civil Procedure

Whenever a Federal Rule of Civil Procedure applicable to adversary proceedings makes reference to another Federal Rule of Civil Procedure, the reference shall be read as a reference to the Federal Rule of Civil Procedure as modified in this Part VII.

Rule 7003. Commencement of Adversary Proceeding

Rule 3 F. R. Civ. P. applies in adversary proceedings.

Rule 7004. Process; Service of Summons, Complaint

(a) SUMMONS; SERVICE; PROOF OF SERVICE. (1) Except as provided in Rule 7004(a)(2), Rule 4(a), (b), (c)(1), (d)(1), (e)-(j), (l), and (m) F.R. Civ. P. applies in adversary proceedings. Personal service under Rule 4(e)-(j) F.R. Civ. P. may be made by any person at least 18 years of age who is not a party, and the summons may be delivered by the clerk to any such person.

(2) The clerk may sign, seal, and issue a summons electronically by putting an "s/" before the clerk's name and including the court's seal on the summons.

(b) SERVICE BY FIRST CLASS MAIL. Except as provided in subdivision (h), in addition to the methods of service authorized by Rule 4(e)-(j) F. R. Civ. P., service may be made within the United States by first class mail postage prepaid as follows:

(1) Upon an individual other than an infant or incompetent, by mailing a copy of the summons and complaint to the individual's dwelling house or usual place of abode or to the place where the individual regularly conducts a business or profession.

(2) Upon an infant or an incompetent person, by mailing a copy of the summons and complaint to the person upon whom process is prescribed to be served by the law of the state in which service is made when an action is brought against such defendant in the courts of general jurisdiction of that state. The summons and complaint in that case shall be addressed to the person required to be served at that person's dwelling house or usual place of abode or at the place where the person regularly conducts a business or profession.

(3) Upon a domestic or foreign corporation or upon a partnership or other unincorporated association, by mailing a copy of the summons and complaint to the attention of an officer, a managing or general agent, or to any other agent authorized by appointment or by law to receive service of process and, if the agent is one authorized by statute to receive service and the statute so requires, by also mailing a copy to the defendant.

(4) Upon the United States, by mailing a copy of the summons and complaint addressed to the civil process clerk at the office of the United States attorney for the district in which the action is brought and by mailing a copy of the summons and complaint to the Attorney General of the United States at Washington, District of Columbia, and in any action attacking the validity of an order of an officer or an agency of the United States not made a party, by also mailing a copy of the summons and complaint to that officer or agency. The court shall allow a reasonable time for service pursuant to this subdivision for the purpose of curing the failure to mail a copy of the summons and complaint to multiple officers, agencies, or corporations of the United States if the plaintiff has mailed a copy of the summons and complaint either to the civil process clerk at the office of the United States attorney or to the Attorney General of the United States.

(5) Upon any officer or agency of the United States, by mailing a copy of the summons and complaint to the United States as prescribed in paragraph (4) of this subdivision and also to the officer or agency. If the agency is a corporation, the mailing shall be as prescribed in paragraph (3) of this subdivision of this rule. The court shall allow a reasonable time for service pursuant to this subdivision for the purpose of curing the failure to mail a copy of the summons and complaint to multiple officers, agencies, or corporations of the United States if the plaintiff has mailed a copy of the summons and complaint either to the civil process clerk at the office of the United States attorney or to the Attorney General of the United States. If the United States trustee is the trustee in the case and service is made upon the United States trustee solely as trustee, service may be made as prescribed in paragraph (10) of this subdivision of this rule.

(6) Upon a state or municipal corporation or other governmental organization thereof subject to suit, by mailing a copy of the summons and complaint to the person or office upon whom process is prescribed to be served by the law of the state in which service is made when an action is brought against such a defendant in the courts of general jurisdiction of that state, or in the absence of the designation of any such person or office by state law, then to the chief executive officer thereof.

(7) Upon a defendant of any class referred to in paragraph (1) or (3) of this subdivision of this rule, it is also sufficient if a copy of the summons and complaint is mailed to the entity upon whom service is prescribed to be served by any statute of the United States or by the law of the state in which service is made when an action is brought against such a defendant in the court of general jurisdiction of that state.

(8) Upon any defendant, it is also sufficient if a copy of the summons and complaint is mailed to an agent of such defendant authorized by appointment or by law to receive service of process, at the agent's dwelling house or usual place of abode or at the place where the agent regularly carries on a business or profession and, if the authorization so requires, by mailing also a copy of the summons and complaint to the defendant as provided in this subdivision.

(9) Upon the debtor, after a petition has been filed by or served upon the debtor and until the case is dismissed or closed, by mailing a copy of the summons and complaint to the debtor at the address shown in the petition or to such other address as the debtor may designate in a filed writing.

(10) Upon the United States trustee, when the United States trustee is the trustee in the case and service is made upon the United States trustee solely as trustee, by mailing a copy of the summons and complaint to an office of the United States trustee or another place designated by the United States trustee in the district where the case under the Code is pending.

(c) SERVICE BY PUBLICATION. If a party to an adversary proceeding to determine or protect rights in property in the custody of the court cannot be served as provided in Rule 4(e)-(j) F. R. Civ. P. or subdivision (b) of this rule, the court may order the summons and complaint to be served by mailing copies thereof by first class mail postage prepaid, to the party's last known address and by at least one publication in such manner and form as the court may direct.

(d) NATIONWIDE SERVICE OF PROCESS. The summons and complaint and all other process except a subpoena may be served anywhere in the United States.

(e) SUMMONS: TIME LIMIT FOR SERVICE WITHIN THE UNITED STATES. Service made under Rule 4(e), (g), (h)(1), (i), or (j)(2) F.R.Civ.P. shall be by delivery of the summons and complaint within 7 days after the summons is issued. If service is by any authorized form of mail, the summons and complaint shall be deposited in the mail within 7 days after the summons is issued. If a summons is not timely delivered or mailed, another summons will be issued for service. This subdivision does not apply to service in a foreign country.

(f) PERSONAL JURISDICTION. If the exercise of jurisdiction is consistent with the Constitution and laws of the United States, serving a summons or filing a waiver of service in accordance with this rule or the subdivisions of Rule 4 F.R.Civ.P. made applicable by these rules is effective to establish personal jurisdiction over the person of any defendant with respect to a case under the Code or a civil proceeding arising under the Code, or arising in or related to a case under the Code.

(g) SERVICE ON DEBTOR'S ATTORNEY. If the debtor is represented by an attorney, whenever service is made upon the debtor under this Rule, service shall also be made upon the debtor's attorney by any means authorized under

Rule 5(b) F. R. Civ. P.

(h) SERVICE OF PROCESS ON AN INSURED DEPOSITORY INSTITUTION. Service on an insured depository institution (as defined in section 3 of the Federal Deposit Insurance Act) in a contested matter or adversary proceeding shall be made by certified mail addressed to an officer of the institution unless -

(1) the institution has appeared by its attorney, in which case the attorney shall be served by first class mail;

(2) the court orders otherwise after service upon the institution by certified mail of notice of an application to permit service on the institution by first class mail sent to an officer of the institution designated by the institution; or

(3) the institution has waived in writing its entitlement to service by certified mail by designating an officer to receive service.

Rule 7005. Service and Filing of Pleadings and Other Papers

Rule 5 F. R. Civ. P. applies in adversary proceedings.

Rule 7007. Pleadings Allowed

Rule 7 F. R. Civ. P. applies in adversary proceedings.

Rule 7007.1. Corporate Ownership Statement

(a) REQUIRED DISCLOSURE. Any corporation that is a party to an adversary proceeding, other than the debtor or a governmental unit, shall file two copies of a statement that identifies any corporation, other than a governmental unit, that directly or indirectly owns 10% or more of any class of the corporation's equity interests, or states that there are no entities to report under this subdivision.

(b) TIME FOR FILING. A party shall file the statement required under Rule 7007.1(a) with its first appearance, pleading, motion, response, or other request addressed to the court. A party shall file a supplemental statement promptly upon any change in circumstances that this rule requires the party to identify or disclose.

Rule 7008. General Rules of Pleading

Rule 8 F.R.Civ.P. applies in adversary proceedings. The allegation of jurisdiction required by Rule 8(a) shall also contain a reference to the name, number, and chapter of the case under the Code to which the adversary proceeding relates and to the district and division where the case under the Code is pending. In an adversary proceeding before a bankruptcy judge, the complaint, counterclaim, cross-claim, or third-party complaint shall contain a statement that the proceeding is core or non-core and, if non-core, that the pleader does or does not consent to entry of final orders or judgment by the bankruptcy judge.

Rule 7009. Pleading Special Matters

Rule 9 F. R. Civ. P. applies in adversary proceedings.

Rule 7010. Form of Pleadings

Rule 10 F. R. Civ. P. applies in adversary proceedings, except that the caption of each pleading in such a proceeding shall conform substantially to the appropriate Official Form.

Rule 7012. Defenses and Objections — When and How Presented — By Pleading or Motion — Motion for Judgment on the Pleadings

(a) WHEN PRESENTED. If a complaint is duly served, the defendant shall serve an answer within 30 days after the issuance of the summons, except when a different time is prescribed by the court. The court shall prescribe the time for service of the answer when service of a complaint is made by publication or upon a party in a foreign country. A party served with a pleading stating a cross-claim shall serve an answer thereto within 21 days after service. The plaintiff shall serve a reply to a counterclaim in the answer within 21 days after service of the answer or, if a reply is ordered by the court, within 21 days after service of the order, unless the order otherwise directs. The United States or an officer or agency thereof shall serve an answer to a complaint within 35 days after the issuance of the summons, and shall serve an answer to a cross-claim, or a reply to a counterclaim, within 35 days after service upon the United States attorney of the pleading in which the claim is asserted. The service of a motion permitted under this rule alters these periods of time as follows, unless a different time is fixed by order of the court: (1) if the court denies the motion or postpones its disposition until the trial on the merits, the responsive pleading shall be served within 14 days after notice of the court's action; (2) if the court grants a motion for a more definite statement, the responsive pleading shall be served within 14 days after the service of a more definite statement.

(b) APPLICABILITY OF RULE 12(b)-(i) F.R.CIV.P. Rule 12(b)-(i) F.R.Civ.P. applies in adversary proceedings. A responsive pleading shall admit or deny an allegation that the proceeding is core or non-core. If the response is that the proceeding is non-core, it shall include a statement that the party does or does not consent to entry of final orders or judgment by the bankruptcy judge. In non-core proceedings final orders and judgments shall not be entered on the bankruptcy judge's order except with the express consent of the parties.

Rule 7013. Counterclaim and Cross-Claim

Rule 13 F. R. Civ. P. applies in adversary proceedings, except that a party sued by a trustee or debtor in possession need not state as a counterclaim any claim that the party has against the debtor, the debtor's property, or the estate, unless the claim arose after the entry of an order for relief. A trustee or debtor in possession who fails to plead a counterclaim through oversight, inadvertence, or excusable neglect, or when justice so requires, may by leave of court amend the pleading, or commence a new adversary proceeding or separate action.

Rule 7014. Third-Party Practice

Rule 14 F. R. Civ. P. applies in adversary proceedings.

Rule 7015. Amended and Supplemental Pleadings

Rule 15 F. R. Civ. P. applies in adversary proceedings.

Rule 7016. Pre-Trial Procedure; Formulating Issues

Rule 16 F. R. Civ. P. applies in adversary proceedings.

Rule 7017. Parties Plaintiff and Defendant; Capacity

Rule 17 F. R. Civ. P. applies in adversary proceedings, except as provided in Rule 2010(b).

Rule 7018. Joinder of Claims and Remedies

Rule 18 F. R. Civ. P. applies in adversary proceedings.

Rule 7019. Joinder of Persons Needed for Just Determination

Rule 19 F. R. Civ. P. applies in adversary proceedings, except that (1) if an entity joined as a party raises the defense that the court lacks jurisdiction over the subject matter and the defense is sustained, the court shall dismiss such entity from the adversary proceeding and (2) if an entity joined as a party properly and timely raises the defense of improper venue, the court shall determine, as provided in 28 U. S. C. Section 1412, whether that part of the proceeding involving the joined party shall be transferred to another district, or whether the entire adversary proceeding shall be transferred to another district.

Rule 7020. Permissive Joinder of Parties

Rule 20 F. R. Civ. P. applies in adversary proceedings.

Rule 7021. Misjoinder and Non-Joinder of Parties

Rule 21 F. R. Civ. P. applies in adversary proceedings.

Rule 7022. Interpleader

Rule 22(a) F.R.Civ.P. applies in adversary proceedings. This rule supplements – and does not limit – the joinder of parties allowed by Rule 7020.

Rule 7023. Class Proceedings

Rule 23 F. R. Civ. P. applies in adversary proceedings.

Rule 7023.1. Derivative Actions

Rule 23.1 F. R. Civ. P. applies in adversary proceedings.

Rule 7023.2. Adversary Proceedings Relating to Unincorporated Associations

Rule 23.2 F. R. Civ. P. applies in adversary proceedings.

Rule 7024. Intervention

Rule 24 F. R. Civ. P. applies in adversary proceedings.

Rule 7025. Substitution of Parties

Subject to the provisions of Rule 2012, Rule 25 F. R. Civ. P. applies in adversary proceedings.

Rule 7026. General Provisions Governing Discovery

Rule 26 F. R. Civ. P. applies in adversary proceedings.

Rule 7027. Depositions Before Adversary Proceedings or Pending Appeal

Rule 27 F. R. Civ. P. applies in adversary proceedings.

Rule 7028. Persons Before Whom Depositions May Be Taken

Rule 28 F. R. Civ. P. applies in adversary proceedings.

Rule 7029. Stipulations Regarding Discovery Procedure

Rule 29 F. R. Civ. P. applies in adversary proceedings.

Rule 7030. Depositions Upon Oral Examination

Rule 30 F. R. Civ. P. applies in adversary proceedings.

Rule 7031. Deposition Upon Written Questions

Rule 31 F. R. Civ. P. applies in adversary proceedings.

Rule 7032. Use of Depositions in Adversary Proceedings

Rule 32 F. R. Civ. P. applies in adversary proceedings.

Rule 7033. Interrogatories to Parties

Rule 33 F. R. Civ. P. applies in adversary proceedings.

Rule 7034. Production of Documents and Things and Entry Upon Land for Inspection and Other Purposes

Rule 34 F. R. Civ. P. applies in adversary proceedings.

Rule 7035. Physical and Mental Examination of Persons

Rule 35 F. R. Civ. P. applies in adversary proceedings.

Rule 7036. Requests for Admission

Rule 36 F. R. Civ. P. applies in adversary proceedings.

Rule 7037. Failure to Make Discovery: Sanctions

Rule 37 F. R. Civ. P. applies in adversary proceedings.

Rule 7040. Assignment of Cases for Trial

Rule 40 F. R. Civ. P. applies in adversary proceedings.

Rule 7041. Dismissal of Adversary Proceedings

Rule 41 F. R. Civ. P. applies in adversary proceedings, except that a complaint objecting to the debtor's discharge shall not be dismissed at the plaintiff's instance without notice to the trustee, the United States trustee, and such other persons as the court may direct, and only on order of the court containing terms and conditions which the court deems proper.

Rule 7042. Consolidation of Adversary Proceedings; Separate Trials

Rule 42 F. R. Civ. P. applies in adversary proceedings.

Rule 7052. Findings by the Court

Rule 52 F. R. Civ. P. applies in adversary proceedings, except that any motion under subdivision (b) of that rule for amended or additional findings shall be filed no later than 14 days after entry of judgment. In these proceedings, the reference in Rule 52 F.R. Civ. P. to the entry of judgment under Rule 58 F.R. Civ. P. shall be read as a reference to the entry of a judgment or order under Rule 5003(a).

Rule 7054. Judgments; Costs

(a) JUDGMENTS. Rule 54(a)-(c) F.R.Civ.P. applies in adversary proceedings.

(b) COSTS; ATTORNEY FEES.

(1) Costs Other Than Attorney's Fees. The court may allow costs to the prevailing party except when a statute of the United States or these rules otherwise provides. Costs against the United States, its officers and agencies shall be imposed only to the extent permitted by law. Costs may be taxed by the clerk on 14 days' notice; on motion served within seven days thereafter, the action of the clerk may be reviewed by the court.

(2) Attorney's Fees.

(A) Rule 54(d)(2)(A)-(C) and (E) F.R.Civ.P. applies in adversary proceedings except for the reference in Rule 54(d)(2)(C) to Rule 78.

(B) By local rule, the court may establish special procedures to resolve fee-related issues without extensive evidentiary hearings.

Rule 7055. Default

Rule 55 F. R. Civ. P. applies in adversary proceedings.

Rule 7056. Summary Judgment

Rule 56 F. R. Civ. P. applies in adversary proceedings.

Rule 7058. Entering Judgment in Adversary Proceeding

Rule 58 F.R. Civ. P. applies in adversary proceedings. In these proceedings, the reference in Rule 58 F.R. Civ. P. to the civil docket shall be read as a reference to the docket maintained by the clerk under Rule 5003(a).

Rule 7062. Stay of Proceedings to Enforce a Judgment

Rule 62 F. R. Civ. P. applies in adversary proceedings.

Rule 7064. Seizure of Person or Property

Rule 64 F. R. Civ. P. applies in adversary proceedings.

Rule 7065. Injunctions

Rule 65 F. R. Civ. P. applies in adversary proceedings, except that a temporary restraining order or preliminary injunction may be issued on application of a debtor, trustee, or debtor in possession without compliance with Rule 65(c).

Rule 7067. Deposit in Court

Rule 67 F. R. Civ. P. applies in adversary proceedings.

Rule 7068. Offer of Judgment

Rule 68 F. R. Civ. P. applies in adversary proceedings.

Rule 7069. Execution

Rule 69 F. R. Civ. P. applies in adversary proceedings.

Rule 7070. Judgment for Specific Acts; Vesting Title

Rule 70 F. R. Civ. P. applies in adversary proceedings and the court may enter a judgment divesting the title of any party and vesting title in others whenever the real or personal property involved is within the jurisdiction of the court.

Rule 7071. Process in Behalf of and Against Persons Not Parties

Rule 71 F. R. Civ. P. applies in adversary proceedings.

Rule 7087. Transfer of Adversary Proceeding

On motion and after a hearing, the court may transfer an adversary proceeding or any part thereof to another district pursuant to 28 U. S. C. Section 1412, except as provided in Rule 7019(2).

PART VIII

APPEALS TO DISTRICT COURT OR BANKRUPTCY APPELLATE PANEL

Rule 8001. Scope of Part VIII Rules; Definition of "BAP"; Method of Transmission

(a) GENERAL SCOPE. These Part VIII rules govern the procedure in a United States district court and a bankruptcy appellate panel on appeal from a judgment, order, or decree of a bankruptcy court. They also govern certain procedures on appeal to a United States court of appeals under 28 U.S.C. § 158(d).

(b) DEFINITION OF "BAP." "BAP" means a bankruptcy appellate panel established by a circuit's judicial council and authorized to hear appeals from a bankruptcy court under 28 U.S.C. § 158.

(c) METHOD OF TRANSMITTING DOCUMENTS. A document must be sent electronically under these Part VIII rules, unless it is being sent by or to an individual who is not represented by counsel or the court's governing rules permit or require mailing or other means of delivery.

Rule 8002. Time for Filing Notice of Appeal

(a) IN GENERAL.

(1) Fourteen-Day Period. Except as provided in subdivisions (b) and (c), a notice of appeal must be filed with the bankruptcy clerk within 14 days after entry of the judgment, order, or decree being appealed.

(2) Filing Before the Entry of Judgment. A notice of appeal filed after the bankruptcy court announces a decision or order—but before entry of the judgment, order, or decree—is treated as filed on the date of and after the entry.

(3) Multiple Appeals. If one party files a timely notice of appeal, any other party may file a notice of appeal within 14 days after the date when the first notice was filed, or within the time otherwise allowed by this rule, whichever period ends later.

(4) Mistaken Filing in Another Court. If a notice of appeal is mistakenly filed in a district court, BAP, or court of appeals, the clerk of that court must state on the notice the date on which it was received and transmit it to the bankruptcy clerk. The notice of appeal is then considered filed in the bankruptcy court on the date so stated.

(b) EFFECT OF A MOTION ON THE TIME TO APPEAL.

(1) In General. If a party timely files in the bankruptcy court any of the following motions, the time to file an appeal runs for all parties from the entry of the order disposing of the last such remaining motion:

(A) to amend or make additional findings under Rule 7052, whether or not granting the motion would alter the judgment;

(B) to alter or amend the judgment under Rule 9023;

(C) for a new trial under Rule 9023; or

(D) for relief under Rule 9024 if the motion is filed within 14 days after the judgment is entered.

(2) Filing an Appeal Before the Motion is Decided. If a party files a notice of appeal after the court announces or enters a judgment, order, or decree—but before it disposes of any motion listed in subdivision (b)(1)—the notice becomes effective when the order disposing of the last such remaining motion is entered.

(3) Appealing the Ruling on the Motion. If a party intends to challenge an order disposing of any motion listed in subdivision (b)(1)—or the alteration or amendment of a judgment, order, or decree upon the motion—the party must file a notice of appeal or an amended notice of appeal. The notice or amended notice must comply with Rule 8003 or 8004 and be filed within the time prescribed by this rule, measured from the entry of the order disposing of the last such remaining motion.

(4) No Additional Fee. No additional fee is required to file an amended notice of appeal.

(c) APPEAL BY AN INMATE CONFINED IN AN INSTITUTION.

(1) In General. If an inmate confined in an institution files a notice of appeal from a judgment, order, or decree of a bankruptcy court, the notice is timely if it is deposited in the institution's internal mail system on or before the last day for filing. If the institution has a system designed for legal mail, the inmate must use that system to receive the benefit of this rule. Timely filing may be shown by a declaration in compliance with 28 U.S.C. § 1746 or by a notarized statement, either of which must set forth the date of deposit and state that first-class postage has been prepaid.

(2) Multiple Appeals. If an inmate files under this subdivision the first notice of appeal, the 14-day period provided in subdivision (a)(3) for another party to file a notice of appeal runs from the date when the bankruptcy clerk dockets the first notice.

(d) EXTENDING THE TIME TO APPEAL.

(1) When the Time May be Extended. Except as provided in subdivision (d)(2), the bankruptcy court may extend the time to file a notice of appeal upon a party's motion that is filed:

(A) within the time prescribed by this rule; or

(B) within 21 days after that time, if the party shows excusable neglect.

(2) When the Time May Not be Extended. The bankruptcy court may not extend the time to file a notice of appeal if the judgment, order, or decree appealed from:

(A) grants relief from an automatic stay under § 362, 922, 1201, or 1301 of the Code;

(B) authorizes the sale or lease of property or the use of cash collateral under § 363 of the Code;

(C) authorizes the obtaining of credit under § 364 of the Code;

(D) authorizes the assumption or assignment of an executory contract or unexpired lease under § 365 of the Code;

(E) approves a disclosure statement under § 1125 of the Code; or

(F) confirms a plan under § 943, 1129, 1225, or 1325 of the Code.

(3) Time Limits on an Extension. No extension of time may exceed 21 days after the time prescribed by this rule, or 14 days after the order granting the motion to extend time is entered, whichever is later.

Rule 8003. Appeal as of Right—How Taken; Docketing the Appeal

(a) FILING THE NOTICE OF APPEAL.

(1) In General. An appeal from a judgment, order, or decree of a bankruptcy court to a district court or BAP under 28 U.S.C. § 158(a)(1) or (a)(2) may be taken only by filing a notice of appeal with the bankruptcy clerk within the time allowed by Rule 8002.

(2) Effect of Not Taking Other Steps. An appellant's failure to take any step other than the timely filing of a notice of appeal does not affect the validity of the appeal, but is ground only for the district court or BAP to act as it considers appropriate, including dismissing the appeal.

(3) Contents. The notice of appeal must:

(A) conform substantially to the appropriate

Official Form;

(B) be accompanied by the judgment, order, or decree, or the part of it, being appealed; and

(C) be accompanied by the prescribed fee.

(4) Additional Copies. If requested to do so, the appellant must furnish the bankruptcy clerk with enough copies of the notice to enable the clerk to comply with subdivision (c).

(b) JOINT OR CONSOLIDATED APPEALS.

(1) Joint Notice of Appeal. When two or more parties are entitled to appeal from a judgment, order, or decree of a bankruptcy court and their interests make joinder practicable, they may file a joint notice of appeal. They may then proceed on appeal as a single appellant.

(2) Consolidating Appeals. When parties have separately filed timely notices of appeal, the district court or BAP may join or consolidate the appeals.

(c) SERVING THE NOTICE OF APPEAL.

(1) Serving Parties and Transmitting to the United States Trustee. The bankruptcy clerk must serve the notice of appeal on counsel of record for each party to the appeal, excluding the appellant, and transmit it to the United States trustee. If a party is proceeding pro se, the clerk must send the notice of appeal to the party's last known address. The clerk must note, on each copy, the date when the notice of appeal was filed.

(2) Effect of Failing to Serve or Transmit Notice. The bankruptcy clerk's failure to serve notice on a party or transmit notice to the United States trustee does not affect the validity of the appeal.

(3) Noting Service on the Docket. The clerk must note on the docket the names of the parties served and the date and method of the service.

(d) TRANSMITTING THE NOTICE OF APPEAL TO THE DISTRICT COURT OR BAP; DOCKETING THE APPEAL.

(1) Transmitting the Notice. The bankruptcy clerk must promptly transmit the notice of appeal to the BAP clerk if a BAP has been established for appeals from that district and the appellant has not elected to have the district court hear the appeal. Otherwise, the bankruptcy clerk must promptly transmit the notice to the district clerk.

(2) Docketing in the District Court or BAP. Upon receiving the notice of appeal, the district or BAP clerk must docket the appeal under the title of the bankruptcy case and the title of any adversary proceeding, and must identify the appellant, adding the appellant's name if necessary.

Rule 8004. Appeal by Leave—How Taken; Docketing the Appeal

(a) NOTICE OF APPEAL AND MOTION FOR LEAVE TO APPEAL. To appeal from an interlocutory order or decree of a bankruptcy court under 28 U.S.C. § 158(a)(3), a party must file with the bankruptcy clerk a notice of appeal as prescribed by Rule 8003(a). The notice must:

(1) be filed within the time allowed by Rule 8002;

(2) be accompanied by a motion for leave to appeal prepared in accordance with subdivision (b); and

(3) unless served electronically using the court's transmission equipment, include proof of service in accordance with Rule 8011(d).

(b) CONTENTS OF THE MOTION; RESPONSE.

(1) Contents. A motion for leave to appeal under 28 U.S.C. § 158(a)(3) must include the following:

(A) the facts necessary to understand the question presented;

(B) the question itself;

(C) the relief sought;

(D) the reasons why leave to appeal should be granted; and

(E) a copy of the interlocutory order or decree and any related opinion or memorandum.

(2) Response. A party may file with the district or BAP clerk a response in opposition or a cross-motion within 14 days after the motion is served.

(c) TRANSMITTING THE NOTICE OF APPEAL AND THE MOTION; DOCKETING THE APPEAL; DETERMINING THE MOTION.

(1) Transmitting to the District Court or BAP. The bankruptcy clerk must promptly transmit the notice of appeal and the motion for leave to the BAP clerk if a BAP has been established for appeals from that district and the appellant has not elected to have the district court hear the appeal. Otherwise, the bankruptcy clerk must promptly transmit the notice and motion to the district clerk.

(2) Docketing in the District Court or BAP. Upon receiving the notice and motion, the district or BAP clerk must docket the appeal under the title of the bankruptcy case and the title of any adversary proceeding, and must identify the appellant, adding the appellant's name if necessary.

(3) Oral Argument Not Required. The motion and any response or cross-motion are submitted without oral argument unless the district court or BAP orders otherwise.

(d) FAILURE TO FILE A MOTION WITH A NOTICE OF APPEAL. If an appellant timely files a notice of appeal under this rule but does not include a motion for leave, the district court or BAP may order the appellant to file a motion for leave, or treat the notice of appeal as a motion for leave and either grant or deny it. If the court orders that a motion for leave be filed, the appellant must do so within 14 days after the order is entered, unless the order provides otherwise.

(e) DIRECT APPEAL TO A COURT OF APPEALS. If leave to appeal an interlocutory order or decree is required under 28 U.S.C. § 158(a)(3), an authorization of a direct appeal by the court of appeals under 28 U.S.C. § 158(d)(2) satisfies the requirement.

Rule 8005. Election to Have an Appeal Heard by the District Court Instead of the BAP

(a) FILING OF A STATEMENT OF ELECTION. To elect to have an appeal heard by the district court, a party must:

(1) file a statement of election that conforms substantially to the appropriate Official Form; and

(2) do so within the time prescribed by 28 U.S.C. § 158(c)(1).

(b) TRANSMITTING THE DOCUMENTS RELATED TO THE APPEAL. Upon receiving an appellant's timely statement of election, the bankruptcy clerk must transmit to the district clerk all documents related to the appeal. Upon receiving a timely statement of election by a party other than the appellant, the BAP clerk must transmit to the district clerk all documents related to the appeal and notify the bankruptcy clerk of the transmission.

(c) DETERMINING THE VALIDITY OF AN ELECTION. A party seeking a determination of the validity of an election must file a motion in the court where the appeal is then pending. The motion must be filed within 14 days after the statement of election is filed.

(d) MOTION FOR LEAVE WITHOUT A NOTICE OF APPEAL—EFFECT ON THE TIMING OF AN ELECTION. If an appellant moves for leave to appeal under Rule 8004 but fails to file a separate notice of appeal with the motion, the motion must be treated as a notice of appeal for purposes of determining the timeliness of a statement of election.

Rule 8006. Certifying a Direct Appeal to the Court of Appeals

(a) EFFECTIVE DATE OF A CERTIFICATION. A certification of a judgment, order, or decree of a bankruptcy court for direct review in a court of appeals under 28 U.S.C. § 158(d)(2) is effective when:

(1) the certification has been filed;

(2) a timely appeal has been taken under Rule 8003 or 8004; and

(3) the notice of appeal has become effective under Rule 8002.

(b) FILING THE CERTIFICATION. The certification must be filed with the clerk of the court where the matter is pending. For purposes of this rule, a matter remains pending in the bankruptcy court for 30 days after the effective date under Rule 8002 of the first notice of appeal from the judgment, order, or decree for which direct review is sought. A matter is pending in the district court or BAP thereafter.

(c) JOINT CERTIFICATION BY ALL APPELLANTS AND APPELLEES. A joint certification by all the appellants and appellees under 28 U.S.C. § 158(d)(2)(A) must be made by using the appropriate Official Form. The parties may supplement the certification with a short statement of the basis for the certification, which may include the information listed in subdivision (f)(2).

(d) THE COURT THAT MAY MAKE THE CERTIFICATION. Only the court where the matter is pending, as provided in subdivision (b), may certify a direct review on request of parties or on its own motion.

(e) CERTIFICATION ON THE COURT'S OWN MOTION.

(1) How Accomplished. A certification on the court's own motion must be set forth in a separate document. The clerk of the certifying court must serve it on the parties to the appeal in the manner required for service of a notice of appeal under Rule 8003(c)(1). The certification must be accompanied by an opinion or memorandum that contains the information required by subdivision (f)(2)(A)-(D).

(2) Supplemental Statement by a Party. Within 14 days after

the court's certification, a party may file with the clerk of the certifying court a short supplemental statement regarding the merits of certification.

(f) CERTIFICATION BY THE COURT ON REQUEST.

(1) How Requested. A request by a party for certification that a circumstance specified in 28 U.S.C. §158(d)(2)(A)(i)-(iii) applies—or a request by a majority of the appellants and a majority of the appellees—must be filed with the clerk of the court where the matter is pending within 60 days after the entry of the judgment, order, or decree.

(2) Service and Contents. The request must be served on all parties to the appeal in the manner required for service of a notice of appeal under Rule 8003(c)(1), and it must include the following:

(A) the facts necessary to understand the question presented;

(B) the question itself;

(C) the relief sought;

(D) the reasons why the direct appeal should be allowed, including which circumstance specified in 28 U.S.C. § 158(d)(2)(A)(i)-(iii) applies; and

(E) a copy of the judgment, order, or decree and any related opinion or memorandum.

(3) Time to File a Response or a Cross-Request. A party may file a response to the request within 14 days after the request is served, or such other time as the court where the matter is pending allows. A party may file a cross-request for certification within 14 days after the request is served, or within 60 days after the entry of the judgment, order, or decree, whichever occurs first.

(4) Oral Argument Not Required. The request, cross-request, and any response are submitted without oral argument unless the court where the matter is pending orders otherwise.

(5) Form and Service of the Certification. If the court certifies a direct appeal in response to the request, it must do so in a separate document. The certification must be served on the parties to the appeal in the manner required for service of a notice of appeal under Rule 8003(c)(1).

(g) PROCEEDING IN THE COURT OF APPEALS FOLLOWING A CERTIFICATION. Within 30 days after the date the certification becomes effective under subdivision (a), a request for permission to take a direct appeal to the court of appeals must be filed with the circuit clerk in accordance with F.R.App.P. 6(c).

Rule 8007. Stay Pending Appeal; Bonds; Suspension of Proceedings

(a) INITIAL MOTION IN THE BANKRUPTCY COURT.

(1) In General. Ordinarily, a party must move first in the bankruptcy court for the following relief:

(A) a stay of a judgment, order, or decree of the bankruptcy court pending appeal;

(B) the approval of a supersedeas bond;

(C) an order suspending, modifying, restoring, or granting an injunction while an appeal is pending; or

(D) the suspension or continuation of proceedings in a case or other relief permitted by subdivision (e).

(2) Time to File. The motion may be made either before or after the notice of appeal is filed.

(b) MOTION IN THE DISTRICT COURT, THE BAP, OR THE COURT OF APPEALS ON DIRECT APPEAL.

(1) Request for Relief. A motion for the relief specified in subdivision (a)(1)—or to vacate or modify a bankruptcy court's order granting such relief—may be made in the court where the appeal is pending.

(2) Showing or Statement Required. The motion must:

(A) show that moving first in the bankruptcy court would be impracticable; or

(B) if a motion was made in the bankruptcy court, either state that the court has not yet ruled on the motion, or state that the court has ruled and set out any reasons given for the ruling.

(3) Additional Content. The motion must also include:

(A) the reasons for granting the relief requested and the facts relied upon;

(B) affidavits or other sworn statements supporting facts subject to dispute; and

(C) relevant parts of the record.

(4) Serving Notice. The movant must give reasonable notice of the motion to all parties.

(c) FILING A BOND OR OTHER SECURITY. The district court, BAP, or court of appeals may condition relief on filing a bond or other appropriate security with the bankruptcy court.

(d) BOND FOR A TRUSTEE OR THE UNITED STATES. The court may require a trustee to file a bond or other appropriate security when the trustee appeals. A bond or other security is not required when an appeal is taken by the United States, its officer, or its agency or by direction of any department of the federal government.

(e) CONTINUATION OF PROCEEDINGS IN THE BANKRUPTCY COURT. Despite Rule 7062 and subject to the authority of the district court, BAP, or court of appeals, the bankruptcy court may:

(1) suspend or order the continuation of other proceedings in the case; or

(2) issue any other appropriate orders during the pendency of an appeal to protect the rights of all parties in interest.

Rule 8008. Indicative Rulings

(a) RELIEF PENDING APPEAL. If a party files a timely motion in the bankruptcy court for relief that the court lacks authority to grant because of an appeal that has been docketed and is pending, the bankruptcy court may:

(1) defer considering the motion;

(2) deny the motion; or

(3) state that the court would grant the motion if the court where the appeal is pending remands for that purpose, or state that the motion raises a substantial issue.

(b) NOTICE TO THE COURT WHERE THE APPEAL IS PENDING. The movant must promptly notify the clerk of the court where the appeal is pending if the bankruptcy court states that it would grant the motion or that the motion raises a substantial issue.

(c) REMAND AFTER AN INDICATIVE RULING. If the bankruptcy court states that it would grant the motion or that the motion raises a substantial issue, the district court or BAP may remand for further proceedings, but it retains jurisdiction unless it expressly dismisses the appeal. If the district court or BAP remands but retains jurisdiction, the parties must promptly notify the clerk of that court when the bankruptcy court has decided the motion on remand.

Rule 8009. Record on Appeal; Sealed Documents

(a) DESIGNATING THE RECORD ON APPEAL; STATEMENT OF THE ISSUES.

(1) Appellant.

(A) The appellant must file with the bankruptcy clerk and serve on the appellee a designation of the items to be included in the record on appeal and a statement of the issues to be presented.

(B) The appellant must file and serve the designation and statement within 14 days after:

(i) the appellant's notice of appeal as of right becomes effective under Rule 8002; or

(ii) an order granting leave to appeal is entered.

A designation and statement served prematurely must be treated as served on the first day on which filing is timely.

(2) Appellee and Cross-Appellant. Within 14 days after being served, the appellee may file with the bankruptcy clerk and serve on the appellant a designation of additional items to be included in the record. An appellee who files a cross-appeal must file and serve a designation of additional items to be included in the record and a statement of the issues to be presented on the cross-appeal.

(3) Cross-Appellee. Within 14 days after service of the cross-appellant's designation and statement, a cross-appellee may file with the bankruptcy clerk and serve on the cross-appellant a designation of additional items to be included in the record.

(4) Record on Appeal. The record on appeal must include the following:

- docket entries kept by the bankruptcy clerk;
- items designated by the parties;
- the notice of appeal;
- the judgment, order, or decree being appealed;
- any order granting leave to appeal;
- any certification required for a direct appeal to the court of appeals;

- any opinion, findings of fact, and conclusions of law relating to the issues on appeal, including transcripts of all oral rulings;
- any transcript ordered under subdivision (b);
- any statement required by subdivision (c); and
- any additional items from the record that the court where the appeal is pending orders.

(5) Copies for the Bankruptcy Clerk. If paper copies are needed, a party filing a designation of items must provide a copy of any of those items that the bankruptcy clerk requests. If the party fails to do so, the bankruptcy clerk must prepare the copy at the party's expense.

(b) TRANSCRIPT OF PROCEEDINGS.

(1) Appellant's Duty to Order. Within the time period prescribed by subdivision (a)(1), the appellant must:

(A) order in writing from the reporter, as defined in Rule 8010(a)(1), a transcript of such parts of the proceedings not already on file as the appellant considers necessary for the appeal, and file a copy of the order with the bankruptcy clerk; or

(B) file with the bankruptcy clerk a certificate stating that the appellant is not ordering a transcript.

(2) Cross-Appellant's Duty to Order. Within 14 days after the appellant files a copy of the transcript order or a certificate of not ordering a transcript, the appellee as cross-appellant must:

(A) order in writing from the reporter, as defined in Rule 8010(a)(1), a transcript of such additional parts of the proceedings as the cross-appellant considers necessary for the appeal, and file a copy of the order with the bankruptcy clerk; or

(B) file with the bankruptcy clerk a certificate stating that the cross-appellant is not ordering a transcript.

(3) Appellee's or Cross-Appellee's Right to Order. Within 14 days after the appellant or cross-appellant files a copy of a transcript order or certificate of not ordering a transcript, the appellee or cross-appellee may order in writing from the reporter a transcript of such additional parts of the proceedings as the appellee or cross-appellee considers necessary for the appeal. A copy of the order must be filed with the bankruptcy clerk.

(4) Payment. At the time of ordering, a party must make satisfactory arrangements with the reporter for paying the cost of the transcript.

(5) Unsupported Finding or Conclusion. If the appellant intends to argue on appeal that a finding or conclusion is unsupported by the evidence or is contrary to the evidence, the appellant must include in the record a transcript of all relevant testimony and copies of all relevant exhibits.

(c) STATEMENT OF THE EVIDENCE WHEN A TRANSCRIPT IS UNAVAILABLE. If a transcript of a hearing or trial is unavailable, the appellant may prepare a statement of the evidence or proceedings from the best available means, including the appellant's recollection. The statement must be filed within the time prescribed by subdivision (a)(1) and served on the appellee, who may serve objections or proposed amendments within 14 days after being served. The statement and any objections or proposed amendments must then be submitted to the bankruptcy court for settlement and approval. As settled and approved, the statement must be included by the bankruptcy clerk in the record on appeal.

(d) AGREED STATEMENT AS THE RECORD ON APPEAL. Instead of the record on appeal as defined in subdivision (a), the parties may prepare, sign, and submit to the bankruptcy court a statement of the case showing how the issues presented by the appeal arose and were decided in the bankruptcy court. The statement must set forth only those facts alleged and proved or sought to be proved that are essential to the court's resolution of the issues. If the statement is accurate, it—together with any additions that the bankruptcy court may consider necessary to a full presentation of the issues on appeal—must be approved by the bankruptcy court and must then be certified to the court where the appeal is pending as the record on appeal. The bankruptcy clerk must then transmit it to the clerk of that court within the time provided by Rule 8010. A copy of the agreed statement may be filed in place of the appendix required by Rule 8018(b) or, in the case of a direct appeal to the court of appeals, by F.R.App.P. 30.

(e) CORRECTING OR MODIFYING THE RECORD.

(1) Submitting to the Bankruptcy Court. If any difference arises about whether the record accurately discloses what occurred in the bankruptcy court, the difference must be submitted to and settled by the bankruptcy court and the record conformed accordingly. If an item has been improperly designated as part of the record on appeal, a party may move to strike that item.

(2) Correcting in Other Ways. If anything material to either party is omitted from or misstated in the record by error or accident, the omission or misstatement may be corrected, and a supplemental record may be certified and transmitted:

(A) on stipulation of the parties;

(B) by the bankruptcy court before or after the record has been forwarded; or

(C) by the court where the appeal is pending.

(3) Remaining Questions. All other questions as to the form and content of the record must be presented to the court where the appeal is pending.

(f) SEALED DOCUMENTS. A document placed under seal by the bankruptcy court may be designated as part of the record on appeal. In doing so, a party must identify it without revealing confidential or secret information, but the bankruptcy clerk must not transmit it to the clerk of the court where the appeal is pending as part of the record. Instead, a party must file a motion with the court where the appeal is pending to accept the document under seal. If the motion is granted, the movant must notify the bankruptcy court of the ruling, and the bankruptcy clerk must promptly transmit the sealed document to the clerk of the court where the appeal is pending.

(g) OTHER NECESSARY ACTIONS. All parties to an appeal must take any other action necessary to enable the bankruptcy clerk to assemble and transmit the record.

Rule 8010. Completing and Transmitting the Record

(a) REPORTER'S DUTIES.

(1) Proceedings Recorded Without a Reporter Present. If proceedings were recorded without a reporter being present, the person or service selected under bankruptcy court procedures to transcribe the recording is the reporter for purposes of this rule.

(2) Preparing and Filing the Transcript. The reporter must prepare and file a transcript as follows:

(A) Upon receiving an order for a transcript in accordance with Rule 8009(b), the reporter must file in the bankruptcy court an acknowledgment of the request that shows when it was received, and when the reporter expects to have the transcript completed.

(B) After completing the transcript, the reporter must file it with the bankruptcy clerk, who will notify the district, BAP, or circuit clerk of its filing.

(C) If the transcript cannot be completed within 30 days after receiving the order, the reporter must request an extension of time from the bankruptcy clerk. The clerk must enter on the docket and notify the parties whether the extension is granted.

(D) If the reporter does not file the transcript on time, the bankruptcy clerk must notify the bankruptcy judge.

(b) CLERK'S DUTIES.

(1) Transmitting the Record—In General. Subject to Rule 8009(f) and subdivision (b)(5) of this rule, when the record is complete, the bankruptcy clerk must transmit to the clerk of the court where the appeal is pending either the record or a notice that the record is available electronically.

(2) Multiple Appeals. If there are multiple appeals from a judgment, order, or decree, the bankruptcy clerk must transmit a single record.

(3) Receiving the Record. Upon receiving the record or notice that it is available electronically, the district, BAP, or circuit clerk must enter that information on the docket and promptly notify all parties to the appeal.

(4) If Paper Copies Are Ordered. If the court where the appeal is pending directs that paper copies of the record be provided, the clerk of that court must so notify the appellant. If the appellant fails to provide them, the bankruptcy clerk must prepare them at the appellant's expense.

(5) When Leave to Appeal is Requested. Subject to subdivision (c), if a motion for leave to appeal has been filed under Rule 8004, the bankruptcy clerk must prepare and transmit the record only after the district court, BAP, or court of appeals grants leave.

(c) RECORD FOR A PRELIMINARY MOTION IN THE DISTRICT COURT, BAP, OR COURT OF APPEALS. This subdivision (c) applies if, before the record is transmitted, a party moves in the district court, BAP, or court of appeals for any of the following relief:

- leave to appeal;
- dismissal;
- a stay pending appeal;
- approval of a supersedeas bond, or additional security on a bond or undertaking on appeal; or
- any other intermediate order.

The bankruptcy clerk must then transmit to the clerk of the court where the relief is sought any parts of the record designated by a party to the appeal or a notice that those parts are available electronically.

Rule 8011. Filing and Service; Signature

(a) FILING.

(1) With the Clerk. A document required or permitted to be filed in a district court or BAP must be filed with the clerk of that court.

(2) Method and Timeliness.

(A) In General. Filing may be accomplished by transmission to the clerk of the district court or BAP. Except as provided in subdivision (a)(2)(B) and (C), filing is timely only if the clerk receives the document within the time fixed for filing.

(B) Brief or Appendix. A brief or appendix is also timely filed if, on or before the last day for filing, it is:

(i) mailed to the clerk by first-class mail—or other class of mail that is at least as expeditious—postage prepaid, if the district court's or BAP's procedures permit or require a brief or appendix to be filed by mailing; or

(ii) dispatched to a third-party commercial carrier for delivery within 3 days to the clerk, if the court's procedures so permit or require.

(C) Inmate Filing. A document filed by an inmate confined in an institution is timely if deposited in the institution's internal mailing system on or before the last day for filing. If the institution has a system designed for legal mail, the inmate must use that system to receive the benefit of this rule. Timely filing may be shown by a declaration in compliance with 28 U.S.C. § 1746 or by a notarized statement, either of which must set forth the date of deposit and state that first-class postage has been prepaid.

(D) Copies. If a document is filed electronically, no paper copy is required. If a document is filed by mail or delivery to the district court or BAP, no additional copies are required. But the district court or BAP may require by local rule or by order in a particular case the filing or furnishing of a specified number of paper copies.

(3) Clerk's Refusal of Documents. The court's clerk must not refuse to accept for filing any document transmitted for that purpose solely because it is not presented in proper form as required by these rules or by any local rule or practice.

(b) SERVICE OF ALL DOCUMENTS REQUIRED. Unless a rule requires service by the clerk, a party must, at or before the time of the filing of a document, serve it on the other parties to the appeal. Service on a party represented by counsel must be made on the party's counsel.

(c) MANNER OF SERVICE.

(1) Methods. Service must be made electronically, unless it is being made by or on an individual who is not represented by counsel or the court's governing rules permit or require service by mail or other means of delivery. Service may be made by or on an unrepresented party by any of the following methods:

(A) personal delivery;

(B) mail; or

(C) third-party commercial carrier for delivery within 3 days.

(2) When Service is Complete. Service by electronic means is complete on transmission, unless the party making service receives notice that the document was not transmitted successfully. Service by mail or by commercial carrier is complete on mailing or delivery to the carrier.

(d) PROOF OF SERVICE.

(1) What is Required. A document presented for filing must contain either:

(A) an acknowledgment of service by the person served; or

(B) proof of service consisting of a statement by the person who made service certifying:

(i) the date and manner of service;

(ii) the names of the persons served; and

(iii) the mail or electronic address, the fax number, or the address of the place of delivery, as appropriate for the manner of service, for each person served.

(2) Delayed Proof. The district or BAP clerk may permit documents to be filed without acknowledgment or proof of service, but must require the acknowledgment or proof to be filed promptly thereafter.

(3) Brief or Appendix. When a brief or appendix is filed, the proof of service must also state the date and manner by which it was filed.

(e) SIGNATURE. Every document filed electronically must include the electronic signature of the person filing it or, if the person is represented, the electronic signature of counsel. The electronic signature must be provided by electronic means that are consistent with any technical standards that the Judicial Conference of the United States establishes. Every document filed in paper form must be signed by the person filing the document or, if the person is represented, by counsel.

Rule 8012. Corporate Disclosure Statement

(a) WHO MUST FILE. Any nongovernmental corporate party appearing in the district court or BAP must file a statement that identifies any parent corporation and any publicly held corporation that owns 10% or more of its stock or states that there is no such corporation.

(b) TIME TO FILE; SUPPLEMENTAL FILING. A party must file the statement with its principal brief or upon filing a motion, response, petition, or answer in the district court or BAP, whichever occurs first, unless a local rule requires earlier filing. Even if the statement has already been filed, the party's principal brief must include a statement before the table of contents. A party must supplement its statement whenever the required information changes.

Rule 8013. Motions; Intervention

(a) CONTENTS OF A MOTION; RESPONSE; REPLY.

(1) Request for Relief. A request for an order or other relief is made by filing a motion with the district or BAP clerk, with proof of service on the other parties to the appeal.

(2) Contents of a Motion.

(A) Grounds and the Relief Sought. A motion must state with particularity the grounds for the motion, the relief sought, and the legal argument necessary to support it.

(B) Motion to Expedite an Appeal. A motion to expedite an appeal must explain what justifies considering the appeal ahead of other matters. If the district court or BAP grants the motion, it may accelerate the time to transmit the record, the deadline for filing briefs and other documents, oral argument, and the resolution of the appeal. A motion to expedite an appeal may be filed as an emergency motion under subdivision (d).

(C) Accompanying Documents.

(i) Any affidavit or other document necessary to support a motion must be served and filed with the motion.

(ii) An affidavit must contain only factual information, not legal argument.

(iii) A motion seeking substantive relief must include a copy of the bankruptcy court's judgment, order, or decree, and any accompanying opinion as a separate exhibit.

(D) Documents Barred or Not Required.

(i) A separate brief supporting or responding to a motion must not be filed.

(ii) Unless the court orders otherwise, a notice of motion or a proposed order is not required.

(3) Response and Reply; Time to File. Unless the district court or BAP orders otherwise,

(A) any party to the appeal may file a response to the motion within 7 days after service of the motion; and

(B) the movant may file a reply to a response within 7 days after service of the response, but may only address matters raised in the response.

(b) DISPOSITION OF A MOTION FOR A PROCEDURAL ORDER. The district court or BAP may rule on a motion for a procedural order—including a motion under Rule 9006(b) or (c)—at any time without awaiting a response. A party adversely affected by the ruling may move to reconsider, vacate, or modify it within 7 days after the procedural order is served.

(c) ORAL ARGUMENT. A motion will be decided without oral argument unless the district court or BAP orders otherwise.

(d) EMERGENCY MOTION.

(1) Noting the Emergency. When a movant requests expedited action on a motion because irreparable harm would occur during the time needed to consider a response, the movant must insert the word "Emergency" before the title of the motion.

(2) Contents of the Motion. The emergency motion must

(A) be accompanied by an affidavit setting out the

nature of the emergency;

(B) state whether all grounds for it were submitted to the bankruptcy court and, if not, why the motion should not be remanded for the bankruptcy court to consider;

(C) include the e-mail addresses, office addresses, and telephone numbers of moving counsel and, when known, of opposing counsel and any unrepresented parties to the appeal; and

(D) be served as prescribed by Rule 8011.

(3) Notifying Opposing Parties. Before filing an emergency motion, the movant must make every practicable effort to notify opposing counsel and any unrepresented parties in time for them to respond. The affidavit accompanying the emergency motion must state when and how notice was given or state why giving it was impracticable.

(e) POWER OF A SINGLE BAP JUDGE TO ENTERTAIN A MOTION.

(1) Single Judge's Authority. A BAP judge may act alone on any motion, but may not dismiss or otherwise determine an appeal, deny a motion for leave to appeal, or deny a motion for a stay pending appeal if denial would make the appeal moot.

(2) Reviewing a Single Judge's Action. The BAP may review a single judge's action, either on its own motion or on a party's motion.

(f) FORM OF DOCUMENTS; PAGE LIMITS; NUMBER OF COPIES.

(1) Format of a Paper Document. Rule 27(d)(1) F.R.App.P. applies in the district court or BAP to a paper version of a motion, response, or reply.

(2) Format of an Electronically Filed Document. A motion, response, or reply filed electronically must comply with the requirements for a paper version regarding covers, line spacing, margins, typeface, and type style. It must also comply with the page limits under paragraph (3).

(3) Page Limits. Unless the district court or BAP orders otherwise:

(A) a motion or a response to a motion must not exceed 20 pages, exclusive of the corporate disclosure statement and accompanying documents authorized by subdivision (a)(2)(C); and

(B) a reply to a response must not exceed 10 pages.

(4) Paper Copies. Paper copies must be provided only if required by local rule or by an order in a particular case.

(g) INTERVENING IN AN APPEAL. Unless a statute provides otherwise, an entity that seeks to intervene in an appeal pending in the district court or BAP must move for leave to intervene and serve a copy of the motion on the parties to the appeal. The motion or other notice of intervention authorized by statute must be filed within 30 days after the appeal is docketed. It must concisely state the movant's interest, the grounds for intervention, whether intervention was sought in the bankruptcy court, why intervention is being sought at this stage of the proceeding, and why participating as an amicus curiae would not be adequate.

Rule 8014. Briefs

(a) APPELLANT'S BRIEF. The appellant's brief must contain the following under appropriate headings and in the order indicated:

(1) a corporate disclosure statement, if required by Rule 8012;

(2) a table of contents, with page references;

(3) a table of authorities—cases (alphabetically arranged), statutes, and other authorities—with references to the pages of the brief where they are cited;

(4) a jurisdictional statement, including:

(A) the basis for the bankruptcy court's subject-matter jurisdiction, with citations to applicable statutory provisions and stating relevant facts establishing jurisdiction;

(B) the basis for the district court's or BAP's jurisdiction, with citations to applicable statutory provisions and stating relevant facts establishing jurisdiction;

(C) the filing dates establishing the timeliness of the appeal; and

(D) an assertion that the appeal is from a final judgment, order, or decree, or information establishing the district court's or BAP's jurisdiction on another basis;

(5) a statement of the issues presented and, for each one, a concise statement of the applicable standard of appellate review;

(6) a concise statement of the case setting out the facts relevant to the issues submitted for review, describing the relevant procedural history, and identifying the rulings presented for review, with appropriate references to the record;

(7) a summary of the argument, which must contain a succinct, clear, and accurate statement of the arguments made in the body of the brief, and which must not merely repeat the argument headings;

(8) the argument, which must contain the appellant's contentions and the reasons for them, with citations to the authorities and parts of the record on which the appellant relies;

(9) a short conclusion stating the precise relief sought; and

(10) the certificate of compliance, if required by Rule 8015(a)(7) or (b).

(b) APPELLEE'S BRIEF. The appellee's brief must conform to the requirements of subdivision (a)(1)-(8) and (10), except that none of the following need appear unless the appellee is dissatisfied with the appellant's statement:

(1) the jurisdictional statement;

(2) the statement of the issues and the applicable standard of appellate review; and

(3) the statement of the case.

(c) REPLY BRIEF. The appellant may file a brief in reply to the appellee's brief. A reply brief must comply with the requirements of subdivision (a)(2)-(3).

(d) STATUTES, RULES, REGULATIONS, OR SIMILAR AUTHORITY. If the court's determination of the issues presented requires the study of the Code or other statutes, rules, regulations, or similar authority, the relevant parts must be set out in the brief or in an addendum.

(e) BRIEFS IN A CASE INVOLVING MULTIPLE APPELLANTS OR APPELLEES. In a case involving more than one appellant or appellee, including consolidated cases, any number of appellants or appellees may join in a brief, and any party may adopt by reference a part of another's brief. Parties may also join in reply briefs.

(f) CITATION OF SUPPLEMENTAL AUTHORITIES. If pertinent and significant authorities come to a party's attention after the party's brief has been filed—or after oral argument but before a decision—a party may promptly advise the district or BAP clerk by a signed submission setting forth the citations. The submission, which must be served on the other parties to the appeal, must state the reasons for the supplemental citations, referring either to the pertinent page of a brief or to a point argued orally. The body of the submission must not exceed 350 words. Any response must be made within 7 days after the party is served, unless the court orders otherwise, and must be similarly limited.

Rule 8015. Form and Length of Briefs; Form of Appendices and Other Papers

(a) PAPER COPIES OF A BRIEF. If a paper copy of a brief may or must be filed, the following provisions apply:

(1) Reproduction.

(A) A brief may be reproduced by any process that yields a clear black image on light paper. The paper must be opaque and unglazed. Only one side of the paper may be used.

(B) Text must be reproduced with a clarity that equals or exceeds the output of a laser printer.

(C) Photographs, illustrations, and tables may be reproduced by any method that results in a good copy of the original. A glossy finish is acceptable if the original is glossy.

(2) Cover. The front cover of a brief must contain:

(A) the number of the case centered at the top;

(B) the name of the court;

(C) the title of the case as prescribed by Rule 8003(d)(2) or 8004(c)(2);

(D) the nature of the proceeding and the name of the court below;

(E) the title of the brief, identifying the party or parties for whom the brief is filed; and

(F) the name, office address, telephone number, and e-mail address of counsel representing the party for whom the brief is filed.

(3) Binding. The brief must be bound in any manner that is secure, does not obscure the text, and permits the brief to lie reasonably flat when open.

(4) Paper Size, Line Spacing, and Margins. The brief must be on 8½-by-11 inch paper. The text must be double-spaced, but quotations more than two lines long may be indented and single-spaced. Headings and footnotes may be single-spaced. Margins must be at least one inch on all four sides. Page numbers may be placed in the margins, but no text may appear there.

(5) Typeface. Either a proportionally spaced or monospaced face may be used.

(A) A proportionally spaced face must include serifs, but sans-serif type may be used in headings and captions. A proportionally spaced face must be 14-point or larger.

(B) A monospaced face may not contain more than 10½ characters per inch.

(6) Type Styles. A brief must be set in plain, roman style, although italics or boldface may be used for emphasis. Case names must be italicized or underlined.

(7) Length.

(A) Page limitation. A principal brief must not exceed 30 pages, or a reply brief 15 pages, unless it complies with (B) and (C).

(B) Type-volume limitation.

(i) A principal brief is acceptable if:

- it contains no more than 14,000 words; or
- it uses a monospaced face and contains no more than 1,300 lines of text.

(ii) A reply brief is acceptable if it contains no more than half of the type volume specified in item (i).

(iii) Headings, footnotes, and quotations count toward the word and line limitations. The corporate disclosure statement, table of contents, table of citations, statement with respect to oral argument, any addendum containing statutes, rules, or regulations, and any certificates of counsel do not count toward the limitation.

(C) Certificate of Compliance.

(i) A brief submitted under subdivision (a)(7)(B) must include a certificate signed by the attorney, or an unrepresented party, that the brief complies with the type-volume limitation. The person preparing the certificate may rely on the word or line count of the word-processing system used to prepare the brief. The certificate must state either:

- the number of words in the brief; or
- the number of lines of monospaced type in the brief.

(ii) The certification requirement is satisfied by a certificate of compliance that conforms substantially to the appropriate Official Form.

(b) ELECTRONICALLY FILED BRIEFS. A brief filed electronically must comply with subdivision (a), except for (a)(1), (a)(3), and the paper requirement of (a)(4).

(c) PAPER COPIES OF APPENDICES. A paper copy of an appendix must comply with subdivision (a)(1), (2), (3), and (4), with the following exceptions:

(1) An appendix may include a legible photocopy of any document found in the record or of a printed decision.

(2) When necessary to facilitate inclusion of odd-sized documents such as technical drawings, an appendix may be a size other than 8½-by-11 inches, and need not lie reasonably flat when opened.

(d) ELECTRONICALLY FILED APPENDICES. An appendix filed electronically must comply with subdivision (a)(2) and (4), except for the paper requirement of (a)(4).

(e) OTHER DOCUMENTS.

(1) Motion. Rule 8013(f) governs the form of a motion, response, or reply.

(2) Paper Copies of Other Documents. A paper copy of any other document, other than a submission under Rule 8014(f), must comply with subdivision (a), with the following exceptions:

(A) A cover is not necessary if the caption and signature page together contain the information required by subdivision (a)(2).

(B) Subdivision (a)(7) does not apply.

(3) Other Documents Filed Electronically. Any other document filed electronically, other than a submission under Rule 8014(f), must comply with the appearance requirements of paragraph (2).

(f) LOCAL VARIATION. A district court or BAP must accept documents that comply with the applicable requirements of this rule. By local rule, a district court or BAP may accept documents that do not meet all of the requirements of this rule.

Rule 8016. Cross-Appeals

(a) APPLICABILITY. This rule applies to a case in which a cross-appeal is filed. Rules 8014(a)-(c), 8015(a)(7)(A)-(B), and 8018(a)(1)-(3) do not apply to such a case, except as otherwise provided in this rule.

(b) DESIGNATION OF APPELLANT. The party who files a notice of appeal first is the appellant for purposes of this rule and Rule 8018(a)(4) and (b) and Rule 8019. If notices are filed on the same day, the plaintiff, petitioner, applicant, or movant in the proceeding below is the appellant. These designations may be modified by the parties' agreement or by court order.

(c) BRIEFS. In a case involving a cross-appeal:

(1) Appellant's Principal Brief. The appellant must file a principal brief in the appeal. That brief must comply with Rule 8014(a).

(2) Appellee's Principal and Response Brief. The appellee must file a principal brief in the cross-appeal and must, in the same brief, respond to the principal brief in the appeal. That brief must comply with Rule 8014(a), except that the brief need not include a statement of the case unless the appellee is dissatisfied with the appellant's statement.

(3) Appellant's Response and Reply Brief. The appellant must file a brief that responds to the principal brief in the cross-appeal and may, in the same brief, reply to the response in the appeal. That brief must comply with Rule 8014(a)(2)-(8) and (10), except that none of the following need appear unless the appellant is dissatisfied with the appellee's statement in the cross-appeal:

(A) the jurisdictional statement;

(B) the statement of the issues and the applicable standard of appellate review; and

(C) the statement of the case.

(4) Appellee's Reply Brief. The appellee may file a brief in reply to the response in the cross-appeal. That brief must comply with Rule 8014(a)(2)-(3) and (10) and must be limited to the issues presented by the cross-appeal.

(d) LENGTH.

(1) Page Limitation. Unless it complies with paragraphs (2) and (3), the appellant's principal brief must not exceed 30 pages; the appellee's principal and response brief, 35 pages; the appellant's response and reply brief, 30 pages; and the appellee's reply brief, 15 pages.

(2) Type-Volume Limitation.

(A) The appellant's principal brief or the appellant's response and reply brief is acceptable if:

(i) it contains no more than 14,000 words; or

(ii) it uses a monospaced face and contains no more than 1,300 lines of text.

(B) The appellee's principal and response brief is acceptable if:

(i) it contains no more than 16,500 words; or

(ii) it uses a monospaced face and contains no more than 1,500 lines of text.

(C) The appellee's reply brief is acceptable if it contains no more than half of the type volume specified in subparagraph (A).

(D) Headings, footnotes, and quotations count toward the word and line limitations. The corporate disclosure statement, table of contents, table of citations, statement with respect to oral argument, any addendum containing statutes, rules, or regulations, and any certificates of counsel do not count toward the limitation.

(3) Certificate of Compliance. A brief submitted either electronically or in paper form under paragraph (2) must comply with Rule 8015(a)(7)(C).

(e) TIME TO SERVE AND FILE A BRIEF. Briefs must be served and filed as follows, unless the district court or BAP by order in a particular case excuses the filing of briefs or specifies different time limits:

(1) the appellant's principal brief, within 30 days after the docketing of notice that the record has been transmitted or is available electronically;

(2) the appellee's principal and response brief, within 30 days after the appellant's principal brief is served;

(3) the appellant's response and reply brief, within 30 days after the appellee's principal and response brief is served; and

(4) the appellee's reply brief, within 14 days after the appellant's response and reply brief is served, but at least 7 days before scheduled argument unless the district court or BAP, for good cause, allows a later filing.

Rule 8017. Brief of an Amicus Curiae

(a) WHEN PERMITTED. The United States or its officer or agency or a state may file an amicus-curiae brief without the consent of the parties or leave of court. Any other amicus curiae may file a brief only by leave of court or if the brief states that all parties have consented to its filing. On its own motion, and with notice to all parties to an appeal, the district court or BAP may request a brief by an amicus curiae.

(b) MOTION FOR LEAVE TO FILE. The motion must be accompanied by the proposed brief and state:

(1) the movant's interest; and

(2) the reason why an amicus brief is desirable and why the matters asserted are relevant to the disposition of the appeal.

(c) CONTENTS AND FORM. An amicus brief must comply with Rule 8015. In addition to the requirements of Rule 8015, the cover must identify the party or parties supported and indicate whether the brief supports affirmance or reversal. If an amicus curiae is a corporation, the brief must include a disclosure statement like that required of parties by Rule 8012. An amicus brief need not comply with Rule 8014, but must include the following:

(1) a table of contents, with page references;

(2) a table of authorities—cases (alphabetically arranged), statutes, and other authorities—with references to the pages of the brief where they are cited;

(3) a concise statement of the identity of the amicus curiae, its interest in the case, and the source of its authority to file;

(4) unless the amicus curiae is one listed in the first sentence of subdivision (a), a statement that indicates whether:

(A) a party's counsel authored the brief in whole or in part;

(B) a party or a party's counsel contributed money that was intended to fund preparing or submitting the brief; and

(C) a person—other than the amicus curiae, its members, or its counsel—contributed money that was intended to fund preparing or submitting the brief and, if so, identifies each such person;

(5) an argument, which may be preceded by a summary and need not include a statement of the applicable standard of review; and

(6) a certificate of compliance, if required by Rule 8015(a)(7)(C) or 8015(b).

(d) LENGTH. Except by the district court's or BAP's permission, an amicus brief must be no more than one-half the maximum length authorized by these rules for a party's principal brief. If the court grants a party permission to file a longer brief, that extension does not affect the length of an amicus brief.

(e) TIME FOR FILING. An amicus curiae must file its brief, accompanied by a motion for filing when necessary, no later than 7 days after the principal brief of the party being supported is filed. An amicus curiae that does not support either party must file its brief no later than 7 days after the appellant's principal brief is filed. The district court or BAP may grant leave for later filing, specifying the time within which an opposing party may answer.

(f) REPLY BRIEF. Except by the district court's or BAP's permission, an amicus curiae may not file a reply brief.

(g) ORAL ARGUMENT. An amicus curiae may participate in oral argument only with the district court's or BAP's permission.

Rule 8018. Serving and Filing Briefs; Appendices

(a) TIME TO SERVE AND FILE A BRIEF. The following rules apply unless the district court or BAP by order in a particular case excuses the filing of briefs or specifies different time limits:

(1) The appellant must serve and file a brief within 30 days after the docketing of notice that the record has been transmitted or is available electronically.

(2) The appellee must serve and file a brief within 30 days after service of the appellant's brief.

(3) The appellant may serve and file a reply brief within 14 days after service of the appellee's brief, but a reply brief must be filed at least 7 days before scheduled argument unless the district court or BAP, for good cause, allows a later filing.

(4) If an appellant fails to file a brief on time or within an extended time authorized by the district court or BAP, an appellee may move to dismiss the appeal—or the district court or BAP, after notice, may dismiss the appeal on its own motion. An appellee who fails to file a brief will not be heard at oral argument unless the district court or BAP grants permission.

(b) DUTY TO SERVE AND FILE AN APPENDIX TO THE BRIEF.

(1) Appellant. Subject to subdivision (e) and Rule 8009(d), the appellant must serve and file with its principal brief excerpts of the record as an appendix. It must contain the following:

(A) the relevant entries in the bankruptcy docket;

(B) the complaint and answer, or other equivalent filings;

(C) the judgment, order, or decree from which the appeal is taken;

(D) any other orders, pleadings, jury instructions, findings, conclusions, or opinions relevant to the appeal;

(E) the notice of appeal; and

(F) any relevant transcript or portion of it.

(2) Appellee. The appellee may also serve and file with its brief an appendix that contains material required to be included by the appellant or relevant to the appeal or cross-appeal, but omitted by the appellant.

(3) Cross-Appellee. The appellant as cross-appellee may also serve and file with its response an appendix that contains material relevant to matters raised initially by the principal brief in the cross-appeal, but omitted by the cross-appellant.

(c) FORMAT OF THE APPENDIX. The appendix must begin with a table of contents identifying the page at which each part begins. The relevant docket entries must follow the table of contents. Other parts of the record must follow chronologically. When pages from the transcript of proceedings are placed in the appendix, the transcript page numbers must be shown in brackets immediately before the included pages. Omissions in the text of documents or of the transcript must be indicated by asterisks. Immaterial formal matters (captions, subscriptions, acknowledgments, and the like) should be omitted.

(d) EXHIBITS. Exhibits designated for inclusion in the appendix may be reproduced in a separate volume or volumes, suitably indexed.

(e) APPEAL ON THE ORIGINAL RECORD WITHOUT AN APPENDIX. The district court or BAP may, either by rule for all cases or classes of cases or by order in a particular case, dispense with the appendix and permit an appeal to proceed on the original record, with the submission of any relevant parts of the record that the district court or BAP orders the parties to file.

Rule 8019. Oral Argument

(a) PARTY'S STATEMENT. Any party may file, or a district court or BAP may require, a statement explaining why oral argument should, or need not, be permitted.

(b) PRESUMPTION OF ORAL ARGUMENT AND EXCEPTIONS. Oral argument must be allowed in every case unless the district judge—or all the BAP judges assigned to hear the appeal—examine the briefs and record and determine that oral argument is unnecessary because

(1) the appeal is frivolous;

(2) the dispositive issue or issues have been authoritatively decided; or

(3) the facts and legal arguments are adequately presented in the briefs and record, and the decisional process would not be significantly aided by oral argument.

(c) NOTICE OF ARGUMENT; POSTPONEMENT. The district court or BAP must advise all parties of the date, time, and place for oral argument, and the time allowed for each side. A motion to postpone the argument or to allow longer argument must be filed reasonably in advance of the hearing date.

(d) ORDER AND CONTENTS OF ARGUMENT. The appellant opens and concludes the argument. Counsel must not read at length from briefs, the record, or authorities.

(e) CROSS-APPEALS AND SEPARATE APPEALS. If there is a cross-appeal, Rule 8016(b) determines which party is the appellant and which is the appellee for the purposes of oral argument. Unless the district court or BAP directs otherwise, a cross-appeal or separate appeal must be argued when the initial appeal is argued. Separate parties should avoid duplicative argument.

(f) NONAPPEARANCE OF A PARTY. If the appellee fails to appear for argument, the district court or BAP may hear the appellant's argument. If the appellant fails to appear for argument, the district court or BAP may hear the appellee's argument. If neither party appears, the case will be decided on the briefs unless the district court or BAP orders otherwise.

(g) SUBMISSION ON BRIEFS. The parties may agree to submit a case for decision on the briefs, but the district court or BAP may direct that the case be argued.

(h) USE OF PHYSICAL EXHIBITS AT ARGUMENT; REMOVAL. Counsel intending to use physical exhibits other than documents at the argument must arrange to place them in the courtroom on the day of the argument before the court convenes. After the argument, counsel must remove the exhibits from the courtroom unless the district court or BAP directs otherwise. The clerk may destroy or dispose of the exhibits if counsel does not reclaim them within a reasonable time after the clerk gives notice to remove them.

Rule 8020. Frivolous Appeal and Other Misconduct

(a) FRIVOLOUS APPEAL—DAMAGES AND COSTS. If the district court or BAP determines that an appeal is frivolous, it may, after a separately filed motion or notice from the court and reasonable opportunity to respond, award just damages and single or double costs to the appellee.

(b) OTHER MISCONDUCT. The district court or BAP may discipline or sanction an attorney or party appearing before it for other misconduct, including failure to comply with any court order. First, however, the court must afford the attorney or party reasonable notice, an opportunity to show cause to the contrary, and, if requested, a hearing.

Rule 8021. Costs

(a) AGAINST WHOM ASSESSED. The following rules apply unless the law provides or the district court or BAP orders otherwise:

(1) if an appeal is dismissed, costs are taxed against the appellant, unless the parties agree otherwise;

(2) if a judgment, order, or decree is affirmed, costs are taxed against the appellant;

(3) if a judgment, order, or decree is reversed, costs are taxed against the appellee;

(4) if a judgment, order, or decree is affirmed or reversed in part, modified, or vacated, costs are taxed only as the district court or BAP orders.

(b) COSTS FOR AND AGAINST THE UNITED STATES. Costs for or against the United States, its agency, or its officer may be assessed under subdivision (a) only if authorized by law.

(c) COSTS ON APPEAL TAXABLE IN THE BANKRUPTCY COURT. The following costs on appeal are taxable in the bankruptcy court for the benefit of the party entitled to costs under this rule:

(1) the production of any required copies of a brief, appendix, exhibit, or the record;

(2) the preparation and transmission of the record;

(3) the reporter's transcript, if needed to determine the appeal;

(4) premiums paid for a supersedeas bond or other bonds to preserve rights pending appeal; and

(5) the fee for filing the notice of appeal.

(d) BILL OF COSTS; OBJECTIONS. A party who wants costs taxed must, within 14 days after entry of judgment on appeal, file with the bankruptcy clerk, with proof of service, an itemized and verified bill of costs. Objections must be filed within 14 days after service of the bill of costs, unless the bankruptcy court extends the time.

Rule 8022. Motion for Rehearing

(a) TIME TO FILE; CONTENTS; RESPONSE; ACTION BY THE DISTRICT COURT OR BAP IF GRANTED.

(1) Time. Unless the time is shortened or extended by order or local rule, any motion for rehearing by the district court or BAP must be filed within 14 days after entry of judgment on appeal.

(2) Contents. The motion must state with particularity each point of law or fact that the movant believes the district court or BAP has overlooked or misapprehended and must argue in support of the motion. Oral argument is not permitted.

(3) Response. Unless the district court or BAP requests, no response to a motion for rehearing is permitted. But ordinarily, rehearing will not be granted in the absence of such a request.

(4) Action by the District Court or BAP. If a motion for rehearing is granted, the district court or BAP may do any of the following:

(A) make a final disposition of the appeal without reargument;

(B) restore the case to the calendar for reargument or resubmission; or

(C) issue any other appropriate order.

(b) FORM OF THE MOTION; LENGTH. The motion must comply in form with Rule 8013(f)(1) and (2). Copies must be served and filed as provided by Rule 8011. Unless the district court or BAP orders otherwise, a motion for rehearing must not exceed 15 pages.

Rule 8023. Voluntary Dismissal

The clerk of the district court or BAP must dismiss an appeal if the parties file a signed dismissal agreement specifying how costs are to be paid and pay any fees that are due. An appeal may be dismissed on the appellant's motion on terms agreed to by the parties or fixed by the district court or BAP.

Rule 8024. Clerk's Duties on Disposition of the Appeal

(a) JUDGMENT ON APPEAL. The district or BAP clerk must prepare, sign, and enter the judgment after receiving the court's opinion or, if there is no opinion, as the court instructs. Noting the judgment on the docket constitutes entry of judgment.

(b) NOTICE OF A JUDGMENT. Immediately upon the entry of a judgment, the district or BAP clerk must:

(1) transmit a notice of the entry to each party to the appeal, to the United States trustee, and to the bankruptcy clerk, together with a copy of any opinion; and

(2) note the date of the transmission on the docket.

(c) RETURNING PHYSICAL ITEMS. If any physical items were transmitted as the record on appeal, they must be returned to the bankruptcy clerk on disposition of the appeal.

Rule 8025. Stay of a District Court or BAP Judgment

(a) AUTOMATIC STAY OF JUDGMENT ON APPEAL. Unless the district court or BAP orders otherwise, its judgment is stayed for 14 days after entry.

(b) STAY PENDING APPEAL TO THE COURT OF APPEALS.

(1) In General. On a party's motion and notice to all other parties to the appeal, the district court or BAP may stay its judgment pending an appeal to the court of appeals.

(2) Time Limit. The stay must not exceed 30 days after the judgment is entered, except for cause shown.

(3) Stay Continued. If, before a stay expires, the party who obtained the stay appeals to the court of appeals, the stay continues until final disposition by the court of appeals.

(4) Bond or Other Security. A bond or other security may be required as a condition for granting or continuing a stay of the judgment. A bond or other security may be required if a trustee obtains a stay, but not if a stay is obtained by the United States or its officer or agency or at the direction of any department of the United States government.

(c) AUTOMATIC STAY OF AN ORDER, JUDGMENT, OR DECREE OF A BANKRUPTCY COURT. If the district court or BAP enters a judgment affirming an order, judgment, or decree of the bankruptcy court, a stay of the district court's or BAP's judgment automatically stays the bankruptcy court's order, judgment, or decree for the duration of the appellate stay.

(d) POWER OF A COURT OF APPEALS NOT LIMITED. This rule does not limit the power of a court of appeals or any of its judges to do the following:

(1) stay a judgment pending appeal;

(2) stay proceedings while an appeal is pending;

(3) suspend, modify, restore, vacate, or grant a stay or an injunction while an appeal is pending; or

(4) issue any order appropriate to preserve the status quo or the effectiveness of any judgment to be entered.

Rule 8026. Rules by Circuit Councils and District Courts; Procedure When There is No Controlling Law

(a) LOCAL RULES BY CIRCUIT COUNCILS AND DISTRICT COURTS.

(1) Adopting Local Rules. A circuit council that has authorized a BAP under 28 U.S.C. § 158(b) may make and amend rules governing the practice and procedure on appeal from a judgment, order, or decree of a bankruptcy court to the BAP. A district court may make and amend rules governing the practice and procedure on appeal from a judgment, order, or decree of a bankruptcy court to the district court. Local rules must be consistent with, but not duplicative of, Acts of Congress and these Part VIII rules. Rule 83 F.R.Civ.P. governs the procedure for making and amending rules to govern appeals.

(2) Numbering. Local rules must conform to any uniform numbering system prescribed by the Judicial Conference of the United States.

(3) Limitation on Imposing Requirements of Form. A local rule imposing a requirement of form must not be enforced in a way that causes a party to lose any right because of a nonwillful failure to comply.

(b) PROCEDURE WHEN THERE IS NO CONTROLLING LAW.

(1) In General. A district court or BAP may regulate practice in any manner consistent with federal law, applicable federal rules, the Official Forms, and local rules.

(2) Limitation on Sanctions. No sanction or other disadvantage may be imposed for noncompliance with any requirement not in federal law, applicable federal rules, the Official Forms, or local rules unless the alleged violator has been furnished in the particular case with actual notice of the requirement.

Rule 8027. Notice of a Mediation Procedure

If the district court or BAP has a mediation procedure applicable to bankruptcy appeals, the clerk must notify the parties promptly after docketing the appeal of:

(a) the requirements of the mediation procedure; and

(b) any effect the mediation procedure has on the time to file briefs.

Rule 8028. Suspension of Rules in Part VIII

In the interest of expediting decision or for other cause in a particular case, the district court or BAP, or where appropriate the court of appeals, may suspend the requirements or provisions of the rules in Part VIII, except Rules 8001, 8002, 8003, 8004, 8005, 8006, 8007, 8012, 8020, 8024, 8025, 8026, and 8028.

PART IX

GENERAL PROVISIONS

Rule 9001. General Definitions

The definitions of words and phrases in §§ 101, 902, 1101, and 1502 of the Code, and the rules of construction in § 102 govern their use in these rules. In addition, the following words and phrases used in these rules have the meanings indicated:

(1) "Bankruptcy clerk" means a clerk appointed pursuant to 28 U. S. C. Section 156(b).

(2) "Bankruptcy Code" or "Code" means title 11 of the United States Code.

(3) "Clerk" means bankruptcy clerk, if one has been appointed, otherwise clerk of the district court.

(4) "Court" or "judge" means the judicial officer before whom a case or proceeding is pending.

(5) "Debtor." When any act is required by these rules to be performed by a debtor or when it is necessary to compel attendance of a debtor for examination and the debtor is not a natural person: (A) if the debtor is a corporation, "debtor" includes, if designated by the court, any or all of its officers, members of its board of directors or trustees or of a similar controlling body, a controlling stockholder or member, or any other person in control; (B) if the debtor is a partnership, "debtor" includes any or all of its general partners or, if designated by the court, any other person in control.

(6) "Firm" includes a partnership or professional corporation of attorneys or accountants.

(7) "Judgment" means any appealable order.

(8) "Mail" means first class, postage prepaid.

(9) "Notice provider" means any entity approved by the Administrative Office of the United States Courts to give notice to creditors under Rule 2002(g)(4).

(10) "Regular associate" means any attorney regularly employed by, associated with, or counsel to an individual or firm.

(11) "Trustee" includes a debtor in possession in a chapter 11 case.

(12) "United States trustee" includes an assistant United States trustee and any designee of the United States trustee.

Rule 9002. Meanings of Words in the Federal Rules of Civil Procedure When Applicable to Cases Under The Code

The following words and phrases used in the Federal Rules of Civil Procedure made applicable to cases under the Code by these rules have the meanings indicated unless they are inconsistent with the context:

(1) "Action" or "civil action" means an adversary proceeding or, when appropriate, a contested petition, or proceedings to vacate an order for relief or to determine any other contested matter.

(2) "Appeal" means an appeal as provided by 28 U. S. C. Section 158.

(3) "Clerk" or "clerk of the district court" means the court officer responsible for the bankruptcy records in the district.

(4) "District court," "trial court," "court," "district judge," or "judge" means bankruptcy judge if the case or proceeding is pending before a bankruptcy judge.

(5) "Judgment" includes any order appealable to an appellate court.

Rule 9003. Prohibition of Ex Parte Contacts

(a) GENERAL PROHIBITION. Except as otherwise permitted by applicable law, any examiner, any party in interest, and any attorney, accountant, or employee of a party in interest shall refrain from ex parte meetings and communications with the court concerning matters affecting a particular case or proceeding.

(b) UNITED STATES TRUSTEE. Except as otherwise permitted by applicable law, the United States trustee and assistants to and employees or agents of the United States trustee shall refrain from ex parte meetings and communications with the court concerning matters affecting a particular case or proceeding. This rule does not preclude communications with the court to discuss general problems of administration and improvement of bankruptcy administration, including the operation of the United States trustee system.

Rule 9004. General Requirements of Form

(a) LEGIBILITY; ABBREVIATIONS. All petitions, pleadings, schedules and other papers shall be clearly legible. Abbreviations in common use in the English language may be used.

(b) CAPTION. Each paper filed shall contain a caption setting forth the name of the court, the title of the case, the bankruptcy docket number, and a brief designation of the character of the paper.

Rule 9005. Harmless Error

Rule 61 F. R. Civ. P. applies in cases under the Code. When appropriate, the court may order the correction of any error or defect or the cure of any omission which does not affect substantial rights.

Rule 9005.1. Constitutional Challenge to a Statute – Notice, Certification, and Intervention

Rule 5.1 F.R.Civ.P. applies in cases under the Code.

Rule 9006. Computing and Extending Time

(a) COMPUTING TIME. The following rules apply in computing any time period specified in these rules, in the Federal Rules of Civil Procedure, in any local rule or court order, or in any statute that does not specify a method of computing time.

(1) Period Stated in Days or a Longer Unit. When the period is stated in days or a longer unit of time:

(A) exclude the day of the event that triggers the period;

(B) count every day, including intermediate Saturdays, Sundays, and legal holidays; and

(C) include the last day of the period, but if the last day is a Saturday, Sunday, or legal holiday, the period continues to run until the end of the next day that is not a Saturday, Sunday, or legal holiday.

(2) Period Stated in Hours. When the period is stated in hours:

(A) begin counting immediately on the occurrence of the event that triggers the period;

(B) count every hour, including hours during intermediate Saturdays, Sundays, and legal holidays; and

(C) if the period would end on a Saturday, Sunday, or legal holiday, then continue the period until the same time on the next day that is not a Saturday, Sunday, or legal holiday.

(3) Inaccessibility of Clerk's Office. Unless the court orders otherwise, if the clerk's office is inaccessible:

(A) on the last day for filing under Rule 9006(a)(1), then the time for filing is extended to the first accessible day that is not a Saturday, Sunday, or legal holiday; or

(B) during the last hour for filing under Rule 9006(a)(2), then the time for filing is extended to the same time on the first accessible day that is not a Saturday, Sunday, or legal holiday.

(4) "Last Day" Defined. Unless a different time is set by a statute, local rule, or order in the case, the last day ends:

(A) for electronic filing, at midnight in the court's time zone; and

(B) for filing by other means, when the clerk's office is scheduled to close.

(5) "Next Day" Defined. The "next day" is determined by continuing to count forward when the period is measured after an event and backward when measured before an event.

(6) "Legal Holiday" Defined. "Legal holiday" means:

(A) the day set aside by statute for observing New Year's Day, Martin Luther King Jr.'s Birthday, Washington's Birthday, Memorial Day, Independence Day, Labor Day, Columbus Day, Veterans' Day, Thanksgiving Day, or Christmas Day;

(B) any day declared a holiday by the President or Congress; and

(C) for periods that are measured after an event, any other day declared a holiday by the state where the district court is located. (In this rule, "state" includes the District of Columbia and any United States commonwealth or territory.)

(b) ENLARGEMENT.

(1) In General. Except as provided in paragraphs (2) and (3) of this subdivision, when an act is required or allowed to be done at or within a specified period by these rules or by a notice given thereunder or by order of court, the court for cause shown may at any time in its discretion (1) with or without motion or notice order the period enlarged if the request therefor is made before the expiration of the period originally prescribed or as extended by a previous order or (2) on motion made after the expiration of the specified period permit the act to be done where the failure to act was the result of excusable neglect.

(2) Enlargement Not Permitted. The court may not enlarge the time for taking action under Rules 1007(d), 2003(a) and (d), 7052, 9023, and 9024.

(3) Enlargement Governed By Other Rules. The court may enlarge the time for taking action under Rules 1006(b)(2), 1017(e), 3002(c), 4003(b), 4004(a), 4007(c), 4008(a), 8002, and 9033, only to the extent and under the conditions stated in those rules. In addition, the court may enlarge the time to file the statement required under Rule 1007(b)(7), and to file schedules and statements in a small business case under § 1116(3) of the Code, only to the extent and under the conditions stated in Rule 1007(c).

(c) REDUCTION.

(1) In General. Except as provided in paragraph (2) of this subdivision, when an act is required or allowed to be done at or within a specified time by these rules or by a notice given thereunder or by order of court, the court for cause shown may in its discretion with or without motion or notice order the period reduced.

(2) Reduction Not Permitted. The court may not reduce the time for taking action under Rules 2002(a)(7), 2003(a), 3002(c), 3014, 3015, 4001(b)(2), (c)(2), 4003(a), 4004(a), 4007(c), 4008(a), 8002, and 9033(b). In addition, the court may not reduce the time under Rule 1007(c) to file the statement required by Rule 1007(b)(7).

(d) MOTION PAPERS. A written motion, other than one which may be heard ex parte, and notice of any hearing shall be served not later than seven days before the time specified for such hearing, unless a different period is fixed by these rules or by order of the court. Such an order may for cause shown be made on ex parte application. When a motion is supported by affidavit, the affidavit shall be served with the motion. Except as otherwise provided in Rule 9023, any written response shall be served not later than one day before the hearing, unless the court permits otherwise.

(e) TIME OF SERVICE. Service of process and service of any paper other than process or of notice by mail is complete on mailing.

(f) ADDITIONAL TIME AFTER SERVICE BY MAIL OR UNDER RULE 5(b)(2)(D), (E), or (F) F.R.Civ.P. When there is a right or requirement to act or undertake some proceedings within a prescribed period after service and that service is by mail or under Rule 5(b)(2) (D), (E), or (F) F.R. Civ. P., three days are added after the prescribed period would otherwise expire under Rule 9006(a).

(g) GRAIN STORAGE FACILITY CASES. This rule shall not limit the court's authority under Section 557 of the Code to enter orders governing procedures in cases in which the debtor is an owner or operator of a grain storage facility.

Rule 9007. General Authority to Regulate Notices

When notice is to be given under these rules, the court shall designate, if not otherwise specified herein, the time within which, the entities to whom, and the form and manner in which the notice shall be given. When feasible, the court may order any notices under these rules to be combined.

Rule 9008. Service or Notice by Publication

Whenever these rules require or authorize service or notice by publication, the court shall, to the extent not otherwise specified in these rules, determine the form and manner thereof, including the newspaper or other medium to be used and the number of publications.

Rule 9009. Forms

Except as otherwise provided in Rule 3016(d), the Official Forms prescribed by the Judicial Conference of the United States shall be observed and used with alterations as may be appropriate. Forms may be combined and their contents rearranged to permit economies in their use. The Director of the Administrative Office of the United States Courts may issue additional forms for use under the Code. The forms shall be construed to be consistent with these rules and the Code.

Rule 9010. Representation and Appearances; Powers of Attorney

(a) AUTHORITY TO ACT PERSONALLY OR BY ATTORNEY. A debtor, creditor, equity security holder, indenture trustee, committee or other party may (1) appear in a case under the Code and act either in the entity's own behalf or by an attorney authorized to practice in the court, and (2) perform any act not constituting the practice of law, by an authorized agent, attorney in fact, or proxy.

(b) NOTICE OF APPEARANCE. An attorney appearing for a party in a case under the Code shall file a notice of appearance with the attorney's name, office address and telephone number, unless the attorney's appearance is otherwise noted in the record.

(c) POWER OF ATTORNEY. The authority of any agent, attorney in fact, or proxy to represent a creditor for any purpose other than the execution and filing of a proof of claim or the acceptance or rejection of a plan shall be evidenced by a power of attorney conforming substantially to the appropriate Official Form. The execution of any such power of attorney shall be acknowledged before one of the officers enumerated in 28 U. S. C. Section 459, Section 953, Rule 9012, or a person authorized to administer oaths under the laws of the state where the oath is administered.

Rule 9011. Signing of Papers; Representations to the Court; Sanctions; Verification and Copies of Papers

(a) SIGNING OF PAPERS. Every petition, pleading, written motion, and other paper, except a list, schedule, or statement, or amendments thereto, shall be signed by at least one attorney of record in the attorney's individual name. A party who is not represented by an attorney shall sign all papers. Each paper shall state the signer's address and telephone number, if any. An unsigned paper shall be stricken unless omission of the signature is corrected promptly after being called to the attention of the attorney or party.

(b) REPRESENTATIONS TO THE COURT. By presenting to the court (whether by signing, filing, submitting, or later advocating) a petition, pleading, written motion, or other paper, an attorney or unrepresented party is certifying that to the best of the person's knowledge, information, and belief, formed after an inquiry reasonable under the circumstances,-

(1) it is not being presented for any improper purpose, such as to harass or to cause unnecessary delay or needless increase in the cost of litigation;

(2) the claims, defenses, and other legal contentions therein are warranted by existing law or by a nonfrivolous argument for the extension, modification, or reversal of existing law or the establishment of new law;

(3) the allegations and other factual contentions have evidentiary support or, if specifically so identified, are likely to have evidentiary support after a reasonable opportunity for further investigation or discovery; and

(4) the denials of factual contentions are warranted on the evidence or, if specifically so identified, are reasonably based on a lack of information or belief.

(c) SANCTIONS. If, after notice and a reasonable opportunity to respond, the court determines that subdivision (b) has been violated, the court may, subject to the conditions stated below, impose an appropriate sanction upon the attorneys, law firms, or parties that have violated subdivision (b) or are responsible for the violation.

(1) How Initiated.

(A) By Motion. A motion for sanctions under this rule shall be made separately from other motions or requests and shall describe the specific conduct alleged to violate subdivision (b). It shall be served as provided in Rule 7004. The motion for sanctions may not be filed with or presented to the court unless, within 21 days after service of the motion (or such other period as the court may prescribe), the challenged paper, claim, defense, contention, allegation, or denial is not withdrawn or appropriately corrected, except that this limitation shall not apply if the conduct alleged is the filing of a petition in violation of subdivision (b). If warranted, the court may award to the party prevailing on the motion the reasonable expenses and attorney's fees incurred in presenting or opposing the motion. Absent exceptional circumstances, a law firm shall be held jointly responsible for violations committed by its partners, associates, and employees.

(B) On Court's Initiative. On its own initiative, the court may enter an order describing the specific conduct that appears to violate subdivision (b) and directing an attorney, law firm, or party to show cause why it has not violated subdivision (b) with respect thereto.

(2) Nature of Sanction; Limitations. A sanction imposed for violation of this rule shall be limited to what is sufficient to deter repetition of such conduct or comparable conduct by others similarly situated. Subject to the limitations in subparagraphs (A) and (B), the sanction may consist of, or include, directives of a nonmonetary nature, an order to pay a penalty into court, or, if imposed on motion and warranted for effective deterrence, an order directing payment to the movant of some or all of the reasonable attorneys' fees and other expenses incurred as a direct result of the violation.

(A) Monetary sanctions may not be awarded against a represented party for a violation of subdivision (b)(2).

(B) Monetary sanctions may not be awarded on the court's initiative unless the court issues its order to show cause before a voluntary dismissal or settlement of the claims made by or against the party which is, or whose attorneys are, to be sanctioned.

(3) Order. When imposing sanctions, the court shall describe the conduct determined to constitute a violation of this rule and explain the basis for the sanction imposed.

(d) INAPPLICABILITY TO DISCOVERY. Subdivisions (a) through (c) of this rule do not apply to disclosures and discovery requests, responses, objections, and motions that are subject to the provisions of Rules 7026 through 7037.

(e) VERIFICATION. Except as otherwise specifically provided by these rules, papers filed in a case under the Code need not be verified. Whenever verification is required by these rules, an unsworn declaration as provided in 28 U. S. C. Section 1746 satisfies the requirement of verification.

(f) COPIES OF SIGNED OR VERIFIED PAPERS. When these rules require copies of a signed or verified paper, it shall suffice if the original is signed or verified and the copies are conformed to the original.

Rule 9012. Oaths and Affirmations

(a) PERSONS AUTHORIZED TO ADMINISTER OATHS. The following persons may administer oaths and affirmations and take acknowledgements: a bankruptcy judge, clerk, deputy clerk, United States trustee, officer authorized to administer oaths in proceedings before the courts of the United States or under the laws of the state where the oath is to be taken, or a diplomatic or consular officer of the United States in any foreign country.

(b) AFFIRMATION IN LIEU OF OATH. When in a case under the Code an oath is required to be taken, a solemn affirmation may be accepted in lieu thereof.

Rule 9013. Motions: Form and Service

A request for an order, except when an application is authorized by the rules, shall be by written motion, unless made during a hearing. The motion shall state with particularity the grounds therefor, and shall set forth the relief or order sought. Every written motion, other than one which may be considered ex parte, shall be served by the moving party within the time determined under Rule 9006(d). The moving party shall serve the motion on:

(a) the trustee or debtor in possession and on those entities specified by these rules; or

(b) the entities the court directs if these rules do not require service or specify the entities to be served.

Rule 9014. Contested Matters

(a) MOTION. In a contested matter not otherwise governed by these rules, relief shall be requested by motion, and reasonable notice and opportunity for hearing shall be afforded the party against whom relief is sought. No response is required under this rule unless the court directs otherwise.

(b) SERVICE. The motion shall be served in the manner provided for service of a summons and complaint by Rule 7004 and within the time determined under Rule 9006(d). Any written response to the motion shall be served within the time determined under Rule 9006(d). Any paper served after the motion shall be served in the manner provided by Rule 5(b) F.R. Civ. P.

(c) APPLICATION OF PART VII RULES. Except as otherwise provided in this rule, and unless the court directs otherwise, the following rules shall apply: 7009, 7017, 7021, 7025, 7026, 7028-7037, 7041, 7042, 7052, 7054-7056, 7064, 7069, anD 7071. The following subdivisions of Fed. R. Civ. P. 26, as incorporated by Rule 7026, shall not apply in a contested matter unless the court directs otherwise: 26(a)(1) (mandatory disclosure), 26(a)(2) (disclosures regarding expert testimony) and 26(a)(3) (additional pre-trial disclosure), and 26(f) (mandatory meeting before scheduling conference/discovery plan). An entity that desires to perpetuate testimony may proceed in the same manner as provided in Rule 7027 for the taking of a deposition before an adversary proceeding. The court may at any stage in a particular matter direct that one or more of the other rules in Part VII shall apply. The court shall give the parties notice of any order issued under this paragraph to afford them a reasonable opportunity to comply with the procedures prescribed by the order.

(d) TESTIMONY OF WITNESSES. Testimony of witnesses with respect to disputed material factual issues shall be taken in the same manner as testimony in an adversary proceeding.

(e) ATTENDANCE OF WITNESSES. The court shall provide procedures that enable parties to ascertain at a reasonable time before any scheduled hearing whether the hearing will be an evidentiary hearing at which witnesses may testify.

Rule 9015. Jury Trials.

(a) APPLICABILITY OF CERTAIN FEDERAL RULES OF CIVIL PROCEDURE. Rules 38, 39, 47, 49, and 51, F.R.Civ.P., and Rule 81(c) F.R.Civ.P. insofar as it applies to jury trials, apply in cases and proceedings, except that a demand made under Rule 38(b) F.R.Civ.P. shall be filed in accordance with Rule 5005.

(b) CONSENT TO HAVE TRIAL CONDUCTED BY BANKRUPTCY JUDGE. If the right to a jury trial applies, a timely demand has been filed pursuant to Rule 38(b) F.R.Civ.P., and the bankruptcy judge has been specially designated to conduct the jury trial, the parties may consent to have a jury trial conducted by a bankruptcy judge under 28 U.S.C. §157(e) by jointly or separately filing a statement of consent within any applicable time limits specified by local rule.

(c) APPLICABILITY OF RULE 50 F.R. CIV. P. Rule 50 F.R. Civ. P. applies in cases and proceedings, except that any renewed motion for judgment or request for a new trial shall be filed no later than 14 days after the entry of judgment.

Rule 9016. Subpoena

Rule 45 F. R. Civ. P. applies in cases under the Code.

Rule 9017. Evidence

The Federal Rules of Evidence and Rules 43, 44, and 44.1 F. R. Civ. P. apply in cases under the Code.

Rule 9018. Secret, Confidential, Scandalous, or Defamatory Matter

On motion or on its own initiative, with or without notice, the court may make any order which justice requires (1) to protect the estate or any entity in respect of a trade secret or other confidential research, development, or commercial information, (2) to protect any entity against scandalous or defamatory matter contained in any paper filed in a case under the Code, or (3)to protect governmental matters that are made confidential by statute or regulation. If an order is entered under this rule without notice, any entity affected thereby may move to vacate or modify the order, and after a hearing on notice the court shall determine the motion.

Rule 9019. Compromise and Arbitration

(a) COMPROMISE. On motion by the trustee and after notice and a hearing, the court may approve a compromise or settlement. Notice shall be given to creditors, the United States trustee, the debtor, and indenture trustees as provided in Rule 2002 and to any other entity as the court may direct.

(b) AUTHORITY TO COMPROMISE OR SETTLE CONTROVERSIES WITHIN CLASSES. After a hearing on such notice as the court may direct, the court may fix a class or classes of controversies and authorize the trustee to compromise or settle controversies within such class or classes without further hearing or notice.

(c) ARBITRATION. On stipulation of the parties to any controversy affecting the estate the court may authorize the matter to be submitted to final and binding arbitration.

Rule 9020. Contempt Proceedings

Rule 9014 governs a motion for an order of contempt made by the United States trustee or a party in interest.

Rule 9021. Entry of Judgment

A judgment or order is effective when entered under Rule 5003.

Rule 9022. Notice of Judgment or Order

(a) JUDGMENT OR ORDER OF BANKRUPTCY JUDGE. Immediately on the entry of a judgment or order the clerk shall serve a notice of entry in the manner provided in Rule 5(b) F.R.Civ.P. on the contesting parties and on other entities as the court directs. Unless the case is a chapter 9 municipality case, the clerk shall forthwith transmit to the United States trustee a copy of the judgment or order. Service of the notice shall be noted in the docket. Lack of notice of the entry does not affect the time to appeal or relieve or authorize the court to relieve a party for failure to appeal within the time allowed, except as permitted in Rule 8002.

(b) JUDGMENT OR ORDER OF DISTRICT JUDGE. Notice of a judgment or order entered by a district judge is governed by Rule 77(d) F. R. Civ. P. Unless the case is a chapter 9 municipality case, the clerk shall forthwith transmit to the United States trustee a copy of a judgment or order entered by a district judge.

Rule 9023. New Trials; Amendment Of Judgments

Except as provided in this rule and Rule 3008, Rule 59 F.R.Civ.P. applies in cases under the Code. A motion for a new trial or to alter or amend a judgment shall be filed, and a court may on its own order a new trial, no later than 14 days after entry of judgment. In some circumstances, Rule 8008 governs post-judgment motion practice after an appeal has been docketed and is pending.

Rule 9024. Relief from Judgment or Order

Rule 60 F.R.Civ.P. applies in cases under the Code except that (1) a motion to reopen a case under the Code or for the reconsideration of an order allowing or disallowing a claim against the estate entered without a contest is not subject to the one year limitation prescribed in Rule 60(c), (2) a complaint to revoke a discharge in a chapter 7 liquidation case may be filed only within the time allowed by § 727(e) of the Code, and (3) a complaint to revoke an order confirming a plan may be filed only within the time allowed by § 1144, § 1230, or § 1330. In some circumstances, Rule 8008 governs post-judgment motion practice after an appeal has been docketed and is pending.

Rule 9025. Security: Proceedings Against Sureties

Whenever the Code or these rules require or permit the giving of security by a party, and security is given in the form of a bond or stipulation or other undertaking with one or more sureties, each surety submits to the jurisdiction of the court, and liability may be determined in an adversary proceeding governed by the rules in Part VII.

Rule 9026. Exceptions Unnecessary

Rule 46 F. R. Civ. P. applies in cases under the Code.

Rule 9027. Removal

(a) NOTICE OF REMOVAL.

(1) WHERE FILED; FORM AND CONTENT. A notice of removal shall be filed with the clerk for the district and division within which is located the state or federal court where the civil action is pending. The notice shall be signed pursuant to Rule 9011 and contain a short and plain statement of the facts which entitle the party filing the notice to remove, contain a statement that upon removal of the claim or cause of action the proceeding is core or non-core and, if non-core, that the party filing the notice does or does not consent to entry of final orders or judgment by the bankruptcy judge, and be accompanied by a copy of all process and pleadings.

(2) TIME FOR FILING; CIVIL ACTION INITIATED BEFORE COMMENCEMENT OF THE CASE UNDER THE CODE. If the claim or cause of action in a civil action is pending when a case under the Code is commenced, a notice of removal may be filed only within the longest of (A) 90 days after the order for relief in the case under the Code, (B) 30 days after entry of an order terminating a stay, if the claim or cause of action in a civil action has been stayed under Section 362 of the Code, or (C) 30 days after a trustee qualifies in a chapter 11 reorganization case but not later than 180 days after the order for relief.

(3) TIME FOR FILING; CIVIL ACTION INITIATED AFTER COMMENCEMENT OF THE CASE UNDER THE CODE. If a claim or cause of action is asserted in another court after the commencement of a case under the Code, a notice of removal may be filed with the clerk only within the shorter of (A) 30 days after receipt, through service or otherwise, of a copy of the initial pleading setting forth the claim or cause of action sought to be removed or (B) 30 days after receipt of the summons if the initial pleading has been filed with the court but not served with the summons.

(b) NOTICE. Promptly after filing the notice of removal, the party filing the notice shall serve a copy of it on all parties to the removed claim or cause of action.

(c) FILING IN NON-BANKRUPTCY COURT. Promptly after filing the notice of removal, the party filing the notice shall file a copy of it with the clerk of the court from which the claim or cause of action is removed. Removal of the claim or cause of action is effected on such filing of a copy of the notice of removal. The parties shall proceed no further in that court unless and until the claim or cause of action is remanded.

(d) REMAND. A motion for remand of the removed claim or cause of action shall be governed by Rule 9014 and served on the parties to the removed claim or cause of action.

(e) PROCEDURE AFTER REMOVAL.

(1) After removal of a claim or cause of action to a district court the district court or, if the case under the Code has been referred to a bankruptcy judge of the district, the bankruptcy judge, may issue all necessary orders and process to bring before it all proper parties whether served by process issued by the court from which the claim or cause of action was removed or otherwise.

(2) The district court or, if the case under the Code has been referred to a bankruptcy judge of the district, the bankruptcy judge, may require the party filing the notice of removal to file with the clerk copies of all records and proceedings relating to the claim or cause of action in the court from which the claim or cause of action was removed.

(3) Any party who has filed a pleading in connection with the removed claim or cause of action, other than the party filing the notice of removal, shall file a statement admitting or denying any allegation in the notice of removal that upon removal of the claim or cause of action the proceeding is core or non-core. If the statement alleges that the proceeding is non-core, it shall state that the party does or does not consent to entry of final orders or judgment by the bankruptcy judge. A statement required by this paragraph shall be signed pursuant to Rule 9011 and shall be filed not later than 14 days after the filing of the notice of removal. Any party who files a statement pursuant to this paragraph shall mail a copy to every other party to the removed claim or cause of action.

(f) PROCESS AFTER REMOVAL. If one or more of the defendants has not been served with process, the service has not been perfected prior to removal, or the process served proves to be defective, such process or service may be completed or new process issued pursuant to Part VII of these rules.

This subdivision shall not deprive any defendant on whom process is served after removal of the defendant's right to move to remand the case.

(g) APPLICABILITY OF PART VII. The rules of Part VII apply to a claim or cause of action removed to a district court from a federal or state court and govern procedure after removal. Repleading is not necessary unless the court so orders. In a removed action in which the defendant has not answered, the defendant shall answer or present the other defenses or objections available under the rules of Part VII within 21 days following the receipt through service or otherwise of a copy of the initial pleading setting forth the claim for relief on which the action or proceeding is based, or within 21 days following the service of summons on such initial pleading, or within seven days following the filing of the notice of removal, whichever period is longest.

(h) RECORD SUPPLIED. When a party is entitled to copies of the records and proceedings in any civil action or proceeding in a federal or state court, to be used in the removed civil action or proceeding, and the clerk of the federal or state court, on demand accompanied by payment or tender of the lawful fees, fails to deliver certified copies, the court may, on affidavit reciting the facts, direct such record to be supplied by affidavit or otherwise. Thereupon the proceedings, trial and judgment may be had in the court, and all process awarded, as if certified copies had been filed.

(i) ATTACHMENT OR SEQUESTRATION; SECURITIES. When a claim or cause of action is removed to a district court, any attachment or sequestration of property in the court from which the claim or cause of action was removed shall hold the property to answer the final judgment or decree in the same manner as the property would have been held to answer final judgment or decree had it been rendered by the court from which the claim or cause of action was removed. All bonds, undertakings, or security given by either party to the claim or cause of action prior to its removal shall remain valid and effectual notwithstanding such removal. All injunctions issued, orders entered and other proceedings had prior to removal shall remain in full force and effect until dissolved or modified by the court.

Rule 9028. Disability of a Judge

Rule 63 F.R. Civ. P. applies in cases under the Code.

Rule 9029. Local Bankruptcy Rules; Procedure When There is No Controlling Law

(a) LOCAL BANKRUPTCY RULES.

(1) Each district court acting by a majority of its district judges may make and amend rules governing practice and procedure in all cases and proceedings within the district court's bankruptcy jurisdiction which are consistent with - but not duplicative of - Acts of Congress and these rules and which do not prohibit or limit the use of the Official Forms. Rule 83 F.R.Civ.P. governs the procedure for making local rules. A district court may authorize the bankruptcy judges of the district, subject to any limitation or condition it may prescribe and the requirements of 83 F.R.Civ.P., to make and amend rules of practice and procedure which are consistent with - but not duplicative of - Acts of Congress and these rules and which do not prohibit or limit the use of the Official Forms. Local rules shall conform to any uniform numbering system prescribed by the Judicial Conference of the United States.

(2) A local rule imposing a requirement of form shall not be enforced in a manner that causes a party to lose rights because of a nonwillful failure to comply with the requirement.

(b) PROCEDURE WHEN THERE IS NO CONTROLLING LAW. A judge may regulate practice in any manner consistent with federal law, these rules, Official Forms, and local rules of the district. No sanction or other disadvantage may be imposed for noncompliance with any requirement not in federal law, federal rules, Official Forms, or the local rules of the district unless the alleged violator has been furnished in the particular case with actual notice of the requirement.

Rule 9030. Jurisdiction and Venue Unaffected

These rules shall not be construed to extend or limit the jurisdiction of the courts or the venue of any matters therein.

Rule 9031. Masters Not Authorized

Rule 53 F. R. Civ. P. does not apply in cases under the Code.

Rule 9032. Effect of Amendment of Federal Rules of Civil Procedure

The Federal Rules of Civil Procedure which are incorporated by reference and made applicable by these rules shall be the Federal Rules of Civil Procedure in effect on the effective date of these rules and as thereafter amended, unless otherwise provided by such amendment or by these rules.

Rule 9033. Review of Proposed Findings of Fact and Conclusions of Law in Non-Core Proceedings

(a) SERVICE. In non-core proceedings heard pursuant to 28 U. S. C. Section 157(c)(1), the bankruptcy judge shall file proposed findings of fact and conclusions of law. The clerk shall serve forthwith copies on all parties by mail and note the date of mailing on the docket.

(b) OBJECTIONS: TIME FOR FILING. Within 14 days after being served with a copy of the proposed findings of fact and conclusions of law a party may serve and file with the clerk written objections which identify the specific proposed findings or conclusions objected to and state the grounds for such objection. A party may respond to another party's objections within 14 days after being served with a copy thereof. A party objecting to the bankruptcy judge's proposed findings or conclusions shall arrange promptly for the transcription of the record, or such portions of it as all parties may agree upon or the bankruptcy judge deems sufficient, unless the district judge otherwise directs.

(c) EXTENSION OF TIME. The bankruptcy judge may for cause extend the time for filing objections by any party for a period not to exceed 21 days from the expiration of the time otherwise prescribed by this rule. A request to extend the time for filing objections must be made before the time for filing objections has expired, except that a request made no more than 21 days after the expiration of the time for filing objections may be granted upon a showing of excusable neglect.

(d) STANDARD OF REVIEW. The district judge shall make a de novo review upon the record or, after additional evidence, of any portion of the bankruptcy judge's findings of fact or conclusions of law to which specific written objection has been made in accordance with this rule. The district judge may accept, reject, or modify the proposed findings of fact or conclusions of law, receive further evidence, or recommit the matter to the bankruptcy judge with instructions.

Rule 9034. Transmittal of Pleadings, Motion Papers, Objections, and Other Papers to the United States Trustee

Unless the United States trustee requests otherwise or the case is a chapter 9 municipality case, any entity that files a pleading, motion, objection, or similar paper relating to any of the following matters shall transmit a copy thereof to the United States trustee within the time required by these rules for service of the paper:

(a) a proposed use, sale, or lease of property of the estate other than in the ordinary course of business;

(b) the approval of a compromise or settlement of a controversy;

(c) the dismissal or conversion of a case to another chapter;

(d) the employment of professional persons;

(e) an application for compensation or reimbursement of expenses;

(f) a motion for, or approval of an agreement relating to, the use of cash collateral or authority to obtain credit;

(g) the appointment of a trustee or examiner in a chapter 11 reorganization case;

(h) the approval of a disclosure statement;

(i) the confirmation of a plan;

(j) an objection to, or waiver or revocation of, the debtor's discharge;

(k) any other matter in which the United States trustee requests copies of filed papers or the court orders copies transmitted to the United States trustee.

Rule 9035. Applicability of Rules in Judicial Districts in Alabama and North Carolina

In any case under the Code that is filed in or transferred to a district in the State of Alabama or the State of North Carolina and in which a United States trustee is not authorized to act, these rules apply to the extent that they are not inconsistent with any federal statute effective in the case.

Rule 9036. Notice by Electronic Transmission

Whenever the clerk or some other person as directed by the court is required to send notice by mail and the entity entitled to receive the notice requests in writing that, instead of notice by mail, all or part of the information required to be contained in the notice be sent by a specified type of electronic transmission, the court may direct the clerk or other person to send the information by such electronic transmission. Notice by electronic means is complete on transmission

Rule 9037. Privacy Protection For Filings Made with the Court

(a) REDACTED FILINGS. Unless the court orders otherwise, in an electronic or paper filing made with the court that contains an individual's social-security number, taxpayer-identification number, or birth date, the name of an individual, other than the debtor, known to be and identified as a minor, or a financial-account number, a party or nonparty making the filing may include only:

(1) the last four digits of the social-security number and taxpayer-identification number;

(2) the year of the individual's birth;

(3) the minor's initials; and

(4) the last four digits of the financial-account number.

(b) EXEMPTIONS FROM THE REDACTION REQUIREMENT. The redaction requirement does not apply to the following:

(1) a financial-account number that identifies the property allegedly subject to forfeiture in a forfeiture proceeding;

(2) the record of an administrative or agency proceeding unless filed with a proof of claim;

(3) the official record of a state-court proceeding;

(4) the record of a court or tribunal, if that record was not subject to the redaction requirement when originally filed;

(5) a filing covered by subdivision (c) of this rule; and

(6) a filing that is subject to § 110 of the Code.

(c) FILINGS MADE UNDER SEAL. The court may order that a filing be made under seal without redaction. The court may later unseal the filing or order the entity that made the filing to file a redacted version for the public record.

(d) PROTECTIVE ORDERS. For cause, the court may by order in a case under the Code:

(1) require redaction of additional information; or

(2) limit or prohibit a nonparty's remote electronic access to a document filed with the court.

(e) OPTION FOR ADDITIONAL UNREDACTED FILING UNDER SEAL. An entity making a redacted filing may also file an unredacted copy under seal. The court must retain the unredacted copy as part of the record.

(f) OPTION FOR FILING A REFERENCE LIST. A filing that contains redacted information may be filed together with a reference list that identifies each item of redacted information and specifies an appropriate identifier that uniquely corresponds to each item listed. The list must be filed under seal and may be amended as of right. Any reference in the case to a listed identifier will be construed to refer to the corresponding item of information.

(g) WAIVER OF PROTECTION OF IDENTIFIERS. An entity waives the protection of subdivision (a) as to the entity's own information by filing it without redaction and not under seal.

PART X [Abrogated]

SUBJECT INDEX

SUBJECT INDEX

www.ingramcontent.com/pod-product-compliance
Lightning Source LLC
LaVergne TN
LVHW080017210926
848481LV00011B/3043
9781880730461